THE CULTS

OF

THE GREEK STATES

BY

LEWIS RICHARD FARNELL, M.A.

FELLOW AND TUTOR OF EXETER COLLEGE, OXFORD

IN THREE VOLUMES

VOL. II

WITH ILLUSTRATIONS

CARATZAS BROTHERS, PUBLISHERS
NEW ROCHELLE, NEW YORK

1977

292
F23c
10 1178
May 1977

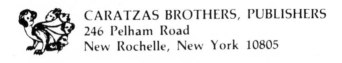

CARATZAS BROTHERS, PUBLISHERS
246 Pelham Road
New Rochelle, New York 10805

CONTENTS OF VOL. II

---++---

CHAPTER XIII.

CHAPTER XVIII.

CHAPTER XIX.

CHAPTER XX.

CHAPTER XXI.

LIST OF PLATES IN VOL. II

           (*b*) Aphrodite and Poseidon on vase.

      XLV.   Bronze statuette of Aphrodite, Bibliothèque Nationale, Paris.

      XLVI.   Venus Genetrix, Louvre.

      XLVII.   Limestone statuette of Aphrodite in Louvre.

      XLVIII. Relief of Hermes, Aphrodite, and Eros from Calabria.

      XLIX. (*a*) Bust of Aphrodite.
            (*b*) Aphrodite with Gorgoneium.

        L. (*a*) Aphrodite and Ares on vase in British Museum.
           (*b*) Aphrodite and Ares on relief in Venice.

       LI. (*a*) Aphrodite, limestone head from Cyprus.
           (*b*) Aphrodite with Eros, terracotta in Louvre.

      LII.   Head of Aphrodite in Holkham Hall.

      LIII.   Head of Aphrodite in Louvre.

      LIV.   Cnidian Aphrodite, statue in Munich.

      LV.   Head of Aphrodite in Brocklesby Hall.

      LVI.   Head of Aphrodite, in possession of Lord Ronald Gower.

      LVII.   Head of Aphrodite in Smyrna.

      LVIII.   Statue of Aphrodite in Syracuse.

      LIX.   Bronze figure of Eileithyia in British Museum.

               Coin-Plate A.

               Coin-Plate B.

THE CULTS OF THE GREEK STATES

CHAPTER XIII.

ARTEMIS.

THE female divinities of the Greek religion have so much of common character as to suggest the belief that they are all different forms under different names of the same divine personage. Such a theory can only be criticized *a posteriori*, after a minute examination of the various cults and the various ideas attaching to those cults. And it is at any rate convenient to study side by side such cognate forms as Artemis, Hekate, Demeter, Persephone, and Aphrodite. Of these the most prominent among the scattered tribes and communities of the Greek world was Artemis. Perhaps no other figure in the Greek Pantheon is so difficult to understand and explain, not because the conceptions that grew up in her worship are mystic and profound, but because they are, or at first sight appear, confusing and contradictory.

Most of her cult is genuinely Hellenic, although in some places we can discover Oriental influences and ideas. We can trace it back to a prehistoric period, and it is found in all the chief places of prehistoric Greek settlement ; in Thessaly, Euboea, Boeotia, Phocis, Locris, Aetolia, Sicyon, Achaea, Elis, Argolis, and, in its most primitive form, in Attica Laconia and Arcadia. Partly from its wide prevalence, and partly from certain most primitive features that it possessed, we must hold that this cult was either an aboriginal heritage

of the Greek nation, or that it was borrowed by all the tribes
at some very remote time, and as no trace or remembrance of
its foreign origin has been preserved in the earliest traditions
that were rife in the chief centres of the worship, the latter
supposition appears idle and gratuitous. Again, the various
streams of Greek colonization in the Mediterranean diffused
the worship of Artemis, and we find it more widely spread
than that of any other Hellenic goddess; it was implanted
at an early time in Lemnos, in the Tauric Chersonese, and
along the coasts of Asia Minor; it was established in the
Greek colonies of Sicily, especially at Syracuse; from Aetolia
it passed up the Hadriatic and the Phocian emigrants brought
it to Massilia. Perhaps it was from this city that it spread to
Spain, where we find undoubted traces of it [a].

Proofs of its early existence in Africa are not easy to discover; for the records of the cult at Cyrene and Alexandria are
comparatively late. It is probable that it was overshadowed
at Cyrene by the more prominent state-worship of the nymph
of that name, the subduer of lions, beloved by Apollo, a deity
of vegetation who, as Studniczka has ably shown, was a
primitive Aeolic form of Artemis [b].

In many of these places, where the new settlers came into
contact with an earlier population, we cannot strictly say that
they introduced the worship as a new cult, but we have
reasons for supposing that they found an indigenous goddess
who bore a certain resemblance to their Artemis and with whom
they therefore identified her. And it is just because she was
so easily confused with foreign and Oriental goddesses, that
the difficulty is so great of defining her original significance for
the Greeks. The name Artemis or Artamis gives us no clue,
for the philological attempts to explain it have led to nothing.

We must have recourse to the various records of her worship
in those parts of Greece where Oriental influences were least
likely to have penetrated in early days, and where the myths
and cult have a character that we have the right to call most
primitive. On comparing these with the later and more

[a] Vide *Geographical Register*, p. 603.   *chische Göttin*, Leipzig, 1890, and the
[b] Studniczka, *Kyrene, eine altgrie-*   article 'Cyrene' in Roscher's *Lexicon.*

advanced, we may not succeed in finding any single conception that can explain the manifold character of Artemis,
but we may be able to group together many cult-names and
beliefs according as they refer to the same part of the original
nature of the goddess, and we can trace a very interesting
succession of ideas that throw light on the earlier stages of
development in Greek society.

The poems of Homer represent Artemis not at all as a lunar
goddess or a divinity of any special department of the natural
world, but as the chaste huntress, most beautiful among her
nymphs, the sister of Apollo, the goddess who sends a gentle
death to women. But his portrait of Artemis gives us not the
first but the last point in the development of her character;
and the conception of her in later Greek literature is not more
advanced or more spiritual than his.

A different aspect of her is presented in the Arcadian and
Athenian rites and legends, which provide us with testimony
much earlier than Homer's; and from these and other fragments of evidence it appears probable that the aboriginal
Artemis was not a goddess of chastity, nor a goddess of the
moon, nor the twin-sister of Apollo, but an independent
divinity connected with the waters and with wild vegetation and beasts; reflecting in her character the life of her
worshippers who were still in the savage stage, supporting
themselves by hunting and fishing rather than by agriculture,
possessing primitive marriage customs and giving a peculiar
status to women, and whose religion was full of ideas relating to
totemism and to the sacred character of the clan-animal. And
even in the later and civilized period her personality retains
more traces of savagery than that of any other Greek divinity.

The most primitive traits in her cult, those at least that
correspond to the most primitive life of man, are expressed
by such cult-titles as refer to the water, the trees, and woodland life. In Arcadia, Laconia, and Sicyon, she was worshipped as Λιμνᾶτις and Λιμναία [1,2], 'the lady of the lake';
near the lake of Stymphalus as Στυμφαλία [3], the goddess who
bred the deadly birds which Heracles slew; and Ἑλεία, the
goddess of the marsh, appears to have been one of her cult-

names in Arcadia and Messene [5]. She was associated frequently with rivers, as in Elis, where she received the names
'Αλφειαία and 'Αλφειωνία [4], and where she was worshipped under
these titles at an altar by the side of the Cladeus and at the
mouth of the Alpheus ; with these names is connected the
ancient legend of the love of Alpheus for Artemis, a legend
transplanted from Elis to Syracuse, where the name Ortygia
proves the old association of the locality with the goddess [a].
The antiquity of this worship of Artemis 'Αλφειαία and of the
combined cult of the goddess and the river-god is indicated by
the curious legend given in Pausanias [b], how, to secure herself
from the pursuit of Alpheus, Artemis celebrated with her
nymphs a festival in the night by Letrinoe, where Alpheus
joins the sea, and how she daubed the faces of her attendants
with clay to prevent him recognizing them. As clay-daubing
is a common practice in savage rites of initiation and purification, we may believe this to be an aetiological myth invented
to explain some primitive ceremony performed by the worshippers of Artemis on the banks of the river.

The goddess of still and running water is also naturally
a goddess of trees and fish. The strange worship of Artemis
'Απαγχομένη, the 'hanging Artemis,' at Kaphyae in Arcadia [6]
must have originally been consecrated to the goddess of vegetation. Pausanias tells us a curious story concerning it which
conceals the meaning of the ritual : once upon a time certain
children in play attached a noose to the neck of her idol and
said that they were hanging Artemis ; whereupon the men of
Kaphyae stoned them, but the angry divinity smote their
wives with a disease, and the oracle bade them atone for
the innocents' death ; the Kaphyans obeyed its injunction, and
instituted the cult of the 'hanging Artemis.' The custom of
hanging the mask or image of the divinity of vegetation on a
tree to secure fertility, of which other instances will be noted [c],
sufficiently explains these and similar stories ; and we may

[a] Vide p. 432. The connexion
between Syracuse and Delos, between
Alpheus, Arethusa, and Artemis, is
illustrated by the passage in Pindar [4],

and by the statement of Pindar's scholiast
that a temple of Artemis 'Αλφειώα stood
in Ortygia [4].   [b] 6. 22, 5.
[c] Aphrodite-chapter, p. 634.

illustrate the ritual of Kaphyae by a relief found at Thyrea showing the image of Artemis hanging on a garlanded tree [a].

The tree-goddess was worshipped in Arcadia with epithets such as Καρυᾶτις[7] and Κεδρεᾶτις[8], the goddess of the nut-tree and the cedar, and we may suppose the title Δαφναία[9], the goddess of the laurel, which was attached to her in Laconia, to be derived from her original character and not to have been borrowed from her later association with Apollo. In the Laconian legend and cult of Boiae she appears to have been identified with the myrtle[11 a]; and these records attest that in Lacedaemon tree-worship was especially prominent in the religion of Artemis.

It is noteworthy that there are no cultivated trees associated with the goddess[b]; and we may compare with the facts just mentioned the story that her idol at Sparta was found in a willow-brake, and was bound round with withies[c]; hence came the title Ἄρτεμις Λυγοδέσμα[10]. The close relation between her and the nymphs of the wood may have arisen from their common connexion with trees. Thus at Teuthea in Achaea she was worshipped under the general name of Νεμιδία or Νεμυδία[12], the goddess of the woodland pasture[d]. As with the trees of the wood, so, at least in one instance, she is associated with the wild flowers ; for it was probably not merely as a sister of Apollo, but by the right of her own nature, that she was called Ὑακινθοτρόφος, 'the nurturer of the hyacinth,' at Cnidus[13].

Though none of her titles expressly designate her as a fish-goddess, yet the strange form of Eurynome in the Arcadian worship[14] seems to indicate that this conception was not alien to the earliest character of Artemis in this country. We learn from Pausanias that at Phigaleia a mysterious goddess was worshipped at the junction of two streams, in a temple which was opened once a year only and which was surrounded with a grove of cypresses : the image in the temple was chained

[a] *Ann. dell' Inst.* 1829, Tav. c.

[b] We find the fir-cone a badge of Artemis on a coin of Perge, according to Mionnet, *Suppl.* 5. 439.

[c] The epithet Φακελῖτις[11] given her at Syracuse probably alludes to the custom of wrapping the idol round with branches.

[d] We may compare with this title her association with the nymphs of the river Amnisus in Crete ; Callim. *Dian.* 15 ; Apoll. Rhod. 3. 877. Cf.[25].

to its place, and had the upper parts of a woman and the lower of a fish : to the popular mind, he tells us, this was another form of Artemis ; but the learned knew that the goddess of the temple and the image was Eurynome, the daughter of Oceanus, the sea-goddess mentioned by Hesiod and Homer. In Roscher's *Lexicon* the latter view is accepted as correct ; but Preller and Welcker, without much discussion, take what appears to have been the view of the people [a]. Much may be urged in favour of the popular belief. In the first place, why should a scarcely known sea-goddess receive so strange a worship in a place so far inland as Phigaleia, where the inhabitants were landsmen of a very primitive kind ? And why should her temple be planted round with cypresses, which as wild trees might belong naturally to Artemis [b]?

Again, the title Εὐρυνόμη seems to be one of the descriptive and general appellatives, like Καλλιστώ and Δέσποινα, used to denote one of the goddesses pre-eminent in the land. Now in Arcadia this must either have been Artemis, or Demeter, or Persephone ; but the fish-form would be appropriate to neither of the two latter, but only to Artemis Λιμνᾶτις. And even if we took the other view, we should have to say on the evidence of Pausanias that the popular imagination associated Artemis so closely with the waters and the life of the waters that it could see their native Artemis in a statue of a goddess of the sea [c].

It is doubtful whether we are to consider such titles as Νηοσσόος[15], Ἐκβατηρία[17], Εὐπορία[16], which designate the goddess who brings the mariner to the haven where he would be, to have come to her through a natural extension of the notion and functions of the water-goddess, or whether she gained them from her relations with Apollo, or from her association with the Oriental goddess of Phoenicia, Asia Minor, and

[a] Roscher's *Lexicon, s. v.* Eurynome ; Preller-Robert, *Griechische Myth.* 1. p. 318 ; Welcker, *Griech. Götterl.* 1. p. 651. The affinity of the Phigaleian goddess with Artemis Limnatis is assumed by Immerwahr, *Kulte und Mythen Arkadiens*, p. 155.

[b] Vide Bötticher, *Baumcultus*, p. 493.

[c] It might be believed that Eurynome was one of the titles that Artemis borrowed from the Oriental Aphrodite, as we hear of Eurynome the wife of Adonis in Servius (*Eclog.* 10. 18). But Arcadia lies remote from Oriental influences and was scarcely touched by the legend of Aphrodite.

Cyprus, whose maritime character was recognized. At Troezen the temple of Poseidon was shared by Artemis Aeginaea, and at Eleusis we hear of the common temple of Artemis Propylaea and Poseidon the Father; his statue stood in the temple of Artemis Iphigenia at Hermione[18]. But whether they belong to the Greek Artemis proper or not, these sea-titles are certainly of more recent date than the very early period with which we are still concerned.

The worship of Artemis at Munychia, in its primitive form at least, seems to have had no reference to the sea. And it is unnecessary to regard the Artemis at Aulis as a maritime goddess merely because she sent contrary winds; for, as has been often remarked, any deity or any departed hero might do this: and the legend of the anger of Artemis against the Atridae is connected with an incident of the chase.

In certain cases these titles may have come to her by a natural process of development; for as the tribes of shepherds and hunters who worshipped her became seafarers, the goddess herself might be supposed to take to the sea.

Still more light is thrown on the early character of Artemis by considering what animals were habitually regarded as sacred to her: it is rare and exceptional to find her related by way of sacrifice, legend, or cult-name with the animals of the higher agricultural community, with the ox or the horse or the domestic pig; and in certain localities the calf and the sheep were tabooed in her ritual[51]. She is rather the patroness of the wild beasts of the field, the animals of the chase, with which—as will be soon mentioned—her life is connected by the mysterious tie which in very early religions binds the deity to the animal world. The hare, the wolf, the hind, the wild boar, and the bear are consecrated to her by sacrifice or legend; and we may take the description of the yearly offerings to Artemis Λαφρία at Patrae[19] as best illustrating her nature as a goddess of the wild life of the woods. The priestess, a maiden regarded probably as the human counterpart of the goddess, was drawn in a chariot by stags; and Pausanias speaks of the great holocaust of stags and fawns, wolves and bears, and birds which were all thrown or

driven into the flames of a great fire; we gather also that
tame animals and cultivated fruit were offered, as was natural
in the later period. It may have been the costliness of this sacrifice that gave her the name Βαθύπλουτος recorded by Suidas [19] [e].
The title Λαφρία, signifying possibly 'the devourer,' is proper
to the Calydonian goddess, and it was from Calydon that the
worship of Artemis Λαφρία probably spread to Phocis, Doris,
and Cephallenia, and certainly to Patrae and Messene [19].

In the legend of the colonization of Boiae, the hare appears
to be the embodiment or representative of Artemis; for the
oracle had said that the goddess would show the settlers where
they should dwell, and a hare suddenly appeared and, having
guided them to the spot, disappeared into a myrtle-tree [a].

The close connexion between Artemis and the wild boar is
illustrated by the story of Meleager, as sketched by the *Iliad*:
it was Artemis herself, for a reason that will concern us later,
who sent the boar; and the strife that ensues between the
Kouretes and the Aetolians over the possession of his head
and skin is an indication of the divine character of the beast.
Much later and historical illustration may be offered of this
association of the boar with Artemis: a fragment of Diodorus
Siculus [b] contains the story that Phintias, the tyrant of Acragas,
dreamed that while hunting the wild boar he was attacked and
slain by the wild sow; and he appears to have appealed to
the protection of Artemis Σώτειρα by striking coins with the
head of the goddess under this designation on the obverse,
and a wild boar's head on the other side [c]. The title Καπροφάγος [20], by which the goddess was known in Samos, refers
probably to the sacrificial offering of the wild boar, at which
she was supposed to partake of his flesh or blood.

That the lion and the wolf were sacred to Artemis is proved
by the Syracusan custom, referred to by Theocritus, of leading
a lioness in certain festal processions instituted in her honour [21],
and by the cult-epithet Λυκεία which attached to her at
Troezen [22]; and it is unreasonable to say that such a title
came to her merely from her later connexion with Apollo,
the wolf-god, as it belongs even more naturally to her than

[a] Paus. 3. 22, 12.   [b] 22. 5.   [c] Head, *Hist. Num.* p. 108.

to him[a]. But the wild animals with which she was most
frequently associated in cult and in legend[b] were the boar
and the stag or fawn ; in the records of literature and in the
monuments of art, the latter appears as her most familiar
companion, and two at least of her cult-names were derived
from it : we hear of Artemis Ἐλαφία[4] in Elis, and Ἐλαφηβόλος
in Pamphylia[24a], and we could infer that the latter was one of
her common sacred titles, both from the frequency of its use
in the older and later poetry and from the name of the Attic
month Ἐλαφηβολιών, which, like most of the other months,
derived its name from a sacred title of a divinity; sacrifice
being offered in this month, according to the author of the
Etymologicum Magnum, to Artemis Ἐλαφηβόλος. A month
of the same name occurred in the calendar of Iasos and
Apollonia[24b] in Chalcidice ; and we hear of the festival of the
Ἐλαφηβόλια, celebrated with great pomp down to the time of
Plutarch, at Hyampolis, to commemorate a Phocian victory
over the Thessalians[24c].

Finally, in this connexion it may be mentioned that the
quail, the bird of spring, that migrated in the early months of
the year from Africa to Greece, was in some way consecrated
to Artemis. Ortygia, near Syracuse, near Delos, near Ephesus,
and in Aetolia[25], probably means the place of the quail-
goddess, and from an expression in a line of Aristophanes'
Birds, in which Leto is called 'the mother of the quail[c],' we
gather that Artemis was herself at some time vaguely conceived of as a quail, though the bird is not found as her emblem
in any of the artistic representations. We have little direct
evidence that Ortygia was a common sacred title, but we
gather from Sophocles that she was thus styled in Euboean
worship[25]. And we may believe that this association between
the goddess and the bird was derived from some primitive
cult-idea, for we note that in other parts of the Mediterranean

[a] Artemis is seen on coins of Troezen
of the imperial period holding the head
of a wolf. Her title Λυκοᾶτις was
derived from the Arcadian Λυκόα, the
'wolf-city[22].'

[b] The mysterious stag with golden

horns, captured by Heracles, was perhaps an ancient form of Artemis herself,
and, according to Pindar, was sacred to
Artemis Orthosia[23].

[c] *Av.* 870.

and in another religion the quail appears to have been a sacred and mystic bird; for instance, there was an annual sacrifice of the quail at Tyre in commemoration of the resurrection of Heracles[a].

All these special relations and affinities are comprised under the title of Artemis Ἀγροτέρα[26], which Homer gives her, and under which she was worshipped in Athens, Laconia, Megara, Olympia, Achaea, Megalopolis, and elsewhere[26 a–h]. The sacrifice at Agrae in Attica was of special importance; five hundred she-goats were offered annually by the polemarch to Artemis Ἀγροτέρα as a thanksgiving for the victory of Marathon, and it was one of the special duties of the ephebi to assist in the ritual[26 f]. Spartan religion prescribed the sacrifice of a she-goat to Agrotera before the king began the campaign or the battle[26 b].

As regards the relations between the goddess of the wild and the animal world, it is important to observe that while Greek poetry and art more usually describe her as the huntress and destroyer, the older religion was more familiar with the conception of her as the protector and patroness of wild animals, and especially of those that were with young[b]. According to Xenophon, the true sportsman would spare the very young hare for the sake of Artemis[26 k]. 'Very kindly is the fair goddess to the tender whelps of ravening lions, and to the sucking young of all the beasts of the field '; 'she loathes the banquet of the eagles' who 'devoured the pregnant hare.' These striking words of Aeschylus[c], which might seem to anticipate the modern sentiment of kindness to animals, really express the view of very primitive religion, in which that sentiment was in some cases a sacred belief and possessed far greater force than it possesses now.

In fact these features of the earliest worship of Artemis suggest a cult which, though it had already advanced beyond totemism, yet retained traces of totemistic ideas. We may thus explain the legend and ritual in which the animal is in

---

[a] Athenae. p. 392. Vide Robertson Smith's *Religion of the Semites*, p. 449.

[b] The only cult-titles that designated her as the destroyer are Ἐλαφηβόλος and probably Λαφρία, and Ποδάγρα in Laconia[26 i].   [c] *Ag.* 138. 135.

some way identified with the deity or with the worshipper, and on rare and solemn occasions is eaten in the sacrificial meal in which the deity and his people are drawn more closely together. Now the early myths and cults of Artemis furnish evidence of this stage of religious thought. The above-mentioned epithet of Leto 'Ορτυγομήτρα would suggest that there was once a belief that the quail was another form of Artemis; a legend is given by Apollodorus that she ran between the Aloades in the form of a hind, and on a coin which Müller quotes, and which he ascribes to Delos, the goddess appears to have been represented with stag's horns [a]. And we have the story mentioned by Pausanias [b] that she guided the new settlers to the site of Boiae, a town of Laconia, in the form of a hare.

But it is the legends of Arcadia and Attica that best reveal the strange bond that once existed between Artemis and the animal world. In the old Arcadian myth of Arcas and Callisto we have a confused story, which has been well interpreted by Müller [c], and which contains vague allusions to a very ancient cult-form that deserve notice. The evidence that he puts together makes it certain that in this story Callisto, the beloved of Zeus, the mother of Arcas and of the Arcadian race, the nymph who was the comrade of Artemis, wearing the same dress and sharing her pursuits, and who was changed into a she-bear, is none other than Artemis herself [d]: he notices that Καλλίστη is a frequent poetical title of Artemis, and was used at Athens as a term of cult [27], and that on the very hill where the nymph Callisto was supposed to be buried a temple was raised to Artemis Καλλίστη [27].

From this myth alone, then, we might conclude that the bear was regarded sometimes as the very goddess; and this becomes clearer still by comparing the Arcadian legend with the worship of Artemis Βραυρωνία at Brauron, Athens, and Munychia [30, 31].

[a] *Dorians*, p. 379, note 1, quoted from the collection of Payne Knight; I have been unable to trace this coin further.

[b] 3. 22, 9.

[c] *Proleg.* pp. 73-76.

[d] Other evidence for this view is given by the fact that her other names appear to have been Μεγιστώ and Θεμιστώ, evidently titles of a divinity, and that she was called the daughter of Lycaon, a title probably of the Arcadian Zeus [29].

of which the significance from this point of view has been well shown by Mr. Lang [a]. It is important to put together the passages from which we obtain our knowledge of this ritual [32], which presents a very interesting problem, but one that is often evaded in the study of Greek religion [b]. We learn from Aristophanes that it was the custom for young maidens, clothed in a saffron robe, to dance in the Brauronian ceremonies of Artemis, and that in this dance they, as well as the priestess, were called 'bears'; the saffron robe was possibly worn in order to imitate the tawny skin of the bear [c], and probably in the earliest times of the rite an actual bear-skin was worn by the dancers. The dance was called ἀρκτεία, and the maidens who took part in it were between five and ten years of age. Various explanations are given of this strange ritual by the scholiast on the passage in the *Lysistrate*, by Suidas, and by the writer in Bekker's *Anecdota* : the bear was once a tame bear who lived amongst them : or a wild bear appeared in the Peiraeeus and did much damage ; some one slew it and a pestilence followed, whereupon Apollo ordered the people to sacrifice a maiden to the 'bear Artemis [d],' but a goat was offered instead by a man who called it his daughter. The scholiast merely says that Artemis was angry, and ordered every maiden by way of propitiation to dance the bear-dance before marriage and to pass round the temple wearing the saffron robe. The festival of the Brauronia acquired considerable public importance, and was organized every five years by the ἱεροποιοί.

[a] *Myth, Ritual, and Religion*, 2. pp. 212-215.

[b] In Roscher's *Lexicon* there is no critical reference to these Brauronian ceremonies that is of any value ; they are collected without much criticism by Welcker, I. pp. 571-574, and by Preller-Robert, *Griech. Mythol.* I. pp. 312-315. Schömann, *Griechische Alterth.* 2. p. 458, merely repeats an impossible theory of Lobeck's (*Aglaoph.* p. 74) concerning the meaning of ἄρκτοι.

[c] This seems to be implied by the scholiast on the passage, and is taken

for granted by Welcker. But the explanation is certainly doubtful ; for though the difference between saffron and tawny is not great, the usual bear-skin is brown. The saffron robe might have come to be worn merely as a sacred adornment, and to admit this would not invalidate the argument in the text.

[d] The phraseology in Bekk. *Anecd.* I. p. 444, is quite correct—τιμᾶν τὴν Ἄρτεμιν καὶ θῦσαι κόρην τῇ Ἀρκτῷ—but is misunderstood and regarded with suspicion by Welcker, *Griech. Götterl.* I. p. 574, n. 16.

Two things are clear from these accounts : (*a*) that the dance was a kind of initiation by which the young girls before arriving at puberty were consecrated to the goddess [a] ; (*b*) that the goddess and her worshippers and the bear were considered as of one nature, and called by the same name [b]. All this accords exactly with the many illustrations offered by totemistic religions of the belief that the tribe draw nearer to their deity by assuming the form or skin of the beast which they consider to be mysteriously related to themselves, and to be an embodiment of their god or goddess. It would be consonant with this belief if we found that at Brauron the bear was offered in a sacrificial meal to the goddess on solemn occasions : but the authorities make it clear that a goat or hind was usually the animal of sacrifice. Weight, however, must be given to the observation made by the scholiast on the passage in the *Lysistrate*, that a bear and not a hind was sacrificed in place of Iphigenia, and that the offering took place at Brauron [c]. It is probable that we have here a real local tradition, and the Brauronian sacrifice would be thus completely in accordance with ancient totemistic ideas : the maidens dressed up as bears assist at the sacrifice to the bear-goddess of an animal considered as akin to her and to themselves, and thus, if the sacrificial meal followed upon the act of oblation, they would be recruiting their physical life and reviving the communion between themselves and their divinity. At the same time the feeling of kinship with the bear would easily lead to the belief at a later time that the goddess was angry because her animal was killed. The substitution of the goat for the bear was a violation of the logic of the ceremony, and due probably to the great difficulty of procuring the larger animal in the later periods of the Attic sacrifice ; perhaps also to the chance that may have put the ritual into the hands of a goat-tribe,

[a] Vide Robertson Smith, *Religion of the Semites*, pp. 304, 309, for other instances of sacrifices upon initiation, showing the same principle as the Brauronian bear-dance.

[b] This view that the ἄρκτοι who danced were considered to represent the goddess may be illustrated by the dance of the Caryatides, the maidens who impersonated Ἀρτεμις Καρυᾶτις.

[c] The authority for the statement was probably Phanodemus in his *Atthis*.

for we have the legend that the female goat was treated as a kinswoman.

As illustrating this ceremonial sacrifice of a bear, which I have assumed to have been part of the original Brauronian ritual, we have the Arcadian myth of Callisto, which we may believe to be based on certain ancient cult-practices. That legend clearly attests the divinity of the bear [a], and yet the animal comes to be regarded as hostile to Artemis, and in certain versions of the story is finally slain. But in one most important account the animal is not slain in the ordinary secular manner, but is sacrificially offered, or comes near to being so offered, to a divinity, namely, to Zeus Λυκεῖος, into whose holy precincts she had accidentally strayed [b]. Although the bear has no real connexion with Zeus Lyceius, yet we seem to light again upon the traces of the same strange fact, concealed in doubtful myth, which we note in the cult of Brauron ; namely, the offering up of a holy animal, to a divinity the same in kind, by a tribe of worshippers who were united to both by blood-relationship.

The main part of the mysterious Arcadian story may be explained, if we suppose that the cult of Artemis Καλλιστώ, the bear-goddess, had died out, and nothing remained but the memory that the bear, a holy and peculiar animal, had been offered up to a divinity: the nearest analogies would be supplied by the existing ceremonies of the worship of Zeus Λυκεῖος, and this alien trait might have come into the story to explain the fact of the sacrificial offering; then it would become difficult to understand why, if the animal had been once beloved by Artemis, it should have been put to death at all in her name. The bear, therefore, was supposed to have incurred the enmity of the goddess, and, to explain the reason, reference was made to the probably later notion of the goddess's chastity [c].

[a] We have also a possible allusion to an Arcadian bear-dance, performed in the worship of Demeter or Artemis at Lycosura, in the human figure with the bear's head wrought on Damophon's peplos of Demeter.

[b] Hygin. *Poet. Astron.* 2. 1.

[c] Many instances might be given of this change in the point of view, whereby the animal that was once the favourite and the kinsman of the divinity, and therefore on rare occasions

With this stage of ritual the tradition of human sacrifice is closely connected; and it has been often supposed that even in historical times this rite, or a modification of it, survived in the worship of Artemis. But there is no clear and special evidence that this was ever the case. In the Thargelia at Athens two human καθάρματα, being probably criminals, were sacrificed in a sort of religious execution; but though Artemis, from her later connexion with Apollo [56], came to obtain a place in that festival worship, yet it does not appear that the καθάρματα were devoted to her. Again, the flagellation of the Spartan ephebi before the altar of Artemis ʹΟρθία [53 e], which has been almost always regarded as a modification of an earlier religious act of human oblation [a], is much more naturally explained by Prof. Robertson Smith as a ceremony of initiation, in which the youth is admitted into the full status of tribesman, and in which the altar or the sacred idol must be touched with his blood in order that the physical bond between him and his divinity may be strengthened [b]. At the same time this strange rite, which seems to have been still in vogue in the time of Philostratus, was intended also, no doubt, as a test of the youth's endurance; it is called a ἅμιλλα, a contest of fortitude, by Plutarch [53 e], and such cruel tests have been frequently imposed by savage tribes before the tribesman was admitted to the privileges of manhood. If it had been merely a fiction put in place of the primitive fact of a human sacrifice, it is not likely that the logic of the ceremony would have demanded the fictitious immolation of all the ephebi *en masse.*

But though we may not find much clear survival of actual or fictitious human sacrifice in the Artemis-worship of the historical periods, yet it might be thought that the traditions clearly imply its practice in the prehistoric age, and we are often obliged to regard tradition as actual evidence of

sacrificed, becomes regarded as hostile to that divinity. The same change happened in the relations of Bacchus and the goat.

[a] For instance by the Laconians themselves, according to Pausanias [53 c].

[b] Vide *Religion of the Semites,* pp. 303, 304; it was in accordance with the same notion that boys' hair was shorn and offered to Artemis at the Ionic festival of the Apaturia [74].

a prehistoric fact. But here it is quite possible that tradition, in one important case at least, has been misinterpreted. The crucial case is the legend of the sacrifice of Iphigenia at Aulis. With this is connected the Brauronian cult and the worship of the Tauric Artemis [31, 32, 52 b]; for Euripides, in bringing Iphigenia and the image to the shores of Brauron, is certainly following some local legend, and he is very explicit in his account of the local ritual[a]; also the scholiast on the passage in the *Lysistrate* says, ' Some declare that the events connected with Iphigenia took place in Brauron and not in Aulis [32].'

Moreover, the legend of the Tauric goddess speaks much about human sacrifice [35, 52], and we may believe that this rite was actually practised in the locality that was the original seat of the cult, whether Attica, Lemnos, or the Tauric Chersonese. Euripides makes Athena herself institute the ritual of the Tauric-Brauronian Artemis at Halae, and she ordains by way of ransom to the goddess for Orestes' life, that in the yearly sacrifice there the sword should be held to a man's throat and some blood should be drawn, 'for the sake of righteousness and that the goddess might have honour.' That warriors before a campaign require a sacrifice of peculiar efficacy to bring them into the closest communion with the divinity is quite in accord with primitive religious thought; and if a human victim were demanded, a kinsman or kinswoman would be required rather than an alien. Agamemnon, therefore, may have sacrificed his own daughter before setting out from the same motive that prompted Jephthah to offer his own on his return. But the only historical instance, if we could trust the record in Clemens[b],

---

[a] We should certainly gather from the passage at the close of the *Iphigenia in Tauris* that there were not two separate cults—one of Artemis Βραυρωνία at Brauron and one of Tauropolos at Halae—but only one, namely of Artemis Βραυρωνία worshipped at Halae near Brauron under the name Tauropolos. But Strabo mentions two temples, the one at Brauron the other at Halae,

probably erroneously, though Euripides' words are not quite conclusive; vide Wilamowitz, *Hermes*, 18. 254.

[b] Hiller, in *Hermes*, 21. p. 127, questions the authenticity of the citation. The citation from Πυθοκλῆς περὶ ὁμονοίας may be fictitious, but the explicit statement about the Phocian sacrifice is not likely to have been wholly imaginary.

of human sacrifice to Artemis, would be the sacrifice in her worship at Phocaea, where the human victim is said to have been burnt alive [35]. As regards what we can gather from tradition, the cult-legends of Brauron and Aulis may be explained otherwise. The central idea in them is that an animal-sacrifice was a substitution for an earlier human victim; but this theory of substitution could have been suggested by the mere form of the ritual itself, if the sacred animal was offered sacramentally as being akin to the tribe and the tribal divinity; for instance, if it was partially dressed up in human clothing, like the bull-calf of Dionysos in Tenedos, or if it was called by a human name. Now we have the right to infer that this was actually the case at one time in the Brauronian ceremonies, as the legend says expressly that the man who offered the goat ' called it his daughter [32].' A mass of evidence has been collected and interpreted by Prof. Robertson Smith on this primitive form of sacrifice, the sacramental offering of the ' theanthropic ' animal. This ritual which seems very strange to us, but was quite natural from the totemistic point of view, was certain to be misunderstood in the later period; the mysterious sacrificial animal, which was treated as if it were man, was supposed to be treated thus, because it was a mere make-belief for the human offering which the goddess originally demanded. But this may be really a ὕστερον πρότερον: the human sacrifice—where it actually was in vogue—may have been an outgrowth from the earlier offering of the quasi-human animal. And if human life was at any time offered up in the Brauronian rite, it would be probably truer to say, so to speak, that Iphigenia was a substitute for the doe than that the doe was a substitute for Iphigenia [a]. In either case there was a close affinity between the victim and the goddess; for we have abundant proof [34] that Iphigenia, like Callisto, is an appellative or a local cult-name of Artemis [b].

Among these legends of human sacrifice that admit of

---

[a] The theory by which I have tried to explain the Brauronian cult is merely that which has been very skilfully set forth by Prof. Robertson Smith in re-gard to other primitive sacrifices; vide especially *Religion of the Semites*, pp. 345, 346.

[b] Vide Müller, *Dorians*, p. 383.

the explanation suggested above may be placed the record in Porphyry concerning the sacrifice at Laodicea[a]; he tells us that originally a maiden had there been sacrificed annually to Athena, but that in his day a hind was substituted. As this animal is sacred to Artemis and has little or nothing to do with Athena, and as the Laodiceans claimed to possess the original image of the Brauronian Artemis-cult, and we find an armed figure of this goddess standing between two stags on the coins of the city[b], it is almost certain that Porphyry has given the wrong name to this armed divinity, who was really Artemis. And we may suppose that this sacrifice of the hind at Laodicea, belonging really to the Brauronian goddess, was accompanied by ritual that suggested an actual human offering, and hence the story may easily have arisen that the more cruel custom had once prevailed. Where the view prevailed that the animal took the place of the human life, we can believe that in times of great peril the latter might actually be offered as the more real and acceptable sacrifice, and this might grow to be even the customary rite[c].

Before passing on to the more advanced ideas in the worship of Artemis, we might consider the question whether in this earliest period we already find the maidenly character of the goddess recognized. It might be thought that this, which is her sole quality of great importance for a higher and more spiritual religion, must necessarily have been a virtue with which the imagination of a more advanced age endowed her. But though in one sense this is true, yet it is probable that the germ of the idea was to be found in the primitive period. In the first place, the Arcadian myth of Arcas and Callisto appears inconsistent in its earliest form with the character of the chaste goddess. A closely parallel myth is that which deals with the birth of Telephos, who is sprung from Auge the priestess, not indeed of Artemis, but of Athena Alea: it may be only an accident of local worship that brings the

[a] Athena[1a].
[b] Head, *Hist. Num.* p. 660.
[c] Vide pp. 453, 455 for further evidence of human sacrifice in the Artemis-cult. At Tegea, at the festival of Apollo and Artemis, the priestess pursued one of the worshippers with the pretended intention of slaying him[35].

latter goddess into the story, for the traces of Artemis are
clearly in the background. We find that Telephos was born
on Mount Parthenion, and we hear of a Τηλέφου ἑστία in the
neighbourhood of Artemisium near Oenoe; he was suckled
by the hind, the familiar animal of the goddess [a]. It seems,
then, most probable that the name Auge is an equivalent for
Artemis; and this belief receives further support from the
statement of Pausanias that the mother of Telephos was
worshipped at Tegea under the title of Αὔγη ἐν γόνασιν [b], and
was identified with Eileithyia, a goddess who was frequently
regarded as another form of Artemis. It may also be more
than a mere coincidence that both Telephos and Arcas come
near in the legend to slaying their own mother. The same
view of the primitive character of Artemis is presented by
another myth, the story of Atalanta and Meilanion, or Hip-
pomenes [c]. It becomes quite clear that Atalanta is Artemis
under another name, when we examine certain particulars
of the legend of her life [d]. She was fabled to have been
exposed as a new-born child by a spring on Mount Parthenion, and to have been nursed by a bear; she becomes
the mighty and swift-footed huntress who refuses marriage,
which had been forbidden her by an oracle; but she unites
herself with Meilanion, and Parthenopaios is their son, the
'child born out of wedlock': the head and skin of the boar
were offered to her by Meleager, and, like Artemis, she possessed a certain association with springs, as on the east coast
of Laconia a fountain was pointed out to Pausanias which had
been called forth by Atalanta [e]. In these myths, then, we
see obscure traces of a primitive goddess who is only maidenly
in the sense that she rejects marriage. Now when we look at
the manifold worships of Artemis in historic Greece, and consider how the cult-names interpret them to us, we are struck
with an apparent contradiction : whereas in the earliest poetry
and in many of the early myths the most prominent quality

[a] Paus. 8. 54, 5 ; Apollod. 1. 8, 6.
[b] Paus. 8. 48, 7.
[c] Vide Roscher, *s. v.* Atalanta.
[d] Vide Callimachus, *Hymn to Diana*,

221, &c.; Paus. 3. 12,9 ; Hyg. *Fab.* 270
(' Parthenopaius Meleagri et Atalantes
filius '); Ov. *Metam.* 10. 560, &c.
[e] Paus. 3. 24, 1.

in the goddess is her chastity, this is never presented to us in cult ; there is no public worship of Artemis the chaste. The term Παρθένος, where it is applied to Artemis, does not appear to have been a cult-epithet, and the worship of Artemis Κορία in Arcadia [38], about which Callimachus informs us, seems wrongly understood by Welcker[a] as devoted to Artemis the virgin : for κόρη does not mean virgin, and κορία might merely mean the goddess who assists girls ; and the legend that explains the title refers to the madness of the Proetides, who lead a wild life and reject marriage, until they are tamed at last by Artemis Ἡμερασία[38]. It appears, in fact, from those of her sacred titles that allude to the relation of the sexes, that she was especially concerned with the loss of virginity and with child-bearing ; for she was worshipped and invoked as λυσίζωνος[43], λοχεία[40], σοωδῖνα[42] ; maidens of marriageable age did certain honours to Artemis as κανηφόροι, and women in travail called upon Artemis for aid[39]. And she not only assisted but even encouraged child-birth ; for, as Euripides naïvely says, 'Artemis Λοχία would not speak to childless women[b].' In some communities she was identified with Eileithyia[41], and the title of Artemis Χιτωνέα or Χιτώνη[44], by which she was worshipped in Miletus and Syracuse, was explained as derived from the offerings of women's robes made to her after child-birth, or, as Euripides implies[32], made in behalf of those who had died in child-birth ; certain epigrams in the *Anthology* refer to these dedications[44]. And what is still more important is that, while such titles and the allusions to these functions are numerous, we can find scarcely any that recognize her as a goddess of marriage, though we must raise the question in regard to epithets such as Ἄρτεμις Πειθώ, Ἡγεμόνη, and Εὔκλεια. On the other hand, as will be noticed, she takes a special interest in the rearing of children, and certain ceremonies connected with their nurture are consecrated to her.

[a] *Griech. Gotterlehre*, 2. p. 393.
[b] The passage[39] quoted by the scholiast on Theocritus from Menander implies that women in travail called upon Artemis to forgive them for being no longer virgins ; but Artemis Λοχία would require no such apology.

But there is another feature occasionally discernible in her worship which seems still more alien to the character of the Greek Artemis, namely, orgiastic and lascivious dances and the use of phallic emblems in the ritual. At Elis we hear of the temple of Artemis Κορδάκα, the worship being accompanied with the dance that Pausanias considers to be native to the region of Sipylos and to have been brought into the Elean cult by the followers of Pelops [46]; and at Derrha on Taygetus, where Artemis was worshipped, we hear of a dance of the same character, called Καλλαβίδες [46], performed in her honour; while Hesychius mentions the λόμβαι [46] that were used in one of her cults, and which he describes as having a phallic significance [a].

It may be said, and by way of apology it was said by the worshippers of Elis and Laconia, that this ritual which had an orgiastic taint upon it was a foreign, an Oriental, innovation; for the Eleans attributed the worship of Artemis Κορδάκα to Pelops, and the procession that closed the festival of Artemis Ὀρθία was called Λυδῶν πομπή [46]. This may be true in the main, as much may have been borrowed across the sea for the Greek worship from the closely related goddess of Asia Minor. But these facts of ritual would in any case illustrate the point upon which stress is being laid, that the earliest worship of Artemis in Greece admitted ideas that were alien to the purity of the later conception. Now if we suppose this higher idea to have been prominent in the primitive period to which myth and cult bring us back, in the first place how could the virgin Artemis' have been so frequently identified with the various forms of the Asiatic goddess, whose worship in many details showed an impure character? Again, how was it that the virgin-goddess had so much to do with the processes of maternity? The cult of the primitive divinity usually reflects the present or past life of the worshipper, and human acts and states are attributed to the deity according to his or her special character and range of functions.

[a] It has been suggested that the ancient title of Artemis Ὀρθία in Laconia contained a similar allusion; yet this interpretation seems very far-fetched, and the term may be otherwise explained (vide p. 453, note b).

The idol of Αὔγη ἐν γόνασιν worshipped at Tegea no doubt represented the goddess of child-birth, who was closely akin to the Arcadian Artemis, as herself in the pangs of travail.

We have then abundant evidence, both from cult and myth, that the primitive Greek did not necessarily conceive of Artemis as a virgin-goddess, and that the cults of historical times scarcely, if ever, take notice of this side of her character[a]. In fact, on general grounds, it would be hard to show why a goddess of a primitive hunting and pastoral tribe, a divinity of the fertilizing waters, who fostered the wild growths of the earth and the sucklings of the beasts of the field, should have been naturally regarded by them as a virgin ; though a goddess whose character was derived from that period might easily fail to become a divinity of settled married life.

But, on the other hand, the belief in her virginal nature must have become a dogma at a comparatively early time. It is prominent in Homer, and it explains why the early myths of the Arcadians were careful to detach such figures as Callisto and Auge and Atalanta from Artemis herself, and to make them, rather than the goddess who had come to be regarded as virginal, the ancestresses of certain Arcadian stocks. Moreover, in certain myths that are probably pre-Homeric, the chastity of Artemis is plainly considered essential ; there is the well-known Actaeon story, and the special form of it preserved by Stesichorus[b], that Actaeon's love for Semele was thwarted by Artemis, a peculiar version

[a] There were certain rules of monastic severity and chastity imposed upon the priest and priestess of Artemis Ὑμνία worshipped at the Arcadian Orchomenos[124]; and this was undoubtedly a very ancient cult. But we cannot always argue from the character of the priesthood to that of the divinity ; for we find the necessity of chastity in the priest of one of the worships of Heracles. The priestess of Artemis Τρικλαρία in Achaea at Patrae[35], as of Ἀγροτέρα at Aegira[26], was a maiden ; whether this was the case in most centres of the Greek worship is doubtful. The priestess of Artemis Ὑμνία was necessarily a virgin, until the Arcadians found it advisable to alter this rule and select a married woman: ὁμιλίας ἀνδρῶν ἀποχρώντως ἔχουσα. We hear of Artemis Βραυρωνία being served by married priestesses. According to Artemidorus an ἑταίρα would not enter the temple of Artemis[36].

[b] Paus. 9. 2, 3.

which has been pressed to an unnatural interpretation by Klaus [a].

And that this is pre-eminently her character in the earliest literature must be due to some conception deeply rooted in the popular worship. How then is this strange contradiction to be explained? The usual solution of it, that Artemis became virginal through her close connexion with the Apolline worship, seems idle ; for the Apolline worship, though we may find certain high and spiritual conceptions in it, contained no essential idea of sexual purity: the sister of Apollo need not by any means have been a chaste goddess [b]. And it is much more unreasonable to say that she became pure when she became recognized as the moon ; for, in the first place, her lunar character, though very prominent in modern accounts of her, has no clear recognition in the more ancient and genuine legend and cult ; and, secondly, there is neither reason nor analogy for the supposition that in early mythology and worship the moon was necessarily a virgin.

A different explanation may be hazarded. In the period of the most primitive religion of Artemis the goddess was considered and addressed as Παρθένος, and this title would explain many geographical names in Greece, in the islands, and on the coasts of the Mediterranean [c]; and it seems

[a] *De Dianae antiquissima Naturâ,* Wratislaviae, 1881, p. 26 : Actaeon is considered by him to be another form of Zeus ; Artemis is his wife and jealous of Semele.

[b] We may add also that if the nymph Cyrene is rightly interpreted as an older form of Artemis, the relations between Apollo and Artemis were not always regarded as chaste and fraternal ; vide Roscher's *Lexicon, s. v.* Kurene.

[c] The ancient name of Samos was Parthenia, the island of the goddess Parthenos, given it, according to Strabo, by the Carians [36]: we have Mount Parthenion in Arcadia ; the city Parthenion in Euboea ; a river Parthenius in Paphlagonia associated by legend with Artemis, Steph. Byz. *s. v.* Παρθένιον and

Παρθένιος. The goddess in the Tauric Chersonese bore the name of Παρθένος, and the inscription from the Chersonese published in the *Revue des Études Grecques* contains the formula of the oath taken by the magistrates (circ. 150 B.C.) in her name; a goddess Παρθένος was worshipped at Neapolis in Thrace [36]. The same idea of a goddess who was at once Παρθένος and Μήτηρ existed in Phrygian religion ; vide Ramsay, *Hellenic Journal,* 10. 229. From the story told by Diodorus Siculus (5. 62), which is very full of aetiological fancy, we gather that there was a worship on the Carian Chersonese of a goddess Παρθένος, with surnames such as Μολπαδία, Ῥοιώ, Ἡμιθέα [125], and not originally regarded as virginal. Swine

probable that the term was widely prevalent in Asia Minor, especially in Caria, designating a goddess who was closely akin to Artemis and the Oriental Aphrodite[37]. But the oldest sense of Parthenos was not 'virginal' but 'unmarried,' as we might gather from the Carian legend alone; and in this sense her Oriental equivalent, a goddess of impure character and worship, was also Παρθένος[a]. In fact, Artemis Παρθένος may have been originally the goddess of a people who had not yet the advanced Hellenic institutions of settled marriage, who may have reckoned their descent through the female, and among whom women were proportionately powerful. Then when society developed the later family system the goddess remained celibate though not opposed to child-birth; and we may thus understand why she was always pre-eminently the goddess of women, and why maidens before marriage should offer their girdles and perform other probably piacular rites to Artemis[b]. Finally, as it was always necessary to consider the goddess unmarried, and at the same time her worship became more spiritual, the title Παρθένος may

are tabooed in her worship as in the cult of Aphrodite and Adonis; the story of her leap into the sea is the same as that told of Dictynna and Derketo the Syrian fish-goddess (Diod. Sic. 2. 4). She is connected with Apollo and the art of healing, and she aids women in travail. We have here a Carian-Cretan religion of an Artemis-Aphrodite; vide Aphrodite, pp. 637, 646.

[a] Vide Aphrodite-chapter, pp. 629, 657.

[b] There are two important Greek myths in which the leading motive is the rebellion of women against the married state, and both of them seem to have some relation to the worship of Artemis: (a) the myth of the daughters of Proetus, who, according to one version, treat the temple of Hera, the goddess of marriage, with contempt (Pherecydes ap. Schol. Od. 15. 225; Acusilaus ap. Apollod. 2. 2, 2), were punished by

Aphrodite and roamed in madness about the country, and whose example induced the other Argive women to desert their husbands and to slay their children; the Proetides are pursued by Melampus and a band of young men who are taught to dance a religious kind of dance as a curative for the women; they are finally healed in the temple of Artemis Ἡμερασία, and the temple of Artemis Κορία is consecrated in their memory[38]. Perhaps the pursuit of the young men was a ceremony connected with primitive marriage-customs and parallel to the race of armed youths in the wooing of Atalanta. (b) The myth of the Lemnian women who despise Aphrodite and slay their husbands. The whole island was sacred to the Tauric Artemis, and the legend indirectly connects this slaying with the spread of the Lemnian worship to the Tauric Chersonese; cf. Hygin. Fab. 15.

thus have acquired the higher sense, and expressed the stainless and chaste goddess. such as she came to be recognized, not expressly in cult, but in the imagination of the Greek world. It would on this theory have been the progress from the non-moral idea of the unmarried goddess to the moral conception of the virgin Artemis, a progress carried out by the change in the meaning of Παρθένος, that was of the greatest import for the Greek religious sense. For it was the personality of Artemis rather than of Athena that consecrated that idea of the beauty of purity, the ideal of the life unsullied by passion, which received here and there a rare expression in Greek literature and more frequently inspired the forms of art. The drama of the *Hippolytos* is unique in Greek, and perhaps in any literature; for here the law of chastity is a spiritual law, presented with no ascetic or unnatural sanction, but united with a genial delight in pure forms of life and action. And the poet conceives that such life is approved by Artemis. But in this play, as elsewhere, he shows himself above the religious thought of his age; for neither in the popular religion, nor in the general literature, is there any view clearly expressed that purity in the abstract was consecrated by any divine sanction, although unchastity under certain special conditions, and sometimes the breach of the marriage vow, were regarded as incurring divine reprobation [a].

In tracing the development of the worship of Artemis from the savage to the more settled and civilized period, we may first notice that she comes to have some connexion with agriculture and the breeding of the domestic animals. The goat was the animal most commonly used in her sacrifices [47], and it is possible that she acquired some of her cult-titles from it [b]; the local legend of the city Αἴγειρα in Achaea

---

[a] Vide Hera-chapter, p. 197. Cf. the story in Pausanias 8. 47, 4, that the tyrant of Orchomenos, having purposed to violate a maiden who destroyed herself to preserve her chastity, was slain by a Tegean whom Artemis stirred up in a dream.

[b] Αἰγιναία[18]—a doubtful title of Arte-mis, sometimes supposed to designate the goat-goddess—was connected in the local legend of Laconia with the Cretan goddess Britomartis, and was more probably derived from the island Aegina, where the Cretan cult had settled. Κνακεᾶτις, Κνακαλησία, Κναγία, are appellatives [47] that have been supposed to refer to the

connected the name with the goats to whose horns the natives on one occasion attached torches and thus scared away the invading army of the Sicyonians [a]; a temple was then founded near Aegira to Artemis Ἀγροτέρα [26], on the spot where the fairest she-goat, the leader of the flock, rested on the ground, the influence of the goddess being supposed to be working in her favourite animal.

In Sparta, as has been mentioned above, the custom prevailed of the king sacrificing a goat to Artemis in front of the army before charging the enemy, and we hear frequently of the great annual sacrifice in Attica of five hundred she-goats as a thank-offering to the goddess for the victory of Marathon.

Once, at least, we may believe that Artemis, like Athena, was associated, if only accidentally, with the breeding of horses [b]. In Arcadia, in the territory of the Pheneatae, was the worship and temple of Artemis Εὐρίππα [48], and near it was a bronze statue of Poseidon Hippios of mythical dedication; the local legend explained the statue and the temple by saying that Odysseus' horses had strayed, and the hero found them here. In this instance the local legend has probably interpreted a cult-name correctly; for εὐρίππα could not mean 'the inventor of the use of horses,' but simply 'the finder of them'; and it was natural for those who followed them and found them when they strayed into the wilds to give thanks to the goddess of the wilds, who led the owners to their lost property. It is possible that this cult at Pheneos was introduced by a Lapith-Thessalian immigration, and may have been derived from that of Artemis Pheraea in Thessaly, who, like her sister Hekate, was for some reason connected with horses [c]. In any case the association of the Greek Artemis with horses is slight enough, and it is hard to say why Pindar once or twice speaks of her as 'the driver of the steed.'

goat Artemis, but the interpretation of them is doubtful, and Pausanias' statements about the local cults are not helpful. The only reason for this explanation is that κνηκός means pale yellow, and κνάκων is a term applied to the goat by Theocritus.

[a] Paus. 7. 26, 2–3.

[b] Vide Fraser, *The Golden Bough*, vol. 1, p. 6, for the myth of Hippolytus and the significance of the horse in the Artemis-cult.

[c] Vide Immerwahr, *Kulte und Mythen Arkadiens*, p. 40.

It is not improbable that the epithet Ἡμερασία [38], which attached to Artemis and was explained by the legend of the taming of the Proetides, referred originally to the domestication of animals. We may conclude that the breeding of cattle was in some places consecrated to Artemis ; for the natural meaning of the epithet Ταυροπόλος is the ' bull-tender,' and thus it becomes equivalent to the name Πολυβοία [49], which Hesychius found in some of his authorities as a title of Artemis. The worship of Artemis Ταυροπόλος is proved to have existed in Attica, in the island Ikaria near Samos, at Phocaea, Pergamon, Smyrna, Magnesia on the Maeander, and Amphipolis, in Paros and Andros [50]. The name of the city Ταυρόπολις in Caria is probably of the same origin. We have a right to interpret this cult-name of the goddess, which was rather widely diffused among the Ionic communities, by simply referring it to her more advanced pastoral and agricultural functions, although it has been supposed to have a lunar reference. For, though the later tendency of Greek religious exegesis was to give to names and persons of divinities a celestial meaning where this was possible [a], we find no expression of the lunar character of Tauropolos in ancient cult and in the older literature and art. In the passage in the *Ajax* of Sophocles, the chorus surmise that the madness of Ajax may have been sent him from Artemis Tauropolos, because it turned him against the cattle [50 l]. The coins of Amphipolis, where this worship had been implanted from Athens, and where the goddess was honoured by a λαμπαδηφορία, display her wearing the polos on her head and riding on a bull with a torch in each hand ; and this emblem, as will be noticed below, need have no reference to the moon, although it might seem natural to interpret the horns that are seen rising from

[a] For instance, vide the scholiast, *ad Soph. Aj.* 172 Ταυροπόλος ἡ αὐτὴ τῇ Σελήνῃ ἐστὶ καὶ ἐποχεῖται ταύροις, ἣν καὶ ταυρωπὸν ὀνομάζουσι ; Porph. *de Lun.* ch. 18 ; Suchier, *de Dian. Brauron.* p. 50, and Preller, 1. p. 252 ; vide Suidas, *s. v.* Ταυροπόλος. If the bull-riding Europa were certainly a type of the moon-goddess (and this is by no means certain, vide p. 479), it would not follow that ταυροπόλος must be the same ; the bull appears in the worship or representations of many divinities that have no lunar character at all, such as Themis, Dionysos, Demeter, Hestia, Τύχη, Apollo, Poseidon.

her shoulders on another coin of this city which bears the inscription Ταυροπόλος as the crescent of the moon [a]. The cult of Munychia, which was connected with Artemis Tauropolos and the Brauronian worship [32], spread to Pygela on the Ionian coast [30b] from Ephesus or Miletus, and on one of the coins of Pygela [b] we have the head of Artemis Munychia on the obverse, on the reverse the figure of a bull charging.

In connexion with the cult which has just been examined, we must notice the obscure and almost legendary account of the Tauric Artemis, and the chief localities of this worship, Lemnos, Attica, and the Crimea [52]. The Brauronian worship is associated, as has been shown, with the legend of Artemis Ταυρική, of Orestes and Iphigenia, with the bear-dance, and with a ritual that seems to point to a primitive practice of human sacrifice. We have also the legend that the Tyrrhenian Pelasgi bore away the Brauronian image and the sacred maidens to Lemnos [32], and we hear of the μεγάλη θεός in this island to whom maidens were sacrificed [52b], and who was called Chryse, the sister of Iphigenia according to the later genealogists; we have reason to think that the ἀρκτεία or bear-dance was practised in Lemnos as in Attica; and, finally, Lemnos, as well as Brauron, is connected with the Tauric Chersonese by the tradition that its king Thoas migrated thence to the Crimea [c]. The question as to the original home of this worship has been much debated, and cannot be decided on the evidence; and it is needless here to discuss Müller's plausible theory [d] that it originated in Lemnos as a Minyan worship, and spread thence to Byzantium and the Black Sea; we may also hold that it was aboriginal in Attica, and that the earliest Greek adventurers in the Black Sea found in the Crimea a goddess whose name and whose rites reminded them of the Tauric. It cannot, at least, have come from the Black Sea originally, for the cults of Brauron and Lemnos point to a very early period, and the Crimea was opened to Greek colonization at a comparatively late time. All that

[a] But vide *Artemis - Monuments,* p. 529.
[b] Head, *Hist. Num.* p. 508.
[c] Hygin. *Fab.* 15.

[d] *Orchomenos,* pp. 304–306; *Dorians,* I. 384; he conjectures that Ταυρική was the original name of Lemnos.

we can gather about this Artemis Ταυρώ or Ταυρική is that this cult was associated with a vague legend of bloodshed[a], with the name of Iphigenia, and with a certain type of primitive idol to which the title 'Ορθία was given. Where this type prevailed in the Artemis-cults of various parts of Greece, the legend that it was brought by Orestes and Iphigenia was likely to spring up; and we cannot find any other ground for the connexion between Artemis 'Ορθία or 'Ορθωσία, in Laconia and other places, and the Tauric Artemis, than the similarity of the traditional shape of their images and the survival of certain cruel rites[b]. The question of interest is whether Artemis Ταυρική and Artemis Ταυροπόλος, who were connected in the legends of Brauron and Aricia [53 i],

[a] It is only in regard to the Chersonese that we can speak positively of human sacrifice in historical times, which seems to have continued till a late period, the second century A. D., if we can trust the words of Scymnus Chius [35].

[b] We find the worship of Artemis 'Ορθία or 'Ορθωσία in Athens, Megara, Sparta, on Mount Lycone in the Argolid, in Arcadia, Elis, and Epidauros, and at Byzantium [53]. We hear most of the Laconian cult [53 c], and we gather that in spite of its more humane features, the musical contests and the procession of the maidens bearing the sacred robe, a singularly wild and barbaric character attached to the worship and the idol. The men who first found the idol in a withy-bed went mad, and the earliest worshippers came to blows and slew each other on the altar, and the idea always prevailed that this goddess craved human blood. For this reason Pausanias considers that the Spartan image had the best right of any to be considered the actual idol brought from the savage Tauri by Orestes and Iphigenia, although Attica, Cappadocia, and Lydia claimed this honour. We can understand why so many places in the Mediterranean should have made this claim for their sacred image [53] if we interpret the title 'Ορθία as designating nothing more than a primitive type of the erect wooden idol; and this is the most natural explanation: the phallic sense which Schreiber (Roscher's *Lexicon*, ss. 586, 587) imputes to the word is quite impossible; and the moral sense of 'upright' is most unlikely when we consider the primitive age to which the worship belonged; although in later times the term may have advanced to a higher meaning, as in Epidauros, where, according to a late inscription [53 f], it denoted the healing-goddess who makes the sick man arise and walk. Schreiber's objection that most primitive idols were of the erect type, and therefore the name 'Ορθία would not have been used to designate a particular one, is no real objection; the worshipper of one locality may name his image without regard to those elsewhere; just as all goddesses were beautiful, but one was specially called 'the beautiful' in a local cult. Then if, as seems likely, the Laconian idol called 'Ορθία was the most famous, its title and its legend of Orestes would come to be attached elsewhere to other idols of Artemis of the same type and perhaps of the same savage character.

are really cognate.   They are pronounced to have been originally quite distinct by Preller, Welcker, and Schreiber, for reasons that seem insufficient to prove distinctness of cult. Schreiber relies on the argument that the Samian ritual of Artemis Tauropolos was genuinely Greek and harmless, being innocently maintained with cakes and honey, while the Tauric was a bloodthirsty goddess, whose ritual demanded human victims, and whose character was vicious and orgiastic. But a different ritual might be consecrated in different places to a divinity whose worship nevertheless expressed the same idea ; and we do not know that the difference was so great as he asserts ; for, on the one hand, that innocent Samian sacrifice described by Herodotus[54] was offered to Artemis, but not, so far as we know, to Artemis Tauropolos, whose cult was found in Icaria but not in Samos[a], and, on the other hand, we hear, though on doubtful authority, that human sacrifices were offered to Artemis Tauropolos at Phocaea[b].

The Attic-Lemnian worship of Artemis Ταυρική may have sprung up quite independently of the Tauropolos cult, but it seems reasonable to suppose that it contained the same reference to the agricultural functions of the goddess.   For if Ταυρώ is not a name of Artemis that has been derived from the Black Sea, a theory impossible to accept, what else could it mean in its application to her but the 'bull-goddess'?   The Greeks of the fifth century certainly understood it as such ; for Euripides speaks of the worship imported by Orestes and Iphigenia to the coast of Attica, not far from Brauron, as that of Ταυροπόλος, and from the natural connexion of the two terms Nikander invented the story that it was a bull, and not a hind, that was sacrificed as substitute for Iphigenia[32].   We do not hear, indeed, that the bull was an animal ever consecrated by sacrifice to the Tauric goddess in Attica or Lemnos, yet the term Ταυροφάγος[32], the bull-devourer, applied by Nikander to Artemis of Aulis, is not likely to have been invented by him, and it is analogous to the title καπροφάγος noted above[c];

---

[a] Schreiber (Roscher's *Lexicon*, p. 568) makes the same mistake as Stephanus of Byzantium, who quotes carelessly

from Strabo (*s. v.* Ταυροπόλιον).
[b] Vide pp. 439, 440.
[c] P. 431.

and a singular story is preserved by Aristotle[53 k] that a golden bull stood on the altar of Artemis Orthosia, who, at Sparta at least, was identified with the Tauric goddess. Whether the ritual of Artemis Munychia, who was closely associated with the Brauronian goddess, contained an allusion to the agricultural Tauropolos is uncertain; we only hear of sacred ἀμφιφῶντες used in the Munychian sacrifice, which appear to have been cheese-cakes stamped with torches [30 a].

We have also an allusion to Artemis as a goddess of agriculture in the legends at Patrae about Artemis Τρικλαρία; when her temple was polluted by the unchastity of Comaetho, the goddess refused to give the fruits of the soil: human victims were led to the river for sacrifice, 'crowned with wheat-stalks.' We have here probably a ritual designed to produce crops [a], and this is afterwards connected with the worship of Dionysos Aesymnetes, who came in from the North and caused the cruel practice to cease [35]. The chief goddess of Hyampolis in Phocis was Artemis, and part of the flocks were consecrated to her, and the fattest of the beasts were those that she reared [54 e].

The deity of agriculture and vegetation confronts us again and still more clearly in the Arcadian worship of Artemis, where she enters into very close association with Demeter and Despoina[55]. At Akakesion, before the temple of Despoina was a shrine of Artemis Hegemone, and on one side of the throne on which sat the two mysterious goddesses, Demeter and Despoina, the statue of Artemis was placed, clad in a fawn's skin, with the quiver on her shoulders, and in her hands a torch and two serpents. The details of the worship and of the artistic representation which are given by Pausanias, the association recognized here between these goddesses and Cybele, the mythic connexion of Despoina with the water-god, are facts enough to prove that we have here a primitive cult of the earth-goddesses, regarded as deities of vegetation; and that Despoina, whose real name Pausanias was shy to pronounce,

---

[a] For instances of the human victim used for agricultural purposes, vide Fraser's *Golden Bough*, vol. 1, p. 242–ʼ 249, 389–392; Mannhardt's *Baumkultus*, pp. 363, 364.

was originally Persephone, akin to the great Arcadian goddess Artemis. Elsewhere in Arcadia we find Artemis associated with Demeter and her daughter [55 b], and she enjoyed an altar in common with the Despoinae in the Altis of Olympia [55 c]. The serpents which she bore in her hand are the emblem of the earth-goddess, and give to Artemis something of the character of Hekate in this Akakesian cult; at Lycosura, on the other hand, the familiar animal of Artemis, the fawn, was consecrated to Despoina [55 d]. It was probably this Arcadian worship that led Aeschylus to call Artemis 'the daughter of Demeter [55]'; and it is this same more advanced aspect of her as a goddess of cultivated fruits that is illustrated by her later participation in the Attic Apolline feast of Thargelia [56], and perhaps by the legend that she was born in the spring-month of Thargelion [79 a].

From the facts that have been examined hitherto that relate for the most part to primitive conceptions and cults, it seems reasonable to conclude that Artemis in the earliest Greek religion was an earth-goddess, associated essentially and chiefly with the wild life and growth of the field, and with human birth. It was natural enough that the goddess of vegetative nature and fructifying water should become also a goddess of herds and cattle and agriculture[a]. But this advance was not carried far in the religious conception of Artemis, and it rarely appears in literature. The goat that feeds in wild places, rather than the cattle that graze in the field, was her pastoral animal; in the worship of Tauropolos it seems that the bull or the cow was rarely sacrificed to her, and Cicero [51] tells us that it was expressly forbidden to offer the calf to Artemis[b]. The interesting myth given us in the *Iliad*, that when the father of Meleager in Calydon was offering θαλύσια, or the first-fruits of the harvest, to the gods, he neglected Artemis and thus incurred her wrath, may

[a] We may suppose the same development in the functions and character of the local Semitic Baalim; vide Robertson Smith, *Rel. of the Sem.* p. 100.

[b] We may doubt whether this rule held everywhere; at Hyampolis in Phocis.[54c], where Artemis was especially worshipped, cattle in general seem to have been put under protection. Sacrifice was made to Artemis Λαφρία at Patrae of ἱερεῖα ἅπαντα[19], which appear from the context to be domesticated animals.

illustrate the fact that she was only received among the agricultural divinities with difficulty and at a comparatively late time. Callimachus tells us that the man on whom Artemis looks with 'smiling face and kindly heart' is blessed with increase of crops and herds[54e]; but 'the peaceful sway over man's harvesting' was mainly appropriated by Demeter, Persephone, and Dionysos : while Artemis, in regard to her physical functions and character, was never completely civilized.

The view that has here been taken about the original character of this divinity is opposed to the older and traditional theory which has been maintained by Welcker and Preller, namely, that she was originally a lunar goddess. To maintain this is to go beyond the evidence and to confuse the latest with the earliest period of the cult. It is obvious that Homer does not know her as a goddess of the moon ; neither was she known as such in the earliest centres of her worship. And some of her cult-titles, which have been supposed to have reference to the moon, have been misinterpreted or are of doubtful interpretation. For instance, the epithet Μουνυχία has been supposed by Welcker to stand for Μουνορυχία, ' she who walks alone at night ' ; but, though later writers have countenanced it, this is entirely pre-scientific etymology[a], and the word seems to have merely designated the harbour near the Peiraeeus from which the goddess was named, and is possibly derivable from a Phoenician term signifying ' the haven of rest.' Another title has been regarded as containing a clear reference to the moon, namely Αἰθοπία[57], by which she was known on the Euripus, and perhaps at Amphipolis : the word certainly means the 'burning-faced one'; but it is hazardous to refer all words that denote fire or brightness to the celestial bodies offhand, and to conclude that Αἰθοπία must mean the ' bright-faced' goddess of the moon. We cannot trace the origin of the name, which may have arisen from some peculiarity of an Artemis-idol[b], or in other conceivable

---

[a] Even if the etymology were better, it would take much to persuade us that the early Greek would apply such a phrase to the moon.

[b] Cf. Dionysos Μόρυχος and Κεχηνώς, names which probably arose from certain features of the local idol.

ways; and if we could interpret it with certainty, even then it would throw little light on the primitive period of worship, as we do not know when it came to be applied to the goddess. It seems to have been used by Anacreon as an epithet of Semele, who was certainly no moon-goddess, and may have alluded to the story of her fiery death.

There are other epithets which attach to Artemis, and which have some reference to fire. She was worshipped as Φωσφόρος in Messenia, Munychia, and Byzantium [58]; as Σελασία in Laconia [60]; as Σελασφόρος [59] in Attica. On Mount Krathis, on the borders of Arcadia and Achaea, there was a temple of Artemis Πυρωνία [61], from which the Argives fetched fire for the Lernaean festival. But none of these worships reveal an aboriginal lunar goddess; for in the first place we have no proof that they are very early, and in the earliest literature in which Artemis is pourtrayed neither torch nor fire is spoken of as her attribute; the passage in Sophocles which speaks of the 'gleaming torches of Artemis, wherewith she speeds over the Lycian mountain [62],' and which is the first, so far as I am aware, that refers to the fire-bearing goddess [a], certainly does not show that the poet regarded her as a lunar power [b]. As regards the representations in art, the torch does not appear in the hands of Artemis before the fifth century [c]; the first certain instance would be the torch-bearing figure on the Parthenon frieze, if the view now prevalent that this is Artemis be correct; and from the fourth century onward this is a common form.

In the next place, the cults of Σελασφόρος and Φωσφόρος are

[a] Neither in the lines descriptive of Artemis in the Homeric hymn to Aphrodite [125], nor in the smaller hymns to Artemis and Selene, nor in Hesiod's *Theogony* has she any association with the moon or fire: vide *Theog.* 371; *Hom. Hymn to Helios,* 6. 31; *Hymn to Herm.* 1. 100.

[b] We may suppose that the poet alludes to the fact mentioned in Max. Tyr. *Dissert.* 8 Λυκίοις ὁ Ὄλυμπος πῦρ ἐκδιδοῖ . . . καὶ ἔστιν αὐτοῖς τὸ πῦρ τοῦτο καὶ ἱερὸν καὶ ἄγαλμα.

[c] Welcker sees Artemis in the new-born child who holds two torches and stands on the knees of Zeus beneath the inscription Διὸς φῶς on a black-figured vase published by Minervini; *Mon. Inéd.* 1852, Taf. 1; but he has mistaken a male for a female child: the babe is undoubtedly Dionysos, and Διὸς φῶς, 'the light of God,' is a free interpretation of his name.

not known to have associated Artemis with the moon-goddess ; in the former she was combined with Apollo Διονυσόδοτος, and the legend that explained the Attic cult of Φωσφόρος at Munychia told how Thrasybulus, when marching from Phyle, was guided by a pillar of fire, and an altar was afterwards raised to ἡ Φωσφόρος[a]. Again, when the torch had come to be used in the ritual or to appear in the representations of Artemis, it is very doubtful whether it was primarily intended to designate the moon-goddess. For it belongs quite as naturally to the huntress who roams the woods by night or to the divinity of the earth, and it is still more frequently an attribute of Demeter and Persephone and of the company of Dionysos[b]; and Dr. Schreiber[c] seems right in comparing a religious idol of the torch-bearing Artemis preserved on an altar of the Museo Chiaramonti with a type of Demeter on Attic votive-reliefs. The character that Artemis bears in the worship of Despoina has been already examined, and it is clear that the torch which she carries in the group of Damophon is a badge of the chthonian divinity. The ceremonious or magical use of fire in the ritual of divinities who have power over vegetative nature is well known; the torch borne over the land is supposed to evoke by sympathy the fructifying warmth of the earth[d]. This would be the meaning of the practice which appears to have been observed in the cult of Artemis Ἀγροτέρα at Aegira, of binding lighted torches to the horns of goats[e], which receives striking illustration from the ceremony performed in the spring outside the temple of the great Syrian goddess at Hierapolis, the sacrifice called the πυρή or λαμπάς, in which trees laden with animals were set on fire[f]. The

[a] There is another context where φωσφόρος is applied to Artemis with a particular meaning—an epigram in the *Anthology* in which Artemis is praised as the goddess who gives children to the childless and sight to the blind, and is therefore called 'the bringer of light[62].'

[b] Of Artemis' association with Dionysos in cult we have no explicit proof except the account in Pausanias of the ritual of Artemis Triclaria and Dionysos Aesymnetes in Achaea[35]. She appears to have shared a temple with him and Asclepios at Corone in Messenia[70].

[c] Roscher's *Lexicon*, p. 595.

[d] Vide Mannhardt, *Wald- und Feld-Kulte*, I. pp. 521–525.

[e] The legend explained the custom as a *ruse de guerre*; vide p. 450.

[f] Luc. *de Dea Syr.* 49.

temple and statue of Artemis Προσηῴα, the goddess 'who faces the rising sun,' on the promontory of Artemision in Euboea [63], need not be supposed to have been consecrated to the moon-divinity, although Hesychius gives ἀνθήλιος as an epithet of Selene; for it was natural and common for statues to face in this direction, and the divinities to whom the herald in the *Agamemnon* goes to offer prayer are called the δαίμονες ἀντήλιοι.

Again, we cannot conclude that the Greek Artemis was from an early period recognized as lunar merely because she was associated with Hekate in the poems of Hesiod and in the Homeric hymn to Demeter; for there is no proof that Hekate herself, when she was first adopted into the Greek religion, was regarded clearly or solely as a lunar goddess. Nor, lastly, is Artemis to be called the moon-goddess because she was from of old a goddess of child-birth: for the functions of Λοχεία belong quite as naturally to the earth-goddess as to the moon, although Plutarch chose to interpret Artemis Eileithyia as identical with Selene [64].

The first evidence that we have of this lunar character of Artemis is the fragment of Aeschylus' *Xantriae*, containing the strange words, 'whom neither the ray of the sun beholds nor the starry eye of Leto's daughter,' if we suppose, as is natural, that 'Leto's daughter' is Artemis[a]. This misconception about the goddess, which the learned Alexandrine poets avoid, is rife in later Roman literature and later art which sets the crescent on her forehead [b].

How it is to be explained is a question upon which it is not necessary to dwell here. It seems to have arisen first from her close connexion with Hekate, and, secondly, from the

[a] It is true that Euripides calls Hekate also the daughter of Leto, but an Attic audience would certainly interpret Λητῴα κόρη as Artemis; vide Hekate [3].

[b] It appears that Plutarch [30] supposes that the Greeks at the time of the battle of Salamis already worshipped Artemis as a lunar deity, for he states that they consecrated the 16th of Munychion to her, the day 'on which the Greeks conquered at Salamis and the goddess shone with full moon.' Mommsen (*Heort.* p. 404, note) points out the absurdity of this statement; Plutarch is quite wrong in his chronology of the battle, and the 16th of Munychion, which had probably always been consecrated to Artemis. was not necessarily a full-moon day.

greater clearness with which the fifth century had come to recognize Hekate as a goddess of the moon. We may also suppose that Artemis acquired this character partly from her association with Apollo; for though she already appears as his sister in Homer, and there is no trace in his poems of the lunar Artemis, yet the belief that Apollo was identical with Helios comes into prominence about the same time as the conception of the moon-goddess Artemis [a].

It may be from her affinity to Hekate and the deities of the under-world, or from the early belief that it was Artemis who sent untimely or mysterious death, that we find her form appearing occasionally on grave-monuments; a relief [b] of a late period has been found in Thrace showing the figures of two dead children apotheosized as Apollo and Artemis. The stories of Hekaerge in Delos and Aspalis in Phthia, which will be afterwards examined, of Eucleia and Iphinoe mentioned below, seem to reveal the goddess as a deity of death and the lower world, who herself dies [c]. But her chthonian functions were not at all prominent in belief or worship.

Turning now from the physical side of her character, we find that her cult has some few relations with social and political life. As regards the institution of the family, we have seen that she has more to do with child-birth than with marriage. None of her cult-titles have any clear reference to a goddess of wedlock. We hear of the worship of Eucleia at Thebes, 'the goddess of fair report,' to whom a preliminary sacrifice was offered by bride and bridegroom [66a]: 'the people,' says Plutarch, 'call and consider Eucleia Artemis; others consider her to be a maiden who died unmarried, the daughter of Heracles and Myrto [d].' No doubt 'the people'

[a] For the recognition of Apollo as the sun-god, which is at least very obscure in the older literature, cf. the fragment of Timotheus, Bergk, *Fr.* 13, and Plutarch, *de defec. Orac.* p. 433 D and 434 E

[b] *Gazette Archéol.* 1878, Pl. 2, and *Rev. Arch.* 1870, p. 248.

[c] In primitive cult the deity of vegetation is naturally supposed to die and be buried at certain seasons; we find this trait in the legend of the Cretan Zeus, of Dionysos and Adonis, of Oriental Aphrodite and her Cretan and Cypriote counterparts.

[d] We may compare with this the ritual and story at Megara, where maidens before their marriage offered

were right, but the sacrifice may have been propitiatory of the unmarried goddess, and we cannot say with certainty that this title designated her as the divinity who brought about and protected the 'honourable estate of matrimony'; for elsewhere, as will be noticed below, it is attached to her with reference to the glory of war.

The other titles which, as Dr. Schreiber supposes [a], may have referred to wedlock are more than doubtful; namely, Ἡγεμόνη, 'the leader'; Πειθώ, 'the persuasive'; Εὐπραξία, 'the giver of good fortune.' We hear of the shrine of Artemis 'the leader' at Akakesion, in Arcadia [67 a], before the great temple of Despoina; and of her bronze statue that held torches. But it is impossible to be sure that this title there designated her as a goddess 'who led the bridal procession,' although in Sparta Artemis Hegemone and Apollo Karneios shared the temple of Eileithyia [67 c]. In Callimachus the epithet is applied to her as the divinity who led Neleus to the site of Miletus, which he founded [44 a]; a temple mentioned by Pausanias at Tegea was said to have been consecrated to this cult by the man who at the bidding of Artemis slew the tyrant of Orchomenos and escaped to Tegea [67 b]; and we have a very similar story about Artemis Hegemone, who freed the Ambraciots from the tyranny of Phalaecus, narrated by Antoninus Liberalis [67 e]. We might believe that in these cults the goddess was regarded simply as 'she who shows the way [b],' as in the story of Artemis Phosphorus and Thrasybulus, and the title Ἡγεμόνη may have arisen from the widespread artistic type of the running goddess with the torches in her hand [c].

An Artemis Πειθώ [68] is known to us only through Pausanias, who mentions her temple in or near the ἀγορά at

libations and locks of their hair to a maiden named Ἰφινόη, a mythical personage who had died unmarried. There can be no doubt but that Iphinoe is a forgotten cult-name of Artemis [79 a].

[a] Roscher's *Lexicon*, p. 574.

[b] In Orphic literature Artemis Ἡγεμόνη becomes one with Τύχη—as the

goddess who leads men's lives: Τύχη is called Μειλιχίην, Ἐνοδῖτιν, . . . Ἄρτεμιν ἡγεμόνην; *Orph. Hymn*, 72. 3.

[c] The Hegemone who occurs in the oath taken by the ephebi at Athens is probably Aphrodite Pandemos [67 f]; vide Aphrodite, p. 662.

Argos, and connects it with the legend of Hypermnestra and the trial in which she defended herself against her father [a]. The title, then, has probably a juridical sense, and we may compare it with 'Αγοραία mentioned below. As regards Εὐπραξία [45], a term which is found applied to Artemis on a relief from Tyndaris in Sicily, it is probable that it alludes to the goddess who gives women safety and success in child-birth; it need not primarily denote the marriage divinity [b].

Still, though in ordinary cult there is no direct evidence of the worship of Artemis as a recognized goddess of marriage, and we have seen reason for supposing that the primitive conception of Artemis was opposed to this, it would be quite natural that the goddess of child-birth and the goddess who had special charge of the lives of women should come to be associated with the rites of wedlock; and we may find occasional testimony to this conception of her in literature and art [c]. But that this conception was rare we can conclude from the hymn of Callimachus, who nowhere mentions it.

Her relations to the family-life are expressed by the titles Παιδοτρόφος [70], the rearer of children, and Κορυθαλία [72]; the former was attached to her in the cult at Corone in Messenia, where she shared her temple with Dionysos and Asclepios; and the temple of Artemis Κορυθαλία stood by a stream outside Sparta, where the nurses brought boy-children and consecrated them to her, and the feast of Τιθηνίδια was celebrated with dance and masquerade and a sacrifice of sucking-pigs and loaves. It was Artemis to whom boys offered the locks of their hair on the Κουρεῶτις, one of the days of the Attic 'Απατούρια, and who aided the growth of girls and the athletic exercises of youth [71, 74]. The cherishing of children may have become assigned to her either as a

---

[a] It may be that the temple of Peitho, standing in the market-place at Sicyon, and connected with the myth that Apollo and Artemis had departed from the land and were persuaded to return, may have had some association with an Artemis Πειθώ, a goddess of the ἀγορά; Paus. 2. 7, 7–8.

[b] Vide *Artemis-Monuments*, p. 531.

[c] Prayer was occasionally made to her for a happy marriage [68]. Plutarch's statement that those who are marrying need the favour of Artemis above all may allude to the propitiatory rites which she claimed and to her function as the goddess of child-birth [45].

primitive goddess of the earth and water, or as the sister of Apollo Κουροτρόφος ; and either view could be illustrated by a line in Hesiod, who says of the water-goddesses—

ἄνδρας κουρίζουσι σὺν ᾿Απόλλωνι ἄνακτι[a].

With the higher social organization based on relationship Artemis had little to do, and was very rarely recognized as the ancestral divinity of the community. We hear, indeed, of Artemis Πατρῴα, 'the ancestress,' at Sicyon[76], and of Πατριῶτις at Pleiae in Laconia, and a late inscription seems to attest the existence of the same cult at Amyclae[77]. The Sicyon cult must have been ancient, as the image of Artemis was aniconic; but we know nothing about its institution, and we cannot explain the origin of this strange title of hers, which does not accord with her character in the popular belief, unless we suppose it came to her from her association with Apollo Patrous, whose cult she seems to have shared at Athens[76]. Only at Epidaurus does she appear to have been associated in public cult with the tribal organization ; a single inscription of the early Roman period from that place preserves the interesting and unique title Artemis Παμφυλαία[78], which stands near in meaning to that of Aphrodite Pandemos.

In considering the relations of Artemis to the higher life of the individual and the state, we may suppose that she came into some of them through her relationship with Apollo, and that others she acquired by a natural development of her character. But it is difficult to estimate exactly how much has been derived from the Apolline worship ; for the association of the two divinities, though not aboriginal, is certainly old, and came to be recognized, after the Homeric period, far and wide throughout the Greek world[b]. We find it in Homer, and we may conclude that his poems reflect the religious ideas

[a] *Theog.* 347. It has been suggested by Robert (*Griech. Mythol.* Robert-Preller, p. 780, 2) that ἡ Κουροτρόφος, mentioned in the prayer of the women in the *Thesmophoriazusae,* and in an inscription concerning the ephebi sacrifice, is Artemis[73] ; but as no instance has yet been found in which this title has been applied to Artemis, it is better in these cases to interpret it as an epithet of Gaea.

[b] The references showing a joint worship of Apollo and Artemis given by Müller, *Dorians,* 2. p. 368, are not all relevant ; and few of them prove that it belonged to an early period. For a more complete list vide[79].

of the Aeolic shore of Asia Minor : and we might assign to the Homeric age the joint worship at Sicyon [79 s], Megara [79 r], and Delos [79 a]. But the figure of Apollo plays no part in the earliest cults and cult-legends of Artemis ; for instance, the primitive Arcadian, the Calydonian, those of Tauropolos and Orthia : nor, on the other hand, does Artemis appear in the earliest legends of the temple and oracle of Delphi. In what way the later association came about has never been satis-factorily explained ; we cannot simply enumerate the points of affinity between the two divinities and give these as the reason, since many of them are probably merely the result of that association. And the union may have arisen with as much likelihood from some local connexion of the two cults and from the fusion of local myths as from some original logical connexion of ideas.

The place where the two deities were first closely asso-ciated, and whence the belief in their twinship spread, was probably Delos [79 a]. For the legends that connected their birth with Delos or the neighbouring island of Rheneia are ancient, and the antiquity of the Artemis-cult in these waters seems partly attested by the very ancient cult-name Ortygia, which appears twice in the *Odyssey* to be attached to Delos, and to Rheneia in the Homeric hymn to Apollo [a]. Again, the hyperborean offerings at Delos were mythically connected, not only with Apollo, but with Artemis and the names of Oupis or Opis and Hekaerge and Arge [b]. These titles are applied to the maidens who brought the offerings from the North, and dying in Delos were buried in or behind the temple of Artemis and received honours at their tomb, the Delian maidens consecrating to them their locks before marriage [79 a]. Now Hekaerge and Opis are known to be names of the goddess [c], and the ritual at their tomb has no

[a] *Od.* 5. 123 ; 15. 402 ; *Hom. Hymn to Apoll.* 16.

[b] Herodotus gives the names Ἄργη (? the swift-footed one) and Opis, but Hekaerge has as good authority; in Claudian Hekaerge and Opis are de-scribed as Scythian divinities of the chase [79 a].

[c] Ἑκαέργη is a term applied to Artemis in an ancient hymn, quoted by Clemens and ascribed to Bran-chos [79 a] ; her connexion with the name Ὦπις will be mentioned below.

meaning except as performed to Artemis herself[a]; and divine epithets such as these, and such as Callisto and Iphigenia, which have become detached from the divinity and have changed their designation, must, for this very reason, be considered ancient.

Therefore as one of these terms, Ἑκαέργη, certainly associates the goddess with Apollo, we have a proof of the antiquity of this association at Delos. And we know of the early fame and splendour of the Pan-Ionic festival held in that island, where hymns were sung to the twin divinities. It seems reasonable, then, to believe that it was from that locality and that worship that the idea of the close relation between Artemis and Apollo was diffused.

The two cult-names which she undoubtedly borrowed from this connexion are Δελφινία[73 b] and Πυθίη[79 i]. As regards the first, by which she was known in Attica and Thessaly, there are other titles mentioned already that show her as a goddess of harbours and maritime life, and this title of her brother's could the more easily be attached to her. But the second, which was in vogue at Miletus, and which refers to Delphi and oracular powers, finds very little illustration in actual cult and belief. The doubtful designation of Artemis as Σίβυλλα[79 k] may be compared with the vague stories about the Sibyl recorded by Pausanias, who mentions a Delian hymn in which she called herself Artemis[b], the wife, the sister, and daughter of Apollo : 'these things she invented as one mad and inspired.' We hear also of an oracle of Apollo and Artemis at

[a] With the ceremonies at Delos in honour of the maidens we may compare the rites practised in honour of Aspalis, who, according to the legend given by Antoninus Liberalis[65], slew herself to preserve her chastity from the tyrant of Phthia; her body disappeared, but her statue was miraculously found near the statue of Artemis, and she became worshipped under the title of Ἀμειλήτη Ἑκαέργη. It is clear that Ἀσπαλίς is a forgotten name of the Artemis of Phthia; there is a hint in the story of the chthonian character of the goddess, who dies and is born again (the tyrant's name is Tartarus). We need not see in the Phthian the influence of the Thessalian worship of Artemis Hekate; for the main point of the legend of Phthia is the virginity of the goddess, and this is the special mark of the Greek Artemis rather than Hekate. The name Ἑκαέργη occurs also in the worship of Ctesulla at Ceos, who, like Ariadne, was supposed to have died in travail, and who was a disguised form of Artemis Aphrodite; vide Aphrodite[72].

[b] Paus. 10. 12, 1.

Adrastea[79l], and an Artemis-oracle in Cilicia[79m]; but it is doubtful if these are genuine Hellenic cult-names. And where she
was united in worship with Apollo Pythius, as at Anaphe,
Pheneos, and perhaps Sparta[79 f, g, h], we do not hear that she
shared his prophetic power. At Delphi the oracle remained
exclusively Apolline; and we have few traces of a cult of
Artemis, beyond an inscription[79 e] from which it appears that
the emancipation of slaves was sometimes performed in her
name as well as the god's[a]. Her occasional association with
her brother in vase-representations that refer to the consultation of the Delphic oracle is an artistic motive, and is
no proof of actual cult.

Whether the name of Artemis Οὐλία[79n], to whom, according
to Pherecydes, Theseus sacrificed before his journey against
the Minotaur, is derived from Apollo Οὔλιος, with whom she
was associated at Lindos[102], or whether it comes to be attached
to the goddess independently, is a doubtful question. The
titles belong to both as divinities of health: and Artemis, the
goddess of waters, who produced the hot spring, might
naturally be invested with these powers, as the epithets
εὐάκοος and ἐπήκοος expressed that she listened to the prayers
of the sick[b]. Generally speaking, it may be said that any
prominent divinity of a community, whatever was his or her
original nature, might be regarded and invoked as the giver
of health and life, just as we have seen Athena worshipped as
Hygiaea at Athens. It was probably as the sister of Apollo
that Artemis became a goddess of purification, as Arctinos
in the *Aithiopis* mentions that Achilles was purified from
the blood of Thersites by ceremonies performed in Lesbos to
Apollo and Artemis, whose title Λύη or Λυαία[79o] perhaps expresses this idea.

The comparatively few cult-titles of Artemis that refer to
civic or civilized life cannot be clearly deduced from any more

[a] It is possible that the Lycian cult
of Artemis Ἐλευθέρα[79o] drew its name
from the protection and asylum which
her temple afforded to the slave and
the criminal.

[b] Ἄρτεμις Λουσιᾶτις[79p] occurs in an

inscription of the fourth century B.C. on
the rim of a bronze vessel from Achaea;
Ἄρτεμις Θερμία and Εὐάκοος[79q] in an inscription of the third century B. C., found
in some baths at Mitylene, dedicating
an aqueduct to her.

primitive idea nor from association with other deities. She
had little to do with property, or the acquisition or allotment
of land; although she was worshipped as Τρικλαρία at Patrae[35],
and this name may have arisen from some tripartite division of
the land, which was given a religious sanctity, or, as Müller
supposes [a], from the chance that this temple at Patrae was
the central shrine of three old village communities.

The worship of Artemis had an important political bearing
in Euboea, where she was the presiding deity of the Euboean
league, and we find that the temple of Artemis Ἀμαρυσία [80]
was the place of a Pan-Ionic meeting. The cult existed in
Attica also, being especially prevalent in the deme of Ath-
monum, and the festival at Athens rivalled the Euboean in
splendour.

Her relation to the life of the city is expressed chiefly by the
titles Βουλαία [81] and Βουληφόρος [82], by which she was addressed
at Athens and Miletus; though, as far as we know, these are
late, nor was she so essentially a deity of the βουλή as Zeus
and Athena. It may be that this designation of her at
Athens arose from some statue that stood before the council-
chamber; for in the Attic inscriptions, mostly of the first
century B.C., we find her in constant conjunction with Apollo
Προστατήριος [81 a]. Once at least she was recognized as
a divinity of the market-place, namely, at Olympia [55], and
with this cult of Artemis Ἀγοραία we may, perhaps, associate
the Argive worship of Artemis Πειθώ [68].

Such political titles of Artemis are rare and of slight prevalence. Even at Athens, in spite of her title Βουλαία, we can
gather from the non-occurrence of her name in the formulae
of the state-oaths and the oath of the jurors that her religion
reflected but little of the civic life and government [b]. The

---

[a] *Dorians*, 2. p. 374, n. 8.

[b] The witness in the law-courts of
Plato's ideal state might swear by Zeus,
Apollo, and Themis; the Athenian jury-
man swore by Zeus, Poseidon, and Demeter; *Laws*, p. 936 E; Dem. Κ. Τιμοκρ.,
p. 747. In an inscription belonging
to the time of the second maritime con-

federacy of Athens, the deities invoked
in the treaty of alliance between Corcyra
and Athens are Zeus, Demeter, Apollo
(*Bull. de Corr. Hell.* 1889, p. 357).
The name of Artemis occurs in the
formula of the oath of alliance in two
Cretan inscriptions, and the treaty between Smyrna and Magnesia is ratified

practice at Pellene in Achaea, where the oath was taken in matters of the greatest concern to Artemis Soteira, appears to have been exceptional [123 f].

We may note also, that though there are very many localities that gave a title to or borrowed one from Artemis [84-117], scarcely any of these, where the worship was purely Greek[a], were actual cities, except the small community of Selasia [69] in Laconia, the city Lycoas in Arcadia, 'the wolf city,' which was a ruin in the time of Pausanias, and Aptera in Crete [90]. The rest are country districts, islands, rivers, or heights. It is true that Zeus promises to give her, in the hymn of Callimachus, 'thirty cities which shall cherish no other deity, but only thee, and shall be called of Artemis'; but either these πτολίεθρα are not Greek cities proper or are unknown to us. The epithet πολιῆοχος, which Apollonius Rhodius [b] attaches to her, is not known to have belonged to actual cult. We hear in Strabo and Pausanias of Artemis Aetolis [85], the goddess of Aetolia, the least civilized of the Greek communities, and the chief divinity of Calydon was Artemis Λαφρία, the wild goddess. It is, in fact, not the Hellenic, but chiefly the half-foreign goddess of Asia Minor, who was worshipped as the patron deity of the city.

The district and city of Perge [111], in Lycia, was sacred to Artemis Περγαία, and her image in Cicero's time was embellished with gold; a yearly πανήγυρις was held there in her honour, and mendicant priests appear to have been attached to her as they were to Cybele. Astyrene, Mindos of Halicarnassus, Sardis, Tauropolis in Caria, and pre-eminently Ephesus, were associated with her name; and the various

---

in the name of Artemis Tauropolos [59 g]. For the mock-treaty in the *Lysistrate*, 1262, Artemis is invoked by the Spartan woman, but it is the wild Artemis, 'the slayer of beasts'; in the Gortynian inscription we find that Artemis was invoked in the formula of the oath by which a woman could clear herself before a court of law [81]. On the other hand, we cannot always conclude that all the deities mentioned in the public oath of

the Greek cities were necessarily prominent divinities of the πόλις; the chief deity of the country, whatever his or her character was, would generally be mentioned, and certain nature-powers like Helios.

[a] Artemis Φεραία of Pherae is probably not the Greek Artemis pure and simple, but Artemis combined with the later goddess Hekate.

[b] *Argon.* 1. 312.

cities called Hierapolis in Asia Minor usually derived their name from the worship of the Oriental goddess[a]. We find Artemis as a city-goddess under the name of 'Αστίας[91] in an inscription from Iasos of Caria, a city which worshipped her as its προκαθηγεμών, or foundress. Possibly the title Προηγέτις, by which she was united in the Lycian worship with Apollo Προηγέτης, may have been attached to her as the leader of the migrations of peoples[91]. But even in Asia Minor she was very rarely identified, as in various places Isis and Hera were, with the Τύχη of the city. Perhaps the only instance is the city of Gerasa[118] in the Syrian Decapolis, which inscribed the title of Artemis Tyche upon its coins of the second century A. D. The naïve words that Callimachus puts into the mouth of the girl Artemis[b], who prays for the possession of mountains rather than cities—the latter she will only visit when women in travail invoke her aid—are quite in accord with the character of the goddess in the public religion of Greece proper.

She is slightly more prominent as a goddess of battle, or as a divinity who aided the fight. In many cases this function may have been attributed to her from the fact that the battle occurred in a locality, often wild ground, where Artemis was supposed to be powerful[c]. Thus the Greeks brought thank-offerings to her in commemoration of the battle of Artemision, and the epigram of Simonides refers to these[119]; the annual sacrifice of goats, offered by the Athenians for the victory of Marathon, was due to the goddess of the mountain or the marsh, who might be naturally supposed to have aided them[26 f]. The Spartan sacrifice before joining battle has been mentioned[26 b]; and, according to Pollux, the Athenian polemarch made a joint offering to her and the war-god[26 f]. She was also recognized as a deity who inspired the leader with wise counsel, as 'Αριστοβούλη, to whom Themistocles erected a temple on Melita after the battle of Salamis[120].

---

[a] E. g. Hierapolis, another name for Bambyce, derived from the worship of the Syrian goddess Atargatis; Strabo, 748.

[b] Callim. *Hymn to Art.* ll. 18–22.

[c] We might explain in the same way the sacrifice to the nymphs of Cithaeron—νύμφαις Σφραγίτισι—before the battle of Plataea; Plut. *Arist.* 11.

The association of Artemis with war was sometimes expressed by the title Εὔκλεια [a]—for instance the monument of the lion that stood without the temple of Artemis Εὔκλεια at Thebes was supposed to commemorate a legendary victory of Heracles [66 b]—also by a special application of the epithet Σώτειρα, which she shared with many other divinities, and which in Megara [123 a] was explained by reference to the destruction of a band of Persians; in Megalopolis it probably conveyed an allusion to the victories of Epaminondas [123 b]. No doubt the title often had a wider application, referring perhaps to safety in child-birth.

It is possible that Λαφρία was an epithet of Artemis that referred as much to war as to the chase; and the common type of the running goddess may represent the huntress or the warlike deity [122]. Although in mythological scenes Artemis appears not infrequently engaged in combat, for instance against Tityos and the giants, yet this aspect of her is very rarely presented in the temple ἀγάλματα. But a statue of Artemis existed in Messenia bearing shield and spear, and there is reason for supposing the images of the Brauronian and the Tauric Artemis represented her as armed [b].

It is rare to find the worship of Artemis associated with any of the arts of life, and none of them are attributed to her discovery or teaching. But Homer and the author of the Homeric hymn to Aphrodite knew of her as a goddess who delights in the dance and song and the lyre [125]. No doubt we must here reckon with the influence of the Delian festival and her connexion with Apollo; but in Arcadia, where this connexion was least recognized [c], the musical character of Artemis was acknowledged in an independent cult. The worship of Artemis Ὑμνία [124], common to the Orchomenians and Mantineans, was among the most important in Arcadia, and though Pausanias tells us nothing

---

[a] The cult of Eucleia at Athens appears to have commemorated the battle of Marathon; but it is doubtful whether this figure was Artemis, or a mere personification like Εὔνοια and Εὐνομία, with whom she was coupled in Attic cult [66 d].

[b] Vide *Artemis-Monuments*, p. 527.

[c] We only have two records of a joint worship of Apollo and Artemis in Arcadia, [79 g] and [79 w].

about the significance of the name, it must surely refer to the hymns sung at her yearly festival, and it recalls the παρθένια, the maidens' songs sung at Sparta in honour of the maiden-goddess. We may also explain the worship of Artemis Χελῦτις in Sparta [125] as paid to the goddess who loved the music of the tortoise-shell lyre; and it was in Sparta also where she was worshipped with a special dance performed by the maidens of Caryae. We gather, too, from a passage in the *Phoenissae* that on Parnassos a maidens' chorus danced in honour of the ἀθάνατος θεά, who from the context appears to be Artemis. The goddess worshipped on the Carian Chersonese, who may be called Artemis Aphrodite, was known as Μολπαδίας, 'the songful one [125].' In fact, the dance and song were indispensable in Greek religious service, and no cult remained so backward as not to reflect some light from Hellenic civilization. Even the bear-goddess of Brauron was supposed to delight in the recitations of the Homeric poems in her festival [a].

Such is the main account of the Greek worship of Artemis; and it appears from it that, while in the imagination of the poet and artist the character of the goddess possessed a high spiritual value, the cults have comparatively little connexion with the moral and intellectual or even the higher material life of the nation and individual. The conceptions of purification from sin, of legal trial and satisfaction for homicide, of the sanctity of the suppliant and the stranger, which fostered the growth of early Greek law and religion, and which we find in the worships of Zeus and Athena, play little or no part in this. Greek religious philosophy, in its attempt to idealize the leading personages of the religion, to make each the embodiment of an intellectual or spiritual abstraction, scarcely touches Artemis; nor had she a very prominent place in the later mystic and Orphic literature [b], except under the form of Hekate.

[a] Vide [52]. This recitation is often associated with the supposed festival of Dionysos at Brauron; but there is no proof that there was any festival of Dionysos called Βραυρώνια: the only authority for it is the scholiast on Arist. *Pax* 874, who is followed by Suidas, and it is probable that he invented it himself out of a misunderstanding of Aristophanes, who is really referring to the festival of Artemis.

[b] *Orphic Hymn to Artemis*, l. 36

The Greek cult of this latter goddess must be separately described with some detail. It remains to notice here what we can find of non-Hellenic or Oriental influence in the worship of Artemis, and to trace its fusion with foreign but cognate cults. And, first, we note a combination in which she is identified or associated with a divinity whose worship may have spread through Phrygia and Thrace to North Greece, and probably through Caria to Crete, and of whom Cybele, Bendis, Semele, Dictynna, Britomartis, and possibly Ariadne and Europa, are the various local names; secondly, a tendency to attach the name of Artemis to Semitic goddesses, such as Astarte, Derceto, Atargatis. It is with the first of these combinations that we are here most concerned; for it is not only prior, but it reaches further throughout the various areas of Greek religion. The view implied by Strabo [126] that Cybele, the goddess of Asia Minor, was identical or closely connected with the Thracian Bendis, Kotys, or Hekate, seems to be warranted by the facts that we can gather of North Greek and Phrygian worship; and that this goddess was, in regard to her main character at least, an earth-goddess or a divinity of vegetation seems proved by the nature of the myths and rites of Cybele, her close association with Dionysos, and by the newly discovered interpretation of the name Semele [a], which is closely cognate to a Phrygian word for earth. The details of this Cybele-worship must be given in a later chapter. It is enough here to show its points of connexion with that of Artemis, and the common idea from which that connexion arose.

The direct and clear recognition in the earlier literature of Artemis and Cybele as kindred divinities appears but rarely[b]: a striking instance of it is a fragment of Diogenes ὁ τραγικός, quoted by Athenaeus: 'I hear that the Bacchic maidens of

---

ἐλθὲ θεὰ σώτειρα φίλη μύστῃσιν ἅπασι: but it is not the Artemis of the old Greek religion that the hymn celebrates, but the goddess confused with Hekate and Eileithyia; cf. Orph. Argon. l. 905, for the mystic rites of initiation connected with Artemis Hekate.

[a] Vide article by Kretschmer, Aus der Anomia, p. 17.

[b] We find Artemis Munychia worshipped near Cyzicus in association with the 'mother-goddess,' who in this locality must have been Cybele [20 d].

Lydia, dwelling by the river Halys, honour Artemis the goddess of Tmolus in a laurel-shaded grove [127].' The goddess of Tmolus worshipped by maenads is certainly Cybele, but is here given the name of the Greek goddess, and the laurel-grove, sacred properly to the latter, is associated with the goddess of Asia Minor.

Another form of Cybele was the armed Cappadocian Mâ, the mother-goddess, who came, perhaps in the later period, to be identified with the Tauric Artemis [128], owing probably to the influence diffused through the Euxine of the Dindymene and Pessinuntian rites, as these would naturally attract the legend of the Tauric cult [a].

The Thracian Bendis [129] was probably in origin and character the same as the great mother of Phrygia, and was worshipped, according to Strabo, with the same orgiastic rites ; her cult spread through Thessaly to Athens probably about the time when that of Cybele had acquired public prevalence there. We hear also of Bendis as the 'great goddess of Lemnos' to whom human victims were offered, and she may well have been recognized there as cognate to the Tauric Artemis [52 b]. And though of close affinity to Cybele and Hekate, she was received into Greek religion chiefly as a Thracian form of Artemis. Herodotus speaks of the 'queen Artemis [54 g],' to whom the Thracians and Paeonians sacrificed, the 'queen' being probably one of her native titles [b]. The reasons for this association of the Greek maidenly goddess with the Bendis-Hekate-Brimo, the patroness of savage magic and terrifying superstition, may have been some external resemblance of attributes, but also, probably, some consanguinity of character. Like Artemis Ταυροπόλος, the Thracian divinity was supposed to ride on bulls ; like Artemis, she was a mighty huntress, though her weapon was not the bow, but the spear in each hand [129]. We find the feast of Bendis formally established at Athens

[a] The legend of Orestes and the Tauric Artemis penetrated as far south as Cilicia into the worship of Artemis Περασία at Castabala, whose ritual, so far as Strabo describes it, appears to be certainly un-Hellenic [128].

[b] As the queen-goddess, the Thracian divinity appears to have been once at least identified with Hera ; Polyaen. *Strat.* 7. 22.

by the time of Plato[a], and the worship must have been known
to the Athenians at an earlier date through the Θρᾶτται, the
comedy of Cratinus. The well-known scene in the opening of
the *Republic* speaks of the torch-races on horseback held in
her honour at the Peiraeeus, the vantage-ground in Attica of
foreign cults. And this ceremony may perhaps explain why
Bendis was identified with Artemis; for the two Greek
goddesses, in whose rites and legends from the fifth century
onwards the torch is a specially prominent symbol, are
Demeter and Artemis; but the wild Thracian huntress was
more naturally associated with the latter than with the
divinity of settled agricultural life, although Bendis also,
like the Greek Artemis, had some connexion with agriculture, as cereal offerings were brought to her and the bull
appears to have been one of her sacred animals. It was
in Thessaly, and especially at Pherae, that this association
with Artemis took place. The cult and legends of Pherae,
where Admetus was probably a name for the god of the lower
world who, like Dionysos, yoked wild beasts to his chariot,
and where Hekate or Bendis was regarded as his daughter,
have a certain chthonian character; and this was found in the
worship of Artemis Φεραία, which was the chief Thessalian
worship of the goddess, and which spread to Acarnania,
Sicyon, and Argos [117, 120]. The legend of Medea, the devotee
of Hekate and the Tauric goddess, and the part she played
in Thessaly seem to indicate that from an early time in
this land the cult of Artemis was infected with sorcery and
superstitious rites. As the worshippers of Bendis in the
Peiraeeus rode with torches on horseback, so the goddess of
Pherae was herself figured on coins mounted on a horse and
with a torch in her hand; Millingen has published a relief
from Crannon[b] with a torch-bearing Artemis standing by her
horse and hound; and we gather from Lycophron that 'the
goddess of Strymon,' whom he identifies with Brimo and
Pheraea, was honoured with torches. We may see also an

---

[a] An Attic inscription, circ. 429 B.C., dealing with the temple-moneys associates
Bendis with Adrasteia in the state-cult [138 b].

[b] *Uned. Mon.* 2. 16.

allusion to Bendis and Artemis on the coin of the Thracian Aenos, which displays a goat bending over a torch set in a socket as for a lampadephoria [a].

Finally, we can trace in Crete the close affinity between Artemis and the goddess of a Cretan pre-Hellenic people who in blood or religion were probably akin to the worshippers of Cybele in Asia Minor. The Cretan goddess was Britomartis [131], known especially in the western part of the island, and generally in the Hellenic world, as Dictynna, and associated with the Thracian goddess [129, 131 k], but more closely still with Artemis. 'The Cretans worship Diana most religiously, naming her by the national name of Britomartis,' says Solinus [131a]; and Pausanias supposes that she was originally a nymph who rejoiced in hunting and the chase, and was especially dear to Artemis. The worship spread to Delos, to Aegina, where her cult-title was Ἀφαία, and where she may have been identified with Hekate, who was prominent in the local cult [b], and to Sparta, where her temple stood nearest to the wall [c]. Euripides, in the *Hippolytus*, appears to attest a worship of Dictynna near Troezen; we have evidence of its existence in Phocis, Astypalaea, and Cephallenia, and of a feast of Artemis Britomartis in Delos, and an inscription of the Roman period proves that the public worship of the θεὰ Δικτύα spread as far north as Massilia. The name Βριτόμαρτις is explained by ancient lexicographers as meaning 'sweet maid,' and Δίκτυννα was of course connected with the Greek word for a net. As philology has not yet settled to what group of languages these words belong, we might think they were titles attached to Artemis by the early Hellenic settlers in Crete. But the statement of Strabo is against this, who says that the Dictynnaeon, or temple of

[a] Head, *Hist. Num.* p. 214, Fig. 157.

[b] Steph. Byz. gives Ἀφαία as a cult-name of Hekate in a confused note; probably Ἀφαία should be read.

[c] If we accepted Pausanias' statement, we should have to believe that the Cretan goddess was also worshipped on the south coast of Laconia under the titles of Artemis Ἰσσωρία and Λιμναία [131d];

but Wide, in *Lakonische Kulte*, p. 109, shows good reason for doubting his testimony on this point. Stephanus of Byzantium and Hesychius do not appear to have known the Cretan origin of Artemis Issoria, and as her temple stood on the height, it is not probable that she would be identified with Artemis of the marsh.

Dictynna, was in the territory of the Cydonians, an aboriginal Cretan population; and though, according to Herodotus, it was built by the Samians in the time of Polycrates, yet we cannot suppose that they introduced the worship, for the legend is entirely Cretan. Originally independent, she became regarded in the fifth century as a personality scarcely distinct from Artemis: like her, she was worshipped as a mighty huntress with her hounds, as πολύθηρος, the divinity of the beasts of the wild; and Λαφρία, the prevalent title of Artemis in Aetolia, is mentioned as an epithet of Britomartis Dictynna in Cephallenian cult. In Crete itself, where her worship was of national importance, she does not seem to have been actually identified in the cult of the autonomous cities with her sister-goddess of the Hellenic religion, for in the treaty of alliance between the men of Latos and Olus inscribed about 200 B.C., and in the oath that bound the citizens of Cnossus to those of Dreros, the two divinities are mentioned separately [131 a]; but on the Cretan coins of the imperial period Dictynna appears altogether in the guise of Artemis. It concerns us to examine the grounds of this association. It would have doubtless come about, if the Greeks had only known Dictynna as a divine huntress, and had heard the Cretan myth that she had plunged into the water to preserve her chastity from the pursuit of Minos. But, besides this, there is reason to think that her significance for the old Cretan worship was essentially the same as that of Artemis for the Arcadian. The legend concerning her rescue in the fishers' nets might perhaps have arisen from the popular derivation of the name Δίκτυννα; yet even if Pausanias was wrong in supposing that the title Λιμναία was given her in Spartan cult, it is still probable that she, like Artemis, had some real connexion with the waters. This would arise naturally from the seafaring character of her worshippers, and the statement in Plutarch is of importance, that she was constantly associated in cult with Apollo Delphinios [131 i], in whose legend the Cretan mariner plays a part. And there is evidence that, like Artemis, Aphrodite, and Cybele, she was a divinity connected with the earth and its vegetative powers.

In her ritual the wild trees appear to have been consecrated to her as to Artemis. The story of the leap into the sea was told not only of Dictynna, but of Aphrodite herself, the fish-goddess Derketo, and the Carian maiden Rhoio, another form of Artemis Aphrodite, and may have arisen from some ritual practised in the worship of the divinity of vegetation[a]. Her name Δίκτυννα, as the writer in Roscher's *Lexicon* (p. 822) remarks, may have been derived from some locality in the west of Crete, and at any rate is probably connected with the name of Mount Dicte in the east, where, according to one legend, Zeus was born, and whence he took his title Δικταῖος[b]. And we might suppose that the relation between the Zeus of Crete and Dictynna was different from that which appears in the genealogical account of the goddess's origin, and that originally she was scarcely distinct from Amalthea, or the sacred goat-mother who nourished Zeus ; in the Cretan legend of the god, the goat and the bee are his sacred animals, the one being usually consecrated to the Hellenic Artemis, the other to the Ephesian. Possibly the Cydonian legend, of which we have some numismatic evidence[c], concerning the nurture of Zeus by a dog, may be derived from some association of the infant-god with Dictynna, with whom this animal was associated. It is at least certain that this character of Dictynna as κουροτρόφος and as the nurse of Zeus was recognized in the later period, for on coins of the early imperial epoch we see Dictynna 'seated on a rock holding a javelin and the infant Zeus on her arm, and guarded on either side by the Curetes[d].'

The conception which we can trace in Thracian-Phrygian worship, and which penetrated into Hellas, of an earth-goddess and a god of vegetation who is sometimes her son or fosterling, sometimes her lover, who suffers and is born again, can be detected also in the religion of Crete, having reached the island from Asia Minor, perhaps through Caria.

---

[a] Vide chapter on Aphrodite, p. 638 ; on Artemis, p. 447 note [c].

[b] This view was held by Callimachus, *Hymn. Dian.* 199. Strabo's objections (p. 479) are not very weighty.

[c] Vide *Ephem. Archaeol.* 1892, p. 7 ; Zeus-chapter, p. 109.

[d] Head, *Hist. Num.* p. 384.

The solar element in that religion appears to me to have been much exaggerated [a]. The Cretan story and cult of Zeus, who is born and dies, whose foster-mother was the goat or Amalthea or Rhea, and whose body-guard were the Curetes, and whose religion there and there only was mystic and orgiastic, must be attached, as has been already remarked, by a close link to the cycle of the myths and cults of Dionysos, Altis, Sabazios, and Cybele [b]. In Ariadne the Greeks recognized occasionally an Aphrodite, but more generally a female counterpart of Dionysos; Europa riding on the sacred bull may be regarded as a personage of the Dionysiac circle, the Cretan equivalent of Artemis Tauropolos, and her name was probably that by which the Greeks designated the Cretan earth-goddess [c], just as in Boeotia they spoke of Demeter Εὐρώπη; and as the Cretan god dies, so his spouse, the earth-goddess, dies, for we hear of the funeral rites of Europa in the Corinthian festival of Ἑλλώτια [d]. Into this Cretan circle, then, of divinities of vegetation, Dictynna Britomartis must be placed; and thus she could be rightly associated with Cybele on the one hand, and Artemis on the other: with the latter all the more naturally because she was a huntress connected in some way with the water and the wilds, and, unlike the Thracian-Phrygian goddess, necessarily a virgin [e].

It was through these half-foreign influences that the worship of Artemis in Aegina, Crete, and Thessaly became tinged with the ideas proper to a primitive and orgiastic nature-

---

[a] The Labyrinth and Minotaur and Europa riding on the bull have no clear solar reference; the name of Pasiphae and her legendary connexion with Aeëtes, and thus with Helios, is the one atom of fact in this solar theory about the Cretan religion.

[b] The very name of the Cretan Nymphs, the Μητέρες, recalls that of the Μεγάλη Μήτηρ of Phrygia. They are especially mentioned by Diodorus Siculus (bk. 4, chs. 79, 80) as the Cretan nurses of Zeus, and worshipped with great reverence at Agrigentum down to late times. We may note also that the name Δίκτη occurred in the region of Mount Ida in the Troad.

[c] Europa seated on the tree on Cretan coins may be a representation expressing her half-forgotten association with the earth. It is of course true that the Cretan myth points to Phoenician influences, and according to Lucian, *de Dea Syria.* 72, the coin-stamp of Sidon was Europa seated on the bull: this would show that in later times she was identified with Astarte; vide Aphrodite-chapter, pp. 632, 633.

[d] Vide Athena-references, [20 b].

[e] For Preller (*Griech. Myth.* 1,

worship, of which the main area was Thrace, Phrygia, Lydia, and some of the Eastern islands. The unmixed Hellenic worship had not been wholly innocent in certain localities; but in ordinary Greek cult Artemis had not been hitherto recognized as the Bacchic and Corybantic personage whom Timotheus celebrated in his verse, calling her 'the raving frenzied Thyiad,' an emotional and questionable divinity, against whom the saner Cinesias publicly protested [a].

The worship of Artemis at Ephesus is a conspicuous instance of the fusion of Eastern and Western religious ideas; and of all these hybrid cults this is the most important for the student of Greek religion, since, according to Pausanias, it was known in every Greek city, and it spread to the westernmost parts of the Mediterranean. The Massilians inherited it from the original Phocian settlers, and were zealous propagandists, as they succeeded in planting it in all their colonies and even in Rome itself [133]. Besides Ephesus, the cities of Pergamon, Smyrna, Sardis, Adramytteum, Prusa, Cyzicus, and Astyra in Antandros stamped their coins with the figure of the Ephesian goddess [b]. At Ephesus, in the Artemision, the goddess was worshipped as πρωτοθρονία, supreme in divine power and place; and although she came to acquire a Hellenic genealogy and some of the honours of the Hellenic goddess [c], the ancients themselves rightly regarded her as in origin a non-Hellenic divinity. According to the view expressed in Pausanias, she was the aboriginal deity of a population consisting of Leleges and Lydians; and Tacitus records the priestly tradition concerning the association of the

---

p. 252) Dictynna personifies the moon; Rapp, in Roscher's *Lexicon*, regards her as a cloud-maiden (*s. v.* Britomartis). To say that any concrete figure of primitive religion is a personification of anything is always a very doubtful expression; my statement is not that either Artemis or Dictynna was a personification of the earth, but that Artemis certainly, and Dictynna probably, possessed much of the character of a deity of vegetation.

[a] 'May your daughter turn out just such a character' was the exclamation of Cinesias; Plut. *de audiend. poet.* c. 4.

[b] *Brit. Mus. Cat.*, coins of Astyra; *Zeitsch. für Numism.* 1880, Taf. 1, 14.

[c] Ortygia was localized near Ephesus, and the Ephesians plead for their goddess before Tiberius as though she were the sister of Apollo and daughter of Leto. We hear of musical contests in honour of the Ephesian as of the Delian goddess [133].

cult with the Lydian Heracles. Accepting this theory of its origin, we should expect to find marks of close kinship with 'the Great Mother' of Phrygia and Lydia, the area of whose worship has been traced above. And in fact we detect in the Ephesian Artemis few or none of the characteristics of a lunar divinity, but all those of a goddess of generation and vegetation, possessing the powers of the life-giving earth. The best evidence of this is the traditional form of the Ephesian idol[a], the great antiquity of which is proved by its semi-aniconic style: the many breasts are the uncouth symbol of fertility, the lions the rams, and the bulls wrought in relief upon her shoulders and legs denote the goddess who fosters the life of the wilds and the fields; the bee which is wrought just above her feet, a frequent symbol on the coins of Ephesus[b], and possibly of some religious significance in the worship[133], figures also in the cognate Cretan worship of Zeus with which Rhea Cybele is associated.

Her affinity to Cybele is still more marked by the turret-crown that she wears on her head, which is the badge of the city-goddess, and by the orgiastic rites practised by the eunuch-priests, whose name Μεγάβυζοι seems to point to the influence of the Persian worship of Artemis[c]. We hear of hierodulae serving in the precincts of the Artemision as in the worship of Mylitta and Ishtar, but we are not told that temple-prostitution was a religious rite at Ephesus. In fact the Ephesian religion, in spite of its orgiastic elements, appears to have been in some respects of an austere character; rigid rules of chastity and purity were imposed on the Essenes[124], a priestly society that was attached to the temple; and if the statement of Artemidorus is correct, no woman was allowed under pain of death to enter the temple, and the functions of the priestesses of various grades must have been confined to its precincts. We cannot estimate exactly how far the original worship was modified or purified by

---

[a] Vide coins of Ephesus, *Brit. Mus. Cat. Ionia*, Nos. 71, 72, 73, 76; alabaster statuette in Naples, Roscher, *Lexicon*, p. 588. Cp. an archaic terracotta in Dresden, with many breasts, head, sleeves, outlines of arms given, the rest aniconic.

[b] Vide A. B. Cook, *Hell. Journ.* 1895, p. 12.

[c] The strong Persian influence in Ephesus is attested by Plutarch, *Lysander*, 3.

Hellenic influences; but in any case it does not seem to have been borrowed mainly from the Semitic people, but rather to express the religious ideas of the ancient races in Asia Minor who were nearer to the Hellenic stock, the Phrygians, Lydians, Carians. The legends of the Amazons and of their close relation with the Artemis of Ephesus appear to point to the north of Asia Minor as the original home of this cult. According to Hyginus[a] the temple itself was built by one of the Amazons, and Callimachus records the story that the ancient idol was set up by the Amazons in the trunk of a tree, and there is frequent reference in Greek myth to the protection which the defeated female warriors sought and found in the Artemision. Both in cult and in legend she was recognized as the divinity of the suppliant, and, according to the author of the *Etymologicum Magnum*, sheep were never sacrificed to her because of the sanctity of the woollen fillet which the suppliant bore. The fact may be accepted without the explanation. In purely Hellenic worship Artemis is not conspicuously the deity of supplication; and, on the other hand, the conception of the huntress-goddess so prominent in Greece does not appear in the Ephesian religion. We may conclude that the early Greek settlers of the country of Ephesus, as those of Crete, found established there the worship of an indigenous goddess, to whom they applied the name and some of the titles of the Greek Artemis; and that the character of the Ephesian and Cretan goddess was identical or of close affinity with that of Cybele. With the Ephesian we may probably associate the Artemis of Perge, a city-goddess whose cult, briefly mentioned above, appears in one important respect, namely in the institution of mendicant priests, to have been influenced by the Phrygian religion.

Next perhaps to these in prominence was the cult of Artemis Λευκοφρυήνη at Magnesia on the Maeander[134], which again brings Crete into connexion with Phrygia. The ancient city with its temples had been destroyed by the Cimmerians, but had been afterwards restored by the Ephesians, who rebuilt the temple with such architectural skill and on

[a] *Fab.* 237.

such a scale that it became famous in the ancient world. The local worship of the Phrygian Cybele, which existed there till some time after the residence of Themistocles, appears to have died out, absorbed perhaps by the cult of Artemis Leucophryene, who was probably akin to her. We hear little of the details of the Magnesian cult; but as the Ephesians were its second founders, and as the type of Artemis Leucophryene on later coins of the city resembles that of the Ephesian goddess [a], the conception of the divinity came probably to be very similar in both worships. It is true that we hear of no un-Hellenic features in the worship of the goddess of Magnesia, who, like the Greek Artemis, appears to have been associated with the lake and the hot spring. But it is probable that she was originally a Cretan goddess, and that the cult belonged to the Carian-Cretan group; for the Cretans claimed to have had a share in the colonization of Magnesia, and the worship is proved by inscriptions to have existed in Crete. An image of the goddess was carved for Amyclae by Bathycles of Magnesia, and the sons of Themistocles are said to have set up her statue in Athens.

To this class we may also assign the worship of Artemis Κολοηνή [103], that was in great repute by the lake Coloe in the neighbourhood of Sardis. Strabo tells us a strange story about the miraculous dance of the sacred κάλαθοι, the baskets that contained the cereal offerings consecrated to her, and Pausanias speaks of certain lascivious dances that were brought from Sipylos to Elis by the followers of Pelops and performed in honour of Ἄρτεμις Κόρδαξ. The calathos-dance was probably nothing more mysterious than the dance of the maidens representing Artemis with the basket on their heads, as we find similar figures dancing round the column of Hekate. The Artemis of Sipylos and Coloe was probably a Hellenized form of the great mother-goddess of Phrygia and Lydia.

Lastly, there is archaeological [b] evidence of a goddess of similar character worshipped at Lampsacus on the Hellespont. A silver patera has been found on that site containing a curious

---

[a] Vide Head, *Hist. Num.* p. 502; *Brit. Mus. Cat. Ionia*, p. 163.

[b] *Gazette Archéol.* 1877, p. 119.

representation of a female divinity with stag's horns on her forehead, who holds a bow in her left hand and makes a gesture with her right that signifies fertility; on each side of the throne on which she sits are dogs, and below negresses leading lions—a strange medley of attributes that allude to Artemis, Hekate, and Cybele.

We have finally to notice the purely Oriental divinities with whom Artemis became identified or associated. The grounds of this association may often be uncertain, and the interpretation often shifted: the Cappadocian goddess Mâ, for instance, was regarded as Selene, Athena, or Enyo; the Syrian goddess of Hierapolis, whom the pseudo-Lucian usually calls Hera, had also something of the character of Athena, Aphrodite, Selene, Rhea, Artemis, Nemesis, and the Fates[a]. We may believe that wherever the Greeks found in the East a prominent goddess who was regarded as a huntress and controller of wild beasts, or as a goddess of vegetation, or as an unmarried divinity, they would be inclined to name her Artemis; and in some cases the name might be given because of certain details in the ritual[b]. What at first sight is surprising is that it is attached to divinities of the East whose rites were notoriously impure.

The old Persian goddess Anaitis, a divinity of the water and vegetation and originally distinct, as Meyer[c] maintains, from the similar female deity of so many Semitic cults, came in a later period into close contact with the Babylonian Nana; and this may have happened before the cult of the Persian goddess was established by Artaxerxes II in Babylon, Susa, Ecbatana, Damascus, and Sardes. And in Armenia the same impure rites were practised in the temple of Anaitis as Herodotus records of the Babylonian worship. Strabo vouches for the same practice at Zela in Pontus, where the Persian goddess became powerful. It was for this reason, perhaps that Herodotus and Berosus were led to identify her with

[a] *De Dea Syr.* p. 32 ; Plut. *Sull.* ch. 9.
[b] For instance, the practice of dedicating the hair of boys and maidens to the Syrian goddess at Bambyce occurs also in the worship of the Greek Artemis; *de Dea Syr.* p. 60 ; *C. I. G. Att.* 3, no. 131.
[c] Roscher's *Lexicon*, p. 330.

Aphrodite. But usually she was regarded as the counterpart of Artemis in the Greek theocrasy, and the worship of the Persian Artemis[132] was specially in vogue in the cities of Lydia, particularly at Hierocaesarea, where her temple claimed a peculiar sanctity. We have also archaeological proof of the long-continued prevalence throughout the Roman empire of the worship of the Hellenized goddess of Persia ; for instance, several votive reliefs have 'been found in Holland, and are now in the Museum of Leyden, bearing Greek inscriptions to Artemis Anaeitis and often associating her with the Phrygian moon-god Men. She is usually represented with peplos, chiton, and pointed shoes, and holding up her right hand. In Lydia her image appears to have borne the typical form of the Tauric goddess[53 c]. How far the character of the Persian and the Hellenic divinity really coincided is difficult to determine precisely ; that both were divinities of vegetation powerful over the animal world, and that the torch was used in the ritual of both, may have been sufficient reasons for their *rapprochement*. And their association may have also led to the occasional identification of Artemis with the Babylonian Nana.

For the Semitic goddess the most common name was Astarte, or some form of this, and in the theocrasy of the Hellenistic period Artemis sometimes appears as her Greek equivalent, though much less frequently than Aphrodite. A very curious legendary indication of the early existence of an Artemis-Astarte worship in Greece proper is offered by the story in Pausanias about the temple of Artemis Ἀστρατεία[79 u] at Pyrrhichos in Laconia. The natives appear to have believed that it was founded to commemorate the incursion of the Amazons and their 'ceasing from the campaign' at this place: near it was the temple of Apollo Ἀμαζόνιος, and the images in both temples were dedicated by the Amazons. We have here the usual popular explanation of a perverted and misunderstood title. Ἀστρατεία is a comparatively late word of the Athenian law-courts, denoting the offence of evading military service, and is quite meaningless when applied to the goddess. The cult is evidently from Asia Minor, and I would suggest that Artemis Ἀστρατεία is a corruption for Ἀστάρτη. Her connexion with Astarte probably arose from the same grounds as her association with the Persian goddess; and it cannot be taken as evidence of the early lunar character of Artemis. For as E. Meyer maintains [a], this Babylonian-Semitic goddess is originally not a divinity of the moon, this planet being regarded as male both by the Babylonians and Semites; and although the Babylonian deity sometimes appears represented with the crescent moon upon her forehead, this is probably due to her late association with Isis, and to the misunderstanding of the symbol of the sun which Isis bore on her forehead. Even in the late account given by the pseudo-Lucian of the worship of the great goddess of the Syrian Hierapolis, properly Atargatis, but associated by the narrator with Aphrodite, Rhea, Artemis, and other Greek goddesses, it is specially said that there were no statues here to the sun or the moon. It is true that in the later period of Greek religious thought Artemis was regarded as a lunar divinity, and in the latest Graeco-Asiatic religious system she came to be closely associated with the Phrygian moon-god Men [b]. But this lunar character of the Greek and Semitic goddess was certainly not recognized in the seventh century B.C.; and before this period the Oriental goddess had probably been adopted as Artemis in more than one Hellenic locality.

To those who regard Artemis simply as the pure virgin of Greek religion, innocent of all orgiastic extravagance, it may seem strange that her maidenly character could not save her from this later association with the Oriental goddess of generation, with a Semitic divinity whose worship was solemnized by temple-harlots. But it has been shown that that ideal aspect of Artemis was the fair outgrowth of the popular imagination in literature, legend, and art, and was not her aspect in the primitive rite and conservative cult of Greece. The worships of Arcadia and Brauron contained many ideas not alien to those expressed in the rites and symbols of the earth-goddess of Phrygia and Lydia and the Semitic divinity of Hierapolis.

[a] Roscher's *Lexicon*, s. v. Astarte and Atargatis.

[b] 132. Similarly, in Phrygian cult Apollo Lairbenos was identified with or closely assimilated to Helios and Men; vide inscription published by Ramsay, *Hellenic Journal*, 10. 217.

CHAPTER XIV.

THE idea of the righteous control of human life, which did not conspicuously appear in the cults that have just been examined, essentially belonged to the worship of Nemesis. This figure lost much of its personal force in proportion as it developed in moral significance. In the beginning the name denoted more than a mere moral abstraction; for there is reason to suppose that both Nemesis and Upis were connected titles or surnames of Artemis or Artemis Aphrodite. In regard to the latter, of which the Doric form is ᾿Ωπις, the Ionic Οὖπις, there is no doubt; its usual explicit reference is to Artemis [a], who was worshipped by this title in Lacedaemon and probably Troezen. We have, indeed, only the testimony of late and learned writers such as Callimachus and the lexicographers; but this was drawn either from earlier literature or from knowledge of actual legend and cult. And we have indirect evidence that is even more trustworthy: we hear in Athenaeus of the οὔπιγγοι, the sacred formulae or hymns by which Artemis was addressed at Troezen, the name implying the invocation and the worship of Artemis Upis; and mention has already been made of the Delian maiden Upis who with Arge first brought the Hyperborean offerings to the island, and arrived there in company with the divinities themselves, as Herodotus emphatically says. The sacred rites performed to her, the ceremonious

---

[a] Bergk's proposed emendation of the line in the epigram attributed to Simonides—
(libri, Ωπις 'Αθήνης)
Πατρίδα κυδαίνων ἱερὴν πόλιν ᾿Ωπίας 'Αθηνᾶς

(*Poet. Lyr. Graec.* 3. p. 499) has no probability, and we know nothing of an Athena Upia.

offering made to her of the maidens' hair wound about a spindle, make it certain that Upis was an ancient and half-forgotten name of Artemis. It was resuscitated by later poetry and attached vaguely to the Ephesian Artemis, to the Rhamnusian goddess, and, in a doubtful fragment quoted by Hesychius, to Artemis Hekate [a].

It is important to find the right interpretation of this title. It is impossible perhaps to decide about its original meaning and to say whether this was moral or physical; but it is clear that the Greeks themselves interpreted it as the 'watcher,' connecting it probably with ὀπίζεσθαι. But of what was the goddess regarded as the 'watcher'? Of women in travail, according to the authority from whom the explanation in the *Etymologicum Magnum* is drawn; and this limitation of the reference of the word, though probably groundless, is of some interest as showing that it did not at once seem to accord with the traditional and accepted character of Artemis that she should be addressed as the 'watcher' or overseer of right and wrong, of human life and conduct in general. Yet the title Οὖπις must have come to acquire this broader sense in the later period, for it occurs as a synonym of Nemesis, the Rhamnusian goddess, who 'gazes at the deeds of men [135].' This application of the title, as we know the moral connotation of Nemesis, not only serves to decide what was the received significance of Οὖπις, but also illustrates the connexion surviving in a late period of Nemesis and Artemis.

It is the origin and the ground of this latter association that we have now to consider.

The goddess Νέμεσις may be studied from two different points of view: as a mere personification of the moral idea of retribution, or on the other hand as a concrete figure of ancient Attic religion, identical with a primitive goddess of Rhamnus, to whom this exceptional title was attached, and who was probably a form of Artemis Aphrodite. In the first character she

---

[a] We may thus explain the epithet Ὀπωτῆρος, which, according to Hesychius (*s. v.* Ὀπωτῆρε), appears to have been attached to Hekate; and we may compare the epithet Ὀπιταίς in the worship of Artemis at Zacynthus [136].

will be noticed in a later chapter ; it is the other aspect of her that concerns us here[a]. And we have to consider, first, what evidence there is of the existence of this concrete goddess in Attic or Greek religion of an early period; secondly, whether and on what ground the surname Νέμεσις was ever applied to Artemis or Aphrodite. In Homer, Nemesis is not a personal figure ; in Hesiod she is, but probably only as a mere personification, such as Αἰδώς[b]. But in the fragment of the *Cypria*[137] her figure has life and vivid personality. She flies over land and sea, like Dictynna of Crete, to escape her lover, and assumes different shapes of animals ; Zeus overtakes her in Rhamnus and in the form of a swan becomes the father of Helen. The locality and this latter transformation is not indeed mentioned in the lines of the *Cypria* ; but we have fair reason for supposing, as the account given by Cratinus agrees in most details with the story of the *Cypria*, that it agreed also in the close of the legend, which has not been preserved in the epic fragment. This, then, is the myth which Dr. Furtwängler supposes[c] to have been afterwards in its main features transferred to Leda by Euripides, while Herr Posnanzky[d] maintains that the legend which makes Leda the mother of Helen is the oldest, and that the author of the *Cypria* for a moral epic purpose chose to make her the daughter of a personified abstraction, the daughter of Retribution. The question whether the myth that makes Leda or that which makes Nemesis the parent is the older, is not of importance here. But it is certainly an error to say that the Nemesis in the *Cypria* or in the comedy of Cratinus is as abstract a notion, or is as weakly personified, as

[a] The most modern literature on the subject gives either an incomplete or an unsatisfactory account: *Némésie et la jalousie des Dieux*, by Tournier, deals chiefly with the personification and the abstract idea ; *Nemesis und Adrasteia*, by Hermann Posnanzky (Breslau, 1890), is more useful for the archaeology and the account of Adrasteia than for its statements and conclusions about Nemesis. He nowhere raises the question why it was that a mere personification, which he seems to consider Nemesis to

have originally been, became identified with a goddess of Attica.

[b] She is clearly so in the *Works and Days*, 739, 754, and she is very probably so in the passage of the *Theogony* in which she is made the daughter of Night[137]; for Hesiod is fond of giving this sort of cosmic origin to the abstractions which he wishes to make divinities.

[c] *Collection Sabouroff*, note complémentaire à la planche 71[2].

[d] Op. cit.

the Nemesis in Hesiod. For the sake of moral allegory a poet might call Helen the daughter of Retribution, just as Aeschylus called her 'bride of battle'; but he would scarcely be likely to depict at great length the coyness of Retribution, and to draw her through a series of transformation-scenes which have the stamp of vivid primitive fancy upon them. It might seem quite natural to a primitive Greek that his goddess should assume the form of a goose, but he could hardly conceive of an abstract moral idea in this form. The whole story which Cratinus and the author of the *Cypria* give and the mention of the locality of Rhamnus would be altogether ridiculous, unless the poets had known of a real goddess worshipped at that spot in Attica, one of whose names was Nemesis, and who was supposed capable of bona-fide maternity[a]. We can conclude also from the form of the legend that, like Artemis and Dictynna, this divinity was naturally regarded as chaste.

This, then, is one proof drawn from ancient authority of the existence of a real and concrete goddess known by this moral title. Of no personified moral abstraction in the Greek language is so personal a story told, and none of them had any deep roots in local worship.

A second proof might be derived from the funeral cere-mony or feast of the Νεμέσια at Athens [137]. It might be sup-posed that as the omission of any of the necessary funereal rites might draw retribution or nemesis upon the kinsmen, the name of this ritual might have simply arisen from this feeling; yet it would be much more naturally given to a celebration which was consecrated to a goddess who, like Aphrodite, was a goddess of birth and death, and who was considered to have power in the underworld. Perhaps from this character of the Rhamnusian goddess arose the idea of the Νέμεσις of the dead, and the association of Nemesis with the θεοὶ παλαμναῖοι and χθόνιοι in the Locrian Timaeus[b]; though here the force of the personified moral idea is felt also, as these are the powers that are said to note and punish wrong-doing.

[a] Otto Keller, *Thiere des Klassischen Alterthums* (p. 288), also regards the Nemesis of Rhamnus as a concrete divinity, akin to Aphrodite Astarte.

[b] Pp. 104 E, 105.

Further evidence of the reality of the cult is gained from the account of the famous statue at Rhamnus [137] [a], which was assigned by some to Pheidias, by others, more correctly, to Agoracritus [a]. From the description of Pausanias we do not gather that there was any trait of the figure itself which had an allegorical meaning ; and whether the moral idea of Nemesis was expressed in the face we cannot say, for the fragment preserved in the British Museum of the right upper part of the visage is too small to bear witness to anything more than the excellence and Pheidian character of the work. It is clear that the sculptor, though he may have remembered Marathon and the 'nemesis' that overtook the Persians there, and may have wrought the victories upon her crown with allusion to that, yet thought of her, not as Hesiod thought of αἰδώς and δίκη, but as an actual territorial divinity akin to Aphrodite and Artemis ; and therefore he set the spray of the apple-tree, the symbol of the former, in her hand, and the stag, the sacred animal of the latter, as an ornament on her crown. The cup in her hand may denote the goddess who dispenses blessing or who receives libation ; the mysterious Aethiopians wrought on the cup have not yet been explained [b]; the representation of the negresses below the throne of the statue of Lampsacus mentioned above is not a parallel, for there we may suppose a reference to Isis and Africa, which is inconceivable in the Rhamnusian work. It is unnecessary to suppose that the main work was inspired by the *Cypria* story ; if it had been we should have expected in the decoration of the crown and the base some allusion to the egg and the swan. Even the scene on the base of the statue can be at most a mere allusion to the legend of Helen's birth given in the *Cypria* : according to the words

[a] There is some force in the argument of Posnanzky, p. 95, that if the statue were by Agoracritus, the Rhamnusians would be tempted to attribute it to Pheidias ; while the reverse would scarcely be natural.

[b] Fürtwangler (op. cit.) regards the Aethiopians as the emblems of light,

an allusion to the celestial character of the goddess ; but this significance nowhere else belongs to them in Greek literature and art. Perhaps the Homeric notion of the 'blameless' people was in the mind of the sculptor of the just goddess.

of Pausanias, which need awake no suspicion, the scene represented Leda leading back Helen to Nemesis, and no doubt implies the tradition which the epic poet had followed, that Nemesis, not Leda, was her mother. The statue was probably inspired by the local belief of Rhamnus, where, as may have often happened when an epithet of a divinity had for a long period been detached and had long passed current as the proper name, the worshippers were no longer certain about the precise character and original name of the divinity. If Nemesis of Rhamnus—as is perhaps the most likely view— were originally an ancient Artemis akin to the Brauronian, it was not at all unnatural that she should be partly confused with Aphrodite [a] : we have seen how in the earliest cults the functions of Artemis overlap those of the other goddess who is generally regarded as her opposite ; and we have reason to think that the Rhamnusian deity was a goddess of birth and a goddess of death, being the mother of Helen Aphrodite, and the divinity to whom the Νεμέσια were consecrated. Hence she would have sympathies both with Aphrodite and Artemis ; and hence may have arisen the myth of her birth from the ocean [b]. And this double character can be illustrated by the work of Agoracritus.

But on the whole this Rhamnusian goddess was more often regarded as the double of Artemis than of Aphrodite. Ἀριστοβούλη, an epithet of the former, is connected by Arte-midorus [137 a] with Νέμεσις [c] ; we have seen how Artemis Upis becomes localized in the later literature at Rhamnus; and it will be noticed later how Adrasteia became regarded

---

[a] At Patrae there was a temple of Nemesis near to Aphrodite's [137 b], and a statement in Photius connects Nemesis with Aphrodite and the marriage-ritual ; and in a later Attic inscription Neme-sis enjoys the Aphrodite-appellative Ourania [137 a].

[b] Posnanzky's statement (p. 12), 'doch wird sich schwerlich eine tiefere aus dem Wesen beider Gottheiten (Aphrodite und Nemesis) geschöpfte Deutung finden,' has only some point if by Nemesis he

means the personification of retribution ; but the difficulty vanishes if we regard Νέμεσις as an appellative given for some special reason to the primitive goddess of Rhamnus who possessed the character described in the text.

[c] He seems to be referring to the Hours or the Nymphs who are men-tioned in the immediate context; but Ἀριστοβούλη is only known as an epithet of Artemis.

as one both with Nemesis and Artemis. How strong was this syncrasy of the two divinities is shown by Solinus, who speaks in an incorrect fashion of Rhamnus as the place where stood the ' Pheidian statue of Diana '; and one of the special characteristics of Artemis, namely, her maidenhood, becomes assigned to Nemesis also [138 c].

Like the Rhamnusian divinity, the Nemesis of Smyrna must be regarded as an actual and personal goddess, not as a mere personification, though in this case, as in the other, the latter view predominates in the later period. What is peculiar to the Smyrniote cult is that there were two divinities of this name, and that they were regarded as the daughters of Night [137 c]. It was they who appeared to Alexander in a dream as he was sleeping under a plane-tree before their temple, and advised him to remove the city to its later site [a]. Above their heads, or above their throne, in the temple of the new city were placed statues of the Charites, archaic works of the sculptor Boupalos. As the Charites were their attendants, and as the plane-tree appears to have been consecrated to them, we may conjecture of them, as of the ancient Rhamnusian goddess, that they were divinities of nature connected with the vegetative world. Whatever view was taken of the Nemesis of Rhamnus came to be taken of the Smyrniote figures also, but there is no special mention of their association with Artemis; they seem closer akin to Aphrodite, being like her divinities of the state and attended by the Charites, and the pig appears to have been a sacred animal in their worship as occasionally it was in hers. As earth-goddesses they may also have had some connexion in cult with Dionysos. On late coins of Smyrna they are represented wearing the mural crown and drawn by griffins [b], the animals of Oriental cult that became associated at times with Aphrodite and Artemis, and frequently in the later period with Nemesis.

The question arises, why at Smyrna only there were two Nemeseis and not one. Posnanzky [c] may be right in objecting to Gerhard's explanation, who regards the one as expressing

[a] Paus. 7. 5, 2.   [b] Head, *Hist. Num.* p. 510.
[c] Op. cit. pp. 61, 62.

the good side of the goddess, the other the evil; but he himself has no solution to offer, and is content with Welcker's suggestion [a] that Nemesis became double at Smyrna because 'Dämonen' tend to become multiplied.

Perhaps a more natural reason for the duality was the change of the city's site, as Pausanias' words imply that the Smyrniotes made two Nemeseis because they had removed from their ancient abode. We may suppose that the older Smyrna had its Νέμεσις, the goddess who was the luck of the city, and that she was retained and a new one created for the new settlement.

It is perhaps through her early relations with Nemesis that Artemis came to have some affinity with the Moirae; this is true at least of Artemis Ὀρθία, who in a Greek inscription of the Roman period is mentioned as receiving worship side by side with Moira the Lacheseis and Asclepios [53 c]: but it may only have been the stress of some casual occurrence that brought her into this company of divinities. For on the whole the association with Nemesis, who, as will be shown in a later chapter, becomes more and more a mere personification, has scarcely affected the character of Artemis.

A question remains which is of special interest, and which has scarcely been noticed by those who have dealt with this subject: on what grounds and with what meaning was the appellative which has been discussed attached to the Rhamnusian goddess? The question is beset with the difficulties which often embarrass the student of ancient religions. No doubt many of the divine epithets which were in vogue in local cults may be derived from some fundamental conception of the divinity; and others were applied as the worshippers advanced in their modes of life and thought, and regarded their deity as their guide and helper. But others may have been gathered and absorbed by the local god or goddess from some alien worship that could not hold its own; there might be no logical reason but mere contiguity, or some accidental special circumstance that gave rise to a peculiar myth and hence to a peculiar epithet. The difficulty of offering a probable

[a] *Götterlehre*, 3. p. 34.

explanation becomes of course all the greater when we are not sure of the meaning of the name ; and we are not quite sure of the meaning borne by the term Νέμεσις when it was first applied to the Rhamnusian goddess.

If we knew that it was not applied to her before the Homeric period, then we should say that she was regarded by the men of Rhamnus as the goddess who feels righteous indignation at evil acts and evil words, and hence, by a natural transition, as the goddess who punishes men for these[a].

It would then remain to ask, why did the Rhamnusian divinity, whom we have seen reason for supposing to have been an ancient Artemis-Aphrodite, come to acquire this high moral function? It may have come about owing to the impression produced by some historical event of which we know nothing. We cannot, at all events, say that it was derived from the recognized character of Artemis or Aphrodite as the punisher of evil-doers. For such a character was not specially acknowledged as theirs in general Greek religion ; in the mythic account of Artemis her punishments appear often capricious or non-moral, and are very limited in their visitation. It may be that we here have an instance of a moral idea that gained strong hold over a particular society, and craved religious expression, and so became attached mechanically, as it were, to the chief divinity of that community. Though we may not explain it, we may find a parallel to this development of an Artemis-Aphrodite, a divinity akin to the earth-goddess, into a moral and retributive power, the guardian of right ; for we find that Ge herself developed into a Ge Themis, and thence into Themis alone[b].

---

[a] This is on the whole the Homeric meaning, and it is this meaning that Hesiod personifies ; vide the passages collected in Posnanzky, pp. 1–4.

[b] This suggested equation, between Ge = Ge Themis = Themis and Artemis = Artemis Nemesis = Nemesis, is curiously illustrated by a legend preserved in Suidas, *s. v.* βούχετα· πόλις ἐστὶ τῆς 'Ηπείρου, ἥν φησι Φιλόχορος ὠνομάσθαι διὰ τὸ τὴν Θέμιν ἐπὶ βοὸς ὀχουμένην ἐλθεῖν ἐκεῖ κατὰ τὸν Δευκαλίωνος κατακλυσμόν. Here is an allusion to a Θέμις ταυροπόλος, a type which recalls the 'Άρτεμις ταυροπόλος. An Attic inscription proves the association of Themis with Nemesis at Rhamnus ; and this is proved also by the statue dedicated to Themis found in Rhamnus and now in Athens; *Eph. Arch.* 1891, Πίν. 1, pp. 54–63.

But it is quite possible that the goddess of Rhamnus was called ·Nemesis before the time of Homer; for, as has been maintained already, the peculiar form of the story in the *Cypria* about the birth of Helen implies a pre-existing belief in a real goddess Nemesis, who probably became real and concrete through the word being attached as an epithet to the Rhamnusian· divinity. We are thus carried back to an indefinitely remote period in order to allow time for the name that was thus attached to have become detached, and to have acquired vogue beyond its own locality as the actual name of a goddess. And perhaps in this early period the word νέμεσις, if, as is generally agreed, it is to be derived from the root meaning 'distribution,' was not limited to the evil sense, but denoted distribution of any lot, the lot of life to which each is born.

It may have originally designated the Rhamnusian Artemis-Aphrodite naturally and properly as a goddess of birth ; as time went on and νέμεσις had its meaning changed and nar-rowed in the ordinary language, the cult-title too would get this new moral significance, and Artemis or Aphrodite Nemesis would come to mean the goddess who distributes evil for evil done. At last, when the proper name was dropped and the appellative took its place, doubt might arise whether this really designated either the one or the other of these two divinities, whose ordinary worship and legend did not well accord with the idea conveyed by the epithet.

As regards the representations of Nemesis, by far the greater number deal only with Nemesis the personification. The monuments of actual cult are few and doubtful. Of the Rhamnusian statue nothing has survived save the beautiful fragment in the Elgin room of the British Museum, and the base, with some part of the relief-work, now in the Central Museum of Athens. It has been supposed by Dr. Furt-wängler[a] and M. Six[b] that a copy of the statue of Agora-critus survives in the representation on a Cypriote coin

[a] Op. cit.
[b] *Numism. Chron.* 1882, p. 89, Pl. 5.

of the fifth century B.C.[a]; a tall and stately female figure, resembling in her drapery the type of the Athena Parthenos of Pheidias, holding in her right hand a phiale over a thymaterion, and a branch in her left. The theory is attractive but by no means convincing; there is no trace of the crown, and the phiale and bough appear so frequently in representations of a religious act that they are not by themselves sufficient to prove that this figure is a direct copy of the Rhamnusian. Dr. Furtwängler tries to clinch the argument by pointing to the brooch which secures her chiton on her right shoulder, and in which he, like M. Six, recognizes the shape of a griffin. Their interpretation of this detail appears to be correct. But the griffin-shape really proves nothing, for we do not hear that this animal was associated at all with the Nemesis of Rhamnus, and we cannot argue that it was simply on the evidence of monuments of the later period. As an Oriental symbol the griffin could designate Aphrodite, and it is found also with Artemis because of her connexion with Apollo[b]. The goddess on the Aeginetan relief, drawn in a car by griffins and accompanied by Eros, must surely be no other than Aphrodite, as Dr. Furtwängler, who first named her Artemis Nemesis, has since recognized in his article on Eros in Roscher's *Lexicon*[c]. The griffin probably came into vogue in the representations of Nemesis through the cult of Smyrna, and it was perhaps associated with the Smyrniote divinity through her close relationship with Aphrodite.

We may conclude from the evidence of the coins of Smyrna that the mere abstract idea of right and retribution entered far more into the representation of the Nemeseis of Smyrna than into that of the Rhamnusian deity. They appear not so much as divinities of real flesh and blood, but as forms of moral allegory, bearing in their hands the staff and bridle, the symbols of order and control[d]. But we cannot say that these coin-representations express the ideas of the genuine ancient cult.

[a] Gardner, *Types of Greek Coins,* 10. 27, with description, p. 170; Head, *Hist. Num.* p. 625, who names the figure Aphrodite.

[b] Vide *Artemis-Monuments,* p. 533.

[c] P. 1352.

[d] Head, *Hist. Num.* p. 510.

In the large series of monuments of the legend and cult of Nemesis examined by Dr. Furtwängler in the article already quoted, few could be supposed to have any direct connexion with local worship, and of these few none are with certainty to be interpreted as representations of Nemesis. The question might be raised about the terracotta in the Museum of Syracuse published by Kekulé[a], showing an enthroned goddess who wears a turret-shaped crown, a diploidion, and large himation, a fold of which she raises above her head as a veil with her right hand, while her left hand rests on a swan that sits on the left arm of the throne. The solemnity of the representation suggests a monument of cult ; but, as far as we know, Rhamnus and Smyrna were the only sites of the actual cult of Nemesis, and their cult-monuments do not seem to have employed the swan as a symbol of the divinity. The bird is still more appropriate to Aphrodite, and it is her name that this enthroned figure suggests, with its rich flowing hair, matronly form, and earnest expression.

[a] *Terracotten von Sicilien*, 2. 3.

CHAPTER XV.

ADRASTEIA.

ADRASTEIA, understood in the later period as the goddess of inevitable fate, came to be a sort of twin-sister of Nemesis, and so was occasionally connected with Artemis [138 b]. At Andros and Cos there was a joint worship of Adrasteia and Nemesis [138 c], and we find the two connected by Anti-machus, the learned epic poet of the latter part of the fifth century, quoted by Strabo ; in the drama of the fifth century, in the younger Attic comedy, in passages of the *Anthology* and of Lucian, the functions of the one goddess cannot easily be distinguished from those of the other [a] ; and in the later literature the identity is completely established. We need not look further than this for an explanation of the statement in Harpocration that Demetrius of Scepsis identified Adrasteia with Artemis, and for the presence of the statue of the former in the temple of Artemis Leto and Apollo at Cirrha, the divinities who brought down the due 'nemesis' on the Cirrhaeans.

But the origin of 'Αδράστεια, which can be clearly traced, is independent of Nemesis. There is no doubt that it was a cult-name and probably a local title of Cybele detached at an early period [138 a]. It was near Priapus, Cyzicus, and in the Troad, localities where Cybele was especially worshipped, that the cult of Adrasteia was established ; in a fragment of the *Phoronis* she is scarcely distinguished from Cybele, being

---

[a] This is not the view of Posnanzky, op. cit. pp. 75–77, who thinks that 'Αδρά-στεια is appealed to in order to avert the evil consequences of speech, Nemesis to punish ῞Υβρις ; but the passages he quotes do not seem to bear out this dis-tinction. The question will be further discussed in a later chapter on per-sonification of abstract ideas.

described as the mountain-goddess whose attendants were the Idaean Dactyli. Later on, men came to know her not so much as the great mother herself, but as a mountain-nymph, and in Crete as the nymph who nursed Zeus; while in Orphic literature her close relation with Cybele was recognized. As early as the Peloponnesian war the worship of Adrasteia had become established on the Acropolis of Athens, probably in some association with Cybele and Bendis, who had gained public recognition in Athens in the fifth century [138 b].

How then did Cybele acquire this character of a stern goddess of inevitable fate and justice? There is certainly but little essential connexion of nature between the Phrygian goddess of wild orgies and impure rites and the lofty and austere impersonation of righteous judgement, such as was the Ἀδράστεια of Plato and the Stoics. The explanation is probably due merely to a misunderstanding of the name.

Cybele Ἀδράστεια meant the goddess of the city or locality in Phrygia that took its name from the Phrygian hero Adrastus [a]. Then when the title was detached, it came to be interpreted as 'the goddess from whom one cannot run away'; and this meaning may have been assisted by the confusion between the Phrygian Adrastus and the Argive hero, whose legend was a picture of inevitable fate. When afterwards this new sense of Ἀδράστεια came into vogue, she naturally became connected with Nemesis, and so accidentally with Artemis. But the general character of the latter goddess in Greece was, as we have seen, scarcely touched by this association with these powers of retribution and righteous judgement. It is more important to consider her relations with Hekate, in order to understand the part played by Artemis in later Greek religion.

[a] This on the whole is the view taken by Posnanzky, pp. 83, 84.

CHAPTER XVI.

HEKATE.

A GREAT obscurity hangs about the name, the origin, and the character of this goddess. The name at least seems to be Greek, and to be an epithet that may signify the 'far-off one,' or the 'far-darting one,' if we consider it as a shortened form of ἑκατηβόλος; but no explanation that has been offered is very certain or significant[a].

As to her origin, she is usually accepted as a Hellenic divinity, and the question has scarcely been discussed by modern writers. If this view is correct[b], she was one whose worship must have been obscured in the earliest period among the leading Greek tribes, and have revived later. For there is no mention of her in the *Iliad* and *Odyssey*, nor in any fragment of the 'Homeric' epic; although, had the epic poets of the eighth or seventh century known of her as she was known to the later Greek, she would probably have been noticed in such a passage, for instance, as Odysseus' descent to Hades. Again, neither early nor late did any real mythology

[a] The derivation from ἑκατηβόλος, an epithet of the archer-god Apollo, is not satisfactory — for Hekate was never imagined to carry bow or spear; there is only one statue of a very late period showing a quiver on her shoulders. Another theory is that, as ἕκατος was an adjective sometimes attached to Apollo, so ἑκάτη might have been the feminine form of it and applied to Artemis, and subsequently, becoming personal, might have been detached from her and regarded as the name of a separate goddess; but ἑκάτη is never found applied to Artemis as a common adjective.

[b] This is the view tacitly taken by Steuding in Roscher's *Lexicon* (*s. v.* Hekate), by Petersen in his articles in the *Archaeologisch-epigraphische Mittheilungen aus Wien*, 4 and 5, by Schoemann in his *Opuscula Academica* —*de Hekate Hesiodea*, 2. pp. 215–249, and by Köppen, *Die dreigestaltete Hekate*. Preller and Welcker appear to believe in the foreign origin of the cult.

grow up about her: we find nothing but a few stories of
little value or credit, invented sometimes to explain some of
her obscure titles, such as Ἄγγελος; and only once does she
play some part in a dramatic myth, namely, in the Gigantomachy as described by Apollodorus, as the legends of the
later period bring all the deities into the action and Hekate
is named among them, though she is not found in the early
accounts of the battle. In fact, the importance and reality
that she came to have in Greek religion may for the most
part have come to her through her association with Demeter
and Artemis.

Not only has she little legend, but there is no fixed and
accepted genealogy for her: she was regarded by Hesiod and
others as the daughter of the Titan Perses and Asterie [1], by
Musaeus as the daughter of Asterie and Zeus [2], by Bacchylides
as sprung from Night [3], by Euripides as the daughter of Leto [3];
and in a Thessalian legend she was said to be the daughter of
Admetus and a Pheraean woman; also she was believed to be
close of kin to Aeëtes and Circe of Colchis. In the Hesiodic
fragment she is emphatically called μουνογενής, having neither
brother nor sister [a]; and no clan or tribe claimed descent from
her. Neither her temple nor her images were associated with
a prehistoric period or legend, and the magic practices performed in the name of Hekate, and the sorcery that made her
a form of terror, seem to us more savage or mediaeval than
Hellenic. There was, indeed, a certain part of true Greek
ritual that was tainted with magic, but no such atmosphere
of evil and debased superstition gathered around any figure
of the Hellenic religion as around Hekate.

These various facts suggest that this personage was not
Greek at all, but borrowed from a neighbouring people; and
it may be that her cult invaded Greece, starting from the
same land and following the same track as that of Dionysos.

[a] Μουνογενής, in the two places where it
occurs in that passage, would make better
sense if understood as sprung from one
parent only—μουνογενὴς ἐκ μητρὸς ἐοῦσα
(Theog. 448); Zeus honours her especially, though μουνογενής, which might
mean though no one knows who was her
father. This sense of the word is found in
the later Orphic literature, being applied
to Athene, as sprung from Zeus alone, in
Hymn 32. 1; but in early Greek the
word could hardly bear this meaning.

At first sight such a theory may seem to be contradicted
by the evidence that we have of the very wide prevalence of
the worship of Hekate throughout the Greek world; we find
it in the central northern and southern islands of the Aegean,
on the coast and in the interior of Asia Minor, in Italy and
Sicily; but this of course proves nothing, as the same is true
of the late worships of Mithras and Isis, which, like the
worship of Hekate, spread far beyond the limits of the ancient
classical world[a]. What is more important is that she was
less frequently found in the more secluded parts of Greece,
scarcely, for instance, at all in Arcadia, where we have only
a doubtful allusion to her worship in a passage quoted by
Porphyry from Theopompus [13c], and that she had nothing to
do with the primitive cults of those divinities with whom she
afterwards became associated. Thus she does not appear in
the Arcadian worship of Despoina[b] and Demeter Erinys; nor
had she place in Eleusinian legend, nor in the ancient
Brauronian cult of Artemis.

The earliest literary record, and the Thessalian and
Aeginetan worships, give some support to the theory suggested above, that we must trace back this goddess to some
land beyond the boundaries of Greece, lying probably to the
north[c]. The earliest references to her in literature are—(a) The
quotation in Pausanias from the κατάλογος γυναικῶν attributed
to Hesiod, showing that the poet connected Hekate with
Artemis and Iphigenia[4]: we may regard this as an early
Boeotian version which tries to adapt a Greek myth to a new
cult, and to discover the new goddess, who came from the
North and who, perhaps through Medea, had some connexions
with the Euxine, in the local Artemis Iphigenia of Aulis and
Tauris. (b) The well-known passage in Hesiod's *Theogony*,
which can scarcely be the composition of the author of the
κατάλογος γυναικῶν, and is probably an earlier account, the
earliest in Greek literature, of Hekate[1]; for it connects

[a] Vide Geographical Register of
Hekate-Cults, p. 606.

[b] The supposition of Köppen (*Die
dreigestaltete Hekate*, Vienna, 1823, p. 6)
that Despoina was Hekate is perfectly

baseless.

[c] This view has been already taken
by Voss in his *Mythologische Briefe*, 3.
190, 194, 212.

her with no figure of Greek religion at all, except Zeus; she has no ties at present with Artemis or any other divinity. These lines may be regarded as an interpolation in the poem, which makes no other mention of Hekate, and which devotes to no other divinity such an emphatic record of function and rank. But they are a valuable fragment of Boeotian poetry[a]: the lines show something of the zeal of the propagandist who wishes to obtain recognition for a new cult, and are of the first importance as evidence of the original character that Hekate possessed. The poet regards her as Titan-born and belonging to the older world, which may be a way of saying that she had no recognized place at that time in the Hellenic Pantheon: Zeus maintains her in her rights and gives her a share in Olympus and the 'earth and the unvintaged sea'; she gives men aid in war, and sits by kings in their judgement-seat; she brings honour to the horse-men and to the athlete in the contest; she gives the hunter or the fisher his prey, and works with Hermes to increase the herds of bullocks, goats, and sheep in the stall: lastly, she is κουροτρόφος, the foster-mother of children.

Many of these ideas reappear in later cults, but the poet claims more than the Greek communities that received the worship of Hekate were ever willing to accord to her, and he probably omits certain darker traits of her original character, such as her association with the lower world, with magic, and with the cross-ways. We may notice that he nowhere hints at any connexion between her and the moon.

The poem then seems to suggest that the cult was a new importation into Boeotia; and we should then naturally think of it as coming from the North. Of this there is certain other evidence. It has been noticed above[b] that there is a close con-nexion between the Thessalian Artemis Pheraea and Hekate, and the most striking illustration of this is the Thessalian

---

[a] The Boeotian style is seen in the use of the picturesque epithet for the personal noun. Schoemann, in his trea-tise *de Hekate Hesiodea*, may be right in rejecting the theory that the fragment has an Orphic or mystic origin, although its tone is not unlike that of the later Orphic hymn, and its main idea, namely that Hekate is of omnipresent power, is that which is tediously applied to all the divinities of later Orphism.

[b] P. 474.

story that Hekate was the daughter of Pheraea, and as
a newly-born infant was thrown out into the cross-roads, but
rescued and brought up by shepherds[5]. The Artemis of
Iolchos, with whom the legend couples the name of Medea, is
a goddess of magical incantations and of the arts of poisoning.
In the narrative of Diodorus Siculus[a], Medea tells Pelias that
her tutelary goddess has come to him from Colchis 'riding
upon serpents'; and she names her Artemis, though this
mode of travelling is suitable only for Hekate, of whom
Medea is the priestess and perhaps the 'double'[b]. And the
evil reputation for witchcraft which attached to the whole
land of Thessaly can be best explained by supposing that the
worship of Hekate, bringing its original taint with it, struck
deep roots upon this soil. It is true that the superstitious
terrors that were connected with the name of this divinity
and with the practices of her votaries seem to have been felt
more in the later ages; but supposing they were not there in
the beginning, we cannot easily explain how they grew up;
for they could not have naturally come from the association
of this worship with that of Artemis or Persephone.

A locality which was particularly noted for the honour paid
to Hekate was Aegina[7]: her mysteries were in vogue in that
island at least as early as the fifth century, and are often
mentioned by later writers, the institution of them being
attributed to the Thracian Orpheus. This name, and the
prehistoric connexion between the heroic family of the
land, the Aeacidae, and Phthia, seem to suggest once more
that the worship travelled down from the North. Again, we
find it in the islands of the Thracian Sea, and in Samothrace
amalgamated with the mystic rites of the Cabiri[7]. And
if Thrace had been its original home we should expect
it to have crossed the Hellespont as naturally as it travelled
southwards into Greece; and in fact we find it in the Troad,
in Paphlagonia, Galatia, Lydia, Caria, Lycia, Pamphylia. Or
we may of course say that it passed over to the east side of

[a] 4. 51.
[b] The Thessalian ἱέρεια τῆς Ἐνοδίας,
who poisoned the flesh of a mad bull

for a strategic purpose, was keeping up
the tradition of Medea; Polyaen. *Strat.*
8. 42.

the Aegean directly from Greece, at some time when the affinity between Artemis and Hekate had become so recognized that any centre of the cult of Artemis was likely to attract the worship of the kindred goddess. We may thus explain its existence at Ephesus[9], to account for which a curious story was invented telling how Artemis was inhospitably received there by the wife of Ephesus, and how by way of punishment the goddess changed her into a dog, but repenting at last restored her to her human form: the woman then went and hanged herself for shame, but was raised to life again and appeared in the costume of Artemis and received the name of Hekate. We see why the dog comes into the story, and we should understand the matter of the hanging if Hekate were worshipped under the title of ἀπαγχομένη, as Artemis was. All that we know is that there was a statue, possibly more than one, of Hekate behind or near the temple of the great Ephesian goddess.

In certain parts of Caria the worship appears to have struck deep root. The original name of the city of Idrias was Hekatesia, and the worship of Hekate Λαγινῖτις was maintained there. The name was popularly derived from the hare that fled to the site of the town, but in reality referred to the neighbouring city of Lagina, the chief centre, at least in late times, of Hekate-worship in Asia Minor. The cult of this latter city[a] associated the goddess so intimately with the Carian Zeus Panamerios, that we may suppose that she there took the place of the great goddess of Asia Minor and was probably regarded as his spouse. We hear of the annual festival 'of the key,' the κλειδὸς πομπή, alluding to the mysteries of the lower world; the divinities were partly served by eunuchs, and choirs of boys were trained under the supervision of the state to sing a traditional hymn of praise. The part played by the eunuch in the ritual reminds us of the Cybele cult, and some ancient mythographers appear to have associated the Corybantes with the service of Hekate[11,16], and we have seen that the orgiastic mysteries of Samothrace were devoted to her as well as to the Cabiri[7].

[a] Vide Geographical Register, s. v. Lagina, p. 607.

There seems, then, some ground for the belief expressed in Strabo[a] that Hekate belongs to that circle of Phrygian-Thracian cults of which the chief figure is an earth-goddess, and the orgiastic ritual a marked characteristic. And we find that Hekate comes to be related to Cybele, and plainly identified with the Cretan Britomartis, whose name itself was explained in reference to an ancient prophecy concerning the birth of Hekate[b]: in Aegina itself the worship and mysteries of Hekate may not have been altogether distinct from that of the Cretan goddess who came to the island at an early period.

The theory that Thrace was her native country becomes the stronger as we find the undoubtedly Thracian goddess Bendis with many points of likeness to Hekate. The epithet Δίλογχος that belonged to the former is explained by Hesychius as describing the goddess who, like Hekate, had power in more than one sphere of nature; and the torch seems to have been the special symbol of both. The Thracian goddess—whatever was her real name—whom the Greeks called Artemis Basileia or βούσβατος[c] was connected with herds and the fruits of the soil, and Hekate also was concerned with these, as we find in the Hesiodic description and in later Greek legend and ritual. A strong reason for believing that Hekate was an intruder in the Hellenic world is that the hound was her familiar and sacrificial animal, and that this sacred character belonged to him scarcely anywhere else in genuinely Greek religion or ritual[d]. For Artemis he was

[a] P. 473.

[b] Artemis [131 k].

[c] Ib. [54 g], [129].

[d] Plutarch tells us that generally in Greek religion the hound was regarded as unclean, and yet that he was used in rites of purification in Boeotia; he is probably referring to the rites of Hekate, as Boeotia was an ancient home of her worship [12]. A sacred character attached to this animal also in the worship of Asclepios at Epidauros; but Asclepios does not belong to the ancient Greek religion, and himself also came from the north of Greece, and possibly from Thrace. By becoming the son of Apollo he is adopted into Greek religion. The goddess of child-birth to whom, according to Socrates, the Argives offered a dog, διὰ τὴν ῥαστώνην τῆς λοχείας, was called Εἰλιόνεια, but may be regarded as Ἑκάτη Εἰλείθυια [12]. The Spartan ephebi sacrificed a young hound to the war-god; whether this was a foreign element in the cult of Ares or not may be doubted.

a purely secular beast, useful for the hunt ; she never assumes
his shape and he is never offered to her. But we have evidence
that he was regularly sacrificed to Hekate [12], and the goddess
herself is clearly supposed to take his form in that Ephesian
legend mentioned above ; and in the ghostly stories such as
those that amused Lucian, he probably often figured as her
'manifestation' or her 'sending.' The dog was also the
animal used for purification in the rites of Hekate [12]. It is
true that we have no direct proof of the sacred character
of the dog in the religion of Thrace ; but in certain legends
the metamorphosed Hecuba, 'the dog with fiery eyes,' was
supposed to join the following of Hekate and to roam howling
through the Thracian forests [a] ; and the statue of Hekate
Lampadephorus at Byzantium was supposed to commemorate
the good service of the dogs who aroused the citizens when
Philip of Macedon attacked them by night [b].

Accepting this theory of the origin of the cult, we should
say that Hekate was the Greek term corresponding to some
Thracian title of this goddess, and that it obtained vogue first
in Thessaly, Boeotia, and Aegina at a much earlier period than
that at which the name of Bendis was received in Greece.
From Aegina or Boeotia it may have passed to Athens, perhaps not earlier than the middle of the sixth century [10]. She
appears in the Homeric hymn to Demeter which is often
attributed to the age of the Peisistratidae [13 a]. According to
one account, which however is questionable, it was to Hekate
that the Athenians offered sacrifice after Marathon at Agrae [c],
and it may be that her worship, like that of Pan, was for the
first time publicly instituted in Attica after this great event,
although we have proof of its earlier private recognition in
a terracotta of the sixth century B. C. [d] A fifth-century
inscription from Eleusis possibly contains a trace of the name
of Hekate in conjunction with Hermes and the Graces, with
whom she was associated on the Acropolis of Athens, at least

[a] Cf. Artemis [130].

[b] Geograph. Reg. s. v. Byzantium.

[c] Artemis [26 f]. The name of Hekate
has been substituted by the pseudo-
Plutarch for that of Artemis 'Αγροτέρα,
who was the goddess worshipped at
Agrae and to whom the Athenians
vowed sacrifice before Marathon.

[d] *Hekate-Monuments*, p. 549.

in the later period [15]. The statue by Alcamenes that stood
by the temple of Nike Apteros at the top of the Propylaea
was called Hekate Ἐπιπυργιδία, or Artemis Hekate, or
Artemis Ἐπιπυργιδία, and a later Attic inscription com-
bines her with Hermes, and another mentions her torch-
bearer in company with the priest of the Graces [10, 15]. We
know also that some time before the Peloponnesian war her
images were common in Athens, placed before the doors as
charms to avert evil [23 b], and she had become especially
a woman's goddess and identified with Artemis [10].

We have now to explain why it was that she was identified
with this particular Greek goddess, or at least more closely
related to her than to any other. The usual reason given is
very simple: namely, that both were merely different names
for the moon-goddess. But this view—which is not often
challenged—rests on a misconception of the original nature
of Artemis, and a very questionable interpretation of the
original character of Hekate. For the two goddesses had been
connected as early as Hesiod, as the passage quoted by
Pausanias from the κατάλογος γυναικῶν proves [4] ; but at this
period, as has been shown, we can find no lunar element in the
character of Artemis ; on the contrary, there are reasons for
thinking that this view of her came later into vogue through
her association with Hekate, and therefore should not be
regarded as the ground of that association. On the other
hand, the belief that Hekate herself was pre-eminently and
originally a moon-goddess approves itself only to those who do
not pay sufficient attention to the Hesiodic fragment, and who
apply the logical deductive method of Roscher to primitive
forms of religion [a]. The theory for which reasons have been
given above, that Hekate is one of many forms of a Thracian-
Phrygian divinity, brings with it the belief that she would
derive most of her functions from the earth rather than the
moon. Her torches and her interest in child-birth are thus
quite as well explained, and her care for the crops and the
herds, the hunter and the fisher, much better. The hound may

[a] Vide Steuding on Hekate in Ros-   view as Preller, Welcker, and Petersen
cher's *Lexicon*, who takes the same   (*Arch. Epigr. Mitt.* 4).

have become her familiar, not because it was regarded as the animal 'who bays the moon,' but because it was the natural follower of the goddess who haunts the wilds, and because in many legends the dog has an 'uncanny' and infernal character. We may thus best understand her affinity with Artemis, which was recognized in an early period; for the latter goddess drew most of her nature from the earth and from the life of the wilds, and most of the description in the Hesiodic passage would apply to Artemis as well. And apart from any deep essential affinity, her torches and her hounds and her wild nature would be enough to persuade the Greeks that Hekate was a sort of 'double' of the Hellenic goddess.

Nevertheless it is also true that from the fifth century onwards we have clear proof that the imagination of poets and artists, and perhaps also the view of those who offered sacrifice to Hekate, did connect her in some way with the moon [13]; and in this there is something of genuine and popular belief that cannot be ignored, and which is of more value than the philosophic theory that begins as early as the sixth century to resolve deities into elements—Hera, for instance, into the air.

In the Homeric hymn to Demeter, Hekate is said to have been hiding in a cave when she witnessed the rape of Proserpine, and to have come to meet the bereaved mother with torches in her hands. Possibly the poet is thinking of her as a moon-goddess, but it is an illusion to suppose that only a moon-goddess could hide in a cave and could witness things: the infernal divinities might also be thought to be witnesses and to lurk underground. It is in the Attic drama that she first emerges plainly in her lunar character, and at the same time is so closely combined with Artemis that she is called the daughter of Leto. Euripides addresses her as ' Hekate, child of Leto [3]'; and when Aeschylus, in the fragment already quoted, speaks of the ἀστερωπὸν ὄμμα Λητῴας Κόρης, which the context shows to be the moon, he is perhaps thinking of Artemis Hekate, to whom he refers by name in the *Supplices* [23 k]. The sun and the moon are clearly combined as Helios and Hekate in the fragment of Sophocles'

'Ριζοτόμοι [13 a] ; and this view must have become popular, for sometimes the vase-painting of the fourth century plainly characterized Hekate as the moon-goddess [a]. There were also certain ritual-practices consecrated to Hekate when the moon was new or full ; the ' suppers of Hekate ' were offered by rich people, and little round cakes set with candles were placed in the cross-roads, and sacred both to her and to Artemis [13 b] ; but we cannot take this as certain evidence, nor conclude at once that a divinity was recognized as lunar because the phases of the moon marked the time when oblation was to be made ; just as we must not offhand regard a deity to whom prayers or sacrifice were addressed at sunrise as a personification of the dawn. ' The banquets of Hekate' seem to have been offerings made, not to the lunar goddess, but rather to the mistress of spirits, in order to avert evil phantoms from the house. None of the household would touch the food [13 b, c]. It was offered on the thirtieth day, which was sacred to the dead.

However, we find a genuine lunar element in Hekate recognized in popular belief and in the later public monuments : and some of the later scholiasts and expounders of mythology, who were in no better position to judge than we are, seem to have regarded this element as the essential and original one in her nature. It very probably was original, in the sense that she had it before she became a Greek divinity ; for it is difficult to see, on the theory of her foreign origin, how she could have acquired this character in Greece, where the moon-goddess received such slight recognition. But we need not say that it ever constituted the whole of her nature, unless we are bound to follow the method prevalent in the German interpretation of myths and to trace the manifold character and functions of a divinity deductively back to a single concept or idea. On the other theory, which might be called the theory of local ' contagion ' or assimilation, an earth-goddess could ' catch,' inherit, or usurp certain qualities or features of a moon-goddess, or vice versa. And the Hesiodic fragment

[a] The question as to the meaning of the triple-shaped Hekate of Alcamenes will be discussed later.

and other evidence allow us to believe that Hekate came down into Greece as an earth-goddess with the usual interest that such a divinity always had in vegetation and nutrition, in wild and human life, but possessing also a certain attraction for the moon, and trailing with her a very pernicious cloud of superstition and sorcery. That her lunar aspect became afterwards so prominent may be owing to the religious economy of the Greeks, who had earth-goddesses in plenty, and whose Selene, a retiring and faded divinity, may have seemed to want new support.

But the Greeks themselves were much perplexed about her, and knew that she was other than Selene and Artemis; in fact, the complexity of the Hesiodic portrait corresponds in some measure to the later belief and cult. She became associated, for instance, almost as closely with Demeter and Persephone as with Artemis, and this by right of her original character as a divinity who had power on the surface of the earth and underground [14]. The Hekate of Sophocles' ' root-gatherers ' seems to have drawn her attributes and nature from the moon, the earth, and the lower world ; for the moon-light was her spear, and her brows were bound with oak-leaves and serpents. Euripides, who spoke of her as the daughter of Leto, called her also the εἰνοδία θυγάτηρ Δήμητρος, the queen of the phantom-world ; and on black-figured vases she appears in company with Persephone, Demeter, and Hermes. It accords with the wider character of her presented in the Hesiodic poem, that, like Demeter and Ge, she was Κουροτρόφος [23 k], and an ancient inscription from Selinus possibly contains the prayer made to her by a mother for her child. The Gauls found her in Galatia, and learned to pray to her for themselves and their crops[a]. In a late Greek inscription from Cilicia she is regarded as one with Artemis Εὔπλοια, Selene, and Gaia [21], and in a late oracle quoted by Eusebius [14] Hekate, who demands a statue, declares that her shape is that of Demeter, ' the fair goddess of fruits.' We find her also allied with the lesser powers that had some connexion with the earth,

---

[a] Vide Geographical Register, _s. v._ Galatia.

vegetation and the life of the woods; we find her with Pan [a] and the Corybantes and Cybele, deities who, like Hekate, inspired madness [16] ; with Priapus at Tralles [17] ; in Athens with Hermes and the Charites, who must have been regarded in this association as divinities of increase and growth. Also the maritime character of the goddess claimed for her in the *Theogony* was not altogether forgotten [21] ; and as we have such early testimony for it, we may regard it as original, and not derived from Artemis Εὔπλοια, nor arising necessarily from any view about the earth or the moon, but possibly only from the seafaring habits of her worshippers [b]. Her ghostly character also, which becomes very prominent in later times, but was probably always recognized, must have kept her chthonian nature clearly before men's minds ; for sorcery and magic belong more naturally to the lower world, at least from the Greek point of view, than to the Moon, who seems to have been considered a fairly harmless divinity in Greece, being occasionally a passive victim of sorcery when a Thessalian witch laid her foaming and sick on the grass, but not being herself a great sorceress. And so the mocking Lucian, when Mithrobarzanes is preparing to go down into hell, makes him dig a pit and invoke the powers from below, the Furies and the Poenae, 'nightly Hekate and praiseworthy Persephone [c].' And the magician in his *Philopseudes* brings up Hekate from below in the form of a woman, half a furlong high, snake-footed and with snakes in her hair and on her shoulders, with a torch in her left hand and a sword in her right; while Selene comes down from the sky in the shapes of a woman, an ox, and a dog ; we may suppose the latter form to have been assumed out of compliment to the other goddess.

In fact Hekate appealed to the later imagination more as an infernal power than as a lunar ; she borrows her whip and cord from the Furies, and her serpents made her an image of fear like the Gorgon. But though such a character was likely

[a] Hekate is classed with Pan among the θεοὶ ἐπίγειοι by Artemidorus; *Oneirocr.* 2. 34.
[b] The mullet was sacred to Hekate; and, according to a legend preserved by the scholiast on Apoll. Rhod. 4. 826, she was the mother of Scylla.
[c] *Nekyomant.* 9.

to be impressive in the ages of decay and debased religion, it probably influenced secret practice more than the public cult[a], and it never, as Welcker wrongly supposes[b], altogether obscured the early Hesiodic conception of a Hekate powerful on earth and sea and beneficent to men in certain parts of life. Many details of this conception have been already shown to have survived to a late period ; and Plutarch, Porphyry, and the later Orphic literature express the same thought in formal or philosophic terms : she had for them something of the same cosmic power, though her importance is evidently slight, as she had for the early Boeotian poet[24].

But the high moral functions that the latter claims for her were never given her in Greek religion : she never ' sat in the judgement-seat of kings,' and her mysteries are not known to have had any moral or spiritual significance at all. Her association with Zeus Meilichios at Athens, of which we have some slight evidence[c], does not prove that any of the moral ideas which were infused into that worship attached themselves to her; the casual conjunction of the two divinities arose merely from the chthonian character of both. In the inscription that dedicates the late Capitoline statue she is called Μεισοπόνηρος[22], and this, which is the one moral epithet

[a] There are only two titles by which Hekate was probably known in public cult as a goddess of mystery and fear[22]— ἄφραττος at Tarentum (Hesych. *s. v.*), an epithet of the 'unspeakable one,' and ἀνταία, of which the meaning is disputed. The passage in Hesychius (*s. v.* ἀνταία), which is made clear by Lobeck's emendation of δαιμόνια for δαίμονα (*Aglaoph.* p. 121), interprets the word as ' hostile,' being applied to Hekate as sending visions of ill, and so the author of the *Etymologicum Magnum* explains the word ἄντιος as αἴτιος βλάβης; but Hesychius states that Aeschylus in the *Semele* used the word as ἱκέσιος, and this agrees with the interpretation given by the scholiast on the *Iliad*, 22. 113, and with its use in Apoll. Rhod. I. 1141, and in the *Orphic Hymn*, 40. 1, where it is an epithet of Demeter. But the former interpretation is more probably correct, the word ἐξάντης having the opposite sense, ' free of evil '; Plat. *Phaedr.* 244 E. The epithet ΠΑΝΔΙΝΑ attached to a goddess on fourth-century coins of Terina and Hipponium has been regarded as a title of Hekate and interpreted as Πανδείνη, the 'all-terrible' (*Rev. Arch.* 1848, p. 159; cf. Millingen, *Considérations sur la Numismatique de l'ancienne Italie*, Florence, 1841, p. 72) : but the inscription is perfectly legible and certain, and cannot be a miswriting for Πανδείνη; nor does the figure hold a whip or any other attribute of Hekate. Probably the name is not Greek and denotes a local nymph.

[b] *Griech. Götterl.* I. 567.

[c] Vide Zeus[138 a].

ever attached to her in cult, does not come to very much : it may allude to her whip and her cord, or it may designate the goddess who controls evil spirits. Her chthonian associations may have suggested some vague belief in her as a goddess who punished certain kinds of guilt, and in the *Antigone* Creon's sin against the body of Polyneikes is supposed to have incurred the wrath of Pluto and the θεὰ ἐνοδία; but we cannot further illustrate this belief, except with the slight instance of a late inscription from Phrygia, in which the disturber of a grave is threatened with the wrath of Hekate [20].

The household purifications, called ὀξυθύμια [22], performed in the name of Hekate do not seem to have had any reference at all to moral stain or evil [a]. The house was swept and smoked, and the pollutions were carried away in a potsherd, apparently to the cross-roads, and then thrown away while the bearer's back was turned. If these were connected with the sacrifice of a dog at the cross-roads, of which we hear, we may regard the dog as a κάθαρμα, and the purifications as having some reference to child-birth in the house. Also, they may have been supposed to purge the household of ghosts, who were taken thus to the cross-roads, and committed to the keeping of the infernal goddess [b].

As there is very little morality that we can discover in her religion, so the occasions on which appeal might be made to her appear to have been few: it was good to invoke her in haunted places, because she could send up forms of terror or benign apparitions [c]; it was important to have her image at the cross-ways, probably because they were considered likely places for ghosts, and before the threshold of the

---

[a] The δεισιδαίμων of Theophrastus purifies his house as an ἐπαγωγὴ τῆς Ἑκάτης [22].

[b] In Plato's State (*Laws* 873 b) the body of the murderer must be thrown out after execution, unburied, at the cross-roads. Why these places were of such evil character is hard to say; their gloomy associations were no doubt enhanced by the images of Hekate, the way-goddess that stood there; but it is possible that these were originally placed there because of the ill omen that attached to the cross-ways in the popular belief of Greece and other nations.

[c] In the *Helena* of Euripides (569) Helen exclaims when she sees Menelaos, ὦ φωσφόρ' Ἑκάτη, πέμπε φάσματ' εὐμενῆ, to which Menelaos replies, οὐ νυκτίφαντον πρόπολον Ἐνοδίας μ' ὁρᾷς.

house, lest ghosts might enter. But in spite of the Boeotian poet's assurances, the warrior in battle and the athlete and horseman in the race do not appear to have often invoked the aid of Hekate [a].

It is a question how far her association with Artemis affected the traditional character of either of the two goddesses. In certain details we may suppose there was mutual borrowing. The torch in the hands of Artemis is supposed by Petersen to have come from Hekate or Hekate Eileithyia [b]; his argument rests on the fact that Artemis is not designated or represented as Πυρφόρος, or the torch-bearer, till a comparatively late period, the latter part of the fifth century, by which time her connexion with Hekate had been generally recognized; and the torch had been no doubt an aboriginal property of the latter goddess.

A certain type of Artemis, the representation of her speeding along with two torches in her hands, is almost certainly borrowed, as we find in North Greece a similar type of Hekate in swift motion with her torches raised and her wild hounds at her side [c].

Again, the connexion of Hekate with the cross-ways was no doubt primitive, although it does not appear in the fragment of the *Theogony*, and probably both at the cross-ways and before the house her image was intended to scare away evil spirits; it seems likely, then, that it was only as a double of Hekate that Artemis was regarded as a προθυραία or ἐνοδία [d]. But Artemis was in her own right, like Apollo Ἀγυιεύς, a leader of the path; and there is no reason for supposing that she borrowed from the other goddess such titles as Ἡγεμόνη [e]. And on the other hand Hekate, being often represented hurrying along with torches, may have been considered

[a] There were games in her honour at Stratonicea; *Bull. de Corr. Hell.* 1881, 236.

[b] *Arch. Epigr. Mitt.* 4. p. 142.

[c] Vide *Hekate-Monuments*, p. 551.

[d] Hekate [23] b, e.

[e] Στροφαία is an epithet applied to Artemis (Hekate [23] c), and is of doubtful sense: if it refers to the cross-ways it must have come from Hekate; but it is not known to have been a title of the latter goddess: it is attached also to Hermes, not apparently as a deity of the cross-ways, but as the divinity whose image stood within the house and 'turned back' the evil-doer.

as a leader of the ways in the Lycian˙worship of Hekate Προκαθηγέτις [23 d], independently of Artemis.

The place before the gate of the temple, or city, or house was consecrated to Hekate[a]; and it is only by confusion that the Ἑκάτειον standing before the door was called an Artemision [23 b]; for Artemis in herself had no natural association with such places. It was perhaps only a local accident that gave the latter goddess the name of Προθυραία at Eleusis[b] where she was worshipped before the great temple of the mysteries, as for a similar reason Athene was called Προναία at Thebes and Delphi[c].

The titles which she may be supposed to have borrowed from Hekate are Ἄγγελος [23 f], Κελκαία [23 g], and perhaps Εὐρίππα[d]. As regards the title Ἄγγελος we have the curious story narrated by Sophron and mentioned in the chapter on Hera[e]: the maiden Ἄγγελος, to escape her mother's wrath, takes refuge in places that were polluted by child-birth or the presence of a corpse; she was purified by the Cabiri by the lake of Acheron, and was afterwards given a position in the lower world. This quaint legend receives some light from the gloss in Hesychius, from whom we learn that Ἄγγελος was a title of Artemis in Syracuse; and we gather from Theocritus that she and Hekate were sometimes identified there[f]. Thus the story may illustrate the character of the latter as a divinity of the lower world, and her connexion with child-birth; while the purification of Ἄγγελος by the Cabiri may allude to the Samothracian mysteries, in which, as we have seen, Hekate has a part.

But why she should be called 'the messenger' is doubtful: an imaginative Greek might have regarded the moon as a messenger, but there is nothing in the very eccentric

[a] It may be that Antigone, in her appeal to Hekate, when she sees 'all the plain glittering with brazen arms,' is thinking of the goddess who guards the gate (Eur. *Phoen.* 110); her titles Κλειδοῦχος, Φυλακή, Πρόπολις[2 a, b], refer to the keeper of the gates; in the *Aeneid* she is mentioned as standing by the gates of hell.

[b] Artemis [18].

[c] In Aesch. *Suppl.* 449 προστατηρίας Ἀρτέμιδος εὐνοίαισι: the title has no local sense.

[d] P. 449.

[e] P. 184; Schol. Theocr. 2. 12.

[f] *Id.* 2. 12, 33.

behaviour of Angelos which suggests the moon at all, and others prefer to explain the title as denoting the goddess who reported to Demeter the fate of her daughter. This is probable enough, as the Demeter-legend was so rife in Sicily; perhaps also the application of the title was assisted by the common representation of the goddess speeding with a torch in each hand. If this Syracusan legend has been properly interpreted, we have evidence of a peculiar local genealogy invented for Hekate; for she is made the daughter of Zeus and Hera, a parentage which may perhaps have been suggested by her association with Eileithyia.

The inexplicable epithet Κελκαία, which was attached to Artemis in Attica, may have come to her from Hekate; for Petersen calls attention to a late statue dedicated by an inscription to Artemis Κελκαία, and showing her triple-formed [a].

On the whole, then, the proved influence of Hekate on the traditional public cult of Artemis does not appear very important; but it was an innovation which caused the figure of the Greek goddess to lose its clearness of outline and her character to become confused and bizarre. And being now more closely associated with the moon and with unhellenic superstitions, she became more exposed to the contagion of Oriental cult.

As regards the other question, how much Hekate may have borrowed of the character and functions of Artemis, little can be said. Though the later Orphic literature scarcely distinguishes between the two divinities in regard to their titles and powers, the literature, cults, and monuments of the classical period fail to show that Hekate usurped any considerable part of the functions or legends or even appeared at all in the guise of Artemis. She does not seem to have taken to hunting or the bow [b], and she holds aloof from Apollo; nor was her virginity insisted upon, nor was she received, as Artemis was, by the Eleusinian divinities. It is possible that the title Σωτείρη, which she enjoyed in Phrygia [23h], and that of Καλλίστη [23 i], which appears to have been attached to her at Athens, were

---

[a] *Arch. Epigr. Mitth.* 5.p.22; 4.Taf.5   the quiver (in Rome, Matz-Duhn, *Antike*
[b] There is one statue of Hekate with   *Bildwerke*, p. 617).

derived from the worship of her sister-goddess. And it is not impossible that she became interested in child-birth through her association with Artemis or Eileithyia, with whom at Argos she probably had some relations [23 k] ; for such interest is not attributed to her in the passage in the *Theogony*, and is only slightly and occasionally manifested. The first mention of it occurs in the *Supplices* of Aeschylus [23 k], in a line which speaks of her as one with Artemis. Yet reasons might be brought in favour of the belief that Hekate was regarded from the beginning as a divinity of child-birth, either in her own original right as an earth-goddess, or because her torches suggested the torches of Eileithyia and were taken as a sign that she had the same office, or because her hound was really regarded by the Greeks as a symbol of easy delivery. For the Genetyllides, the divine mid-wives, who, like most alien divinities, won favour with Attic women, and over whose worship Aristophanes and Lucian made merry, were sometimes identified[a] with Hekate[23 k] : but if it were thought necessary to attach them to some higher power in the same profession, one would have expected that they would have been attached to Artemis, unless Hekate were recognized as of the same character and there-fore a fitter 'proxenos' for these questionable goddesses, being herself of foreign extraction. Again, in the *Troades* of Euripides, Cassandra in her fine frenzy invokes the aid of Hekate for her approaching marriage [23 k] ; and it is hard to see why she should here have appealed to this divinity, unless as a recognized goddess of marriage. And the divine powers of marriage might easily be considered also powers of birth[b].

But neither as a goddess of marriage or birth or agriculture was Hekate of any real national importance in Greece ; her worship was without morality, and displayed energy only in sorcery and imposture. It was one of the evil things that grew up into prominence with the decline of Hellenism.

[a] They are also confused with Aphro-dite ; vide Aphrodite [118 g].

[b] Like Artemis, Hekate is especially a women's goddess ; in the *Lysistrate* before coming to the meeting the wife of Theogenes has to consult her ἑκά-τειον [10].

CHAPTER XVII.

MONUMENTS OF THE CULT OF ARTEMIS.

AS we can trace very primitive elements in the worship of Artemis, so in her earliest monuments we find the very ancient type of the religious emblem, the rude stock or the shaped stone without any human semblance. The Artemis of Icaria was represented by a piece of unhewn wood according to Arnobius [50 b], and Pausanias describes the emblem of the Artemis Patroa of Sicyon as a pillar of stone [a]. A cone-shaped stone, decorated below with metal bands and surmounted with a human head, was the form under which she was worshipped in her temple at Perge, which is represented with the idol inside on coins of the city [b], and we see an Artemis-idol of similar shape on a Neapolitan vase [c]. The temple-statue of the Ephesian goddess of many breasts also preserves in the treatment of the lower limbs much of the aniconic form ; and it is not unlikely that the statue of Artemis Μονογισήνη, which the legend ascribed to Daedalus [108 a], was of the same type, showing the transition from the pillar to the human likeness. It is an interesting fact that the most primitive representation of the human form which has come down to us from the beginnings of Greek sculpture, and which illustrates that transition, is an image of Artemis found in Delos, and now in Athens, and dedicated according to the inscription by Nicandra of Naxos ' to the far-darting one, the lover of the bow ' (Pl. XXVIII). She wears a long chiton, from beneath which the toes and sandals just appear ; the arms are held down and pressed against the sides with scarcely an

[a] Zeus [138 b].   [b] Gerhard, *Akad. Abhandl.* Taf. 59. 2, 3.
[c] *Arch. Zeit.* 1853, Taf. 55.

PLATE XXVIII

To face page 520

interval; and the body has more of the columnar than the human shape, only the breasts and hips being faintly indicated. The face, which is much disfigured, seems worked out in very low relief. The hands are clenched, but there is a slight opening through them which suggests that she was holding some emblem, possibly an arrow or bow. It is clear that so immobile and indefinite a form as this could express but little of the character with which the cults invested her; the idea of the huntress-goddess, for instance, could scarcely be clearly given until the sculptor could show more movement in the limbs.

The earliest monuments of the period when art had gained power of expression speak clearly of her close association with wild places and with the beasts of the wild; for one of the types that came very early into vogue in Greece and the islands was that of the winged Artemis, who holds in each hand a lion, having seized it by the hind paw head downwards. Pausanias saw her thus represented on that very primitive monument of Greek metal-work, the chest of Cypselus [132], and we see the same form on a bronze-relief from Olympia [a] and on a 'Melian' amphora in Berlin [b]. The conception of Artemis as the πότνια θηρῶν is Greek, but it is likely that this type of the winged goddess came from the East, probably from the cult of Anaitis. Some writers indeed regard it as genuinely Hellenic in its origin, and handed down from the Mycenaean period [c]; we find a female form somewhat similar, only without wings, holding water-birds by the neck or a goat by the horns, on gems of the 'island' style found in the tomb of Vaphio [d], but it is open to question whether this type was created entirely apart from Oriental influences. At any rate the later form of this cult-figure, with its wings and with the heraldic arrange-

[a] Pl. XXIX. b. Curtius, *Ausgrabungen zu Olympia*, Abbild. 3, Taf. 2, 3.

[b] Roscher, p. 1751; *Arch. Zeit.* 1854, Taf. 61.

[c] Curtius, *Sitzungsber. der Berl. Akad.* 1887, p. 1172; Milchöfer, *Anfänge*, p. 86; Studniczka, *Kyrene eine*

alt-griechische Göttin, p. 153: in his article in Roscher, p. 1752, he has somewhat modified this opinion.

[d] *Eph. Arch.* 1889, Πίν. 10, nos. 5, 13, 33, 34; cf. Milchöfer, *Anfänge*, p. 86.

ment of the lions, seems to point clearly to the East. There
is a marked Oriental style in the representation on the Berlin
amphora ; and a wingless goddess holding lions in this hieratic
fashion occurs on an ivory relief in the British Museum from
the palace in Nimrud[a]. And the Oriental origin of the type
has been recently strongly maintained by MM. Radet and
Ouvré, on the ground of a recent discovery at Dorylaeum in
Phrygia, a stone relief showing the winged goddess holding
a small lion by the front paws and wearing a Persian tiara on
her head[b]. Perhaps derived from this early type, and at all
events inspired by the same idea, are those representations
of Artemis, of which the recently discovered terracottas in
Corfu are examples[c], which show her holding the stag and
the lion, and with the hare leaping from her shoulder into her
hand. They may be as late as the fifth century, but preserve
the archaic form and the hieratic style.

As the primitive cults often recognized in her a goddess
of the lake and the stream, we might look for some allusion to
this aspect of her in the earliest monuments. But it is difficult
to find. We are told only of the mysterious image of the
divinity, half-woman half-fish, that Pausanias saw at Phigaleia,
and which was popularly regarded as a form of Artemis[d].
But there is no surviving trace of this uncouth representation ;
and perhaps the only monument that has come down to us
from a very early period which recognizes Artemis as a fish-
goddess is the strange vase wrought with figures in relief,
recently found in Boeotia (Pl. XXIX a). It belongs to the vases
of the geometrical style, and it exhibits a type of Artemis
closely akin to the 'Persian '; the goddess, a stiff hieratic
form, stands with her arms extended over two lions, two
water-birds are symmetrically placed on each side of her
head, and the head and shoulders of a bull are drawn under
her right arm[e]. The vase-painter has thus given very manifold

[a] Published by Roscher, p. 1753.
[b] *Bull. de Corr. Hell.* 1894, Pl. 4.
p. 129.
[c] *Ib.* 1891, pp. 1-117. An archaic
terracotta of similar type has been found
on the Acropolis; *Arch. Anzeig.* 1893,
p. 146, Fig. 24.
[d] P. 428.
[e] *Eph. Arch.* 1892, Πίν. 10. 1, p. 2·2.

PLATE XXIX

a

b

expression to the idea of the divine ' mistress of animals,' and has added also a clear allusion to the ' lady of the lake'; for on the lower field of her close-fitting robe he has drawn a large fish. As regards the later periods, it is only in very few monuments that this association of her with the waters is hinted at [a].

The aspect of Artemis that is far the most prevalent in the earliest and latest periods of Greek art is that of Artemis Ἀγροτέρα, the goddess who fostered the life of the wood and the wild. We have traces among the monuments of an early cult-type of Artemis Ἐνδενδρος, the divinity of the tree, who was worshipped once at least under the actual form of the myrtle-tree. On a coin of Myra we see the primitive figure of Artemis-Aphrodite appearing in the midst of a cleft trunk (Coin Pl. B 29) from which two serpents are starting, the symbols of the earth-goddess ; and on a coin of Perge she appears to be holding a fir-apple [b], the wild trees being those which are specially associated with her. On a fragment of a beautiful Attic vase of the transitional period, found on the Acropolis, she is holding a flower before her face [c]. Her character as a divinity of vegetation is sometimes shown by the symbol of the calathus which she wears on her head, and she commonly appears in the monuments of all periods as the goddess to whom the animal and the tree of the wood are equally sacred. Thus on a coin of Flaviopolis of the time of Marcus Aurelius we see a very primitive form of the goddess, derived probably from some semi-iconic cult-statue, with the calathus on her head and with two stags symmetrically arranged by two pine-trees at each side of her [d]; and we may compare the form of Artemis on a vase published by Gerhard, where she stands in a rigid and hieratic pose, with her forearms held out parallel from her body, and a torch in each hand ; above her is a wild fig-tree, from which a sort of game-

[a] On a coin of Pherae we see the Pheraean Artemis riding on a horse past a lion-headed fountain from which water flows (Müller-Wieseler, *Denkm. d. Alt. Kunst*, 2, no. 173); on a fourth-century coin of Stymphalus, where she was worshipped as the goddess of the lake, we find a head of Artemis, but with no peculiar emblem (Coin Pl. B 38).

[b] Mionnet, *Suppl.* 5. p. 439.

[c] *Mitt. d. deutsch. Inst. Ath.* 5. Taf. 10.

[d] Coin Pl. B 31.

bag containing a hare is hung as a votive-offering [a]. A small marble representation of Artemis was found at Larnaka in Cyprus, and is now in the Museum of Vienna, which shows Artemis leaning on her own ancient idol that wears the calathus as the emblem of fruitfulness; a coin of the city of Eucarpia in Phrygia [b] reproduces the type exactly, and proves that the larger figure was holding a bow in her left hand over the idol, and was raising her right hand to her quiver behind, while at her right stands a stag looking up to her face (Pl. XXX. a).

To this series of monuments belongs the Artemis-statue from Gabii now in Munich (Pl. XXXIII), probably a temple-statue or copy of one as Wieseler [c] supposes. The exact interpretation of its meaning is not easy. The goddess is moving rapidly forward bearing a shut quiver on her back, and something in her left hand, a torch more probably than a bow, and holding in her right hand the paws of a roe that has just sprung up caressingly towards her. On her head is a crown and a veil; her gaze is fixed upon the distance, and her expression is earnest but indifferent. Her long girded diploidion is flapping about her in the wind, yet something of the solemnity and precision proper to the temple-statue is retained in some part of the drapery as well as in the treatment of the hair. It cannot be a momentary action that is here represented ; she is not striking down her prey or protecting her favourite animal from any immediate peril. If we explain the whole work, as Wieseler would, as showing Artemis returning homeward through the woods at night by the light of her torch, while the roe runs to her and leaps up to be caressed, we might still regard the representation as typical, and believe that the intention of the sculptor was not so much to render a motive of merely passing interest, as to express the manifold character of the earth-goddess, the huntress, and the protectress of animals.

This last function of hers is most commonly expressed by

[a] *Antike Bildwerke*, Taf. 42; Bötticher, *Baumcultus*, Fig. 26.
[b] *Arch. Zeit.* 1880, Taf. 17.
[c] Müller-Wieseler, *Denkm. d. Alt.
Kunst*, 2. 168.

PLATE XXX

a

b

PLATE XXXIII

93

the symbol of the stag standing peacefully by her side, and sometimes gazing up at her face ; as on the coins of Perge (Coin Pl. B 33) and Abdera[a], on those of the Syrian Laodicea (Coin Pl. B 32) that present us with a strange representation of Artemis bearing the calathus and armed with the shield, with two stags by her side; and on coins of Athens[b] that contain the figure of the goddess wearing the calathus and holding the bow in her left hand and the patera in her right, with the stag looking up. We have also an archaic representation of Artemis on a gem in St. Petersburg[c], standing by a laurel-tree and holding an arrow in her left, while her right hand rests upon an altar and a fawn gazes up at her; and we may regard this as a traditional motive, derived from temple-sculpture.

The intimate association through ritual and sacrifice between Artemis and the stag or fawn has been noticed already: it is illustrated by such representations as the vase-painting that depicts her riding on a roe (Pl. XXX. b), and indirectly by the statue in Arcadia carved by Damophon with a fawn's skin over her shoulders.

The representations that show her merely as the huntress, and that can be directly or indirectly connected with public cult, are not very frequent. The statue in her shrine at Epidauros was of this type, but we only know it through Pausanias' record[:61]. The cult-type of the huntress-goddess, carved for her shrine at Pellene[26], is perhaps preserved on coins of that city[d]; and the same form appears inside a temple on the coins of Corinth[e]. The image of Artemis Laphria[19a], which was carved by the Naupactian Menaechmus and Soidas in the earlier part of the fifth century, presented her in the act of hunting; and we find the figure of the huntress-goddess on many coins that allude undoubtedly to the worship of Artemis Laphria, whose title and cult in Calydon and Patrae had special reference to the chase and the life of the wild-wood. On a coin of Patrae struck under Luqius Verus[f], we see the

[a] Gardner, *Types*, Pl. 3. 31.
[b] *Num. Comm. Paus.* BB. 5 and 6.
[c] *Compte-Rendu*, 1873, Pl. 3. no. 9.
[d] *Num. Comm. Paus.* S. 12, p. 92.
[e] *Ib.* D. 68.
[f] *Brit. Mus. Cat. Pelop.* Pl. 6. 1.

figure of Artemis facing, with her right hand on her hip holding her bow and arrow, and standing by an altar with her hound near her ; and a similar type appears on two coins of Nero and Domitian, with the title of Artemis Laphria[a]; but we have a different type on an Aetolian gold coin that has on its obverse the figure of Aetolia seated on shields, and Artemis standing before her with her left leg advanced and with a bow in her left hand and a torch in her right[b].

It is open to question whether either of these types repro- duces the temple-statue of gold and ivory carved by the Naupactian sculptors. Both show slight traces of an archaism that may naturally have attached to the work of Soidas and Menaechmus ; Professor Gardner makes out a strong case for the claim of the former to reproduce the temple-image, as it is of frequent occurrence, but, on the other hand, it is natural to believe that the Artemis standing by the figure of Aetolia should bear something of the semblance of the great national image of Calydon. Doubt is all the more legitimate because neither of them exactly conforms to Pausanias' description of that statue (τὸ μὲν σχῆμα θηρεύουσά ἐστι).

Many cities took the type of Artemis the huntress as their coin-device ; she appears on a coin of Syracuse, wearing the short diploidion and buskins, discharging an arrow, with her hound running at her side (Coin Pl. B 37), and on a coin of the Tauric Chersonese, kneeling on a stag and transfixing it with a spear[c]. Such representations, in which she appears merely as the destroyer of beasts, while never very common in religious monuments, had more vogue than any in the later secular art; they are by no means adequate to the earlier ideas in her worship.

Much has been said of the very interesting primitive thought surviving in the Brauronian ritual of Attica and the Callisto myth of Arcadia. But the monuments give no illus- tration at all of this; a votive-offering of a bear carved in marble, found on the Acropolis, is the only object of art

[a] *Num. Comm. Paus.* Q. 9; see
Gardner, *ib.* p. 77.
[b] Müller-Wieseler, *Denkm. d. Alt.*

Kunst, 2. 165.
[c] *Brit. Mus. Cat. Thrace,* Tauric
Chers. no. 7.

that alludes to the bear-goddess and the bear-dance of the maidens. But as regards the type of the Brauronian goddess we have some slight numismatic evidence; for Pausanias tells us that the ancient image was carried off by the Persians from Brauron to Susa [31, 32], and was afterwards given by Seleucus to the men of the Syrian Laodicea. Now Prof. Robert[a] has shown weighty reasons for disbelieving this statement, and suggests that the story was invented in the time of Seleucus by the Laodiceans, who may have been jealous of the pretensions of the Brauronian image; still the story would scarcely have arisen unless the idols of Brauron and Laodicea were of similar type. And this latter city's coins—as has been mentioned above—show us a strange figure of Artemis bearing an uplifted shield and battle-axe (Coin Pl. B 32). It is more probable, as Prof. Gardner argues[b] on the strength of Pausanias' statement, that this is approximately the type of the ancient Brauron-image than that Beulé is right in supposing that we have that image reproduced on the archaic coin of Athens mentioned above, that shows the goddess with the patera and bow. The Attic image would scarcely have held the axe; but it may well have been armed, as we have instances elsewhere in Greece of an armed Artemis; and if we suppose that the Brauronian divinity stood armed in her temple on the Attic shore, we may suggest another reason besides those which I have mentioned in a former chapter[c] for the association of Brauron with Orestes and the Tauric Chersonese: namely, if the early Greek settlers spread the story of the maiden-goddess of the Crimea, whose image was armed like the Palladion[d], we can better understand why the armed Artemis Parthenos of Brauron should have been identified with her; especially if, as we have reason to suppose, her cult-name

[a] *Archaeologische Märchen,* p. 144. He points out that the closing words of Euripides' *Iphigenia in Tauris* are utterly inconsistent with Pausanias' statement; the ancient idol which Pausanias mentions as still existing at Brauron was the aboriginal one.

[b] *Num. Comm. Paus.* pp 57 and 139.
[c] Pp. 451, 452.
[d] The idol in the arms of Iphigenia had at times the exact form of the Palladion; vide Gerhard, *Arch. Zeit.* 1849, Pl. 7. p. 70.

at Brauron was Tauropolos, and the name of the Chersonese resembled this in sound.

Of the original significance of the Arcadian Callisto-myth we have no monumental illustration whatever, and the only public recognition that it received from any Arcadian state, so far as the monuments show, was the coin-device of Orchomenos ; on fourth-century coins of that state we find on the obverse Artemis kneeling and drawing her bow, and on the reverse Callisto pierced and falling with the young Arcas behind her[a].

It has been shown that in the Arcadian and other worships there were ideas alien to the virginal character of Artemis. But Greek art gives no expression to these : there is no artistic type of Artemis Λοχία and the other kindred titles[b], no representation at all of the orgiastic and lascivious dances practised at times in her worship; for the 'calathiscus,' the dance of the women with baskets on their heads, which appears on one of the terracottas of Corfu and perhaps on one marble relief[c], was not of this character.

The domesticated animals, and those of the agricultural community which appear to have been rarely associated with the goddess in cult, are also rarely connected with her in art. The sacrificial importance of the goat in her worship can scarcely be illustrated by any surviving monuments of the state-religion; for we cannot regard as such the silver medallion from Herculaneum presenting the head and shoulders of Artemis and two goats bounding above her shoulders[d]. A late coin of the Arcadian Kaphya[e], where Artemis Κνακαλησία[47], a title believed to refer to the goat-goddess, was worshipped, shows the figure of the goddess merely bearing two torches, and does not support that interpretation.

---

[a] *Brit. Mus. Cat. Peloponnese*, 35. 15.

[b] The Artemis figure on one of the very early Boeotian vases recently discovered (*Eph. Arch.* 1892, Πίν. 8, 9) has been interpreted by Wolters (*ib.*) as if the goddess was represented in the pangs of travail; but the interpretation appears to me most improbable.

[c] *Denkm. d. Alt. Kunst*, 2. 188.

[d] Vide Roscher, p. 566 : the goat on the coin of Aenos bending over a torch refers probably to Artemis; vide supra, p. 475.

[e] Head, *Hist. Num.* p. 374.

PLATE XXXI

a

b

To face page 529

Of Artemis Tauropolos, the 'bull-goddess,' we have a few certain representations, chiefly on coins. The most important of these are the coins of Amphipolis (Coin Pl. B 34), which have already been briefly mentioned[a]; on one of these the figure of Tauropolos has the calathus on her head, the torch and spear in her hand, and the solemn hieratic pose of the temple-idol. The horns behind her shoulders are usually supposed to refer to the moon, and certainly much the same symbol appears in representations of Selene; if this is its meaning here, we must suppose that the Attic worship of Tauropolos, when transplanted to Amphipolis, acquired a certain lunar character from the neighbouring worship of Hekate: but the horns may equally well be regarded as a symbol of Tauropolos in the literal sense of the word. Again, we find the bull-riding goddess, holding an inflated veil, on a coin of Hadrianopolis[b] struck in the reign of Caracalla; and on the coins of Eretria, Phigela, and Phocaea the bull on the obverse is probably a symbol of this worship in those cities[c].

A relief from Andros is mentioned by Stuart[d], with a representation of Artemis and a bull standing by her; and a figure in the British Museum, clad in chiton and mantle, with a bull's head carved at her feet[e], must be a fragment of a statue of Artemis Tauropolos, standing on the bull and carrying a torch (Pl. XXXI. a). We may give this name also to the Artemis on a relief published in the *Annali dell' Instituto*[f], representing her by the side of Dionysos in a chariot drawn by bulls. She seems also to have had this character in Ephesian worship, for we find bulls' heads carved in relief on the lower part of the Ephesian idol, and we can thus explain the curious statement in Plutarch that the horns of an ox were hung in the temple of Diana on the Aventine[g]; for Strabo tells us that that temple

[a] Pp. 451-2.
[b] *Brit. Mus. Cat. Thrace, &c.*, p. 118.
[c] Head, *Hist. Num.* pp. 306, 307; Mionnet, *Suppl.* Pl. 72. 4.
[d] *Antiquities of Athens*, vol. 4. ch. 6, Pl. 5.

[e] It was found at Woodchester, and shows fairly good style of the Roman period.
[f] 1881, Tav. E.
[g] *Quaest. Roman.* 4.

borrowed the type of its goddess from the Ephesian idol
at Marseilles [133 c].

The divinities whose functions refer to the vegetative and
animal life of the earth often become regarded also as powers
of the lower world, and it has been noticed that Artemis
acquired this character indirectly in the Arcadian worship
of Despoina, into which she was brought. The statue by
Damophon of the goddess holding two serpents, which he
carved for this cult, has been mentioned already [55 a]; we find
serpents starting from the cleft tree in which the image of
Artemis appears on the coin of Myra described above [a].
The serpent is proper to the earth-goddess and the divinities
of the lower world, and probably this is its meaning in these
representations; while in a later period it becomes the badge
of Artemis Hekate [b].

It has been shown that the literature and cult very rarely
indeed associated Artemis with the cultivation of the land and
with the harvest: she was the earth-goddess of the wilds
rather than of the tilth. The only representation, so far as
I am aware, that gives her something of the character of
Demeter is on a late Roman carneole, where she is figured in
a chariot drawn by stags, and turning round and giving
ears of corn to a peasant [c]. Wieseler explains this as an
allusion to the lunar aspect of the goddess, and to the
fertilizing effects of the nightly dew, noticing that Selene
is called Φερέκαρπος, 'the corn-giver,' in an Orphic hymn [d].
As the work is of so late a period, this is possible. It
is also possible that it expresses simply the agricultural
character that may have belonged to her worship in
certain localities, and which certainly attached to her cult
in Calydon.

[a] P. 523.

[b] Panofka rightly regarded the cult-title of Artemis Ἄγγελος as denoting a goddess of the lower world (vide supra, p. 517); but he ought not to have given this name to the winged goddess on a vase who holds a κηρυκεῖον and gives a libation to Apollo, for this would more naturally be interpreted as Iris ; *Annali dell' Inst.* 1833, pp. 173, 174, Taf. d'Agg. B. and C.

[c] *Denkm. d. Alt. Kunst*, 2. 171 b.

[d] *Orph. Hymn*, 9. 5 ; cf. Catullus, *Eleg.* 34. 17.

a

b

Enough has perhaps been said already to show how comparatively late and scanty is the evidence for the lunar theory about Artemis, and how the art of the early and of the greatest period does not recognize her as a goddess of the moon. The only certain symbol of Artemis Selene is the crescent, and this only comes into use in the later epoch. It designates the moon-goddess on a coin of the Roman period on which Artemis of the Ephesians is represented, and where stars are seen in the field [a] ; and it would be safe to say that all the monuments of Graeco-Roman art which place the crescent on the forehead of Artemis express the Roman idea of the identity of the two divinities, but it is doubtful if any of these are derived from any cult.

In regard to her relations with the life of the family, the institutions of marriage and the clan, the monuments tell us very little indeed. We have no sure representation of Artemis Κουροτρόφος, the cherisher of children; and if she appears in vase-scenes in the bridal procession [b], it is not necessarily as a goddess of wedlock who encouraged conjugal fidelity, but as she to whom propitiatory sacrifices must be made before marriage, or as the goddess who aided child-birth. This is probably her character in the interesting votive-relief from Tyndaris, dedicated to Artemis Εὐπραξία [45], which has been mentioned in a former chapter, and which has been well interpreted by Brunn [c]; the goddess is clad in a short chiton which leaves her right breast bare, and she stands holding a sacrificial basket over an altar, and in her right hand a lowered torch with which to kindle the altar-flame; as Brunn remarks, the 'priestess Artemis' of Arcadia [d] might have been thus represented. The worshippers that approach her appear to be father, mother, and daughter, and the parents may be praying for their daughter's fruitfulness in marriage.

Among the monuments that illustrate the more advanced

[a] *Denkm. d. Alt. Kunst*, 2. 163 b, with inscription Ἄρτεμις Ἐφεσίων.

[b] For instance on a vase published *ib.* 2. 182, where Artemis appears at the head of the bridal procession arrayed in matronly fashion in mantle and coif; cf. *ib.* 1. 42.

[c] P. 463.

[d] For Artemis Ἱέρεια at Oresthasion vide Geographical Register, Arcadia.

and spiritual character of Artemis, those are perhaps the most important that associate her with Apollo. But as their association in cult was not original or primitive, and her state-worship was on the whole independent of the Apolline, so none of these monuments go back to a very early period. Of the groups of the two divinities in Greece mentioned by Pausanias[79], only two need be supposed to belong to the archaic period, the groups at Olympia[79 v] and at Pyrrhichos in South Laconia[79 u], and not all of them belong to temple-worship.

The only coins on which Apollo and Artemis are found together, so far as I have been able to discover, are those of Megara, Rhegium, Leontini, Alexandria, Germe in Mysia, Byzantium, Calchedon, Trajanopolis; in this last-mentioned city we may certainly suppose a close community of cult, for the twin deities are clasping hands over an altar on which the sacrificial fire is burning (Coin Pl. B 39). A bronze coin of Megara of the period of Septimius Severus gives us a free reproduction, we may believe, of the group of Leto and her children that Praxiteles carved for the temple of Apollo in that city; Artemis is clad in a long chiton and is raising her hand to her quiver, and holds, according to Prof. Gardner's interpretation[a], a plectrum in her left hand. We have also a fairly large number of representations on vases and reliefs in which the brother and sister appear side by side, either alone or in large groups. Most of these are inspired merely by the poetic imagination of the artists, who invented pleasing and characteristic motives to express the idea of the union and love of brother and sister, or who dealt with the many myths that associated them in some action or event, such as the slaughter of the Niobids, of Tityos, or of Python. Among the most beautiful representations of Artemis are those of which instances will be given below, in which she is pouring a libation to her brother. In fact, wherever Apollo appears, an artist would be likely to put Artemis by his side; and only a very few of these representations have any cult-significance. But a relief in the Villa

[a] *Num. Comm. Paus.* i. p. 6, Pl. A. 10.

Albani may be mentioned that no doubt alludes to their common worship at Delphi. It was first published by Welcker, and represents Artemis holding a torch and wearing a bow and quiver on her back, Leto standing behind her, on the right Nike pouring a libation to Apollo Citharoedus, and the Delphic temple in the background. The style is hieratic and affectedly archaistic (Pl. XXXI. b).

We have scarcely any direct monumental reference to their common cult at Delos and the Hyperborean offerings ; a 'pinax' in the Louvre on which Artemis is seen riding on a swan contains probably an allusion to this, for in the usual legend this was the bird that conveyed Apollo back from the northern regions in spring. The occasional association of Artemis with the griffin probably arose in the same way ; as this fabulous animal of Oriental cult had been transplanted in Greek legend to the northern shores of the Black Sea, and figures as the convoy of Apollo in the representations of his return. And Artemis herself was sometimes depicted riding on the griffin, as in the painting mentioned by Strabo in her temple on the Alpheus [4].

We have no representations that refer clearly and definitely to any oracular powers exercised by Artemis through association with her brother ; it is only possible that the coin of Perge already mentioned (Coin Pl. B 33), on which she appears in a short chiton, holding a sceptre in her left hand and a laurel crown [a] in her right, with the fawn gazing up into her face, may refer to an oracle in that city; but the laurel need not refer to Apolline functions, but perhaps alludes to the city games or to the woodland character of the goddess, to whom all wild trees were sacred.

As Artemis Οὐλία, or the goddess of health, she is associated with Apollo at least once, namely, on a coin of Germe in Mysia, on which she appears standing by him and Asclepios ; but this is of a very late period and illustrates merely an isolated local cult.

[a] It does not seem quite clear from the coin that the crown is laurel ; but it is all the more probable because she wears the laurel crown herself on the obverse of the same coin; Head, *Hist. Num.* p. 584, Fig. 321.

Neither in the literature nor the art does Artemis appear prominently as the city-goddess. Her figure is indeed the usual or occasional coin-device of a very large number of cities, yet only in a very few instances can she be supposed to personify the city-community or its fortune. She wears the turret-crown as the city-goddess on coins of the Tauric Chersonese [a] after the period of Alexander, and on a late coin of Amphipolis we see the figure that personifies the state seated and holding in her hand a small statue of Artemis Tauropolos [b]. It is usual to find the turret-crown on the head of the Ephesian goddess. We have also on Milesian coins of the Roman period a temple-type of Artemis, whose worship was here combined with Apollo's, wearing the modius and veil and holding in her hands the patera and bow, with her stag standing by her feet; the style points to a work of fifth-century sculpture [c]. But we cannot quote monuments of the autonomous period of unmixed Hellenic worship that recognize her clearly as the patron goddess of the state, as Hera was recognized at Argos and Samos, and Athena at Athens. Where we find her head on coins, we may assume with some probability that she was worshipped in those cities, but we cannot conclude that she was in any special sense the city-goddess [d].

The worship of Artemis Βουλαία was, as has been shown,

[a] *Brit. Mus. Cat. Thrace*, p. 2.

[b] *Ib. Macedon*, p. 60.

[c] Head, *Hist. Num.* p. 505.

[d] The following is a geographical list of coin-representations of Artemis, so far as I have been able to collect them :—

In Sicily and Magna Graecia : Paestum, Thurii, Bruttii, Rhegium, Leontini, Larinum, Capua, Neapolis, Agrigentum, Amestratus, Centuripae, ? Iaeta, Mamertini, Morgantia.

In North Greece, Thrace, and Macedon : Abdera, Adrianopolis, Perinthus, Tauric Chersonese, Marcianopolis, Tomi, Anchialus, Deultum, Pantalia, Serdica, Trajanopolis, Coela, Lysimachia, Olbia, Byzantium, Thasos, Bizya, Amphipolis, Bottiaei, Chalcidice, Orthagoria, Thessalonica, Dium.

In Thessaly and Central Greece : Apollonia, Demetrias, Phoenike, Pherae, Epirus (coins of Pyrrhus), Nicopolis, Zacynthus, Tanagra, Athens, Megara, Corinth.

Peloponnese : Methana, Caphyae, Orchomenos, Phigaleia, Alea, Pheneus, Stymphalus, Aegira, Patrae, Pellene, Heraea, Aegium.

The islands : Icaria.

Asia Minor : Parium, Pitane, Cyzicus, Miletopolis, Apollonia, Germe, Pergamum, Adramytteum, Perge, Amisus, Sinope, Phanagoria, Prusa, Creteia, Flaviopolis, Zeleia, Colophon, Magnesia, Phocaea, Oenoe, Miletus, Ephesus, Phigela.

important in Athens, but of this or of Artemis Agoraia we have no characteristic representation. An attempt has been made by Wieseler to discover the goddess of the moral law, Artemis Upis, on a gem[a] that presents her standing by a pillar with her feet crossed, holding a branch in her hand, with a roe standing by her; the attitude expresses meditation, but it is very hazardous to say that it is specially appropriate to any particular cult.

The armed Artemis was as rare a type in the temples of Greece as the armed Aphrodite. It is possible, as has been already suggested, that the Tauropolos of Attica was armed, and Pausanias speaks of a bronze statue of Artemis bearing arms in Messene[121], whose shield fell from her arm as a sign of the disastrous end of the Messenian war of independence[b]. But this is not the usual representation of Artemis Σώτειρα, the saviour in war. On the coins of Pagae and Megara (Coin Pl. B 35) that reproduce the type of Strongylion's statue carved for the latter city[123], we see the figure of the goddess in short chiton and buskins, hurrying along with a torch in each hand; the altar and the temple that appear on some of the coins of this type make it clear that the figure is derived from the temple-statue of Soteira, as Prof. Gardner has pointed out[c]. The torch alludes to the story of the night when Artemis bewildered the retreating Persians, and it is probably to some such type as this that the line in the *Anthology* refers—' Artemis hot with speed is the herald of the coming war[d].'

A statuette in the British Museum of fourth-century style, dedicated to Artemis Soteira (Pl. XXXII. a), shows a very similar figure of the goddess clad in short chiton and fawn-skin, striding quickly forward. We have also the Syracusan coins[e] from 345 to 317 B.C., that commemorate the restoration

[a] Müller-Wieseler, *Denkm. d. Alt. Kunst*, 2. 172 a.
[b] She has the lance in her hand in a few vase-paintings; Lenormant, *Él. Céramogr.* 1. Pl. 97, 100, 103; *Denkm. d. Alt. Kunst*, 1. 2, 11; on a relief from Asopus, *Arch. Zeit.* 1882, Taf. 6. 1.

[c] *Num. Comm. Paus.* pp. 4, 8.
[d] 9. 534: Ἄρτεμις ἱδρώουσα προάγγελός ἐστι Κυδοιμοῦ.
[e] *Brit. Mus. Cat. Sicily*, p. 183, no. 252 (Fig.); *Denkm. d. Alt. Kunst.* 2. 163.

of the democracy and Timoleon's successes, and bear the head of Artemis Soteira with the strung bow behind her or with the shut quiver, and with the lyre or cithar that alludes to the festal celebration of the triumph (Coin Pl. B 36). We may lastly notice here a coin of Demetrias in Thessaly, of the second century B. C., which contains the figure of Artemis seated on a galley, probably alluding to her help in naval warfare[a].

The monuments that in any way associate Artemis with the arts are very rare indeed, and the few vases on which she is found listening to the music of Apollo Citharoedus or herself playing the lyre have no proved connexion with any worship. Her statue in Praxiteles' group at Megara, if it held the plectrum in the hand, as the Artemis on the coin that reproduces this group appears to do, would appropriately express the title of Artemis 'Υμνία, but could have had no direct reference to the Arcadian cult. Nor is there any Arcadian coin that clearly expresses the idea of this worship; for the head of Artemis of semi-archaic style wearing her hair in a net, which we see on a coin of Arcadia[b], and which Imhoof-Blumer would interpret as the head of Artemis 'Υμνία, has nothing characteristic about it at all.

These, on the whole, are the chief monuments which can be associated directly or indirectly with the cult of Artemis, though theories might be advanced about the cult-significance of many others; and we see how far more meagre is this source of our information about the ritual and ideas of her worship than the literary evidence is : we can scarcely doubt that much of the thought that was embodied in her religion had ceased to have much meaning by the time that art was developed enough to tell its own story.

[a] *Brit. Mus. Cat. Thessaly*, p. 34.   [b] *Denkm. Alt. Kunst*, 2. 156 e.

CHAPTER XVIII.

IDEAL TYPES OF ARTEMIS.

THE Hellenic ideal of the virgin-huntress, the goddess kindly to boys and maidens and to the living things of the wood, as it was perfected in the religious hymn and the Euripidean drama, was not fully embodied in Greek art until the age of Praxiteles and the great painters of Alexander's period. Yet the developed archaic art had done something for the expression of the Artemis-type, and had given it movement and life. The fragment of an Attic vase quoted above[a] shows a very striking representation of the divinity which we may date about 470 B.C. She is clad in Ionic chiton and mantle with a panther's skin over her shoulders, holding in her left hand the bow and raising in her right hand a flower towards her lips. The golden-coloured drapery and the white flesh suggest a cult-image of chryselephantine technique, and the figure may be a copy of the older image in the Brauronian temple on the Acropolis.

Of considerable importance also for character and style is the Pompeian statuette in the Museum of Naples (Pl. XXXII. b), representing Artemis striding forward, clad in a chiton with sleeves and a finely textured mantle, with a quiver at her back ; the fingers are restored, but the one hand must have been holding a bow or torch, the other holding up the skirt of her dress ; a diadem adorned with rosettes crowns her head, of which the hair has been given a golden tinge. The maidenly character is clearly expressed in the bright face and the dimpled chin. The later copyist shows his hand in the soft

[a] Vide p. 523; Hirschfeld, *Arch. Zeit.* 1873, p. 109.

treatment of the flesh and the rendering of the eyelids, but on the whole the spirit and style of genuine archaism survive in the work [a].

The period of transitional art has left us one interesting representation of Artemis, the Actaeon-metope from the younger temple of Selinus, on which she stands hounding on the dogs against Actaeon. She wears a chiton with sleeves and with the upper part falling over so as to conceal the girdling; above her forehead is a diadem, and the hair is severely drawn away from the face and secured in a long plait behind. The features are broad and strong, of the maidenly type, and with the expression of sombre earnestness common on the faces of this period.

When we look for the form of Artemis in the great periods of Greek art, we find that no statue of her is ascribed to Pheidias or to any of his school, nor has any original survived that we can attribute directly to him or his pupils. We may believe that Artemis would be represented on the Parthenon frieze in the assembly of divinities, but we cannot discover her figure with any certainty there [b]. Nor can we quote with any conviction a head which has been regarded as that of Artemis, and once as an actual fragment of the Parthenon gable-sculpture, and shows certainly the Pheidian style [c]. We hear of an Artemis wrought for the group in the pediment of the Delphic temple by Praxias the Athenian, a pupil of Calamis; but we know nothing of him or his work.

[a] Vide a long article by Graef in the *Mitt. d. deutsch. Inst.* (*Röm. Abth.*), 3. p. 280, who compares a bronze in Berlin from Thresprotis, and who considers that the Pompeian statuette may represent something of the style and form of the Artemis Laphria carved for Pagae by Soidas and Menaechmus.

[b] It is almost hopeless to expect that certainty will ever be attained as regards the names of all the divinities on the frieze. As regards probabilities, it is very difficult to believe with Flasch and many recent writers that the torch-bearing figure of the matronly form is Artemis;

there is reason for thinking that at the time of Pheidias the torch was by no means the common and accepted symbol of Artemis, as it was of Demeter and Persephone; and if he intended this figure for Artemis, we may doubt if the Athenian public would discover his intention; still less would they be likely to recognize her, as Dr. Furtwängler does (*Meisterwerke*, p. 431, Engl. ed.), in the goddess whose drapery is slipping from her shoulder and who is seated next to Aphrodite.

[c] *Mon. dell' Inst.* 11. Tav. 16; *Gazette Archéol.* 1875, Pl. 1.

PLATE XXXIV

To face page 539

The statue in Lansdowne House (Pl. XXXIV) shows us a conception of the goddess that may have been prevalent in the Periclean age, though it is merely a Roman copy: the drapery, a Doric double chiton, displays something of the earlier Pheidian style in its arrangement of the folds, but the face, though it preserves to some extent the breadth of the fifth-century heads, shows for the most part the forms of the first decade of the fourth century. The expression is thoughtful, but not without brightness [a].

The Artemis of the Phigalean frieze, which is a work of provincial sculpture executed probably from Attic drawings, and on which she appears as her brother's charioteer, is a figure full of life and elasticity; she has bare arms and wears a single chiton that flaps about her limbs and is secured by a double cross-band that passes over her shoulders and round her breasts. But this is merely a dramatic figure in a mythological scene.

The solemnity of the religious sculpture of the fifth century is better preserved in the statue in the Villa Albani of Artemis holding a young calf: she is clad in a single Ionic chiton girt round the waist, that leaves her arms and neck bare and falls to the feet in austere columnar folds ; the pose of the lower limbs reminds us of the Pheidian Parthenos [b].

Turning to the monuments of Peloponnesian art we find a group of Artemis Leto and Apollo, attributed to Polyclitus, who carved it for the temple of Artemis Orthia on the summit of Mount Lycone ; but it is doubtful whether the elder or younger sculptor of this name was the author of the work, and we can say nothing of its character.

The most striking Peloponnesian representation of the goddess is on a very beautiful Argive relief dedicated by Polystrata (Pl. XXXV. a). She stands in profile towards the right, holding a bow in her left hand and a half-sunk torch in her right, with her quiver at her back ; she wears nothing but

[a] Vide Michaelis, *Ancient Marbles*, Lansdowne House, no. 67.

[b] Gerhard's *Antike Bildwerke*, Taf. 12; Roscher's *Lexicon*, p. 562. Cf. the

terracotta in Berlin, Artemis holding torch and cup in double Doric chiton of later fifth-century style ; *Archaeol. Anz.* 1892, p. 103.

a Doric chiton that falls to her feet in severe folds, the girdling being concealed under the diploidion ; the hair is pressed over the head in vertical plaits and gathered up in a knot behind ; the face wears a bright smile, and the features are most pure and maidenly, and the style of the whole work is strong and noble. We may ascribe the monument to the end of the fifth century. With this we may compare the type of Artemis on some red-figured vases of the perfected style ; for instance, on two vases, one in the Cabinet des Médailles of the Louvre, the other in Carlsruhe, on both of which Apollo is represented receiving a libation from Artemis : the drawing of the figures on both is very beautiful, and the expression of the faces is solemn and profound.

The fourth century is of more importance for this chapter of Greek religious art, and nearly all its most famous sculptors dealt with this theme. We have record of the Artemis Soteira of Strongylion, whose figure we see on the coins of Megara moving swiftly along in Amazonian attire[a] with a torch in each hand (Coin Pl. B 35), of the Artemis Soteira carved by Cephissodotus for Megalopolis[123 b], and of the Artemis Εὔκλεια that Scopas wrought for Thebes. As an instance of the type prevalent in the earlier half of the fourth century, we may note the head of Artemis on the coins of Stymphalus (Coin Pl. B 38) ; the countenance has something of the breadth and fullness of the older style of religious sculpture, the cheek is broad and the chin large ; the delicate fineness of the maidenly type presented on the Syracusan coins mentioned below is not yet attained.

The statues of Artemis by Praxiteles were of even greater

---

[a] The Amazonian attire of the goddess, in short chiton and buskins, goes back to the middle of the fifth century : we find her thus on the rude Laconian relief which is earlier than 450 B.C. (*Arch. Zeit.* 1882, Pl. 6), and on coins of Patrae that probably reproduce the type of the statue carved by Menaechmus and*Soidas of Naupactus. But before the fourth century she usually wears the long Ionic or Doric chiton with an upper fold falling over, and this austerer style is preserved in some of the later monuments. From the fourth century onwards, the light drapery of the huntress, the short chiton with the mantle rolled round the breast, becomes her usual costume. Cf. Claud. *de Rapt. Proserp.* 2. 33 :—

'Crispatur gemino vestis Gortynia cinctu
    Poplite fusa tenus.'

PLATE XXXV

a

b

importance, we may believe, than those just mentioned. The charm of the maiden goddess and of the woodland secluded life that she impersonated would seem to have had special fascination for him ; she must have appeared among the twelve divinities that he carved for the temple of Artemis Soteira in Megara [a], and that city possessed another group by his hand of Leto Apollo and his sister [79 r]. We hear of a group of the same divinities wrought by him for Mantinea [79 w], of his statue of Artemis Brauronia on the Acropolis of Athens [b], and of the temple-image of the goddess at Anticyra by him, or more probably by his sons [c]. We have only the badly preserved coins of Anticyra and Megara [d] that may show us something of the motive and costume of the Praxitelean statues in those cities, but of their style and expression we know nothing. Yet we may believe that it was this sculptor, more than any other, who defined the ideal

[a] Paus. I. 40, 3.

[b] Prof. Kekulé (*Ath. Mitt.* 5. 256) and Prof. Robert (*Archaeol. Märchen,* p. 157) believe that the Brauronian image was the work of the elder Praxiteles ; yet the inscriptions which Michaelis has published (*Parthenon,* p. 307 ; cf. *C. I. A.* 2. 744–758) appear to support Studniczka's view (*Vermutungen zur Griechischen Kunstgeschichte,* 18) that the Praxitelean statue, which was evidently placed by the side of an older one, was erected in 346–345 B.C. The inscriptions, with their confusing descriptions of two different statues, do not seem to me to bear out Prof. Robert's conclusions, namely that the Praxitelean statue was of wood and a standing figure, and that the older image, dedicated perhaps soon after the shrine was built in the time of the Peisistratidae, was of stone and represented the seated goddess. A seated Artemis in the archaic period, as a cult-figure, is, so far as I am aware, an unknown type ; it was very rare in any period. It is more likely that Praxiteles made the innovation than that the

archaic sculptor should have changed the traditional form. We know from the inscriptions that one statue in the shrine was standing and the other seated ; it seems to me more probable that τὸ ἄγαλμα τὸ ἑστηκός is the same as τὸ ἕδος τὸ ἀρχαῖον.

[c] The text in Pausanias 10. 37, I (reading ἔργον τῶν Πραξιτέλους instead of ἔργων τῶν Πραξιτέλους, which can scarcely be grammatically translated) ought more naturally to mean a 'work of the sons of Praxiteles' ; for there is no evidence that Pausanias could use such a phrase for 'a Praxitelean work.' The other instance often quoted to support this meaning is not really parallel : ἔργον τῶν Μύρωνος θέας μάλιστα ἄξιον (9. 30, 1) ; for there the genitive depends on the comparative phrase that follows. A coin of Anticyra presents us with an Artemis that corresponds closely with the description in Pausanias, but we cannot judge of the style of the original by its help and we cannot say how far it reproduces the pose.

[d] *Num. Comm. Paus.* A. 10, Y. 17.

of Artemis for the Greek imagination. For Petronius, in praising a woman's beauty, speaks of her small lips as such as those 'which Praxiteles believed Diana to have.' It is a slight phrase, but it proves that it was the Praxitelean Artemis that would first occur to an appreciative writer when speaking of the goddess ; and it suggests that the form of the mouth was that which gave character to the whole countenance. Now the Hermes of Olympia, the Cnidian Aphrodite of Munich, and the relief of the Muses at Athens show how much of the peculiar spiritual quality that belongs to the Praxitelean countenance was derived from his treatment of the mouth, to which he gave that strange half-smile and expression of dreamy self-consciousness. But we cannot suppose that he would lend such expression to the face of Artemis, to whom it would be quite inappropriate. An epigram of Diotimus speaks of her proud and spirited look [a], and we find this not infrequently on works that belong to fourth-century art or are descended from it. But this is not the Praxitelean expression that hitherto we have known ; and we are left without sufficient criteria for identifying among existing monuments those that may have been derived from his originals ; for the figure on the coin of Anticyra, even if we allow that it is a superficial reproduction of a Praxitelean work, is of little use to us, for it does not agree with the figure on the coins of Megara in pose or drapery or treatment of the hair.

One or two representations of Artemis may be here mentioned that show much of the spirit and feeling of Praxitelean sculpture. The marble statuette in the Vienna Museum (Pl. XXX. a), of which the motive has already been described, is probably a work of the younger Attic school, and claims a high place among the monuments of the goddess for the beautiful rendering of the flesh and for the expression of character in the face. Her drapery, which preserves traces of colour, is a high-girt Doric diplois open at the right side, and a mantle which is brought in a thick narrow fold across her body and falls over her left arm. The face is high, the features maidenly and noble. The hair is carefully drawn

[a] *Anth. Pal.* 2. p. 674, no. 158.

away from the forehead and temples, the eyes are long and
rather narrow, the line of the eyebrows is straight and pure ;
the wall of the nose near the eyes is very large, as it is in the
Hermes' head ; the upper lip is slightly curved and the lower
lip is very full ; the chin is large and the cheeks are broad.
The eyes are full of thought, with a distant inscrutable look
in them, and the proud reserved expression accords with the
self-centred life of the goddess.   This is a figure of the
temple-worship, but it is also the Artemis of the popular
poetic imagination.

    To this period belongs a marble life-size figure in the
Louvre [a] of a maiden securing the ends of her mantle over her
right shoulder in a clasp.   It was found at Gabii, and may be
regarded with some probability as a representation of the
girl-Artemis ; for though the genre action would be suitable
enough to a nymph or an Attic maiden arranging her dress,
we have one undoubted figure of the young goddess with
her hair arranged in the same fashion as we see in this [b].
The face, although the deadness of the surface shows
the hand of the Roman copyist, preserves something of
Praxitelean form and expression ; and the romantic or genre
treatment of a divine theme is in accordance with the
practice of Praxiteles.   If this is Artemis, it is the girl-
goddess in solitude, absorbed in her own woodland life, and
naively indifferent to worship.

    The coins of Syracuse which have already been mentioned,
and of which a specimen is given on Coin Pl. B 36, struck
not much later than the middle of the fourth century,
present an interesting and characteristic type of the Artemis-
head.   The forms of the countenance resemble those of
Apollo in contemporary art, but the expression is colder and
more reserved.   The arrangement of the hair is simple and
displays the height of the forehead ; the features are broad
and strong and of a noble type.   We may believe that this
resemblance to Apollo noted here became part of the received
ideal of Artemis from now onwards ; for we find it as the chief

[a] *Denkm. d. Alt. Kunst*, 2. 180.
[b] Kekulé, *Griech. Thonfigur. aus Tanagra*, Taf. 17.

feature in Claudian's description of her, which is perhaps inspired by some representation of Alexandrine art: 'there was much of her brother in her face, and you might deem her cheeks the cheeks of Phoebus, her eyes his eyes[a].' This family likeness appears strongly impressed upon the countenances of the twin divinities on the cameo published by Prof. Overbeck, a work of the Alexandrine period[b]; it is recognizable in the Artemis of Versailles and the Apollo Belvidere.

It may be that some work of the younger Attic school is the source whence the Artemis Colonna in Berlin (Pl. XXXVI) has been derived[c]. The statue is a Graeco-Roman copy of average merit, but without much vitality. The pose and action are somewhat difficult to explain. She is hurrying forward, with both arms partly stretched out; the right hand certainly held nothing, but the left was grasping something that must have been either a torch or a bow. The expression is one of proud indifference, and the eyes are fixed upon some distant object; we might suppose that she has just discharged an arrow and is gazing upon the distant quarry, and that the action of the archer still lingers, so to speak, in the hands, the right still holding out the bow and the left just drawn back after releasing the string. Her drapery is a long Doric diplois without girdle. The features are pure and maidenly, the forehead rather high, the lips thin and half open.

We cannot say with certainty that the development and perfecting of the ideal of Artemis was the achievement of sculpture alone; for Pliny places among the masterpieces of Apelles[d] a picture of Artemis in the midst of a group of

[a] 'At Triviae lenis species, et multus
   in ore
Frater erat, Phoebique genas et lumina Phoebi
Esse putes, solusque dabat discrimina sexus.
Brachia nuda nitent, levibus proiecerat auris
Indociles errare comas, arcuque remisso
Otia nervus agit, pendent post terga sagittae.'—*De Rapt. Proserp.* 2. 27.

[b] Overbeck, *Kunst-Mythologie*, Gemmentafel no. 7.

[c] Wieseler (*Denkm. d. Alt. Kunst*, 2. 167) after a long discussion refers it to the younger Attic school; Friederichs to a Praxitelean original (*Praxiteles und die Niobe-Gruppe*). The quaint arrangement of the hair, which is twisted round the quiver and supports it, is probably an affectation of the later copyist.

[d] Pliny, *N. H.* 35. 96: 'Peritiores

PLATE XXXVI

To face page 544

maidens sacrificing; and the names of other painters also are recorded, Nicomachus [a], Timotheus [b], Timarete [c], who worked on this theme.

From the Hellenistic period two monuments may be selected as typical of the later style. The Artemis of Versailles has sometimes been wrongly regarded as intended to be grouped with Apollo Belvidere: the style of the features shows much resemblance, but the countenance of Artemis expresses no anger or excitement, but only earnestness ; she is equipped as the huntress, in short chiton with the mantle wrapped round her body, but she is conceived by the sculptor not as the capturer of the hind whose horns she is holding, but as its protector against some beast of prey, towards which she hurries while she draws the arrow from the quiver ; the idea of the slim and strong maiden-divinity is well expressed in the limbs and the details of the head [d]. The Artemis of the Pergamene frieze (Pl. XXXVII. a) is a figure which shows some external affinity to the Versailles figure : here also she appears in the character of the huntress, wearing a short woollen chiton which leaves the shoulders bare, and which is bound round her waist by a scarf that is drawn across the breast ; the features are fresh and delicate, and do not wholly conform to the usual Pergamene type, for the face has not the fullness nor the protuberance of the forehead in the middle above the eyes, that we usually find in the other faces on the frieze ; the lines about the mouth remind us slightly of the style of Praxiteles ; the hair is drawn back so as fully to reveal the face, and is bound up in a high knot behind. For vigour of movement and warm treatment of the surface, this frieze-figure surpasses any other repre-

artis praeferunt omnibus eius operibus . . . Dianam sacrificantium choro virginum mixtam, quibus vicisse Homeri versus videtur id ipsum describentis ' (cf. *Od.* 6. 102 ; Hom. *Hymn to Artemis*, l. 16 : Ἡγεῖται χαρίεντα περὶ χροΐ κόσμον ἔχουσα ἐξάρχουσα χορούς). The text of Pliny is doubtful, but its difficulties cannot be here discussed.

[a] Pliny, *N. H.* 35. 108.

[b] *Id.* 36. 32.

[c] *Id.* 35. 147.

[d] There is a close parallel between the Versailles figure and the representation on a gem published from Millin in Müller-Wieseler's *Denkmäler* (no. 157 a), only that here the figure of Artemis has still more of the Amazonian character, the right breast being exposed.

sentation of the goddess that has come down to us from the Hellenistic age.

In the later period many of the earlier types may have often been successfully reproduced. A striking example is the statue in Dresden (Pl. XXXV. b) of the Graeco-Roman age, but derived perhaps from some original of the earlier Attic period [a], representing the goddess in long Doric double chiton that falls in austere folds down to the feet; there is no girdle visible, but the quiver-band presses the light raiment over the breast. The arms and hands are antique, with the exception of the finger-tips, and it is clear that she was holding the bow in a peaceful way against her left side, and her right hand was raised to the quiver. But as the whole pose of upper and lower limbs is most tranquil, we must believe that this hand is lifted not to draw an arrow but to close the quiver, and this motive would agree with the mild gentleness that appears in the face. In drapery and pose it shows something of the solemnity of temple-sculpture, and it expresses the ancient idea of the goddess who was friendly to the beasts of the field and to the children of men.

The survey of the chief monuments that express the ideal of Artemis may close with a notice of the singular work of the Messenian sculptor Damiphon. We have record of three statues of the goddess carved by his hand, an Artemis Laphria at Messene [19 b], an Artemis Phosphorus in the same city, probably belonging to a group of which Tyche, Epaminondas, and the City of Thebes were the other figures [58], and an Artemis in the temple of Despoina at Lycosura, standing near the two divinities of the temple, Demeter and Despoina, bearing a doe-skin on her shoulders, a quiver on her back, in one hand a torch, and two serpents in the other [55 a]. Until recently all writers were agreed in reckoning Damophon among the sculptors of the middle of the fourth century; and in the absence of direct evidence this would be the natural view. We might suppose with Brunn that he was an artist who maintained the tradition of the religious sculpture of the fifth century; and as his chief works were in Messenia and Arcadia,

[a] Dr. Furtwängler, in *Meisterwerke*, p. 324, maintains its Praxitelean origin.

PLATE XXXVII *b*

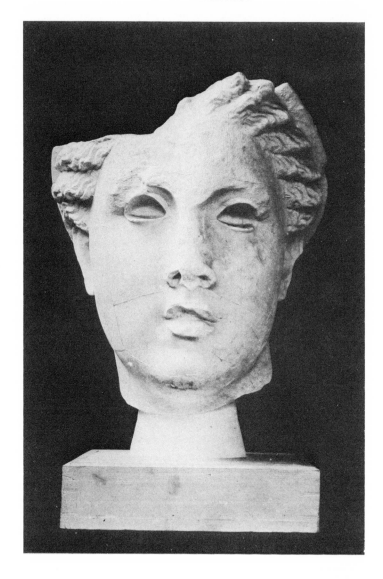

and as the group for which he carved the Artemis Phosphorus commemorated the glory of Thebes and Epaminondas, it might be concluded positively that he flourished about the time of the building of Megalopolis and the restoration of Messene. But in 1889 the shrine at Lycosura was discovered, together with much of the sculpture by Damophon, and one is now compelled to assign him to a later date. For Dr. Dörpfeld [a], whose authority on architectural questions is very weighty, maintains that the excavated temple shows the bad work-manship of the later period, and that the temple was built and the sculpture carved of the same material and at the same time. He determines that the building cannot be earlier than the second, and may be as late as the first century B. C.

If the temple is to be assigned to the second century, it is quite possible to reconcile the style of the sculpture with the acceptance of that date. The heads of Demeter, Artemis, and Anytos display neither the forms nor the purity of fourth-century sculpture. But, on the other hand, few who have seen and carefully studied the originals could believe with Prof. Overbeck [b] that they are as late as Hadrian's period. For no work of this later age of Graeco-Roman art displays such warm treatment of the surface, such soft modulation of the flesh, or such exuberant life as these fragments of Damo-phon's works. The monuments which they vividly recall are those of the second Pergamene period ; the sculpture of the altar-frieze displays the same warmth and the same exuber-ance in handling and working out the forms. And the type of Damophon's heads agrees in many essentials with the Pergamene type [c]. The height of the skull is greater than the depth ; there is little or no marking of the bone-structure, but the chief emphasis is on the flesh ; the breadth between the eyes and the depth of the eye-sockets is very great. These are Pergamene traits ; but what chiefly reminds us of the Pergamene style in the heads of Demeter and Artemis is

[a] *Athen. Mittheil.* 1890 and 1893.

[b] *Gesch. d. Griech. Plast.* (4th ed.), vol. 2. p. 488 : his account of the heads seems to imply that he has not seen the originals.

[c] Vide my analysis of the Perga-mene head in *Hellenic Journal,* 1890, p. 183.

the treatment of the mouth and the full lips, which as it were pout forward, and the strange convex shape of Demeter's eyeball ; this last detail of form the Pergamene school inherited from Scopas. We may also note the close affinity between the head of Anytos and some of the giants' heads on the Pergamene frieze; his beard, for example, shows a singular resemblance to that of the giant confronting Hekate.

We may take, then, this head of Artemis (Pl. XXXVII b) as one of the last among the monuments of the goddess belonging to the Greek period. The religious severity and purity of the older style are gone ; but the freshness and warmth of life still remains. In spite of its colossal size, it impresses us rather as the face of a healthy girl, joyous and eager, than as the face of a goddess.

PLATE XXXVIII

a

b

CHAPTER XIX.

HEKATE : REPRESENTATIONS IN ART.

THE evidence of the monuments as to the character and significance of Hekate is almost as full as that of the literature. But it is only in the later period that they come to express her manifold and mystic nature. Before the fifth century there is little doubt that she was usually represented as of single form like any other divinity, and it was thus that the Boeotian poet imagined her, as nothing in his verses contains any allusion to a triple-formed goddess. The earliest known monument is a small terracotta found in Athens, with a dedication to Hekate (Pl. XXXVIII. a), in writing of the style of the sixth century. The goddess is seated on a throne with a chaplet bound round her head ; she is altogether without attributes and character, and the only value of this work, which is evidently of quite a general type and gets a special reference and name merely from the inscription [a], is that it proves the single shape to be her earlier form, and her recognition at Athens to be earlier than the Persian invasion.

With this single exception, the black-figured and earlier red-figured vases are the only monuments that show us the figure of Hekate in the archaic and transitional periods [b] ; and on these, as well as on the vases of the later time, her form is single, and her usual attribute is the double torch. Also, so far as we can define the significance that she has

[a] As Fränkel (*Arch. Zeit.* 1882, p. 265) points out, it is not distinguishable in form from the seated Athena found in Athens.

[b] The goddess on the Aeginetan relief in the chariot with Eros cannot

be Hekate, as Welcker supposes, *Annali*, 2, p. 70. No Greek could have put that interpretation upon the figure, which has no attribute of Hekate, nor has Hekate any right to be associated with Eros.

in these early representations, we must say that there is no reference to her lunar character, but clear reference to her as a goddess of the lower world, or of the earth.

Thus on a black-figured vase of Berlin [a] we see Hekate with torches, standing over against Cora, and between them the chthonian Hermes riding on a goat [b]; and with the same form and attributes she is present on a Nolan vase in a representation of the setting forth of Triptolemos with the gifts of corn [c]. The other persons present are Demeter, Proserpine, probably Artemis, and Hades, so that Hekate is here associated with the Eleusinian divinities of vegetation and the lower world.

But on the evidence of this and one or two other similar vase-paintings we have no right, in the absence of any literary evidence, to assume with Steuding [d] that the goddess was ever received into the mystic cult at Eleusis: it is a common thing for the vase-painters to amplify their groups with cognate or appropriate figures without any express sanction of cult or legend.

Other vase-representations in which Hekate appears clearly designated as a divinity of the lower world are very rare, and the interpretation which discovers her in these is often very doubtful. Thus in the various paintings of the carrying off of Proserpine, a figure that has often been called Hekate [e] may be a torch-bearing Demeter. The only certain instance that

[a] Pl. XXXVIII. b (*Arch. Zeit.* 1868, Taf. 9).

[b] We find Hekate again with Hermes and in company with Demeter on a vase of the fifth century, published in Gerhard, *Auserles. Vasenb.* 1. 217.

[c] *Mon. dell' Inst.* 1. Tav. 4. But we cannot always give the name of Hekate to the goddess with two torches in vase-representations of this myth: the name might suit this figure on the Louvre vase (Overbeck, *Kunst-Mythol. Atlas*, 15. 20), but on the vase of the Duc de Luynes (*ib.* no. 13) a similar figure must be called Persephone or Demeter; in all other cases, except where an inscription gives the name of Hekate, it may as well be Artemis.

[d] Roscher, *Lexicon*, p. 1893.

[e] Overbeck, *Kunst-Mythologie*, 2. pp. 601–608. On a vase (published *Mon. dell' Inst.* 2. Tav. 49) that represents Heracles capturing Cerberus, there is a figure which is sometimes called Hekate thrusting a torch into his face; but it may be a Fury. And the statement that Hekate was regarded as the ἄγγελος or the Iris of Hell rests on the interpretation of a figure holding a torch and standing by Hades on a vase published in the *Bulletino Nap.* vol. 3. Tav. 3: this again is very probably a Fury.

may be quoted is a representation of this scene on a vase of the fourth century, of South Italian style, in the British Museum. We see a goddess with a circle of rays round her head and torches in her hand preceding the chariot that bears Hades and Proserpine. It is impossible that this figure should be Selene or Demeter or a Fury, or any other than Hekate, who here appears as a lunar and also as a nether divinity, possibly also a divinity of marriage, as in the *Troades* of Euripides.

This is almost all that we can gather about Hekate from the vase-paintings of any period; there is nothing distinctive in her form or drapery, and even the two torches are no sure clue to recognize her by. We have accounts of the form of Hekate in painting which give us certain details that the vases fail to supply: according to the extract quoted by Eusebius from Porphyry [13g], she was represented with a white robe and golden sandals on one of her shapes, and bronze sandals on another; but probably this is a type belonging to a late period of art.

Among the works of sculpture of the fifth century, the chief representation of Hekate was Myron's; unfortunately all that we are told of this statue is that it showed the goddess in single form, and that it was wrought for the Aeginetan worship. If Myron in this work indulged his ruling passion for dramatic movement, then we might illustrate his Hekate by the relief which Dr. Conze discovered in Thasos (Pl. XXXIX. a) and published, on which the goddess is seen sweeping along in long chiton holding two torches, with her wild hounds leaping at her side [a].

From Alcamenes onwards the triple form of Hekate is more common than the single, although this latter never entirely dies out. Pausanias in a well-known passage attributes to Alcamenes himself the invention of this new type; but all that we have the right to conclude from his words is that he was the first sculptor of eminence who carved a triple statue of the goddess. It is probable that the triple form had been seen in monuments before Alcamenes' work was

[a] Conze, *Reise auf den Inseln d. thrakischen Meeres,* Taf. 10. 4.

produced. But the question what this triplicity meant must be first discussed. Some of the late writers on mythology, such as Cornutus and Cleomedes [13 i, k], and some of the modern, such as Preller and the writer in Roscher's *Lexicon* and Petersen, explain the three figures as symbols of the three phases of the moon. But very little can be said in favour of this, and very much against it. In the first place, the statue of Alcamenes represented Hekate 'Επιπυργιδία, whom the Athenian of that period regarded as the warder of the gate of his Acropolis [10], and as associated in this particular spot with the Charites [15], deities of the life that blossoms and yields fruit. Neither in this place nor before the door of the citizen's house did she appear as a lunar goddess.

We may also ask, Why should a divinity who was sometimes regarded as the moon, but had many other and even more important connexions, be given three forms to mark the three phases of the moon, and why should Greek sculpture have been in this solitary instance guilty of a frigid astronomical symbolism, while Selene, who was obviously the moon and nothing else, was never treated in this way? With as much taste and propriety Helios might have been given twelve heads.

If this had been actually the intention of Alcamenes, it is difficult to know how he could make the Athenian public discover it in his figure ; and we too often forget to ask how the ordinary Greek would naturally regard a monument. It is fairly certain that unless Alcamenes put a crescent over the forehead of each of his figures they would not be all clearly recognized as 'moon-phases': he may have done this, or anything else, as we know nothing at all of the details of his work; but, as it is only the latest monuments that show the crescent at all, and these only over one of the heads, it is not probable that Alcamenes placed this badge over each. In the relief found in Aegina (Pl. XXXIX. c) we see that the one figure holds the torches, the second a pitcher, and the third a cup ; and Petersen supposes that all these things alluded to the moon, who sheds the gracious dew on the herbs [a]. The

[a] *Arch. Epigr. Mittheil. aus Oesterreich*, 4. p. 167.

PLATE XXXIX

a

b

c

d

To face page 552

torch would occasionally, though not always, suggest to a Greek that the person bearing it was Selene. But what evidence have we that the pitcher and the cup allude to dew, and that these are the ordinary symbols of the moon-goddess? For the figure that bore these could only be certainly recognized as Selene if Selene were *par excellence* a cup-bearer ; but she is not. Therefore if Alcamenes' figures merely carried torch, cup, and pitcher, his great idea that the triple shape should symbolize the three phases of the dewy moon would have been scarcely revealed to the public.

In fact, among the many late monuments that represent the triple Hekate, there is none of which two of the figures do not carry some attribute or property that cannot designate Selene [a]. We can apply the name with certainty, then, to one only of such figures [b].

A second explanation which rests also on ancient authority is that the triple shape has reference to the Hesiodic idea of a goddess whose divinity is of many elements ; that the Hekateion is in fact a trinity of Selene, Persephone, and Artemis, or represents the κόρη φωσφόρος in shapes and with attributes that are drawn from the moon, the lower world, and the earth. Such an explanation may be supported by the analogy of such figures as the double-headed Zeus, Zeus Τριόφθαλμος, and perhaps the two-headed Boreas on the vase representing the pursuit of Oreithyia [c].

[a] In the description given by the scholiast on Theocritus 2. 12, some of the attributes have evidently no reference to the moon, for instance the calathus ; cf. [13 k].

[b] The most curious argument in favour of the equation of the triple Hekate to the three periods of the moon is advanced by Steuding in his article in Roscher, p. 1890. Alcamenes, he maintains, must have been thinking of the three phases of the moon because he has grouped his three figures in so peculiar a manner that wherever you stand you see a middle one *en face* which equals the full moon, and left and right profiles which correspond to the curves of the waxing and waning moon respectively. Perhaps it is only an accident that the writer has got the curves of the waxing and waning moon wrong, or has put right for left; the flaw in the argument is that the arrangement is not peculiar, as three figures cannot be placed back to back in any other way. Also it is asking a great deal to ask us to believe that the Greek, when gazing at his statues, was in the habit of comparing the human profiles with curves of astral bodies.

[c] One of his faces is dark, the other light ; it may be that he is thus characterized as a divinity of the upper and lower world.

The objection to this view is rather that it is insufficient than incorrect. Artemis, Demeter, Hermes, Aphrodite have each many natures and different spheres in which they act: but the idea of representing any one of these as a multiplicity or trinity of figures never occurred to any Greek artist. And though Hekate may have been ordinarily recognized as a goddess of three worlds, having associations with Selene, Artemis, and Persephone, a triple shape would scarcely have been given her for this reason only, had not her figure for practical purposes already been made triple at the cross-roads. It is true that we have no certain proof that this had happened before the time of Alcamenes, but it is the only reasonable motive for the shape of his statue at the entrance to the Acropolis. All that we need suppose is that the Ἑκάτεια at the cross-roads or before the houses had already been given three heads [a]. This would suggest to Alcamenes to enlarge upon this type that had been invented for practical convenience only, and to group together three figures around a column or back to back, as well as to invest each figure with attributes that alluded to the complex nature of the divinity, so that the triplicity was no longer merely a convenience but an expression of essential character.

After Alcamenes there was no great sculptor to whom a triple Hekate is attributed [b]. Among the many representations that have come down to us, then, we might expect to find some traces of the influence of his work. It is quite gratuitous to regard such works as the Hekate of the Capito-

[a] We know there were Ἑκάτεια before the doors in the time of the Peloponnesian war; and both here and at the cross-roads there was a motive for tripling the heads at least, namely that the countenance might guard egress and approach from either direction, or make the path of the traveller lucky whichever way he took. But the monuments fail to prove this, all the three-headed Hermae of Hekate being late.

[b] The two statues of Hekate at Argos, wrought by Naukydes and Polycleitus [23 k] (whether the older or the younger is uncertain), cannot with certainty be regarded as forming a group of three with the temple-statue of Scopas, so as to express the triple idea. We do not know when they were wrought or whether they stood in the same temple as the image by Scopas; for Pausanias' words, τὰ ἀπαντικρύ, may refer to statues on the other side of the road, and do not seem naturally to apply to a group, especially as they were of bronze while Scopas' work was of marble.

line [a] or the Leyden Museum [b] as copies ; there is nothing in the style of these that has any far-off association with the age of Alcamenes. But the claim of the relief found in Aegina, and now in Königswart in Bohemia (Pl. XXXIX. c), to represent something of the spirit of the original work is certainly greater [c]. The work appears to be of the fourth century B. C., and to possess considerable artistic merit; so far as can be judged from the publications of it, the faces have a dignity and breadth that recall the older style, the hair is drawn away from the cheek, and the expression is austere and solemn. But the archaism in the treatment of the drapery is not what would be expected from a pupil of Pheidias, unless it were retained as a tradition of hieratic sculpture ; and Petersen may be right in regarding a lately found fragment of a Hekateion, which he has published in the *Römische Mittheilungen des deutschen Institutes* [d], as standing nearer to the work of Alcamenes (Pl. XXXIX. b). Unfortunately nothing is preserved but the three torsos, set back to back ; from the position of the arms we can conjecture that the hands held such attributes as pitcher, cup, or torch. What is most important in the fragment is the treatment of the drapery, which shows the folds and the arrangement common in works of the Pheidian school, the girdle hidden, and the upper fold of the chiton drawn down so as to form a rich border across the waist.

Among the later monuments representing the triple Hekate we find illustration of nearly all the religious ideas that have been already examined.

Her connexion with the Charites at Athens explains those works on which, under the Hermae of the triple goddess, three maidens are represented dancing hand in hand around the shaft [e]: the maidens bear the calathus—the emblem of fruitfulness—on their heads, and themselves have something of the form of Hekate.

[a] Published in Roscher, p. 1905.

[b] *Arch. Zeit.* i. Taf. 8.

[c] The grouping of the figures cannot make for or against the theory, for Pausanias' words describing the work of Alcamenes, ἀγάλματα τρία προσεχόμενα ἀλλήλοις, are not altogether clear.

[d] 4. p. 73.

[e] Gerhard, *Akad. Abhandl.* Taf. 32, 4.

The same idea, her association with the fruitfulness of the earth, is expressed by the symbol of the apple which one or more figures of the triple group is often holding in her hand, as on the monument from Catajo in Vienna[a]; and by the fruits that are sometimes carved on the shaft of the Hekate column. Between the shoulders of the figures on the monument just mentioned we see a small statue of Pan ; and some association of her with the Phrygian worship may explain the Phrygian cap which one of her figures wears in the bronze of the Capitoline[b] and another bronze of the British Museum.

The character of Hekate Κλειδοῦχος[24], the guardian of the gate, is shown by the key which appears in the hands of many of her figures ; and possibly this alludes not only to the gate of the house and the city, but to the gate of hell, which she might be supposed to keep : as the key is known to have been also the badge of Hades[c].

The later coins and gems and works of sculpture afford ample illustration of her infernal and terrifying aspect ; her hair is sometimes wreathed with serpents, like the Gorgon's ; or the snake appears in her hand, a symbol of the same significance as the whip and cord which she borrows from the Furies ; the sword or the dagger which she often holds refers to the goddess of retribution.

A monument full of archaeological illustration of the bizarre ideas in this worship is the marble Hekateion of the Bruckenthal collection at Hermanstadt (Pl. XXXIX. d). The body of the front form is divided by parallel lines into different fields[d]. On her shoulders are carved in low relief two figures, the one being Tyche holding a horn, the other perhaps Nemesis ; on her breast is a rising sun: on the second field women with children, and Hermes with caduceus, and two animals— probably hounds : on the third the scene may probably be interpreted as the initiation of a child ; there is the triple image of Hekate on the left, and on the right a woman is

[a] Gerhard, *Akad. Abhandl.* Taf. 32. I, 2.

[b] Roscher, p. 1906.

[c] There was a statue of Plouton with

a key at Olympia (Paus. 5. 20).

[d] Vide more detailed account in Harrison and Verrall's *Myths and Monuments of Ancient Athens,* p. 381.

PLATE XL

To face page 557

holding a knife over an animal that seems to be a small dog[a].

In the latest gems we sometimes find her lunar character very clearly shown, as on a gem published by Müller[b], on which the moon is seen looking out of a cloud above Hekate. This representation shows a different treatment of the triple form : we see three heads and shoulders and six hands, but the lower part of her body is single, and closely resembles that of the Ephesian Artemis. We have probably here a real reminiscence of this cognate cult, and as we find bulls' heads wrought on the idol of Ephesus, so here on the gem we see bulls at the feet of Hekate.

This type of the single body with the three heads and shoulders may have descended from the earlier Hermae of the street and the cross-ways, and it existed by the side of the full triple form in late times, though it was probably far less commonly used for temple-monuments. But where Hekate was represented in dramatic action, the former type was more likely to be used, as it could be shown in much more natural movement than the trinity of three complete figures. The most memorable instance of the single body with the six arms and three heads is found on the Pergamene frieze (Pl. XL.), where she is armed with spear, sword, shield and torch, and is engaged in conflict with a serpent-footed giant. It is interesting to see that the form of the goddess in this last monument of genuinely Greek sculpture is free from the terrifying traits and the turgid symbolism with which later literature and art had invested her. The deity of the nether world is marked by the protruding forehead, the forward fall of the hair, the earnest and fixed expression, and the solemnity given by the shadows into which the profiles are cast ; and here, as in the earlier vase-paintings and in the Aeginetan relief, the forms and the drapery are such as are proper to the maidenly goddess.

[a] An initiation to Hekate might be alluded to in a vase-painting published in the *Annali del' Instituto,* 1865, Tav. d'Agg. F (p. 95), representing two youths seated before a table, above which is the inscription MVЅTΑ ; but the interpretation given of it there seems to me very doubtful.

[b] *Denkm. d. alt. Kunst,* 2. 888.

558   GREEK RELIGION.

REFERENCES FOR CHAPTERS XIII–XIX.

Artemis of the water.

[1] Artemis Λιμνᾶτις at Limnae on the borders of Messenia and Laconia: Paus. 4. 4, 2 ἔστιν ἐπὶ τοῖς ὅροις τῆς Μεσσηνίας ἱερὸν Ἀρτέμιδος καλουμένης Λιμνάτιδος, μετεῖχον δὲ αὐτοῦ μόνοι Δωριέων οἵ τε Μεσσήνιοι καὶ οἱ Λακεδαιμόνιοι. Strabo, 362 τὸ δ᾽ ἐν Λίμναις τῆς Ἀρτέμιδος ἱερὸν . . . ἐν μεθορίοις ἐστὶ τῆς τε Λακωνικῆς καὶ τῆς Μεσσηνίας ὅπου κοινὴν συνετέλουν πανήγυριν καὶ θυσίαν ἀμφότεροι . . . ἀπὸ δὲ τῶν Λιμνῶν τούτων καὶ τὸ ἐν τῇ Σπάρτῃ Λιμναῖον εἴρηται τῆς Ἀρτέμιδος ἱερόν. Tac. Ann. 4. 43 Auditae de hinc Lacedaemoniorum et Messeniorum legationes de iure templi Dianae Limnatidis quod suis a maioribus suaque in terra dicatum Lacedaemonii firmabant annalium memoria vatumque carminibus. Cf. inscription published Arch. Zeit 1876, p. 130; Roehl, Ins. Graec. Ant. 50 archaic dedication Λιμνᾶτις on a brazen cymbal. Cf. ib. 61. 73. Vide also Arch. Zeit. 1876, Tat. v.

[2] Artemis Λιμναία at Sicyon: Paus. 2. 7, 6 βαδίζουσιν ἐς τὴν ἀγοράν ἐστι ναὸς Ἀρτέμιδος ἐν δεξιᾷ Λιμναίας. Λιμνᾶτις in Epidaurus: Paus. 3. 23, 10 κατὰ τὴν ὁδὸν τὴν ἐκ Βοιῶν ἐς Ἐπίδαυρον ἄγουσαν Ἀρτέμιδος ἱερόν ἐστιν ἐν τῇ Ἐπιδαυρίων Λιμνάτιδος. At Patrae: Paus. 7. 20, 7–8 τῆς δὲ ἀγορᾶς ἄντικρυς κατ᾽ αὐτὴν τὴν διέξοδον τέμενός ἐστιν Ἀρτέμιδος καὶ ναὸς Λιμνάτιδος. ἐχόντων δὲ ἤδη Λακεδαίμονα καὶ Ἄργος Δωριέων ὑφελέσθαι Πρευγένην τῆς Λιμνάτιδος τὸ ἄγαλμα κατὰ ὄψιν ὀνείρατος λέγουσιν ἐκ Σπάρτης . . . τὸ δὲ ἄγαλμα τὸ ἐκ τῆς Λακεδαίμονος τὸν μὲν ἄλλον χρόνον ἔχουσιν ἐν Μεσόᾳ . . . ἐπειδὰν δὲ τῇ Λιμνάτιδι τὴν ἑορτὴν ἄγωσι, τῆς θεοῦ τις τῶν οἰκετῶν ἐκ Μεσόας ἔρχεται τὸ ξόανον κομίζων τὸ ἀρχαῖον ἐς τὸ τέμενος τὸ ἐν τῇ πόλει. Near Tegea: Paus. 8. 53, 11 ἱερὸν Ἀρτέμιδος ἐπίκλησιν Λιμνάτιδος καὶ ἄγαλμά ἐστιν ἐβένου ξύλου· τρόπος δὲ τῆς ἐργασίας ὁ Αἰγιναῖος καλούμενος ὑπὸ Ἑλλήνων. Eur. Hipp. 228 δέσποιν᾽ ἁλίας Ἄρτεμι λίμνας καὶ γυμνασίων τῶν ἱπποκρότων.

[3] Artemis Στυμφηλία at Stymphelus in Arcadia: Paus. 8. 22, 7 ἐν Στυμφήλῳ δὲ καὶ ἱερὸν Ἀρτέμιδός ἐστιν ἀρχαῖον Στυμφηλίας· τὸ δὲ ἄγαλμα ξόανόν ἐστι τὰ πολλὰ ἐπίχρυσον. πρὸς δὲ τοῦ ναοῦ τῷ ὀρόφῳ πεποιημέναι καὶ αἱ Στυμφηλίδες εἰσὶν ὄρνιθες.

[4] Artemis Ἀλφειαία at Letrini in Elis: Paus. 6. 22, 8 ἐπ᾽ ἐμοῦ δὲ οἰκήματά

τε ἐλείπετο ὀλίγα καὶ 'Αλφειαίας 'Αρτέμιδος ἄγαλμα ἐν ναῷ . . . *id.* § 10 οἱ δὲ 'Ηλεῖοι . . . τὰ παρὰ σφίσιν 'Αρτέμιδι ἐς τιμὴν τῇ 'Ελαφιαίᾳ καθεστηκότα ἐς Λετρίνους τε μετήγαγον καὶ τῇ 'Αρτέμιδι ἐνόμισαν τῇ 'Αλφειαίᾳ δρᾶν, καὶ οὕτω τὴν 'Αλφειαίαν θεὸν 'Ελαφιαίαν ἀνὰ χρόνον ἐξενίκησεν ὀνομασθῆναι. Paus. 5. 14, 6, at Olympia, 'Αλφειῷ καὶ 'Αρτέμιδι θύουσιν ἐπὶ ἑνὸς βωμοῦ. Cf. Schol. Pind. *Ol.* 5. 8. Strabo, 343 πρὸς δὲ τῇ ἐκβολῇ (τοῦ 'Αλφειοῦ) τὸ τῆς 'Αλφειωνίας 'Αρτέμιδος ἢ 'Αλφειούσης ἄλσος ἐστὶ . . . ταύτῃ δὲ τῇ θεῷ καὶ ἐν 'Ολυμπίᾳ κατ' ἔτος συντελεῖται πανήγυρις, καθάπερ καὶ τῇ 'Ελαφίᾳ καὶ τῇ Δαφνίᾳ . . . ἐν δὲ τῷ τῆς 'Αλφειωνίας ἱερῷ γραφαὶ Κλεάνθους τε καὶ 'Αρήγοντος, ἀνδρῶν Κορινθίων, τοῦ μὲν Τροίας ἅλωσις καὶ 'Αθηνᾶς γοναί, τοῦ δ' "Αρτεμις ἀναφερομένη ἐπὶ γρυπός, σφόδρα εὐδόκιμοι. Pind. *Nem.* 1. 1–6 "Αμπνευμα σεμνὸν 'Αλφεοῦ κλεινᾶν Συρακοσσᾶν θάλος 'Ορτυγία, δέμνιον 'Αρτέμιδος, Δάλου Κασιγνήτα. In Ortygia : Schol. Pind. *Pyth.* 2. 12 ὅθεν 'Αλφείωας 'Αρτέμιδος ἐκεῖ φασὶν εἶναι ἱερόν . . . ἵδρυται γὰρ ἄγαλμα 'Αρτέμιδος ἐπὶ τῇ 'Αρεθούσῃ. Pind. *Pyth.* 2. 12 'Ορτυγίαν . . . ποταμίας ἔδος 'Αρτέμιδος. Diod. Sic. 5. 3 τὴν δ' "Αρτεμιν τὴν ἐν ταῖς Συρακούσαις νῆσον λαβεῖν παρὰ τῶν θεῶν τὴν ἀπ' ἐκείνης . . . 'Ορτυγίαν ὀνομασθεῖσαν. Athen. p. 346 b οἶδα δὲ καὶ τὴν ἐν τῇ Πισάτιδι γραφὴν ἀνακειμένην ἐν τῷ τῆς 'Αλφειώσας 'Αρτέμιδος ἱερῷ.

⁵ Artemis 'Ελεία : Strabo, 350 "Ελος δ' οἱ μὲν περὶ τὸν 'Αλφειὸν χώριν τινά φασιν . . . οἱ δὲ περὶ τὸ 'Αλώριον ἕλος, οὗ τὸ τῆς 'Ελείας 'Αρτέμιδος ἱερὸν τῆς ὑπὸ τοῖς 'Αρκάσιν· ἐκεῖνοι γὰρ ἔσχον τὴν ἱερωσύνην. Cf. Hesych. *s. v* "Αρτεμις ἐν Μεσσήνῃ.

⁶ Artemis 'Απαγχομένη : Paus. 8. 23, 6, near Kaphyae, Κονδυλέα χωρίον, καὶ 'Αρτέμιδος ἄλσος' καὶ ναός ἐστιν ἐνταῦθα καλουμένης Κονδυλεάτιδος τὸ ἀρχαῖον· μετονομασθῆναι δὲ ἐπ' αἰτίᾳ τὴν θεόν φασι τοιαύτῃ. παιδία περὶ τὸ ἱερὸν παίζοντα . . . ἐπέτυχε καλῳδίῳ, δήσαντα δὲ τὸ καλῴδιον τοῦ ἀγάλματος περὶ τὸν τράχηλον ἐπέλεγεν ὡς ἀπάγχοιτο ἡ "Αρτεμις . . . Καφυεῖς δὲ . . . τὴν ἐν ταῖς Κονδυλέαις θεόν . . . καλοῦσιν 'Απαγχομένην ἐξ ἐκείνου. Cf. Clem. *Protrept.* 32 P "Αρτεμιν δὲ 'Αρκάδες 'Απαγχομένην καλουμένην προστρέπονται, ὥς φησι Καλλίμαχος ἐν Αἰτίοις.

⁷ Artemis Καρυᾶτις at Karyae in Laconia : Paus. 3. 10, 7 τὸ γὰρ χωρίον 'Αρτέμιδος καὶ Νυμφῶν ἐστὶν αἱ Κάρυαι, καὶ ἄγαλμα ἕστηκεν 'Αρτέμιδος ἐν ὑπαίθρῳ Καρυάτιδος· χοροὺς δὲ ἐνταῦθα αἱ Λακεδαιμονίων παρθένοι κατὰ ἔτος ἱστᾶσι, καὶ ἐπιχώριος αὐταῖς καθέστηκεν ὄρχησις. Luc. περὶ ὀρχ. 10 Λακεδαιμόνιοι . . . παρὰ Πολυδεύκους καὶ Κάστορος καρυατίζειν μαθόντες—ὀρχήσεως δὲ καὶ τοῦτο εἶδος ἐν Καρύαις τῆς Λακωνικῆς διδασκόμενον. Pollux, 4. 104 ἦν δέ τινα καὶ Λακωνικὰ ὀρχήματα . . . Καρυάτιδες ἐπὶ 'Αρτέμιδι. Photius, *s. v.* Καρυάτεια· ἑορτὴ 'Αρτέμιδος. Cf. Serv. *Ecl.* 8. 29 templum Caryatidae Dianae a Lacedaemonibus consecratum.

⁸ Artemis Κεδρεᾶτις at Orchomenos in Arcadia : Paus. 8. 13, 2 πρὸς

560   GREEK RELIGION.

δὲ τῇ πόλει ξόανόν ἐστιν Ἀρτέμιδος· ἵδρυται δὲ ἐν κέδρῳ μεγάλῃ, καὶ τὴν θεὸν ὀνομάζουσιν ἀπὸ τῆς κέδρου Κεδρεάτιν.

⁹ Artemis Δαφναία at Hypsoi on the Laconian mountains : Paus. 3. 24, 8 ἱερὸν Ἀσκληπιοῦ καὶ Ἀρτέμιδος ἐπίκλησιν Δαφναίας. At Olympia, vide ⁴.

¹⁰ Artemis Λυγοδέσμα at Sparta : Paus. 3. 16, 11 καλοῦσι δὲ οὐκ Ὀρθίαν μόνον, ἀλλὰ καὶ Λυγοδέσμαν τὴν αὐτήν, ὅτι ἐν θάμνῳ λύγων εὑρέθη, περιειληθεῖσα δὲ ἡ λύγος ἐποίησε τὸ ἄγαλμα ὀρθόν.

¹¹ Artemis Φακελῖτις at Syracuse : Prob. Verg. *Ecl.* p. 3 (ed. Keil) Orestes . . . iuxta Syracusas somnio admonitus simulacrum Deae quod secum de Tauricâ advexerat, templo posito consecravit, quam appellavit Facelitim, sive quod fasce lignorum tectum de Taurica simulacrum extulisset.

¹¹ᵃ At Boiae in Laconia : Paus. 3. 22, 12 τὸ δένδρον ἔτι ἐκείνην σέβουσι τὴν μυρσίνην καὶ Ἄρτεμιν ὀνομάζουσι Σώτειραν.

¹² Artemis Νεμιδία (?) at Teuthea in Achaea : Strabo, 342 ὅπου τὸ τῆς Νεμυδίας Ἀρτέμιδος ἱερόν.

¹³ Artemis Ὑακινθοτρόφος at Cnidus : Collitz. *Dialect. Inscriften.* No. 3502 Ἀρτάμιτι Ὑακινθοτρόφῳ καὶ Ἐπιφανεῖ, ἃς καὶ αὐτᾶς ἱερεὺς ὑπάρχει διὰ βίου.

¹⁴ Artemis Εὐρυνόμη near Phigaleia : Paus. 8. 41, 4 ἔστι τῆς Εὐρυνόμης τὸ ἱερόν, ἅγιόν τε ἐκ παλαιοῦ καὶ ὑπὸ τραχύτητος τοῦ χωρίου δυσπρόσοδον· περὶ αὐτὸ καὶ κυπάρισσοι πεφύκασι πολλαί τε καὶ ἀλλήλαις συνεχεῖς· τὴν μὲν Εὐρυνόμην ὁ μὲν τῶν Φιγαλέων δῆμος ἐπίκλησιν εἶναι πεπίστευκεν Ἀρτέμιδος. ὅσοι δὲ αὐτῶν παρειλήφασιν ὑπομνήματα ἀρχαῖα θυγατέρα Ὠκεανοῦ φασὶν εἶναι τὴν Εὐρυνόμην . . . ἡμέρᾳ δὲ τῇ αὐτῇ κατὰ ἔτος ἕκαστον τὸ ἱερὸν ἀνοιγνύουσι τῆς Εὐρυνόμης· τὸν δὲ ἄλλον χρόνον οὔ σφισιν ἀνοιγνύναι καθέστηκεν. τηνικαῦτα δὲ καὶ θυσίας δημοσίᾳ τε καὶ ἰδιῶται θύουσιν . . . τῶν Φιγαλέων δὲ ἤκουσα ὡς χρυσαῖ τε τὸ ξόανον συνδέουσιν ἁλύσεις καὶ εἰκὼν γυναικὸς τὰ ἄχρι τῶν γλουτῶν, τὸ ἀπὸ τούτου δέ ἐστιν ἰχθύς. Cf. Athenae. p. 325 c Ἡγήσανδρος δ' ὁ Δελφὸς τρίγλην παραφέρεσθαι (φησὶ) ἐν τοῖς ἀρτεμισίοις.

¹⁵ ? Artemis Νηοσσόος : Ap. Rhod. 1. 569 τοῖσι δὲ φορμίζων εὐθήμονι μέλπεν ἀοιδῇ Οἰάγροιο πάϊς νηοσσόον εὐπατέρειαν Ἄρτεμιν, ἣ κείνας σκοπίας ἅλος ἀμφιέπεσκεν Ῥυομένη καὶ γαῖαν Ἰωλκίδα.

¹⁶ Artemis Εὐπορία : Hesych. *s. v.* Ἄρτεμις ἐν Ῥόδῳ.

¹⁷ Artemis Ἐκβατηρία : Hesych. *s. v.* Ἐκβατηρίας· Ἄρτεμις ἐν Σίφνῳ.

¹⁸ Artemis Αἰγιναία at Sparta : Paus. 3. 14, 2 θεῶν δὲ ἱερὰ Ποσειδῶνός ἐστιν Ἱπποκουρίου καὶ Ἀρτέμιδος Αἰγιναίας. Cf. Paus. 1. 38, 6 Ἐλευσινίοις

... ἔστι ... Προπυλαίας Ἀρτέμιδος καὶ Ποσειδῶνος πατρός. Cf. Artemis Εὐρίππα [48] and [34]. At Calauria worship of Artemis (?) connected with Poseidon : Rang. *Ant. Hell.* 821 b.

Titles of the goddess of the wilds.

[19] Artemis Λαφρία[a] at Patrae : Paus. 7. 18, 8 Πατρεῦσι δὲ ἐν ἄκρᾳ τῇ πόλει Λαφρίας ἱερόν ἐστιν Ἀρτέμιδος· ξενικὸν μὲν τῇ θεῷ τὸ ὄνομα, ἐσηγμένον δὲ ἑτέρωθεν καὶ τὸ ἄγαλμα. Καλυδῶνος καὶ Αἰτωλίας τῆς ἄλλης ὑπὸ Αὐγούστου τοῦ βασιλέως ἐρημωθείσης, οὕτω τὸ ἄγαλμα τῆς Λαφρίας οἱ Πατρεῖς ἔσχον ... τὸ μὲν σχῆμα τοῦ ἀγάλματος θηρεύουσά ἐστι, ἐλέφαντος δὲ καὶ χρυσοῦ πεποίηται, Ναυπάκτιοι δὲ Μέναιχμος καὶ Σοΐδας εἰργάσαντο ... Ἄγουσι δὲ καὶ Λάφρια ἑορτὴν τῇ Ἀρτέμιδι ἀνὰ πᾶν ἔτος, ἐν ᾗ τρόπος ἐπιχώριος θυσίας ἐστὶν αὐτοῖς ... πρῶτα μὲν δὴ πομπὴν μεγαλοπρεπεστάτην τῇ Ἀρτέμιδι πομπεύουσι, καὶ ἡ ἱερωμένη παρθένος ὀχεῖται τελευταία τῆς πομπῆς ἐπὶ ἐλάφων ὑπὸ τὸ ἅρμα ἐζευγμένων ... ἐσβάλλουσι ζῶντας ἐς τὸν βωμὸν ὄρνιθάς τε τοὺς ἐδωδίμους καὶ ἱερεῖα ὁμοίως ἅπαντα, ἔτι δὲ ὗς ἀγρίους καὶ ἐλάφους τε καὶ δορκάδας, οἱ δὲ καὶ λύκων καὶ ἄρκτων σκύμνους, οἱ δὲ καὶ τὰ τέλεια τῶν θηρίων. κατατιθέασι δὲ ἐπὶ τὸν βωμὸν καὶ δένδρων καρπὸν τῶν ἡμέρων. τὰ δὲ ἀπὸ τούτου πῦρ ἐνιᾶσιν ἐς τὰ ξύλα.

[b] In Messenia at Ithome : Paus. 4. 31, 7 Δαμοφῶντος δέ ἐστι τούτου καὶ ἡ Λαφρία καλουμένη παρὰ Μεσσηνίοις ... Καλυδωνίοις ἡ Ἄρτεμις, ταύτην γὰρ θεὸν μάλιστα ἔσεβον, ἐπίκλησιν εἶχε Λαφρία. Μεσσηνίων δὲ οἱ λαβόντες Ναύπακτον ... παρὰ Καλυδωνίων ἔλαβον.

[c] Artemis in Cephallenia, [131][g]. Cf. Heracleides, Müller, *Frag. Hist. Graec.* 2. p. 217, frag. 17.

[d] The month Λάφριος in Phocis and Doris: Le Bas, *Boeotie* 920.

[e] Suidas, p. 702 B, *s. v.* βαθεῖα· βαθύπλουτον εἶναι τὴν Λαφρίαν Ἄρτεμιν.

[20] Artemis Καπροφάγος : Hesych. *s. v.* Ἄρτεμις ἐν Σάμῳ. Cf. Hom. *Od.* 6. 104 τερπομένη κάπροισι καὶ ὠκείῃς ἐλάφοισι.

[21] Sacrifice at Syracuse : Theocr. 2. 66 :

ἦνθ' ἁ τωὔβούλοιο κανηφόρος ἄμμιν Ἀναξὼ
ἄλσος ἐς Ἀρτέμιδος, τᾷ δὴ τόκα πολλὰ μὲν ἄλλα
θηρία πομπεύεσκε περισταδὸν ἐν δὲ λέαινα.

[22] Artemis Λυκεία at Troezen : Paus. 2. 31, 4 πλησίον δὲ τοῦ θεάτρου Λυκείας ναὸν Ἀρτέμιδος ἐποίησεν Ἱππόλυτος. Cf. Λυκοᾶτις at Lycoa in Arcadia : Paus. 8. 36, 7 Ἀρτέμιδος ἱερὸν καὶ ἄγαλμά ἐστι χαλκοῦν Λυκοάτιδος.

[23] Artemis Ἐλαφιαία in Elis, vide [4] : Pind. *Ol.* 3. 51 :

χρυσόκερων ἔλαφον θήλειαν ... ἄν ποτε Ταϋγέτα
ἀντιθεῖσ' Ὀρθωσίᾳ ἔγραψεν ἱράν.

[24][a] Artemis Ἐλαφηβόλος in Pamphylia: *Bull. de Corr. Hell.* 1883,

562   GREEK RELIGION.

p. 263, inscription of early Roman period from Attalia, published by Ramsay, ἱερέα διὰ βίου . . . θεᾶς Ἀρτέμιδος Ἐλαφηβόλου.

b The month Ἐλαφηβολιών in Attica and Iasos: C. I. Gr. 2675 b, 2677 b: in Apollonia in the Chalcidic peninsula, Athenae. p. 334 E.

c Ἐλαφηβόλια at Athens and Phocis: Athenae. p. 646 E Ἔλαφος· πλακοῦς ὁ τοῖς ἐλαφηβολίοις ἀναπλασσόμενος διὰ σταιτὸς καὶ μέλιτος καὶ σησάμου : El. Mag. s. v. Ἐλαφηβολιών· μὴν Ἀθηναίων· ἀπὸ τῶν ἐλάφων ὠνόμασται αἱ τῷ μηνὶ ἐθύοντο τῇ ἐλαφηβόλῳ Ἀρτέμιδι. At Hyampolis in Phocis : Plut. de mul. virt. 244 E ἑορτὴν ἐκ πασῶν μεγίστην τὰ Ἐλαφηβόλια μέχρι νῦν τῇ Ἀρτέμιδι τῆς νίκης ἐκείνης ἐν Ὑαμπόλιδι τελοῦσιν (in honour of a victory over the Thessalians).

d Strabo, 215, among the Heneti, δύο ἄλση τὸ μὲν Ἥρας Ἀργείας τὸ δ᾽ Ἀρτέμιδος Αἰτωλίδος. προσμυθεύουσι δ᾽, ὡς εἰκός, τὸ ἐν τοῖς ἄλσεσι τούτοις ἡμεροῦσθαι τὰ θηρία καὶ λύκοις ἐλάφους συναγελάζεσθαι.

e Near Colophon, a small island sacred to Artemis : Strabo, 643 εἰς ὃ διανηχομένας τὰς ἐλάφους τίκτειν.

25 Artemis Ὀρτυγία (? cult-title) : Soph. Trach. 212 :

βοᾶτε τὰν ὁμόσπορον
Ἄρτεμιν Ὀρτυγίαν, ἐλαφαβόλον, ἀμφίπυρον,
γείτονας δὲ Νύμφας.

Tac. Ann. 3. 61 primi omnium Ephesii adiere memorantes . . . esse apud se . . . lucum Ortygium, ubi Latonam partu gravidam . . . edidisse ea numina; deorumque monitu sacratum nemus. Cf. Strabo, 639. Schol. Ap. Rhod. 1. 419 Φανόδικος ἐν τοῖς Δηλιακοῖς ἱστόρηκεν καὶ Νίκανδρος ἐν γ᾽ Αἰτωλικῶν . . . ἐκ τῆς ἐν Αἰτωλίᾳ Ὀρτυγίας κληθῆναι τὴν Δῆλον Ὀρτυγίαν. Athenae. p. 392 D Φανόδημος ἐν δευτέρῳ Ἀτθίδος φησίν . . . Δῆλον τὴν νῆσον τὴν ὑπὸ τῶν ἀρχαίων καλουμένην Ὀρτυγίαν. Cf. ⁴.

26 Artemis Ἀγροτέρα : Hom. Il. 21. 470 πότνια θηρῶν Ἄρτεμις ἀγροτέρη.

a At Aegira : Paus. 7. 26, 3 Ὑπηρησιεῖς δὲ τῇ τε πόλει τὸ ὄνομα τὸ νῦν μετέθεντο ἀπὸ τῶν αἰγῶν, καὶ καθότι αὐτῶν ἡ καλλίστη καὶ ἡγουμένη τῶν ἄλλων ὤκλασεν, Ἀρτέμιδος Ἀγροτέρας ἐποιήσαντο ἱερόν . . . Ἀρτέμιδός τε ναὸς καὶ ἄγαλμα τέχνης τῆς ἐφ᾽ ἡμῶν· ἱερᾶται δὲ παρθένος, ἔστ᾽ ἂν ἐς ὥραν ἀφίκηται γάμου.

b In Lacedaemon : Xen. Hell. 4. 2, 20 σφαγιασάμενοι οἱ Λακεδαιμόνιοι τῇ Ἀγροτέρᾳ, ὥσπερ νομίζεται, τὴν χίμαιραν, ἡγοῦντο ἐπὶ τοὺς ἐναντίους.

c At Megara : Paus. 1. 41, 3 Ἀλκάθουν τὸν Πέλοπος . . . ἱερὸν ποιῆσαι τοῦτο, Ἀγροτέρον Ἄρτεμιν καὶ Ἀπόλλωνα Ἀγραῖον ἐπονομάσαντα.

ᵈ At Megalopolis : Paus. 8. 32, 4 Ἀγροτέρας ναὸς Ἀρτέμιδος ἀνάθημα Ἀριστοδήμου.

ᵉ At Olympia : Paus. 5. 15, 8 πρυτανείου δὲ πρὸ μὲν τῶν θυρῶν βωμός ἐστιν Ἀρτέμιδος Ἀγροτέρας.

ᶠ At Agrae in Attica : Paus. 1. 19, 6 διαβᾶσι δὲ τὸν Εἰλισσὸν χωρίον Ἄγραι καλούμενον καὶ ναὸς ἀγροτέρας ἐστὶν Ἀρτέμιδος. ἐνταῦθα Ἄρτεμιν πρῶτον θηρεῦσαι λέγουσιν ἐλθοῦσαν ἐκ Δήλου. Bekker's Anecdota, p. 326. 28 καὶ Ἀρτέμιδος καὶ Ἀγραίας αὐτόθι τὸ ἱερόν. Schol. Arist. Eq. 657 τῇ Ἀγροτέρᾳ· τῇ Ἀρτέμιδι· ἰδίως γὰρ οἱ Ἀθηναῖοι σέβουσι καὶ τιμῶσι τὴν Ἀγροτέραν Ἄρτεμιν. Ael. Var. Hist. 2. 25 Πέρσαι δὲ ἡττήθησαν τῇ ἡμέρᾳ ταύτῃ (τῇ ἕκτῃ τοῦ Θαργηλιῶνος)· καὶ Ἀθηναῖοι δὲ τῇ Ἀγροτέρᾳ ἀποθύουσι τὰς χιμαίρας τὰς τριακοσίας, κατὰ τὴν εὐχὴν τοῦ Μιλτιάδου δρῶντες τοῦτο. Cf. Xen. Anab. 3. 2, 12. Plut. de malign. Herod. 862 A τὴν πρὸς Ἄγρας πομπήν, ἣν πέμπουσιν ἔτι νῦν τῇ Ἑκάτῃ χαριστήρια τῆς νίκης ἑορτάζοντες. Pollux, 8. 91 ὁ δὲ πολέμαρχος θύει μὲν Ἀρτέμιδι Ἀγροτέρᾳ καὶ τῷ Ἐνυαλίῳ. C. I. A. 2. 467 ἐπειδὴ οἱ ἔφηβοι . . . ἐπόμπευσάν τε τῇ Ἀρτέμιδι τῇ Ἀγροτέρᾳ ἐν ὅπλοις : beginning of first century B. C.

ᵍ At Artamition in Euboea : Mitt. d. deut. Inst. Ath. 1883, p. 202 Πυρριχῇ ἄθλ[ῳ or ων] Παρθένον Ἀγροτέραν : mutilated inscription ? third century B. C.

ʰ In Pontos : C. I. Gr. 2117, inscription found near Phanagoria, fourth century B. C., Ξενοκλείδης Πόσιος ἀνέθηκε τὸν ναὸν Ἀρτέμιδι Ἀγροτέρᾳ ἄρχοντος Παιρισάδους τοῦ Λεύκωνος Βοσπόρου.

ⁱ Artemis Ποδάγρα in Laconia : Clem. Alex. Protrept. 32 P ἔστι δὲ καὶ Ποδάγρας ἄλλης Ἀρτέμιδος ἐν τῇ Λακωνικῇ ἱερόν, ὥς φησι Σωσίβιος.

ᵏ Xenoph. Ven. 5. 14 τὰ μὲν οὖν λίαν νεογνὰ (τῶν λαγίων) οἱ φιλοκυνηγέται ἀφιᾶσι τῇ θεῷ (Ἀρτέμιδι).

ˡ Worshipped as huntress at Epidaurus : Paus. 2. 29, 1 ναοὶ ἐν τῇ πόλει καὶ Διονύσου καὶ Ἀρτέμιδός ἐστιν ἄλλος· εἰκάσαις ἂν θηρευούσῃ τὴν Ἄρτεμιν.

ᵐ At Pellene : Paus. 7. 27, 4 πλησίον δὲ τοῦ Ἀπόλλωνος ναός ἐστιν Ἀρτέμιδος· τοξευούσης δὲ ἡ θεὸς παρέχεται σχῆμα.

²⁷ Artemis Καλλίστη in the Academia near Athens : Paus. 1. 29, 2 κατιοῦσι δὲ ἐς αὐτὴν περίβολός ἐστιν Ἀρτέμιδος καὶ ξόανα Ἀρίστης καὶ Καλλίστης· ὡς μὲν ἐγὼ δοκῶ καὶ ὁμολογεῖ τὰ ἔπη τὰ Σαπφοῦς, τῆς Ἀρτέμιδός εἰσιν ἐπικλήσεις αὗται. Near Tricoloni in Arcadia : Paus. 8. 35, 8 ταφός ἐστι Καλλιστοῦς, χῶμα γῆς ὑψηλόν, . . . ἐπὶ δὲ ἄκρῳ τῷ χώματι ἱερόν ἐστιν Ἀρτέμιδος ἐπίκλησιν Καλλίστης· δοκεῖν δέ μοι καὶ Πάμφως μαθών τι παρὰ Ἀρκάδων πρῶτος Ἄρτεμιν ἐν τοῖς ἔπεσιν ὠνόμασε Καλλίστην. Artemis

Καλλίστη in Syria: *C. I. Gr.* 4445, sepulchral dedication, Ἀρτέμιδι Καλ(λ)ίστῃ . . . χαῖρε.

²⁸ Cf. Artemis Ὡραία, inscription found in the Peiraeeus, Ἱερῶν Ἀρτέμιδι Ὡραίαι: *Eph. Arch.* 1884, p. 69.

²⁹ Artemis Καλλιστώ: Apollod. 3. 8, 2 Εὔμηλος δὲ καί τινες ἕτεροι λέγουσι Λυκάονι καὶ θυγατέρα Καλλιστώ γενέσθαι· αὕτη σύνθηρος Ἀρτέμιδος οὖσα τὴν αὐτὴν ἐκείνῃ στολὴν φοροῦσα. Istros apud Steph. Byz. *s. v.* Ἀρκαδία: Ἴστρος δέ φησι ὅτι Θεμιστοὺς καὶ Διὸς ὁ Ἀρκὰς ἐγένετο, διὰ δὲ τὴν τῆς μητρὸς ἀποθηρίωσιν (ἄρκτῳ γὰρ ὑφ᾿ Ἥρας αὐτὴν ὁμοιασθῆναι) ταύτης τυχεῖν τῆς προσηγορίας. Hygin. *Astron.* 2. 1 Ariethus autem Tegeates historiarum scriptor non Callisto sed Megisto dicit appellatam.

³⁰ Artemis Μουνυχία: ᵃ in the Peiraeeus: Paus. 1. 1, 4 ὁ μὲν ἐπὶ Μουνυχίᾳ λιμὴν καὶ Μουνυχίας ναὸς Ἀρτέμιδος. Plut. *De glor. Atheniens.* p. 349 τὴν δὲ ἕκτην ἐπὶ δέκα τοῦ Μουνυχιῶνος Ἀρτέμιδι καθιέρωσαν, ἐν ᾗ τοῖς Ἕλλησι περὶ Σαλαμῖνα νικῶσι ἐπέλαμψεν ἡ Θεὸς πανσέληνος. Cf. Pollux, 6. 75 ἀμφιφῶντες, ἃς ἔφερον εἰς Μουνυχίας Ἀρτέμιδος, δᾷδας ἡμμένας περιπήξαντες.

ᵇ At Pygela near Ephesus: Strabo, 639 ἱερὸν ἔχον Ἀρτέμιδος Μουνυχίας.

ᶜ In Cyzicus: *C. I. Gr.* 3657 προιερωμένην Ἀρτέμιδος Μουνυχίας.

ᵈ In Placia near Cyzicus: *Mitt. d. d. Inst. Ath.* 1882, 155 ἱερωμένην Μητρὸς Πλακιανῆς . . . καὶ Ἀρτέμιδος Μουνυχίας: ? first century B.C.

³¹ Artemis Βραυρωνία: Paus. 1. 33, 1 Μαραθῶνος δὲ ἀπέχει τῇ μὲν Βραυρὼν ἔνθα Ἰφιγένειαν . . . ἐκ Ταύρων φεύγουσαν τὸ ἄγαλμα ἀγομένην τὸ Ἀρτέμιδος ἀποβῆναι λέγουσι, καταλιποῦσαν δὲ τὸ ἄγαλμα ταύτῃ καὶ ἐς Ἀθήνας καὶ ὕστερον ἐς Ἄργος ἀφικέσθαι· ξόανον μὲν δὴ καὶ αὐτόθι ἐστὶν Ἀρτέμιδος ἀρχαῖον. *Id.* 1. 23, 7, on the Acropolis, Ἀρτέμιδος ἱερόν ἐστι Βραυρωνίας, Πραξιτέλους μὲν τέχνη τὸ ἄγαλμα, τῇ θεῷ δέ ἐστιν ἀπὸ Βραυρῶνος δήμου τὸ ὄνομα. *Id.* 3. 16, 8 τὸ γὰρ ἐκ Βραυρῶνος (ἄγαλμα) ἐκομίσθη τε ἐς Σοῦσα, καὶ ὕστερον Σελεύκου δόντος Σύροι Λαοδικεῖς ἐφ᾿ ἡμῶν ἔχουσι. Strabo, 399 Βραυρὼν ὅπου τὸ τῆς Βραυρωνίας Ἀρτέμιδος ἱερόν, Ἁλαὶ Ἀραφηνίδες, ὅπου τὸ τῆς Ταυροπόλου. Diphilos Ἐλενηφοροῦντες: Athenae. p. 223 A ὦ τόνδ᾿ ἐποπτεύουσα καὶ κεκτημένη Βραυρῶνος ἱεροῦ θεοφιλέστατον τόπον Λητοῦς Διός τε τοξόδαμνε Παρθένε. *C. I. Gr.* 150 a, b.

Ritual of the Brauronian worship.

³² Arist. *Lysistr.* 645 κᾆτ᾿ ἔχουσα τὸν κροκωτὸν ἄρκτος ἦ Βραυρωνίοις. Schol. *ib.* Ἄρκτον μιμούμεναι τὸ μυστήριον ἐξετέλουν. αἱ ἀρκτευόμεναι δὲ τῇ θεῷ κροκωτὸν ἠμφιέννυντο καὶ συνετέλουν τὴν θυσίαν τῇ Βραυρωνίᾳ Ἀρτέμιδι καὶ τῇ Μουνυχίᾳ, ἐπιλεγόμεναι παρθένοι, οὔτε πρεσβεύτεραι δέκα ἐτῶν οὔτ᾿

ἐλάττους πέντε· ἐπετέλουν δὲ τὴν θυσίαν αἱ κόραι ἐκμειλισσόμεναι τὴν θεόν, ἐπειδὴ λιμῷ περιπεπτώκασιν οἱ Ἀθηναῖοι ἄρκτον ἡμέραν ἀνῃρηκότες τῇ θεᾷ· οἱ δὲ τὰ περὶ τὴν Ἰφιγένειαν ἐν Βραυρῶνι φασίν, οὐκ ἐν Αὐλίδι. Εὐφορίων " Ἀρχίαλον Βραυρῶνα κενήριον Ἰφιγενείας." καὶ ἄρκτον ἀντ' αὐτῆς, οὐκ ἔλαφον, φονευθῆναι . . . (δηλωθέντος δὲ τοῦ χρησμοῦ τοῖς Ἀθηναίοις ἐψηφίσαντο μὴ πρότερον συνοικίζεσθαι ἀνδρὶ παρθένον, εἰ μὴ ἀρκτεύσειεν τῇ θεῷ R). Cf. Suidas, s.v. ἄρκτος. Hesych. s.v. Βραυρωνίοις· τὴν Ἰλιάδα ᾖδον ῥαψωδοὶ ἐν Βραυρῶνι τῆς Ἀττικῆς. Βραυρώνια ἑορτή· Ἀρτέμιδι Βραυρώνια ἄγεται καὶ θύεται αἴξ. Hesych. s.v. Ἄρκος . . . καὶ τὸ ζῶον καὶ ἡ ἱέρεια τῆς Ἀρτέμιδος. Harpocr. s.v. ἀρκτεῦσαι· τὸ καθιερωθῆναι πρὸ γάμων τὰς παρθένους τῇ Ἀρτέμιδι τῇ Μουνυχίᾳ ἢ τῇ Βραυρωνίᾳ. Eustath. Il. p. 331. 26 ἱδρύσατο γὰρ . . . Μουνυχίας Ἀρτέμιδος ἱερόν· ἄρκτου δὲ γενομένης ἐν αὐτῷ καὶ ὑπ' Ἀθηναίων ἀναιρεθείσης, λοιμὸς ἐπεγένετο, οὗ ἀπαλλαγὴν ὁ θεὸς ἐχρησμῴδησεν, εἴ τις τὴν θυγατέρα θύσει τῇ Ἀρτέμιδι . . . Ἔμβαρος . . . διακοσμήσας τὴν θυγατέρα, αὐτὴν μὲν ἀπέκρυψεν ἐν τῷ ἀδύτῳ, αἶγα δὲ ἐσθῆτι κοσμήσας ὡς τὴν θυγατέρα ἔθυσεν. Cf. Bekker's Anecd. p. 444 Λυσίας τὸ καθιερωθῆναι πρὸ γάμων τὰς παρθένους τῇ Ἀρτέμιδι ἀρκτεύειν ἔλεγε . . . εἴς τις ἀνὴρ . . . ἔχων αἶγα καὶ ὀνομάζων ταύτην θυγατέρα ἔθυσε λάθρα. Ib. 206 τῇ Ἀρτέμιδι καὶ τῇ ἄρκτῳ ἀφοσιώσασθαι καὶ θῦσαι, ὅπερ ἐποίουν πρὸ τῶν γάμων αἱ κόραι. Et. Mag. p. 747. 56, s.v. Ταυροπόλος. οἱ δὲ λέγουσιν ὅτι τῶν Ἑλλήνων βουλομένων ἀνελεῖν τὴν Ἰφιγένειαν ἐν Αὐλίδι ἡ Ἄρτεμις ἀντέδωκεν ἔλαφον· κατὰ δὲ Φανόδημον ἄρκτον κατὰ δὲ Νίκανδρον, ταῦρον· διὸ καὶ τὴν θεὸν οὐ ταυροπόλον ἀλλὰ ταυροφάγον ὠνόμασαν. Schol. Hom. Il. 1. 594 Φιλόχορός φησι Πελασγοὺς . . . ἐπεὶ πλεύσαντες ἐς Βραυρῶνα κανηφόρους παρθένους ἥρπασαν. Cf. ⁵²b. Arist. Ath. Polit. c. 54 κληροῖ δὲ καὶ ἑτέρους δέκα (ἱεροποιοὺς) οἱ . . . τὰς πεντετηρίδας ἁπάσας διοικοῦσι πλὴν Παναθηναίων. εἰσὶ δὲ πεντετηρίδες . . . δευτέρα δὲ Βραυρωνία. Deinarch. in Aristog. p. 106 ἡ ἱέρεια τῆς Ἀρτέμιδος τῆς Βραυρωνίας. Eur. Iph. Taur. 1450:

χῶρός τίς ἐστιν Ἀτθίδος πρὸς ἐσχάτοις
ὅροισι, γείτων δειράδος Καρυστίας,
ἱερός, Ἁλάς νιν οὑμὸς ὀνομάζει λεώς·
ἐνταῦθα τεύξας ναὸν ἵδρυσαι βρέτας,
ἐπώνυμον γῆς Ταυρικῆς πόνων τε σῶν,

. . . .

. . . . Ἄρτεμιν δέ νιν βροτοὶ
τὸ λοιπὸν ὑμνήσουσι Ταυροπόλον θεάν.
νόμον δὲ θὲς τόνδ'· ὅταν ἑορτάζῃ λεὼς
τῆς σῆς σφαγῆς ἄποιν', ἐπισχέτω ξίφος
δέρῃ πρὸς ἀνδρός, αἷμά τ' ἐξανιέτω
ὁσίας ἕκατι θεά θ' ὅπως τιμὰς ἔχῃ.
σὲ δ' ἀμφὶ σεμνάς, Ἰφιγένεια, κλίμακας
Βραυρωνίας δεῖ τῇσδε κλειδουχεῖν θεᾶς.

οὗ καὶ τεθάψει κατθανοῦσα, καὶ πέπλων
ἄγαλμά σοι θήσουσιν εὐπήνους ὑφάς,
ἂς ἂν γυναῖκες ἐν τόκοις ψυχορραγεῖς
λείπωσ' ἐν οἴκοις.

Cf. Callim. *Dian.* 173.

³³ ? Artemis Βραυρωνὶς Αἰθοπία at Amphipolis: *Anth. Pal.* 7. 705:

Ἀμφίπολι,
λοιπά τοι Αἰθοπίης Βραυρωνίδος ἴχνια νηοῦ
μίμνει

Ἄρτεμις Βραυρωνία at Laodicea ad mare, ³¹: cf. Athena ¹ ᵃ: *C. I. Gr.* 4470, 4471 ἡ κυρία Ἄρτεμις (Roman period).

³⁴ Ἄρτεμις Ἰφιγένεια in Hermione: Paus. 2. 35, 1 Ἀρτέμιδος ἐπίκλησιν Ἰφιγενείας ἐστὶν ἱερὸν καὶ Ποσειδῶν χαλκοῦς τὸν ἕτερον πόδα ἔχων ἐπὶ δελφῖνος. Hesych. *s. v.* Ἰφιγένεια· ἡ Ἄρτεμις.

³⁵ Human sacrifices to Artemis, vide ³²: Clem. Alex. *Protrept.* P. 36 Ταῦροι τὸ ἔθνος, οἱ περὶ τὴν Ταυρικὴν χερρόνησον κατοικοῦντες, οὓς ἂν τῶν ξένων παρ' αὑτοῖς ἕλωσι . . . αὐτίκα μάλα τῇ Ταυρικῇ καταθύουσιν Ἀρτέμιδι. *Ib.* (citation of doubtful authenticity, vide Hiller in *Hermes* 21. p. 127) Πυθοκλῆς ἐν τρίτῳ περὶ ὁμονοίας (Φωκαεῖς) τῇ Ταυροπόλῳ Ἀρτέμιδι ἄνθρωπον ὁλοκαεῖν ἱστορεῖ. Cf. Scymnus Chius, *Perieg.* 861 (οἱ Ταῦροι) ἱλασκόμενοι τὰ θεῖα τοῖς ἀσεβήμασιν. Paus. 7. 19, 1–6 Ἰώνων τοῖς Ἀρόην καὶ Ἄνθειαν καὶ Μεσάτιν οἰκοῦσιν ἦν ἐν κοινῷ τέμενος καὶ ναὸς Ἀρτέμιδος Τρικλαρίας ἐπίκλησιν, καὶ ἑορτὴν οἱ Ἴωνες αὐτῇ καὶ παννυχίδα ἦγον ἀνὰ πᾶν ἔτος· ἱερωσύνην δὲ εἶχε τῆς θεοῦ παρθένος, ἐς ὃ ἀποστέλλεσθαι παρὰ ἄνδρα ἔμελλε . . . ἤλεγχεν ἡ Πυθία Μελάνιππον καὶ Κομαιθώ· καὶ ἐκείνους τε αὐτοὺς μάντευμα ἀφίκετο θῦσαι τῇ Ἀρτέμιδι, καὶ ἀνὰ πᾶν ἔτος παρθένον καὶ παῖδα, οἳ τὸ εἶδος εἶεν κάλλιστοι τῇ θεῷ θύειν· ταύτης μὲν δὴ τῆς θυσίας ἕνεκα ὁ ποταμὸς ὁ πρὸς τῷ ἱερῷ τῆς Τρικλαρίας ἀμείλιχος ἐκλήθη . . . παύσασθαι δὲ οὕτω λέγονται θύοντες τῇ Ἀρτέμιδι ἀνθρώπους: the sacrifice connected with the worship of Dionysos Αἰσυμνήτης. Tatian, *Ad Graec.* Schwartz, p. 30. 1 Λατιάριον Δία . . . τοῖς ἀπὸ τῶν ἀνδροκτασιῶν αἵμασι τερπόμενον· Ἄρτεμιν δὲ οὐ μακρὰν δὲ τῆς Μεγάλης πόλεως τῶν αὐτῶν πράξεων ἐπανῃρημένην τὸ εἶδος. At Tegea: Paus. 8. 53, 1 ἐν τοῦ Ἀγυιέως τῇ ἑορτῇ . . . ἡ τῆς Ἀρτέμιδος ἱέρεια διώκει τινά.

Titles referring to the goddess of women and childbirth.

³⁶ Artemis Παρθένος at Paros: Roehl, *Inscr. Graec. Ant.* 401, poetical title. Artem. *Oneirocr.* 4. 4 ἑταίρα ἔδοξεν εἰς τὸ τῆς Ἀρτέμιδος ἱερὸν εἰσεληλυθέναι. Κατέλυσε τὴν ἑταιρείαν· οὐδὲ γὰρ εἰς τὸ ἱερὸν πρότερον εἰσέλθοι ἄν, εἰ μὴ καταλύσειε τὴν ἑταιρείαν. Cf. Paus. 3. 18, 4 Ἀρτέμιδος τοῖς Κρησὶν ἱερὸν . . . παρθένον τὴν ἱερευομένην. Vide ¹⁹, ²⁶ ᵃ, ³⁵, ¹²⁴, ¹³³ ᵃ.

³⁷ A goddess Παρθένος in the Tauric Chersonese : Herod. 4. 103 θύουσι μὲν (Ταῦροι) τῇ Παρθένῳ τούς τε ναυηγοὺς καὶ τοὺς ἂν λάβωσιν Ἑλλήνων ἐπαναχθέντας . . . τὴν δὲ δαίμονα ταύτην τῇ θύουσι λέγουσιν αὐτοὶ Ταῦροι Ἰφιγένειαν. Cf. Strabo, 308 ἄκρα μεγάλη μέρος οὖσα τῆς ὅλης χερρονήσου . . . ἐν ᾗ τὸ τῆς Παρθένου ἱερόν, δαίμονός τινος, ἧς ἐπώνυμος καὶ ἡ ἄκρα ἡ πρὸ τῆς πόλεως ἐστιν . . . καλουμένη Παρθένιον ἔχον νεὼν τῆς δαίμονος καὶ ξόανον. Inscription from the Tauric Chersonese, containing the formula of the oath taken by magistrates : *Revue des études Grecques*, 1891, p. 388 ὀμνύω Δία Γᾶν Ἅλιον Παρθένον θεοὺς Ὀλυμπίους καὶ Ὀλυμπίας. Cf. Dittenberg. *Syll.* 252. Παρθένος at Neapolis in Thrace : Schöne, *Griechische Reliefs*, No. 48. In Caria : Diod. Sic. 5. 62 τὴν μὲν ὀνομαζομένην Παρθένον ἐν Βυβαστῷ τῆς Χερρονήσου τιμὰς ἔχειν καὶ τέμενος. Cf. Athenae. p. 655 Β Κλύτος δὲ ὁ Μιλήσιος, Ἀριστοτέλους δὲ μαθητής, ἐν τῷ πρώτῳ περὶ Μιλησίων γράφει . . . περὶ δὲ τὸ ἱερὸν τῆς Παρθένου ἐν Λέρῳ εἰσὶν οἱ καλούμενοι ὄρνιθες μελεαγρίδες : the goddess of Leros identified with Artemis, Aelian, *Hist. An.* 4. 42. Strabo, 637 (Σάμος) ἐκαλεῖτο Παρθενία οἰκούντων Καρῶν.

³⁸ Artemis Κορία at Lousoi in Arcadia : Callim. *in Dian.* 234 ἦ μέν τοι Προῖτός γε δύω ἐκαθείσατο νηούς· Ἄλλον μὲν Κορίης, ὅτι οἱ συνελέξαο κούρας Οὔρεα πλαζομένας Ἀζήνια, τὸν δ' ἐπὶ Λούσοις Ἡμέρῃ οὕνεκα θυμὸν ἀπ' ἄγριον εἵλεο παίδων. Polyb. 4. 18, 10 προῆγον (οἱ Αἰτωλοὶ) ὡς ἐπὶ Λούσων· καὶ παραγενόμενοι πρὸς τὸ τῆς Ἀρτέμιδος ἱερόν, ὃ κεῖται μὲν μεταξὺ Κλείτορος καὶ Κυναίθης, ἄσυλον δὲ νενόμισται παρὰ τοῖς Ἕλλησιν, ἀνετείνοντο διαρπάσειν τὰ θρέμματα τῆς θεοῦ. Hesych. *s. v.* ἀκρουχεῖ . . . Ἄκροι, ὄρος τῆς Ἀργείας, ἐφ' οὗ Ἀρτέμιδος ἱερὸν ἱδρύσατο Μελάμπους, καθάρας τὰς Προιτίδας. Paus. 8. 18, 8 τὰς δὲ θυγατέρας τοῦ Προίτου κατήγαγεν ὁ Μελάμπους ἐς τοὺς Λουσοὺς καὶ ἠκέσατο τῆς μανίας ἐν Ἀρτέμιδος ἱερῷ· καὶ ἀπ' ἐκείνου τὴν Ἄρτεμιν ταύτην Ἡμερασίαν καλοῦσιν οἱ Κλειτόριοι.

³⁹ Schol. Theocr. 2. 66 εἰώθασι γὰρ τῇ Ἀρτέμιδι κανηφοροῦν αἱ μέλλουσαι γαμεῖσθαι, ἐπὶ ἀφοσιώσει τῆς παρθενίας, ἵνα μὴ νεμεσηθῶσιν ὑπ' αὐτῆς . . . καὶ παρὰ Μενάνδρῳ· αἱ κυΐσκουσαι ἐπικαλεῖσθε τὴν Ἄρτεμιν, ἀξιοῦσθαι συγγνώμης, ὅτι διεκορήθητε.

⁴⁰ Artemis Λοχεία, Λοχία, Λεχώ : Plut. *Quaest. Symp.* p. 659 A ὅθεν οἶμαι καὶ τὴν Ἄρτεμιν λοχείαν καὶ Εἰλείθυιαν, οὐκ οὖσαν ἑτέραν ἢ τὴν Σελήνην ὠνομάσθαι. Eur. *Supp.* 958 οὐδ' Ἄρτεμις Λοχία προσφθέγξαιτ' ἂν τὰς ἀτέκνους. Λοχεία in Phthiotis : *C. I. Gr.* 1768 Ἀρτέμιδι Λοχείᾳ, private dedication. In Pergamon : *C. I. Gr.* 3562, public inscription from Gambreium in Pergamene territory, ἀναγράψαι τόνδε τὸν νόμον εἰς δύο στήλας καὶ ἀναθεῖναι τὴν μὲν . . . τὴν δὲ πρὸ τοῦ νεὼ τῆς Ἀρτέμιδος τῆς λοχίας.

⁴¹ ᵃArtemis Εἰλείθυια, vide ⁶⁴, at Chaeronea : *C. I. Gr.* 1596 Ἀρτάμιδι Εἰλειθυίᾳ (fourth century B.C.).

568   GREEK RELIGION.

ᵇ At Lebadea : *C. I. Gr.* 1598 Ἀρτέμισιν πράαις χαριστήριον (Roman period).

ᶜ In Thisbe : *Bull. de Corr. Hell.* 1884, p. 402 Πασικρίτα Δωπύραν Ἀρτάμιδι Εἰλειθείῃ ἱαρὰν εἶμεν (act of enfranchisement in the name of Artemis).

ᵈ Orchomenos : *Mitt. d. d. Inst. Ath.* 1882, p. 357 Ἀρτάμιδι Εἰλειθυίῃ (dedication third century B.C.).

ᵉ Thespiae : *ib.* 1880, p. 129 τὴν θυγατέρα Φιλίππην Ἀρτέμιδι Εἰλειθυίᾳ (? second century B.C.).

ᶠ Tanagra : Ἀθην. 4. 294, No. 6 Ἀθανίκκεια Ἵμνω Ἀρτάμιδι Εἰλειθυίῃ, (? pre-Roman period).

ᵍ ? In Euboea : Artemis Βολοσία = Εἰλείθυια : Procop. *Bell. Goth.* 4. 22, inscription at Geraestum, Τύννιχος ἐποίει Ἀρτέμιδι Βολοσίᾳ· οὕτω γὰρ τὴν Εἰλείθυιαν ἐν τοῖς ἄνω χρόνοις ἐκάλουν.

⁴² Artemis Σοωδίνα at Chaeronea : *C. I. Gr.* 1595 Ἀπόλλωνος Λαφναφορίω Ἀρτάμιδος Σοωδίνας.

⁴³ Artemis Λυσίζωνος : Hesych. *s.v.* ἐπίθετον Ἀρτέμιδος. Schol. Ap. Rhod. 1. 288 Λυσιζώνου Ἀρτέμιδος ἱερὸν ἐν Ἀθήναις.

⁴⁴ Artemis Χιτώνη : ᵃ at Miletus : Callim. *in Dian.* 235 πότνια πουλυμέλαθρε πολύπτολι, χαῖρε Χιτώνη, Μιλήτῳ ἐπίδημε· σὲ γὰρ ποιήσατο Νηλεὺς Ἡγεμόνην, ὅτε νηυσὶν ἀνήγετο Κεκροπίηθεν.

ᵇ At Syracuse : Steph. Byz. *s.v.* Χιτώνη· οὕτως ἡ Ἄρτεμις λέγεται, καὶ Χιτωνία, ὡς Παρμένων ὁ Βυζάντιος καὶ Ἐπίχαρμος ἐν Σφιγγί " καὶ τὸ τᾶς Χιτωνίας αὐλησάτω τίς μοι μέλος." Cf. Athenae. 629 E παρὰ δὲ Συρακοσίοις καὶ χιτωνέας Ἀρτέμιδος ὄρχησίς τις ἐστὶν ἴδιος καὶ αὔλησις. Cf. *Anth. Pal.* 6. 201 :

Σάνδαλα καὶ μίτρην περικαλλέα, τόν τε μυρόπνουν
βόστρυχον ὡραίων οὖλον ἀπὸ πλοκάμων,
καὶ ζώνην καὶ λεπτὸν ὑπένδυμα τοῦτο χιτῶνος,
καὶ τὰ περὶ στέρνοις ἀγλαὰ μαστόδετα,
* ἄμβροτον εὐώδινος ἐπεὶ φύγε νηδύος ὄγκον
* εὐφραντῇ νηῷ θῆκεν ὑπ᾽ Ἀρτέμιδος.

Cf. *ib.* 271–273.

⁴⁵ Pollux, 3. 38 ταύτῃ γὰρ (τῇ Ἥρᾳ) τοῖς προτελείοις προυτέλουν τὰς κόρας καὶ Ἀρτέμιδι καὶ Μοίραις. καὶ τῆς κόμης δὲ τότε ἀπήρχοντο ταῖς θεαῖς αἱ κόραι. Plut. *Quaest. Rom.* p. 264 B πέντε δεῖσθαι θεῶν τοὺς γαμοῦντας οἴονται, Διὸς τελείου καὶ Ἥρας τελείας καὶ Ἀφροδίτης καὶ Πειθοῦς ἐπὶ πᾶσι δ᾽ Ἀρτέμιδος. Εὐπραξία at Tyndaris : *C. I. Gr.* 5613 b Πρῶτος καὶ Μενίππη Ἀρτέμιδι Εὐπραξίᾳ (? second century B.C.). Cf. *Annali del Inst.* 1849, Tav. H, p. 264.

⁴⁶ Artemis Κορδάκα in Elis in the Pisatid territory : Paus. 6. 22, 1 σημεῖά ἐστιν ἱεροῦ Κόρδακος ἐπίκλησιν ᾿Αρτέμιδος, ὅτι οἱ τοῦ Πέλοπος ἀκόλουθοι τὰ ἐπινίκια ἤγαγον παρὰ τῇ θεῷ ταύτῃ καὶ ὠρχήσαντο ἐπιχώριον τοῖς περὶ τὸν Σίπυλον Κόρδακα ὄρχησιν. Hesych. *s. v.* Καλαβίς· τὸ περισπᾶν τὰ ἴσχια, καλαβοῦσθαι· ἐν τῷ τῆς Δερεατίδος ἱερῷ ᾿Αρτέμιδος ἀδόμενοι ὕμνοι (? restituendum : Καλαβίδες· ἐν τῷ κ.τ.λ. . . . ἀδόμενοι ὕμνοι· καλαβοῦσθαι, τὸ περισπᾶν τὰ ἴσχια). Cf. Photius, p. 126. 14 Καλλαβίδες· τὸ διαβαίνειν ἀσχημόνως καὶ διέλκειν τὰ ἴσχια ταῖς χερσίν. Paus. 3. 20, 7 ἐν τῷ Ταυγέτῳ . . . Δέρειον, ἔνθα ᾿Αρτέμιδος ἄγαλμα ἐν ὑπαίθρῳ Δερεατίδος. Cf. Steph. Byz. *s.v.* Δέρα. Hesych. *s.v.* Λόμβαι· αἱ τῇ ᾿Αρτέμιδι θυσιῶν ἄρχουσαι ἀπὸ τῆς κατὰ τὴν παιδιὰν σκευῆς· οἱ γὰρ φάλητες οὕτω καλοῦνται. Λυδῶν πομπή in the worship of Artemis ᾿Ορθία in Sparta : Plut. *Arist.* 17 τὰς περὶ τὸν βωμὸν ἐν Σπάρτῃ πληγὰς τῶν ἐφήβων καὶ τὴν μετὰ ταῦτα Λυδῶν πομπὴν συντελεῖσθαι.

⁴⁷ Artemis the goat-goddess : vide Αἰγιναία ¹⁸ ; ᾿Αγροτέρα ²⁶ ᵇ, ᶠ ; Βραυρωνία ³². *C. I. A.* 1. 5 : archaic inscription found at Eleusis ᾿Αρτέμιδι αἶγα. In Phthiotis : Antonin. Liber. 13. 65. Κναγία in Sparta : Paus. 3. 18, 4–5 τὰ δὲ ἐς τὴν Κναγίαν ῎Αρτεμίν ἐστιν οὕτω λεγόμενα. Κνακεᾶτις near Tegea : Paus. 8. 53, 11 ᾿Αρτέμιδος Κνακεάτιδός ἐστι ναοῦ τὰ ἐρείπια. Κνακαλησία at Kaphyae : Paus. 8. 23, 3 Καφυάταις δὲ ἱερὰ θεῶν Ποσειδῶνός ἐστι καὶ ἐπίκλησιν Κνακαλησίας ᾿Αρτέμιδος· ἔστι δὲ αὐτοῖς καὶ ὄρος Κνάκαλος, ἔνθα ἐπέτειον τελετὴν ἄγουσι τῇ ᾿Αρτέμιδι.

⁴⁸ Artemis Εὐρίππα at Pheneos in Arcadia : Paus. 8. 14, 5 ἀπολέσθαι γὰρ ἵππους τῷ ᾿Οδυσσεῖ, καὶ αὐτὸν γῆν τὴν ᾿Ελλάδα κατὰ ζήτησιν ἐπιόντα τῶν ἵππων ἱδρύσασθαι μὲν ἱερὸν ἐνταῦθα ᾿Αρτέμιδος καὶ Εὐρίππαν ὀνομάσαι τὴν θεόν, ἔνθα τῆς Φενεατικῆς χώρας εὗρε τὰς ἵππους, ἀναθεῖναι καὶ τοῦ Ποσειδῶνος τὸ ἄγαλμα τοῦ ῾Ιππίου. Cf. Pind. *Ol.* 3. 26 Λατοῦς ἱπποσόα θυγάτηρ. *Frag.* 59 τί κάλλιον ἀρχομένοισιν ἢ καταπαυομένοισιν ἢ βαθύζωνόν τε Λατὼ καὶ θοᾶν ἵππων ἐλάτειραν ἀεῖσαι ;

Artemis, goddess of cattle.

⁴⁹ Πολυβοία : Hesych. *s.v.* θεός τις, ὑπ᾿ ἐνίων μὲν ῎Αρτεμις, ὑπὸ δὲ ἄλλων, Κόρη.

⁵⁰ Ταυροπόλος : ᵃ in Attica ³².

ᵇ In Icaria near Samos : Strabo, 639 ἔστι δὲ καὶ ᾿Αρτέμιδος ἱερὸν καλούμενον Ταυροπόλιον. Clem. Alex. *Protr.* p. 40 P ἐν ῾Ικάρῳ τῆς ᾿Αρτέμιδος τὸ ἄγαλμα ξύλον ἦν οὐκ εἰργασμένον· cf. Arnob. *adv. gent.* 6. 11.

ᶜ In Icaria in the Persian gulf : Dionys. *Perieg.* 610 ὅθι Ταυροπόλοιο θεοῖο βωμοὶ κνισήεντες ἀδευκέα καπνὸν ἔχουσι.

570   GREEK RELIGION.

^d At Mylasa: *C. I. Gr.* 2699 [ὁ δῆμος ἐτίμησε]ν . . . ἱερέα Ταυροπόλου.

^e At Phocaea: vide supra ³⁵.

^f Pergamon: Fränkel, *Inschr. von Pergamon*, No. 13, l. 24 Ὀμνύω Δία Γῆν . . . Ἀθηνᾶν Ἀρείαν καὶ τὴν Ταυροπόλον.

^g Smyrna and Magnesia: Artemis Ταυροπόλος, invoked in the oath of alliance: *C. I. Gr.* 3137.

^h Amphipolis: Diod. Sic. 18. 4 (after the death of Alexander) τοὺς δὲ . . . ναοὺς ἔδει κατασκευασθῆναι . . . ἐν Ἀμφιπόλει δὲ τῆς Ταυροπόλου. Livy, 44. c. 44 Amphipolim cum iam fama pugnae pervenisset, concursusque matronarum in templum Dianae, quam Tauropolon vocant, ad opem exposcendam fieret.

ⁱ At Andros: vide *Artemis Monuments*, p. 527.

^k Ταυρόπολις: Steph. Byz. *s.v.* πόλις Καρίας.

^l Soph. *Aj.* 172 :

ἦ ῥά σε Ταυροπόλα Διὸς Ἄρτεμις . . .

ὥρμασε πανδάμους ἐπὶ βοῦς ἀγελαίας ;

Schol. *ib.* ταυροπόλος ἡ αὐτὴ τῇ Σελήνῃ ἐστὶ καὶ ἐποχεῖται ταύροις ἦν καὶ ταυρωπὸν ὀνομάζουσι.

^m Ταυροπόλια: Hesych. *s.v.* ἃ εἰς ἑορτὴν ἄγουσιν Ἀρτέμιδι.

ⁿ Hesych. *s. v.* Εὐλακία· Ἄρτεμις ? from Laconian εὐλάκη, a ploughshare.

⁵¹ Artemis Ταυροφάγος,³² : cf. Cic. *De Invent.* 2. 95 apud quosdam lex erat: ne quis Dianae vitulum immolaret.

⁵² Artemis Ταυρώ, Ταυρική, connected with the legend of Orestes: Hesych. *s. v.* Ταυρώ· ἡ ἐν Ταύροις Ἄρτεμις : cf. ³⁵, ³⁷, ¹²⁸.

^a In Attica, ³².

^b In Lemnos: Plut. *de Mul. Virt.* (247 A) Τυρρηνῶν τῶν Λῆμνον καὶ Ἴμβρον κατασχόντων, ἁρπασάντων δὲ Βραυρωνόθεν τὰς Ἀθηναίων γυναῖκας . . . (247 E) τὸ ξόανον τῆς Ἀρτέμιδος ὃ πατρῷον ἦν αὐτοῖς εἰς Λῆμνον ἐκ Βραυρῶνος κομισθὲν ἐκ δὲ Λήμνου πανταχοῦ συμπεριαγόμενον. Harpocr. *s. v.* ἀρκτεῦσαι· ὅτι δὲ αἱ ἀρκτευόμεναι παρθένοι ἄρκτοι καλοῦνται Εὐριπίδης Ὑψιπύλῃ Ἀριστοφάνης Λημνίαις καὶ Λυσιστράτῃ. Steph. Byz. *s. v.* Λῆμνος . . . ἀπὸ τῆς μεγάλης λεγομένης θεοῦ ἦν Λῆμνόν φασι· ταύτῃ δὲ καὶ παρθένους θύεσθαι: from Hekataeus.

^c In Cappadocia, ¹²⁸.

⁵³ Artemis Ὀρθία and Ὀρθωσία: Lampridius Heliogab. c. 7 Orestem quidem ferunt non unum simulacrum Dianae nec uno in loco posuisse, sed multa in multis. Cf. Plut. *de Mul. Virt.* p. 247 D–F.

ᵃ At Megara : *C. I. Gr.* 1064, inscription on basis of statue of priestess, ἀζομένη κούρην Λητωΐδα εἰοχέαιραν Ἄρτεμιν Ὀρθωσίην, πόλεως περὶ τείχεα πάντα.

ᵇ At Byzantium : Herod. 4. 87 τῆσι μὲν νῦν στήλῃσι ταύτῃσι Βυζάντιοι ... ἐχρήσαντο πρὸς τὸν βωμὸν τῆς Ὀρθωσίης Ἀρτέμιδος.

ᶜ At Sparta : Paus. 3. 16, 7–11 τὸ χωρίον τὸ ἐπονομαζόμενον Λιμναῖον Ὀρθίας ἱερόν ἐστιν Ἀρτέμιδος. τὸ ξόανον ἐκεῖνο εἶναι λέγουσιν ὅ ποτε Ὀρέστης καὶ Ἰφιγένεια ἐκ τῆς Ταυρικῆς ἐκκλέπτουσιν . . . διαμεμένηκεν ἔτι καὶ νῦν τηλικοῦτο ὄνομα τῇ Ταυρικῇ θεῷ ὥστε ἀμφισβητοῦσι μὲν οἱ Καππαδόκαι οἱ τὸν Εὔξεινον οἰκοῦντες τὸ ἄγαλμα εἶναι παρὰ σφίσιν, ἀμφισβητοῦσι καὶ Λυδῶν οἷς ἐστιν Ἀρτέμιδος ἱερὸν Ἀναίτιδος . . . μαρτύρια δέ μοι καὶ τάδε τὴν ἐν Λακεδαίμονι Ὀρθίαν τὸ ἐκ τῶν βαρβάρων εἶναι ξόανον· τοῦτο μὲν γὰρ Ἀστράβακος καὶ Ἀλώπεκος . . . τὸ ἄγαλμα εὑρόντες αὐτίκα παρεφρόνησαν· τοῦτο δὲ οἱ Λιμνᾶται Σπαρτιατῶν καὶ Κυνοσουρεῖς καὶ ἐκ Μεσόας τε καὶ Πιτάνης θύοντες τῇ Ἀρτέμιδι ἐς διαφοράν, ἀπὸ δὲ αὐτῆς καὶ ἐς φόνους προήχθησαν. ἀποθανόντων δὲ ἐπὶ τῷ βωμῷ πολλῶν νόσος ἔφθειρε τοὺς λοιπούς· καί σφισιν ἐπὶ τούτῳ γίνεται λόγιον αἵματι ἀνθρώπων τὸν βωμὸν αἱμάσσειν· θυομένου δὲ ὅντινα ὁ κλῆρος ἐπελάμβανε, Λυκοῦργος μετέβαλεν ἐς τὰς ἐπὶ τοῖς ἐφήβοις μάστιγας, ἐμπίμπλαται δὲ οὕτως ἀνθρώπων αἵματι ὁ βωμός. ἡ δὲ ἱέρεια τὸ ξόανον ἔχουσά σφισιν ἐφέστηκε. Plut. *Thes.* 31 τὴν Κόρην ἐν ἱερῷ Ἀρτέμιδος Ὀρθίας χορεύουσαν. Philostrat. *Apoll. Vit.* 6. 20 τὸ τῶν μαστίγων ἔθος τῇ Ἀρτέμιδι τῇ ἀπὸ Σκυθῶν δρᾶται, χρησμῶν, φασιν, ἐξηγουμένων ταῦτα. Plut. *Inst. Lacon.* 239 D καλεῖται δὲ ἡ ἅμιλλα διαμαστίγωσις· γίνεται δὲ καθ᾿ ἕκαστον ἔτος. Sext. Empir. *Pyrrh. Hypot.* 208 Λάκωνες δὲ ἐπὶ τοῦ βωμοῦ τῆς Ὀρθωσίας Ἀρτέμιδος μαστίζονται. *C. I. Gr.* 1416 Δαμοκλείδας . . . νεικάσας τὸ παιδικὸν κέλητι, Ἀρτέμιτι Ὀρθείᾳ. *Id.* 1444 Ἄρτεμις Ὀρθεία· Ἀσκληπιὸς Μοῖρα Λαχέσεις συγκαθιδρυμέναι αὐτῇ. Cauer, *Delect.*² 34 φίλητορ . . . Ἀρτέμιτι βωρσέα ἀνέσηκε (cf. Hesych. βωρθία· Ὀρθία). *Ib.* 37 οἱ Νεικηφόρου νεικάαντερ . . . μῶαν καὶ λόαν Ἀρτέμιδι βωρθέα ἀνέθηκαν (cf. Hesych. μῶα· ᾠδὴ ποιά). Alcm. *Frag.* 23 ἅμιν Ὀρθίᾳ φᾶρος φεροίσαις. Cf. ⁴⁶.

ᵈ In the Argolid on Mount Lycone : Paus. 2. 24, 5 ᾠκοδόμηται δὲ ἐπὶ κορυφῇ τοῦ ὄρους Ἀρτέμιδος Ὀρθίας ἱερόν, καὶ ἀγάλματα Ἀπόλλωνος καὶ Λητοῦς καὶ Ἀρτέμιδος πεποίηται λευκοῦ λίθου. Πολυκλείτου δέ φασιν εἶναι ἔργα.

ᵉ Artemis Ὀρθία in Arcadia : Hesych. *s. v.* Ὀρθία· Ἄρτεμις· οὕτως εἴρηται ἀπὸ τοῦ ἐν Ἀρκαδίᾳ χωρίου, ἔνθα ἱερὸν Ἀρτέμιδος ἵδρυται. Schol. Pind. *Ol.* 3. 54 Ὀρθωσία ἡ Ἄρτεμις παρὰ τὸ Ὀρθώσιον ὅπερ ἐστὶν ὄρος Ἀρκαδίας . . . περὶ τῆς Ἀρτέμιδος Ἀπολλόδωρος γράφει. Ὀρθωσία δέ, ὅτι ὀρθοῖ εἰς σωτηρίαν, ἢ ὀρθοῖ τοὺς γεννωμένους. καὶ ἐν Ἀθήναις ἵδρυται, τὸ ἱερὸν δέ ἐστιν ἐν Κεραμεικῷ. καὶ παρ᾿ Ἠλείοις Ὀρθωσίας Ἀρτέμιδος ἱερόν, ὥς φησι Δίδυμος. Cf. ²³.

ᶠ At Epidaurus: *Eph. Arch.* 1885, p. 195 Ἀρτέμιδι Ὀρθίᾳ Διονύσιος κατ' ὄναρ (? connected with Asclepios Ὄρθιος as divinity of health : vide Cavvadias, *ib.*).

ᵍ In Elis: supra ᵉ. Cf. Paus. 5. 16, 6 δῆμος Ὀρθία in Elis.

ʰ In Athens: supra ᵉ.

ⁱ At Aricia: Solin. *Polyhist.* 2. 11 (Momms. p. 37) Aricia . . . hoc in loco Orestes oraculo monitus simulacrum Scythicae Dianae quod de Taurica extulerat priusquam Argos peteret consecravit. Cf. Strabo, 239 τῆς δ' Ἀρικίνης τὸ ἱερὸν (τοῦ Ἀρτέμιδος) λέγουσιν ἀφίδρυμά τι τῆς Ταυροπόλου.

ᵏ Arist. *Mirab. Ausc.* p. 847 B ἐν Ἀρτέμιδος Ὀρθωσίας βωμῷ ταῦρον ἵστασθαι χρύσειον, ὃς κυνηγῶν εἰσελθόντων φωνὴν ἐπαφίησιν.

⁵⁴ Offerings to Artemis as goddess of agriculture and flocks.

ᵃ Hom. *Il.* 9. 533 :

> καὶ γὰρ τοῖσι κακὸν χρυσόθρονος Ἄρτεμις ὦρσε
> χωσαμένη, ὅ οἱ οὔτε θαλύσια γουνῷ ἀλωῆς
> Οἰνεὺς ῥέξ'.

ᵇ At Samos in the worship of Artemis : Herod. 3. 48 ἱστάντες τοὺς χορούς, τρωκτὰ σησάμου τε καὶ μέλιτος ἐποιήσαντο νόμον φέρεσθαι.

ᶜ At Hyampolis in Phocis : Paus. 10. 35, 7 σέβονται δὲ μάλιστα τὴν Ἄρτεμιν, καὶ ναὸς Ἀρτέμιδός ἐστιν αὐτοῖς . . . δὶς γὰρ καὶ οὐ πλέον ἑκάστου ἐνιαυτοῦ τὸ ἱερὸν ἀνοιγνύναι νομίζουσιν. ὁπόσα δ' ἂν τῶν βοσκημάτων ἱερὰ ἐπονομάσωσιν εἶναι τῇ Ἀρτέμιδι, ἄνευ νόσου ταῦτα καὶ πιότερα τῶν ἄλλων ἐκτρέφεσθαι λέγουσι. Cf. ⁷².

ᵈ At Scillus in Elis, temple of Ephesian Artemis, dedicated by Xenophon, *Anab.* 5. 3, 13, with inscription, ἱερὸς ὁ χῶρος τῆς Ἀρτέμιδος· τὸν ἔχοντα καὶ καρπούμενον τὴν μὲν δεκάτην καταθύειν ἑκάστου ἔτους : vide ¹³³, sub fin. Cf. ⁷⁸.

ᵉ Callim. *in Dian.* 35 οὓς δέ κεν εὐμειδής τε καὶ ἵλαος αὐγάσσηαι κείνοις εὖ μὲν ἄρουρα φέρει στάχυν, εὖ δὲ γενέθλη τετραπόδων.

ᶠ Eur. *Iph. Taur.* 20 :

> ὅ,τι γὰρ ἐνιαυτὸς τέκοι
> κάλλιστον ηὔξω φωσφόρῳ θύσειν θεᾷ (Ἀγαμέμνων).

ᵍ Herod. 4. 33 τὰς Θρηικίας καὶ τὰς Παιονίδας γυναῖκας, ἐπεὰν θύωσι τῇ Ἀρτέμιδι τῇ Βασιληίῃ, οὐκ ἄνευ πυρῶν καλάμης θυούσας τὰ ἱρά.

⁵⁵ Artemis connected with Persephone, Demeter, Dionysos.

ᵃ At Lycosura in Arcadia : Paus. 8. 37, 1 ἀπὸ δὲ Ἀκακησίου τέσσαρας σταδίους ἀπέχει τὸ ἱερὸν τῆς Δεσποίνης· πρῶτα μὲν δὴ αὐτόθι Ἡγεμόνης ναός ἐστιν Ἀρτέμιδος, καὶ χαλκοῦν ἄγαλμα ἔχον δᾷδας· ποδῶν ἐξ εἶναι μάλιστα αὐτὸ εἰκάζομεν· ἐντεῦθεν δὲ ἐς τὸν ἱερὸν περίβολον τῆς Δεσποίνης ἐστὶν ἔσοδος . . . § 4 τοῦ θρόνου (ἐν ᾧ καθέζονται Δέσποινα καὶ ἡ Δημήτηρ) δὲ ἑκατέρωθεν Ἄρτεμις μὲν παρὰ τὴν Δήμητρα ἔστηκεν ἀμπεχομένη δέρμα ἐλάφου καὶ ἐπὶ τῶν ὤμων φαρέτραν ἔχουσα ἐν δὲ ταῖς χερσὶ τῇ μὲν λαμπάδα ἔχει, τῇ δὲ δράκοντας δύο. παρὰ δὲ τὴν Ἄρτεμιν κατάκειται κύων, οἷαι θηρεύειν εἰσὶν ἐπιτήδειοι.

b At Zoitia in Arcadia : Paus. 8. 35, 7 Δήμητρος ναὸς καὶ Ἀρτέμιδος. At Megalopolis : Paus. 8. 31, 1, before the temple of Demeter and Kore, ἐπειργασμένοι ἐπὶ τύπων πρὸ τῆς ἐσόδου τῇ μὲν Ἄρτεμις τῇ δὲ Ἀσκληπιός ἐστι καὶ Ὑγίεια.

c At Olympia in the Altis : Paus. 5. 15, 4 Ἀρτέμιδος Ἀγοραίας βωμός, . . . πεποίηται δὲ καὶ Δεσποίναις. Cf.[79] v.

d At Lycosura : Paus. 8. 10, 10 ἡ ἱερὰ τῆς καλουμένης Δεσποίνης ἔλαφος.

e Herod. 2. 156 Αἰσχύλος ὁ Εὐφορίωνος . . . μοῦνος δὴ ποιητέων τῶν προγεγενημένων· ἐποίησε γὰρ Ἄρτεμιν εἶναι θυγατέρα Δήμητρος. Cf. Hekate, 4 [14, 15].

f ? With Dionysos at Alagonia in West Laconia : Paus. 3. 26, 11 θέας δὲ αὐτόθι ἄξια Διονύσου καὶ Ἀρτέμιδός ἐστιν ἱερά. Cf.[35, 70], *Artemis Monuments*, p. 527.

56 *Et. Mag.* p. 443. 18 Θαργήλια· ἑορτὴ Ἀθήνῃσι . . . Θαργήλια δέ εἰσι πάντες οἱ ἀπὸ γῆς καρποί· ἄγεται δὲ μηνὶ Θαργηλιῶνι, Ἀρτέμιδος καὶ Ἀπόλλωνος.

57 Artemis Αἰθοπία : Steph. Byz. *s. v.* Αἰθόπιον· χωρίον Λυδίας . . . ἡ πλησίον τοῦ Εὐρίπου, ἀφ᾽ οὗ ἡ Ἄρτεμις Αἰθοπία . . . οἱ δὲ τὴν αὐτὴν τῇ Σελήνῃ παρὰ τὸ αἴθειν, ὡς Καλλίμαχος, οἱ δὲ ὅτι ἡ αὐτή ἐστι τῇ Ἑκάτῃ ἥτις ἀεὶ δᾷδας κατέχει ὡς Ἐρατοσθένης. ? At Amphipolis,[33]. Cf. Anacreon, *Fr.* 135, Hesych. Αἰθοπεῖς παῖδα (Bergk, corr. Αἰθοπίης παῖδα) Ἀνακρέων. ἄλλοι τὸν οἶνον, ἄλλοι τὴν Ἄρτεμιν.

58 Artemis Φωσφόρος a in Messene at the city on Ithome : Paus. 4. 31, 10 Τύχη τε καὶ Ἄρτεμις Φωσφόρος. τὰ μὲν δὴ λίθου Δαμοφῶντος.

b In Munychia : Clem. Alex. *Strom.* p. 418 P τῷ Θρασυβούλῳ νύκτωρ . . . πῦρ ἑωρᾶτο προηγούμενον ὅπερ αὐτοὺς ἀπταίστως προπέμψαν κατὰ τὴν Μουνυχίαν ἐξέλιπεν, ἔνθα νῦν ὁ τῆς Φωσφόρου βωμός ἐστι. Cf. *C. I. A.* 2. 432 τῶν θυσιῶν ὧν ἔθυον πρὸ τῶν ἐκκλησιῶν . . . καὶ τῇ Ἀρτέμιδι τῇ Φωσφόρῳ.

c At Byzantium : Dionys. Byz. *Anapl. Fr.* 27 templum Dianae Luciferae et Veneris Placidae =·Ἄρτεμις Φωσφόρος and Ἀφροδίτη Γαληναία. Cf. Hesych. *Miles. Constant.* 16 Ἀρτέμιδος (τέμενος) πρὸς τὸ τῆς Θρᾴκης ὄρος.

^d ? At Segesta: Cic. *Verr.* 4. 33 Fuit apud Segestanos ex aere simulacrum Dianae, quum summa atque antiquissima praeditum religione, tum singulari opere artificioque perfectum. . . . 34 Colebatur a civibus. . . . Erat admodum amplum et excelsum signum cum stola : verum tamen inerat in illa magnitudine aetas atque habitus virginalis ; sagittae pendebant ab humero ; sinistra manu retinebat arcum ; dextra ardentem facem praeferebat.

^e At Anticyra?: Paus. 10. 37, 1 ἱερὸν . . . Ἀρτέμιδος· ἔργον τῶν Πραξιτέλους, δᾷδα ἔχουσα τῇ δεξιᾷ καὶ ὑπὲρ τῶν ὤμων φαρέτραν· παρὰ δὲ αὐτὴν κύων ἐν ἀριστερᾷ.

⁵⁹ Artemis Σελασφόρος at Phlya: Paus. 1. 31, 4 Ἀπόλλωνος Διονυσοδότου καὶ Ἀρτέμιδος Σελασφόρου βωμοί. In Pholegandros: *Rev. Arch.* 1865, 1. 126 ἔδοξε τῷ δήμῳ στεφανῶσαι Μενεκράτην . . . τετράκις ἀρχιερατεύσαντα τῇ Σελασφόρῳ Ἀρτέμιδι.

⁶⁰ Artemis ? Σελασία: Hesych. *s. v.* τόπος τῆς Λακωνικῆς, ὅθεν εἰκὸς κληθῆναι τὴν Ἄρτεμιν.

⁶¹ Artemis Πυρωνία on Mount Κρᾶθις near Pheneos: Paus. 8. 15, 5 ἐν δὲ τῇ Κράθιδι τῷ ὄρει Πυρωνίας ἱερόν ἐστιν Ἀρτέμιδος· καὶ τὰ ἔτι ἀρχαιότερα παρὰ τῆς θεοῦ ταύτης ἐπήγοντο Ἀργεῖοι πῦρ ἐς τὰ Λερναῖα.

⁶² Schol. Theocr. 2. 12 (Ἑκάτη) καὶ νῦν Ἄρτεμις καλεῖται καὶ Φυλακὴ καὶ Δαδοῦχος καὶ Φωσφόρος καὶ Χθονία. Soph. *O. R.* 206 :

> τάς τε πυρφόρους
> Ἀρτέμιδος αἴγλας σὺν αἷς
> Λύκι᾽ ὄρεα διᾴσσει.

Anthol. Pal. 9. 46 :

> Πηρὸς ἄπαις, ἢ φέγγος ἰδεῖν, ἢ παῖδα τεκέσθαι
> εὐξαμένη, δοιῆς ἔμμορεν εὐτυχίης.

> . . . .

> Ἄρτεμις ἀμφοτέροισιν ὑπήκοος, ἥ τε λοχείης
> μαῖα, καὶ ἀργεννῶν φωσφόρος ἢ σελάων.

⁶³ Artemis Προσηῴα on the promontory Artemision in North Euboea: Plut. *Themist.* 8 Ἔχει δὲ ναὸν οὐ μέγαν Ἀρτέμιδος ἐπίκλησιν Προσηῴας : *ib.* inscription on a stele there in honour of the naval victory, σήματα ταῦτ᾽ ἔθεσαν παρθένῳ Ἀρτέμιδι. *Mitt. d. d. Ath. Inst.* 1883, p. 19 οἵδε ἐπηγγείλαντο καὶ εἰσήνεγκαν εἰς τὴν ἐπανόρθωσιν τοῦ ἱεροῦ τῆς Ἀρτέμιδος τῆς Προσηῴας.

⁶⁴ Aesch. *Frag.* 169:

> ᾶς οὔτε πέμφιξ Ἡλίου προσδέρκεται
> οὔτ' ἀστερωπὸν ὄμμα Λητῴας κόρης.

Plut. *Quaest. Conviv.* p. 658 F οἶμαι καὶ τὴν Ἄρτεμιν Λοχείαν καὶ Εἰλείθυιαν, οὐκ οὖσαν ἑτέραν ἢ Σελήνην, ὠνομάσθαι.

? Artemis as death-goddess.

⁶⁵ Hom. *Il.* 21. 483:

> ἐπεί σε λέοντα γυναιξὶ
> Ζεὺς θῆκεν, καὶ ἔδωκε κατακτάμεν ἥν κ' ἐθέλησθα.

Od. 15. 409:

> ἀλλ' ὅτε γηράσκωσι πόλιν κάτα φῦλ' ἀνθρώπων,
> ἐλθὼν ἀργυρότοξος Ἀπόλλων Ἀρτέμιδι ξὺν
> οἷς ἀγανοῖσι βέλεσσιν ἐποιχόμενος κατέπεφνεν.

Strabo, 635 καὶ τὰ λοιμικὰ δὲ πάθη καὶ τοὺς αὐτομάτους θανάτους τούτοις ἀνάπτουσι τοῖς θεοῖς (Ἀπόλλωνι καὶ Ἀρτέμιδι). In Phthiotis: Anton. Liber. 13, Artemis = Ἀσπαλὶς ἀμειλήτη ἑκαέργη: ξόανον παρὰ τὸ τῆς Ἀρτέμιδος ἑστηκός . . . ᾧ καθ' ἕκαστον ἔτος αἱ παρθένοι χίμαρον ἄθορον ἐκρήμνων, ὅτι καὶ ἡ Ἀσπαλὶς παρθένος οὖσα ἑαυτὴν ἀπηγχόνισεν. Cf. the legend of Ctesulla Ἑκαέργη in Anton. Liber. 1, and the story of the Carian Παρθένος, ³⁷.

? Artemis as marriage-goddess.

⁶⁶ *Anth. Pal.* 6. 276 Ἄρτεμι, σῇ δ' ἰότητι γάμος θ' ἅμα καὶ γένος εἴη τῇ Λυκομηδείῳ παιδὶ φιλαστραγάλῃ. Cf.⁴⁵.

Εὔκλεια ᵃ at Plataea: Plut. *Arist.* 20 Ἀγάμενοι δὲ αὐτὸν οἱ Πλαταιεῖς ἔθαψαν ἐν τῷ ἱερῷ τῆς Εὐκλείας Ἀρτέμιδος . . . τὴν δ' Εὔκλειαν οἱ μὲν πολλοὶ καὶ καλοῦσι καὶ νομίζουσιν Ἄρτεμιν, ἔνιοι δέ φασιν Ἡρακλέους μὲν θυγατέρα καὶ Μυρτοῦς γενέσθαι . . . τελευτήσασαν δὲ παρθένον ἔχειν παρά τε Βοιωτοῖς καὶ Λοκροῖς τιμάς. Βωμὸς γὰρ αὐτῇ καὶ ἄγαλμα κατὰ πᾶσαν ἀγορὰν ἵδρυται, καὶ προθύουσιν αἵ τε γαμούμεναι καὶ οἱ γαμοῦντες.

ᵇ At Thebes: Paus. 9. 17, 1 πλησίον δὲ Ἀρτέμιδος ναός ἐστιν Εὐκλείας. ταφῆναι δὲ ἐντὸς τοῦ ἱεροῦ θυγατέρας Ἀντιποίνου λέγουσιν, Ἀνδρόκλειάν τε καὶ Ἀλκίδα . . . τοῦ ναοῦ δὲ . . . λέων ἐστὶν ἔμπροσθεν.

ᶜ At Paros: Le Bas, *Îles* 2062 dedication Στρατηγ[ίδ]ι Ἀφροδίτῃ Διὶ Ἀφροδισίῳ Ἑρμῇ Ἀρτέμιδι Εὐκλείῃ.

ᵈ Εὔκλεια at Athens, ? Artemis: Paus. 1. 14, 5 ναὸς Εὐκλείας ἀνάθημα καὶ τοῦτο ἀπὸ τῶν Μήδων, οἳ τῆς χώρας Μαραθῶνι ἔσχον. *C. I. Gr.* 258 τὸν ἑαυτῆς ἄνδρα Ἱεροκλῆν ἱερατεύσαντα Εὐκλείᾳ καὶ Εὐνοίᾳ ἀνέθηκεν, ? fourth century, B.C. Cf. *C. I. A.* 3. 277 ἱερέως Εὐκλείας καὶ Εὐνομίας, on seat in Attic theatre, late period.

⁶⁷ Artemis Ἡγεμόνη ᵃ at Akakesion in Arcadia, vide ⁵⁵ ᵃ.

ᵇ At Tegea : Paus. 8. 47, 6 ἐς δὲ τὴν Ἄρτεμιν τὴν Ἡγεμόνην τὴν αὐτὴν τοιάδε λέγουσιν. Ὀρχομενίων τῶν ἐν Ἀρκαδίᾳ τυραννίδα ἔσχεν Ἀριστομηλίδας . . . φονεύσας δὲ ἐκεῖνον (Χρόνιος) καὶ ἐς Τέγεαν φυγὼν ἐποίησεν ἱερὸν τῇ Ἀρτέμιδι.

ᶜ At Sparta : Paus. 3. 14, 6 τὸ δὲ Εἰλειθυίας ἐστὶν (ἱερὸν) Ἀπόλλωνός τε Καρνείου καὶ Ἀρτέμιδος Ἡγεμόνης.

ᵈ At Asea : Roehl, Inscr. Graec. Ant. 92 Ἀγημοῖ on base of statue dedicated ? to Artemis Hegemone.

ᵉ In Ambracia : Anton. Liber. 4 τοὺς δὲ Ἀμβρακιώτας ἐκφυγόντας τὴν δουλείαν Ἄρτεμιν Ἡγεμόνην ἱλάσασθαι καὶ ποιησαμένους ἀγροτέρης εἴκασμα παραστήσασθαι χάλκεον αὐτῷ θῆρα. Cf. Polyaen. 8. 52.

ᶠ ? At Athens : Pollux, 8. 106, oath of the Ephebi, ἴστορες θεοί, Ἄγραυλος, Ἐνυάλιος, Ἄρης, Ζεύς, Θαλλώ, Αὐξώ, Ἡγεμόνη. Paus. 9. 35, 1 τιμῶσι γὰρ ἐκ παλαιοῦ καὶ Ἀθηναῖοι Χάριτας Αὐξὼ καὶ Ἡγεμόνην.

ᵍ At Miletus, ⁴⁴ ᵃ : cf. Plut. de Mul. Virt. p. 253 F οὔσης οὖν ἑορτῆς Ἀρτέμιδι καὶ θυσίας παρὰ Μιλησίοις, ἣν Νηληΐδα προσαγορεύουσιν.

ʰ Hesych. s. v. Ἡγεμόνη· Ἄρτεμις καὶ Ἀφροδίτη.

ⁱ Ἀρτέμιτος Ἀγεμόνος, inscription (? second century, B.C.) from Aetolia, Journ. Hell. Stud. 13. p. 353.

⁶⁸ Artemis Πειθώ at Argos : Paus. 2. 21, 1 τραπείσιν εὐθὺς ἐπὶ τὴν ἀγορὰν . . . τὸ δὲ τῆς Ἀρτέμιδος ἱερὸν ἐπίκλησιν Πειθοῦς, Ὑπερμνήστρα καὶ τοῦτο ἀνέθηκε, νικήσασα τῇ δίκῃ τὸν πατέρα.

Artemis the protectress of children.

⁶⁹ Diod. Sic. 5. 73 Ἄρτεμίν φασιν εὑρεῖν τὴν τῶν νηπίων παιδίων θεράπειαν καὶ τροφάς τινας ἁρμοζούσας τῇ φύσει τῶν βρεφῶν, ἀφ' ἧς αἰτίας καὶ κουροτρόφον αὐτὴν ὀνομάζεσθαι. Cf. Hom. Od. 20. 71 μῆκος δ' ἔπορ' Ἄρτεμις ἁγνή.

⁷⁰ Artemis Παιδοτρόφος at Corone in Messenia : Paus. 4. 34, 6 θεῶν δέ ἐστιν ἐνταῦθα Ἀρτέμιδός τε καλουμένης Παιδοτρόφου καὶ Διονύσου καὶ Ἀσκληπιοῦ ναός.

⁷¹ Artemis Φιλομείραξ at Elis : Paus. 6. 23, 6 ἱερὸν τῆς Φιλομείρακός ἐστιν Ἀρτέμιδος. τῇ μὲν δὴ θεῷ γέγονεν ἡ ἐπίκλησις ἅτε τοῦ γυμνασίου γείτονι. Cf. Paus. 2. 10, 7, statue of Artemis, τὰ ἐς ἰξὺν μόνον εἰργασμένη, in the gymnasium at Sicyon.

⁷² Artemis Κορυθαλία at Sparta : Athen. p. 139 A–B κομίζουσι γὰρ αἱ τιτθαὶ τὰ ἄρρενα παιδία κατὰ τὸν καιρὸν τοῦτον εἰς ἀγρὸν καὶ πρὸς τὴν Κορυθαλίαν καλουμένην Ἄρτεμιν, ἧς τὸ ἱερὸν παρὰ τὴν καλουμένην Τίασσάν ἐστι . . . θύουσι δὲ καὶ τοὺς γαλαθηνοὺς ὀρθαγορίσκους καὶ παρατιθέασιν ἐν τῇ θοίνῃ τοὺς ἰπνίτας

ἄρτους ... ταῦτα μὲν ὁ Πολέμων. Cf. Hesych. *s.v.* Κορυθαλλίστριαι· αἱ χορεύουσαι τῇ Κορυθαλλίᾳ θεᾷ. *s. v.* Κυριττοί· οἱ ἔχοντες τὰ ξύλινα πρόσωπα, κατὰ 'Ιταλίαν, καὶ ἑορτάζοντες τῇ Κορυθαλλίᾳ, γελοιασταί. Plut. *Quaest. Conviv.* p. 657 E τοῦ 'Απόλλωνος δύο τιθήνας, τὴν 'Αλήθειαν καὶ τὴν Κορυθάλειαν.

⁷³ ? Κουροτρόφος : Arist. *Thesmoph.* 295 εὔχεσθε ταῖν Θεσμοφόροιν, τῇ Δήμητρι καὶ τῇ Κόρῃ καὶ τῷ Πλούτῳ καὶ τῇ Καλλιγενείᾳ καὶ τῇ Κουροτρόφῳ καὶ τῷ Ἑρμῇ καὶ ταῖς Χάρισιν. *C. I. A.* 2. 481 ἔθυσαν (οἱ ἔφηβοι) τῇ τε 'Αθηνᾷ τῇ Πολιάδι καὶ τῇ Κουροτρόφῳ.

⁷⁴ Hesych. *s.v.* Κουρεῶτις· μηνὸς τοῦ Πυανεψιῶνος ἡμέρα, ἐν ᾗ τὰς ἀπὸ τῆς κεφαλῆς τῶν παίδων ἀποκείροντες τρίχας 'Αρτέμιδι θύουσι. Cf. *Et. Mag.* p. 533. 42 ἑορτή ἐστιν ἐπὶ τρεῖς ἡμέρας τελουμένη ... τῇ δὲ τρίτῃ τοὺς κούρους εἰσάγουσιν εἰς τὴν ἑορτήν, καὶ συνιστῶσι τοῖς συγγενέσι καὶ γνωρίμοις, καὶ ἐγγράφουσιν εἰς τὴν πολιτείαν.

⁷⁵ Artemis ? Ὑπομελάθρα : Hesych. *s.v.* ἐπίθετον 'Αρτέμιδος, ὡς ὁ Μίνδιος (?).

⁷⁶ Artemis Πατρῴα at Sicyon : vide Zeus, ¹³⁸b. Cf. *C. I. A.* 3. 176 'Απόλλωνι πατρῴῳ καὶ 'Αρτέμιδι.

⁷⁷ Artemis Πατριῶτις at Pleiae : *C. I. Gr.* 1444 ἱέρειαν ... 'Αρτέμιδος Πατριώτιδος ἐν Πλείαις. ? At Amyclae : *Eph. Arch.* 1892, p. 23 late inscription found there mentioning ἱερεὺς 'Αρτέμιδος (Πατριώ)τιδος.

⁷⁸ Artemis Παμφυλαία at Epidaurus : *Eph. Arch.* 1883, p. 28 'Αρτέμιδος Παμφυλαίας Εὐκράτης Εὐκράτεος πυροφορήσας.

Common cult of Artemis and Apollo.

⁷⁹ᵃ In Delos : *Journal of Hell. Studies,* 1890, p. 260 ; *C. I Gr.* 2280, 2282, &c. *Bull. de Corr. Hell.* 1882, 48–49 dedications to Artemis Δηλία in the temple of Apollo : cf. 1878, p. 339. *Bull. de Corr. Hell.* 1891, p. 291, Delian inscription found in a small island near Amorgus, ἐς θυσίαν τῷ 'Απόλλωνι καὶ τῇ 'Αρτέμιδι, third century, B.C. Herod. 4. 34 τῇσι δὲ παρθένοισι ταύτῃσι τῇσιν ἐξ Ὑπερβορέων τελευτήσασι ἐν Δήλῳ, κείρονται καὶ αἱ κόραι καὶ οἱ παῖδες οἱ Δηλίων· αἱ μὲν πρὸ γάμου πλόκαμον ἀποτεμόμεναι καὶ περὶ ἄτρακτον εἱλίξασαι, ἐπὶ τὸ σῆμα τιθεῖσι (τὸ δὲ σῆμά ἐστι ἔσω ἐς τὸ 'Αρτεμίσιον ἐσιόντι ...) οἱ δὲ παῖδες τῶν Δηλίων, περὶ χλόην τινὰ εἱλίξαντες τῶν τριχῶν, προτιθεῖσι καὶ οὗτοι ἐπὶ τὸ σῆμα ... ταύτας μὲν οὖν τῇ Εἰλειθυίᾳ ἀποφερούσας ἀντὶ τοῦ ὠκυτόκου τὸν ἐτάξαντο φόρον ἀπικέσθαι· τὴν δὲ Ἄργην τε καὶ τὴν Ὦπιν ἅμα αὐτοῖσι τοῖσι θεοῖσι ἀπικέσθαι λέγουσι καί σφι τιμὰς ἄλλας δεδόσθαι πρὸς σφέων· καὶ γὰρ ἀγείρειν σφι τὰς γυναῖκας, ἐπονομαζούσας τὰ οὐνόματα ἐν τῷ ὕμνῳ· παρὰ δὲ σφέων μαθόντας νησιώτας τε καὶ Ἴωνας ὑμνέειν Ὦπίν τε καὶ Ἄργην· καὶ τῶν μηρίων καταγιζομένων

578   GREEK RELIGION.

ἐπὶ τῷ βωμῷ τὴν σποδόν, ταύτην ἐπὶ τὴν θήκην τῆς Ὠπιός τε καὶ Ἄργης ἀναισι-
μοῦσθαι ἐπιβαλλομένην. ἡ δὲ θήκη αὐτέων ἐστὶ ὄπισθε τοῦ Ἀρτεμισίου.
Arnob. *Adv. Gent.* 6. 6 Non in Dianae delubro, quod in Apollinis
constitutum est Delii, Hyperoche Laodikeque (humationis habuisse
perhibentur officia)? Paus. 1. 43, 4, at Megara, τὸ μνῆμα Ἰφινόης Ἀλκάθου
θυγατρός· ἀποθανεῖν δὲ αὐτήν φασιν ἔτι παρθένον. καθέστηκε δὲ ταῖς κόραις
χοὰς πρὸς τὸ τῆς Ἰφινόης μνῆμα προσφέρειν πρὸ γάμου καὶ ἀπάρχεσθαι τῶν
τριχῶν, καθὰ καὶ τῇ Ἑκαέργῃ καὶ Ὤπιδι αἱ θυγατέρες ποτὲ ἀπεκείροντο αἱ Δηλίων.
Id. 5. 7, 8 ἐπεὶ δὲ ᾠδὴν Μελάνωπος Κυμαῖος ἐς Ὦπιν καὶ Ἑκαέργην ᾖσεν,
ὡς ἐκ τῶν Ὑπερβορέων . . . ἀφίκοντο ἐς Δῆλον. *Et. Mag.* p. 641. 55 Οὖπις
ἐπίθετον Ἀρτέμιδος, ἢ παρὰ τὸ ὀπίζεσθαι τὰς τικτούσας αὐτήν . . . ἢ διὰ τὰς
ὑπερβορέας κόρας, Οὖπιν, Ἑκαέργην, Λοξώ. Plato, Ἀξιοχ. p. 371 A χαλκέων
δέλτων, ἃς ἐξ Ὑπερβορέων ἐκόμισαν Ὦπίς τε καὶ Ἑκαέργη. Claud. *de Cons.
Stilich.* 3. 253 Iungunt se geminae metuenda feris Hekaerge, et soror,
optatum numen venantibus, Opis, progenies Scythiae.   Clem. Alex.
Strom. p. 674 P ὁ μὲν γὰρ (Βράγχος ὁ μάντις) ἐπιρραίνων τὸ πλῆθος δάφνης
κλάδοις προκατήρχετο τοῦ ὕμνου ὧδέ πως· μέλπετε ὦ παῖδες ἑκάεργον καὶ
ἑκαέργαν.   Athenag. *Leg. pro Christ.* 14. p. 61 (Dechair) καὶ ὁ Δῆλος
καὶ ἡ Ἄρτεμις Τεκταίου καὶ Ἀγγελίωνος τέχνη.   Anonym. *Vit. Plat.* p. 6
Cobet ἐν τῇ ζ´ τοῦ Θαργηλιῶνος μηνός, ἐν ᾗ ἑορτὴν ἐπιτελοῦσιν οἱ Δήλιοι τοῦ
Ἀπόλλωνος, ἐν δὲ τῇ ς´ τοῦ αὐτοῦ μηνός, . . . ἐν ᾗ γενεθλιακὴν ἑορτὴν Ἀρτέμιδος
ἐπετέλουν.

b At Athens, common cult of Apollo Προστατήριος and Artemis
Βουλαία, [81]. Cf. [76], [56]. Artemis Δελφινία at Athens: Pollux, 8. 119 τὸ
ἐπὶ Δελφινίῳ (δικαστήριον) ἱδρύθη μὲν ὑπὸ τοῦ Αἰγέως λέγεται δὲ Ἀπόλλωνι
Δελφινίῳ καὶ Ἀρτέμιδι Δελφινίᾳ. Cf. [131]. Demosth. κ. Ἀριστοκρ. 74.
p. 644 δικαστήριον, ὃ πάντων ἁγιώτατα τούτων ἔχει καὶ φρικωδέστατα, ἄν τις
ὁμολογῇ μὲν κτεῖναι, ἐννόμως δὲ φῇ δεδρακέναι· τοῦτο δ' ἐστὶ τὸ ἐπὶ Δελφινίῳ.
C. I. A. 3. 77, calendar of sacrifices (Roman period) Πυανεψιῶνος
Ἀπόλλωνι καὶ Ἀρτέμιδι ζ πόπανον.

c Artemis Δελφινία in Thessaly: *Eph. Arch.* 1884, p. 221 Ἀρτέμιδι
Δελφινίᾳ Αἰσχυλὶς . . . λειτορεύσασα (? second century B. C.).

d Artemis Σελασφόρος with Apollo at Phlya in Attica, [59].

e Artemis with Apollo at Delphi: Collitz, *Dialect. Inschr.* No. 1810
ἀπέδοτο Μνασίλαος . . . τῷ Ἀπόλλωνι τῷ Πυθίῳ καὶ Ἀρτέμιτι σῶμα γυναικεῖον.
Cf. *C. I. Gr.* 1688, inscription B.c. 379 containing Amphictyonic oath,
Ὀμνύω κατὰ τοῦ Ἀπόλλωνος τοῦ Πυθίου καὶ τᾶς Λατοῦς καὶ τᾶς Ἀρτάμιτος.
Cf. joint worship at Cyrrha, [138].

f Artemis Σώτειρα with Apollo Πύθιος at Anaphe: *C. I. Gr.* 2481.

ᵍ Near Pheneos: Paus. 8. 15, 5 Ἀπόλλωνί ἐστι Πυθίου ναός . . .
ἐνταῦθα ἔτι καὶ νῦν Ἀπόλλωνι Φενεᾶται καὶ Ἀρτέμιδι θύουσιν.

ʰ Paus. 3. 11, 9 Σπαρτιάταις δὲ ἐπὶ τῆς ἀγορᾶς Πυθαέως τέ ἐστιν
Ἀπόλλωνος καὶ Ἀρτέμιδος καὶ Λητοῦς ἀγάλματα.

ⁱ Artemis Πυθίη at Miletus: *C. I. Gr.* 2866 Ἀρτέμιδι Πυθίῃ καὶ Αὐτοκράτορι Καίσαρι Σεβαστῷ. *Ib.* 2885 Ὑδροφόρος Ἀρτέμιδος Πυθίης Μαλία
Ῥουφεῖνα. Cf. ⁸¹ᵇ.

ᵏ Clem. Alex. *Strom.* 1. p. 384 P λέγεται (τὴν Σίβυλλαν) . . . Φρυγίαν
τε οὖσαν κεκλῆσθαι Ἄρτεμιν καὶ ταύτην παραγενομένην εἰς Δελφοὺς ᾆσαι.

ˡ Strabo, 588 ἡ μὲν οὖν πόλις (Ἀδράστεια) μεταξὺ Πριάπου καὶ Παρίου
ἔχουσα ὑποκείμενον πεδίον ὁμώνυμον ἐν ᾧ καὶ μαντεῖον ἦν Ἀπόλλωνος Ἀκταίου
καὶ Ἀρτέμιδος.

ᵐ Strabo, 676 ἐν δὲ τῇ Κιλικίᾳ ἐστὶ καὶ τὸ τῆς Σαρπηδονίας Ἀρτέμιδος καὶ
μαντεῖον, τοὺς δὲ χρησμοὺς ἔνθεοι προθεσπίζουσι.

ⁿ Artemis Οὐλία: Macr. *Saturn.* 1. 17, 21 Pherecydes refert Thesea
cum in Cretam ad Minotaurum duceretur vovisse pro salute atque
reditu suo Ἀπόλλωνι Οὐλίῳ καὶ Ἀρτέμιδι Οὐλίᾳ. ? At Lindos: Artemis with
Apollo Οὔλιος ¹⁰².

ᵒ Artemis Λύη: Diomed. Bk. 3. p. 484 ed. Putsch. Morbo Sicilia
laborabat. Variis et assiduis ceremoniis Dianam placantes, finem
malis invenerunt, eandem Lyen cognominaverunt. Cf. Artemis Ἐλευθέρα
in Lycia: Artemid. *Oneirocr.* 2. 35 ἡ λεγομένη παρὰ Λυκίοις Ἐλευθέρα
Ἄρτεμις. Arctinus, *Aethiopis Düntzer, Ep. Poes.* p. 16 (Photius)
Ἀχιλλεὺς εἰς Λέσβον πλεῖ καὶ θύσας Ἀπόλλωνι καὶ Ἀρτέμιδι καὶ Λητοῖ
καθαίρεται τοῦ φόνου (Θερσίτου) ὑπ' Ὀδυσσέως.

ᵖ Artemis Λουσιᾶτις: Collitz, *Dial. Inschr.* 1601 ἱαρὸν ἀνέθηκε τᾶι
Ἀρτέμιδι Λουσιάτι. ? Achaean inscription of fourth century B.C.

ᑫ Artemis Θερμία, εὐάκοος, ἐπήκοος: *C. I. Gr.* 2172, inscription from
baths in Mitylene, τὰν κράνναν καὶ τὸ ὑδραγώγιον ἀπὸ Κεγχρεᾶν Ἀρτέμιδι
Θερμίᾳ εὐακόῳ. On basis found at Mitylene Μεγάλη Ἄρτεμις Θερμία
Bull. de Corr. Hell. 1880, 430, No. 14. Aristid. 1. p. 503, Dind. τὴν
Θερμαίαν Ἄρτεμιν, ἣ τὰς πηγὰς τὰς θερμὰς ἔχει. Cf. Paus. 5. 15, 7 τέταρτος
δὲ βωμὸς Ἀρτέμιδος ἐπίκλησιν Κοκκώκας· καὶ Ἀπόλλωνος πέμπτος Θερμίου . . .
ἀνθ' ὅτου δὲ Ἄρτεμιν ἐπονομάζουσιν Κοκκώκαν, οὐχ οἷά τε ἦν μοι διδαχθῆναι.
Εὐάκοος in Crete: *C. I. Gr.* 2566 Ἀρχονίκα Ζαύλω . . . ἀναζῶσα Ἀρτέμιδι
εὐακόῳ εὐξαμένα ὑπὲρ ἑαυτᾶς εὐχάν. Ἐπήκοος at Rome: *C. I. Gr.* 5941
Θεᾷ ἐπηκόῳ Ἀρτέμιδι Αὐλίδι Σωτείρᾳ Αὐρ. Ἐλπινείκη. At Epidaurus: *Eph.
Arch.* 1883, 3 Ἀρτέμιδι Ἑκάτῃ ἐπηκόῳ, inscription of Roman period.
Samothrace inscription of late Roman period Ἀρτέμιδι Ἐπηκόῳ *Athen.
Mittheil.* 1893, p. 377.

ʳ At Megara : Paus. ι. 44, 2 Ἀπόλλωνος ἱερὸν ... Προστατηρίου ...
Ἀπόλλων δὲ ἐν αὐτῷ κεῖται θέας ἄξιος καὶ Ἄρτεμις καὶ Λητὼ καὶ ἄλλα ἀγάλματά
ἐστι, Πραξιτέλους ποιήσαντος Λητὼ καὶ οἱ παῖδες. Cf. Artemis Ἀγροτέρα with
Apollo Ἀγραῖος, ²⁶ c.

ˢ At Sicyon : Paus. 2. 11, 1 Ἐπωπέα δὲ καὶ Ἀρτέμιδι καὶ Ἀπόλλωνι τὸ
πλησίον ἱερὸν ποιῆσαι λέγουσι. Cf. 2. 7, 8.

ᵗ In the Argolid, ⁵³ d : C. I. Gr. 1173 Ἀρτέμιδος Ἀπόλλωνος
Στατείλιος ἱεροπολήσας.

ᵘ At Pyrrhichus in South Laconia : Paus. 3. 25, 3 θεῶν δὲ ἐν τῇ γῇ
σφίσιν ἱερά ἐστιν Ἀρτέμιδός τε ἐπίκλησιν Ἀστρατείας, ὅτι τῆς ἐς τὸ πρόσω
στρατείας ἐνταῦθα ἐπαύσαντο Ἀμαζόνες, καὶ Ἀπόλλων Ἀμαζόνιος· ξόανα μὲν
ἀμφότερα ἀναθεῖναι δὲ λέγουσιν αὐτὰ τὰς ἀπὸ Θερμώδοντος γυναῖκας. Cf. ⁶⁷ c.

ᵛ At Olympia in the temple of Hera : Paus. 5. 17, 3 Κόρη δὲ καὶ
Δημήτηρ καὶ Ἀπόλλων καὶ Ἄρτεμις, αἱ μὲν ἀλλήλων εἰσὶν ἀπαντικρὺ καθήμεναι,
Ἀπόλλων δὲ ἐναντίος ἐστώσῃ τῇ Ἀρτέμιδι ἕστηκεν.

ʷ At Mantinea : Paus. 8. 9, 1 Ἔστι δὲ Μαντινεῦσι ναὸς διπλοῦς ... τοῦ
ναοῦ δὲ τῇ μὲν ἄγαλμά ἐστιν Ἀσκληπιοῦ τέχνη Ἀλκαμένους, τὸ δὲ ἕτερον Λητοῦς
ἐστιν ἱερὸν καὶ τῶν παίδων· Πραξιτέλης δὲ τὰ ἀγάλματα εἰργάσατο.

ˣ At Tanagra : Paus. 9. 22, 1 ἐν Τανάγρᾳ ... ὁ τρίτος τῶν ναῶν Ἀπόλλωνος, ὁμοῦ δὲ αὐτῷ Ἄρτεμίς τε καὶ Λητώ.

ʸ At Abae in Phocis : Paus. 10. 35, 3 παρὰ τὸν ναὸν τὸν μέγαν ἐστὶν ἄλλος
ναός ... βασιλεὺς δὲ Ἀδριανὸς ἐποίησε τῷ Ἀπόλλωνι· τὰ δὲ ἀγάλματα ἀρχαιό-
τερα καὶ αὐτῶν ἐστιν Ἀβαίων ἀνάθημα χαλκοῦ δὲ εἴργασται καὶ ὁμοίως ἐστὶν
ὀρθά, Ἀπόλλων καὶ Λητώ τε καὶ Ἄρτεμις.

ᶻ At Eretria : Rang. Ant. Hellén. 1242 ὁ δῆμος Ἐρετριέων Στήσιππον
ἀρετῆς ἕνεκα ... Ἀρτέμιδι Ἀπόλλωνι Λητοῖ (fourth century B. c.).

ᵃᵃ At Mylasa : C. I. Gr. 2694 ἱερέα Ἀπόλλωνος καὶ Ἀρτέμιδος.

ᵇᵇ At Araxa in Lycia : Bennd. Reisen in Lykien, vol. ι, p. 77, Inscr.
53 b ἀναφυούσης τῆς θεοτόκου γῆς λαινέους μορφὰς ... Ἄρτεμίν τε καὶ
Ἀπόλλωνα.

ᶜᶜ Artemis Προηγέτις with Apollo in Lycia : Bennd. Reisen in Lykien,
Inscr. 45 τῶν προηγετῶν Ἀρτέμιδος καὶ Ἀπόλλωνος.

ᵈᵈ Artemis Κλαρία and Apollo Κλάριος on late coins of Colophon :
Head, Hist. Num. p. 494. Brit. Mus. Cat. Ionia, p. 42.

ᵉᵉ Artemis Καυκασίς with Apollo Καυκασεύς in Chios : Rev. Arch.
1877, p. 107 τὴν ἱερητείαν Ἀπόλλωνος Καυκασέως καὶ Ἀρτέμιδος Καυκα-
σίδος.

ᶠᶠ Artemis Ephesia with Apollo, ¹³³ᵃ (not in public cult); at Massilia, ¹³³ᵇ.

ᵍᵍ With Apollo Μαλεάτας in Cynuria: *C. I. Gr.* 1173 Ἀρτέμιδος Ἀπ(όλλωνος) Στατείλιος . . . ἱεραπολήσας (Roman period).

ʰʰ With Apollo Ἀγυιεύς at Tegea, ³⁵.

ⁱⁱ In Cyrene: Athenae. p. 549 E, F, quoting Ptolemaeus Euerg. (Müll. *Frag. Hist.* 3. 187, 6) Ἀρτεμίτια μεγίστη ἑορτὴ ἐν Κυρήνῃ, ἐν ᾗ ὁ ἱερεὺς τοῦ Ἀπόλλωνος (ἐνιαύσιος δ' ἐστὶ) δειπνίζει τοὺς πρὸ αὐτοῦ ἱερευσαμένους. Cf. Inscr. Smith-Porcher, *Discoveries at Cyrene*, Pl. 80, 8, p. 112.

Artemis as city-goddess.

⁸⁰ Artemis Ἀμαρυνθία or Ἀμαρυσία ᵃ at Eretria : Livy, 35. 38 sacrum anniversarium eo forte tempore Eretriae Amarynthidis Dianae erat, quod non popularium modo sed Carystiorum etiam coetu celebratur. Strabo, 448 τὴν δὲ δύναμιν τὴν Ἐρετριέων ἣν ἔσχον ποτὲ μαρτυρεῖ ἡ στήλη, ἣν ἀνέθεσάν ποτε ἐν τῷ ἱερῷ τῆς Ἀμαρυνθίας Ἀρτέμιδος. Cf. Rang. *Ant. Hellén.* 689 τὴν μὲν μίαν (εἰκόνα) στῆσαι ἐν τῷ ἱερῷ τῆς Ἀρτέμιδος τῆς Ἀμαρυσίας . . . ἀναγορεύεσθαι δὲ τὰς τιμὰς Ἀρτεμισίων τῷ ἀγῶνι τῆς πυρρίχης. Cf. ⁸⁹.

ᵇ. In Attica: Paus. 1. 31, 4–5 Ἀθμονεῖς δὲ τιμῶσιν Ἀμαρυσίαν Ἄρτεμιν . . . ἑορτὴν δὲ καὶ Ἀθηναῖοι τῆς Ἀμαρυσίας ἄγουσι οὐδέν τι Εὐβοέων ἀφανέστερον. *C. I. A.* 1. 526 ὅρος Ἀρτέμιδος τεμένους Ἀμαρυσίας (archaic period). Cf. *ib.* 4. 521 h.

⁸¹ Artemis Βουλαία ᵃ at Athens: *C. I. Gr.* 112, 113 τῶν θυσιῶν ὧν ἔθυον τὰ πρὸ τῶν ἐκκλησιῶν ὡς τῷ Ἀπόλλωνι τῷ προστατηρίῳ καὶ τῇ Ἀρτέμιδι τῇ Βουλαίᾳ. Cf. *C. I. A.* 2. 390, 392, 408, 417, 431, 432, containing the same formula. Cf. Aesch. *Sept.* 449 προστατηρίας Ἀρτέμιδος εὐνοίαισι.

ᵇ At Mi¹etus: *Bull. de Corr. Hell.* 1877, p. 287 Ἀρτεμὼ τὴν ὑδροφόρον τῆς Πυθίης Ἀρτέμιδος καὶ ἱέρειαν διὰ βίου τῆς Βουλαίας Ἀρτέμιδος (inscription of Roman period).

⁸² Artemis Βουληφόρος at Miletus: Dittenb. *Syllog.* 391. *Rev. Arch.* 1874², p. 104 τῇ Θεῷ κεχαρισμένως ἕξει καὶ τῷ δήμῳ. συμφερόντως καὶ νῦν καὶ ἐς τὸν ἔπειτε (*sic*) χρόνον συντελοῦντι τὰς ἀγέρσεις Ἀρτέμιδι Βουληφόρῳ Σκίριδι καθότι Σκίριδαι ἐξηγούμενοι εἰσφέρουσι.

⁸³ Artemis Ἀγοραία, ⁵⁵ᶜ.
The name of Artemis in the formulae of public oaths: *C. I. Gr.* 2554, alliance between Latus and Olus in Crete. Cf. ⁵⁰ᵍ, ¹²³f. In the Gortynian inscription the woman takes the oath in the name of Artemis on a question of property, vide *Hell. Journ.* 1892, p. 65.

At Dreros in Crete, Artemis associated with Leto and Apollo in the public oath, Cauer, *Delect.*² 121.

Titles taken from cities and localities.

⁸⁴ Callim. *in Dian.* 33:

τρὶς δέκα τοι πτολίεθρα, τὰ μὴ θεὸν ἄλλον ἀέξειν
εἴσεται ἀλλὰ μόνην σέ, καὶ 'Αρτέμιδος καλέεσθαι.

Ib. 188 :

νήσων μὲν Δολίχη, πολίων δέ τοι εὔαδε Πέργη,
τηΰγετον δ' ὀρέων, λιμένες γε μὲν Εὐρίποιο.

⁸⁵ Αἰτωλή in Naupactus : Paus. 10. 38, 12 ἔστι μὲν ἐπὶ θαλάσσῃ ναὸς Ποσειδῶνος . . . ἔστι δὲ καὶ ἱερὸν 'Αρτέμιδος καὶ ἄγαλμα λευκοῦ λίθου· σχῆμα δὲ ἀκοντιζούσης παρέχεται, καὶ ἐπίκλησιν εἴληφεν Αἰτωλή, among the Heneti.

⁸⁶ Αἰγιναία, ¹⁸.

⁸⁷ Artemis 'Ακρία : Hesych. *s. v.* ἔστι δὲ καὶ ἡ Ἥρα καὶ Ἄρτεμις καὶ 'Αφροδίτη προσαγορευομένη ἐν Ἄργει, κατὰ τὸ ὅμοιον ἐπ' ἄκρῳ ἱδρυμέναι. Cf. Artemis Κορυφαία on Mount Coryphon near Epidaurus, Paus. 2. 28. 2.

⁸⁸ Artemis 'Αλφειαία, ⁴.

⁸⁹ Artemis 'Αμαρυνθία : Steph. Byz. *s. v.* 'Αμάρυνθος· νῆσος Εὐβοίας, ἀπό τινος κυνηγοῦ 'Αρτέμιδος 'Αμαρύνθου. Cf. ⁸⁰.

⁹⁰ Artemis 'Απτέρα in Crete : Cauer, *Delect.*² 128, treaty of alliance between Aptera and Teos, ἀναγραψῶμεν δὲ καὶ ἁμὲς τό τε πρότερον δόγμα καὶ τὰν ἀνανέωσιν ἐς τὸ ἱερὸν τὸ τᾶς 'Αρτέμιδος τᾶς 'Απτέρας.

⁹¹ Artemis 'Αστίας at Iasos in Caria : *C. I. Gr.* 2683 'Αρτέμιδι 'Αστιάδι καὶ Αὐτοκράτορι Καίσαρι Μ. Αὐρηλίῳ Κωμόδῳ 'Αντωνίνῳ Σεβαστῷ. στεφανη-φόρος τῆς προκαθηγεμόνος τῆς πόλεως ἡμῶν 'Αρτέμιδος 'Αστιάδος, inscription of first century A. D. (?), *Rev. des Études Grecques*, 1893, p. 157. Polyb. 16. 12 παρὰ τοῖς 'Ιασσεῦσι, τὸ τῆς 'Εστιάδος (leg. 'Αστιάδος).

⁹² Artemis 'Αστυρηνή : Strabo, 606, in Antandros, Ἄστυρα, κώμη καὶ ἄλσος τῆς 'Αστυρηνῆς 'Αρτέμιδος ἅγιον. Cf. 613.

⁹³ Artemis Αὐλιδεία at Tanagra : *Bull. de Corr. Hell.* 1879, 385, No. 32, inscription at Tanagra, ἡ βουλὴ καὶ ὁ δῆμος 'Ολυππίχην . . . ἱερατεύσασαν 'Αρτέμιδι Αὐλιδεί(ᾳ), ? second century B.C. Cf. *I. G. A.* 170.

⁹⁴ Artemis Βορειτηνή in Thyatira : *C. I. Gr.* 3477 'Αρτέμιδι Βορειτηνῇ καὶ τῇ πατρίδι Γλύκων . . . ἀνέθηκε. Cf. 3507.

⁹⁵ Artemis Δηλία in Delos, ⁷⁹ᵃ.

⁹⁶ Δηλιάς in Halicarnassus : Newton, *Halic.* 2. 698, No. 6 a ὁ δῆμος Τιβερίῳ Κλαυδίῳ Καίσαρι Σεβαστῷ Γερμανικῷ . . . 'Αρτέμιδι Δηλιάδι.

⁹⁷ Artemis Δερεᾶτις, ⁴⁶. Cf. *C. I. Gr.* 4300 A.

⁹⁸ Artemis Ἐλευσινία: Hesych. *s. v.* καὶ ἐν Σικελίᾳ τιμᾶται ″Αρτεμις. Cf. ἡ Ἐλευσίνα, ¹³¹ᵃ.

⁹⁹ Artemis Ἐφεσία, ¹³³.

¹⁰⁰ ? Ἰσσωρία, ¹³¹d.

¹⁰¹ Καυκασίς, ⁷⁹ee.

¹⁰² ? Κεκοία in Rhodes: *Bull. de Corr. Hell.* 1885, 100 τὸν ἱερῆ Ἀρτάμιτος Κεκοίας Δαμάτριον. Ross, *Inscr. Inéd.* 3. 272 Ξέναρχος . . . ἱερατεύσας Ἀπόλλωνος Πυθαέως καὶ Ἀπόλλωνος Ὀλίου Ἀρτέμιδος τᾶς ἐν Κεκοίᾳ θεοῖς. Ross, *Arch. Aufsätze,* 2. 594 Ἀριστολόχος . . . ἱερατεύσας Ἀθαναίας Λινδίας καὶ Διὸς Πολιέως καὶ Ἀρτάμιτος τᾶς ἐν Κεκοίᾳ θεοῖς, ? third century B. C.

¹⁰³ Artemis Κολοηνή near Sardis: Strabo, 626 ἐν δὲ σταδίοις τετταρά-κοντα ἀπὸ τῆς πόλεως ἔστιν ἡ Γυγαία μὲν ὑπὸ τοῦ ποιητοῦ λεγομένη (λίμνη), Κολόη δ᾿ ὕστερον μετονομασθεῖσα, ὅπου τὸ ἱερὸν τῆς Κολοηνῆς Ἀρτέμιδος μεγά-λην ἁγιστείαν ἔχον. φασὶ δ᾿ ἐνταῦθα χορεύειν τοὺς καλάθους κατὰ τὰς ἑορτάς.

¹⁰⁴ Artemis Κονδυλεᾶτις, ⁶.

¹⁰⁵ Artemis Κινδυάς: Strabo, 658, on the Carian coast, πλησίον δ᾿ ἐστὶ τῶν Βαργυλίων τὸ τῆς Ἀρτέμιδος ἱερὸν τὸ τῆς Κινδυάδος . . . ἦν δέ ποτε καὶ χωρίον Κινδύη. Cf. Polyb. 16. 12. Cf. *Classical Review,* 1894, p. 217 ἐὰν δέ τις παρὰ ταῦτα ποιήσῃ ἀποτείσει Ἀρτέμιδι Κινδυάδι, sepulchral inscription with fine, ? found near Kindya.

¹⁰⁶ Artemis Κλαρία at Colophon. Cf. ⁷⁹dl.

¹⁰⁶a Κρησία: Diod. Sic. 5. 77. Cf. ¹³³a.

¹⁰⁷ Artemis Λυκοᾶτις, ²².

¹⁰⁸a Artemis Μονογισηνή: Steph. Byz. *s. v.* Μονόγισα· (πόλις Καρίας ὅθεν) ″Αρτεμις Μονογισηνή, ἵδρυμα Δαιδάλου . . . γίσσα γὰρ τῇ Καρῶν φωνῇ λίθος ἑρμηνεύεται.

b Artemis Μυνδία on coins of Myndus in Caria, Roman period: Head, *Hist. Num.* p. 529.

c Artemis Μυσία near Sparta: Paus. 3. 20, 9 Μυσίας ἱερὸν Ἀρτέμιδος.

¹⁰⁹ Artemis Οἰνωᾶτις in Argolis: Paus. 2. 25, 3 Οἰνόη χωρίον ἐστιν Ἀρτεμίσιον, καὶ ἱερὸν Ἀρτέμιδος ἐπὶ κορυφῇ τοῦ ὄρους. Steph. Byz. *s. v.* Οὔνη· πόλις Ἄργους· . . . Οἰνωᾶτις ″Αρτεμις, ἡ ἐν Οἰνόῃ τῆς Ἀργείας ἱδρυμένη ὑπὸ Προίτου. Cf. Eur. *Herc. Fur.* 375:

> τάν τε χρυσοκάρανον
> δόρκα . . . .
> κτείνας, θηροφόνον θεὰν
> Οἰνωᾶτιν ἀγάλλει.

584   GREEK RELIGION.

¹¹⁰ Artemis Οἰναία in Attic deme Οἰνόη: *C. I. A.* 1. 534 Οἰνόησι
'Αρτ[έμιδι?]. *Ib.* 3. 336 'Αρτέμιδος Οἰναίας.

¹¹⁰a Artemis 'Ολυμπία from the mountain north of Eretria: *Eph.
Arch.* 1892, p. 141 Χρυσαλλὶς Σημίου 'Αρτέμιδι 'Ολυμπία. Cf. *ib.* p. 126,
fourth-century inscription from Eretria, ἀναγράψαι ἐν στήλῃ λιθίνῃ τὴν
προξενίαν καὶ στῆσαι ἐν τῷ τῆς 'Αρτέμιδος ἱερῷ.

¹¹¹ Artemis Περγαία at Perge in Pamphylia, ¹³³: Strabo, 667 Πέργη
πόλις καὶ πλησίον ἐπὶ μετεώρου τόπου τὸ τῆς Περγαίας 'Αρτέμιδος ἱερόν, ἐν ᾧ
πανήγυρις κατ' ἔτος συντελεῖται. Cic. *in Verr.* 2. 1, 54 Pergae fanum
antiquissimum et sanctissimum Dianae . . . ex ipsa Diana, quod
habebat auri, detractum. Phot. *s. v.* ἡ Περγαία "Αρτεμις· τάσσεται ἐπὶ
τῶν ἀγυρτῶν καὶ πλανητῶν· παρόσον καὶ ἡ θεὸς ἐν αὐτῇ. At Halicarnassus:
C. I. Gr. 2656 ἔδοξε τῇ βουλῇ καὶ τῷ δήμῳ . . . πριαμένη τὴν ἱερητείαν τῆς
'Αρτέμιδος τῆς Περγαίας παρέξεται ἱέρειαν ἀστὴν ἐξ ἀστῶν ἀμφοτέρων ἐπὶ τρεῖς
γενεὰς γεγενημένην καὶ πρὸς πατρὸς καὶ πρὸς μητρός· ἡ δὲ πριαμένη . . . θύσει
τὰ ἱερὰ τὰ δημοτελέα καὶ τὰ ἰδιωτικά . . . ἐν ᾧ δὲ μηνὶ ἡ θυσία συντελεῖται
ἡ δημοτελὴς ἀγειρέτω πρὸ νήσου τὰς ἡμέρας τρεῖς, ἐπ' οἰκίαν μὴ πορευομένη,
ὁ δὲ ἀγερμὸς ἔστω τῆς ἱερείας. At Lindos: *Rev. Arch.* 1867², p. 25,
No. 67 'Αρτάμιτι Περγαίαι.

¹¹² Artemis Πριαπίνη ? at Priapus: Plut. *Lucull.* 13 λέγεται γὰρ 'Αρτέ-
μιδος χόλῳ Πριαπίνης ὁ χειμὼν ἐμπεσεῖν τοῖς Ποντικοῖς συλήσασιν αὐτῆς τὸ
ἱερὸν καὶ τὸ ξόανον ἀνασπάσασι.

¹¹³ Artemis Σαρδιανή at Sardis: *C. I. Gr.* 3459 'Απολλώνιος ἀρχιερεὺς
. . . τὴν ἱερέαν τῆς Σαρδιανῆς 'Αρτέμιδος ἀνῆκεν τοῦ φόρου 'Αθηνᾶς (? third
century B.C.).

¹¹⁴ Artemis Σαρωνία on the coast near Troezen: Paus. 2. 32, 10
στρεπτὸν δὲ ἐπονομάζουσι τοῦτον, ὅτι . . . ἀνετράπη 'Ιππολύτου τὸ ἅρμα, τούτου
δὲ οὐ πολὺ τῆς Σαρωνίας 'Αρτέμιδος ἀφέστηκε τὸ ἱερόν . . . Σαρώνια γὰρ δὴ κατὰ
ἔτος τῇ 'Αρτέμιδι ἑορτὴν ἄγουσι. Eur. *Hipp.* 1126:

ὦ ψάμαθοι πολιήτιδος ἀκτᾶς
δρυμός τ' ὄρειος, ὅθι κυνῶν
ὠκυπόδων μέτα θῆρας ἔναιρεν
Δίκτυνναν ἀμφὶ σεμνάν.

^{1 5} Artemis Σελασία ?, ⁶⁰.

¹¹⁶ Artemis Σκιαδῖτις near Megalopolis: Paus. 8. 35, 5 Σκιάδις καλού-
μενον χωρίον καὶ 'Αρτέμιδος Σκιαδίτιδος ἐρείπιά ἐστιν ἱεροῦ.

¹¹⁷ Artemis Φεραία: Callim. *in Dian.* 259 Πότνια Μουνυχίη λιμενοσκόπε,
χαῖρε, Φεραίη. At Sicyon: Paus. 2. 10, 7 Φεραίας ἱερὸν 'Αρτέμιδος.
κομισθῆναι δὲ τὸ ξόανον λέγουσιν ἐκ Φερῶν. At Argos: *id.* 2. 23, 5 τῆς δὲ
'Αρτέμιδος τῆς Φεραίας, σέβουσι γὰρ καὶ 'Αργεῖοι Φεραίαν "Αρτεμιν κατὰ ταὐτὰ

Ἀθηναίοις καὶ Σικυωνίοις, τὸ ἄγαλμα καὶ οὗτοί φασιν ἐκ Φερῶν τῶν ἐν Θεσσαλίᾳ κομισθῆναι. At Athens : Hesych. *s. v.* Φεραία· Ἀθήνῃσι ξενικὴ θεός· οἱ δὲ τὴν Ἑκάτην : *ib.* Ἀδμήτου κόρη· Ἑκάτη, τινὲς δὲ τὴν Βενδῖν : vide [130]. In Acarnania : *C. I. Gr.* 1837 Ἀρτέμιδι Φεραίᾳ (Roman period).

[118] Artemis Τύχη on Imperial coins of Gerasa in the Syrian Dekapolis : Head, *Hist. Num.* p. 665 Ἄρτεμις Τύχη Γερασῶν.

Artemis as goddess of war.

[119] Vide [26b],[f] : Epigram of Simonides, Bergk, 135 :

Παντοδαπῶν ἀνδρῶν γενεὰς Ἀσίας ἀπὸ χώρας
παῖδες Ἀθηναίων τῷδε ποτ᾽ ἐν πελάγει
ναυμαχίᾳ δαμάσαντες ἐπεὶ στράτος ὤλετο Μήδων
σήματα ταῦτ᾽ ἀνέθεν παρθένῳ Ἀρτέμιδι.

[120] Artemis Ἀριστοβούλη : Plut. *de Herod. Malign.* 869 τοῦ Θεμιστοκλέους βουλεύματος, ὁ βουλεύσας τῇ Ἑλλάδι ναυμαχῆσαι πρὸ τῆς Σαλαμῖνος, ἱδρύσατο ναὸν Ἀριστοβούλης Ἀρτέμιδος ἐν Μελίτῃ, τοῦ βαρβάρου καταπολεμηθέντος. Cf. Plut. *Themist.* 22 ἔκειτο δὲ καὶ τοῦ Θεμιστοκλέους εἰκόνιον ἐν τῷ ναῷ τῆς Ἀριστοβούλης ἔτι καθ᾽ ἡμᾶς. ? At Rhodes : Porph. *de Abstin.* 2. 54 ἐνστάσης δὲ τῆς ἑορτῆς προαγαγόντες τὸν ἄνθρωπον ἔξω πυλῶν ἄντικρυς τοῦ Ἀριστοβούλης ἕδους, οἴνου ποτίσαντες ἔσφαττον.

[121] In Messenia : Paus. 4. 13, 1 τὸ τῆς Ἀρτέμιδος ἄγαλμα, ὃν χαλκοῦν καὶ αὐτὸ καὶ τὰ ὅπλα παρῆκε τὴν ἀσπίδα.

[122] *Anth. Pal.* 9. 534 Ἄρτεμις ἱδρώουσα προάγγελός ἐστι κυδοιμοῦ.

[123] Artemis Σώτειρα [a] at Megara : Paus. τ. 40, 2 ἀρχαῖόν ἐστιν ἱερόν, ... καὶ ἄγαλμά τε κεῖται χαλκοῦν Ἀρτέμιδος ἐπίκλησιν Σωτείρας. At Pagae in Megara : *id.* 1. 44, 4 ἐν δὲ ταῖς Παγαῖς θέας ὑπελείπετο ἄξιον Ἀρτέμιδος Σωτείρας ἐπίκλησιν χαλκοῦν ἄγαλμα, μεγέθει τῷ παρὰ Μεγαρεῦσιν ἴσον καὶ σχῆμα οὐδὲν διαφόρως ἔχον. *C. I. Gr.* 1052b, 1063 ἡ βουλὴ καὶ ὁ δῆμος Φαυστεῖναν Φαυστείνου ἱέρειαν Ἀρτέμιδος Σωτείρας.

[b] At Megalopolis : Paus. 8. 30, 10 καθεζομένῳ δὲ τῷ Διὶ ἐν θρόνῳ παρεστήκασι τῇ μὲν ἡ Μεγάλη πόλις, ἐν ἀριστερᾷ δὲ Ἀρτέμιδος Σωτείρας ἄγαλμα. ταῦτα μὲν λίθου τοῦ Πεντελησίου Ἀθηναῖοι Κηφισόδοτος καὶ Ξενοφῶν εἰργάσαντο.

[c] At Phigaleia : Paus. 8. 39, 5 ἔστι δὲ Σωτείρας τε ἱερὸν ἐνταῦθα Ἀρτέμιδος καὶ ἄγαλμα ὀρθὸν λίθου· ἐκ τούτου δὲ τοῦ ἱεροῦ καὶ τὰς πομπάς σφισι πέμπειν κατέστη.

[d] At Troezen : Paus. 2. 31, 1 ἐν τῇ ἀγορᾷ Τροιζηνίων ναὸς καὶ ἀγάλματα Ἀρτέμιδός ἐστι Σωτείρας. Θησέα δὲ ἐλέγετο ἱδρύσασθαι καὶ ὀνομάσαι Σώτειραν, ἥνικα Ἀστερίωνα τὸν Μίνω καταγωνισάμενος ἀνέστρεψεν ἐκ τῆς Κρήτης. Cf. *Bull. de Corr. Hell.* 1893, p. 93, inscription from Troezen, fourth century B.C., Ἀρχέστρατος ... Ἀρτάμιτι Σωτείρᾳ.

e At Boiae, ¹¹a.

f At Pellene: Paus. 7. 27, 3 ὑπὲρ δὲ τὸν ναὸν τῆς ᾿Αθηνᾶς ἐστὶν ἄλσος περιῳκοδομημένον τείχει Σωτείρας ἐπίκλησιν ᾿Αρτέμιδος, καὶ ὀμνύουσιν ἐπὶ μεγίστοις αὐτήν· ἔσοδός τε πλὴν τοῖς ἱερεῦσιν, ἄλλῳ γε οὐδενί ἐστιν ἀνθρώπων. ἱερεῖς δὲ ἄνδρες τῶν ἐπιχωρίων εἰσὶ κατὰ δόξαν γένους μάλιστα αἱρούμενοι. Plut. Arat. 32 αὐτοὶ δὲ Πελληνεῖς λέγουσι τὸ βρέτας τῆς θεοῦ τὸν μὲν ἄλλον ἀποκεῖσθαι χρόνον ἄψαυστον, ὅταν δὲ κινηθὲν ὑπὸ τῆς ἱερείας ἐκφέρηται, μηδένα προσβλέπειν ἐναντίον . . . οὐ γὰρ ἀνθρώποις μόνον ὅραμα φρικτὸν εἶναι καὶ χαλεπόν, ἀλλὰ καὶ δένδρα ποιεῖν ἄφορα καὶ καρποὺς ἀπαμβλίσκειν.

g In Thisbe: Bull. de Corr. Hell. 1884, 401, 402 Θοινίας . . . ᾿Αρτάμιδι Σωτείρῃ (fourth century B.C.).

h At Anaphe, ⁷⁹f.

i At Athens: Eph. Arch. 1893, p. 59 ᾿Αρτέμιδι Σωτείρᾳ Μάρων ἀνέθηκε: cf. inscription of first century B.C.(?). Ib. pp. 52–54, inscription mentioning ἡ Σώτειρα and οἱ Σωτηριασταί. Cf. ib. 1883, p. 205, No. 5 Σώτειρα inscribed on a terracotta representing Artemis holding a hare and resting her hand on the head of a fawn.

k At Anaphe: Collitz, Dialect-inschriften, 3433 ὁ δᾶμος ὁ ᾿Αναφαίων . . . ᾿Απόλλωνι Πυθίῳ ᾿Αρτέμιδι Σωτείραι. Cf. 3449–3451.

l Anth. Pal. 6. 267 Φωσφόρος, ὦ Σώτειρ᾿, ἐπὶ Παλλάδος ἵσταθι κλήρων, ῎Αρτεμι, καὶ χαρίεν φῶς ἐὸν ἀνδρὶ δίδου.

¹²⁴ Artemis ῾Υμνία in Arcadia: Paus. 8. 5, 11 ἔστιν ᾿Αρτέμιδος ἱερὸν ῾Υμνίας ἐπίκλησιν· τοῦτο ἐν ὅροις μέν ἐστιν ᾿Ορχομενίων, πρὸς δὲ τῇ Μαντινικῇ· σέβουσι καὶ ἐκ παλαιοτάτου καὶ οἱ πάντες ᾿Αρκάδες ῾Υμνίαν ῎Αρτεμιν. ἐλάμβανε δὲ τὴν ἱερωσύνην τῆς θεοῦ τότε ἔτι κόρη παρθένος . . . μετεβλήθη δὲ ἐξ ἐκείνου καὶ ὁ νόμος. ἀντὶ γὰρ παρθένου διδόασι τῇ ᾿Αρτέμιδι ἱέρειαν γυναῖκα, ὁμιλίας ἀνδρῶν ἀποχρώντως ἔχουσαν. Id. 8. 13, 1 ἐν ὑπτίῳ τοῦ ὄρους ἱερόν ἐστι τῆς ῾Υμνίας ᾿Αρτέμιδος· μέτεστι δὲ αὐτοῦ καὶ Μαντινεῦσι * * * καὶ ἱέρειαν καὶ ἄνδρα ἱερέα· τούτοις οὐ μόνον τὰ ἐς τὰς μίξεις ἀλλὰ καὶ ἐς τὰ ἄλλα ἁγιστεύειν καθέστηκε τὸν χρόνον τοῦ βίου πάντα, καὶ οὔτε λουτρὰ οὔτε δίαιτα λοιπὴ κατὰ τὰ αὐτὰ σφίσι καθὰ καὶ τοῖς πολλοῖς ἐστίν, οὐδὲ ἐς οἰκίαν παρίασιν ἀνδρὸς ἰδιώτου. τοιαῦτα οἶδα ἕτερα ἐνιαυτὸν καὶ οὐ πρόσω ᾿Εφεσίων ἐπιτηδεύοντας τοὺς τῇ ᾿Αρτέμιδι ἱστιάτορας τῇ ᾿Εφεσίᾳ γινομένους· καλουμένους δὲ ὑπὸ τῶν πολιτῶν ᾿Εσσῆνας· τῇ δὲ ᾿Αρτέμιδι τῇ ῾Υμνίᾳ καὶ ἑορτὴν ἄγουσιν ἐπέτειον.

¹²⁵ Artemis Χελῦτις at Sparta: Clem. Alex. 33 P Χελύτιδα δὲ ῎Αρτεμιν Σπαρτιᾶται σέβουσι. Homeric hymn to Aphrodite, 18:

καὶ γὰρ τῇ (᾿Αρτέμιδι) ἅδε τόξα, καὶ οὔρεσι θῆρας ἐναίρειν,
φόρμιγγές τε χοροί τε διαπρύσιοί τ᾿ ὀλολυγαί,
ἄλσεά τε σκιόεντα δικαίων τε πτόλις ἀνδρῶν.

Cf. Eur. *Phoen.* 234. Cf. the Carian worship of Μολπαδίας Ἡμιθέα : Diod. Sic. 5.62–63 Μολπαδίαν δὲ (the sister of Παρθένος) Ἡμιθέαν ὠνομάσθαι καὶ τιμᾶσθαι παρὰ πᾶσι τοῖς ἐν Χερρονήσῳ. ἐν δὲ ταῖς θυσίαις αὐτῆς ... τὰς μὲν σπονδὰς μελικράτῳ ποιοῦσι, τὸν δὲ ἀψάμενον ἢ φαγόντα ὑὸς οὐ νόμιμον προσελθεῖν πρὸς τὸ τέμενος ... τὰς δυστοκούσας τῶν γυναικῶν τῆς ἐν ταῖς ὠδῖσι ταλαιπωρίας καὶ κινδύνων ἀπαλλάττειν τὴν θεόν.

Artemis associated with Cybele, Bendis, Britomartis, Dictynna.

[126] Strabo, 470 Τούτοις δ' (the rites of Rhea-Cybele) ἔοικε καὶ τὰ παρὰ τοῖς Θρᾳξὶ τά τε Κοτύττια καὶ τὰ Βενδίδεια, παρ' οἷς καὶ τὰ Ὀρφικὰ τὴν καταρχὴν ἔσχε.

[127] Athenae. 14. p. 636 Διογένης ὁ τραγικὸς ... ἐν τῇ Σεμέλῃ :

κλύω δὲ Λυδὰς Βακχίας τε παρθένους
ποταμῷ παροίκους Ἅλυϊ Τμωλίαν θεὸν
δαφνόσκιον κατ' ἄλσος Ἄρτεμιν σέβειν.

[128] Steph. Byz. *s. v.* Μάσταυρα· πόλις Λυδίας ἀπὸ Μᾶς ... ἐκαλεῖτο δὲ καὶ ἡ Ῥέα Μᾶ καὶ ταῦρος αὐτῇ ἐθύετο παρὰ Λυδοῖς. Strabo, 535 τὰ Κόμανα καὶ τὸ τῆς Ἐννοῦς ἱερὸν ἦν ἐκεῖνοι Μᾶ ὀνομάζουσι ... τὰ δὲ ἱερὰ ταῦτα δοκεῖ Ὀρέστης μετὰ τῆς ἀδελφῆς Ἰφιγενείας κομίσαι δεῦρο ἀπὸ τῆς Ταυρικῆς Σκυθίας, τὰ τῆς Ταυροπόλου Ἀρτέμιδος. Cf. Paus. 3. 16, 8 ; Dio. Cass. 36. 13 (Dind.) τὰ δὲ δὴ Κόμανα τῆς τε νῦν Καππαδοκίας ἐστὶ καὶ ἐδόκει τό τε τῆς Ἀρτέμιδος τὸ Ταυρικὸν βρέτας καὶ·τὸ γένος τὸ Ἀγαμεμνόνειον δεῦρο ἀεὶ ἔχειν. Artemis Περασία at Castabala in Cilicia identified with the Tauric goddess : Strabo, 537 ἐν τοῖς Κασταβάλοις ἐστὶ τὸ τῆς Περασίας Ἀρτέμιδος ἱερόν, ὅπου φασὶ τὰς ἱερείας τοῖς ποσὶ δι' ἀνθρακιᾶς βαδίζειν ἀπαθεῖς· κἀνταῦθα δέ τινες τὴν αὐτὴν θρυλοῦσιν ἱστορίαν τὴν περὶ τοῦ Ὀρέστου καὶ τῆς Ταυροπόλου. Inscription from Byzantium Μητρὶ θεῶν Μᾶ, Mordtmann und Dethier, *Epigraphik von Byzantium*, Taf. 6. 8.

Artemis-Bendis.

[129] Hesych. Βενδῖς· ἡ Ἄρτεμις, Θρακιστί. Palaeph. *de Incred.* 32 καλοῦσι τὴν Ἄρτεμιν Θρᾷκες Βένδειαν Κρῆτες δὲ Δίκτυνναν, Λακεδαιμόνιοι δὲ Οὖπιν. Plat. *Rep.* 327 A κατέβην χθὲς ἐς Πειραιᾶ ... προσευξόμενός τε τῇ θεῷ (Βενδῖδι) ... 328 A οὐδ' ἴστε ὅτι λαμπὰς ἔσται πρὸς ἑσπέραν ἀφ' ἵππων τῇ θεῷ. At Salamis : Foucart, *Associations Religieuses*, 209. Hesych. *s. v.* Βούσβατον· τὴν Ἄρτεμιν Θρᾷκες. *Id. s. v.* Δίλογχος· τὴν Βενδῖν οὕτω Κρατῖνος ἐν Θρᾴτταις ἐκάλεσεν, ἤτοι ὅτι δύο τιμὰς ἐκληρώσατο οὐρανίαν τε καὶ χθονίαν ... ἢ ὅτι δύο λόγχας φέρει, κυνηγετικὴ οὖσα ... τὴν γὰρ Σελήνην Βενδῖν καὶ Ἄρτεμιν νομίζουσι. *Id. s. v.* Μεγάλη θεός· Ἀριστοφάνης ἔφη τὴν Βενδῖν. Θρᾳκία γὰρ ἡ θεός. Cf. Photius, *Lex.* Μεγάλην θεόν· Ἀριστοφάνης ἐν Ληΐ νίαις· ἴσως τὴν Βενδῖν. Strabo, 466 ὥστε καὶ τὰ ἱερὰ τρόπον τινὰ

κοινοποιεῖσθαι ταῦτά τε (the Corybantic rites of Crete) καὶ τῶν Σαμοθρᾴκων καὶ τὰ ἐν Λήμνῳ.

[130] Artemis Φεραία and Bendis [117] : Lycoph. *Cass.* 1174–1180:

> ὦ μῆτερ, ὦ δύσμητερ, οὐδὲ σὸν κλέος
> ἄπυστον ἔσται, Περσέως δὲ παρθένος
> Βριμὼ τρίμορφος θήσεταί σ᾿ ἐπωπίδα
> κλαγγαῖσι ταρβήσουσαν ἐννύχοις βροτούς,
> ὅσοι μεδούσης Στρυμόνος Ζηρυνθίας
> δείκηλα μὴ σέβουσι λαμπαδουχίαις
> θύσθλοις Φεραίαν ἐξακεύμενοι θεάν.

At Alexandria τὸ Βενδιδεῖον mentioned by Synesius, *Epist.* 4 ad init.

Artemis Dictynna-Britomartis.

[131] Diod. Sic. 5. 76 Βριτόμαρτιν τὴν προσαγορευομένην Δίκτυνναν μυθολογοῦσι γενέσθαι μὲν ἐν Καινοῖ τῆς Κρήτης ἐκ Διὸς καὶ Κάρμης τῆς Εὐβούλου τοῦ γεννηθέντος ἐκ Δήμητρος. ταύτην εὑρέτιν γενομένην δικτύων εἰς κυνηγίαν προσαγορευθῆναι Δίκτυνναν. καὶ τὰς μὲν διατριβὰς ποιήσασθαι μετὰ τῆς Ἀρτέμιδος, ἀφ᾿ ἧς αἰτίας ἐνίους δοκεῖν τὴν αὐτὴν εἶναι Δίκτυνναν τε καὶ Ἄρτεμιν. Arist. *Ran.* 1359:

> ἅμα δὲ Δίκτυννα παῖς,
> Ἄρτεμις καλά,
> τὰς κυνίσκας ἔχουσ᾿ ἐλθέτω.

a In Crete: Strabo, 479 τῆς μέντοι Κυδωνίας ὄρος ἐστὶ Τίτυρος, ἐν ᾧ ἱερόν ἐστιν οὐ Δικταῖον, ἀλλὰ Δικτυνναῖον. Herod. 3. 59 τὰ ἱρὰ τὰ ἐν Κυδωνίῃ ἐόντα νῦν οὗτοί (οἱ Σάμιοι) εἰσι οἱ ποιήσαντες, καὶ τὸν τῆς Δικτύνης νηόν (in the time of Polycrates). At Phalasarna in the west of Crete: Dicaearch. 118 :

> φασὶ δ᾿ ἐν Κρήτῃ πόλιν
> εἶναι Φαλάσαρνα κειμένην πρὸς ἥλιον
> δύνοντα, κλειστὸν λιμέν᾿ ἔχουσαν καὶ ἱερὸν
> Ἀρτέμιδος ἅγιον, καλεῖσθαι τὴν θεὸν Δίκτυναν.

At Olus: Paus. 9. 40, 3 ἕτερα ξόανα (Δαιδάλου) ἐν Κρήτῃ, Βριτόμαρτις ἐν Ὀλοῦντι. Cf. *C. I. Gr.* 2554 (alliance between Latus and Olus) Ὅρκος Λατίων· Ὀμνύω τὰν Ἑστίαν καὶ τὸν Ζῆνα τὸν Κρητογενία . . . καὶ τὰν Ἐλευσίναν καὶ τὰν Βριτόμαρτιν. Cauer, *Delect. Inscr. Graec.*² 121 (oath between Cnossus and Dreros) Ὀμνύω τὰν Ἑστίαν καὶ τὸν Δῆνα . . . τὸν Ἀπέλλωνα τὸν Ποίτιον καὶ τὰν Λατοῦν καὶ τὰν Ἄρτεμιν . . . καὶ τὰν Βριτόμαρτιν. Solinus, 11. 8 Cretes Dianam religiosissime venerantur, Britomartem gentiliter nominantes, quod sermone nostro sonat virginem dulcem. Hesych. Βριτόμαρτις· ἐν Κρήτῃ ἡ Ἄρτεμις. *Id. s. v.* Βριτύ· γλυκὺ Κρῆτες. Callim. *in Dian.* 200 (at the feast of Britomartis in Crete) τὸ δὲ στέφος ἤματι κείνῳ ἢ πίτυς ἢ σχῖνος· μύρτοιο δὲ χεῖρες ἄθικτοι.

ᵇ In Aegina: Paus. 2. 30, 3 ἐν Αἰγίνῃ δὲ πρὸς τὸ ὄρος τοῦ Πανελληνίου Διὸς ἰοῦσίν ἐστιν Ἀφαίας ἱερόν, ἐς ἣν καὶ Πίνδαρος ᾆσμα Αἰγινήταις ἐποίησε. Φασὶ δὲ οἱ Κρῆτες, τούτοις γάρ ἐστι τὰ ἐς αὐτὴν ἐπιχώρια, . . . Διὸς δὲ καὶ Κάρμης τῆς Εὐβούλου Βριτόμαρτιν γενέσθαι· χαίρειν δὲ αὐτὴν δρόμοις τε καὶ θήραις, καὶ Ἀρτέμιδι μάλιστα φίλην εἶναι· Μίνω δὲ ἐρασθέντα φεύγουσα ἔρριψεν ἑαυτὴν ἐς δίκτυα ἀφειμένα ἐπ᾽ ἰχθύων θήρᾳ. ταύτην μὲν θεὸν ἐποίησεν Ἄρτεμις, σέβουσι δὲ οὐ Κρῆτες μόνον ἀλλὰ καὶ Αἰγινῆται, λέγοντες φαίνεσθαί σφισιν ἐν τῇ νήσῳ τὴν Βριτόμαρτιν. ἐπίκλησις δέ οἱ παρά τε Αἰγινήταις ἐστὶν Ἀφαία καὶ Δίκτυννα ἐν Κρήτῃ. Steph. Byz. s. v. Ἀφθαία . . . καὶ Ἀφθαία ἡ Ἑκάτη· ? Ἀφαία. Cf. Callim. in Dian. 189.

ᶜ At Sparta : Paus. 3. 12, 8 ἐπὶ δὲ τῷ πέρατι Ἀφεταΐδος, ἐγγύτατα ἤδη τοῦ τείχους, Δικτύννης ἐστὶν ἱερόν, καὶ βασίλειοι τάφοι τῶν καλουμένων Εὐρυπωντιδῶν.

ᵈ On the south coast of Laconia : Paus. 3. 14, 2 ἐπανελθοῦσιν ὀπίσω πρὸς τὴν λέσχην ἐστὶν Ἀρτέμιδος Ἰσσώρας ἱερόν· ἐπονομάζουσι δὲ αὐτὴν καὶ Λιμναίαν, οὖσαν οὐκ Ἄρτεμιν, Βριτόμαρτιν δὲ τὴν Κρητῶν. Hesych. s. v. Ἰσσωρία· ἡ Ἄρτεμις. καὶ ἑορτή· καὶ τόπος ἐν Σπάρτῃ. Steph. Byz. s. v. Ἰσσώριον· ὄρος τῆς Λακωνικῆς, ἀφ᾽ οὗ ἡ Ἄρτεμις Ἰσσωρία. Cf. Plut. Ages. 32.

ᵉ In Delos : Bull. de Corr. Hell. 1882, p. 23, inscription concerning the treasure in Apollo's temple mentions τοὺς χοροὺς Ἀρτεμισίοις Βριταμαρτίοις.

ᶠ ? Near Troezen : Eur. Hipp. 145 :

οὐδ᾽ ἀμφὶ τὰν πολύθηρον
Δίκτυνναν ἀμπλακίαις
ἀνίερος ἀθύτων πελάνων τρύχει

(Schol. ib. τινὲς δὲ τὴν αὐτὴν εἶναι (τὴν Δίκτυνναν) τῇ Ἑκάτῃ). Cf. ¹¹⁴.

ᵍ ? In Cephallenia : Ant. Lib. Trans. 40 ἔπειτα δὲ ἐκ τοῦ Ἄργους εἰς Κεφαλληνίαν ἀνέβη (Βριτόμαρτις) καὶ αὐτὴν ὠνόμασαν οἱ Κεφαλλῆνες Λαφρίαν· καὶ ἱερὸν ἤγαγεν ὡς θεῷ.

ʰ In Massilia : C. I. Gr. 6764 θεᾷ Δικτύᾳ δῆμος Μασσ[ιλιωτῶν].

ⁱ Connected with Apollo Delphinios : Plut. de Soll. Anim. p. 984 B Ἀρτέμιδός γε Δικτύννης Δελφινίου τε Ἀπόλλωνος ἱερὰ καὶ βωμοὶ παρὰ πολλοῖς Ἑλλήνων εἰσίν.

ᵏ ? Connected with Hekate in Crete : Et. Mag. 214. 26, s. v. Βριτόμαρτις. Νεάνθης ἐν τῷ πρώτῳ περὶ τελετῶν φησὶ χρησμὸν Διὶ δοθῆναι ὅτι ἐκ τῆς μήτρας τῆς Ἑκάτης γεννησόμενος μεταστήσει τῆς βασιλείας αὐτόν. γεννηθείσης δὲ τῆς Ἑκάτης, τὰς συμπαρούσας κόρας τῇ λεχοῖ ἀναβοῆσαι, Βρίτον, τουτέστιν ἀγαθόν.

ˡ Artemis Δικτυνναία near Ambrosus in Phocis : Paus. 10. 36, 5 Δικτυνναίας ἐπίκλησιν ἱερόν ἐστιν Ἀρτέμιδος. ταύτην οἱ Ἀμβρωσεῖς ἄγουσι μάλιστα ἐν τιμῇ· τῷ δὲ ἀγάλματι ἐργασία τέ ἐστιν Αἰγιναία καὶ μέλανος τοῦ λίθου πεποίηται.

590   GREEK RELIGION.

^m ? At Astypalaea : Rang. *Antiq. Hellén.* inscr. No. 1199 Τιμόκλεια Σινάνδρου Δικτύννα (? fourth century B.C.).

ⁿ Strabo, 472 Δίκτη τόπος ἐν τῇ Σκηψίᾳ καὶ ὄρος ἐν Κρήτῃ.

¹³² The Persian Artemis-Aphrodite, vide Aphrodite ⁹⁶ ^b : ? on the chest of Cypselus, Paus. 5. 19, 5 Ἄρτεμις δὲ οὐκ οἶδα ἐφ' ὅτῳ λόγῳ πτέρυγας ἔχουσά ἐστιν ἐπὶ τῶν ὤμων, καὶ τῇ μὲν δεξιᾷ κατέχει πάρδαλιν, τῇ δὲ ἑτέρᾳ τῶν χειρῶν λέοντα. Diod. Sic. 5. 77 τιμᾶται δὲ καὶ παρὰ τοῖς Πέρσαις ἡ θεὸς αὕτη διαφερόντως καὶ μυστήρια ποιοῦσιν οἱ βάρβαροι τὰ παρ' ἑτέροις συντελούμενα μέχρι τῶν νῦν χρόνων Ἀρτέμιδι Περσίᾳ. Strabo, 532 ἅπαντα μὲν οὖν τὰ τῶν Περσῶν ἱερὰ καὶ Μῆδοι καὶ Ἀρμένιοι τετιμήκασι, τὰ δὲ τῆς Ἀναίτιδος διαφερόντως Ἀρμένιοι . . . καὶ θυγατέρας οἱ ἐπιφανέστατοι τοῦ ἔθνους ἀνιεροῦσι παρθένους, αἷς νόμος ἐστὶ καταπορνευθείσαις πολὺν χρόνον παρὰ τῇ θεῷ μετὰ ταῦτα δίδοσθαι πρὸς γάμον. Plut. *Lucull.* 24 βόες ἱεραὶ νέμονται Περσίας Ἀρτέμιδος, ἣν μάλιστα θεῶν οἱ πέραν Εὐφράτου βάρβαροι τιμῶσι· χρῶνται δὲ ταῖς βουσὶ πρὸς θυσίαν μόνον, ἄλλως δὲ πλάζονται κατὰ τὴν χώραν ἄφετοι, χαράγματα φέρουσαι τῆς θεοῦ λαμπάδα. Polyb. 31. 11 κατὰ τὴν Συρίαν Ἀντίοχος ὁ βασιλεὺς βουλόμενος εὐπορῆσαι χρημάτων, προέθετο στρατεύειν ἐπὶ τὸ τῆς Ἀρτέμιδος ἱερὸν εἰς τὴν Ἐλυμαΐδα. Clem. Alex. *Protrept.* p. 57 P (from Berosus) Ἀρταξέρξου τοῦ Δαρείου τοῦ Ὤχου . . . ὃς πρῶτος τῆς Ἀφροδίτης Ταναΐδος τὸ ἄγαλμα ἀναστήσας ἐν Βαβυλῶνι καὶ Σούσοις καὶ Ἐκβατάνοις Πέρσαις καὶ Βάκτροις καὶ Δαμάσκῳ καὶ Σάρδεσιν ὑπέδειξε σέβειν. Plut. *Artax.* 27 τῆς Ἀρτέμιδος τῆς ἐν Ἐκβατάνοις, ἣν Ἀναΐτην καλοῦσιν, ἱέρειαν ἀνέδειξεν αὐτὴν ὅπως ἁγνὸν διάγῃ τὸν ἐπίλοιπον βίον. At Zela : Strabo, 512. At Hierocaesarea and Hypaepa in Lydia : Tac. *Ann.* 3. 62 Altius Hierocaesarienses exposuere Persicam apud se Dianam delubrum rege Cyro dicatum. Cf. ⁵³c. Paus. 5. 27, 5 : *id.* 7. 6, 6 τοῦ δὲ Ἀδράστου τούτου χαλκῆν εἰκόνα ἀνέθεσαν οἱ Λυδοὶ πρὸ ἱεροῦ Περσικῆς Ἀρτέμιδος. At Philadelphia : *Bull. de Corr. Hell.* 1884, p. 376 Μητρὶ Ἀναείτιδι. Cf. *C. I. Gr.* 3422 ἱερέα τῆς Ἀρτέμιδος. At Koloe : *Bull. de Corr. Hell.* 1880, 128 Ἀρτέμιδι Ἀναείτι καὶ Μηνὶ Τιάμου. Cf. Μουσ. καὶ Βιβλ. Σμύρν. 1875, p. 47 ἄγαλμα Ἀρτέμιδος . . . καὶ Μηνὸς ἄγαλμα. Artemis Νάνα in the Peiraeeus : *C. I. A.* 3. 131 Ἄξιος καὶ Κλεὼ Ἀρτέμιδι Νάνᾳ εὐξάμενοι ἀνέθηκαν (? third century B.C.). Philo, Bybl. *Frag.* 2. 20 (Müller, *Frag. Hist. Graec.* vol. 3, p. 568) Κρόνῳ ἐγένοντο ἀπὸ Ἀστάρτης θυγατέρες ἑπτὰ Τιτανίδες ἢ Ἀρτέμιδες. At Attaleia in Lydia : Μουσ. καὶ Βιβλ. Σμύρν. 1885–1886, p. 51 Ἀρτέμιδι Περσικῇ καὶ τῷ δήμῳ Γλύκων, &c. Cf. *C. I. Gr.* 3424 τὰ μεγάλα Σεβαστὰ Ἀναείτεια.

¹³³ Artemis of Ephesus ^a : Paus. 7. 2, 4 πολλῷ πρεσβύτερα ἢ κατὰ Ἴωνας τὰ ἐς τὴν Ἄρτεμιν τὴν Ἐφεσίαν εἶναι . . . Λέλεγες δὲ τοῦ Καρικοῦ μοῖρα καὶ Λυδῶν τὸ πολὺ οἱ νεμόμενοι τὴν χώραν ἦσαν. ᾤκουν δὲ καὶ περὶ τὸ ἱερὸν ἄλλοι τε

ἱκεσίας ἕνεκα καὶ γυναῖκες τοῦ Ἀμαζόνων γένους. Id. 4. 31, 8 Ἐφεσίαν δὲ Ἄρτεμιν πόλεις τε νομίζουσιν αἱ πᾶσαι καὶ ἄνδρες ἰδίᾳ θεῶν μάλιστα ἄγουσιν ἐν τιμῇ. τὰ δὲ αἴτια ἐμοὶ δοκεῖν ἐστὶν Ἀμαζόνων τὸ κλέος, αἱ φήμην τὸ ἄγαλμα ἔχουσιν ἱδρύσασθαι, καὶ ὅτι ἐκ παλαιοτάτου τὸ ἱερὸν τοῦτο ἐποιήθη. τρία δὲ ἄλλα ἐπὶ τούτοις συνετέλεσεν ἐς δόξαν, μέγεθός τε τοῦ ναοῦ τὰ παρὰ πᾶσιν ἀνθρώποις κατασκευάσματα ὑπερηρκότος, καὶ Ἐφεσίων τῆς πόλεως ἡ ἀκμή, καὶ ἐν αὐτῇ τὸ ἐπιφανὲς τῆς θεοῦ. Callim. in Dian. 237 Σοὶ καὶ Ἀμαζονίδες ... ἔν κοτε παρραλίῃ Ἐφέσῳ βρέτας ἱδρύσαντο φηγῷ ὑπ' εὐπρέμνῳ. Tac. Ann. 3. 61 Primi omnium Ephesii adiere, memorantes non, ut vulgus crederet, Dianam atque Apollinem Delo genitos : esse apud se Cenchrium amnem, lucum Ortygiam, ubi Latonam partu gravidam et oleae, quae tum etiam maneat, adnisam, edidisse ea numina ... Mox Liberum patrem, bello victorem supplicibus Amazonum, quae aram insederant, ignovisse. Auctam hinc concessu Herculis, cum Lydia poteretur, caerimoniam templo. Strabo, 639 εἶτα λιμὴν Πάνορμος καλούμενος ἔχων ἱερὸν τῆς Ἐφεσίας Ἀρτέμιδος· εἶθ' ἡ πόλις. ἐν δὲ τῇ αὐτῇ παραλίᾳ ... ἐστὶ καὶ ἡ Ὀρτυγία, διαπρεπὲς ἄλσος. Thuc. 3. 104 ἦν δέ ποτε καὶ τὸ πάλαι μεγάλη σύνοδος ἐς τὴν Δῆλον τῶν Ἰώνων ... ξύν τε γὰρ γυναιξὶ καὶ παισὶν ἐθεώρουν, ὥσπερ νῦν ἐς Ἐφέσια Ἴωνες. Paus. 10. 38, 6 ἐν δὲ Ἀρτέμιδος τῆς Ἐφεσίας ... ὑπὲρ τοῦ βωμοῦ τῆς Πρωτοθρονίας καλουμένης Ἀρτέμιδος. Dion. Halic. Ant. Rom. 4. 25 Ἴωνες μέν, ἐν Ἐφέσῳ, τὸ τῆς Ἀρτέμιδος (ἱερὸν κατεσκεύασαν) ... ἔνθα συνιόντες ... ἀγῶνας ἐπετέλουν ἱππικοὺς καὶ γυμνικούς, καὶ τῶν περὶ μουσικὴν ἀκουσμάτων. C. I. Gr. 2954, a fragment of an Ephesian decree, Πανταχοῦ ἀνεῖσθαι αὐτῆς ἱερὰ ... αὐτή τε εἰδρύσθαι καὶ βωμοὺς ἀνακεῖσθαι διὰ τὰς ὑπ' αὐτῆς γεινομένας ἐναργεῖς ἐπιφανείας ... διὸ δεδόχθαι ὅλον τὸν μῆνα τὸν Ἀρτεμισιῶνα εἶναι [ἱερὸν πάσας τ]ὰς ἡμέρας, ἄγεσθαι δὲ ἐπ' αὐταῖς τὰς ἑορτὰς καὶ τὴν τῶν Ἀρτεμ[ισίων πανήγ]υριν. Et. Mag. 383. 30 Ἐσσήν· ὁ βασιλεὺς κατὰ Ἐφεσίους· ἀπὸ μεταφορᾶς τοῦ μελισσῶν βασιλέως, ὃς εἴρηται ἐσσήν: vide [124]. Strabo, 641 ἱερέας δ' εὐνούχους εἶχον οὓς ἐκάλουν Μεγαβύζους ... καὶ ἦγον ἐν τιμῇ μεγάλῃ· συνιερᾶσθαι δὲ τούτοις ἐχρῆν παρθένους ... ἄσυλον δὲ μένει τὸ ἱερὸν καὶ νῦν καὶ πρότερον. Cf. Xen. Anab. 5. 3, 6 Μεγαβύζῳ τῷ τῆς Ἀρτέμιδος νεωκόρῳ. Plut. An. sen. sit ger. resp. p. 795 D τῶν ἐν Ἐφέσῳ περὶ τὴν Ἄρτεμιν, ὁμοίως ἑκάστην Μελλιέρην τοπρῶτον εἶτα Ἱέρην, τὸ δὲ τρίτον Παριέρην καλοῦσιν: priestess of Artemis, Heliod. Aeth. 1. 12. Et. Mag. p. 402. 20 ἱκεσία γὰρ ἡ θεός (ἡ Ἐφεσία Ἄρτεμις) στεφάνοις δὲ διὰ θαλλῶν τὰς ἱκεσίας ποιοῦσιν· ὅθεν οὐδὲ πρόβατα αὐτῇ θύουσι διὰ τὸ τοὺς ἱκέτας μαλλοὺς προσφέρειν. C. I. Gr. 2955 ἐπὶ πρυτανέως Τιβ. Κλαυδίου Τιτιανοῦ, ... ἀρχιερέως, ἱερατεύοντος Σοσσιανοῦ ... ναυβατούντων Χαριδήμου. ... C. I. Gr. 6797 :

Ἰητῆρι νόσων, φαεσιμβρότῳ Ἀπόλλωνι
ἄνασσαν Ἐφέσου Κρησίαν φαεσφόρον
εὐχὴν ἔθηκεν Εὐτύχης (? third century B.C.).

Artem. *Oneirocr.* 4. 4 γυνὴ ἔδοξεν εἰς τὸν νεὼν τῆς Ἀρτέμιδος τῆς Ἐφεσίας εἰσεληλυθέναι· οὐκ ἐς μακρὰν ἀπέθανε· θάνατος γὰρ ἡ ζημία τῇ εἰσελθούσῃ ἐκεῖ γυναικί. *Ib.* 2. 35 τοῖς δὲ τὸν σεμνότερον ἐπανῃρημένοις βίον ἡ κατεσταλμένη τῷ σχήματι (Ἄρτεμις) ἀμείνων, οἷον ἡ Ἐφεσία καὶ ἡ Περγαία καὶ ἡ λεγομένη παρὰ Λυκίοις Ἐλευθέρα. Hesych. *s. v.* Ἐλουσία· Ἄρτεμις παρὰ Ἐφεσίοις.

b At Massilia: Strabo, 179 ἐν δὲ τῇ ἄκρᾳ τὸ Ἐφέσιον ἵδρυται καὶ τὸ τοῦ Δελφινίου Ἀπόλλωνος ἱερόν . . . ἀπαίρουσι γὰρ τοῖς Φωκαιεῦσιν ἐκ τῆς οἰκείας λόγιον ἐκπεσεῖν φασιν ἡγεμόνι χρήσασθαι τοῦ πλοῦ παρὰ τῆς Ἐφεσίας Ἀρτέμιδος λαβοῦσι . . . ἔν δέ τε ταῖς ἀποίκοις πόλεσι πανταχοῦ τιμᾶν ἐν τοῖς πρώτοις ταύτην τὴν θεὸν καὶ τοῦ ξοάνου τὴν διάθεσιν τὴν αὐτὴν καὶ τἄλλα νόμιμα φυλάττειν τὰ αὐτὰ ἄπερ ἐν τῇ μητροπόλει νενόμισται. Another temple at the mouth of the Rhone, *id.* 184.

c In Rome: Strabo, 180 καὶ δὴ καὶ τὸ ξόανον τῆς Ἀρτέμιδος τῆς ἐν τῷ Ἀβεντίνῳ οἱ Ῥωμαῖοι τὴν αὐτὴν διάθεσιν ἔχον τῷ παρὰ τοῖς Μασσαλιώταις ἀνέθεσαν. Cf. 159, in Spain, τρία πολίχνια Μασσιλιωτῶν ἔστιν οὐ πολὺ ἄπωθεν τοῦ ποταμοῦ· τούτων δ᾽ ἐστὶ γνωριμώτατον τὸ Ἡμεροσκοπεῖον ἔχον ἐπὶ τῇ ἄκρᾳ τῆς Ἐφεσίας Ἀρτέμιδος ἱερὸν σφόδρα τιμώμενον. At Emporiae: *id.* 160.

d In the territory of Scillus in Elis: Xen. *An.* 5. 3, 7 Ξενοφῶν δὲ λαβὼν χωρίον ὠνεῖται τῇ θεῷ . . . ὁ δὲ ναὸς ὡς μικρὸς μεγάλῳ τῷ ἐν Ἐφέσῳ εἴκασται, καὶ τὸ ξόανον ἔοικεν ὡς κυπαρίττινον χρυσῷ ὄντι τῷ ἐν Ἐφέσῳ : vide ⁵⁴d. Cf. Paus. 5. 6, 5.

e At Alea in Arcadia: Paus. 5. 23, 1 (ἱερὸν) Ἀρτέμιδός ἐστιν Ἐφεσίας.

f At Megalopolis: Paus. 8. 30, 6 Ἐφεσίας ἄγαλμα Ἀρτέμιδος.

g At Corinth: Paus. 2. 2, 5 ἔστιν οὖν ἐπὶ τῆς ἀγορᾶς . . . Ἄρτεμίς τε ἐπίκλησιν Ἐφεσία.

h Smyrna: *C. I. Gr.* 3155 οἵδε ἱδρύσαντο τὸ τέμενος Ἀρτέμιδι Ἐφεσίᾳ (early Roman period.)

i Aphrodisias: *C. I. Gr.* 2823 Αἰλίαν Λαβίλλαν, Ἀσίας ἀρχιέρειαν, καὶ κοσμήτειραν τῆς Ἐφεσίας Ἀρτέμιδος καὶ ἀρχιέρειαν τῆς λαμπροτάτης Ἀφροδισιέων πόλεως.

k At Panticapaeum: *C. I. Gr.* 2104b (ὁ δεῖνα) ὑπὲρ τῆς θυγατρὸς Ἰτίης Ἀρτέμιδι Ἐφεσείῃ (fourth century B. C.).

l At Chios: *C. I. Gr.* 2228, private dedication.

134a Artemis Λευκοφρυηνή at Magnesia on the Maeander: Xen. *Hell.* 3. 2, 19 τὰ μὲν στρατεύματα ἀπῆλθε . . . τὸ δ᾽ Ἑλληνικὸν εἰς Λευκοφρύν, ἔνθα ἦν Ἀρτέμιδός τε ἱερὸν μάλα ἅγιον, καὶ λίμνη πλέον ἢ σταδίου ὑπόψαμμος ἀέναος ποτίμου καὶ θερμοῦ ὕδατος. Tac. *Ann.* 3. 62 Proximi Magnetes

REFERENCES FOR CHAPTERS XIII–XIX. 593

L. Scipionis et L. Sullae constitutis nitebantur ut Dianae Leucophrynae perfugium inviolabile foret. Strabo, 647 ἐνταῦθα δ' ἦν καὶ τὸ τῆς Δινδυμήνης ἱερὸν μητρὸς θεῶν· ἱεράσασθαι δ' αὐτοῦ τὴν Θεμιστοκλέους γυναῖκα. νῦν δ' οὐκ ἔστι τὸ ἱερὸν διὰ τὸ τὴν πόλιν εἰς ἄλλον μετῳκίσθαι τόπον· ἐν δὲ τῇ νῦν πόλει τὸ τῆς Λευκοφρυηνῆς ἱερὸν ἔστιν Ἀρτέμιδος, ὃ τῷ μὲν μεγέθει τοῦ ναοῦ καὶ τῷ πλήθει τῶν ἀναθημάτων λείπεται τοῦ ἐν Ἐφέσῳ, τῇ δὲ εὐρυθμίᾳ καὶ τῇ τέχνῃ . . . πολὺ διαφέρει. καὶ τῷ μεγέθει ὑπεραίρει πάντας τοὺς ἐν Ἀσίᾳ πλὴν δυεῖν, τοῦ ἐν Ἐφέσῳ καὶ τοῦ ἐν Διδύμοις. καὶ τὸ παλαιὸν δὲ συνέβη τοῖς Μάγνησιν ὑπὸ Τρηρῶν ἄρδην ἀναιρεθῆναι, Κιμμερικοῦ ἔθνους, . . . τὸ δὲ ἑξῆς τοὺς Ἐφεσίους κατασχεῖν τὸν τόπον. *Bull. de Corr. Hell.* 1891, p. 539, inscription of (?) first century B.C. found on the site, ἡ βουλὴ καὶ ὁ δῆμος καὶ ἡ γερουσία ἐτίμησαν Νεμέριον Κλούιον Μαν(ί)ου υἱὸν . . . εὐσεβῶς μὲν διακείμενον πρὸς τὴν Ἄρτεμιν τὴν Λευκοφρυηνήν.

b In Crete: *C. I. Gr.* 2561 b, l. 25 ἀποδειχθέντες οὖν καὶ αὐτοὶ κριταὶ παραχρῆμα ἀναβάντες ἐπὶ τὸν βωμὸν τῆς Ἀρτέμιδος τῆς Λευκοφρυηνῆς . . . ὠμόσαμεν καθ' ἱερῶν : ? towards the end of second century B.C. Cf. Strabo, 636 Μαγνησία ἡ πρὸς Μαιάνδρῳ Μαγνήτων ἀποικία τῶν ἐν Θετταλίᾳ καὶ Κρητῶν.

c At Amyclae: Paus. 3. 18, 9 Βαθυκλέους δὲ Μάγνητος ὃς τὸν θρόνον ἐποίησε ἀναθήματα ἐπ' ἐξεργασμένῳ τῷ θρόνῳ Χάριτες καὶ ἄγαλμα δὲ Λευκοφρυηνῆς ἐστιν Ἀρτέμιδος.

d At Athens: Paus. 1. 26, 4 χαλκοῦν Ἀρτέμιδος ἄγαλμα ἔστηκεν ἐπίκλησιν Λευκοφρυηνῆς, ἀνέθεσαν δὲ οἱ παῖδες οἱ Θεμιστοκλέους.

Artemis-Upis.

135 In Lacedaemon, vide 129. At Troezen: Schol. Apollon. 1. 972 ὄρπιγγος (? οὔπιγγος) παρὰ Τροιζηνίοις (ὕμνος) εἰς Ἄρτεμιν. Athenae. p. 619 οὔπιγγοι δὲ (ᾠδαὶ) αἱ εἰς Ἄρτεμιν. In Ephesus, Upis-Artemis: Macr. *Sat.* 5. 22, quoting from Alexander Aetolus, ταχέων Ὦπιν βλήτειραν ὀϊστῶν. Callim. *in Dian.* 204 Ὦπι ἄνασσ' εὐῶπι φαεσφόρε. *Et. Mag.* p. 641. 55 Οὖπις· ἐπίθετον Ἀρτέμιδος ἢ παρὰ τὸ ὀπίζεσθαι τὰς τικτούσας αὐτήν, ἢ παρὰ τὴν θρέψασαν αὐτὴν Οὖπιν. Hesych. *s. v.* Ὦπι ἄνασσα παρὰ προθύροις. Cic. *de Nat. Deor.* 3. 58 Tertiae (Dianae) pater Upis traditur, Glauce mater; eam saepe Graeci Upim paterno nomine appellant. *C. I. Gr.* 6280 ἥ τ' ἐπὶ ἔργα βροτῶν ὁράᾳς Ῥαμνουσιὰς Οὖπι.

136 Artemis Ὀπιταῖς in Zacynthos: *C. I. Gr.* 1934 Ἀρχικλῆς . . . καὶ Ἀλκιδάμα τὰν αὐτῶν θυγατέρα θεοκολήσασαν Ἀρτέμιτι Ὀπιταῖδι.

? Artemis-Nemesis.

137 Hesiod. *Theog.* 223 :

τίκτε δὲ καὶ Νέμεσιν πῆμα θνητοῖσι βροτοῖσι
νὺξ ὀλοή.

Cypria, *Frag.* 5 Düntzer :

τοὺς δὲ μέτα τριτάτην Ἑλένην τρέφε θαῦμα βροτοῖσι,
τήν ποτε καλλίκομος Νέμεσις φιλότητι μιγεῖσα
Ζηνὶ θεῶν βασιλῆι τέκε κρατερῆς ὑπ' ἀνάγκης
φεῦγε γὰρ οὐδ' ἔθελεν μιχθήμεναι ἐν φιλότητι
πατρὶ Διῒ Κρονίωνι· . . .
κατὰ γῆν δὲ καὶ ἀτρύγετον μέλαν ὕδωρ
φεῦγε, Ζεὺς δ' ἐδίωκε. . . .
ἄλλοτε μὲν κατὰ κῦμα πολυφλοίσβοιο θαλάσσης
ἰχθύϊ εἰδομένη· . . . γίγνετο δ' αἰεὶ
θηρί' ὅσ' ἤπειρος αἰνὰ τρέφει, ὄφρα φύγοι νιν.

Eratosth. *Catast.* 25 Κύκνος . . . λέγεται δὲ τὸν Δία ὁμοιωθῆναι τῷ ζῴῳ τούτῳ Νεμέσεως ἐρασθῆναι . . . ὁμοιωθέντα τῇ ὀρνέῳ καταπτῆναι εἰς Ῥαμνοῦντα τῆς Ἀττικῆς κἀκεῖ τὴν Νέμεσιν φθεῖραι· τὴν δὲ τεκεῖν ᾠὸν ἐξ οὗ ἐκκολαφθῆναι καὶ γενέσθαι τὴν Ἑλένην, ὥς φησι Κρατῖνος ὁ ποιητής. Cf. Meineke, *Frag. Com. Graec.* 2. p. 82. Clemens Rom. *Homil.* 5. 13 (Dressel, p. 143. 12) Νεμέσει τῇ Θεσπίου τῇ καὶ Λήδᾳ νομισθείσῃ κύκνος ἢ χὴν γενόμενος Ἑλένην ἐτεκνώσατο. Bekk. *Anecd.* p. 282. 32 Νεμέσια πανήγυρίς τις ἐπὶ τοῖς νεκροῖς ἀγομένη, ἐπεὶ ἡ Νέμεσις ἐπὶ τῶν ἀποθανόντων τέτακται. Demosth. πρὸς Σπουδ. p. 1031 εἰσενεγκούσης τῆς ἐμῆς γυναικὸς εἰς τὰ νεμέσεια τῷ πατρὶ μνᾶν ἀργυρίου. Cf. Soph. *El.* 792 Ἄκουε, Νέμεσι τοῦ θανόντος ἀρτίως. Cf. Tim. Locr. *De An. Mund.* c. 12 ad fin., Mullach, *Frag. Phil. Graec.* 2. p. 46.

a Nemesis at Rhamnus : Paus. 1. 33, 2 δοκεῖ δὲ καὶ τοῖς ἀποβᾶσιν ἐς Μαραθῶνα τῶν βαρβάρων ἀπαντῆσαι μήνιμα ἐκ τοῦ θεοῦ ταύτης (Νεμέσεως) . . . λίθον Πάριον ὡς ἐπ' ἐξειργασμένοις ἦγον ἐς τροπαίου ποίησιν. Τοῦτον Φειδίας τὸν λίθον εἰργάσατο, ἄγαλμα μὲν εἶναι Νεμέσεως, τῇ κεφαλῇ δὲ ἔπεστι τῆς θεοῦ στέφανος ἐλάφους ἔχων καὶ Νίκης ἀγάλματα οὐ μεγάλα· ταῖς δὲ χερσὶν ἔχει τῇ μὲν κλάδον μηλέας, τῇ δεξιᾷ δὲ φιάλην. Αἰθίοπες δὲ ἐπὶ τῇ φιάλῃ πεποίηνται . . . Νεμέσει δὲ εἶναι πατέρα Ὠκεανὸν (φασί) . . . πτερὰ δὲ ἔχον οὔτε τοῦτο τὸ ἄγαλμα Νεμέσεως οὔτε ἄλλο πεποίηται τῶν ἀρχαίων . . . ἐπὶ τῷ βάθρῳ . . . Φειδίας πεποίηκε μὲν Ἑλένην ὑπὸ Λήδας ἀγομένην παρὰ τὴν Νέμεσιν. Zenob. 5. 82 Ῥαμνουσία Νέμεσις· ἐν Ῥαμνοῦντι Νεμέσεως ἵδρυται ἄγαλμα δεκάπηχυ ὁλόλιθον ἔργον Φειδίου, ἔχει δὲ ἐν τῇ χειρὶ μηλέας κλάδον· ἐξ οὗ φησιν Ἀντίγονος ὁ Καρύστιος πτύχιόν τι μικρὸν ἐξηρτῆσθαι τὴν ἐπιγραφὴν ἔχον· Ἀγαρόκριτος Πάριος ἐποίησεν. Phot. *s. v.* Ῥαμνουσία Νέμεσις· αὕτη πρῶτον ἀφίδρυτο ἐν Ἀφροδίτης σχήματι· διὸ καὶ κλάδον εἶχε μηλέας. Plin. 36. 17 Certavere autem inter se ambo discipuli (Alcamenes et Agoracritus) Venere facienda vicitque Alcamenes non opere sed civitatis suffragiis contra peregrinum suo faventis. Quare Agoracritus ea lege signum suum vendidisse traditur ne Athenis esset et appellasse Nemesin : id positum est Rhamnunte pago Atticae. Solinus, *Collect. rer. Memorab.*

7. 26 Ramne quoque in qua . . . Phidiacae signum Dianae. *C. I. A.*
3. 289 ἱερέως Οὐρανίας Νεμέσεως, late period : dedications to Themis and
Nemesis *C. I. A.* 2. 1570 and 1571. Artemid. *Oneir.* 2. 37 Ἀριστοβούλη
καὶ Εὐνομία τὰ αὐτὰ τῇ Νεμέσει σημαίνουσι.

ᵇ At Patrae : Paus. 7. 20, 9 τοῦ θεάτρου δὲ οὐ πόρρω Νεμέσεως ναὸς
καὶ ἕτερος ἔστιν Ἀφροδίτης.

ᶜ At Smyrna : Paus. 7. 5, 3 οὕτω μετῳκίσαντο ἐθελονταί (οἱ Σμυρναῖοι)
καὶ δύο Νεμέσεις νομίζουσιν ἀντὶ μιᾶς. καὶ μητέρα αὐταῖς φασὶν εἶναι Νύκτα.
Id. 9. 35, 6 Σμυρναίοις . . . ἐν τῷ ἱερῷ τῶν Νεμέσεων ὑπὲρ τῶν ἀγαλμάτων
χρυσοῦ Χάριτες ἀνάκεινται, τέχνη Βουπάλου. *C. I. Gr.* 3161, inscription
from Smyrna, ? third century B. C., ἀγαθῇ τύχῃ τὰς Νεμέσεις Μελίτων
ἀνέθηκε θεῷ Βρήσει Διονύσῳ. *Id.* 6280 A : late inscription mentioning
swine-sacrifice to the Nemeseis.

ᵈ Νέμεσις with Πειθώ at Mylasa : *Bull. de Corr. Hell.* 1881, p. 39.

¹³⁸ Adrasteia ᵃ connected with Cybele : Strabo, 588 (in the neighbourhood of Priapus on the Hellespont) ἐκαλεῖτο δ᾽ ἡ χώρα αὕτη Ἀδρά-
στεια καὶ Ἀδραστείας πεδίον . . . φησὶ δὲ Καλλισθένης ὑπὸ Ἀδράστου
βασιλέως, ὃς πρῶτος Νεμέσεως ἱερὸν ἱδρύσατο, καλεῖσθαι Ἀδράστειαν. Aesch.
Niob. Frag. 155 Βερέκυντα χῶρον ἔνθ᾽ Ἀδραστείας ἔδος. Schol. Ap.
Rhod. 1. 1129 (fragment of the Phoronis) ἔνθα γόητες Ἰδαῖοι Φρύγες
ἄνδρες ὀρέστεροι οἰκί᾽, ἔναιον Κέλμις Δαμναμενεύς τε μέγας καὶ ὑπέρβιος Ἄκμων
Εὐπάλαμοι θεράποντες ὀρείης Ἀδρηστείης. Cf. Charax in Müll. *Frag.
Hist. Graec.* 3, p. 637, fr. 2 ἔστι δὲ καὶ Τρωάδος Ἀδράστεια τόπος ἀπὸ
Ἀδραστείας θυγατρὸς Μελίσσου τοῦ Ἴδης. Steph. Byz. *s. v.* Ἀδράστεια·
Διογένης οὕτως ἐν πρώτῃ περὶ Κυζίκου φησὶν ἀπὸ Ἀδραστείας κεκλῆσθαι μιᾶς τῶν
ὀρεστειάδων νυμφῶν. Cf. Strabo, 575 (near Cyzicus) τὸ ἀντικείμενον ὄρος ὃ
καλοῦσιν Ἀδραστείας. *Id.* 588 ἐνταῦθα μὲν οὖν (near Priapus) οὐδὲν ἱερὸν
Ἀδραστείας δείκνυται, οὐδὲ δὴ Νεμέσεως, περὶ δὲ Κύζικον ἔστιν Ἀδραστείας
ἱερόν. Callim. *in Iov.* 47 Ζεῦ σὲ δὲ Κυρβάντων ἕταραι προσεπηχύναντο
Δικταῖαι μελίαι, σὲ δὲ κοίμισεν Ἀδρήστεια λίκνῳ ἔνι χρυσέῳ. Cf. Procl.
Theol. Plat. 4. 16, p. 206 παρ᾽ Ὀρφεῖ καὶ φρουρεῖν λέγεται (Ἀδράστεια)
τὸν ὅλον δημιουργὸν καὶ χάλκεα ῥόπτρα λαβοῦσα καὶ τύμπανον αἴγηκες. Plut.
Quaest. Conviv. 657 E οἱ παλαιοὶ τοῦ μὲν Διὸς δύο ποιεῖν τιθήνας τὴν Ἴτην
καὶ τὴν Ἀδράστειαν.

ᵇ With Artemis : Harpocr. *s. v.* Ἀδράστειαν· οἱ μὲν τὴν αὐτὴν λέγουσι
τῇ Νεμέσει . . . Δημήτριος δὲ ὁ Σκήψιος Ἄρτεμιν φησιν εἶναι τὴν Ἀδράστειαν
ὑπὸ Ἀδράστου τινὸς ἱδρυμένην. *C. I. A.* 1. 210 Ἀδρ[αστείας] καὶ Βε[νδῖδος]
ἐγκυκλ[ίου] καρποῦ ἐκ [τῶν] ἱερῶν. At Cyrrha : Paus. 10. 37, 8 παρέχεται δὲ
καὶ ἐς θέαν Ἀπόλλωνος καὶ Ἀρτέμιδος καὶ Λητοῦς ναόν τε καὶ ἀγάλματα μεγέθει
μεγάλα καὶ ἐργασίας Ἀττικῆς. ἡ δὲ Ἀδράστεια ἵδρυται μὲν ἐν τῷ αὐτῷ σφίσι.

c Ἀδράστεια-Νέμεσις joint worship in Andros : *Mitt. d. d. Ath. Inst.* 1876, p. 243 Νέμεσις καὶ Ἀδράστεια : ? second century B. C.   In Cos : *Bull. de Corr. Hell.* 1881, 223 ἱερὰς Ἀδραστείας καὶ Νεμέσιος : ? first century B. C.   Strabo, 588 Ἀντίμαχος δ᾽ οὕτω φησίν· ἔστι δέ τις Νέμεσις μεγάλη θεός, ἡ τάδε πάντα πρὸς μακαρῶν ἔλαχεν· βωμὸν δέ οἱ εἴσατο πρῶτος Ἄδρηστος, ποταμοῖο παρὰ ῥόον Αἰσήποιο ἔνθα τετίμηταί τε καὶ Ἀδρήστεια καλεῖται. Aesch. *Prom.* 936 οἱ προσκυνοῦντες τὴν Ἀδράστειαν σοφοί. Eur. *Rhes.* 342 Ἀδράστεια μὲν ἁ Διὸς παῖς εἴργοι στομάτων φθόνου : *ib.* 468 σὺν δ᾽ Ἀδραστείᾳ λέγω.   Menander, Koch, *Frag. Com. Attic.* 3, p. 93 Ἀδράστεια καὶ θεὰ σκύθρωπε Νέμεσι συγγινώσκετε.   Nonn. *Dionys.* 48. 451 Παρθένος Ἀδρήστεια μετῆϊε δύσγαμον Αὔρην γρῦπας ἀμιλλητῆρας ὑποζεύξασα χαλινῷ. *Anth. Pal.* 9. 405 Ἀδρήστειά σε δῖα καὶ ἰχναίη σε φυλάσσοι Παρθένος ἡ πολλοὺς ψευσαμένη Νέμεσις.

HEKATE.

1 Hes. *Theog.* 409 :

Ἀστερίην εὐώνυμον ἥν ποτε Πέρσης
ἠγάγετ᾽ ἐς μέγα δῶμα φίλην κεκλῆσθαι ἄκοιτιν.
ἡ δ᾽ ὑποκυσαμένη Ἑκάτην τέκε, τὴν περὶ πάντων
Ζεὺς Κρονίδης τίμησε. πόρεν δέ οἱ ἀγλαὰ δῶρα,
μοῖραν ἔχειν γαίης τε καὶ ἀτρυγέτοιο θαλάσσης.
ἡ δὲ καὶ ἀστερόεντος ἀπ᾽ οὐρανοῦ ἔμμορε τιμῆς . . .
ᾧ δ᾽ ἐθέλει μεγάλως παραγίνεται ἠδ᾽ ὀνίνησιν·
ἔν τ᾽ ἀγορῇ λαοῖσι μεταπρέπει, ὅν κ᾽ ἐθέλῃσιν.
οἱ δ᾽ ὁπότ᾽ ἐς πόλεμον φθισήνορα θωρήσσωνται
ἀνέρες, ἔνθα θεὰ παραγίνεται, οἷς κ᾽ ἐθέλῃσι,
νίκην προφρονέως ὀπάσαι καὶ κῦδος ὀρέξαι·
ἔν τε δίκῃ βασιλεῦσι παρ᾽ αἰδοίοισι καθίζει·
ἐσθλὴ δ᾽ αὖθ᾽, ὁπότ᾽ ἄνδρες ἀγῶνι ἀεθλεύωσιν . . .
καὶ τοῖς οἳ γλαυκὴν δυσπέμφελον ἐργάζονται,
εὔχονται δ᾽ Ἑκάτῃ καὶ ἐρικτύπῳ Ἐννοσιγαίῳ,
ῥηϊδίως δ᾽ ἄγρην κυδὴ θεὸς ὤπασε πολλήν . . .
ἐσθλὴ δ᾽ ἐν σταθμοῖσι σὺν Ἑρμῇ ληΐδ᾽ ἀέξειν . . .
οὕτω τοι καὶ μουνογενὴς ἐκ μητρὸς ἐοῦσα
πᾶσι μετ᾽ ἀθανάτοισι τετίμηται γεράεσσι.
θῆκε δέ μιν Κρονίδης κουροτρόφον.

2 Schol. Ap. Rhod. 3. 467 ἐν δὲ τοῖς Ὀρφικοῖς Δήμητρος γενεαλογεῖται· καὶ τότε δὴ Ἑκάτην Δηὼ τέκεν εὐπατέρειαν . . . Μουσαῖος δὲ Ἀστερίας καὶ Διός. Φερεκύδης δὲ Ἀρισταίου τοῦ Παίωνος· Ἀπολλώνιος δὲ Περσέως.

3 Bacchyl. fr. 40 Bergk Ἑκάτα δᾳδοφόρε Νυκτὸς μελανοκόλπου θύγατερ. Eur. *Phoen.* 108 Παῖ Λατοῦς Ἑκάτα.

4 Paus. 1. 43, 1 οἶδα δὲ Ἡσίοδον ποιήσαντα ἐν καταλόγῳ γυναικῶν Ἰφιγένειαν οὐκ ἀποθανεῖν, γνώμῃ δὲ Ἀρτέμιδος Ἑκάτην εἶναι.

Hekate of Pherae.

⁵ Schol. Lycophr. 1180 Φεραίαν· Ἑκάτη, ἐκ Φεραίας, τῆς Αἰόλου θυγατρός, κἀκ τοῦ Διὸς ἐτέχθη, καὶ ἐν τριόδοις ἐρρίφθη . . . Φεραίαν δὲ ὡς ἐν ταῖς Φεραῖς τιμωμένην. Cf. Artemis [117]; Schol. Theocr. 2. 36.

⁶ Polyaen. *Strat.* 8. 42 ἱέρεια τῆς Ἐνοδίας in Thessaly.

⁷ In Aegina : Paus. 2. 30, 2 θεῶν δὲ Αἰγινῆται τιμῶσιν Ἑκάτην μάλιστα καὶ τελετὴν ἄγουσιν ἀνὰ πᾶν ἔτος Ἑκάτης, Ὀρφέα σφίσι τὸν Θρᾶκα καταστήσασθαι τὴν τελετὴν λέγοντες. τοῦ περιβόλου δὲ ἐντὸς ναός ἐστι· ξόανον δὲ ἔργον Μύρωνος, ὁμοίως ἓν πρόσωπόν τε καὶ τὸ λοιπὸν σῶμα. Cf. Liban. ὑπὲρ Ἀριστ. p. 426 R φίλος Ἑκάτῃ καὶ Ποσειδῶνι πλέων μὲν ἐς Αἴγιναν ὑπὲρ τῶν ἐκείνης ὀργίων. Cf. Lucian, *Navig.* 15. Schol. Arist. *Pax* 276 ἐν Σαμοθράκῃ ἦσαν τελεταί τινες ἃς ἐδόκουν τελεῖσθαι πρὸς ἀλεξιφάρμακά τινα κινδύνων· ἐν δὲ τῇ Σαμοθράκῃ τὰ τῶν Κορυβάντων ἦν μυστήρια καὶ τὰ τῆς Ἑκάτης καὶ διαβόητον ἦν τὸ Ζήρινθον ἄντρον ἔνθα τὴν Ἑκάτην ὀργιάζειν ἐλέγετο καὶ τελετὰς ἦγον αὐτῇ τινὰς καὶ κύνας ἔθυον. καὶ ὁ τὴν Ἀλεξάνδραν πεποιηκὼς μέμνηται " Ζήρινθον ἄντρον καὶ κυνοσφαγοῦς θεᾶς λιπὼν ἐρυμνὸν κτίσμα Κυρβάντων Σάον."

⁸ At Delos: *Bull. de Corr. Hell.* 1882, p. 48 (list of treasures in the temple of Apollo) ἄλλο ποτήριον . . . ἐπιγραφὴν ἔχον. ἐπ' ἄρχοντος Πολύβου Τιμοκράτης Ἀντιγόνου Ἀρτέμιδι Ἑκάτει. Cf. *ib.* 1882, p. 344 Ἀθηναγόρας Ἀθηναγόρου Ἀθηναῖος Ἀρτέμιδι Ἑκάτει.

⁹ At Ephesus : Eustath. Hom. *Od.* p. 1714. 41 Καλλίμαχος οὖν ἐν ὑπομνήμασι τὴν Ἄρτεμιν ἐπιξενωθῆναί φησιν Ἐφέσῳ υἱῷ Καΰστρου, ἐκβαλλομένην δὲ ὑπὸ τῆς γυναικός, τὸ μὲν πρῶτον μεταβαλεῖν αὐτὴν εἰς κύνα, εἶτ' αὖθις ἐλεήσασαν ἀποκαταστῆσαι εἰς ἄνθρωπον· καὶ αὐτὴν μὲν αἰσχυνθεῖσαν ἐπὶ τῷ συμβεβηκότι ἀπάγξασθαι, τὴν δὲ θεὸν περιθεῖσαν αὐτῇ τὸν οἰκεῖον κόσμον Ἑκάτην ὀνομάσαι. Strabo, 641 ἡμῖν δὲ ἐδείκνυτο καὶ τῶν Θράσωνός τινα, οὗπερ καὶ τὸ Ἑκατήσιόν ἐστι. Plin. *N. H.* 36. 32 Menestrati Ephesi Hekate in templo Dianae post aedem.

¹⁰ At Athens: Arist. *Lys.* 63 ἡ γοῦν Θεογένους ὡς δεῦρ' ἰοῦσα θοὐκάτειον ἤρετο. Cf. 700. *C. I. A.* 1. 208 Ἄρτεμις Ἑκάτη (fifth century B. C.). Paus. 2. 30, 2 Ἀλκαμένης δέ, ἐμοὶ δοκεῖν, πρῶτος ἀγάλματα Ἑκάτης τρία ἐποίησε προσεχόμενα ἀλλήλοις, ἣν Ἀθηναῖοι καλοῦσιν Ἐπιπυργιδίαν· ἕστηκε δὲ παρὰ τῆς Ἀπτέρου Νίκης τὸν ναόν.

¹¹ Strabo, 472 οἱ δὲ Ἑκάτης προπόλους νομίζουσι τοὺς Κουρῆτας τοὺς αὐτοὺς τοῖς Κορύβασιν ὄντας.

Animals associated with Hekate.

¹² Porph. *de Abst.* 3. 17 ἡ δὲ Ἑκάτη ταῦρος κύων λέαινα ἀκούουσα μᾶλλον ὑπακούει. *Ib.* 4. 16 τὴν δ' Ἑκάτην ἵππον, ταῦρον, λέαιναν κύνα (προσηγόρευσαν). Plut. *Quaest. Rom.* 52. p. 277 ὥσπερ οὖν οἱ Ἕλληνες τῇ Ἑκάτῃ, καὶ τῇ

Γενείτῃ (Μάνῃ) κύνα 'Ρωμαῖοι θύουσιν ὑπὲρ τῶν οἰκογενῶν· 'Αργείους δὲ Σωκράτης φησὶ τῇ Εἰλιονείᾳ κύνα θύειν διὰ τὴν ῥαστώνην τῆς λοχείας. Ib. 68 τῷ δὲ κυνὶ πάντες, ὡς ἔπος εἰπεῖν, Ἕλληνες ἐχρῶντο καὶ χρῶνταί γε μέχρι νῦν ἔνιοι σφαγίῳ πρὸς τοὺς καθαρμούς· καὶ τῇ Ἑκάτῃ σκυλάκια . . . ἐκφέρουσι καὶ περιμάττουσι σκυλακίοις τοὺς ἁγνισμοῦ δεομένους, περισκυλακισμὸν τὸ τοιοῦτον γένος τοῦ καθαρμοῦ καλοῦντες. Cf.ib. 111 οὐ μὴν οὐδὲ καθαρεύειν ᾤοντο παντάπασιν οἱ παλαιοὶ τὸ ζῷον· 'Ολυμπίων μὲν γὰρ οὐδενὶ θεῶν καθιέρωται, Χθονίᾳ δὲ δεῖπνον Ἑκάτῃ πεμπόμενος ἐς τριόδους . . . ἐν δὲ Λακεδαίμονι τῷ φονικωτάτῳ θεῶν 'Ενναλίῳ, σκύλακας ἐντέμνουσι· Βοιωτοῖς δὲ δημοσίᾳ καθαρμός ἐστι, κυνὸς διχοτομηθέντος τῶν μερῶν διεξελθεῖν. Cf. Artemis [130]: Artemis Φεραία associated with the dog-shaped Hecuba. Paus. 3. 14, 9 κυνὸς δὲ σκύλακας οὐδένας ἄλλους οἶδα Ἑλλήνων νομίζοντας θύειν ὅτι μὴ Κολοφωνίους· θύουσι γὰρ καὶ Κολοφώνιοι μέλαιναν τῇ 'Ενοδίῳ σκύλακα.

Hekate a lunar goddess.

[13] a Hom. *Hymn to Demeter*, l. 52 ἤντετό οἱ Ἑκάτη σέλας ἐν χείρεσσιν ἔχουσα. Soph. 'Ριζοτόμοι, fr. 490 Ἥλιε δέσποτα καὶ πῦρ ἱερὸν τῆς εἰνοδίας Ἑκάτης ἔγχος τὸ δι' Οὐλύμπου πωλοῦσα φέρει καὶ γῆς ναίουσ' ἱερὰς τριόδους στεφανωσαμένη δρυῒ καὶ πλεκταῖς ὠμῶν σπείραισι δρακόντων.

b Schol. Arist. *Plut.* 594 κατὰ δὲ νουμηνίαν οἱ πλούσιοι ἔπεμπον δεῖπνον ἑσπέρας ὥσπερ θυσίαν τῇ Ἑκάτῃ ἐν ταῖς τριόδοις. Plut. *Quaest. Conviv.* 708 F ὥστε πάσχειν τοὺς δειπνίζοντας, ἃ πάσχουσιν οἱ τῇ Ἑκάτῃ καὶ τοῖς ἀποτροπαίοις ἐκφέροντες τὰ δεῖπνα, μὴ γευομένους αὐτοὺς μηδὲ τοὺς οἴκοι. Athenae. p. 645 A 'Αμφιφῶν· πλακοῦς 'Αρτέμιδι ἀνακείμενος, ἔχει δὲ ἐν κύκλῳ καόμενα δάδια· Φιλήμων ἐν Πτωχῇ ἢ 'Ροδίᾳ . . . μνημονεύει δ' αὐτοῦ καὶ Δίφιλος ἐν Ἑκάτῃ . . . Φιλόχορος . . . φησὶ ἐς τὰ τῆς 'Αρτέμιδος ἱερὰ φέρεσθαι, ἔτι δὲ καὶ ἐς τὰς τριόδους, ἐπεὶ ἐν ἐκείνῃ τῇ ἡμέρᾳ ἐπικαταλαμβάνεται ἡ σελήνη ἐπὶ ταῖς δυσμαῖς ὑπὸ τῆς τοῦ ἡλίου ἀνατολῆς καὶ ὁ οὐρανὸς ἀμφιφῶς γίνεται.

c At Methydrion in Arcadia : Porph. *de Abstin.* 2. 16 (quoting from Theopompus) κατὰ μῆνα ἔκαστον ταῖς νεομηνίαις στεφανοῦντα καὶ φαιδρύνοντα τὸν Ἑρμῆν καὶ τὴν Ἑκάτην.

d Athenae. 325 A καὶ ταῖς τριακάσι δὲ αὐτῇ τὰ δεῖπνα φέρουσι. Harpocr. *s. v.* τριακάς· τοῖς τετελευτηκόσιν ἤγετο ἡ τριακοστὴ ἡμέρα . . . καὶ ἐλέγετο τριακάς.

e Suidas, *s. v.* Ἑκάτη. οἱ μὲν τὴν Ἄρτεμιν, οἱ δὲ τὴν Σελήνην.

f Schol. Eur. *Med.* 396 ὅταν ᾖ τριῶν ἡμερῶν Σελήνη ὀνομάζεται, ὅταν δὲ ἕξ, Ἄρτεμις, ὅταν δὲ δεκάπεντε, Ἑκάτη. Schol. Arist. *Plut.* 591 τὴν Ἑκάτην ἐν ταῖς τριόδοις ἐτίμων διὰ τὸ τὴν αὐτὴν Σελήνην καὶ 'Αρτέμιδα καὶ Ἑκάτην καλεῖσθαι. Plut. *de Defect. Orac.* p. 416 E τὴν σελήνην . . . χθονίας ὁμοῦ καὶ οὐρανίας κλῆρον Ἑκάτης προσεῖπον.

g Porphyr. ap Euseb. *Praep. Evang.* 3. 11, 32 Ἑκάτη ἡ σελήνη πάλιν·
... διὸ τρίμορφος ἡ δύναμις, τῆς μὲν νουμηνίας φέρουσα τὴν λευχείμονα καὶ χρυσοσάνδαλον καὶ τὰς λαμπάδας ἡμμένας· ὁ δὲ κάλαθος ὃν ἐπὶ τοῖς μετεώροις φέρει τῆς τῶν καρπῶν κατεργασίας οὓς ἀνατρέφει κατὰ τὴν τοῦ φωτὸς παραύξησιν· τῆς δ' αὖ πανσελήνου ἡ χαλκοσάνδαλος σύμβολον.

h Serv. Virg. *Aen.* 4. 511 *Tergeminamque Hekaten* quidam Hekaten dictam esse tradunt quod eadem et Diana sit et Proserpina . . . Tria virginis ora Dianae . . . Lunae Dianae Proserpinae : et cum super terras est creditur esse Luna ; cum in terris, Diana ; cum sub terris, Proserpina. Quibusdam ideo triplicem placet, quia Luna tres figuras habet.

i Cleomedes, Μετεωρ. 2. 5, 111 οἱ μὲν οὖν παλαιοὶ τρία εἶναι περὶ τὴν σελήνην ἔφασαν, τὸ μηνοειδές, τὸ διχότομον, τὸ πεπληρωμένον. ὅθεν καὶ τριπρόσωπον τὴν Ἄρτεμιν ποιεῖν ἔθος ἐστίν.

k Cf. Schol. Theocr. 2. 12. Cornutus, p. 208, Osann. οὐχ ἑτέρα οὖσα αὐτῆς (Ἀρτέμιδος) ἡ Ἑκάτη τρίμορφος εἰσῆκται διὰ τὸ τρία σχήματα γενικώτατα ἀποτελεῖν τὴν σελήνην.

l Plut. περὶ τοῦ προσώπ. τῆς σελ. p. 944 C βάθη ταῦτα τῆς σελήνης ἐστὶ καὶ κοιλώματα· καλοῦσι δ' αὐτῶν τὸ μὲν μέγιστον Ἑκάτης μυχόν, ὅπου καὶ δίκας διδόασιν αἱ ψυχαὶ καὶ λαμβάνουσι.

m ? Lunar goddess in Caria, Stratonicea : *C. I. Gr.* 2720 ἱερέα τοῦ παν(αμαρίου Διὸς) καὶ Ἑκάτης τῆς δᾳδοφόρου. Vide Zeus [8].

Hekate connected with Demeter, Persephone, and the lower world.

[14] Cf. Eur. *Ion* 1048 Εἰνοδία θύγατερ Δάματρος. Mullach, *Frag. Phil. Graec.* 1, Orphic. L καὶ τότε δὴ Ἑκάτην Δηὼ τέκεν εὐπατέρειαν. Serv. Virg. *Aen.* 4. 511 nonnulli eandem Lucinam Dianam Hekaten appellant ideo, quia uni deae tres assignant potestates nascendi valendi moriendi, et quidem nascendi Lucinam deam esse dicunt valendi Dianam moriendi Hekaten. Schol. Theocr. 2. 12 τῇ Δήμητρι μιχθεὶς ὁ Ζεὺς τεκνοῖ Ἑκάτην διαφέρουσαν ἰσχύι καὶ μεγέθει, ἣν ὑπὸ γῆν πεμφθῆναί φασιν ὑπὸ τοῦ πατρὸς πρὸς Περσεφόνης ἀναζήτησιν. Clem. Alex. *Protr.* 13 P μῆνις . . . τῆς Δηοῦς, ἧς δὴ χάριν Βριμὼ προσαγορευθῆναι λέγεται. Euseb. *Praep. Evang.* 5. 13 ξοάνῳ δ' ἄρ' ἐν αὐτῷ μορφή μοι πέλεται Δημήτερος ἀγλαοκάρπου, Εἵμασι παλλεύκοις περὶ ποσσὶ δὲ χρυσοπέδιλος· Ἀμφὶ δέ τοι ζώνῃ δολιχοὶ θείουσι δράκοντες (oracle quoted from Porphyry περὶ τῆς ἐκ λογίων φιλοσοφ.).

[15] *C. I. A.* 3. 268 ἱερέως Χαρίτων καὶ Ἀρτέμιδος Ἐπιπυργιδίας πυρφόρου. *Id.* 1. 5 (Ἑκάτ)η (?) Ἑρμῇ ἐναγωνίῳ Χάρισιν αἶγα. *Id.* 2. 208 Ἑρμοῦ καὶ Ἀρτέμιδος Ἑκάτης.

¹⁶ Eur. *Hipp.* 142 :

οὐ γὰρ ἔνθεος, ὦ κούρα,
εἴτ᾽ ἐκ Πανὸς εἴθ᾽ Ἑκάτας
ἢ σεμνῶν Κορυβάντων
φοιτᾶς ἢ ματρὸς ὀρείας (cf. ¹¹).

¹⁷ Inscription from Tralles : *Bull. de Corr. Hell.* 1880, p. 337 Πριάπιον
καὶ Ἑκατέου αὐλή (second or third century A. D.). .

¹⁸ Thera : *C. I. Gr.* 465 b Εἴσατο τήνδ᾽ Ἑκάτην πολυώνυμον Ἀρτεμίδωρος
Φωσφόρον, ἣν τιμῶσιν ὅσοι χώραν κατέχουσιν Μνημοσύνην θήρας πόλεως παριοῦ-
σιν ἔτευξεν Βάθρα τάδ᾽ (? third century B. c.).   Cf. Artemis ⁵⁸.

¹⁹ Ἑκάτης νῆσος : Suidas, *s. v.* πρὸ τῆς Δήλου κεῖταί τι νησύδριον ὃ ὑπ᾽
ἐνίων Ψαμίτη καλεῖται· καλεῖσθαι δὲ οὕτως φασὶν αὐτὴν διὰ τὸ τοῖς ψαμίτοις
τιμᾶσθαι τὴν θεόν· ψάμιτον δέ ἐστι ψαιστῶν τις ἰδέα.   Cf. Athenae. 645 B,
quoting Semos, mentioning Iris as the divinity on the island.

²⁰ Diod. Sic. 1. 96 εἶναι δὲ λέγουσι πλησίον τῶν τόπων τούτων καὶ σκοτίας
Ἑκάτης ἱερὸν καὶ πύλας Κωκυτοῦ.   *C. I. Gr.* 3857 K ὃς ἂν προσοίσει χεῖρα
τὴν βαρύφθονον Ἑκάτης μελαίνης περιπέσοιτο δαίμοσιν : inscription on a tomb,
late period, Phrygia.   Cf. Soph. *Ant.* 1199.

²¹ Athenae. 325 B Ἀπολλόδωρος δὲ ἐν τοῖς περὶ θεῶν τῇ Ἑκάτῃ φησὶ
θύεσθαι τρίγλην διὰ τὴν τοῦ ὀνόματος οἰκειότητα· τρίμορφος γὰρ ἡ θεός·
Μελάνθιος δ᾽ ἐν τῷ περὶ τῶν ἐν Ἐλευσῖνι μυστηρίων καὶ τρίγλην καὶ μαινίδα, ὅτι
καὶ θαλάττιος ἡ Ἑκάτη. . . . Ἀθήνησι δὲ καὶ τόπος τις Τρίγλα καλεῖται, καὶ
αὐτόθι ἐστὶν ἀνάθημα τῇ Ἑκάτῃ τριγλανθίνῃ. διὸ καὶ Χαρικλείδης ἐν Ἁλύσει
φησὶ " δέσποιν᾽ Ἑκάτα τριοδῖτι τρίμορφε τριπρόσωπε τρίγλαις κηλευμένα." Cf.
late inscription from Cilicia : *Hell. Journ.* 1890, p. 252 εἴτε Σεληναίην,
εἴτ᾽ Ἄρτεμιν, εἴτε σέ, δαίμον Πυρφόρον, ἐν τριόδῳ Γῆν σεβόμεσθ᾽ Ἑκάτην.

²² Hekate Ἀνταία : Hesych. *s. v.* ἀνταία· ἐναντία, ἱκέσιος, σημαίνει δὲ
καὶ δαίμονα (leg. δαιμόνια), καὶ τὴν Ἑκάτην δὲ ἀνταίαν λέγουσιν ἀπὸ τοῦ
ἐπιπέμπειν αὐτά. *Id. s. v.* ἄφραττος· ἡ Ἑκάτη, παρὰ Ταραντίνοις.   Schol.
Arist. *Ran.* 295 Ἔμπουσα . . . Φάντασμα δαιμονιῶδες ὑπὸ Ἑκάτης
ἐπιπεμπόμενον καὶ φαινόμενον τοῖς δυστυχοῦσι . . . δοκεῖ δὲ καὶ ταῖς μεσημβρίαις
φαντάζεσθαι, ὅταν τοῖς κατοιχομένοις ἐναγίζωσι. ἔνιοι δὲ τὴν αὐτὴν τῇ Ἑκάτῃ,
ὡς Ἀριστοφάνης ἐν τοῖς Ταγηνισταῖς " χθονία θ᾽ Ἑκάτη σπείρας ὄφεων
ἐλελιζομένη." εἶτα ἐπιφέρει "τί καλεῖς τὴν Ἔμπουσαν ; " Suidas, *s. v.*
Ἑκάτη· ἐν φάσμασιν ἐκτόποις φαινομένη τοῖς καταρωμένοις, τὰ δὲ φάσματα
αὐτῆς δρακοντοκέφαλοι ἄνθρωποι καὶ ὑπερμεγέθεις.   Theophr. *Charact.* 16
περὶ δεισιδαιμ. καὶ πυκνὰ δὲ τὴν οἰκίαν καθᾶραι δεινός, Ἑκάτης φάσκων
ἐπαγωγὴν γεγονέναι.   Dio Chrys. 4. p. 168 R ὡς εἰώθασιν ἔνιοι τῶν περὶ
τὰς τελετὰς καὶ τὰ καθάρσια μῆνιν Ἑκάτης ἱλασκόμενοί τε καὶ ἐξάντη φάσκοντες
ποιήσειν, ἔπειτα οἶμαι φάσματα πολλὰ πρὸ τῶν καθαρμῶν ἐξηγούμενοι καὶ

ἐπιδεικνύντες, ἅ φασιν ἐπιπέμπειν χολουμένην τὴν θεόν. Harpocr. *s. v.*
ὀξυθύμια Δίδυμος . . . ἐν τῷ ὑπομνήματι ἐς τὸν κατὰ Δημάδου τὰ ἐν ταῖς τριόδοις
φησὶν Ἑκαταῖα, ὅπου τὰ καθάρσια ἔφερόν τινες ἃ ὀξυθύμια καλεῖται. Εὔπολις
Δήμοις "ὃν χρῆν ἔν τε ταῖς τριόδοις κἂν τοῖς ὀξυθυμίοις προστρόπαιον τῆς
πόλεως κάεσθαι τετριγότα." Suidas, *s. v.* ὀξυθύμια· τὰ καθάρματα· ταῦτα γὰρ
ἀποφέρεσθαι εἰς τὰς τριόδους, ὅταν τὰς οἰκίας καθαίρωσιν. Cf. Zeus [138 a].
Ἑκάτη μεισοπόνηρος *C. I. Gr.* 5950.

Common or cognate titles of Artemis and Hekate.

[23 a] Schol. Theocr. 2. 12 τῇ Δήμητρι μιχθεὶς ὁ Ζεὺς τεκνοῖ Ἑκάτην . . .
καὶ νῦν Ἄρτεμις καλεῖται καὶ Φυλακὴ καὶ Δαδοῦχος καὶ Φωσφόρος καὶ Χθονία.

[b] Hekate Προπυλαία : Hesych. *s. v.* προπύλα (leg. προπυλαία). Cf.
Arist. *Vesp.* 804 ὥσπερ Ἑκαταῖον πανταχοῦ πρὸ τῶν θυρῶν. Aesch. *Frag.*
386 δέσποιν' Ἑκάτη βασιλείων πρόδρομος μελάθρων. *C. I. Gr.* 2796, inscrip-
tion third century B. C., Ἑκάτη πρόπολις, at Aphrodisias in Caria.
Hesych. *s. v.* Φυλάδα· ἡ Ἑκάτη (? Φυλακά or Φυλάκα, Lob. Aglaoph. p. 545).
Diphilus, *Frag.* 42, Meineke κεφαλὰς ἔχοντες τρεῖς ὥσπερ Ἀρτεμίσιον.
Ἄρτεμις προθυραία in Eleusis, Artemis [18]. Cf. inscription of late period
from Epidaurus : *Eph. Arch.* 1884, p. 27 Ἀρτάμιτος προθυραίας.
C. I. Gr. 2661 Ἄρτεμιν εὐόλβῳ τῷδε παρὰ προπύλῳ (from Halicarnassus).

[c] Artemis Στροφαία, ? 'the goddess who stands by the hinge of the
door,' at Erythrae : Athenae. 259 B ἦν ἑορτὴ καὶ πανήγυρις ἀγομένη Ἀρτέμιδι
Στοφέα (leg. Στροφαίᾳ). Schol. Pind. *Ol.* 7. 95 Πολέμων γάρ φησι . . . παρ'
Ἐρυθραίοις δὲ τὸ ἕδος τῆς Ἀρτέμιδος δεδέσθαι. Cf. στροφαῖος Hermes.

[d] Hekate Προκαθηγέτις : Benndorf, *Reisen in Lykien*, 68. No. 43
τῆς προκαθηγέτιδος θεοῦ Ἑκάτης (Roman period). Cf. [79] cc.

[e] Artemis Ἐνοδία : Hesych. *s. v.* Ἐνοδία· ἡ Ἄρτεμις. In Thessaly :
Bull. de Corr. Hell. 1883, p. 60. No. 14, inscription from Pherae
(private dedication to Ἐνοδία) : in Euboea *ib.* 1891, p. 412, private
dedication, ? third century B. C. Artemis φωσφόρος ἐνοδία : Robert-
Preller, *Griech. Mythol.* p. 870. Sext. Emp. πρὸς φυσικούς A, § 185
εἴγε μὴν ἡ Ἄρτεμις θεός ἐστιν καὶ ἡ ἐνοδία τις ἂν εἴη θεός· ἐπ' ἴσης γὰρ ἐκείνη
καὶ αὕτη δεδόξασται εἶναι θεά. Hekate ἐνοδία, [13 a] (Soph. *Frag.* 490).
Steph. Byz. *s. v.* τρίοδος· αὕτη (ἡ Ἑκάτη) καὶ ἐνοδία ἐκλήθη ὅτι ἐν τῇ ὁδῷ
εὑρέθη ὑπὸ Ἰνάχου.

[f] Artemis Ἄγγελος : Hesych. *s. v.* Ἄγγελον· Συρακούσιοι τὴν Ἄρτεμιν
λέγουσι = Hekate Ἄγγελος.

[g] Artemis Κελκαία = Hekate : Arr. *Anab.* 7. 19 ἀπενεχθῆναι ὀπίσω ἐς
Ἀθήνας καὶ τῆς Ἀρτέμιδος τῆς Κελκαίας τὸ ἕδος. *C. I. Gr.* 1947 Ἀρτέμιδι
Κελκαίᾳ (private dedication) : inscription of late period, probably found
at Athens.

h Hekate Σωτείρη in Phrygia: *C. I. Gr.* 3827 Q Ἀγαθῇ τύχῃ Σωτείρης Ἑκάτης . . . Δημοσθένη τὸν ἑαυτῶν υἱόν, τειμηθέντα ὑπὸ Σωτείρης Ἑκάτης, κατειέρωσαν (Roman period). Cf. Ἑκάτῃ ἐπηκόῳ on late gem. *C. I. Gr.* 7321 b and vide Artemis [79 q].

i Hekate Καλλίστη in Athens: Hesych. *s. v.* Καλλίστη· . . . καὶ ἡ ἐν τῷ Κεραμεικῷ ἱδρυμένη Ἑκάτη, ἣν ἔνιοι Ἄρτεμιν λέγουσι. Cf. Artemis [27], *ad fin.*

k Aesch. *Supp.* 676 Ἄρτεμιν δ' Ἑκάταν γυναικῶν λόχους ἐφορεύειν. Roehl, *Inscrip. Graec. Antiq.* 517 [ἐπὶ τέκν]ῳ? τᾷ Ἑκάτᾳ (from Selinus). Hekate Εὐκολίνη: Callim. *Frag.* 82 D (Schneider). *Et. Mag.* p. 392. 27 Εὐκολίνη ἡ Ἑκάτη λέγεται παρὰ Καλλιμάχῳ κατ' ἀντίφασιν, ἡ μὴ οὖσα εὔκολος. Eur. *Troad.* 323:

> δίδου δ', ὦ Ἑκάτα, φάος,
> παρθένων ἐπὶ λέκτροις, ἃ νόμος ἔχει.

Herodas, 7. 85 τῇ γὰρ εἰκοστῇ τοῦ Ταυρεῶνος ἡ Ἑκάτη γάμον ποιεῖ τῆς Ἀρτακηνῆς. Hesych. *s. v.* γενετυλλίς· γυναικεία θεὸς πεποιημένου τοῦ ὀνόματος παρὰ τὰς γενέσεις, ἐοικυῖα τῇ Ἑκάτῃ· διὸ καὶ ταύτῃ κύνας προετίθεσαν· ἐστὶ δὲ ξενικὴ ἡ θεὸς καὶ ἑορτὴ τῶν γυναικῶν. Cf. Aphrodite [118 g]. ? Connected with Eileithyia at Argos: Paus. 2. 22, 7 τοῦ δὲ ἱεροῦ τῆς Εἰλειθυίας πέραν ἐστὶν Ἑκάτης ναός, Σκόπα δὲ τὸ ἄγαλμα ἔργον· τοῦτο μὲν λίθου, τὰ δὲ ἀπαντικρὺ χαλκᾶ· Ἑκάτης καὶ ταῦτα ἀγάλματα, τὸ μὲν Πολύκλειτος ἐποίησε, τὸ δὲ ἀδελφὸς Πολυκλείτου Ναυκύδης Μόθωνος. ? Κουροτρόφος at Samos: Plut. *Vita Hom.* 30 ἐγχρίμπτεται γυναιξὶ Κουροτρόφῳ θυούσαις ἐν τῇ τριόδῳ. At Athens: Schol. Arist. *Vesp.* 800 Ἑκάταιον, ἱερὸν Ἑκάτης, ὡς τῶν Ἀθηναίων πανταχοῦ ἱδρυομένων αὐτήν, ὡς ἔφορον πάντων καὶ Κουροτρόφον.

[24] *Orph. Argon.* 979–983:

> τρισσοκάρηνος ἰδεῖν ὀλοὸν τέρας οὔτε δαικτὸν
> ταρταρόπαις Ἑκάτη· λαιοῦ δέ οἱ ἔσσυτ' ἐπ' ὤμου
> ἵππος χαιτήεις· κατὰ δεξιὰ δ' ἦεν ἀθρῆσαι
> λυσσῶπις σκυλάκαινα· μέση δ' ὄφις ἀγριόμορφος
> χερσὶν δ' ἀμφοτέραις ἔχεν ἄορα κωπήεντα.

Orph. Hymn, Hekate, I.:

> Εἰνοδίην Ἑκάτην κλῄζω τριοδῖτιν ἐραννήν,
> οὐρανίην χθονίην τε καὶ εἰναλίην κροκόπεπλον,
> τυμβιδίην, ψυχαῖς νεκύων μέτα βακχεύουσαν
> . . . . ἀγαλλομένην ἐλάφοισιν,
> ταυροπόλον, παντὸς κοσμοῦ κλειδοῦχον ἄνασσαν,
> ἡγεμόνην νύμφην κουροτρόφον οὐρεσιφοῖτιν.

Cf. oracle quoted by Porphyry: Euseb. *Praep. Evang.* 4. 23.

GEOGRAPHICAL REGISTER OF THE CULTS OF ARTEMIS.

Abydos: Polyb. 16. 31, 2.

Achaea, [35], [79p] :

Patrae, [2], [19a]; Aegira, [26a]; Pellene, [26n], [123f]; Teuthea, [12].

Adrasteia on the Propontis, [79l].

Aegina, [131b].

Aetolia, [67i].

Alexandria, [130].

Ambracia, [67e].

Amphipolis, [23], [50h].

Anaphe, [79f], [123k].

Antandros, [92].

Anticyra, [58e].

Apollonia in Chalcidice, [24b].

Arcadia, [5], [27], [29], [53e].

Kaphyae, [6], [47]; Orchomenos, [8], [124]; Lycoa, [22]; Alea, [133]; Megalopolis, [26d], [35], [55b], [116], [123b], [133]; Mantinea, [79w], [124], Paus. 8. 12, 5. Pheneus, [48], [61], [79g]; Stymphelus, [3]; Tegea, [2], [35], [47], [67b]; Oresthasion, Paus. 8. 44, 2 Ἀρτέμιδος Ἱερείας ἱερόν; Lousoi, [38]; Zoitia, [55b]; Lycosura, [55a], [55d]; Phigalea, [14], [123c]; Asea, [67d]; Teuthis, Paus. 8. 28, 6 Ἀφροδίτης τε ἱερὸν καὶ Ἀρτέμιδός ἐστι.

Argolis and Argos, [38], [53d], [68], [79t], [87], [109], [117].

Aricia, [53i].

Armenia, [132].

Astypalaea, [131m] : ? the month Ἀρταμίτιος, *Bull. de Corr. Hell.* 1884, p. 26. Cf. [131m].

Attica.

Athens, [24b,c], [27], [28], [32], [43], [53e], [56], [67f], [79b], [81a], [117], [123i], [129] (Artemis-Bendis), [131] (Dictynna), [134]; Agrae, [26f]; Athmonia, [80b]; Brauron, [32]; Eleusis, [18], [47]; Halae, [32]; Melite, [120]; Munychia, [31], [58b]. Myrrhinus, Artemis Κολαινίς: Paus. 1. 31, 4-5. *C. I. A.* 3. 216 Δέσποινα

Ἄρτεμι Κολαινί (late period) : *ib.* 275 ἱερέως ᾿Αρτέμιδος Κολαινίδος (on a seat in the theatre): cf. 360. Cf. frag. 4, Metagenes, Mein. *Frag. Com.* 2. p. 752. Oinoe, [110]; Peiraeeus, [30], [132]; Phlya, [59].

Boeotia.

Aulis : Paus. 9. 19, 6 Ναὸς ᾿Αρτέμιδός ἐστιν ἐνταῦθα καὶ ἀγάλματα λίθου λευκοῦ, τὸ μὲν δᾷδας φέρον τὸ δὲ ἔοικε τοξευούσῃ. Chaeronea, [41a], [42]; Lebadea, [41b]; Orchomenus, [41d]; Plataea, [66a]; Tanagra, [41f], [79x], [93]; Thebes, [66b]. Therapne : Solin. Polyhist. 7. 8 Therapne unde primum cultus Dianae. Thespiae, [41e]; Thisbe, [41c], [123g].

Byzantium, [53b], [58c]; Hesych. Miles. (Müller, *Frag. Hist. Graec.* 4, p. 152, § 33) τὸν ἐπὶ τῷ Φρίξου λεγομένῳ λιμένι τῆς ᾿Αρτέμιδος οἶκον ἀνεκαίνισεν (Τιμήσιος), in the fourth century B. C.

Calauria, [18].

Calydon, [19b], [54a].

Calymna, the month ᾿Αρταμίτιος : *Bull. de Corr. Hell.* 1884, p. 35.

Cappadocia, [128].

Capua : Athenae. 489 A ἐν Καπύῃ πόλει τῆς Καμπανίας ἀνακείμενον τῇ ᾿Αρτέμιδι ποτήριον.

Caria, [125].

Aphrodisias, [133]; Cnidus, [13]; Iasos, [24b], [91]; Kindye, [105]; Magnesia, [134]; Myndus, [08b]; Mylasa, [50a], [50d], [79aa]; Halicarnassus and Miletus, vide infra. Near Calynda : Strabo, 650 ᾿Αρτεμίσιον ἄκρα καὶ ἱερόν.

Carthaea : Anton. Liberal. 1.

Cephallenia, [19c], [131g].

Chios, [79ee].

Cilicia, [79m], [128].

Colophon, [79dd], [24e].

Corcyra, the month ᾿Αρτέμιτιος : *C. I. Gr.* 1845.

Corinth, [133]: Paus. 2. 2, 3 τὴν δὲ ἐς Κεγχρέας ἰόντων ἐξ ᾿Ισθμοῦ ναὸς ᾿Αρτέμιδος καὶ ξόανον ἀρχαῖον. *C. I. Gr.* 1104, inscription of Roman period, mentioning temple of Artemis.

Crete, [36], [37], [79q], [90], [131a], [134].

Gortys, [83]; Dreros, [83]; Latus and Olus, [83].

Cynuria, [79gg].

Cyrene, [79ii].

Cyrrha, [138].

Cyzicus, [30c], [d].

Delos, [25], [79a], [131e]; Hekate, [8].

Delphi, [79e].

Doris, [19d].

Dyrrhachium : App. *Bell. Civ.* 2. 60 ἱερὸν ᾿Αρτέμιδος.

Elis, [4], [46], [53]e, g, [54]d, [71]; Olympia, [4], [26]e, [79]v, q.

Ephesus, [25], [30]b, [124], [133], [135].

Epidaurus, [2], [26]m, [53]f, [78], [79]q, [87]; Hekate, [23]b.

Erythrae (Ionia); Hekate, [23]c.

Euboea, [26]g, [63]; Hecate, [23]e; Eretria, [79]z, [80]a.

Halicarnassus, [96], [111].

Heneti, [24]d.

Hermione, [34].

Icaria (near Samos), [50]b.

Koloe in Lydia, [132], [103].

Laconia, [1], [2], [26]b, [26]k, [46], [60], [131]d.

  Amyclae, [77], [134]c; Alagonia, [55]f; Boiae, [11]a; Caryae, [7]; Hypsoi, [9]; Pleiae, [77]; Pyrrhichus, [79]u; Sparta, *s. v.*

Lampsacus, the month Ἀρτεμισιών: *C. I. Gr.* 3641 b.

Lemnos, [52]b, [129].

Lycia, [79]o, [79]bb, [79]cc.

Lydia, [57], [127], [128].

  Sardis, [103], [113], [132]; Hierocaesarea, [132]; Thyatira, [94]; Philadelphia, [132].

Macedon, the month Ἀρταμίσιος: Plut. *Alex.* 16.

Magnesia on Sipylus, [50]g.

Massilia, [77]ff, [131]h, [133].

Megara, [26]c, [53]a, [79]r, [123]a.

Messenia, [1], [5], [19]b, [58]a, [70], [121].

Miletus, [37], [44]a, [67]g, [79]i, [81]b, [82].

Mitylene, [79]q.

Mysia, [108]a.

Naupactus, [85].

Naxos, the month Ἀρτεμισιών: *C. I. Gr.* 2416 b.

Pamphylia, Attalia, [24]a, [132]; Perge, [111], [133].

Panticaepaeum, [133].

Paros, [66]c.

Pergamon, [40], [50]f.

Persia, [132].

Phanagoria, [26]i.

Phocaea, [35], [50]e.

Phocis, [19]d, [24]c.

  Abae, [79]y, inscription found near the supposed site of Abae: *Bull. de Corr. Hell.* 1881, p. 449, private dedication to Artemis.

  Hyampolis, [54]c; Ambrosus, [131]l.

Phthiotis, [65], [40].

Pisa, [4].

Pisidia, Termessus: *C. I. Gr.* 4362 ἡ βουλὴ καὶ ὁ δῆμος . . . κανηφόρον θεᾶς Ἀρτέμιδος (late period).

Priapus, [112].

Rhodes, [16], [102], [120]; Lindos, [79]n, [111].

Rome, [79]q, [133].

Samos, [20], [54]b.

Samothrace, [79]q.

Sicily, [79]o, [98].

Acrae: *C. I. Gr.* 5430, inscription mentioning τὸ Ἀρτεμίτιον. Syracuse, [4], [21], [44]b; Tyndaris, [45]; Segesta, [58]d.

Sicyon, [2], [11], [71], [76], [79]s, [117].

Siphnus, [17].

Smyrna, [50]g, [132], [133].

Spain, [133].

Sparta, [10], [18], [46], [47], [53]c, [67]c, [72], [79]h, [125], [131]c.

Syria, [27], [132]; Laodicea ad Mare, [33].

Tauric Chersonese, [35], [37], [52].

Tauromenium, the month Ἀρτεμίσιος: *C. I. Gr.* 5640.

Tenos, the month Ἀρτεμισιών: *C. I. Gr.* 2338.

Thera, the month Ἀρτεμίσιος: *C. I. Gr.* 2465 f.

Thessaly, [79]c; Pherae, [117], [130]; Hekate, [23]e.

Thrace, [54]g, [129]; Neapolis, [37].

Troezen, [22], [114], [123]d, [135], [131]f.

Zacynthos, [136].

CULTS OF HEKATE.

Aegina, [7]; cf. Artemis [131].

Aphrodisias, [23]b.

Arcadia, [13]c.

Argos, [12].

Athens, [10], [13], [15], [21], [22], [23]b, g, i: Hesych. *s. v.* Ζέα· ἡ Ἑκάτη, παρ' Ἀθηναίοις. Byzantium : Hesych. Miles. (Müller, *Frag. Hist. Graec.* 4. p. 149) Ἑκάτης τέμενος κατὰ τὸν τοῦ ἱπποδρομίου τόπον : *ib.* p. 151 λαμπαδηφόρου Ἑκάτης ἀναστήσαντες ἄγαλμα. Cf. Codinus, *De Origin. Constant.* p. 9.

Caria, [13], *sub fin.* : vide Lagina, Stratonicea.

Cos, ? [23]k.

Crete, ? Artemis [131]k.

Cyrene: *Arch. Epigr. Mittheil. aus Oesterreich*, 4, p. 154 (Petersen): Hekateion found in the temple of Aphrodite.

Delos, [8]. Cf. Athenae. 645 B Ἑκάτης νῆσος (near Delos): Harpocrat. *s. v.*

Eleusis, [18].

Ephesus, [9].

Epidaurus, [23b]. Cf. Artemis [79q].

Euboea, [23e].

Galatia: *C. I. Gr.* 4121 Ἐγοισοκομῆται ὑπὲρ ἑαυτῶν καὶ τῶν καρπῶν Μητρὶ (τρι)κράνῳ μεγάλῃ εὐχήν (late period).

Heraclea in Latmos: *C. I. Gr.* 2897 Ἡρακλείδης Σωτάδου νεωκόρος Ἑκάτῃ (? third century, B. c.).

Lagina in Caria: Le Bas-Waddington, *Asie Mineure*, 519, 520 (*C. I. Gr.* 2715), inscription describing the Κλειδὸς πομπή in honour of Hekate; regulations concerning the ritual of Zeus Panamerios and Hekate, τὸν καθ' ἕκαστον ἐνιαυτὸν γεινόμενον ἱερέα τῆς Ἑκάτης καταλέγειν ἐν τῷ περιπολίῳ τῆς θεοῦ καὶ τῶν σύνεγγυς παῖδας ... καὶ αὐτοὺς ᾄσοντας τὸν συνήθη ὕμνον τῇ θεῷ ... διδόντος τοῦ ἱερέως καὶ τ[οῦ ῥαβδού]χου εὐνούχου τὰ ὀνόματα τῷ (παιδονόμῳ). Cf. *ib.* 542. Steph. Byz. *s. v.* Ἑκατησία· οὕτως ἡ Ἰδριὰς πόλις ἐκαλεῖτο Καρίας· ναὸν γὰρ τεύξαντες οἱ Κᾶρες τὴν θεὸν Λαγινίτιν ἐκάλεσαν ἀπὸ τοῦ φυγόντος ζῴου ἐκεῖ, καὶ τὰ Ἑκατήσια τελοῦντες οὕτως ὠνόμασαν.

Lycia, [23d].

Lydia, on coins of Mastaura: Müller, *Denkm. d. a. Kunst*, 2. No. 883.

Miletus: Hesych. *s. v.* ὑπολάμπτειρα· Ἑκάτη ἐν Μιλήτῳ. Cf. *C. I. Gr.* 2852. 37.

Pamphylia, on coins of Aspendus : Head, *Hist. Num.* p. 583.

Paphlagonia: Müller, *Frag. Hist. Graec.* 3, p. 15 (Schol. Ap. Rhod. 4. 247) Νύμφις ἐν τῷ ἕκτῳ περὶ Ἡρακλείας Ἑκάτης φησὶν ἱερὸν εἶναι ἐν τῇ Παφλαγονίᾳ, Μηδείας ἱδρυσαμένης.

Phrygia, [20], [23h].

Samos, [23k].

Samothrace, [7].

Sicily, ? on the river Elorus, Lyc. Cass. 1174 : at Syracuse,[23f]; Selinus, [23k].

Stratonicea, [13].

Tarentum, [22].

Thera, [18].

Thessaly, [6]; Pherae [5], Artemis [117].

Tralles, [17].

CHAPTER XX.

THE figure of Eileithyia, whose worship was ancient and widely prevalent, illustrates the strong tendency in the Greek polytheism towards the multiplicity of personages; for while Hera and Artemis were pre-eminently goddesses of child-birth, the goddess Eileithyia was developed to take special charge of this department, and to play a direct physical part in assisting the processes of birth. She was developed in all probability out of Hera herself, and is identified most frequently with her, though sometimes also with Artemis. ˙ The name—whatever its exact original sense may have been—has an adjectival form, and was primarily, we may believe, an epithet of Hera, and then detached from her and treated as the name of a separate divinity[a]. We hear of the worship of Hera Eileithyia in Attica, and there is some reason for believing that it existed in Argos also ; a passage in Hesychius seems to explain Εἰλείθυια as the Argive Hera[1], and Suidas mentions a strange statue of Hera at Argos which represented her with a pair of shears in her hand[1], an emblem which can scarcely belong to her as an agricultural goddess, and which can only be interpreted as alluding to the cutting of the umbilical cord[b].

It is true also that the assimilation of the goddess of birth

[a] We have the same process in the case of Adrasteia and Peitho, titles that were detached from Cybele and Aphrodite.

[b] Welcker, *Kleine Schriften*, 3. 199. Vide *Arch. Epigr. Mittheil. aus Oesterreich*, 7. (1883), s. 153–167, Taf. 3.

EILEITHYIA. 609

to Artemis seems to have been no less frequent. Plutarch speaks of the worship of Artemis Eileithyia, and inscriptions prove that it existed at Chaeronea and elsewhere in Boeotia, and on an inscription from Lebadea we find a woman returning thanks to ' the gentle Eileithyiae,' whom she calls 'Αρτέμιδες[2]. We may conjecture, too, that in Attica also the two divinities were occasionally worshipped as one ; for an inscription found in the theatre of Dionysos at Athens speaks of the Arrhephoroi of the goddess Εἰλείθυια ἐν Ἄγραις[2] ; but this is a locality of which Pausanias mentions one worship only, that of Artemis 'Αγροτέρα, whose statue carried a bow[a]. Women in travail invoked Artemis Λοχεία, and very many of the titles of Artemis express the functions of Eileithyia ; the two goddesses were not infrequently worshipped in the same temple, and in some representations their symbols and their features are not distinct. Even at Argos, where the goddess of child-birth was more closely associated with Hera, she bears on Argive coins the quiver of Artemis (Coin Pl. B 51).

There might, then, seem more reason for deriving Eileithyia from Artemis rather than from Hera ; but the most ancient tradition makes for the view expressed above. For we find both in Homer and Hesiod that Eileithyia is regarded as the daughter of Hera, and is sent or kept back at Hera's command[1]; and the legend in Crete gave her the same genealogy. Being developed, then, from the conception of Hera as a goddess of marriage who had power over the lives of women, and being associated with Artemis, she cannot be explained away as a lunar goddess ; for it has been shown that neither Hera nor Artemis had originally any proved connexion with the moon. And though a very late writer misnames Eileithyia Selene[2], and some Greek writers believed that the moon affected the processes and conditions necessary to child-birth[b], there is no proof that any genuine Greek cult gave her that name or adopted that physical theory.

[a] Cf. the quiver-bearing Eileithyiae on coins of Argos (Coin Pl. B 51.)
[b] Vide Artemis [40].

As Hera-worship prevailed throughout the whole of Greece, we should expect to find the cult of her daughter Eileithyia prevalent also, and we hear of it in Athens, Boeotia, Arcadia, Argos, Sparta, Messene, Elis, and Achaea, in the Greek islands Crete and Delos, and in Italy [3-24]. It is impossible to fix upon any single locality as the cradle of the cult, and the reasons seem insufficient for accepting Müller's theory that it spread from Crete to Delos, and thence to Attica [a]. There certainly appears to have been a vague Attic tradition pointing to the great antiquity of the worship of the goddess in Delos, and to its connexion with the Attic, while two of her primitive xoana in Athens are connected with Crete [5]. And the influence of the Attic-Delian cult may have propagated the worship in certain places. The temple of Eileithyia in Argolis was connected with the return of Helen from Attica and with the probably Attic myth that Helen was the mother of Iphigenia by Theseus [b].

In the Delian worship [4], so far as the hymn of Olen expressed it, she was more than a divinity of childbirth : the poet invoked her as a primaeval goddess, older than Cronos, a dispenser of destiny, and the mother of Eros. Whether these ideas were inspired, as Welcker supposes, by the influence of the Samothracian belief that Eros was the son of earth, and by a certain affinity between Eileithyia and the earth-goddess [c], or whether Eileithyia had for Olen and the Delian belief something of the character of Aphrodite-Moira, it is clear that the goddess who brings life into the world was, in Delos at least, a divinity of ancient cult, and allied to the highest of the Olympians. This more august conception of her is presented also in the stately lines of Pindar's ode [4].

We can thus understand the special sanctity that in certain places attached to her shrine ; as at Hermione, where none but the priestess might approach her statue [12], and at Sparta, where she was worshipped in company with Apollo Καρνεῖος and Artemis Ἡγεμόνη [d], and at Bura in Achaea, where her

[a] Müller, *Dorians*, 1. p. 312.
[b] Paus. 2. 22, 6.
[c] Welcker, *Griech. Götterl.* 1. p. 359,

although on p. 128 of vol. 3 he regards her as a lunar goddess.
[d] Artemis [67 c].

shrine was next to those of Demeter, Aphrodite, and Dionysos[20]. In Crete and probably elsewhere she acquired a political significance as a city-goddess, in whose temple state decrees and inscribed treaties might be treasured[3]; and we may find the same idea in the Elean worship on the hill of Cronos at Olympia, of which Pausanias gives us a very curious account[18]. Under the name of Εἰλείθυια ’Ολυμπία she was invoked in hymns and attended by a yearly priestess ; and she shared her temple with a mysterious divinity called Sosipolis, ‘ the saviour of the city,’ who was imagined to take the form of a serpent or a little child[a] and to whom the greatest reverence was paid. For of the double temple that part which contained the altar of Eileithyia was accessible to the crowd; but none might enter the inner part, the shrine of Sosipolis, except the priestess, and she only with veiled head ; in the outer shrine the maidens and married women waited and sang the hymn ; in matters of the greatest import oaths were taken in the name of Sosipolis. The mystery and sanctity of this worship and its connexion with Eileithyia were explained by the local legend, which recounted how, just before a great battle between the men of Elis and Arcadia, an Elean woman arrived bringing a new-born babe in her arms, saying that she had been bidden in a dream to take it to her countrymen’s aid. The trustful Elean generals thereupon placed the infant in the forefront of the battle; when the Arcadians charged, the babe turned into a serpent before their eyes, and in their dismay they were routed with great slaughter by the men of Elis, who, after the battle, raised the temple on the spot where the serpent disappeared. The story explains, and was perhaps invented to explain, the meaning of the name Σωσί-πολις, and the form of his manifestation.

The question who this infant-god really was concerns our

---

[a] I would suggest that the female head, inscribed ’Ολυμπία, on fourth-century coins of Elis is not that of an ordinary nymph as Dr. Head supposes (*Hist. Num.* p. 356), but represents Εἰλείθυια ’Ολυμπία: and that the snake seen on some of the Elean coins set over against the eagle is the animal form of Sosipolis.

view about the character of Eileithyia in this worship. Some light is thrown on Sosipolis from another passage in Pausanias' description of Elis, where he mentions a temple of Τύχη, in or near which was a small shrine of 'the saviour of the city'; the deity of the shrine was represented under the form in which he appeared to some one in a dream, as a young boy clad in a star-bespangled cloak and holding in his hand the horn of plenty. The Sosipolis of Elis is probably the Zeus-Dionysos of Crete in the form of infant or boy[a], and Eileithyia was regarded as his foster-mother and as the Τύχη of the state[b]. We may note that at Elis the altar of Pan and Aphrodite[c] was shared by Tyche, whom Pindar calls Φερέπολις.

This development of the character of Eileithyia may have been very ancient, and yet need not have been deduced from the primary idea of a Hera Eileithyia ; it may be due merely to the conception of the birth-goddess who through her function had relation with Aphrodite and the deities of growth and vegetation on the one hand, and with the Fates on the other, and who therefore would aid the growth of the state and personify its fate.

As regards the representation of Eileithyia in monuments, Pausanias supplies us with some evidence. We find that the torch was her frequent emblem and was sometimes held in such a way as to distinguish her statues from those of Artemis: thus her image in the temple at Aegium repre-sented her with one hand stretched out straight before her, and holding up a torch with the other[19]. This enables us, as Professor Gardner has pointed out[d], to interpret as Εἰλείθυια the figure or two figures on coins of Argos holding in each hand a torch, one raised, one lowered (Coin Pl. B 51); and we find on coins of Bura a similar figure with one hand raised and a torch in the other hand[e].

---

[a] Vide Zeus-chapter, p. 38.

[b] Gerhard's view (*Ueber Agatho-daemon und Bona Dea*) that Sosipolis is an Ἀγαθὸς δαίμων is open to the objection pointed out by O. Kern (*Ath. Mittheil.* 1891, p. 24) that we have no certified representation of a child Ἀγαθὸς δαίμων.

[c] Paus. 5. 15, 4.

[d] *Num. Com. Paus.* p. 39.

[e] *Ib.* S. 1.

Besides the torch there is no traditional attribute by which we can recognize the goddess. The treatment of the drapery, for instance, is not at all uniform in the various representations[a]; although on many of the vases we see her clad in a single sleeveless chiton, and Pausanias describes the statue at Aegium as covered from the head to the feet with a lightly woven garment, which might seem to be a natural characteristic of the goddess of child-birth. But on some of the coins she has the chiton and himation; and we can draw no conclusion from the account of the various statues in Pausanias; for though he says that only at Athens were the ξόανα of Eileithyia enveloped in drapery from head to foot, he contradicts this by his account of the figure at Aegium.

As the goddess was an austere divinity, the daughter of Hera, and associated with Artemis and the Moirae and the fortune of the state, her form was always draped, and a nude Eileithyia is an inconceivable representation; although it has been supposed that her statue, the work of the Athenian Euclides, in her temple at Bura[20] was undraped. As I have elsewhere suggested[b], this incongruity only arises from a misunderstanding of Pausanias' phrase: if the last sentence quoted in the note must mean 'and Demeter is clad,' the statement can have no point unless it implies that the other figures were naked, and we should have the absurdity of a nude Eileithyia, the goddess of Bura, who appears on the coins of the city in full attire. But we avoid the difficulty if we interpret the words to mean 'Demeter has a sacred robe,' perhaps a woven peplos, such as was often laid on the images of goddesses.

That which is most significant of Eileithyia is the gesture of the hands, one of which in many representations of coins and vases is upraised with the palm opened outwards,

[a] Vide Müller-Wieseler, *Denkm. d. alt. Kunst*, 2. 229, 228, 393, 729; Baumeister, p. 218.

[b] Vide note in the *Classical Review*, 1888, p. 324. I was wrong in saying that the phrase καὶ τῇ Δήμητρί ἐστιν ἐσθής could not possibly mean 'and Demeter is draped'; for in another passage, 2. 30, 1, Pausanias does use this clumsy expression for the description of a draped statue; but this does not concern the rest of my argument.

a gesture which belonged to a sort of natural magic or mesmerism, and was supposed to assist child-birth[a]. The lifting of the torch, which in itself was the emblem of light and life, had probably the same intention.

As regards the expression and treatment of the face, little can be said; for no great plastic representation of Eileithyia has come down to us[b], while the faces of the vase-figures lack meaning and character, and the coin-types are mostly late and bad. If the head on the Elean coins, inscribed Ὀλυμπία, is as I have suggested the head of Eileithyia, we can only say that the Eleans in the fifth century represented her with the forms of Artemis or the nymphs; we should have expected to find a certain solemnity and matronly character, as in heads of Hera; an archaic bronze of the British Museum (Pl. LIX) gives her something of the form and character of Aphrodite.

The only famous name among those of the artists to whom statues of Eileithyia are attributed is Damophon's, who carved an acrolithic statue of her for her temple at Aegium[19]; we are told that her form was covered with a finely woven garment, and that she held one hand straight out and a torch in the other; but as regards its general character and expression we have no grounds for conjecture.

---

[a] Vide coins of Bura, *Num. Comm.* *Paus.* S. I, and compare Eileithyia standing with upraised hand behind Zeus at the birth of Athena; Gerhard, *Auserles. Vasenb.* vol. I. Taf. 3, 4. The reverse gesture, which retarded birth, was the 'digiti inter se pectine iuncti' (Ovid, *Met.* 9. 299).

[b] Of the very archaic period there are certain kneeling and naked female figures which are of the same type as the Αὔγη ἐν γόνασιν[13]: but we can scarcely call these Εἰλείθυιαι. They are more probably Genetyllides, inferior δαίμονες that watched over child-birth. Kekulé discovers an Εἰλείθυια in a relief found at

Athens and now in private possession, described and represented in *Annali del Inst.* 1864, Taf. d'Agg. 8. p. 108. We see a tall female figure, clad in a high-girt chiton and himation, holding in one hand what seems to be a torch, and in the other something which Kekulé interprets as swaddling-clothes; she is resting this hand on the head of a male person whose diadem and drapery show to be Asclepios, and he argues that there is no other divinity to whom Asclepios could be thus subordinated but Eileithyia. The style appears to be of the fourth century B.C.

REFERENCES FOR CHAPTER XX.

[1] Eileithyia connected with Hera : [a] in Attica, vide Hera, [28] c.

[b] In Argos, vide Hera, [39].

[c] In Crete : Paus. i. 18, 5 Κρῆτες δὲ χώρας τῆς Κνωσίας ἐν ᾽Αμνισῷ γενέσθαι νομίζουσιν Εἰλείθυιαν καὶ παῖδα ῞Ηρας εἶναι. Hom. *Od.* 19. 188 ἐν ᾽Αμνισῷ, ὅθι τε σπέος Εἰλειθυίης. Strabo, 476 Μίνω δέ φασιν ἐπινείῳ χρήσασθαι τῷ ᾽Αμνισῷ, ὅπου τὸ τῆς Εἰλειθυίας ἱερόν. Hom. *Il.* 11. 270:

μογοστόκοι Εἰλείθυιαι,
῞Ηρης θυγατέρες πικρὰς ὠδῖνας ἔχουσαι.

Hes. *Theog.* 922 ἣ δ᾽ (῞Ηρα) ῞Ηβην καὶ ῎Αρηα καὶ Εἰλείθυιαν ἔτικτε. Cf. [4] (Pindar, *Nem.* 7. 1).

[2] Connected with Artemis: Artemis, [64]: Diod. Sic. 5. 72 Διὸς ἐκγόνους φασὶ (οἱ Κρῆτες) γενέσθαι . . . Εἰλείθυιαν καὶ τὴν ταύτης συνεργὸν ῎Αρτεμιν. At Chaeronea, Orchomenos, Thisbe, Thespiae, Tanagra, vide Artemis, [41]. Cf. Nonn. Dionys. 38. 150 Εἰλείθυια Σελήνη. At Agrae in Attica : *C. I. A.* 3. 319 ἐρσηφόροι β᾽ Εἰλιθυίας ἐν῎Αγραις. Bekker's *Anecd.* p. 326. 30 Κλειδῆμος ἐν πρώτῳ ᾽Ατθίδος· τὰ μὲν οὖν ἄνω τὰ τοῦ ᾽Ιλισοῦ πρὸς ἀγορὰν Εἰλήθυια· τῷ δὲ ὄχθῳ πάλαι ὄνομα τούτῳ ὃς νῦν ῎Αγρα καλεῖται, ῾Ελικών. At Sparta, vide Artemis, [67] c.

Localities of her cult.

[3] Crete, [1] c. In Einatos: Steph. Byz. *s. v.* Εἴνατος. Πόλις Κρήτης, ὡς Ξενίων φησί . . . τινὲς δὲ ὄρος καὶ ποταμός, ἐν ᾧ τιμᾶσθαι τὴν Εἰλείθυιαν Εἰνατίην. At Latus: *C. I. Gr.* 3058 (public decree) ἀγγράψαι δὲ καὶ τὸ δόγμα εἰς τὸ ἱερὸν τᾶς ᾽Ελευθύας. Macedonian period.

[4] Delos: Herod. 4. 35 τὴν ῎Αργην τε καὶ τὴν ῎Ωπιν . . . ἀπικέσθαι ἐς Δῆλον ἔτι πρότερον ῾Υπερόχης τε καὶ Λαοδίκης. ταύτας μέν νυν τῇ Εἰλειθυίῃ ἀποφερούσας ἀντὶ τοῦ ὠκυτόκου τὸν ἐτάξαντο φόρον ἀπικέσθαι. Paus. 1. 18, 5 καὶ θύουσί τε Εἰλειθυίᾳ Δήλιοι καὶ ὕμνον ᾄδουσιν ᾽Ωλῆνος. *Id.* 8. 21, 3 Λύκιος δὲ ᾽Ωλὴν . . . Δηλίοις ὕμνους καὶ ἄλλους ποιήσας καὶ ἐς Εἰλείθυιαν, εὔλινόν τε

αὐτὴν ἀνακαλεῖ, δῆλον ὡς τῇ Πεπρωμένῃ τὴν αὐτήν, καὶ Κρόνου πρεσβυτέραν φησὶν εἶναι. *Id.* 9. 27, 2 οὗτος ὁ ᾽Ωλὴν ἐν Εἰλειθυίας ὕμνῳ μητέρα ᾽Ερωτος τὴν Εἰλείθυιάν φησιν εἶναι. Cf. Pind. *Nem.* 7. 1 :

᾽Ελείθυια πάρεδρε Μοιρᾶν βαθυφρόνων,
παῖ μεγαλοσθενέος, ἄκουσον, ῞Ηρας, γενέτειρα τέκνων, ἄνευ σέθεν
οὐ φάος, οὐ μέλαιναν δρακέντες εὐφρόναν
τεὰν ἀδελφεὰν ἐλάχομεν ἀγλαόγυιον ῞Ηβαν.

⁵ Athens, ¹ᵃ, ² : Paus. 1. 18, 4 τοῦ δὲ ἱεροῦ τοῦ Σαράπιδος οὐ πόρρω χωρίον ἐστὶν . . . πλησίον δὲ ᾠκοδόμητο ναὸς Εἰλειθυίας . . . μόνοις δὲ ᾽Αθηναίοις τῆς Εἰλειθυίας κεκάλυπται τὰ ξόανα ἐς ἄκρους τοὺς πόδας. τὰ μὲν δὴ δύο εἶναι Κρητικὰ καὶ Φαίδρας ἀναθήματα ἔλεγον αἱ γυναῖκες, τὸ δὲ ἀρχαιότατον ᾽Ερυσίχθονα ἐκ Δήλου κομίσαι. *C. I. A.* 3. 836 a Πωλ[λα] . . . υὸν βάσσον . . . Εἰλειθυίᾳ ἀνέθηκεν. Cf. 925, 926.

Boeotia.

⁶ Orchomenos, Artemis, ⁴¹.

⁷ Chaeronea, Artemis, ⁴¹.

⁸ Tanagra, Artemis, ⁴¹.

⁹ Thespiae, Artemis, ⁴¹.

¹⁰ Thisbe, Artemis, ⁴¹.

¹¹ Argos, ¹ᵇ : Paus. 2. 22, 6 πλησίον δὲ τῶν ᾽Ανάκτων Εἰληθυίας ἐστὶν ἱερὸν ἀνάθημα ῾Ελένης, ὅτε σὺν Πειρίθῳ Θησέως ἀπελθόντος ἐς Θεσπρωτοὺς ᾽Αφίδνά τε ὑπὸ Διοσκούρων ἑάλω καὶ ἤγετο ἐς Λακεδαίμονα ῾Ελένη. *Id.* 2. 18, 3 (by the gate) τὸ ἱερόν ἐστιν Εἰλειθυίας. ? Εἰλιονεία = Eileithyia : vide Hekate, ².

¹² Hermione : Paus. 2. 35, 11 πρὸς δὲ τῇ πύλῃ . . . Εἰλειθυίας ἐστὶν ἐντὸς τοῦ τείχους ἱερόν. ἄλλως μὲν δὴ κατὰ ἡμέραν ἑκάστην καὶ θυσίαις καὶ θυμιάμασι μεγάλως τὴν θεὸν ἱλάσκονται, καὶ ἀναθήματα δίδοται πλεῖστα τῇ Εἰλειθυίᾳ· τὸ δὲ ἄγαλμα οὐδενὶ πλὴν εἰ μὴ ἄρα ταῖς ἱερείαις ἐστὶν ἰδεῖν.

¹³ Tegea : Paus. 8. 48, 7 τὴν δὲ Εἰλείθυιαν οἱ Τεγεᾶται, καὶ γὰρ ταύτης ἔχουσιν ἐν τῇ ἀγορᾷ ναὸν καὶ ἄγαλμα, ἐπονομάζουσιν Αὔγην ἐν γόνασι, λέγοντες ὡς Ναυπλίῳ παραδοίη τὴν θυγατέρα ῞Αλεος ἐντειλάμενος ἐπανάγοντα αὐτὴν ἐς θάλασσαν καταποντῶσαι· τὴν δέ, ὡς ἤγετο, πεσεῖν ἐς τὰ γόνατα καὶ οὕτω τεκεῖν τὸν παῖδα ἔνθα τῆς Εἰλειθυίας ἐστὶ τὸ ἱερόν.

¹⁴ Cleitor : Paus. 8. 21, 3 Κλειτορίοις δὲ ἱερὰ τὰ ἐπιφανέστατα . . . τρίτον δέ ἐστιν Εἰλειθυίας.

¹⁵ Megalopolis : Paus. 8. 32, 4, herme-formed image of Eileithyia.

¹⁶ Sparta, ² : Paus. 3. 17, 1 οὐ πόρρω δὲ τῆς ᾽Ορθίας ἐστὶν Εἰλειθυίας ἱερόν· οἰκοδομῆσαι δέ φασιν αὐτὸ καὶ Εἰλείθυιαν νομίσαι θεὸν γενομένου σφίσιν

ἐκ Δελφῶν μαντεύματος. Ross, *Arch. Aufsätze*, 2. 667 Μαχανίδας ἀνέθηκε τᾷ Ἐλευσίᾳ (close of third century B. C.). Roehl, *Inscr. Graec. Ant.* 52 Λεχοῖ : ? Εἰλειθυίᾳ (Archaic).

[17] Messene : Paus. 4. 31, 9 πεποίηται δὲ καὶ Εἰλειθυίας Μεσσηνίοις ναὸς καὶ ἄγαλμα λίθου.

[18] Olympia : Paus. 6. 20, 2 ἐν δὲ τοῖς πέρασι τοῦ Κρονίου κατὰ τὸ πρὸς τὴν ἄρκτον ἐστὶν ἐν μέσῳ τῶν θησαυρῶν καὶ τοῦ ὄρους ἱερὸν Εἰλειθυίας, ἐν δὲ αὐτῷ Σωσίπολις Ἠλείοις ἐπιχώριος δαίμων ἔχει τιμάς. τὴν μὲν δὴ Εἰλείθυιαν ἐπονομάζοντες Ὀλυμπίαν, ἱερασομένην αἱροῦνται τῇ θεῷ κατὰ ἔτος ἕκαστον, ἡ δὲ πρεσβῦτις ἡ θεραπεύουσα τὸν Σωσίπολιν νόμῳ τε ἁγιστεύει τῷ Ἠλείων καὶ αὐτή, λουτρά τε ἐσφέρει τῷ θεῷ καὶ μάζας κατατίθησιν αὐτῷ μεμαγμένας μέλιτι· ἐν μὲν δὴ τῷ ἔμπροσθεν τοῦ ναοῦ, διπλοῦς γὰρ δὴ πεποίηται, τῆς τε Εἰλειθυίας βωμὸς καὶ ἔσοδος ἐς αὐτό ἐστιν ἀνθρώποις· ἐν δὲ τῷ ἐντὸς ὁ Σωσίπολις ἔχει τιμάς, καὶ ἐς αὐτὸ ἔσοδος οὐκ ἔστι πλὴν τῇ θεραπευούσῃ τὸν θεόν, ἐπὶ τὴν κεφαλὴν καὶ τὸ πρόσωπον ἐφειλκυσμένη ὕφος λευκόν. παρθένοι δὲ ἐν τῷ τῆς Εἰλειθυίας ἐπιμένουσαι καὶ γυναῖκες ὕμνον ᾄδουσι· καθαγίζουσι δὲ καὶ θυμιάματα παντοῖα αὐτῷ, ... ἐπισπένδειν οὐ νομίζουσιν οἶνον. καὶ ὅρκος παρὰ τῷ Σωσιπόλιδι ἐπὶ μεγίστοις καθέστηκε. Cf. 6. 25, 4 τοῖς δὲ Ἠλείοις καὶ Τύχης ἱερόν ἐστιν ... ἐνταῦθα ἔχει τιμὰς καὶ ὁ Σωσίπολις ἐν ἀριστερᾷ τῆς Τύχης, ἐν οἰκήματι οὐ μεγάλῳ. κατὰ δὲ ὄψιν ὀνείρατος γραφῇ μεμιμημένος ἐστὶν ὁ θεός, παῖς μὲν ἡλικίαν, ἀμπέχεται δὲ χλαμύδα ποικίλην ὑπὸ ἀστέρων, τῇ χειρὶ δὲ ἔχει τῇ ἑτέρᾳ τὸ κέρας τῆς Ἀμαλθείας.

Achaea. [19]Aegium : Paus. 7. 23, 5 Αἰγιεῦσι δὲ Εἰλειθυίας ἱερόν ἐστιν ἀρχαῖον, καὶ ἡ Εἰλείθυια ἐς ἄκρους ἐκ κεφαλῆς τοὺς πόδας ὑφάσματι κεκάλυπται λεπτῷ, ξόανον πλὴν προσώπου τε καὶ χειρῶν ἄκρων καὶ ποδῶν· ταῦτα δὲ τοῦ Πεντελησίου λίθου πεποίηται. καὶ ταῖς χερσὶ τῇ μὲν ἐς εὐθὺ ἐκτέταται, τῇ δὲ ἀνέχει δᾷδα ... ἔργον δὲ τοῦ Μεσσηνίου Δαμοφῶντός ἐστι τὸ ἄγαλμα·

[20] Bura : Paus. 7. 25, 9, vide Aphrodite, [32 a].

[21] Pellene : Paus. 7. 27, 8 ἔστι δὲ καὶ Εἰλειθυίας Πελληνεῦσιν ἱερόν.

[22] ? Paros : *C. I. Gr.* 2389 Φιλουμένη Σεληνῆς Εἰλειθυίῃ εὐχήν.

[23] Pyrgoi, port of Caere : Strabo, 226 ἔχει δὲ Εἰληθυίας ἱερόν, Πελασγῶν ἵδρυμα, πλούσιόν ποτε γενόμενον.

[24] In the Aegyptian Thebaid : Strabo, 817 Εἰλειθυίας πόλις καὶ ἱερόν.

CHAPTER XXI.

APHRODITE-WORSHIP.

THE worship of Aphrodite was perhaps as widely diffused around the Mediterranean lands as that of any other Hellenic divinity. We find it in North Greece, and in especial honour at Thebes; in the country of Attica, in the city, and the coast; in Megara, Corinth, and the Corinthian colonies; in Sicyon, Hermione, Epidauros, and Argos; in Laconia there was a special and important form of the worship; there are comparatively slight traces of it in Arcadia, but abundant testimony of its prevalence in Elis and on the coast of Achaea. The most famous centres of the cult were the Greek islands, Cyprus, Cythera, and Crete. It spread with Greek colonization over the shores of the Black Sea, to Phanagoria for example; and it was one of the chief public worships in most of the Greek cities of the coast of Asia Minor, notably at Cnidos; while from the Troad issued the worship of Aphrodite, that was associated with the name of her favourite hero Aeneas, and was borne to the mainland of Greece, to Sicily, and Italy. Finally we have proofs of the worship of the goddess at Naucratis and Saguntum [1-19].

But in spite of its wide prevalence in the Hellenic world, there is no valid evidence that the cult of Aphrodite belonged to the aboriginal religion of the Hellenic nation. The comparison of the texts and the monuments leads to the conclusion that she was originally an Oriental divinity, and that after her adoption into Greece she retained in many local worships many traits of her Oriental character.

But this view has not been always accepted; some writers [a]

[a] E.g. Preller, *Griech. Mythol.* I. pp. 404, 405; on the other hand, 271³; Roscher, Aphrodite—*Lexicon*, Welcker (*Griechische Götterlehre*, I.

on Greek religion holding the opinion that, though for the most part the goddess appears as an Oriental or Graeco-Oriental personage, yet there was a primitive Hellenic divinity who became merged in this. This opinion is sometimes put forth without any statement of evidence, and it is a necessary question what the evidence is that might be stated in its favour. Now the criteria for judging that any given worship was aboriginal Hellenic are such as these : the evidence of the name, where the interpretation of the name shows clearly its Greek origin or its origin among the larger race to whom the Hellenic family belonged ; the existence of the worship, and the traditional antiquity attaching to it, among those tribes whose seats were especially remote from foreign influence ; its association with certain ritual and ideas of a primitive Hellenic cast ; or, lastly, the prevalence of ancient tradition connecting by lineal descent certain Hellenic stocks with the divinity in question.

We have such proofs as these of the aboriginal character of the leading worships that have been examined hitherto ; but these tests applied to the origin of the Aphrodite-cult lead to a different result.

The name tells us nothing [a] ; so far as philology has hitherto attempted to explain it, it may be Aryan or Semitic. To explain the name Κύπρις as a Greek form of the Sabine goddess Kupra [b] is altogether unnatural, for the Sabine goddess so far as we know her bears no relation to Aphrodite, and Κύπρις is undoubtedly a Greek local title of the goddess

pp. 608 and 666) maintains the wholly Oriental character of the goddess, and finds no place for a goddess of love in the older Hellenic system ; and this view is tacitly accepted in the last edition of Preller : Preller-Robert, I. p. 345. The only recent attempt to disprove the Oriental origin of the cult, and to claim it entirely for the primitive Greek religion, has been made by Enman (*Mém. de l'Acad. d. St. Pétersbourg,* 34. 1886), who ignores much of the evidence; one of his chief premises, 'Aphrodite erscheint unter den gleichen Bedingungen wie Athene und Artemis in allen Landschaften als Göttin,' p. 17, is demonstrably untrue. For the susceptibility of early Hellas to Oriental influences vide Otto Gruppe, *Die griechischen Culte,* pp. 156, 157.

[a] An ingenious attempt has been made to explain the name as a Greek mispronunciation of Ashtoret by F. Hommel in Fleckeisen's *Neue Jahrbücher für Philologie,* 1882, p. 176 ; but philological analogies are wanting.

[b] Vide Enman, *op. cit.*

of Cyprus, whom no one could maintain to be Hellenic in her origin.

When we examine the centres of this worship in Greece, we find nowhere attaching to it such autochthonous sanctity as for instance attached to Demeter at Eleusis, to Athena on the Acropolis of Athens and at Alalcomenae, or to Artemis in Arcadia. In the last-named region, of all Hellas the land of most primitive cult, the only two temples of Aphrodite that might according to the record have been ancient, were that on Mount Cotilum, above Bassae, and that of the Paphian Aphrodite at Tegea [23], [28]; the worship of Aphrodite Erycine at Psophis was evidently a late importation [29]. In Attica and at Athens the older cults of Aphrodite betray their direct or indirect connexion with the East in the names, or traditions, or practices associated with them. Such religious titles as Οὐρανία, Ἐπιτραγία, ἐν Κήποις are to be referred to the Oriental goddess; in the Attic deme Athmon, the rites of Aphrodite Ourania were said to be introduced by King Porphyrion, who may be regarded as the personification of Phoenician commerce [12], and at Phalerum and Athens the goddess was connected with the immigrant Theseus [14 b] and her Cretan double Ariadne, and her ritual at Athens illustrated the curious Oriental idea of the confusion of the sexes [104]. In fact, whenever an Aphrodite-cult in any Greek state claimed to be of remote antiquity, its foreign origin usually stood confessed.

In no Hellenic community was Aphrodite regarded as the divine ancestress, with one salient exception, which itself strongly supports the view here maintained. At Thebes she was closely related to Cadmus [9], the mythic founder of the city; and it is probable that the name Harmonia was a title of the goddess herself, as we hear of an Aphrodite Ἄρμα at Delphi [7]. Therefore the chorus of women in the *Septem contra Thebas* appeal to Cypris for aid as 'the first mother of the race, for from thy blood we are sprung [116],' although we do not hear that she was designated even at Thebes as πατρῴα. But Cadmus and Aphrodite were not autochthonous personages of the Theban soil; the stranger hero coming from the

East brings with him the worship of the Eastern divinity, and among the ancient anathemata of Harmonia at Thebes was a statue of Aphrodite Ourania, a title that points always to the East. In Semitic cities, as will be noted, she was prominently a city-goddess; that to some extent she was this at Thebes, bears witness not to any primitive idea of Hellenic religion, but to the surviving influence of Oriental tradition.

Again, her connexion with other genuinely Greek worships was neither so ancient nor so close as to incline us to believe that the cult of Aphrodite belonged from the beginning to the Greek circle, or grew up spontaneously within it. Because in the *Iliad* Aphrodite is styled the daughter of Zeus and Dione [92], and Dione is a name that belongs to the oldest native religion, we have no right to conclude that we are here on the track of a primitive Greek goddess of love, who faded at the coming of her more powerful sister from the East. The daughter of Dione was never distinguished from the foam-born goddess of Cyprus, except by later mythographers [98], nor have we any evidence that her relationship with Dione was acknowledged in a single Greek cult[a]; so far as we know it was a poetical fiction, or a popular belief that may have arisen at Dodona, and the cause of the fiction or the belief was the desire to admit the Oriental divinity into the Hellenic pantheon by a sort of legal adoption, as we find the later and partly alien deities, Bacchus and Asclepios, were admitted. As Zeus was given her for a father, it is not easy to explain why Dione rather than Hera was selected as her adoptive mother; for we hear of no prominent Dodonean cult of Aphrodite. It may have been due to the epic arrange-

[a] We have no certain trace of any public worship of Aphrodite at Dodona, the chief seat of Dione's cult; Carapanos believes that one of the chapels discovered near the temenos of the great temple was Aphrodite's (Dodone, p. 156), but the single inscription which he found [6a] is not sufficient evidence. Dione was worshipped on the Acropolis of Athens, but not in any connexion with any worship of Aphrodite, as far as is known, but rather with Athena Polias (*Mittheilungen d. deutsch. Inst.* 1889, p. 350); the monuments that show Aphrodite and Dione together are extremely rare and have no discoverable reference to cult; the relief in the Museum of Vienne found in that locality, representing Aphrodite and Dione seated together under an oak, is of a late period (*Gaz. Arch.* 1879, Pl. 12).

ment of the tale of Troy, with its marked antagonism between Aphrodite and Hera. Or it may be supposed that the foreign origin of Aphrodite was too obvious for the early genealogist to affiliate her to any of the leading Olympian goddesses ; and that therefore she was made the daughter of the faded divinity Dione, whose worship was of scant fame and vogue in Greece. The Homeric genealogy is not mentioned in Hesiod, who speaks only of her birth from the sea, and in Homer generally the Oriental character of the goddess is less clearly presented than it was in contemporary worship, for in his poems she appears merely under the aspect of the effeminate goddess of love. In Eastern and also in Greek religion she was always more than this, and Homer was probably aware of her more manifold aspect; but it suited his epic purpose thus to represent the goddess of Asia Minor, the friend of the heroes of the *Troad* and the enemy of the Greeks ; and after all he clearly recognizes in the daughter of Dione the divinity of Cyprus. Putting together the accounts of Homer and Hesiod, we can conclude that some time before the Homeric period the goddess had become partly Hellenized, but that the foreign elements in the local cults and legends were marked and strongly felt, and that in Homer's time she had no very clearly defined relations with any of the Greek divinities. It has often been observed that the song of Demodocus in the *Odyssey*, in which she appears as the faithless wife of Hephaestos, is inconsistent with the other Homeric passages that mention Charis as his wife ; and Lucian makes merry over the bigamy of the fire-god [95]. The Homeric hymns to Hephaestos and Aphrodite nowhere make mention of these divinities together ; and the later poetical tradition may have been inspired by the lay of Demodocus; or the singer in the *Odyssey*, as well as the later poets such as Apollonius Rhodius, may have been following the religious tradition of Lemnos, the special home of Hephaestos, where possibly the worship of Aphrodite also was indigenous [a].

[a] There has not as yet been found any direct evidence of an Aphrodite-cult in Lemnos; but probably Chryse, the goddess of the island, is only another name for the great goddess of Asia Minor. At Athens, where the cult of

But no other local cult in Greece associated the two divinities; we cannot therefore say that their casual association in literature at all supports the theory that she was a goddess of the primitive Hellenic religion.

Nor is this theory confirmed by her relations in myth and religion with Ares, even if the latter were known to be genuinely Hellenic in his origin[a]. The poetical legends in Homer and Hesiod no doubt point to some real connexion in the local worships of Ares and Aphrodite; we hear of a temple of Ares at Athens near the Council-hall, that contained two images of Aphrodite, and of a temple dedicated to Ares and Aphrodite on the road from Argos to Mantinea; at Latus in Crete the two were invoked together in the formula of a treaty of alliance, and Pindar styles him the 'husband of Aphrodite, the lord of the brazen chariot [96].'

But the occasional combination of two cults, of which one may be native to the soil, is never any reason at all for denying the foreign origin of the other; in fact it was generally through such combination that a foreign worship took root in the new land, according to some affinity of ritual or divine character, or for some local reason. The reason in this case is not hard to suggest, if we suppose that the connexion between the two divinities sprang up at Thebes. For Ares was the prevailing god of the city and land, and with the coming of Cadmus and Harmonia came the worship of the Oriental goddess, and the older and the imported cult may have been reconciled by the fiction of a marriage, of which Harmonia was afterwards regarded as the offspring. This alliance would have been all the more natural, if the Aphrodite of Thebes appeared in the form of the armed goddess, a very common type of the Oriental divinity.

The belief that there must have been a primitive Greek Aphrodite has been often maintained on the ground of the frequent *rapprochement* of her cult to that of Hebe and the Charites, and from her occasional connexion with the Horae.

Hephaestos was probably very ancient, he had a temple in common with Athena; Aug. *de Civ. Dei*, bk. 18.ch. 12.

[a] Vide Tümpel, Ares und Aphrodite, Fleckeisen's *Jahrb. Suppl.* 641.

Certainly these goddesses are often and naturally mentioned together[94]. In the *Iliad* it is the Charites who wove her ambrosial robe; and Demodocus sang of the Charites who washed her and anointed her with oil when she retired to Cyprus. We hear in the Homeric hymn to Apollo of Harmonia, Hebe, and Aphrodite dancing hand in hand. In the Hesiodic description of the creation of Pandora, the πότνια Πειθώ, 'the lady of persuasion,' who with the Charites adorns the dangerous maiden, is probably none other than Aphrodite, who is mentioned also at the beginning of the *Theogony*, together with Themis, Hebe, and Dione, among the divinities of whom Hesiod is going to sing. And the poet of the *Cypria* speaks of the Nymphs and the Graces with golden Aphrodite singing their fair songs about the slopes of Mount Ida. The natural affinity of these goddesses was recognized in more than one public cult[93].

We have also epigraphical evidence that the worship of Aphrodite Colias on the Attic promontory opposite Aegina was connected with a temple of Hebe in that vicinity. At Sparta there was a statue of Aphrodite Ἀμβολογήρα, 'the putter-off of old age,' standing apparently near to the statues of sleep and death, and Plutarch quotes the line from one of the choral hymns, 'Set old age far from us, O fair Aphrodite[25 g].' The relationship of the Charites with the goddess appeared in certain statues of them which Pausanias saw in their temple at Elis, wearing some of the emblems of Aphrodite, the rose and the myrtle, for he says 'of all divinities they are most akin to this goddess,' and the statue of Eros stood by their side on the same base. In the Homeric hymn to Venus, the Hours are said to adorn the goddess with the same golden necklaces as they deck themselves with, and their figures also on later monuments bear close resemblance to Aphrodite's[94, 107 i].

But these facts are explained if we suppose that the great goddess of anterior Asia came at an early date to the shores of Greece with the character of a divinity of vegetation, who had power over the various forms of life and birth in the world, and who was therefore akin to the Charites of ancient worship at Orchomenos and Athens; and that she came also with the aspect and functions of a divinity of love, beauty, and youth, and was thus brought near to the Greek Hebe.

It has been suggested by Kekulé [a] that the last-named goddess who was worshipped at Phlius and Sicyon, under the name of Dia, was originally the Hellenic Aphrodite herself, daughter of Zeus and Hera. But the mere coincidence between the names of Dia and Dione, who was made the mother of Aphrodite, is a very slight argument: his suggestion would have more weight if Hebe, Dione, and Aphrodite were closely associated in ancient myth and widely prevalent cult. But this is by no means the case; in the myths and the monuments of art Hebe approaches nearer to Hera than to Aphrodite; their combination in the Attic worship is an isolated instance, and not known to be very ancient, and Hebe has no prominent function as a goddess of love and marriage.

Nor can we say that the association of Aphrodite and the Charites belongs to a primitive period; in the most ancient and solemn worship of these latter goddesses at the Boeotian Orchomenos, Aphrodite cannot be found to have had any place [b]; and their cult on the Acropolis of Athens seems to have been equally independent of her, nor did she borrow their names or titles.

Nor, lastly, can any proof of the antiquity of her religion in Hellas be derived from her relations with Eros: for as the child and companion of Aphrodite, he figures only in the later literature and occasional later cult [97]. The only ancient centres of Eros-worship were Thespiae and Parion, where he

---

[a] Kekulé, *Hebe* (1867).

[b] Müller, on the contrary, in his *Orchomenos*, p. 173, supposes a close local connexion between Aphrodite and the goddesses of Orchomenos; but the sole evidence is Servius' interpretation of the epithet Acidalia applied to Aphrodite in Virg. *Aen.* 1. 720. He refers this to the fountain near Orchomenos where the Graces were wont to bathe: it is merely an unfortunate literary epithet of Virgil's, and it does not prove that that fountain and that locality were sacred to Venus; it may be that Virgil knew of the fountain as one of the chief haunts of the Graces, with whom in later literature Aphrodite is so closely connected. The writer (Dr. Roscher) of the article on Aphrodite in Roscher's *Lexicon* merely follows Müller. The view expressed in the *Bulletin de Correspondance Hellénique*, 1889, p. 471, about 'Aphrodité, la déesse de qui relèvent les Charites,' is quite untenable.

was regarded probably not merely as the personification of human love, but as a physical and elemental force, a divinity of fertility. With these cults Aphrodite has nothing to do. This itself is a strong negative argument against the aboriginal antiquity of her worship in Hellas; for had it been part of the common religious inheritance of the people, one would suppose that it would have been attracted into the circle of the most ancient cult of Eros, whose character and functions were so like her own.

It does not appear then that the belief in the primitive Hellenic origin of Aphrodite is borne out by her relations with other recognizably Hellenic divinities.

The belief sometimes seems to rest on the difficulty of imagining that the ancient Greeks could have dispensed with a goddess of love ; but this difficulty would be only serious if it were proved that every other old Aryan race had been blessed with such a divinity[a]. But this is by no means certain, and the danger of *a priori* reasoning from one religion to another is now sufficiently recognized.

We can now deal with the question under what form and with what characteristics the goddess of the East was known and worshipped by the earliest Greeks. If her original personality were made clear and precise, we could then estimate how far this was transformed in the later Hellenic imagination. But to give a precise picture of the Oriental goddess is difficult, because, as her names were many, her aspect and functions may have varied even more than we know in the various centres of the Semitic worship. The names Ishtar, Attar Athare, Atargatis-Derceto, Astarte designate the same goddess in the Assyrian, Aramaic, Canaanite, Phoenician tongues. The female Baal, known as Belit and

[a] It is probable that a divinity of human love in the abstract is a creation alien to the spirit of any very ancient religion ; the early Aryan and Semitic races had divinities enough and to spare of vegetation and fertility, and any of these could supervise human love and birth as part of a wider physical law. Therefore it would be unreasonable to suppose that before the arrival of Aphrodite there was a mysterious vacuum in Greek religion which the people would feel. She may have arrived not necessarily because she was wanted, but because she was brought.

to the Greeks as Mylitta, at Carthage as Tanit, was originally in all probability the same divinity, although sometimes distinguished in local worship. The Persian Anaitis,
though naturally and in origin distinct, came to be coloured
with the religious ideas of the Babylonian Nana-worship ;
and these and the name appear in the later Hellenic cult
of Artemis Nanaea[a]. Lastly, we have the Syro-Arabian
Allat, an armed goddess identified sometimes with Athena,
sometimes with Aphrodite Ourania. As regards the character
of this widely worshipped goddess of the Semitic peoples,
there is much obscurity in detail ; but there are certain leading
traits which may be gathered from the cults and myths, and
which may be briefly stated here on account of their importance for the Greek worship, as they reappear in the Hellenic
goddess[99]. In the Assyrian myth of Ishtar who descends
into the lower world, and whose lovers come to an untimely
end, we have a goddess whose myth and cult refers to the
vegetation of the earth, and with whom in some places,
Byblos for example, Adon or Tammuz was associated. It was
easy for such a divinity to come to be considered as a power
of the lower world also, and this may explain why terracotta
images of her were put into Phoenician graves[b], and it probably
explains many of the Greek views and titles of Aphrodite.
It has sometimes been asserted that the Semitic goddess was
a lunar divinity; but that she was originally this is most
improbable, as in the Semitic imagination the moon was
a male power, and the lunar qualities and symbols came to
Astarte from her early connexion with Isis[c]. Under her
Syrian and Phoenician name Atargatis or Derketo, at
Bambyce and Ascalon she was regarded as a divinity of the
waters. But this nature-goddess became a goddess of the
city at Ascalon, Byblos, and Carthage, wearing a mural crown,
and sometimes represented as equipped with bow or spear.
She was also prominently a goddess of love and sexual

---

[a] Vide pp. 484, 485.
[b] Perrot and Chipiez, vol. 3. p. 202.
[c] Vide Baethgen, *Beiträge zur Semi-
tischen Religionsgeschichte*, p. 31, who
explains the form of Astarte on the
stele of Jehav-milk, king of Byblos, as
due to the blending of Phoenician and
Egyptian ideas.

passion, and her rites at Babylon, Byblos, and Bambyce were
notorious for the temple prostitution practised there[99 c].
A different illustration of the prominence of the sexual idea
was the practice of voluntary mutilation of which we hear at
Bambyce, and which found its way into the rites of Cybele.
To the same darker side of this worship belonged that strange
idea of the confusion of sex, the blending of the male and
female natures in one divine person. The usual illustration
of this mysterious Oriental fancy is the description found in
Macrobius of the statue of the Venus Barbata of Cyprus:
'there is in Cyprus a statue of her bearded, but with female
dress, with the sceptre and the signs of the male nature, and
they think that the same goddess is both male and female.
Aristophanes calls her Aphroditos.' This statement which
explains the 'duplex Amathusia' in Catullus' ode, is repeated
by Servius, and is supported by the similar statement of
Joannes Lydus that the 'Pamphylians once paid worship to
a bearded Aphrodite[113 e].' As no such statue has yet with
certainty been found in Cyprus, it has been doubted whether
we can fairly attribute this idea to the Semitic religion at all.
But there is much that is proved by literary evidence that
cannot be attested by archaeological, and the lack of illustration from the monuments ought not to invalidate such
a precise assertion as that of Macrobius about a fact which he
could scarcely have invented, and which explains better than
anything else the origin of the Greek Hermaphrodite[a]. In
fact the Semitic idea of the androgynous divinity is not
attested merely by Macrobius: on a Ninevite inscription preserved in the British Museum there appears to be an allusion
to this double character of Ishtar, just as a later Phoenician
inscription speaks of a 'King Astarte[b].' The same idea
appears in the legends of Semiramis, the warlike goddess-
queen who wears male attire and repudiates marriage[c]. This

[a] It seems more reasonable to derive
this abnormal type from certain religious
ideas than from the observation of certain abnormal phenomena in nature.

[b] Vide letter from Mansell to Lenormant, *Gazette Archéol.* 1879, p. 62; cf.

the double Herme of male and female
divinity on a late Chaldean (?) relief;
Lajard, *Culte de Vénus en Orient*,
Pl. 1. 1.

[c] Diod. Sicul. 2. chs. 6 and 14.

strange conception may have had its origin in a theological dogma: that the divinity being perfect must possess all the powers—passive and active—of creation; but the forms in which the idea was expressed were likely to be tainted with sensuality.

A no less remarkable belief was that which, according to some authorities, prevailed in certain communities devoted to the Semitic goddess : namely, that though a mother, she was also a virgin [119] o. At least, we hear of the 'virgo caelestis' at Carthage[a], the virgin-Allat in Arabia[b], the virgin-mother ta Petra ; and the same contradiction has been found in the cult and legends of Phrygia and Caria[c]. Whether this is a development and a purification of an older and grosser conception of Ishtar, regarded in the Babylonian legend as a mother-goddess but unmarried, or choosing her temporary partners at will, does not concern us here ; the same perplexing double character of the divinity has been noticed in the Artemis-worship, and it has been supposed to have left traces even in the Hellenic Aphrodite.

Such in very brief outline are the main recognized traits of the Oriental goddess ; and it remains to trace her forms and further development in Greece. We may distinguish between those Aphrodite-cults which preserved in name or rite clear traces of their Oriental origin, and those which had become fully Hellenized, and we shall find even in the latter very few ideas that may not have been developed from the original character of the Semitic divinity.

The clearest sign of the Eastern goddess in the Greek community is the title Οὐρανία. This was the literal translation for the Semitic title 'Méleket Aschamaim,' 'the queen of the heavens,' which Ezekiel applies to her. Semitic scholars have not been able to give a very precise significance to this phrase, and the Greek term that translates it is also

[a] Aug. *de Civ. Dei*, 2. 4.

[b] Vide Epiphanius, *Panarium*, 51 (vol. 2, p. 483 Dind.), who speaks of the Κόρη or Παρθένος at Alexandria, who brought forth Αἰών, and the 'maiden' divinity among the Arabs, who gave birth to Dusares; it is possible that in these beliefs Παρθένος or Κόρη only meant the 'unmarried' goddess, and that they do not contain any idea of a miraculous conception.

[c] Vide chapter on Artemis, pp. 446, 447.

rather vague. We should be probably wrong in assigning to it any distinct solar or lunar or astral meaning ; it is probably sufficient to interpret it as the name of the goddess whose seat was in heaven, and whose power reached through the world [a]. And the Greek epithet may have been as vague as the title 'Ολυμπία, which was applied to her at Sparta[25 f]. The moral or spiritual intention of the term Οὐρανία is certainly late, being probably derived from the Platonic philosophy and perhaps never recognized in actual cult. Its chief importance for us, in tracing the origin of the Aphrodite cult, is that the title alludes as a rule to the Eastern worship ; the direct and indirect evidence of this is too strong to be questioned[99]. Pausanias tells us that the Assyrians were the first who instituted the worship of Ourania, which was afterwards held in honour by the Cyprians, Paphians, and the Phoenicians of Ascalon ; the goddess of Hierapolis in Syria is regarded as Ourania by Lucian, or the writer whose treatise on the Syrian divinity bears his name. The statement in Pausanias seems mainly derived from Herodotus, who regards the temple at Ascalon as the oldest sanctuary of Ourania, to which the temple in Cyprus was affiliated according to Cypriote belief. The historian adds that the Persians acquired this worship at a later period from the Assyrians and Arabians.

The Carthaginian goddess was also known by this name ; and its non-Hellenic connotation is further attested by the freedom with which the Greeks applied it to the foreign divinities of other nations than the Semitic. Thus the armed goddess of Libya, sometimes identified with Athena, was styled Ourania, and so also was the goddess Artimpasa of the Scythians[99 f] ; we may suppose that the reason of this lay in the likeness these divinities bore to the Asiatic goddess rather than in the purity of the worship.

From the prevalent application, then, of this title to the

[a] In Greek cult it certainly never conveyed any allusion to the moon or stars in Greek religion, which did not recognize any lunar or astral nature in Aphrodite ; this is only assumed in the later physical or theological literature ; the title 'Αστερία is not found in cult, and her association in the cult of Achaea with Zeus Amarios in no way suggests that she was there a divinity of the lights of heaven[102].

foreign divinity, we might fairly conclude that it had the same denotation in the temple-worship of the Greek communities, at least in the earliest periods. And we have more or less direct evidence of this ; for we find the title and the worship especially in those places of which the tradition, the ritual, or the commercial relations suggest a connexion with the East. It was instituted in Cythera [99 b], according to Herodotus and Pausanias, by the Phoenicians, and the diffusion of the cult is here connected in all probability with the purple-trade. We learn further from Pausanias that the temple in Cythera preserved the name of Ourania down to his own day, that of all the temples of Aphrodite in Greece it was regarded as the most sacred and ancient, and that the goddess was here represented as armed. It may be for this reason that Homer calls the island ' divine ' [68].

The worship of Aphrodite Ourania was found in the city of Athens and in the Attic deme of the Athmoneis, where it was associated with the legendary Porphyrion, ' the purple-king.' In the city the temple stood in the Ceramicus, near the temple of Hephaestus, and outside the ancient burgh ; we hear also of a herme-statue of Aphrodite Ourania in the district called Κῆποι, and can conclude that the worship of Aphrodite ἐν Κήποις was closely connected with the former [11 a]. Now with nearly the whole of this religion at Athens the names of Aegeus and Theseus were interwoven, and the foreign character of these heroes and their significance as the propagators in Athens and Attica of new cults has been established in a paper by M. de Tascher [a]. He deals more particularly with the importation of the worships of Poseidon and Apollo ; but the Athenian or Attic cults of Aphrodite are still more closely associated with the early Ionic settlement, with the names of Ariadne, Theseus, and Aegeus, and with a stream of myth that circles round Attica, Delos, Naxos, Crete, Cyprus, Troezen, and Argos, which it will here be convenient to trace [104].

Ariadne or Ἀριάγνη of Crete, who was known there also by

[a] Les cultes ioniens en Attique, *Revue des Études grecques,* 1891, Janvier-Avril, p. 1.

the sacred epithet Ἀρίδηλος, was a name that itself must have been an epithet of the Hellenized goddess of the East. It is true that we have no explicit record of the identification of Ariadne and Aphrodite in Crete itself. But we have proof of a cult of Aphrodite Antheia at Cnossus [59 c], the place of the Labyrinth and the Minotaur ; in the territory of the Latii was an ancient Aphrodision, and its general prevalence in the land is attested by the claim asserted by the Cretans for their island to be regarded as the original home of the Aphrodite-worship [59], though this name was here scarcely so much in vogue as those which we may regard as her sacred epithets, Pasiphae and Ariadne. In fact, there is evidence that in Crete there was a mingling of a Semitic and a Phrygo-Carian current of worship and myth, that the Semitic goddess whose sacred animal was the goat, and whose lover was the bull or the bull-headed god, was here brought into the company of a Zeus-Dionysos, Europa, and Cybele, while a virgin goddess, Britomartis or Dictynna, of probably Carian origin, whose myth and worship were rife in the island, was perhaps herself near of kin to the unmarried goddess of the East [a]. The worship of Pasiphae was found in Laconia, where—as will be shown—we have clear proof of the early admission of the Oriental Aphrodite ; the name Pasiphae itself was a wide-spread local title of the goddess, if we may trust Joannes Lydus ; and Pasiphaessa appears as a synonym of Aphrodite in a verse quoted by Aristotle [103]. The bull that is so conspicuous a figure in the Cretan religious myth may have belonged originally to the Eteocretan earth-goddess Europa [b], and the animal is as closely associated with Hellenic ritual and religion, with the worships of Demeter and Artemis for instance, as with Oriental cult. But taking into account the connexion between Europa and Cadmus, and the statements that the representation of Europa on the bull was one of the types of Sidonian coinage, and that Astarte herself was supposed to assume the bull's head as a symbol of supreme power [c], and comparing these facts with such legends as those

---

[a] Vide chapter on Artemis, pp. 475–478.

[b] Vide p. 478.

[c] Lucian, *de Dea Syr.* 4 Tὸ νόμισμα

concei .ing Pasiphae and the Minotaur, we have grounds for concluding that Europa herself came at least to acquire a close affinity with the chief personage and sacred legends of the Eastern worship. And the story repeated by a scholiast that Ariadne was the mother of a certain Tauropolis[104] comes probably from some association between Ariadne and a bull-riding goddess, who may have been a Cretan equivalent of Artemis Tauropolos.

We find also a worship of Aphrodite Ἐπιτραγία on the Attic coast[14], connected by the legend with Theseus and his voyage to Crete: the Delphic oracle had advised him to make Aphrodite his guide and to invite her to be his fellow-voyager: he was therefore sacrificing to her a she-goat on the shore, which was suddenly transformed into a male, so that the goddess was henceforth known as Aphrodite who rides on the goat. The story does not fully explain the name, and is useful merely as indicating the association of Theseus with Aphrodite and of the goddess with the male animal[a]; and it is to the Oriental Aphrodite that the monuments which represent Ἐπιτραγία seem to point. Her close connexion with Crete, which the Attic legend makes clear, may help to explain the prominence of the goat in the sacred Cretan legend concerning the rearing of the child Zeus: that is, we should understand the meaning of the goat as the foster-mother, if we recognize in the Cretan Aphrodite a divinity closely akin to Cybele, and in the Cretan Zeus a Zeus-Dionysos. Reasons have been already given for the latter view, and for the former some will be mentioned later on[b].

As we follow the voyage of Theseus back to Athens[104] it becomes clear that his beloved whom he leads away and

---

τῷ Σιδώνιοι χρέονται τὴν Εὐρώπην ἐφεζο-μένην ἔχει τῷ ταύρῳ τῷ Διί. Cf. Philo Bybl. 2. 24 (*Frag. Hist. Graec.* 3. p. 569) Ἡ δὲ Ἀστάρτη ἐπέθηκε τῇ ἰδίᾳ κεφαλῇ βασιλείας παράσημον κεφαλὴν ταύρου . . . τὴν δὲ Ἀστάρτην Φοίνικες τὴν Ἀφροδίτην εἶναι λέγουσιν.

[a] The representation of divinities riding on their sacrificial animals, not infrequent both in Hellenic and Oriental religious monuments, was probably in its origin a sacramental symbol from which much misunderstanding and much myth arose (vide Robertson Smith, *Religion of the Semites*, p. 457).

[b] Vide also p. 478.

deserts is Aphrodite herself or her Cretan representative[a]; the divinity of Ariadne and her real personality are betrayed in the Cypriote worship and legend. According to one story of that island, when deserted by her lover, she hanged herself on a tree[b]; or wearied with travail and sickness she was put ashore in Cyprus and died there, and was buried near Amathus in a grove which was called after the name of Ariadne Aphrodite. Sacred rites were instituted there in her honour by Theseus when he returned to the island, and the most curious was the practice of one of the youths 'lying-in' on one of the festival days and imitating the cries of women in travail. At first sight it would seem that we have here a sort of consecration of the 'couvade': but it is less hazardous if we merely regard this rite as an illustration of that idea found in the worship of the Eastern goddess of the unnatural confusion of the sexes. And we find it twice again in the track of Theseus and Ariadne. At the Oschophoria at Athens, an ancient harvest festival with which the names of Theseus and Ariadne and the legend of his Cretan journey became entangled, we hear of chosen boys being dressed up as girls and taught to imitate the gait and voice and bearing of maidens[c].

At Argos also the grave of Ariadne was shown[104], and as the worship of Aphrodite Ourania found its way to these shores[22] we may refer to it the mysterious feast called

[a] Movers (*Die Phönizier*, vol. I. p. 641) holds the opinion that Ariadne is a Cretan form of Aphrodite Astarte.

[b] These 'hanging' stories about divinities come from the custom of hanging up their images or masks on a tree; e.g. the story of Helen and the Rhodian women arose from the sacred title of Helene Δενδρῖτις, 'the goddess whose image hung from the tree'; cf. Artemis Ἀπαγχομένη.

[c] Antoninus Liberalis (c. 17) quotes from Nicander a Cretan legend about a certain Leucippus of Phaestum, who had been born a girl but was transformed into a man through the prayers of the mother; the story is connected with the local feast called ἐκδύσια, and certain preliminary marriage rites were performed by the statue of Leucippus. The latter may possibly be a title of the male Aphrodite, and the feast may have been very similar to the Argive Ὑβριστικά and have belonged in reality to an Aphrodite-cult, though Nicander connected it with Leto Phytia. The story in Herodotus of the Scythian Ἀνδρόγυνοι[99f] who worshipped Aphrodite may be indirectly connected with the androgynous character of the Oriental goddess.

'Υβριστικά [113 f], at which women wore the men's dress and men the women's; the quasi-historical event which Plutarch records by way of explanation is clearly a fiction invented to explain a misunderstood rite. The real significance of it is suggested by the statement of Philochorus, that in Cyprus the two sexes exchanged dresses in the worship of Aphroditos or the Venus Barbata [113].

These facts are sufficient to prove the Oriental origin of the Attic worship of Ourania, and point to the track along which it arrived at the Attic shores. One of its chief points of connexion was Delos, where we come upon traces of the Theseus-Ariadne legend and of the Aphrodite-worship [60]. It penetrated at an early date to Thebes, where Harmonia, probably another form of Aphrodite herself, dedicated three statues of Aphrodite Ourania, Pandemos, and Apostrophia [9]. Whether the two latter titles express characteristics that belong to the Oriental conception of the divinity is a question that will arise later. It is enough to notice here the association of the goddess of Thebes with Cadmus and the East; and her Oriental origin may explain why she was here the goddess of the city and the wife of Ares, as at Sidon and elsewhere in Asia Minor she bore the character of a political and warlike divinity. We have proof that the goddess at Corinth had the same title and was of the same origin [16, 99g]. Euripides celebrates Acrocorinthus as the 'holy hill,' 'the city of Aphrodite' [16 a], and Alciphron gives us the legend that she came up from Cythera, perhaps the earliest home in Greece of this foreign worship, to greet Acrocorinthus. The early commerce with Asia Minor will explain the many Oriental traits that are noticeable in the Corinthian worship; the most striking and un-Hellenic was the practice of religious prostitution, to which we have an unambiguous allusion in that strange fragment of Pindar [99g], in which he employs his best style to glorify the 'hospitable young women, the ministrants of Persuasion in rich Corinth, whose thoughts ofttimes flit towards Ourania Aphrodite,' in whose temple they burned frankincense. They are expressly termed by Strabo ἱερό-δουλοι and 'hetaerae' dedicated to the goddess, and these are

636 *GREEK RELIGION.* [CHAP.

the same characters that figure in the impure worships of Cyprus, Byblos, Babylon, and Armenia; the immorality that Herodotus imputes to the Lydians had probably a religious intention, and we hear of the ἱερόδουλοι γυναῖκες in the Phoenician worship on Mount Eryx [83]; but such practices were certainly excluded from the ordinary Greek worships of Aphrodite, whose ritual seems to have been as austere as any other. The only other Hellenic community besides Corinth wherein we hear of unchastity in the temple-cult of Aphrodite is the city of the Locri Epizephyrii [99c], who, according to the story, to gain the goddess's aid in a war, vowed to consecrate their daughters to this service.

The title of Ourania was also attached to her worship at Aegira [32], in a temple to which access was only allowed to women; at Olympia [34] where a Pheidian masterpiece represented her with her foot upon a tortoise, an Oriental symbol, and at Megalopolis [27]. At Panticapaeum [39], the Milesian colony on the Tauric Chersonese, the worship of the goddess would be likely to have some Oriental character, and the name Ourania is applied to her in two inscriptions of the third and second century B.C. found in this place. And we have the evidence of another inscription of the same cult at Smyrna [99 p]. In regard to the later period to which, for instance, the Roman sepulchral relief at Verona belongs, dedicated to the high-priestess of Aphrodite Ourania [47 a], we may doubt whether the epithet possessed any Oriental connotation or only a vague moral or ritualistic sense.

Even where she is not expressly styled Ourania, we can recognize the Eastern divinity in Greece by many signs. The foam-born goddess is derived from the Semitic religion, and perhaps from the maritime commerce of the East; and the goddess of Cyprus and Cythera is called Ἀφρογενής by Hesiod [101]. But except in the cult-titles Ἀφρία and Ἀρφεία [3], which were probably in vogue at Larissa and in the Thracian Chersonese, there is but little reflection of this story of the birth in Greek public worship. Yet her connexion with the sea and her interest in navigation are attested by a long array of titles. Harbours and rocky promontories were

named from her or gave her names [14 a, 19 a]. At Troezen she
was worshipped as 'the watcher from the sea-cliffs[21]'; in
the Peiraeeus, at Cnidus, Mylasa, and Naucratis, as the
goddess who gave the fair wind [106 h]; she appears as the
saviour from shipwreck in the story told by Athenaeus[90]
of the Greek sailor who was sailing from Paphos to Naucratis
bearing in his ship the little idol of Aphrodite : a great storm
arose, and all the crew ran with prayers to the sacred image :
when suddenly fresh myrtle-boughs grew about the vessel and
a delicious fragrance filled it, and there was a great calm.
We gather that she bore the same character in the maritime
cities of Achaea [31], and we hear of her idol at Patrae [30 a] being
dragged up from the sea in a fisherman's net.

At Panticapaeum, as the ruler of ships, she was worshipped
by the side of Poseidon the Saviour [106 q]; and her title
Hegemone or 'leader' may have alluded originally to this
function of hers[a], and may have arisen from the practice which
the Greeks may have derived from Phoenicia of carrying her
image on board [106 r].

There are two other Greek titles that may with probability
be traced to the Oriental goddess of the sea. Leucothea is
usually interpreted as the name of a Hellenic divinity of the
waters, but when we consider that the chief centre of her
worship was Corinth, and that it was found in many other
districts of the Aphrodite-cult, we might surmise that there
was a close connexion between the goddess and the sea-
nymph; and much stronger evidence is given by Leucothea's
relationship with Cadmus, and with Melicertes the Phoenician
Melkarth, who even when Hellenized seems to have retained
his Phoenician character as a devourer of infants. We meet
also with ceremonies of mourning and sadness in the worship
of Leucothea at Thebes, and perhaps in Crete[b], as we find
them elsewhere in the worships of Aphrodite. Moreover, her
leap into the sea reminds us at once of those divine personages
who haunted Crete and the Carian coast, who leap into the

[a] The context in Hesychius suggests
vaguely that the title is connected with
the sea. It came afterwards to have
a political significance, vide infra,
p. 662.
[b] Plutarch, 228 F.

sea for various reasons, and who seem to have been different forms of an Artemis Aphrodite [a].

Lastly, it is possible that the maritime goddess of the East appeared in the form of Aphrodite Aeneias, the story of the wanderings of Aeneas being the legendary record of the diffusion of this cult [45 c]. To understand the origin of Aeneas and the myth concerning him, we must keep in view the peculiar and sacred character of Aeneas in Homer, and we must consider the meaning of the title Αἰνειάς as applied to the goddess [b]. The Aeneas of Homer is unlike any of the other heroes, Greek or Trojan; he appears as a mysterious religious figure to whom the future rule of the land was reserved by Providence; his character and the prophecy about him are only to be explained if the poet was aware of a family of Aeneadae having power in the land, who themselves or whose mythic ancestor were connected with a certain cult. And this view is supported by the statement of Strabo [c], made probably on the authority of Demetrius of Scepsis, that for many generations there survived in this city the descendants of Aeneas who were still called kings, and who enjoyed certain honours, the kingship probably possessing here as elsewhere a priestly quality. We gather also that Arctinus, the author of the 'Ιλίου πέρσις, was aware of the legendary settlement of the Aeneadae on Mount Ida.

[a] Vide p. 645 and pp. 477, 478. Aphrodite herself, according to a doubtful version of the Adonis-myth (Ptolem. Hephaest. *Nov. Hist.* Bk. 3. p. 198, Westermann) flung herself into the sea in sorrow for his death; human victims to Apollo were thrown from the Leucadian rock and from a promontory in Cyprus (Strabo, pp. 452 and 683); Firmicus Maternus (*de Errore Profan. Relig.* p. 85) records the myth that Dionysius, the god of vegetation, was thrown into the sea by Lycurgus; these myths are probably derived from a very widely spread harvest-ritual, of which an essential feature was the throwing into the water the effigy of the decaying deity of vegetation for the purpose of recovering the lost vigour of the land; vide Fraser, *Golden Bough*, vol. 1, pp. 258–261. Probably the many myths of women being put to sea in a chest are derived from the same ritual; some divinity is disguised under the woman's form and name in such stories. Auge is a forgotten name of either Athena or Artemis; Rhoio is the Carian Aphrodite-Artemis (Diod. Sic. 5. 62); Danaë is probably the title of the Argive Hera.

[b] J. A. Hild. *La légende d'Énée avant Virgile*, Paris, 1883; Klausen, *Aeneas und die Penaten.*

[c] Pp. 607, 608.

And from his evidence and Homer's we can conclude that
the story of the wanderings of Aeneas was of later growth,
and that the Troad was the centre from which the name
of this hero and this worship spread over various parts of
the Mediterranean. But what meaning can we find for the
title Αἰνειάς, which belonged to Aphrodite in her cults at
Actium, in Leucas, and in Sicily ? From its form it might be
a patronymic, but it could not mean the ' mother of Aeneas,'
nor can we suppose it to mean the 'daughter of Aeneas,' though
this would be consistent with the form of the word [a]. The
divinity may have sometimes taken the name of the mortal,
when the clan desired to identify their mythic ancestor or
chieftain with the divinity, and so we may account for the
title of Zeus-Agamemnon. A man however might be identified
with a god but scarcely with a goddess.

It is much more likely that this title of Aphrodite is of
independent origin, indigenous in the Troad and not to be
derived from the later and unimportant city of Aeneia on the
Thermaic gulf; that the goddess lent her title to her particular
clan of worshippers, and that to explain their name and their
position in the country the priestly hero Aeneias was imagined.
If he arose in this manner, as the mythic priest of the goddess
taking her title in a masculine form, we could understand the
mysterious character that attaches to him in the *Iliad*. We
can easily gather instances from Greek myth and religion
of heroes and heroines who are merely the shadows or
emanations of divinities, as Auge, Iphigenia and Atalanta
of Artemis, Trophonius of Zeus-Hades. What would be
exceptional in the present case, if this theory were fully
proved, would be that the hero embodied the title not
of the male but the female divinity. But this would be
especially likely to occur where the goddess was served by
priests ; and while in the native Greek cults it is usual to find
the female ministrant in the ritual of the female divinity [b], it

[a] This has been pointed out by Professor Nettleship in the fourth edition
of Conington's *Virgil*, p. xlvi.
  [b] Examples however are recorded of
the contrary; as for instance at Pellene
Artemis Σώτειρα was served by priests
(Artemis [1,3 f]) and Athena Κραναία at
Elatea was served by boy-priests; Paus.

is not unusual to find the priest attached to the service of the Oriental goddess.

Thus even in late times we hear of the Cinyradae, the priestly family attached to her cult in Cyprus ; the king of Paphos down to the time of Alexander is 'priest of Queen Aphrodite[a],' and according to the legend in the *Theogony* it was the fair Phaethon whom Aphrodite carried off and 'made a secret minister in her holy temples[102].'

The name and hero Aeneas then may have arisen directly from that title of the goddess ; or indirectly from it, if he were the imaginary ancestor of the Aeneadae the priests of Ἀφροδίτη Αἰνειάs. What is the true explanation of the title itself, we shall probably never know : it may be as Wörner ingeniously suggests, a derivative from Αἴνη[b], the name of the goddess of Ecbatana whose temple is described by Polybius, and who was probably closely akin to Anaitis ; or it may denote 'Aphrodite the consenting,' coming from the Greek root. The later story of the wanderings of Aeneas is the story of the diffusion of a cult[c] : and in most places where we find the name of Aeneas we find it in connexion with the worship of Aphrodite[45e]; at Aeneia, in Cythera, at Actium, on the coast north of Buthrotum, on the south-east coast of Italy, and notably in Sicily. His landing at Delos and

10. 34, 4; at Calauria, a young girl officiated in the temple of Poseidon until she was of marriageable age; *ib.* 2. 33, 3. These are certainly exceptional facts ; but where the worship of a god and goddess was combined, a male ministrant was naturally appointed. The chief functionary in the cult of the Ephesian Artemis was a priest, and this again may be due to Oriental influence.

[a] Timocharis Echetimos and Timaï-ros, kings of Paphos, are all ἱερῆς τῆς ἀνάσσης; vide Six, *Revue Numismatique*, 1883, pp. 350, 351, and *Revue des Études grecques*, 1892, pp. 55, 56. As the male-ministrant was sometimes preferred in her worship, so she seems to have exhibited at times a pre-

ference for the male animal in her sacrifices[61, 114]; both facts may be explained by her androgynous character, vide Robertson Smith, *Religion of the Semites*, p. 453. From some of her temples women were excluded, for instance from the temple on the Olympus promontory in Cyprus[65]; and according to Artemidorus it was death for a woman to enter the temple of Artemis at Ephesus, the Ephesian Artemis being a semi-Hellenic form of the goddess of Asia Minor (Artemis[133]).

[b] Roscher, *Lexicon*, p. 173; Polyb. 10. 27.

[c] This is also Wörner's view and on the whole Klausen's, *Aeneas und die Penaten*, pp. 316, 317.

Crete, recorded by Dionysios of Halicarnassus[a] and Virgil, may arise from some legendary association with that Cretan and Delian worship of Aphrodite which has been described. And in Argos, where Pausanias saw a statue of Aeneas, we have noticed traces of the Oriental worship of the goddess.

In Sicily the cult becomes naturally blended with that of the Carthaginian goddess of Eryx, and hence probably arose the legend, which is hardly earlier than the third century, of the relations between Aeneas and Dido[b].

In her own land, the Troad, Aphrodite Aeneias was in all probability another form of the earth-goddess Cybele, and hence we may understand the stories that were told of the burial of Aeneas among the Berecyntes [45 c], the votaries of Cybele, and that connected him and his Penates with Samothrace[c]. But as the divinity of a clan that wandered far over the Mediterranean she would naturally become regarded as a goddess of the sea in this as in many other of her cults. We have a proof of this on a coin of Leucas of the second century B.C., that shows us a figure of Aphrodite, derived probably from a public statue, with an 'aplustre' among her emblems, and a ship's prow upon the reverse (Coin Pl. B 45). This has been rightly connected by Curtius[d] with the statue in the temple of Aphrodite Aeneias which Dionysius mentions as standing on the small island between the canal and the city of Leucas. And her maritime character may possibly be illustrated by the title ἔφιππος, which we may believe she bore in some well-known centre of her worship, although we have only a mysterious allusion made to it by the scholiast of the *Iliad*, who tells us the simple story that when Aeneas had sailed to the west he mounted a horse and commemorated the

[a] Dionysios regards the city called Aeneia on the Thermaic gulf as a foundation of Aeneas; and we find a representation of Aeneas carrying Anchises on its coins of the sixth century B.C.; Head, *Hist. Num.* p. 189; Roscher, *Lexicon*, p. 167.

[b] For the view of Dido as the δαίμων Καρχηδόνιος, another form of Astarte, vide Movers, *Die Phönizier*, vol. I. pp. 609–611. We have no direct evidence about the origin of the Eryx-cult; but it may reasonably be supposed to have been derived from Carthage, for we find in it the Oriental feature of the ἱερόδουλοι γυναῖκες [83].

[c] The connexion between Aeneas and the Cabiri probably explains the picture of Parrhasius. 'Aeneas Castorque ac Pollux in eadem tabula.' Plin. *N. H.* 35. 10, 71.

[d] *Hermes.* 10. 243.

event by dedicating a statue to his mother that represented her on horseback [45 c].

The title and the story are so peculiar that no scholiast could have gratuitously invented it. The term ἔφιππος must have been known to have been somewhere connected with the worship of Aphrodite Aeneias, although there is no other hint at all of her connexion with horses, except that Hesychius identifies Hippodameia with Aphrodite. Now the symbolic sense of the horse in Greek religion was manifold : we find it in the worships of Apollo and Helios, the chthonian divinities and the wind-gods, and especially of Poseidon ' who delights in the neighing of steeds and in the war-ships of dark-blue prow [a].' We might believe, therefore, that the horse comes into the legend and cult of Aphrodite as a symbol of the sea-goddess. But another explanation may be offered, when we consider another and more important aspect of this divinity [b].

The goddess of the waters also had charge of the flowers and growths of the earth, and the Oriental goddess was known as Ἄνθεια 'the flower-goddess' in Crete, and worshipped with offerings of fruits and herbs [59 c].

The name of the locality Ἱεροκηπία [107 d], near Paphos, must be derived from a sacred title of Aphrodite. And her functions as a divinity of vegetation are alluded to by the similar name of her temple in Athens, the temple ' in the gardens,' near which stood the statue of Aphrodite Ourania [11 a]. According to Hesychius, trees were cut down and set up in dedication to Aphrodite by the portal of the house, a custom perhaps confined to Cyprus, and probably connected with the worship of Adonis [107 f].

We may believe that the association of Aphrodite with the Hours, found in a worship at Olympia [107 i], and appearing occasionally in surviving monuments, alluded to the processes of birth and growth which all these divinities protected. The pomegranate was sacred to Aphrodite in Cyprus, and on coins of the Roman period of Magnesia on the Maeander we

[a] Arist. *Equit.* 551.   Cf. Artemid. *Oneirocr.* 1. 56.
[b] Vide infra, p. 650.

find the figure of the goddess with this fruit in her hand and with the inscription Ἀφροδίτη Μηλεία[a]. Therefore when Empedocles and Sophocles describe her as ' the giver of life,' ' the goddess of abundant fruits,' they may have been deriving these epithets from actual cult [107 h].

It is probable that the aspect of the Oriental Aphrodite as the earth-goddess is primitive. The Ishtar-myth is certainly explained most naturally in this way, and the great festal sacrifice offered to the goddess of Hierapolis, called the festival of ' the torch[a],' at which large trees were erected in the court of her temple, and various sacrificial animals were suspended from them and all burnt together [107 e], belongs to that widespread ritual of fire, which was intended to evoke the necessary warmth and heat for the crops. Its efficacy lay partly in the supposed power of sympathetic magic [b], partly in the pleasant oblations to the tree-spirit or earth-spirit ; such festivals have taken place in Europe usually on May-day or on Midsummerday : at Hierapolis it fell on some day in early spring, and in many of its details it resembles the sacrifice offered to Artemis at Patrae, which has been described in a former chapter, and of which the essential parts were the erecting green trees round the altar, the kindling a great fire, and the driving into it droves of wild and tame animals. The divinities to whom these rituals were consecrated must have been closely akin in some parts of their nature [c].

Another worship with which the Oriental goddess, at least at a later stage, was nearly connected was that of Cybele, the great earth-goddess of Phrygia, who herself may be only

---

[a] Head, *Hist. Num.* p. 502.

[b] Vide chapter on Artemis, pp. 430, 458. For parallel practices and their significance among other nations, vide Frazer, *The Golden Bough*, vol. 2. pp. 246- 285 ; Mannhardt, *Baumkultus*, ch. 6. pp. 508–512 ; the kindling of trees, the passing of cattle through or into the flames, the semblance of human sacrifice, occurred in most of these, and at Hierapolis : vide Lucian, *de Dea Syr.* ch. 58.

[c] It has been shown that in the Greek cult of Artemis, the two ideas of a goddess of vegetation and a goddess of fresh water are blended. This was probably also the case in the original cult of Aphrodite in the East ; but in Greek religion it does not appear to have been so ; she is prominently a goddess of vegetation, but the stream, the fountain, and the lake, were not consecrated to her. We hear only of the Aphrodite ἐν καλάμοις or ἐν ἕλει at Samos [75].

another form of Ishtar Astarte. The Galli, who were prominent in the Phrygian rites, seem to have played their part
also in the temple-worship at Hierapolis ; and it would appear
from certain details in Lucian's account of it, that their practice
of self-mutilation was partly for the purpose of securing
fertility either for the family or the fields. The Phrygian
goddess who rides on the lion has her counterpart in the
Babylonian-Assyrian religion ; the armed Cappadocian Mâ—
the mother-goddess, a divinity of like nature with Cybele, is
a type that recalls the armed Astarte of Ascalon ; the bull and
the ram were sacred to Cybele as they were to Aphrodite ;
and as the Eastern goddess showed a predilection for the
priest and Aphrodite is worshipped by her Aeneas, so Cybele
was served by Hermes Cadmilos; as the Semitic goddess was
the tutelary genius of cities, so Cybele came to wear the
turreted crown. Lastly, the lamentations for Thammuz, who
appeared to the Greeks with the form and name of Adonis,
are found in the Phrygian worship as the mourning for Attis.

The character of the Eastern goddess as a divinity of vegetation emerges into the clearest light when we examine the
traits of Attis and Adonis, different local names for the same
personage in her religion [108]. These have been gathered
together and clearly set forth by Mr. Frazer in *The Golden
Bough*[a] ; and his conclusion that Adonis is a form of the spirit
of vegetation, the tree or corn-spirit, seems sufficiently certain.
He is born from the myrtle-tree, which like the rose is his
emblem [108 a]. Autumn-fruits are offered to him, and small
beds of flowers that grow up and wither rapidly, called ' the
gardens of Adonis' [108 b, c]. In Lucian's account of the worship
of the Dea Syria, and in the famous idyl of Theocritus,
describing the ritual at Alexandria, we have the record of the
young god, who dies and lives again ; at the latter city an
essential part of the ritual that refers to his death and
resurrection is his immersion in the sea[b], with which we may

[a] Vol. I, pp. 278–285.

[b] The same idea of a divinity of
vegetation who passes away over the
sea and returns was expressed in the
feasts of ἀναγώγια and καταγώγια in

the worship of Aphrodite at Eryx, who
crosses the sea to Libya and returns
(Aelian, *de Nat. Anim.* 4. 2) ; probably also in the artistic type of Aphrodite riding on a swan over the waves.

compare many instances collected by Mr. Frazer of the
primitive rural practice of throwing the dead and decayed
god into the water[a]. We are told by Firmicus Maternus
that in the Phrygian rites of the mother of the gods a pine-
tree was cut down each year, and in the midst of it was bound
the image of a youth [108 h] : this must have been the image of
Attis, and from Lucian's account of a similar rite at Byblos
we may conclude that the pine-tree and the image were burnt
at the end of the ceremony. The mourning for the dead or
departing god was interpreted by Eusebius [109 c] as alluding to
the fall of the year, the withering of flowers and herbs, and in
this he is followed by most modern writers. But Professor
Robertson Smith [b] expresses the view that ' the mourning for
Adonis was not originally a lament over decaying nature, but
simply the official mourning over the slaughter of the theanthropic victim in whose death the god died.' And he believes
that those who mourned for him had originally pierced him,
but that this part of the rite had been dropped when the
mourners could no longer understand why they should slay
their own god, and when they came to believe that his passing
away was due to the same natural law by which the life of
the fields and woods passed away. The earliest form of the
sacrifice would be the offering of a holy swine to Adonis the
swine-god, in fact the offering of the god to himself, ' a most
ancient form of sacramental and piacular mystery in which
the worshippers attest their kinship with the animal god, and
offer in sacrifice an animal of the same kind, which, except on
these mystical occasions, it would be impious to bring to the
altar [c].' We have the same mysterious idea in the Brauronian
worship of Artemis examined above, in the sacrifice of the
bull-calf to Dionysos at Tenedos, and in the sheep-offering to
Aphrodite in Cyprus, if we accept a convincing and brilliant
emendation made by Professor Robertson Smith in the text
of Joannes Lydus [d]. His view that just as Dionysos was the

---

[a] *The Golden Bough*, vol. 1, pp. 260, 261.

[b] *Religion of the Semites*, p. 392, n. 1.

[c] *Ib.*, p. 460.

[d] P. 451 (Jo. Lydus, *de Mensibus*, 4.

p. 80, Bonn. ed.) : in Cyprus πρόβατον κωδίῳ ἐσκεπασμένον συνέθυον τῇ 'Αφρο-δίτῃ : he points out that the phrase κωδίῳ ἐσκεπασμένον is quite meaning-less, and proposes ἐσκεπασμένοι : the

bull-god, so Adonis was originally the swine, and that 'in this, as in many other cases, the sacred victim has been changed by false interpretation into the enemy of the god,' lacks direct evidence, but the indirect evidence which has been collected by Mr. Frazer is very weighty; and to this may be added the explanation of Adonis' death given in a later version of the myth, namely that the swine who slew Adonis was really the embodiment of the jealous Ares ; for in this version the consciousness of the divine character of the animal seems to be preserved. This story is one of the many that arise from a misunderstanding of sacrificial ritual ; we have a much more absurd myth, arising from the same origin, given us by Diodorus Siculus to explain why swine were sacred or tabooed in the Carian worship of Hemithea, a Carian goddess who may be called Artemis-Aphrodite, and why no wine was used in her worship ; two maidens, Molpadias and Parthenos (whose names are certainly titles of Aphrodite-Artemis herself), were watching their father's wine-pots, when they fell asleep and swine entered and broke the pots ; as he was a man of violent temper, and the loss of the wine was all the more serious as this inestimable boon to mankind had only recently been invented, the maidens flung themselves into the sea, and received divine honours [a]. Wherever the swine were sacred in Aphrodite's worship, we may safely infer that they had some reference to Adonis. Ordinarily in the Greek communities the swine was not offered to this goddess [114 d] as we learn from Aristophanes, and though the Greeks were ignorant of the real reason, we may believe this to have been the peculiar sanctity that belonged to this animal in the Oriental cult, as we hear from Lucian that at Hierapolis the pig was too sacred to be either sacrificed or eaten. But it is probable that the especially sacred beast would be offered on rare occasions by way of solemn expiation [b]; and we hear of such sacrifices at Castniae in Pamphylia [56], at Metropolis in Thessaly [5],

---

sacrificers will then have been arrayed in the skin of the sacred animal, testifying their kinship to it and to their divinity.

[a] Vide Artemis-cult [125], Diod. Sic. 5. 63.

[b] Vide Frazer, *The Golden Bough*, vol. i. p. 52.

and of the offering of wild swine in Cyprus [114 c], where, as
Antiphanes says in a line of his *Corinthia*, 'Aphrodite took
particular pleasure in pigs,' and where we have more than one
proof of the presence of Adonis. The Ὑστήρια, or feast of
pigs at Argos, had reference probably to the cult of Adonis
and Aphrodite, and we have other traces of the Eastern
goddess in that city, such as the Hermaphroditic feast of
Ὑβριστικά [114 c], and also clear record of the worship of Adonis
there [108 i]. Now whether we regard Adonis as the swine-
god and accept Professor Robertson Smith's interpretation of
the sacrifice of the divine animal that embodied him and
of the lamentations for the god's death, or whether we say
that the mourning was only for the passing away of the glory
of the year, we may in either case regard Adonis as the spirit
of vegetation. For we have independent evidence that he was
intimately connected with the growth of the fields and the
woods ; and if we had indubitable proof that he was ever
regarded as incarnate in the swine, this incarnation would
reveal the same character of the god, for among many communities of Northern Europe the boar or the sow is regarded
as the embodiment of the corn-spirit.

Therefore, when the cult and ritual of Adonis came to the
shores of Greece, it must have helped to express more clearly
the character of Aphrodite as a divinity of vegetation. But
the Adonis-cult was a comparatively late importation into the
Greek Peninsula. No doubt it had at a much earlier time
been diffused from its Syrian and Phoenician centres throughout the Greek cities of the Asia Minor coast and to the
Eastern islands ; but two centuries may have passed, since
Sappho sang the dirge of Adonis in Lesbos [108 d], before the
Greek mainland received this strange orgiastic worship. The
earliest allusion to its introduction at Athens is in the fragment of the Βουκόλοι of Cratinus, composed probably before
the Peloponnesian war. The poet is satirizing some archon
who refused a chorus to Sophocles, but granted one to some
poetaster who was not fit 'to train a chorus even for the
Adonis-festival'; when this was written, the Adonia were
probably recent and of small prestige [108 f].

It may be that the introduction of the Phrygian worship of Cybele, which made its way to Athens and Thebes at a not much earlier period[a], either brought with it the ritual of Adonis or prepared the minds of the Greeks to tolerate it. The close affinity between the two worships has been noticed ; and Aristophanes, in the *Lysistrate*, when he inveighs against the 'luxury of the women,' and declares that the cries of lamentation for Adonis disturb the debates in the Ecclesia, speaks in the same context of the Phrygian drums and the Phrygian Sabazius[108 e]. And at a later period Aphrodite is addressed as Cybele, and the figures of Attis, Adonis, and Dionysos are scarcely distinguishable, as we gather from Plutarch's account of the two Atteis, from the lines of an oracle given to the Rhodians, and from a late Orphic hymn[108 h]. But the Greeks who adopted and transformed Dionysos and Aphrodite never completely Hellenized Adonis: the more masculine tempers were averse to the effeminate Eastern god[b], with his train of emasculate priests and a lascivious ritual that the more austere state-religion of Greece probably failed to purify ; the saner minds bred in a religious atmosphere, that was on the whole genial and temperate, revolted from the din of cymbals and drums, the meaningless ecstasies of sorrow and joy that marked the new religion[c]. Yet it won its way, thanks partly to the plague and the Peloponnesian war that lowered the ethos and the intelligence of Greece. We have sufficient proofs of its prevalence at Athens: at the time of the departure of the host for Sicily, the Adonia were being celebrated, the figures of Adonis were laid out on biers before the doors, and the women were performing the pageant of a funeral, smiting their breasts and singing dirges for the dead god ; the omen

[a] Vide Gerhard's *Gesammelte Akademische Abhandlungen*, no. 15: Über das Metroon und die Göttermutter. The importation into Attica of the Syrian worship of Aphrodite from Citium was still later (vide [13 c]).

[b] In a line of the Orphic hymn[108 h] Adonis is addressed as male and female.

[c] The old-fashioned Greek view is expressed by Lucian, who reprobates 'the Phrygian demon, the lascivious orgy over the shepherd; the secret rites of initiation, the disreputable mysteries from which men are excluded . . . mere corruption of the mind'[118 g].

was afterwards understood and long remembered [108 d]. We have mention of the Adonis-gardens in Plato and Theophrastus, and an inscription belonging to the end of the fourth century B.C. speaks of a vote of thanks passed by the company of Aphrodite's worshippers in honour of a certain Stephanos who conducted the procession of the Adonia according to the traditional rites [108 g]; the 'tradition' is Eastern, and we may regard Adonis as a Hellenistic rather than a Hellenic divinity. For the celebrity and nature of his worship at Alexandria, the great centre of the Hellenistic world, we have the evidence of the Theocritean idyl ; although the song of Aphrodite's love is human in its tone and very winning, yet there are no moral or spiritual ideas in the worship at all, no conception of a resurrection that might stir human hopes : in this, as in Bion's verses, Adonis personifies merely the life of the fields and gardens that passes away and blooms again. All that Hellenism could do for this Eastern god was to invest him with the grace of its idyllic poetry.

It seems probable from the evidence that has been given that this function of Aphrodite, the protection of the life and growth of the earth, belongs to the earliest conception that the Eastern peoples formed of her. And this would explain and imply her close connexion with the fertilizing waters; as we have the analogy in the Semitic religion of the Baalim, the gods both of the land and the waters that nourish it [a]. But her maritime character is probably of later and accidental growth, coming to her naturally as her cult was spread by a maritime people from East to West. Nothing is so conservative of primitive ideas as the sacrifice; and, though we hear of her sacred fish in the lake near her temple at Hierapolis, none of the animals sacrificed to her in the Greek, and as far as we know in the Semitic, cults, allude at all to the goddess of the sea [114]. Among birds, the partridge and the goose were offered to her, the sparrow, if not sacrificed, was sacred, the dove was too sacred even to be sacrificed in the

---

[a] Robertson Smith, *Religion of the Semites,* p. 99.

East, but in Greece was certainly offered, as we can conclude from those monuments which represent the worshipper standing before the goddess and holding a dove ; but these animals belong to the goddess of spring or the goddess of fertility. The other animals, of whose sacred character in this worship we have direct or indirect evidence—the swine, ram, goat, bull, kid, lamb—are the natural animals for sacrifice or consecration in an agricultural community. And the horse itself, if this animal also on somewhat scanty evidence may be supposed to have been sacred to Aphrodite, may have alluded to the fruits of the earth at least as naturally as to the waves of the sea. For we have the record of the horse-headed Demeter of Phigaleia, and we see from the evidence collected by Mr. Frazer, that the horse is one of the most common embodiments of the corn-spirit.

We may be sure, then, that the Eastern divinity which spread over the Mediterranean through Cyprus to Greece, came rather as a goddess of the earth, akin to Demeter Proserpine and Dionysos, than as a goddess of the sea, though she always retained her interest in the seafarer.

Both in Greece and the East the connexion between the powers of life and nature and the powers of the lower world and death was natural and close and needed to be expressed in worship.

As Ishtar mourns for the beautiful youth Dumuzi or Tammuz, so among the tribes of the Lebanon we hear of the type of the mourning Aphrodite who sat with head veiled and bowed and the tears streaming down her cheeks[109]. This sorrow Macrobius explains—and in a certain sense he may be right—as the image of the winter. But the myth of the East and the later poetry of Greece interpreted it as her sorrow for the dead Adonis, and Bion calls to her, 'No longer slumber on purple draperies, but rise, sad one, thou of the mourning robe, and smite thy breasts.' And according to another legend, the goddess flings herself down the Leucadian rock in grief for her beloved. This myth may be a meaningless fancy; but it corresponds, as has been partly shown, with certain facts of ritual and with another better known legend. The grave of Ariadne-Aphrodite was actually shown in Cyprus [110 k], as the grave of Zeus in Crete and of Dionysos in Delphi. From the record of the ceremonies performed in the worship of Adonis we gather that the dead body of the god was laid out on the bier [108 b]; we are nowhere told that the dead goddess was placed by his side; but we may well believe that this was the case when we examine the myth of Pygmalion as told by Ovid, and interpret it in reference to the love of Adonis and Aphrodite; Pygmalion loves the dead image which he decks in fine raiment, and which at last gains the breath of life. But, according to Apollodorus, Pygmalion is related to Adonis, and Hesychius gives us the name Πυγμαίων as a Cypriote synonym for Adonis [111 c]; and Clemens Alexandrinus gives us the interesting information that the image which Pygmalion carved and loved, and brought to life by the power of his prayer, was that of Aphrodite herself [111 b]. Through these obscure hints of legend a certain fact seems to be partially revealed; that in Cyprus in some religious ceremony, some scenic representation of the Adonia perhaps, the image of the dead goddess [a] was exposed, and then after due performance of certain rites she was supposed to be restored to life. We have the parallel belief in the Assyrian religion about the descent of Ishtar into hell, and her rescue by the messenger of the gods, who sprinkles her with the waters of life and recovers her [b]; and the legends of the deaths of Semiramis and Dido, if we interpret these as names of the Assyrian and Phoenician divinity, embody the same conception of the divinity that must die. This dual character of the Eastern goddess is summarily expressed in the lines of the pseudo-Plautus, who appeals to 'divine Astarte, the strength, the life, the salvation of men and gods,' and again 'the power of destruction, death and decay [110 a].'

---

[a] There is possibly an allusion to such a form in that mysterious passage [110 i] in Hesychius (s.v. 'Εριννύς), which has never been successfully interpreted, in which the Erinnys is explained as an infernal power or as an 'eidolon' of Aphrodite; 'eidolon' in this context must either mean 'phantom' or image.

[b] Vide *De la Saussaye Religionsgeschichte*, vol. I, pp. 338, 339

Finding then in Greece the frequent worship of Aphrodite
as a divinity of death [110] and the lower world, we can regard
this aspect of her as derived from the original tradition. We
hear of the worship at Delphi of 'Aphrodite on the tomb,'
by whose image the spirits of the dead received libations ;
at Argos, the same cult is attested by the strange title
Τυμβωρύχος, denoting the goddess of graves; at Thespiae,
Corinth, and Mantinea by the name of Μελαινίς, the 'dark '
goddess[a]; and the same allusion was probably conveyed by the
epithets Μυχεία, mentioned and probably wrongly interpreted
by Suidas, Εὐμενής attached to Aphrodite by Hesychius, and
Εὐβούλα a title that appears to belong to her on an inscription
found at Paphos ; both these two latter terms being known
appellatives of the lower gods. The story given in Plutarch
about the funeral ceremonies held in honour of Aphrodite in
Aegina and commemorating the heroes of the island who fell
at Troy, shows us the same character of the goddess[b]. From
an inscription quoted by the author of a work ascribed to
Aristotle, we gather that there was a close cult-relation
between Aphrodite and Persephone at Thebes [110 l].

Other indirect but interesting evidence of a similar worship
can be extracted from the legends given by Ovid, Plutarch,
and Antoninus Liberalis [110 g], of the hard-hearted maiden in
Cyprus, whom Plutarch calls by the impossible name of
' Parakuptousa,' and whom divine retribution turned to stone
because she looked unfeelingly on the corpse of her lover. But
Ovid and Plutarch were both aware that the goddess herself
was called by the same name in Cyprus, and the poet tells us
that there was a statue in Cyprus representing the frozen
petrified form. And when Plutarch goes on to say that a
similar story was told in Crete about a maiden named Gorgo,
who came to a like end, we have an easy clue to these
romantic legends about callous young women with remarkable names ; we detect a worship in both islands of
an Aphrodite Gorgo, a goddess conceived as dead and
represented in frozen slumber ; and we have monumental

---

[a] The Aphrodite Μελαινίς of Thespiae seems also to have had some connexion with the moon: vide next ch., p. 699.

[b] *Quaest. Graec.* 44.

evidence for this[a]. Moreover, this worship must in some way have been combined or confused with another in which Aphrodite was known by the very different name of Παρακύπτουσα, 'the goddess who looks out of the corners of her eyes,' an epithet alluding to the sidelong glances of the lover. As usual, the epithets become detached and the stories about the maidens arise from them.

It may have been from this original belief in her as a power of the shadowy world, the home of destiny and retribution, that an association in cult arose between Aphrodite and the Fates and Furies, who according to Epimenides' genealogy were her sisters; and, again, between Aphrodite and Nemesis, the Rhamnusian goddess, who, as I have tried to show, was no mere personification, but a real divinity akin to Aphrodite, if not another form of her, and possessing a marked character as a goddess of doom or punishment[112 a, b]. It is probable also that the cult-relations of Aphrodite with Hermes, of which we have record at Argos, Megalopolis, Cnidos, and Lesbos, arose from the chthonian aspect of the two divinities[110 m].

So far it is the physical or elemental nature of Aphrodite that has been traced in the cults of the various Greek communities; and it does not appear that the Greeks have added anything new to the tradition which they received.

But we have seen that the Eastern goddess was not merely a 'nature-divinity,' but a divinity of the state and the city[116 a], and at Ascalon a goddess of war. We may believe that the cult of the armed Aphrodite belongs to the first period of her worship in Greece[105]. In Cyprus, if we may look to that as her first Hellenic settlement, we hear of Aphrodite Ἐγχειος, and probably the epithet denotes 'the goddess of the spear.' But in Cythera we have still clearer proof given us by Herodotus of the very ancient worship of the Eastern goddess as a warlike divinity. We may believe it to have existed in Corinth, the ancient home of Aphrodite Ourania[16], and we may suppose that it came at an early time to Thebes, and brought about the close association between her and Ares at that city. But nowhere was it of such repute as among the

---

[a] Vide infra, p. 699.

Spartans, who doubtless derived it from Cythera [a], and who gave to the new goddess the martial epithets of Areia and Ἀριοντία [25]. We have a string of epigrams in the *Anthology* referring to this Spartan worship, and playing in various ways on the idea that the stern Lycurgean constitution would only admit Aphrodite if she put off her effeminacy and learned the use of weapons. This, of course, is a misunderstanding : it was the Phoenician, not the Lycurgean, state-religion that gave her the spear or the bow, and for this reason she was once at least mis-named Athena, at the Syrian Laodicea [105 1], and for this among other reasons was more frequently identified with Artemis. I have already suggested that the cult of Artemis Ἀστρατεία on the Laconian coast preserves in a meaningless title the Phoenician name Astarte [b].

In the later Greek literature, the references to the shield and the spear in the hands of the goddess of love are generally mere playful allusions to her love for Ares. But down to the last period of Greek history she preserved her inherited character as a goddess of war in some of the Greek states. The most famous of these worships was that of Aphrodite Stratonikis at Smyrna [47], whose temple claimed rights of sanctuary ; we gather from Tacitus that this title was of ancient origin in that city, and could not have been attached to her, as has sometimes been supposed, out of mere compliment to Queen Stratonike. At Mylasa, Aphrodite was the goddess 'who goes with the army' (Στρατεία) [51] ; at Amorgus, the locality in which she was worshipped appears to have been called Ἀσπίς, 'the place of a shield' [70], whence she took her title of Ἀφροδίτη Οὐρανία ἣ ἐν ἀσπίδι. At Mantinea, the temple of Aphrodite Συμμαχία commemorated the aid given by the Mantineans to Rome and Augustus at the battle of Actium [24] ; and in the oath of alliance between the Arcadian Orchomenos and the Achaean league we find the name of Aphrodite [33]. At Argos, where the Oriental cult had struck deep roots, the worship of Aphrodite Νικηφόρος must have been inspired by the Eastern idea of the warlike goddess, though the people explained it in another way [22 a].

---

[a] An inscription recently discovered attests the cult of Aphrodite Οὐρανία near Amyclae [25 b].   [b] p. 485.

When Sulla, after his victory at Chaeronea, inscribed his trophy with the names of Ares, Aphrodite, and Nike, it is probable that the association of the two former divinities on such a monument was a recognition of the warlike character which may have belonged to the goddess in certain parts of Boeotia.

But her civic and political functions came to her chiefly through her interest in the family and in births and marriages [118]. She was revered as ' the cherisher of children ' at Cyprus and elsewhere [118 i], and before marriage a kid was sacrificed to her ; while at Paphos, where she was worshipped as a civic divinity by the side of Zeus Polieus and Hera [61], we find that as late as the second century A. D. children were consecrated to her charge [118 b], a custom derived perhaps from the East, as we are informed by Lucian that the young men and girls at Hierapolis were in the habit of offering locks of their hair to the goddess of the city [a] ; and in a late Greek inscription we find Astarte invoked in the same prayer with Eros, Harpocrates, and Apollo as the protectress of the family [b].

The charge of the actual processes of birth was assigned in the Greek states usually to Artemis or Eileithyia ; but it is possible that Aphrodite herself was invoked under the name Genetyllis [118 g], if the view expressed by the scholiast on Aristophanes is correct.   But though we have the Venus Genetrix in Rome, we have no Aphrodite Γενέτειρα in Greece, and no clear proof of an Aphrodite Γενετυλλίς.   The Genetyllides are contemptuously mentioned by Aristophanes and Lucian as powers of doubtful origin and doubtful character, who maintained themselves on the luxury and superstition of married women, and whom the husband regarded with suspicion and dislike.   In her worship on the Attic coast, under the title of Κωλιάς, she may have been regarded as a goddess of child-birth [14 a, 118 g] ; for though the epithet, which has been identified by E. Curtius [c] with the Samothracian epithet Καλιάς ' the goddess in the grotto,' gives us no clue, yet the Koliades are mentioned by the side of the Genetyllides in Lucian's tirade against these expensive

---

[a] *De Dea Syria*, p. 58.   [b] *Athenaion*, 4. p. 458.
[c] *Götting. Gel. Anz.* 1860, p. 418.

divinities of midwifery. In the cult of Aphrodite Ctesylla in Ceos [72] and the legend explaining it, we may see an allusion to the goddess of child-birth, especially as she was evidently related closely in this worship to Artemis Hekaerge. At Oropus [10] she shared an altar with Athena the Healer and the daughters of Asclepios [a], and perhaps we have here an expression of the same idea that gave her the name of Κουροτρόφος [118 i].

Her connexion with marriage is much closer : in fact she appropriates the functions, and at Sparta even the name of Hera [25 e]. We hear of an Aphrodite of the bridal-chamber (Θαλάμων) [118 h]; of an Aphrodite Ἅρμα at Delphi [7], the goddess who joins together in matrimony, a title which gives us perhaps the clue to the real meaning of the name Harmonia, the daughter of Aphrodite, who was originally the goddess herself at Thebes ; we find an Aphrodite Νυμφία, the goddess of the bridal [118 f], on the road between Troezen and Hermione. And among the ideas concerning the character and worship of Aphrodite, to which the later Greek writers give expression, those which are associated with wedlock have most moral interest. Artemidorus in his *Oneirocriticon* maintains that Ourania Aphrodite, using the term in its transformed Hellenic sense, had especial virtue in regard to marriage [118 d]; and Stobaeus exclaims 'What could love, what could Hera or Aphrodite preside over more legitimately than over the lawful intercourse of man and woman? [118 k].' Plutarch comments eloquently on the worship at Delphi, saying 'The honour and charm, and mutual love and trust, that grow up daily (in a happy marriage) prove the wisdom of the Delphians in calling Aphrodite the goddess who joins together.' These passages are the more interesting, because in Greek literature panegyrics on marriage are few ; the romantic aspect of love was more commonly associated with the divine power of Eros ; and the later worships of Aphrodite that refer not to marriage but to free love are sometimes marked, as we shall see, by cult-epithets that are neither spiritual nor pure.

And what is of greatest importance is that this refined cult

---

[a] Cf. the Rhodian worship of Apollo, Asclepios, and Aphrodite [58].

of the goddess, as the patroness of married life, is probably a native development within the Greek religion. The record seems to show that the Eastern religion failed to present her at all, or at least prominently, as the goddess who sanctioned and encouraged lawful union. It is true she was at times regarded as the wife of Baal, and was styled 'Virgin' at Carthage, a title which provokes the indignant sarcasm of an early Christian writer. But so far as we can gather from certain Oriental institutions and legends, she seems to have been regarded as against the purer relations of man and woman. In Hierapolis, Armenia, and probably Lydia, she was supposed to demand the sacrifice of virginity before marriage ; and in the legends of Ishtar and Semiramis the goddess herself was represented as wanton and murderous. Some part of this evil character has been transplanted into Greek legend, but very little into Greek worship, and the few traces of it that we can find belong probably to the later period.

The life of the family was closely associated in the Greek communities with the system of the clan ; and Aphrodite in some of the Ionic settlements was connected with this also ; inscriptions of the second and third, and possibly of the fifth century, B.C., prove the existence of the worship of Aphrodite Ἀπάτουρος or Ἀπατούρη in Phanagoria and Panticapaeum [38, 39]. Strabo gives us a Phanagorian legend, explaining the name by some myth, possibly genuine, of the 'deceit' of Aphrodite who lured the giants to her cave where they were destroyed by Heracles ; and at Troezen[a] the same title, which was there attached to Athena, was explained by a legend arising from the same false derivation of the word from ἀπάτη or deceit. The word is of course derived from the Ionic festival of the Ἀπατούρια and from the system of the phratriae, into which the new-born child of the citizen's family was admitted, and which at Athens, and apparently at Troezen, were sanctioned by the worship of Zeus Phratrios and Athena Apaturia. This association with the clan, even more obviously than her connexion with marriage, came to Aphrodite after her settlement in Greece and not from the Eastern tradition.

[a] Paus. 2. 33, 1.

The highest political idea which attached to the worship of Aphrodite was expressed by the cult-title Πάνδημος, about which, from the time of Plato downwards, there has been a strange misunderstanding, but which now, owing to recent discoveries, can no longer be considered of doubtful meaning[117]. We find the cult of Aphrodite Pandemos at Erythrae [49 a] mentioned in an inscription dealing with the sale of priest-hoods; another inscription proves its existence at Cos[117h]; we have Pausanias' testimony of its establishment at Megalopolis[27], and at Thebes[9] where the legend referred its institution to Harmonia[a]. But its chief importance was at Athens, and it is only from Attic inscriptions and Attic records that we can gain a clue to its meaning. Pausanias, after describing the monuments on the south side of the Acropolis, the temple of Asclepios, the temple of Themis, and the tomb of Hippolytus, states abruptly that Theseus, when he drew the citizens together into one city, instituted the worship of Aphrodite Pandemos and Peitho ; and he adds that their ancient statues no longer existed in his time. The context makes it clear that some way beyond the tomb of Hippolytus was the temple of Aphrodite, to whom Pausanias found the title of Pandemos given. It is also probable that she was connected in the Attic legend with Theseus, as Apollodorus in his treatise ' concerning the gods ' takes the same view as Pausanias about the origin of the cult: and also in some way with the worship and myth of Hippolytus ; for we have epigraphic evidence of the existence of a temple of Aphrodite ἐφ' Ἱππολύτῳ, 'near Hippolytus,' that is, 'near the tomb of Hippolytus.' And this shrine must be the same as that which Euripides in the *Hippolytus*, the scholiast on that passage and the scholiast on the *Odyssey*, all designate by the name ἐφ' Ἱππολύτῳ or ' Hippolyteion[11 d].' Now the Hippolyteion must either be another name for the temple of Aphrodite Pandemos, or Pausanias must have omitted to mention the former in his account. But if we take the view that there were two buildings, the one called the Hippolyteion, the other the temple of Aphrodite

---

[a] At Olympia there is no proof, as has been wrongly supposed, of its recognition by the state. Vide infra, pp. 681–684.

Pandemos [a], there is little doubt but that they were in close vicinity to each other on the south and south-west slope of the Acropolis, for two inscriptions have been found on the south-west slope of the Acropolis relating to the worship of Pandemos ; and this position of the temple is not irreconcileable with Apollodorus' statement in the above treatise, that it stood in the 'ancient agora,' if we suppose the ancient agora to have lain between the Pnyx and the Areopagus, so that it might be said to include in its circuit a temple that stood on the slope of the Burg-Hill [b]. Whatever its exact locality was, it was associated in the local legend with Theseus and Phaedra, that is to say, with that circle of cult which included Crete, Troezen, and Athens.

The question now arises as to the meaning of the word Pandemos ; we have seen that Apollodorus gives it the political meaning which is certainly the true one [117 i]. But Nicander of Colophon, quoted by Athenaeus [117 i], finds for it a very different significance, stating that Solon, to whom writers of the New Comedy ascribe the organization of prostitution at Athens, collected money from this class of women and raised a temple to Aphrodite Pandemos as the

[a] Miss Harrison maintains that there were two separate shrines of Pandemos and ἐφ' Ἱππολύτῳ, on the ground that both titles occur in official inscriptions, and we have no instance of the same temple being called by two official names (*Myth. Mon. Anc. Ath.* p. 334). This is a reasonable but not quite certain argument ; for the inscription mentioning 'Αφροδίτη ἐφ' Ἱππολύτῳ [11 d] refers not to any temple but to a statue, and we have evidence that in these financial inscriptions the same statue was sometimes called by different descriptive names, as in the case of the Artemis Brauronia on the Acropolis.

[b] This is Foucart's view in *Bull. de Corr. Hell.* 1889, pp. 157-161 ; he supposes the Hippolyteion to have stood on the same terrace as the Asclepieion, and the temple to Aphrodite Pandemos somewhat further westward nearer to the entrance to the Acropolis. Lolling, in the Δελτίον 'Αρχαιολογικόν, 1888, p. 187, identifies the two, and places the latter near to the approach to the Acropolis on the west (so also in his article in Iwan Müller's *Handbuch des Classischen Alterthums*, vol. 3, p. 330) ; but in the Δελτίον of 1891, p. 127, he seems to conclude, on the strength of an inscription on an altar found not far from the temple of 'Theseus' in the Ceramicus quarter, that the 'ancient agora' to which Apollodorus refers was in the Ceramicus, and the temple of Aphrodite Pandemos was that which Pausanias wrongly calls a temple of Ourania, and stood near the temple of 'Theseus'; but the existence of an altar does not quite prove the existence of a temple on that very site, and this contradiction in Pausanias is too much to suppose.

goddess of common and venal love. And this is the sense in which Plato in the *Symposium* misunderstood or deliberately misused the word [a]. He there distinguishes between Ourania Aphrodite, the elder goddess, the eternal one without father or mother who personifies the intellectual love of the soul [99 t], and Aphrodite Pandemos, who is the younger, the daughter of Zeus and Dione, who personifies the sensual love of the body. This idea is borrowed by Xenophon or whoever is the author of the *Symposium* attributed to him, and we find the same distinction there between Ourania and Pandemos, though he hints at the possibility of the two terms expressing different sides of the same goddess: but he also attests an important distinction in ritual, saying that he is well aware that Ourania and Pandemos were worshipped at different altars and in different shrines, and with difference of ritual [b], Ourania with the purer, Pandemos with the less pure form [99 s]. This interpretation of the two terms was certainly accepted in the later Greek periods. At Thebes the very archaic images of Aphrodite, supposed to have been dedicated by Harmonia, were called Ourania Pandemos and Apostrophia, and Pausanias interpreted the two former titles as Plato had done [9]. At Olympia Pausanias found the Pheidian statue of Aphrodite called Οὐρανία, another in an adjacent enclosure, called Pandemos [99 r], carved by Scopas and representing her riding on a goat. But it is evident from the phraseology of the text that these distinctions between the two statues were not attested by any inscription. We have in the *Anthology* an epigram, describing a statue of Aphrodite, beginning 'Cypris is not here the goddess of vulgar love (Pandemos); do reverence and call her the heavenly one [99 x].'

Modern writers [c] have accepted too readily this philosophic

[a] It has been suggested that Plato vilified Pandemos through his dislike of the democratic connotation of the name.

[b] ῥᾳδιουργότεραι is contrasted in the sentence with ἁγνότεραι, and is also explained by the use of ῥᾳδιουργία for sensual indulgence in the *Memorabilia*,

2. I, 25.

[c] Even Prof. Robert in his new edition of Preller's *Mythologie*. Miss Harrison, in the *Mythology and Monuments of Ancient Athens*, p. 332, rejects the lower meaning of Πάνδημος, but does not discuss the question what positive significance it might have.

and popular misinterpretation of the terms. There is
certainly sufficient evidence that the people understood
Pandemos, from the fourth century onwards, in the lower
sense ; but there is no evidence that the state-religion of Greece
ever recognized this meaning of the title. The people who
forgot the meaning of the obvious epithet 'Απατουρία might
easily suppose that Pandemos could designate the 'common'
and unclean goddess; and Plato, the arch-juggler in the
interpretation of words, is perhaps answerable in part for
the degradation of this one. The title Οὐρανία had, in the old
religion of Greece and the East, no such high significance ;
the Cypriote Aphrodite was Ourania and by no means austere ;
the Corinthian Aphrodite was Ourania and, here only in
Greece proper, was served by young women of loose reputation, whom Pindar grandiloquently calls 'the daughters of
Persuasion, who lift up their hearts to Ourania Aphrodite' [99g] ;
and it is a curious comment on Plato's interpretation of the
term that the only impure element which we can find in the
Greek state-religion of Aphrodite, before the fourth century,
we find in this worship of the 'heavenly' goddess at
Corinth.

The hetaera in Lucian appears to have been better acquainted
than Plato with the significance of Greek religious terms,
when she offered sacrifice to Pandemos and Ourania impar-
tially [99u]. In fact the title Οὐρανία had in the genuine state-
religion no more definite moral sense than 'Ολυμπία, but denoted
originally the Eastern Aphrodite for good or for evil, and
perhaps afterwards came to mean nothing more than the
'goddess of the ancient worship.' The monuments of her
that have survived, or have been recorded, present us with no
attributes or symbols that have any moral meaning at all ;
nor on the other hand, in the monuments that with any
certainty refer to the cult of Pandemos, is there any hint of
the sensual significance supposed to belong to the title.
There are weighty reasons for saying that this supposition
is entirely errroneous. In the first place, the lower meaning
of Pandemos is always correlate with the higher meaning
of Ourania. But this latter is not known to be older than

Plato, and there is no clear evidence that it ever had this meaning in any state-cult ; for supposing that the statues mentioned at Olympia and Thebes were originally designated by these titles, yet Pausanias cannot be said to be giving us more than the popular and late interpretation of the names. Secondly, the word πάνδημος has always, in other applications, a serious and often a religious sense, being attached to Zeus in Attic and other worships as the guardian of the political community [a]. Therefore, as applied to Aphrodite, it ought to mean the goddess 'worshipped by the whole people,' hence the goddess of the political community, and if there were a festival called πανδήμια it would mean the same for the worship of this goddess as the Panathenaia and Pandia meant for the worship of Athens and Zeus. In the feast of Aphrodite Pandemos, that comes as an episode into Menander's play, *The Flatterer*, the religious-minded cook prays solemnly to all the Olympians for safety and health and all blessings : the phrases are borrowed from the public formula of prayer [117].

This political significance and the serious nature of the cult are attested by the inscriptions found on the Acropolis. On the relief dedicated by Arctinos and Menecratia, in the fourth century B. C., the inscription begins with an address to Aphrodite as 'the great and holy goddess.' The priestess who was given the continual charge of the sacrifice was a state-official, and from time to time the ἀστυνόμοι were directed to cleanse the temple and to superintend the public procession held in her honour [117 i]. And the more recent discovery of the altar, dedicated at the end of the third century to Aphrodite Ἡγεμόνῃ τοῦ δήμου [117 i], 'the leader of the people,' and to the Graces, would be by itself almost conclusive evidence of the political significance of the cult and title of Aphrodite on the Acropolis, and, as Lolling maintains [b], we may now believe that the Hegemone mentioned, together with the Graces, among the divinities by whom the Attic Ephebi swore to defend the country and obey the laws [c] was this Aphrodite Hegemone

---

[a] Zeus [134] ; cf. the phrases πανδημεὶ θύειν and πανδήμιος ἑορτή.

[b] Δελτίον Ἀρχαιολ. 1891, p. 127.

[c] Artemis [67 f].

τοῦ δήμου or Aphrodite Πάνδημος. We can then understand
why this political worship was connected with the name of
Theseus, the mythic founder of the Ionic settlement and the
higher state-organization; and why it was instituted at Thebes,
where Aphrodite was regarded as the ancestress of the race,
and why it was chosen for establishment at Megalopolis as
one of the cults suitable for binding together the new con-
federacy of Arcadia. As the Aphrodite-worship of Theseus
is connected, as we have seen, by so many links with Crete
and the East, the Aphrodite Pandemos may be a Greek
development of the goddess who already at Ascalon had
taken under her patronage the city-life.

It remains to notice the apparently authoritative statement
in Xenophon's Symposium, that vouches for the laxer character of this worship. But we cannot vouch for the author
of 'Xenophon's' *Symposium*. What we know is that until the
declining period of Greek history, the cult of Aphrodite, so far
as it appears in written or monumental record, was as pure and
austere as that of Zeus and Athena, purer than that of Artemis,
in nearly all the Greek communities, rules of chastity being
sometimes imposed upon her priestess [18] ; that the only impure
practices in this worship, of which we have any hint before
the fourth century, were connected with the name of Aphrodite
Ourania at Corinth, and that even in the later period, when
the influence of the 'hetaerae' in the Greek cities had at last
corrupted certain parts of the public religion, and impure
titles seem to have become attached to the goddess with the
sanction of the state, the cult of Pandemos is associated with
none of these.

In fact, it implies an ignorance of the earlier spirit of Greek
worship, and a confusion of a religion which was mainly pure
with a mythology that was often the reverse, to suppose that
a pre-Solonian cult could have given a religious sanction
to practices which endangered family life. The Corinthian
worship being demonstrably Oriental is the exception which
proves the rule.

And the mistake made by the author of 'Xenophon's' *Symposium* may be partly explained. His phrase ῾θυσίαι ῥᾳδιουρ-

γότεραι' is, in any case, obscure, and it is not easy to explain what a pure or impure 'sacrifice' would be. Possibly he may have been aware that at Athens νηφάλια ἱερά, that is libations of water and honey without wine, were offered to Aphrodite Ourania [99 q], and he may have supposed that such libations were ceremoniously purer and implied a purer idea, such, for instance, as was in the mind of Oedipus when he boasts that he comes to the Eumenides of Colonus· as 'a man innocent of strong drink to goddesses who love not wine.' But it is certain that the use of wine, or water and honey in libations, did not originally rest on any moral distinction between one worship and another [a], although Theophrastus and others may have believed that the νηφάλια ἱερά were the more innocent and ancient ritual. Again, the writer may have had in his mind the immorality associated with the worship of the Eastern goddess in certain communities, and arbitrarily attached this to the cult of Pandemos in its vulgar sense ; even then ῥᾳδιουργότεραι θυσίαι is still an inappropriate phrase.

In public worship the distinction did indeed exist in the later times between the goddess of honourable marriage and the goddess of free love, but it is not expressed by the titles just examined.

In the minds of the people, and in most of Greek mythology, no doubt Aphrodite was little more than the power that personified beauty and human love ; and this idea, which receives such glowing expression in the poetry [b], is expressed also by a sufficient number of cult-titles, which are neither moral nor immoral, but refer merely to the power of love in life. The most interesting of these is Peitho, by which title Aphrodite was worshipped at Pharsalus [2] and in Lesbos [119 d] as the goddess of Persuasion. It has been already suggested

---

[a] Vide chapter on Zeus-ritual, pp. 88, 89. Νηφάλια were offered to Zeus Γεωργός, Poseidon, the wind-gods ; at Athens to Mnemosyne, the Muses, Eos, Helios, Selene, the Nymphs, and Aphrodite Οὐρανία, to Sosipolis, the city-genius of Elis (Paus. 6. 20, 2) ; sometimes even to Dionysos. No one explanation suits all these cases.

[b] The words with which the short fragment of an Homeric hymn to Aphrodite begin, give us almost the full picture of the Homeric goddess, ' I will sing of Cytherea of Cyprus, who gives sweet gifts to men, and who wears a smile ever upon her lovely face and brings the flower of loveliness.'

that at the creation of Pandora in the Hesiodic account Peitho takes the place of Aphrodite herself, and it is probable that she whom Sappho styled the 'daughter and the golden-gleaming handmaiden' of Aphrodite, had no original inde-pendent existence as a divinity, but grew up from a title of the latter goddess which became detached and personified.

The statues of Peitho and Paregoros, a synonymous per-sonification, stood in the temple of Aphrodite Πρᾶξις at Megara[15]; the temple-statue was of ivory and earlier than the Praxitelean period. As Πρᾶξις might mean 'result' or 'success,' and Peitho and Paregoros are terms that help to explain it, we can interpret the temple-worship as that of the goddess who gives success in love. A similar term is Μαχανῖτις, by which she was worshipped at Megalopolis as the goddess who con-trives ways and means for lovers [27 b].

The goddess who turns men's hearts to love was also worshipped by the name Ἐπιστροφία[15 b], as at Thebes the goddess 'who turns hearts away[a]' was recognized under the reverse name of Aphrodite Ἀποστροφία[9].

The contrast between the healing and destructive force of love in human lives may be that which is expressed by the two interesting titles ἀνδροφόνος and σωσάνδρα. We are told by Plutarch and Athenaeus, who quotes from Polemon, that Aphrodite was called ἀνδροφόνος or ἀνοσία, the 'slayer of men' or the 'unholy' one, at Pharsalus [119], and this is explained by the story that the famous courtesan Lais was murdered in the temple of Aphrodite by the Thessalian women who feared the effects of her beauty on the men of the country [4]. There may be some truth in the story, but the title is not likely to have arisen from this incident. If the word 'Sosandra,' the saviour of men, which denoted a famous statue, evidently of some divinity, ascribed by Lucian to Calamis, were proved to

---

[a] A writer in the *Gazette Archéologi-que* of 1880 interprets Ἀποστροφία as the goddess who frees men from evil passions ; this special sense of the word rests merely on the popular sense given to the word at Thebes in Pausanias' time : it is probably quite groundless and does not correspond with the part usually played by Aphrodite in Greek mythology; for instance, in the myth of the daughters of Cinyras, Aphrodite Ἐπιστροφία and Ἀποστροφία are equi-valent to Eros and Anteros.

be really an epithet of Aphrodite as has been often supposed [a], then this would be an exact counterpart to the
Thessalian term, and we should have in these two the dual
conception that appears in Plautus' description of Astarte. To
this class belongs the epithets Μανδραγορῖτις [119 e], designating
the goddess who soothes or lulls to sleep, or gives the love-
charm, and Ἐλεήμων [43], the name of the compassionate goddess
of Cyprus. But Hesychius, who is our sole authority for these,
does not say whether they are poetical or cult-terms. There
is the same doubt about the title 'Automata,' by which,
according to Servius [48], the Ephesians designated Aphrodite
as the source of spontaneous love.

The worships in which she appears as a goddess of beauty
merely are very rare. A probable instance is the Spartan cult
of Aphrodite Μορφώ [119 a], as it is difficult to interpret this word
except as the 'shapely' one, the goddess of beautiful form [b],
and the veil which she wore on her head may mark the
goddess of the bridal. The only other name of the same
kind attached to Aphrodite is Βαιῶτις [77 a], the goddess 'of
small ears,' by which, according to Hesychius, she was known
at Syracuse, but whether in public cult or merely popular
language he does not say.

In Greek mythology, the goddess is not only the power
that sends love, but is also herself the lover; and it is

[a] Michaelis, *Arch. Zeit.* 1864, p. 190.
It seems, however, more probable that in
Lucian's treatise (Εἰκόνες, c. 6) it really
designates Hera; for in the next dia-
logue ὑπὲρ τῶν εἰκόνων, he writes as if
he had been making special reference to
Hera in the Εἰκόνες; but if she is not
Sosandra, she is scarcely mentioned at
all.

[b] Görres, in his *Studien zur griechischen Mythologie,* 2, p. 60, explains
Μορφώ as a term of the Aphrodite of
the lower world who sends up dreams
(μορφαί), but Aphrodite was never believed to do this, and Μορφεύς whom he
quotes as a parallel figure does not
belong to Greek religion nor appear at

all in literature before Ovid. Curtius
(*Nuove Memorie dell' Institut.* pp. 374,
375) ingeniously explains the chains
round the feet, which Pausanias mentions, as nothing more than the common
Phoenician ornament of the feet to which
Isaiah refers, and he interprets Μορφώ
as alluding not to the beauty of her
body but to her decorations; but in any
case the epithet would designate the
goddess whose chief concern was
personal beauty. The common explanation given of the chains is that they
were put round the statue, in accordance with the naïve belief of very
primitive times, to prevent it running
away.

probable that the Eastern stories of the goddess whose love was often dangerous to its objects appears in the legends of Hippodameia [119 m] and Phaedra, both of which names there is reason for attaching to Aphrodite. But in Greek religion this aspect of her is presented only by the titles Ψίθυρος and Παρακύπτουσα [119 h, i], the one referring to the whispering voice, the other to the side-long glance.

Although we have no proof of immorality being at any time a common characteristic of the worship of Aphrodite in the Greek states, but, in fact, strong evidence to the contrary, yet we have signs of a degeneracy that belongs probably to the later period. As the influence of the hetaerae spread in the social life, and the national pride sank, we hear of altars and temples dedicated under the name of Aphrodite to the mistresses and wives of the Epigoni and their favourites [120]. The worship of Aphrodite Belestiche at Alexandria excited the indignation of Plutarch, and the blasphemous profligacy of Harpalus was the theme of a letter written by Theopompos to Alexander, in which he denounces Alexander's minister, who, 'despising the divine vengeance,' dared to erect altars and a shrine at Athens to Aphrodite Πυθιονίκη [121 d].

To the same later period[a] may probably be ascribed those few worships in which the goddess was designated by some impure name, or by one that referred to the life of the courtesan [120]. Some of them that Clemens and Hesychius record may have been merely popular epithets, and may have had no place at all in cult. But there is good evidence for the worship of Aphrodite Πόρνη at Abydos [44], and for that of Aphrodite Ἑταίρα [120 a] at Athens and Ephesos, which some ancient apologists try to explain away as referring to the bonds of friendship between comrades, but must certainly designate the goddess of the courtesan-world.

'It is not for nothing,' exclaims the comic poet Philetaerus, 'that everywhere there are temples of Aphrodite the mistress, but nowhere shrines of Aphrodite the married goddess.' The first statement is an exaggeration, the second an untruth;

---

[a] The cult of Aphrodite Μιγωνῖτις [69] at Gythium appears to have been more ancient, and was probably derived from the Oriental worship of Cythera.

and it was probably his own age that was responsible for the base worship which he satirizes.

We have, indeed, no direct evidence for fixing the date of the institution of these cults ; the writers who record them belong to the Alexandrine period, and there is no epigraphical testimony of their public importance. The only place where the hetaerae played any part in the ritual of the state was Corinth, where 'whenever the state prayed to Aphrodite on matters of great import, it took as large a number as possible of the hetaerae to aid in the prayer,' and individuals in private prayer often vowed to consecrate a certain number of these women to the divinity [99 g]. We hear of them as early as the Persian wars, when they put up public petition to Aphrodite for the cause of Hellas. But the recognition of such ' Hierodulae' in the state-religion of Corinth is unique in Greece, and may be ascribed directly to the influence of Phoenicia and the East. As regards the other cults of the class just examined, we have no reason for supposing that even in them there was anything impure in the ritual.

A review of the religion of Aphrodite presents us, then, with a goddess who has less to do than most of the other Greek divinities with the arts of civilization[a] or the conceptions of advanced morality and law; we find her prominent in the public worship as controlling the life of the earth and the waters of the sea, and as ruling in the shadowy land of the dead ; revered also as the goddess of physical beauty and love, though to this aspect of her Greek poetry paid more regard than Greek worship ; finally, we find her cult pure on the whole and austere, and satisfying certain moral and political aims by its connexion with marriage and the community of the people.

[a] An inscription of the Imperial period [11e] has been found in the theatre at Athens containing the title 'Αφρο- δίτη 'Εναγώνιος, which must refer to the dramatic performances. In Cyprus there were musical contests in honour of Aphrodite ; the singer whose short prelude to Aphrodite is preserved among the Homeric hymns prays to the goddess to inspire him and give him victory, and the name of the legendary Cypriote king, 'Cinyras,' is derived from the Phoenician word for a harp. But this proves nothing as regards the general character of the Hellenic goddess.

We can also observe that, for the greater part of this worship and for most of the ideas expressed in it, Greece has been indebted to the East. But though the religion of Greece was conservative of the tradition that it had received, merely purifying the cult from a few touches of Oriental gross-ness, Greek philosophy and poetry showed its constructive power in spiritualizing and transforming certain inherited ideas. The meaning of Ourania is changed and deepened, and the name personifies the power of love that is higher than sense, that inspires wisdom and the purest spirit of life. In that passage of Euripides[115 d] where the physical and spiritual powers of Aphrodite are strikingly combined, the goddess who 'from the streams of the Cephissos breathes over the Attic land the tempered breath of fragrant breezes,' is also she who sends 'the loves that are seated by the throne of wisdom, fellow-workers of all virtue.' By a natural development of ideas, the Oriental 'Queen of the Heavens' has led us up through Greek philosophy and poetry to the modern conception of 'platonic affection.'

Lastly the idea, that undoubtedly grew up on Eastern soil, of a goddess who personified the cosmic power of love in the world of animal and vegetative life, was transplanted to Greece, and received the deepest and most spiritual expression in the national poetry, and even acquired a certain philosophic sig-nificance as a pantheistic doctrine[99 z]. The noble fragment of the *Danaides* of Aeschylus[115 a] shows us the Aphrodite Ourania of the East conceived by the Greek imagination as the power that causes the love that is in heaven and earth, the love that works in the rain, and brings forth cattle and herbs for the use of man. The same idea with more mysticism and less poetry appears in the later Orphic literature[99 w, 122].

CHAPTER XXII.

MONUMENTS OF APHRODITE.

IT has been shown that in the cult of Aphrodite, Greek religion was mainly conservative of Oriental ideas; the ritual, the attributes, and most of the characteristics of the goddess are derived from the East.

On the other hand, the comparison of the monuments of the two nations proves, perhaps more than any other archaeological study, the freedom and the originality of the Hellene. 'La déesse de la fécondité sera devenue pour les contemporains de Scopas et de Praxitele la déesse de la beauté [a].' It was the signal achievement of Greek art to have replaced the Oriental type, of which the forms were often gross and at best had little more than a merely hieratic meaning, with a type that became of significance for religion through its depth of spiritual expression, and of the highest importance for the history of art through its embodiment of the perfected forms of corporeal beauty.

The debt of Greece in this worship to the art of the East, was only superficial; yet the monuments of the Oriental cult are of very great importance in their bearing on the religious question discussed in the preceding chapter; for they strengthen the conclusion derived from other evidence that Aphrodite was of Semitic birth.

It is probable that in many localities of the Semitic worship, the earliest representations of Astarte were aniconic, for we find the conical stone as her symbol on the coins of Mallos, and its reference is often made clearer by the concomitant type of the swan [b]. As regards her representation at

---

[a] Perrot et Chipiez, *Histoire de l'Art Antique,* vol. 3, pp. 626, 627.

[b] Head, *Hist. Num.* p. 606.

Paphos, we are told by Tacitus [61] that her temple-image was not of human form, but simply a conical stone shaped like a Greek meta or goal-post. And on a coin of this city we see this emblem enclosed within temple-walls and pillars that show non-Hellenic forms of architecture [a], and we find it also on a slab from the temple of Tanit in Carthage [b]. It is possible to trace the influence of this very primitive symbol of Astarte, in such representations as the statue of Aphrodite Urania in the 'gardens' at Athens [11 a], which was only partly iconic, and in certain terracotta 'alabastra' from Rhodes, of which the upper portion consists of the head and shoulders of the goddess, and the lower preserves the ordinary form of the vase. But neither of these crude types, nor that of the little wooden idols occasionally found in Cyprus [c], some of which are in Berlin and one at Dresden—thin pieces of wood with head, breast, and arms indicated—seem to have had any vogue in Greece proper.

Looking at the Eastern monuments that present the goddess in complete human form, we notice two main types, the representation of the naked divinity, whose forms and pose express simply the idea of fecundity, and that of the fully-draped figure. The first is of very little importance for the earlier or later monuments of Greek religion [d]; originating at Babylon, and there representing the goddess Nana, it became prevalent in Cyprus, where it was afterwards slightly modified by Greek style, and it penetrated into the Mycenean kingdom at an early date [e]. But it was scarcely ever the theme of genuine Greek art in the archaic period ; and whether it has anything to do with the develop-

[a] Head, *Hist. Num.* p. 628.

[b] *Gazette Archéologique,* 1880, Pl. 3 ; on a Carthaginian metal-band belonging to the worship of Tanit we find a cone with outstretched arms attached ; *id.* 1879, Pl. 21.

[c] Roscher, p. 407, l. 68.

[d] A typical instance is the terracotta idol in the Louvre published by Heuzey (*Les Antiques figurines de terre cuite dans le Musée du Louvre,* Pl. 2, no. 4),

of the naked goddess, with her hands pressed on her breast.

[e] The Cypriote figure published in Roscher, p. 407, may be compared with the Babylonian idol of Nana or Astarte (*id.* p. 647) and the Mycenaean representation on a gold plate of the goddess with the dove on her head and with both hands pressing her breast (Schliemann, *Mycenae,* Figs. 267 and 268).

ment of the type of the undraped Aphrodite of the later age
is an open question. The idea of representing the goddess of
beauty and love as naked may have occurred quite naturally
and spontaneously to the Greek artists of the fourth century, or the Eastern art may have suggested and excused
this unusual freedom. The theory that would trace back
the type of the Cnidian Aphrodite, the perfected ideal of the
Greek goddess, to the rude Semitic form of Astarte with her
hands across her body, has been rejected by MM. Perrot and
Chipiez [a], who maintain that there is no Phoenician or any
Semitic monument earlier than the Cnidian that resembles it
at all, and those that resemble it are of later date and are
merely copies of it in the style of Phoenician art. But this
is not entirely true; the Ashmolean Museum at Oxford
possesses a small bronze figure of the late Mycenaean age,
found in a cave on the mountain in Crete, which the Lyttians
called Mount Dicta, representing the Oriental goddess with
her arms held across her body as the Medicean Venus holds
hers [b]. It is true there are many missing links between this
rude type and the Cnidian Aphrodite. But it is quite conceivable that Praxiteles may have been influenced by an
ancient and vaguely remembered form of hieratic art. The
Babylonian idols of Nana in the Louvre betray rather
the influence of the later Greek style of the Alexandrine age
upon the representations of Semitic divinities. One of the
most striking of these has been published in the *Gazette
Archéologique*, an alabaster idol of Nana [c], undraped but laden
with ornaments, wearing an Oriental head-dress surmounted
with a crescent, and showing nothing of Hellenic character
except in the naturalistic rendering of the flesh. It is probably
intended to represent the Babylonian goddess in the semi-
Hellenic form of Artemis Nanaea.

More important in the archaic Greek art, and in those centres
where Oriental influence was strongest, was the type of the
draped female form, with one hand pressed against her breast

[a] *Histoire de l'Art*, 3. pp. 557–
559.
[b] The Keeper of the Ashmolean,
Mr. Arthur Evans, kindly called my
attention to this work.
[c] 1876, Pl. 4.

PLATE XLI

a

b

c

d

PLATE XLII

a

b

and often holding a dove, the other drawing her robe tightly across her lower limbs and holding it a little away from her side. We have proofs that this representation existed at Ephesus, at Dali and elsewhere in Cyprus, at Rhodes and Camirus[a]; a slight modification of it is shown us in a terra-cotta figure from Corinth, of which both hands are held against the breast, with a dove in the right hand, an apple in the left (Pl. XLI b). And in Etruscan art, we find a similar figure serving as a support to a candelabra, the left hand holding the skirt, the right uplifted, and the feet resting on a tortoise[b].

Now these representations are not the genuine products of the archaic art of Hellas, although the pose of the hand on the drapery reminds us often of the archaic figures found on the Acropolis of Athens. For we notice on many of them an Oriental style of head-dress, especially on the figures from Cyprus[c], and we can discover what is probably the germ of this type in a sacred figure of early Babylonian art, fully draped, wearing a high coif or tiara, with the hands pressed on the breast[d]. It has been often regarded as doubtful whether these figures represent a divinity, or priestesses who by these offerings dedicated themselves to the temple they served ; the latter interpretation may sometimes be true, but it is quite certain that they often are actual idols of the goddess, and it is probable that this was their primary meaning, for in the figures of Semitic, as of Greek art, the divine type was probably fashioned earlier than the human. And many of these statuettes betray their divine character by many infallible signs ; some of those for instance from Dali, now in the British Museum, that bear the dove as an emblem, wear also the diadem on their heads ; nor can we suppose that any other

---

[a] In Marseilles marble torso, Pl. XLI c; terracotta from Rhodes, Pl. XLI a; from Ephesus, marble statuette in British Museum ; from Dali, vide limestone figures in the British Museum. On coins of Aphrodisias an ancient cult-form of an Aphrodite idol is preserved of a somewhat different type ; the goddess wears a calathus and veil, but both hands are outstretched. Coin Pl. 2. 49.

[b] A bronze in Berlin, Gerhard, *Gesammelte Abhandlungen*, Taf. 29. 3.

[c] Vide Cypriote figure in Lajard, *Culte de Vénus en Orient*, Pl. 20. 1.

[d] Roscher, p. 647, Fig. 2.

divinity was originally meant than the Eastern goddess, as the dove and the apple are her fitting emblems ; and the tortoise, which we see under the feet of the Etruscan figure, and which Pheidias carved under the feet of his Aphrodite Urania at Elis—probably without much significance, but simply as a traditional emblem—belongs to Astarte Aphrodite alone [a]. An Attic tetradrachm of the fourth century (?) shows a female figure, wrapped in a long garment, carrying a bird and wearing a modius on her head, which Beulé [b] interprets as Aphrodite and refers to the semi-Oriental Cnidian worship introduced into Attica by Conon [c].

We need not suppose that the type of the draped Eastern goddess was absolutely uniform [d] ; it is enough if the wide prevalence of this special type, which has been briefly examined, shows that the monuments of the Eastern cult were before the eyes and the imagination of the Greek artist when he carved the earliest idols of his Aphrodite. It was possibly he who first gave more life and delicacy to the rigid and rude Oriental idol by the motive of the hand that draws the drapery across and slightly away from the body, a motive which in the later Hellenic period becomes expressive of feminine grace in general, and of Aphrodite's in particular.

Apart from the artistic types, the symbols that appear on the monuments, such as the sacred animals and the inanimate objects consecrated to her, give still stronger support to the theory that this worship travelled to Greece from Semitic lands. The dove, for instance, her most common emblem, denoting probably the goddess of spring, appears in the representation of her temple at Paphos above the side-pillars on

[a] The animal probably alludes to the water-goddess ; but it must have been a rare symbol. It has been found carved on a limestone slab consecrated to Aphrodite in the neighbourhood of Paphos ; vide *Journal of Hellenic Studies*, 1888, p. 253. The tortoise on the coins of Aegina may refer to the local worship of the maritime Aphrodite ; Gardner, *Num. Com. Paus.* p. 45.

[b] *Monnaies d'Athènes*, p. 227.

[c] Professor Gardner believes this personage to be Isis ; *Num. Com. Paus.* p. 138.

[d] The terracotta figures of the goddess of Cyprus show much variety, and Pottier, who has examined them in the *Bull. de Corr. Hell.* 1879, p. 92, considers that we have not yet discovered the canonical type of the Aphrodite Astarte of this island. Perhaps there never was one.

the roof [a] ; a miniature Aphrodite temple, probably an import from Cyprus, has been found at Mycenae [b] ; also a figure of the naked type, already mentioned, who is generally and with great probability interpreted as Astarte, and who is pressing the dove against her breast [c], the holy bird in the ritual of Hierapolis and in the sacred legend of Semiramis [d].

In the legend told by Hyginus, the egg that fell from heaven was hatched by the dove, and from this Aphrodite and apparently the divinities of Syria were born [e]. The egg became an emblem of the Semitic goddess [f], but never was in Greece a recognized symbol of Aphrodite ; but this Oriental fable about the birth of the goddess from the egg plays its part, not only in the wide-spread myth of Helen's birth from Nemesis or Leda, but also in the Laconian worship, as Pausanias speaks of the sacred egg in the temple of Hilaeira and Phoebe, at Sparta [g] ; and Helen is probably one of the many 'doubles' of Aphrodite [h]. The iynx, the wrynecked bird, that was used as a love-charm, and appears in many vase-representations where Aphrodite is found, appears also on some Assyrian reliefs that Lajard has published [i]. And most of the animals known to have been consecrated to the goddess in Hellenic ritual were sacred symbols in the Oriental art that was dedicated to this worship. The goat is seen on certain Chaldean cylinders by the side of the Semitic goddess [k]; the sacred character of the ram in the Eastern ritual explains probably the strange design on the Cypriote coins of Marium or Amathus of a naked goddess clinging to the fleece of a running ram, who is almost certainly Aphrodite [l]. The

[a] Head, *Hist. Num.* p. 628.

[b] Schliemann, *Mycenae*, p. 423.

[c] *Ib.* pp. 267, 268.

[d] For the significance of the dove in the Oriental and Greek religion, vide Perrot and Chipiez, *Histoire de l'Art*, vol. 3, p. 200, n. 2.

[e] Hyg. *Fab.* 197; cf. Arnob. *Adv. Gent.* 1. 36 ' Ovorum progenies Dii Syrii.'

[f] Vide the ornamentation on the silver band found near Batna; *Gazette Archéol.* 1880, p. 23.

[g] Paus. 3. 16, 1.

[h] She was worshipped, for instance, in Rhodes as a deity of vegetation like Aphrodite, and appears like the latter in the legend of Theseus ; in certain localities Helen may also have been worshipped as a divinity of the sea, ναυτίλοις σωτήριος as Euripides calls her, *Orestes*, 1637.

[i] *Culte de Vénus*, Planche 17.

[k] *Ib.* Pl. 4. 12.

[l] Head, *Hist. Num.* p. 623.

fashion of representing divinities riding on their sacrificial animals has been already mentioned [a], as explaining the form of Artemis Tauropolos and the Cretan myth of Europa on the bull. The bull-riding goddess was probably a genuinely Hellenic type; but it was found also in Oriental art, as it was used as a device on the coins of Sidon that must have referred, not to the Cretan myth, but to the Oriental cult. Hence also we can explain the design on a coin of Citium struck about 400 B. C., of a goddess riding on a running bull, whom it is more reasonable to name Astarte Aphrodite than Europa [b]. The ritualistic importance of the bull in the Astarte-worship was probably the cause which led to that strange representation of the goddess of which Philo Byblius speaks [c]: 'Astarte placed upon her head the badge of royalty, the head of the bull'; and on a Cilician coin of the later Imperial period we see the bull-headed Astarte holding a rudder, the sign of her maritime power [d].

It is probable that the horse also was a symbol of the Eastern goddess [e]; for the horse's head was a coin-device of Carthage, and belongs to the legend of the foundation of the city by Dido. Hence may have been derived the cult and title of Aphrodite Ἔφιππος, mentioned in the preceding chapter, as Ἐπιτραγία was derived from the sacred character of the goat in her ritual.

As regards the monuments of the special Greek cults, we need not believe that there was always a cult-image and type appropriate to the special aspect of Aphrodite, and to the special appellative by which she was known and worshipped in this or that locality; and it is often impossible to decide what the distinctive character of the image was. For literary evidence fails us in many cases, and among the many monuments that have come down to us there are comparatively few to which we can give with certainty the fitting name, and which we can attach to a particular cult. And though the statues

[a] P. 450.
[b] Head, p. 622.
[c] Vide p. 632.
[d] Lajard, Pl. 3. 1. One might doubt whether this is a syncretism of Astarte and the cow-headed Isis.
[e] Vide Robertson Smith, *Religion of the Semites*, p. 458.

and other representations of Aphrodite are most numerous, yet most of them have in all probability no religious reference at all, being designed not for any temple or worship, but for decorative purposes and private luxury. It is nevertheless true that most of the ideas in the Aphrodite-worship that are preserved in the literature can be illustrated by the symbols and forms of art.

The first question will be whether we have any monuments that present us with the Ourania Aphrodite of Greek religion ; for this was probably her earliest title among the Hellenic communities. In so far as the term merely denoted the goddess of the East, whose power was omnipresent in the world, most of the ancient representations were those of Ourania ; for most of them in symbol or in type attested her Oriental origin. But those which ancient writers expressly designate by this name have not survived even in copies, so far at least as we can pronounce with certainty. The ancient Ourania of Corinth, for instance, can scarcely be the armed goddess on the coins of that city[a] mentioned below, but might be represented by the other coin-device of the goddess holding out the apple in her right hand and grasping the edge of her garment in the left[b]. We hear of her worship at Megalopolis and of that of Pandemos also ; on a coin of this city we see the naked Aphrodite with her hands held across her body as the Medicean holds hers, and a dolphin at her left side : the latter emblem speaks rather of the maritime goddess of the East, but the nudity and the attitude express the ideas that came to be attached to the term Pandemos[c].

The worship at Eryx had, as has been noted, many links of connexion with the Semitic religion ; and the temple-statue would represent Aphrodite Ourania ; possibly the coin of Eryx struck towards the end of the fifth century, and showing the seated goddess holding the dove with Eros standing before her, presents the form with which this worship invested her (Coin Pl. B 40). We have also an undoubted monument of Ourania in the device on the coins of Ouranopolis (Coin

---

[a] *Num. Com. Paus.* p. 26.		[b] *Ib.* FF. 7 : cf. D. 70.
[c] *Ib.* Pl. V. 8.

Pl. B 41), the city founded by the brother of Cassander on
the peninsula of Acte and named after the ancient title of the
goddess; the *British Museum Catalogue*[a] gives this description
of the type, 'Aphrodite Urania clad in long chiton and peplos
fastened on right shoulder seated, facing, on globe : on her
head a spike surmounted by a star : she holds in right hand
long sceptre ending above in circle (of the universe?), from
which hang two fillets; in field left a pyramidical object
surmounted by a star.' On the reverse is a sun with rays.
We have here then an undoubted representation of the goddess,
and symbols that prove the term Ourania to have been
interpreted at that time and in that city—not indeed in the
spiritual Platonic sense — but as a mystical term denoting
the cosmic power that ruled the sun, stars, and earth. But
the monument scarcely illustrates any genuine and early
idea of Greek religion; it is interesting chiefly as showing
the habit of the Alexandrine age, caught from the contact
with the East, of giving to native and foreign divinities
a solar and astral character. On a few Assyrian monuments
the star is seen and was perhaps occasionally a symbol of the
Semitic goddess, and the rays around the head of an Etruscan
bronze statuette of Aphrodite. express the same idea[b]. But
Etruscan art sometimes misinterpreted divinities as powers
of light; and we have seen that in the Hellenic worship
neither solar, lunar, nor astral character belonged to the
goddess, nor can any such aspect of her be clearly recognized
in the genuine Semitic worship.

The only other monument which external evidence helps us
to name is a statue in Madrid[c], representing the goddess with
veil and diadem-shaped modius, with both hands on her
breast, and inscribed Οὐρανίαν Βουκόλος. Even if the inscription is of doubtful authenticity, the title probably names
her rightly, for as regards the pose the statue recalls the
ancient Semitic type, and the head-dress marks the imperial
divinity.

[a] *Macedon*, p. 133.
[b] Gerhard, *Akademische Abhandlungen*, Taf. 31. 5.
[c] Hübner, *Die antiken Bildwerke*,
p. 552.

It appears, then, that if we leave out of sight the later representations that have nothing to do with public worship, the external evidence of inscriptions or literary record by which we can recognize the Ourania of Greek religion is very slight indeed.

Even the statement in Pausanias about the Pheidian statue called Ourania in the temple at Elis is of no more value than the statement which accompanies it, that Scopas' statue which stood in the enclosure outside represented Pandemos; we cannot gather from this that these images were so designated at the time of their dedication, as it is clear from Pausanias' own words that there was no epigraphical proof.

We have to look then to internal evidence, and especially to the symbols. From the review that has been taken of the character of the Eastern goddess and of those attributes of her which impressed the early Greeks, we might say that, when the representations express something more than the goddess of merely human love and desire, when the symbols allude to her general physical power in the world, or when she appears as the armed divinity that guards the city or wearing a mural crown, we have the Greek conception of the ancient high-placed goddess of the East to whom human love was no more than the power which works in the birth and increase of animals and plants. And we must look to the whole representation, not to one special detail; for many of the symbols, derived as most of them were from the East, had become purely conventional, and might be attached to Aphrodite in any character; and no single one of them, except perhaps the tortoise, is a clear token of Ourania.

We may give this name to the seated figure, the most striking representation of her in the archaic period, which Canachus carved of gold and ivory for that temple in Sicyon which only the priestess and her attendant maiden were allowed to enter [18]. The ritual in one detail at least points to the East; the pig was a sacred animal in the Sicyonic cult, too sacred to be offered [114 c]; and we are reminded of the Semitic goddess by the symbols which Canachus attached to his temple-image. The 'polos' on her head was the badge of the 'queen of

the heavens'; the apple in her hand referred to the processes
of life, the power of fertility in the world of plants and animals
that was her prerogative[a]; the poppy in her other hand may
have been a symbol of Ἀφροδίτη Μανδραγορῖτις, the goddess
who lulls the senses and gives sweet sleep, and may be
supposed to convey also an allusion to the lower world, in
which as we have seen both the Eastern and Hellenic goddess
had her part[b].

It would seem natural that the ancient goddess of earth
and heaven, Ourania or 'Olympia,' should be represented on
her throne, and the enthroned goddess was certainly a prevalent form on Semitic monuments. She may be represented
on the relief of late archaic style in the Villa Albani on which
we see a seated female figure in solemn pose and drapery,
with a hare carved beneath her throne ; the hands and head-
dress are restored, but the hare makes it probable that this is
Aphrodite[c] ; and this reference to her power in the animal
world, together with the solemnity of the whole representation,
gives us some right to style this figure also Aphrodite Ourania
(Pl. XLI d).

With still more right may we apply the term to a most
interesting representation of the goddess on a terracotta relief
from Aegina, in private possession at Naples, on which she
appears drawn in a chariot by griffins, bearing a young roe
in her hands, or rather wearing it as an embroidered badge
on her drapery, and with Eros by her side as charioteer

[a] Bernoulli's perplexity in finding the
right name for the statue of Canachus
('Aphrodite,' p. 61) arises from the error
which runs all through his book in his
interpretation of the terms Ourania and
Pandemos.

[b] We find poppy-stalks in the hand
of Demeter in some of her representations; possibly they may have been
merely a symbol of fertility owing to
the number of the seeds.

[c] The only other divinities with whom
the hare was occasionally connected
were Dionysos and Pan (vide Stephani,
Compte-Rendu, 1862, p. 62, who men-

tions one or two mere genre-represen-
tations). With the Albani relief we
may compare the type on coins of
Nagidos in Cilicia of the latter part
of the fourth century, Head, p. 609,
' Aphrodite seated holding patera,
crowned by flying Eros.' She is half-
draped, but probably Ourania ; the
animal faintly drawn under the throne
is, perhaps, a hare or a rabbit; on one
of these coins of Nagidos the goddess
wears the calathos and a flower, and
fruit that looks like the pomegranate is
one of the symbols.

(Pl. XLII a).   The work is of all the more value as it belongs to the earlier part of the fifth century when the original significance of the goddess was more clearly felt. Once more she appears as the power that rules the animal world, and what is of special interest here is that the griffin and the roe are animals that are characteristic of the Oriental goddess[a]. Perhaps Eros himself in this scene is more than the personification of human love, and has the character of a physical or elemental power which belonged to him in the worship at Thespiae.

The most important temple-image to which antiquity attached the name Ourania was the statue of gold and ivory carved by Pheidias, probably in his later period, for the shrine of Aphrodite in Olympia. We have no monumental illustration of it at all; and Pausanias' account is very meagre. We gather that the goddess was draped and standing with one foot on a tortoise. We may conclude at once that, though there is no trustworthy external evidence for the title, the Eleans were right in giving the name 'Ourania' to the statue. The tortoise was an Oriental symbol of the goddess, alluding perhaps to the firmament or the waters: it certainly could not have referred, as Plutarch supposes, to the housekeeping life of the married woman. The Parthenon sculptures, among which we have probably more than one representation of Aphrodite, teach us much concerning the forms and expression with which the Pheidian school conceived and represented the goddess. We may be sure that the temple-image at Elis displayed the grandeur of style, the dignity and solemn grace, the spiritual quality that belonged to the religious monuments of Pheidias' hand. It is even not unlikely that its ideal character and its celebrity assisted the acceptance in the following generation of the false interpretation put by Plato

---

[a] There are two terracotta representations in the British Museum, brought from Cyprus, showing the goddess with the fawn, one in the style of the later part of the fifth century (Pl. XLII b), an erect figure of the goddess wearing a polos adorned with anthemium and holding a fawn; the other a representation of the seated divinity, holding a patera in her right hand and a fawn in her left, probably a work of the fourth century.

on the terms Ourania and Pandemos; since the Pheidian
work, an austere impersonation of a great elemental power,
would contrast strikingly with the later emotional and sometimes sensuous representations of a goddess of human love
and passion. But it is wholly wrong to suppose that Pheidias
wished to give any expression to the distinction between
spiritual and physical love; which is found in Plato and the
epigrammatists, but not in any genuine Greek cult. The
religion of the Greek states showed itself conscious enough of
the nobler and baser, the broader and narrower, conception
of the love-goddess; but never gave any recognition to the
idea of a love that was beyond sense and transcended the
physical world. Nor again ought we to say that the Pheidian
masterpiece intentionally rendered the higher and purer aspect
of the divinity, so as to contrast with lower and more impure
types of her. For, so far as we know, these latter were not
dealt with by the Pheidian or any contemporary school, nor,
as we have seen, is it certain that any cult-title of impure
significance came into vogue as early as the fifth century.
We may even say that if there had been an Aphrodite
Pandemos, to whose worship that lower sense attached which
was never attached to it by the state, and if Pheidias had
been commissioned to carve her image, the face at least would
have displayed the same earnestness and 'decor' as without
doubt were present in the Olympian statue. For these were
a necessary part of the Pheidian expression of divinity: to
carve upon the features the look of troubled passion and
sense-desire was the gift of later art. We may believe then
that his chryselephantine statue in the temple of Olympia
was a real representation of Ourania, partly because through
a certain symbol it was connected with the East; and for the
more important reason that it probably embodied the idea
which was drawn from the East, but had been given a pro-
founder meaning in the poetry of Aeschylus, of the goddess
of a physical creative power that worked in heaven and earth
and the life of man. And thus this image might be said to
contrast with the Cnidian Aphrodite of Praxiteles, not as
being purer or more spiritual, but simply as belonging to

a worship of broader significance. The Cnidian statue might also be technically called Ourania, because of its allusion to the maritime origin of the goddess. But in regard to its forms and expression the term would be out of place; for the Praxitelean work was not the impersonation of the elemental power of Eastern worship, but of the Hellenic ideal of human love and human beauty.

In its application to later monuments, we cannot be sure that the title Ourania retained its early and historical sense; it seems that when a Greek of the Alexandrine and later period saw a statue of the draped goddess with an austere expression he might give it this name, and with still less historical correctness might call a statue of the opposite character Pandemos. But we do not know that the state-cults or their monuments were affected by this unhistorical use of the terms. Looking at the well-attested public representations we may say that the Ourania of Greek religious worship was portrayed as a draped goddess sometimes seated on a throne and sometimes standing; and her ancient and wider character was expressed by means of symbols, such as animals and flowers that seemed to be most full of her procreative force. It is not easy to say that there is any special arrangement of drapery that is characteristic; we might conclude from Lucian's remark [99 a] that the girdle was usually shown; but the monuments do not confirm this: some have supposed that the mantle arranged crescent-wise round her head, or raised up in her hand, and drawn over her shoulder, is significant of Ourania; but the former is natural to the goddess when riding, the latter is only an instinctive movement of modesty, and a common motive in art[a]. The Herme-form may have also been peculiar to her type; and when we find an Aphrodite of younger form leaning on a herme of the goddess, we may regard the latter as an image of Ourania[b]. The Venus of Pompeii in the museum

---

[a] Aristaen. I. 15 τῆς ἀμπεχόνης ἄκροις δακτύλοις ἐφαπτομένη τῶν κροσσῶν.

[b] See Gerhard, *De Venere Proserpina*, Pl. 7–12, and compare a coin of

Thespiae, *Num. Comm. Paus.* Pl. X. 19. Benndorf und Schöne, *Monuments of Lateran*, Pl. 13. 2.

of Naples (Pl. XLIII a) is leaning on a statuette of archaic form of a goddess in a sea-green chiton and saffron mantle, who is wearing a modius on her head and holding a flower to her breast, and whom we may call Ourania [a].

The Eastern goddess, whose power was pre-eminent in the animal world, was sometimes represented by the Greek artist riding upon her favourite animals, the goat, the ram, and the swan. Of these the last type had nothing, as far as we know, to do with public cult [b]; the most important from this point of view was that of Aphrodite 'Επιτραγία, the 'rider on the goat,' a type that has been much misinterpreted both in ancient and modern times. The most famous instance of it was the bronze statue carved by Scopas and set up in the precincts of the temple at Elis which contained the Ourania of Pheidias. As regards the forms and expression we are told nothing, but from certain surviving monuments and from Pliny's statement that another statue by Scopas was the earliest representation of the naked Aphrodite, we can conclude with certainty that the 'Επιτραγία was draped [c]. The Eleans in the time of Pausanias, and perhaps earlier, called it Pandemos, giving no doubt to this title its lower and fictitious sense : for the false interpretation had become prevalent after the fourth century, and the goat was considered an immoral animal. But it is probable that in the time of Scopas the term Pandemos still retained its political and proper meaning, and, as the goddess was draped, and as the ancient accounts of Scopas' work and the monu-

[a] The triple herme with the 'Medicean' figure of Aphrodite below, published by Gerhard, *Akad. Abhandl.* 31. 3, is of doubtful significance.

[b] Vide Kalkmann, Aphrodite auf dem Schwan, *Jahrbuch des deutschen Instituts*, 1, p. 231. The swan may have appeared in actual cult-monuments of Aphrodite as a subordinate symbol represented at her side, as in the monument mentioned in the chapter on Nemesis (p. 498) ; but Kalkmann seems right in maintaining that we have no literary evidence of a religious connexion between the bird and the goddess ; vide *Eph. Arch.* 1893, Πίν. 15, mirror from Eretria with a very beautiful representation of Aphrodite riding on a swan, and holding a patera before its beak.

[c] There are two Elean coins which present to us in faint outlines the statue of Scopas (Coin Pl. B 42). On both we see the fully draped goddess, with a large veil waving about her head, seated on the back of a goat that is galloping to the right.

Plate XLIII

a

b

ments that survive of his hand and style make it impossible
to imagine that there was any sensual expression in her face,
the traditional theory about this work and its traditional
name are probably wrong.   It is more likely that its original
and proper name was 'Επιτραγία, an ancient cult-title of the
Aphrodite-worship, and that it had no reference to the
immoralities of city-life.   The original meaning of 'Επιτραγία
and the symbolism supposed to attach to this type have
been much debated; one writer regarding the goat as the
symbol of vice[a], another as the sign of the starry heavens.
But facts of ritual are usually of more value than theories
about symbolism.   The goat was a sacred animal in the
Semitic worship of the goddess, being carved on her monuments and offered in sacrifice[b], and may even have been sometimes regarded as the goddess herself, her close association
with the goat being one of the many signs of her power over
the animal world.   Aphrodite riding on the goat is therefore
merely a hieratic or ritualistic motive, and the monuments
help to show, what was partly proved by the legends about
the cult of 'Επιτραγία on the Attic coast, that this is a special
representation of Ourania Aphrodite.   Also, none of the
representations contain any allusion at all to the goddess of
sensual desire, but some of them express clearly enough the
traits of the celestial Eastern divinity.   One of the earliest
representations that may be quoted is an archaic Cypriote
work published by Lajard[c]: but the most interesting is
perhaps that which he published in the *Archaeologische
Zeitung* of 1854[d]; on an oinochoe of fine style we see the
goddess riding on the goat, clad in a star-embroidered peplos,
and playing on the lyre (Pl. XLIII b).   The stars may be

---

[a] E. g. the author of a strange article
in the *Jahrbuch des deutschen Instituts*,
1889, p. 208; who gives to Aphrodite
'Επιτραγία the entirely improved significance of ' eine Göttin der unfruchtbaren
Liebe.'

[b] The sacred character of the animal
in her ritual might explain the mysterious αἴξ οὐρανία, mentioned by Hesy-

chius, and the Cretan story of the goat
that nourished Zeus: and there may be
an obscure allusion to the identity of
the goddess and her animal in the story
of Theseus' sacrifice on the shores of
Attica [14b].

[c] Lajard, *Culte de Vénus*, Pl. 21, 1.

[d] Pl. 71, with account given of it in
1855, p. 263.

a merely conventional ornament, and the lyre may indicate Aphrodite Μολπαδίας [a], if from the legend of the Carian maidens we can conclude that she was somewhere known by this title. Lajard indeed would read a deep cosmic meaning in the attribute of the lyre and the device of the stars ; but whether he is right or not, the austere solemnity of the whole representation excludes the idea of any sensual allusion in Ἐπιτραγία. Another representation of the same type on a terracotta medallion published by Gerhard produces the same impression ; the goddess is here fully draped and has rather a sombre appearance, which suggests to Gerhard the theory that the Aphrodite on the goat is partly a divinity of death and the lower world ; we might thus explain the presence of Hermes in a similar representation on a vase in Berlin [b], where Aphrodite appears riding on the goat, her upper body undraped but a mantle drawn over her head, in company with Hermes and Eros ; but this is not sufficient evidence to show that Aphrodite Ἐπιτραγία had in herself any real chthonian character.

The Oriental colour of the Aphrodite worship in Lacedaemon has been noticed, and at least one monument of the type under discussion comes fiom Laconian territory : namely, a marble relief showing Aphrodite on the goat, clad in a high-girdled under-garment and an upper garment that passes over her shoulders and legs, and holding a large veil crescent-wise about her head, with two small Loves arranging the ends of the veil [c].

A similar representation, having probably the same origin in ritual, is that of Aphrodite borne by the ram. An unique instance is the Cypriote coin-device noticed above [d], the goddess clinging to the fleece. In the other instances that have been collected, the goddess sits in the usual position on the back of the animal. A late, but interesting, illustration

[a] Vide Artemis [125], and p. 646.
[b] Furtwängler, *Beschreibung der Vasensammlung im Antiquarium*, 2635.
[c] *Mitt. d. deutschen Inst.* 2. p. 420. Cf. the small terracotta of rather coarse style found in the neighbourhood of

Kertsch, representing Aphrodite riding on the goat with Eros and dove accompanying her; *Compte-Rendu*, 1859, Pl. 4. 1.
[d] P. 675.

of this [a], with a sufficiently clear allusion to Aphrodite Ourania,
is given us on a bronze patera of perhaps the second century
A. D., showing us the goddess half-clad in a peplos that leaves
the upper part of her body bare, riding on a ram, and holding
a mirror in her hand, and accompanied by her dove ; behind
her are seven stars, doubtless the Pleiades.

We have seen reason to suppose, on the evidence of a scholiast
and a late Byzantine writer, that a type existed of Aphrodite
Ἔφιππος, the goddess on horseback, which would be similar in
idea to the last two that have been examined.   But the
interpretation of the monuments that have been quoted in
illustration of this is very doubtful.   A curious bronze [b] exists
in Paris, found in ' the grave of Achilles ' in the Troad, representing a goddess in a chiton of unusual shape and a peplos,
holding the edge of her drapery in her left hand, and resting
her right arm against her breast ; she wears a strange Egyptian
head-dress flanked by two sphinxes and topped by a lion ;
and she stands on a small pedestal which rests on the back of
two horses, each bearing a rider also.   The chief interest of
this enigmatical monument is its combination of a type
of Aphrodite with some of the symbols of Cybele ; also that
it comes from a locality that gave birth to the cult of
Aphrodite Aeneas, with which the type of Ἔφιππος was closely
associated.

Much evidence has been given of the maritime character
of Aphrodite, which, though perhaps not originally belonging
to her, she brought with her from the East.   The monumental
evidence of this is even clearer than the literary ; but the
representations of the goddess under this respect that can be
closely associated with any public cult are not very many.
We find her figure or her head on the coins of some of the
cities where she was worshipped as a sea-goddess, Aegium [c],
Naucratis [d], and Cnidus for example ; and we may connect

[a] *Jahrbuch des deutschen Instituts,*
1890 (Anzeiger), pp. 27–29.

[b] *Arch. Zeit.* 1862, Taf. 166. 4.

[c] Aegium : coin-device of Aphrodite
arranging her tresses with dolphin at
her feet ; Gardner, *Num. Comm. Paus.*
R. 23.

[d] Naucratis : coin of Ptolemy Soter :
Head, *Hist. Num.* 718, head of Aphrodite with ear-rings and necklace.

these with the public worship and with the cult-image in her temples in these places. Two of them bear express allusion to the sea, a ship's prow appearing on the Cnidian coin (Coin Pl. B 44) behind the head of the goddess, and the coin of Aegium presenting a device that must be associated with a type of Aphrodite Ἀναδυομένη or Ἀφρογενής, and of which there was some celebrated representation in sculpture.

The lines of Ovid,

'Cum fieret lapis asper, nunc nobile signum,
　　Nuda Venus madidas exprimit imbre comas[a],'

refer to a marble statue of which the main motive survives on the last-mentioned coin, on one of Methana[b], and on a Bithynian coin[c]. How far this is related to the famous Anadyomene of Apelles need not be discussed here; for the exact motive of that work is doubtful, and there is no proof that it was painted for any state-worship[d].

An interesting type of the maritime Aphrodite is preserved on the Leucadian coin mentioned above[e] (Coin Pl. B 45), if Curtius' interpretation is correct; and on the whole the name of Aphrodite Aeneas seems to suit the figure better than that of Artemis, which is given it in the *British Museum Catalogue*; for the fawn at her side, the common symbol of Artemis, may also belong to Aphrodite, to whom the aplustre held in the hand, and the bird, which looks like a dove on the top of the column behind, are more appropriate[f]. On some specimens a very much larger bird, a swan or a goose, appears behind her, and both are symbols of Aphrodite rather than Artemis.

Among the larger plastic monuments of some religious importance, that represent her as goddess of the sea, the group in the western gable of the Parthenon, preserved only in

[a] *Ars Amat.* 3. 223. The type penetrated to Carthage, for it is found on a Carthaginian metal-band; *Gaz. Arch.* 1879, Pl. 21.

[b] Head, *Hist. Num.* p. 370; cf. Mionnet, *Supp.* 5. p. 227, no. 1342.

[c] *Catalogue of Greek Coins*, Pontus, p. 194.

[d] It was kept in the Asclepieion at Cos; the cult-relations between Aphrodite and Asclepios were very slight.

[e] P. 641.

[f] On another coin of Leucas we have an undoubted head of Aphrodite with stephane and long hair, large full features and a half smile; *Cat. Greek Coins*, 28. 5.

Carrey's drawing, is of great interest. If Carrey's eyes did
not deceive him, and if the naked figure seated on the lap of
the elder goddess was really female, then she could have been
none other than Aphrodite supported by her mother Thalassa;
and this group was probably copied for the relief-work that
adorned the base of Poseidon's chariot in his temple at Corinth [a].
It has been supposed that this remarkable representation was
suggested by some Attic cult such as that of Aphrodite Colias,
but the motive of the supported and supporting figures would
not be appropriate for the central statue of a temple.

The pre-eminent monument of the maritime goddess was
the Cnidian statue by Praxiteles, which is known to us
through Cnidian coinage and some surviving statues that
are copies of it, and also through a very full literary record.
A detailed account of it will be given below; it is only
mentioned here because it was probably designed for the
temple-worship of Aphrodite Εὔπλοια. It is true that certain
archaeologists maintain that it was wrought simply as a work
of art and not for public worship [b]; but there appears to be
more reason for Welcker's [c] view that Praxiteles' work is the
third and last in that series of statues which were dedicated in
the Cnidian temples of Aphrodite mentioned by Pausanias [54] :
' the Cnidians pay particular reverence to Aphrodite, and
possess certain temples of the goddess; the oldest is the
temple of Aphrodite Doritis (the giver of good things), the
second the temple of the goddess " on the height " (Acraea);
but the youngest is that of the goddess whom most people
call the Cnidian, but the men of Cnidus themselves call
Euploea, the goddess of fair weather.' Now it seems
probable that the masterpiece of Praxiteles was actually the
temple-statue of this last shrine; because 'most people' called
it ' the Cnidian ' *par excellence*, and the great work was known
throughout the whole ancient world as ' the Cnidian' goddess;
because also the smile upon its face and the allusion to
the water and to the bath conveyed by the vase at its

[a] Paus. 2. 1, 7 ἐπείργασται θάλασσα
ἀνέχουσα ᾿Αφροδίτην παῖδα.
[b] Overbeck, for instance, *Geschichte*

der griechischen Plastik, 2. p. 170,
n. 54 ; and Friederichs, *Praxiteles.*
[c] *Griechische Götterlehre*, 2. 705.

side (Coin Pl. B 50) would well express the divinity of the calm
summer sea ; and, lastly, because we hear that it stood on a
high and conspicuous place in a chapel open at both ends [a],
whence it could be seen from afar on the sea. There is no
reason why this chapel should not have been the same as the
'latest temple' mentioned by Pausanias, built specially to pro-
tect and at the same time reveal the temple-image. It may
be that it is this Praxitelean statue of Εὔπλοια that the epigram
of Anyta alludes to : 'This spot is sacred to Cypris ; for
she ever loves to behold from the land the glittering main,
that she may give to the mariners a voyage such as they
desire ; and all the surrounding sea trembles when it sees
the radiant image [b].' And the same function and power is
attributed by Lucian to the Cnidian Aphrodite of Praxiteles [c].
But as the image was more than all monuments in the world
the embodiment of love and loveliness, it is likely that if the
name Εὔπλοια continued long to be attached to it, the title
came to comprise the notion of faring well in love as well as
prosperous voyaging on the sea. For we find this double
meaning in it on a gem that has the word inscribed upon it
and shows us Eros riding on a dolphin [d] ; and an epigram in
the *Anthology*, written as if it were the inscription on one of
her statues, makes her say, 'Do reverence to Cypris; for I will
breathe on thee with a favourable breeze in love or on the
bright-visaged sea [e].'

Of the smaller monuments showing the same aspect of
Aphrodite, two may here be mentioned for the importance
of the religious idea they express, although they are not to be
connected immediately with any public cult. One is the
very beautiful silver medallion in the Louvre (Pl. XLIV. a) that
cannot be later than the end of the fifth century B.C., showing Aphrodite of slim maidenly form rising from the waves

---

[a] 'Aedicula quae tota aperitur,' Pliny,
36. 21 ; νεὼς ἀμφίθυρος, Lucian, *Erotes*,
13 ; περισκέπτῳ ἐνὶ χώρῳ, *Anth. Plan.*
4. 160.

[b] *Anth. Pal.* 9. 144.

[c] *Erotes*, 2.

[d] *C. I. G.* 7369 ; cf. the invocation of

the sea-born Aphrodite as the πόθων
μῆτερ ἀελλοπόδων in the *Anthology*, 10.
21.

[e] *Anthol.* 9, p. 143 :
Ἱλάσκευ τὴν Κύπριν· ἐγὼ δέ σοι ἢ
ἐν ἔρωτι
οὔριος ἢ χαροπῷ πνεύσομαι ἐν πελάγει.

PLATE XLIV

a

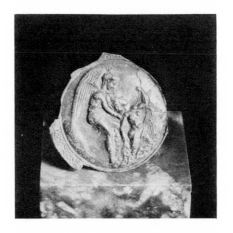

b

To face page 690

Plate XLV

and lifting up her mantle, and Eros, a youth with large wings, who stands behind her and assists her to ascend [a]. No other monument could so well embody the title of ᾿Αφρογενής or ῎Αφριος, the foam-born goddess, or the lines of Hesiod, who tells us that Eros was by her side at the moment of her birth and when she came into the company of the gods [97]. The unique character of the composition, the fineness and nobility of the forms, compel us to believe that this is a direct copy of the same scene carved in relief on the base of the throne of the Zeus Olympios of Pheidias [b].

The other representation is that of a black-figured vase published by Lenormant and De Witte, on which Aphrodite, wearing the aegis, is driving in a chariot with Poseidon. The inscriptions leave us in no doubt about the personages, and the aegis is clearly given (Pl. XLIV. b). There is much that is very remarkable in this. Nowhere else does the goddess wear the emblem of Athena, which cannot be interpreted here as an ordinary goat's fell, appropriate to Aphrodite ᾿Επιτραγία, but is a badge of war marking the Eastern war-goddess; and nowhere else is the warlike Aphrodite represented at the same time as a maritime power, as she certainly is here through her companionship with Poseidon. We know that the goddess at Corinth, as often in the East, was worshipped under her warlike aspect; and we might conclude that in this character she was also closely related by cult with Poseidon, the chief divinity of the land; but even this hypothesis would not fully explain the enigma of this vase-representation.

Generally, as a divinity of vegetation, of fruits and flowers, Aphrodite was, as we have seen, the frequent theme of early art; and the statue of Canachus was a great monumental illustration of this aspect of her. But it is not certain whether any surviving work can be regarded as the cult-image of ' Antheia,' or as the copy of one. This title would be appropriate enough to such an image of her as the bronze in the

---

[a] Cf. the relief published in *Röm. Mitth. d. deut. Inst.* 1892, on which Aphrodite is seen rising and received by the Hours.

[b] Paus. 5. 11, 3 ῎Ερως ἐστὶν ἐκ θαλάσσης ᾿Αφροδίτην ἀνιοῦσαν ὑποδεχόμενος.

Bibliothèque Nationale in Paris, representing her as holding
the hem of her robe in the left hand and an apple in the right,
and wearing a flower-wrought crown (Pl. XLV). The flower
by itself is so common a symbol that it cannot be regarded as
alluding to any special cult of the goddess. But perhaps the
well-known statue called the Venus Genetrix in the Louvre
(Pl. XLVI) reproduces some religious image of the divinity
of vegetation, as we may believe that the hand with the apple
is a correct restoration[a]. The name ' Genetrix' refers to the
mythical descent of the Julian house from Venus, and has, as
we have seen, no exact equivalent among the Greek cult-
titles ; and the type presented by the Louvre statue was certainly used for the Roman goddess, for we find it on a Roman
coin with the title inscribed[b] ; and it was possibly adopted by
Arcesilaus, who carved the statue for the temple of Venus
Genetrix that was dedicated by Julius Caesar B.C. 46[c] ; but
this is uncertain, as other and different types appear on Roman
coins. In any case, the Louvre statue goes back to a much
older original, of which the Greek title is lost to us. The
half-concealed pensive smile on the lips and the sidewards
inclination of the head recall the expression characteristic of
Praxitelean works; and the treatment of the features and hair
displays a pure and almost severe grace. But the broad
cheek and large chin, the large forms of the body and the
noble breadth between the shoulders, show the style of a
period still earlier than that of Praxiteles. And Professor
Furtwängler[d] inclines to believe that Alcamenes, the pupil of
Pheidias, was the author of the original work, as M. Reinach
had already suggested. The chief difficulty in the way of
assigning to it so early a date as the close of the fifth or the
beginning of the fourth century is the treatment of the drapery,
which falls over the limbs like transparent gauze, the surfaces
being traced over with very faint lines. The delicate compli-

---

[a] The terracotta replicas of the statue,
as well as the figure on the Roman coins,
prove this ; vide Fröhner, *Terres-cuites
de l'Asie Mineure*, Pl. 21. 1 ; *Bull. de
Corr. Hell.* 6. Pl. 18.

[b] Coin of Sabina reproduced in

Fröhner, *Sculpture du Louvre*, p. 167.
    [c] Pliny, *N. H.* 35. 155.
    [d] *Ausführliches Lexicon*, p. 413 ; so
also in the *Meisterwerke*; cf. Reinach
in *Gazette Archéologique*, 1887, p. 255.

PLATE XLVI

To face page 692

cation of these cross-folds may have been added by the later copyist, to suit the later taste for mere effect; but the exceeding transparency must have been a quality of the original, and this is generally regarded as a mark of later fourth-century work. But it is beginning to appear in the Victories of the balustrade of the temple of Nike Apteros at Athens, and this voluptuous treatment of the drapery, which Polygnotus introduced into painting, may have come into sculpture earlier than is supposed[a], and expressly for the representations of Aphrodite at a period when the austerity of the fully draped figure was relaxed and the sculptor did not yet venture to represent her unclad. And in one respect the drapery of the Genetrix of the Louvre may incline us, in spite of these doubts, to place it early in the fourth century; for the stately columnar disposition of the folds at her left side reminds us of the 'chiton ποδήρης' of the earlier Pheidian monuments. And this arrangement was especially retained for representations of divinities and statues connected with temple-worship[b]. The 'Venus Genetrix' then may be believed to preserve the type and forms of some temple-monument of the beginning of the fourth century, and expresses the same idea of the goddess as that which probably appeared in the famous Aphrodite ἐν κήποις of Alcamenes.

Her character as a divinity of vegetation was further attested by her associations with the Horae, with Cybele and Dionysos; but the monuments that illustrate this are very rare, and cannot be connected with any known cult[c].

---

[a] The instances which M. Reinach adduces to prove that this style is earlier than is generally supposed are not quite sufficient.

[b] Compare the drapery of the sacred maidens on the Parthenon frieze with that of the Caryatids of the Erechtheum, and the divinity standing amidst the figures on the 'Alcestis' column from Ephesus. Traces of this columnar disposition of the folds appear also on the terracotta figure published by Fröhner mentioned above (p. 692, note a).

[c] The relief published in Stackelberg's *Gräber der Hellenen*, Taf. 29, is the only certain instance I can find of Aphrodite with the Hours: her affinity with Cybele might be illustrated by the bronze from the Troad described above, also possibly by the coin published in Gerhard's *Akademische Abhandlungen*, Taf. 43. 18, on which are seen two goddesses, seated at each side of a temple-door above which is a dove, each with the calathus on her head, the one mounted on two lions, the other on

It is more clearly attested by her association with Adonis; but the surviving monuments that show her in his company refer usually to the story of her love and his death, and have a purely artistic and mythological significance[a]. The most beautiful of these appears to be an Attic aryballos from Kertsch, with figures in relief, recently brought to St. Petersburg and not yet published; the scene clearly alludes to the Cypriote legend, for the group of Aphrodite, Peitho, Adonis, and Eros are combined with the Salaminian hero Teucer, Tecmessa, and Eurysaces. Professor Furtwängler, who is the first who has written an account of it [b], states that the inscriptions on it and the style assign it to the same date as the Parthenon frieze. The vase then has a singular interest as being the first monumental illustration of the introduction of the Adonis-cult into Attica, and also as attesting the influence of the Ajax of Sophocles.

We cannot quote any representations of Adonis that throw light on the ritual connected with him. The beautiful bronze found at Paphos, now in the Bibliothèque Nationale of Paris, is proved to be an Adonis [c], partly by the resemblance between the almost feminine head and the head of Adonis on the coins of Euagoras [d], king of Cyprus, and partly by the remains of a garland of roses wrought in silver upon his hair; in one hand he holds what is probably a grain of incense to be placed in the censer which he carries in his left. The work is of the early Alexandrine period, and embodies the idyllic sentiment that the poetry of that age attached to Adonis.

On the other hand, we have one or two representations of Aphrodite, inspired by the myth and ritual of Adonis, that are of value as illustrations of cult. The story, mentioned before, of the birth of Adonis from the split trunk of the tree into which Myrrha had been transformed, arises probably from the

two bulls. On the relief in *Mus. Chiaram.* (Tav. 36) Aphrodite appears with Eros in company with Maenads.

[a] The group of Aphrodite, Eros, and Adonis described in an epigram of the *Anthology,* 11. 174, is full of the romantic Alexandrine sentiment.

[b] *Meisterwerke,* p. 275 (Engl. ed.), note 10.

[c] *Gazette Archéol.* 1876, Pl. 16.

[d] *Trésor de Numism. des rois Grecs,* Pl. 32, no. 2.

Plate XLVII

664

To face page 695

practice, which was very common in the worship of divinities of vegetation, of hanging his idol from a tree or placing it in the hollow trunk. Now on a Lycian coin struck under Gordian (Coin Pl. B 29) we see the curious type of an idol placed in a hollow tree, from which two serpents are issuing and scaring away two woodcutters who had come to fell it. There is a possible allusion to the Adonis myth, but the idol is a cult image, not of the god but of a veiled goddess wearing the calathus, the symbol of fertility, upon her head, who must be Artemis-Aphrodite and who is here clearly conceived as a divinity of vegetation[a]. The type has much in common with the very archaic type of the draped divinity examined above.

There is another typical representation of Aphrodite that can with more certainty be referred to this subject (Pl. XLVII). A small statuette of limestone in the Louvre presents the figure of a woman seated on the ground, her right hand and arm supporting her, and her left lifted to her face and almost buried in the veil which covers the head. The expression of the face is pensive, and well accords with the pose. In itself the figure would not be recognized as Aphrodite's; but it exactly tallies with the type of the Aphrodite of Libanos described by Macrobius [109] [a]. And reliefs of the Roman period have been found in the same locality, on which the goddess appears in this pose and with this expression. The statuette probably preserves a cult-type, and in cult the mourning Aphrodite would be naturally associated with her dead lover [b].

The monuments that represent Aphrodite as a divinity of the lower world are independent—so far as we can see—of her association with Adonis. The interpretation of many of these is very difficult. None of those published by Gerhard in the *Archäologische Zeitung* [c] have any certain reference to a 'Venus Proserpina'; his supposition that by leaning on

[a] Vide p. 523.

[b] A very similar representation of a mourning female figure is found on a vase in Naples (Heydemann, Beschreibung no. 2900, *Élite Céram.* 4. Pl. 87), which is proved to be Aphro-dite by her *entourage* and the high stephane with anthemion that she wears. Heydemann interprets this as the mourning Aphrodite, without deciding whether there is reference to the Adonis-myth.

[c] 1861, Pl. 146, 147.

a pillar and standing with their legs crossed they proclaim their connexion with the lower world is eccentric enough, and arises from the fallacy of attaching a deep symbolism to details of pose that often arise from merely artistic motives. There is more to be said about another series of figures that are quoted and examined in his treatise on Venus Proserpina, and are put together and briefly described by Bernoulli [a] : the qualities common to this type are (a) the severe hieratic form of idol, (b) the calathus on the head, (c) the left hand holding the edge of the garment and the right pressed against the breast with or without an attribute, (d) dimensions under life-size, so that the idol can serve as a support to a leaning figure. No doubt we have here the forms of an image intended for worship. But what are the signs of Proserpine and what of Venus, and what evidence is there that the type expresses the joint divinity of the two? There is no proof that the hand on the breast alludes in these figures to death and the lower world; it was, as we have seen, a common motive in a very early Aphrodite type derived from the East, in which so far as it had any meaning at all it alluded to fertility; and later it became probably only a conventional motive borrowed from archaic works for hieratic sculpture of archaistic style. The calathus, again, is the emblem of fruitfulness [b], not directly of the lower world. But when any of these figures bears the fruit or the flower of the pomegranate, we have good reason for believing that this is a symbol of the chthonian divinity [c].

[a] Bernoulli, *Aphrodite*, pp. 64–66. Most of them are published in Gerhard's plates to his *Akademische Abhandlungen*, 28–32.

[b] See Euseb. *Praep. Ev.* 3. 11 Κάλαθον ἔχουσι τὸν μὲν τῶν ἀνθέων, σύμβολον τοῦ ἔαρος, τὸν δὲ τῶν σταχύων τοῦ θέρους.

[c] Vide pp. 216, 217. Bötticher, in the *Archäologische Zeitung*, 1856, p. 170, collects many legends proving that the pomegranate was the symbol of strife and death in Greek myth: a pomegranate tree sprang from the blood of Zagreus, from the graves of Eteocles and Polyneices;

Persephone ate of the fruit of the pomegranate and belonged therefore to the lower world: it is never regarded as a token of marriage and fertility, except in a doubtful passage of Antiphanes in Athenaeus, 3. 84: therefore, he concludes, the monuments where the pomegranate is held in the hand, such as the Polycleitean statue of Hera, the Athena Nike in the temple on the Acropolis, are to be interpreted in reference to strife and death. But had the same attribute always the same meaning? We find the pomegranate-fruit and flowers in the hands of one of the

PLATE XLVIII

To face page 697

Thus we may give the name Persephone to the statuette [a] of the
goddess holding the pomegranate flower, on whom Dionysos
leans, she being more usually associated with him than
Aphrodite; and it is scarcely believable that a Greek or
Latin would have been helped to recognize in this idol
Aphrodite Persephone by the fact that the figure happens
to hold her drapery in the same way as Aphrodite often holds
it.   He would only be likely to recognize such a double
divinity when the image combined attributes and tokens of
both personages; and these cases are very few.   The goddess
who holds a dove in her left hand and a pomegranate flower
in her right, and wears a long veil that falls from over a
stephane down her shoulders, may be called the chthonian
Aphrodite [b]; and the Aphrodite on the votive terracotta
tablet from South Italy, who holds out the pomegranate
flower and stands opposite to Hermes, is probably a divinity
of the same character (Pl. XLVIII).   For Hermes himself was
a power of the nether world.   And the solemn and balanced
pose of these figures, as well as of Eros who stands on her
outstretched arm, allows us to believe that these are cult-types
of actual worship.

Where Eros is seen, the goddess whom he accompanies
would be naturally regarded as Aphrodite, unless the representation obviously referred to some well-known myth about
some other divinity.   Therefore such scenes as that on the
fine cylix published by Lenormant and De Witte [c], showing
Eros receiving a goddess who is rising from the earth, must be

Hours on the cup of Sosias (Müller-
Wieseler, 1. 45, 210 a), and we should
naturally interpret it here as a symbol
of fertility; the flower also in the hands
of the running Eros on an archaic Etruscan mirror (Gerhard's *Etrusk. Spieg.* 1.
120, and Roscher, *Lexicon,* p. 1350):
and here it would more naturally be
a symbol of marriage than the lower
world.   Eros indeed is occasionally
associated with death; but the Hours
very rarely.   We may say then that
the pomegranate is a symbol of the
lower world in the hands of Proserpine;
but that it does not always and of
necessity bear this sense: its blood-red
colour could symbolize strife and death,
its seeds life.   The maiden called 'Ροιώ,
who received divine honours in Caria,
was probably another form of the
Asiatic goddess : the legend tells of
her death and divine honours (Diod.
Sic. 5. 62); vide supra, pp. 446, 447.

[a] Gerhard, *Akad. Abhandl.* Taf. 32. 5.

[b] *Id.* Taf. 30. 4.

[c] *Élite Céram.* 4. 34; cf. *Mon. dell'
Inst.* 4. 39, and Fröhner, *Musées de
France,* Pl. 21.

the representations of the return of Aphrodite Kore; and the
connexion, brought about probably through Orphic literature,
between Eros and the divinities of the lower world may have
helped to familiarize the popular imagination with the idea of
a chthonian Aphrodite, one of whose types is probably shown
us in the figure of the goddess who stands in hieratic pose
near to Eros on a terracotta relief found in Italy[a], crowned
with the calathus and holding a poppy-stalk in one hand and
a lowered torch in the other.

The bust or προτομή published in the *Gazette Archéologique*[b] may also be accepted as a representation of the same
goddess (Pl. XLIX. a); the shape of such monuments suggests
that they were intended to be hung up in graves, as were the
images of Astarte in Phoenician tombs. The mitra on her
head and the veil falling down over her shoulders would be
appropriate to a divinity of the lower world, and as the upper
parts of her figure are naked we may believe that the sculptor
intended Aphrodite rather than Persephone. And the Cypriote
idol of archaic type, with the pomegranate flower held in one
hand against its breast, may be brought into this small group
of monuments on account of its *provenance* and this attribute[c]. Whether we can include in this series the small idol
in the Ildefonso group at Madrid[d], as Gerhard and Bernoulli
propose, is very doubtful. If we could with certainty interpret
the two main figures as Antinous and the genius who quenches
the torch, and knew that this interesting group was a monument of the youth's voluntary death, then the goddess whose
image stands near the genius would naturally be of the lower
world, and the motive of the hand that holds her drapery,
combined with the attribute of the apple in her hand and the
calathus upon her head, testifies to Aphrodite. But as excessive
restoration has made the meaning of the whole very uncertain, we are not justified in finding more in the idol-figure
than the ordinary idea of Aphrodite as a goddess of fertility[e].

[a] Gerhard, *Akad. Abhandl.* Taf. 56. 2.   Gerhard, Taf. 33. 1 ; Friederich's *Antike
[b] 1879, Pl. 30.   Bildwerke*, 1665.
[c] Gerhard, Taf. 47 a.   [e] The argument of Bernoulli that this
[d] Vide Bernoulli, *Aphrod.* p. 66 ;   must be the chthonian Aphrodite,

PLATE XLIX a

a

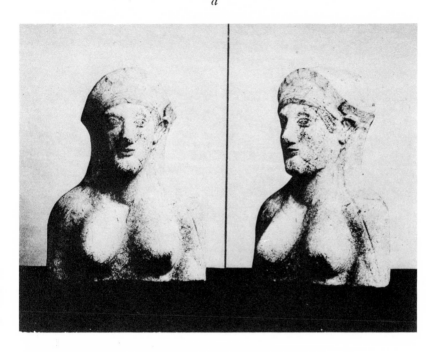

b

These monuments convey the notion by means of external symbols only.   Of far more interest is another work that gives a very different and deeper expression to the same idea : a female head published in the *Archäologische Zeitung*ᵃ, having a striking look of pity and sorrow on the face, and wearing as a kind of head-dress the face of the Gorgon with closed eyes (Pl. XLIX. b).   The head is probably a work of the Alexandrine period, this peculiar expression of pathos being such as we find on many monuments of this period.   But at first sight the work is an enigma ; it cannot represent a mortal, as no woman could wear such a head-dress.   Nor is there any known representation of Athena at all like this, to whom this profound sentiment of pity and sorrow is not appropriate, and who never wears the Gorgoneum as a covering for the head. The writer who published it is no doubt right in connecting it with the legends of Gorgo in Crete and 'Parakuptousa' in Cyprus ᵇ.   But it cannot represent the hard-hearted maiden herself ; for even if a daring sculptor were to give her the frozen Gorgon's head as a coif, he would scarcely spoil the story by giving her that look of compassion.   In fact the head does not refer directly to the story, but to that from which the story was by misinterpretation derived, to the cult of Aphrodite Gorgo, the mourning goddess of the lower world ; hence comes the sorrow in the face and the symbol of death on the head.

The cult of Aphrodite Μελαινίς at Thespiae has been interpreted in the former chapter as referring to the goddess of the under-world ; but on a Thespian coin of the fourth century in the British Museum we see a very striking Aphrodite-head and two crescent moons in the field (Coin Pl. B 48).   If this is the goddess Μελαινίς, we should suppose that her cult came to be associated with a moon-goddess such as Hekate, though it is very unlikely that the epithet originally referred to the moon.

because the same type is used for one of the figures of the triple Hekate, is of little force ; for the shape of the triple Hekate is borrowed partly from 'the fair-fruited' Demeter, and not every one of her three figures is chthonian ; the apple has no reference to the lower world, nor of necessity has the calathus, but these may be the badges of Hekate or Aphrodite as the givers of increase on the earth.

ᵃ 1857, Taf. 1.

ᵇ Vide p. 652.

It has been suggested that from this aspect of Aphrodite as a goddess of death arose her association with Nemesis and the Fates[112 a]. Possibly we have an illustration of this in the bronze, 60 centimetres high, found in perfect preservation in Ostia in the temple of Cybele, representing a naked goddess seated with legs crossed, holding a small object on which to wind thread ; Visconti proposes to call her Aphrodite Κλωθώ[a].

The monuments that may be quoted as illustrating the worship of Aphrodite as a city-goddess fall generally into two groups, the one consisting of those that show her armed as a divinity of war, the other of those that represent her with the turreted crown, the badge of the state, both types being ultimately derived from the East.

In considering the first group we must distinguish between those representations of the armed Aphrodite that are mere caprices of the sculptor's fancy, mere sentimental expressions of her love for Ares, and those on the other hand which are derived from an ancient conception, and seriously express the character of the Eastern goddess of war. Unfortunately the monuments of this latter species are scarcely known to us except through literary record ; nearly all those that have survived have no direct connexion with state-worship. We hear of the statue of the armed goddess of Cythera, and in many epigrams and other literature of the armed Aphrodite of Sparta and the Aphrodite Ἀρεία, whose statue, according to Pausanias, was 'most archaic[25 c].' But we find this type on no coin or monument of Cythera, and not with certainty on any of Lacedaemon. The question however may be raised about the meaning of the figure represented on a Spartan coin of the third century B. C. (Coin Pl. B 43), a divinity who is enveloped from the breast downward in a stiff circular garment that gives to more than half the body the form of an aniconic idol, and who wears a helmet and holds a lance in the right hand, a bow in the left: the right side of the statue is adorned with a cock standing on an aplustre ; at the left side stands a goat[b]. The type corre-

---

[a] *Mon. dell' Inst.* 9. 8; *Annali,* 1869, p. 208.

[b] The replica published by Head, *Hist. Num.* p. 364, Fig. 240, does not

sponds very closely with that of Apollo of Amyclae as described by Pausanias [a], and the figure is given this interpretation by those who have published the coin; but they fail to explain satisfactorily the symbols of the aplustre and the goat. The former might no doubt have been added as an allusion to some naval triumph; but the latter animal can scarcely be shown to belong to the Apolline worship [b]. Prof. Furtwängler [c], therefore, prefers to interpret this figure as the armed Aphrodite of Laconia and Cythera, as we know that the bow and spear were her weapons in the East, and as the goat and aplustre are specially appropriate to her. But we have nowhere any minute description of this warlike Aphrodite, and the figure on the coin undoubtedly corresponds very strikingly with the description of the Amyclaean Apollo.

As regards the statue on the Acrocorinthus which Pausanias saw [16 a], it probably did not belong to the older and genuinely religious type, but was of such form as we see on some of the coins of Corinth (Coin Pl. B 46), that show us the goddess in her temple, naked to the waist and gazing at her reflection in the shield which she holds, as the Capuan statue shows her. The type of the statue and of the coin-figure is a Graeco-Roman or Alexandrine invention, a *jeu d'esprit* referring to her sentiment for Ares [d]. But it possibly replaced

show the cock on the aplustre; but vide Gardner, *Num. Comm. Paus.* N. 16.

[a] 3. 19, 2. Vide Head, op. cit.; Gardner, op. cit. p. 59; Bompois, *Portraits attribués à Cléomène.*

[b] The naked figure on the fourth-century coin of Tylissos of Crete (Head, *Hist. Num.* p. 406) holding a bow and the head of a Cretan goat may be, but is not certainly, an Apollo.

[c] Roscher, p. 408.

[d] Vide Gardner, *Num. Comm. Paus.* p. 27; Bernoulli, p. 161. Compare as a salient instance of the same idea the group in the Louvre of Aphrodite and Eros trying the arms of Ares; Fröhner, *Sculpture du Louvre,* no. 152; Clarac, *Musée,* Pl. 343, n. 1399. A statue

showing much of the type of 'Venus Genetrix,' representing the goddess wearing the sword-belt of Ares and carrying in her left hand not the apple but probably a spear, has been found at Epidauros (*Ephem. Arch.* 1886, Πίν. 13) and mentioned by Reinach in the *Gazette des beaux Arts,* 1888, p. 75: probably a copy made in the first century B.C. of an earlier work of a good period. It is difficult to include among the representations of the armed Aphrodite the strange relief found at Beirut and published in the *Mitt. d. d. Ath. Inst.* 1885, Pl. I, showing a goddess whose drapery and pose are on the whole those of the Athena Parthenos of Pheidias, but who wears the quiver-belt of Artemis and by whose side is on the Acrocorinthus an older image of the armed goddess of Oriental origin.

Among the representations of Ares and Aphrodite it is necessary to mention here those only that refer to the actual cult-relation that, as has been shown, existed in many places between them [96]. The oldest surviving monument that illustrates this association is the François vase [a], where he appears with Aphrodite in the procession of the gods ; next come two vases of the late archaic style, signed by Oltos and Euxitheos [b], and a cylix painted by Sosias [c], on all of which Ares and Aphrodite are seated together in solemn union in the company of the gods. To the finest period of style belongs the representation on the cylix of the British Museum of Ares and Aphrodite amidst other wedded divinities ; she stands erect, wearing a snood and long Ionic chiton, holding a cup in her right hand and raising the left to her chin, as she gazes down on Ares with a profound expression in her face. He is reclining on a couch, wearing a himation round his lower limbs and holding a sceptre (Pl. L. a).

The relief in Venice [d] of early fourth-century style is sometimes quoted among the religious representations of the union of the two divinities (Pl. L. b). On the right stands a bearded warrior in helmet and chiton, with a shield resting at his feet, holding out a cup to receive wine from a female figure arrayed in long chiton and peplos, a fold of which she draws over her head in one hand, while pouring from an oinochoe with the other. Behind her stands a smaller male figure, clad in a himation, in an attitude of adoration. Her pose and solemn expression are in keeping with the style of religious art. The features show many traits of the Pheidian style, but the surfaces of the cheeks are not so broad as on the Parthenon frieze. Now, but for the smaller figure, we should interpret this relief merely as a representation of the leave-taking between the wife and the husband who is departing for battle.

Eros. The writer of the article considers her to be Aphrodite, of a form that shows a reaction against Hellenistic laxness; but any interpretation of the relief must be doubtful, as the details are very incongruous.

[a] *Mon. dell' Inst.* 4. 54.
[b] *Ib.* 10. 23, 24.
[c] Gerhard, *Akad. Abhandl.* Pl. 15.
[d] Roscher's *Lexicon,* p. 406.

PLATE L

a

b

But, looking at the whole group, we must say that the scene has a religious meaning. Can the two main figures be the defunct parents regarded as powers of the lower world? But no other grave reliefs which express this idea with clearness have any resemblance at all to this; the surviving children are only represented of smaller size than the heroic dead, when these latter appear enthroned, as on the Spartan reliefs, or lying on the couch at the family meal, and when the children are bringing their offerings. But here the two larger figures are taking no notice of the worshipper, and the one is offering libation to the other. Therefore it seems impossible to explain them except as divinities; and if divinities they are Ares and Aphrodite, to whom the worshipper is praying, possibly for his own safety on some campaign. But it is necessary to say that this interpretation wants more support from other monuments than it is easy to find.

Many of the other representations in which the two divinities are brought together are 'archaistic,' but probably derived from archaic works that had a serious reference to cult [a].

The only myth of battle in which Aphrodite played a part was the Gigantomachy, and here only in the later representations and descriptions; and it is doubtful whether these are to be taken too seriously, and whether we can say that the ancient idea of the armed goddess at all accounts for her presence in these scenes. On a vase in the Louvre we see her driving with Ares in his chariot against the giants, but the figure of the infant Eros poised above the horses and drawing a tiny bow robs the representation of all serious significance, and shows it to be a mere sport of Alexandrine fancy. She takes a serious part in the action on the Pergamene frieze; and a small bronze found not long ago in Athens of Aphrodite Gigantomachos seems also to represent her in real and earnest conflict, but these representations of her in the battle of the gods may be due merely to the later enlargement of the myth which came to comprise all the Olympians in the struggle.

[a] Vide Bernoulli, *Aphrodite*, p. 144; the Borghese altar, Müller, *Denkmäler* *d. a. Kunst*, 1. 44; puteal in the Capitoline Museum, *ib.* 2. 197.

Among the monuments of the war-goddess we may include a bronze coin from Smyrna, representing Aphrodite, who gave victory in battle, Νικηφόρος or Στρατονικίς, appearing in the form of a cult-statue, clad in a long chiton and wearing the calathus, and supporting Nike on her left arm, which rests on a column[a]. It may well be that we have here a reproduction of the actual temple-statue [47 b].

The monuments of the city-goddess with the turret-crown are less doubtful, though not very numerous. The best illustration of this type comes from Cyprus, whither the Phoenician conception of the city-divinity Astarte, who wears a turreted crown on the coins of Ascalon, was most likely to travel; so that if we find such a goddess in Greek form in Cyprus it is more reasonable to give her the name of Aphrodite than any other. There can be no doubt that it is her head that appears turreted and adorned with earrings on the coins of Salamis of the latter part of the fourth century (Coin Pl. B 47); and two limestone heads found in Cyprus, published by Jahn in the *Archäologische Zeitung*[b], can be proved by the analogies of the coins with which he compares them to be representations of Aphrodite the city-goddess. The larger one (Pl. LI a), about 18 inches in length, belongs to the best period[c]; the goddess wears the turret-crown, and her expression is solemn and appropriate to the city-divinity: the smaller one is of later style, and there is a soft smile on the features, the type being the same as that of the head on the coin of Nicocles[d] of Paphos.

Aphrodite Κουροτρόφος and Aphrodite Hera, the goddess who nurtured children and who encouraged marriage, is not clearly presented to us on any monument. There are many θεαὶ κουροτρόφοι—the title more especially belongs to Demeter and Gaia—and among the many representations of divinities holding children none bear any attribute or symbol that reveals Aphrodite[e]. Nor can we find any clear expression

[a] *Catalogue of Greek Coins, Ionia,* p. 239.

[b] *Arch. Zeit.* 1864, Taf. 188.

[c] *Ib.* Taf. 188 (1); cf. coin 1 b.

[d] *Ib.* Taf. 188 (2); cf. coin 2 c. .

[e] Vide Bernoulli, *Aphrodite,* pp. 121–123: a fragment of an Acropolis vase shows Aphrodite with two little boys

PLATE LI

a

b

except in literature of her functions in regard to marriage. The apple held in the hand of the archaic and later statues may have had some indirect allusion to wedlock, but in itself it was merely a symbol of fertility and increase ; the lifting of the veil or the folds of the peplos upward over the head was a gesture of modesty not peculiar to the bride. Neither have we any sure monumental representation of the goddess of the clan or the civic community, unless we accept as genuine the relief and the inscription found in Sarmatia described already [40].

We should then have to say that the sculptor knew no other way of designating her as the clan-goddess, except by adding the figure of Ares for the idea of marriage and of Eros for the idea of love ; and without the inscription no one would recognize in her the goddess 'Απατούρη. It is equally difficult to say beforehand what expression Greek religious art would be likely to give to Aphrodite Pandemos, the guardian of the state-community; the monuments that are certainly not those of Pandemos in the political and original sense have already been partly discussed. One might think that there would be no better way of revealing the goddess under this aspect to her worshippers than such a representation of her as appears in the group on the Parthenon frieze : where, partly through what remains, partly through Carrey's drawing, Aphrodite is presented with Eros before her, and with the goddess who is probably Peitho at her back, in majestic posture on her throne, witnessing the great religious and political festival of the whole people. And we have record that the worship of Peitho was associated in the legend of Theseus with that of Pandemos [11 c].

It has appeared from the examination of the literature that there is scarcely any record of Aphrodite as a patroness of the arts of civilization, or as a divinity who inspired oracles or who was associated with Apollo [a]. And in the monuments

---

on her arms (or rather on her elbows), both of black colour. Miss Harrison may be right in naming this figure Aphrodite Κουροτρόφος, *Hell. Journ.* vol. 10, Transactions, p. xxxvii.

[a] There are only two inscriptions from Delos and Erythrae that prove a slight connexion between her and Apollo. Vide [49 b], [60].

we find only very scant recognition of these aspects of her. It is true that Gerhard discovers an Aphrodite with Apolline attributes in a statue of the Louvre belonging to the Greek period which has been restored as Euterpe[a]; but he was biassed about Aphrodite, and his interpretation is entirely fanciful[b].

The only monument of importance where she is found with Apollo is in the vase-painting in Vienna, published by Benndorf, and rightly interpreted as the consultation of Apollo by Aphrodite and the other goddesses concerning the fate of Troy[c]; but this alludes to the cyclic version of the myth, not to any cult. Another representation of Aphrodite, expressing probably the same idea, but inspired only by myth, is a bronze relief from Paramythia in Epirus, of very fine style, showing her with Anchises, and in such an attitude as suggests that she is prophesying his future to him[d].

At Salamis the goddess was probably invoked as the patroness of song and the lyric contest; and a few terracottas found in Cyprus, now in the British Museum, show us a female figure, often of Oriental countenance, playing on the lyre; some of them wear the modius, and one a sort of turban bound round with a fillet of wool, and it is probable that they show us a type of the Cypriote Aphrodite[e].

In the later periods the Hellenic goddess became little more than the divinity of love and desire, and a few cult-titles, probably of late origin, designated her thus; in the later monuments this aspect of her predominates, but scarcely any of these that represent her merely as the goddess of sense-beauty can be connected with any cult. But some of those that associate her with Peitho and Eros may be considered as possibly derived from the actual state-religion.

The group of the two goddesses on the Parthenon frieze

[a] Fröhner, *Sculpture du Louvre,* No. 379.

[b] *Arch. Zeit.* 1861, Taf. 147. 2.

[c] *Vorlege Blätter*, E, Taf. 11.

[d] In Bignor Park, Sussex; Müller-Wieseler, 2, Pl. 27, 293: cf. Friederich's *Bausteine*, 1961, who ascribes it to the later period.

[e] Ohnefalsch Richter, *Ancient places of worship in Cyprus*, 12. 5.

mentioned above, though in no sense cult-figures, may have reminded the Athenian of the worship of Aphrodite and Peitho near the Acropolis. Another relief found in Athens, and now in the Central Museum [a], probably represents these two divinities ; we see two female figures in close union, the one with her upper body undraped and with large forms that speak of the earlier style, the other clad in semi-transparent drapery. The composition is full of repose and refined expression, and the relief may belong to the earlier part of the fourth century. A more famous and more certain representation of Aphrodite and Peitho is the beautiful fourth-century relief in Naples, on which Aphrodite is seen seated by Helen and persuading her to give herself to Paris, who stands in converse with Eros [b]. By the goddess is a pillar, on the top of which sits Peitho—the inscription proves the name—clad in ample drapery, and wearing the calathus on her head, her form being perhaps derived from some cult-type. The personification had possibly at Athens a political allusion ; but nearly always in monuments and in literature Peitho is a goddess of love, the power of love's persuasion, and therefore she appears with Aphrodite and wears the calathus, and the earlier and later poets speak of her as if she were herself the Love-goddess.

The very numerous groups of Aphrodite and Eros are almost all 'secular'; for he figures in nearly all of them merely as the personification of human love, and as such he had scarcely any recognition in public worship [c]. Mention has been made of the monuments from South Italy that show him associated with an Aphrodite-Kora ; and it is probable that these correspond to a prevailing religious conception. The figure of Eros on the goddess's extended arm on the

---

[a] Milchhöfer, *Die Museen Athens,* p. 18.

[b] Baumeister, *Denkmäler,* p. 638, Fig. 708.

[c] In Hesiod the cosmogonic and physical character of Eros is combined with the personal and human which in the later lyric poetry prevails. His figure does not appear very early in art, and in his oldest worship—at Thespiae —his idol was not of human form at all, merely an ἀργὸς λίθος (see [118k]). Perhaps one of the earliest examples of Aphrodite associated with Eros is a representation on a mirror-handle in the British Museum.

votive relief from South Italy (Pl. XLVIII) has the severe pose of a temple statue, the hand being outstretched to receive offerings or to give blessing; the lyre may allude to the musical contests in his honour on Helicon. In a terracotta group from Cyrene, now in the Louvre, we may see in the tall figure of Eros, who leans on Aphrodite and wears the calathus on his head, an independent god of ancient cult (Pl. LI b). But in these instances he is probably more than the personal form of the abstract idea of human love; he is the god of Thespiae, a god of birth and increase and probably of death, and very close akin to Hermes.

From the close of the fourth century onwards many representations of Aphrodite have survived that are purely ‘genre,’ some of them frivolous and some sensual, though none actually gross. They are not of direct importance for the history of public cults, with which none of them can have any proved connexion[a]. They illustrate indeed a decadence in art parallel to a certain decadence that has been noticed in the religion; and those who dislike the expression and motive of the Medicean Venus may call her Aphrodite Ἐταίρα; but there is no evidence whatever that a statue of this type was consecrated to the worship of that goddess where such worship existed. These representations of the later period have of course great value for the history of art; for the student of Greek religion they have merely an indirect value as illustrating changes in private sentiment about the gods, important enough, though not necessarily expressing themselves in the public forms and ritual. In the later art, Aphrodite more rarely appears as a goddess than as a woman who gives and requires love and does her best to excite it. But in general worship, even down to the end of paganism, she was always more than this.

---

[a] The statue sometimes called Aphrodite Καλλίπυγος in the Museum at Naples is probably a representation of an ordinary ἑταίρα: it is not necessary to suppose that if a chapel or altar was erected to Aphrodite Καλλίπυγος at Syracuse an image expressing the title was also consecrated to the worship; vide *Jahrbuch des deut. Inst.* 1887, p. 125 (Heydemann).

CHAPTER XXIII.

IDEAL TYPES OF APHRODITE.

WE cannot quote from the period before Pheidias any great monument that presented the inner character of the goddess by means of spiritual expression in the face or whole form. It would be tempting to take as a masterpiece of the religious sculpture of this period the Sosandra of Calamis, the greatest master before Pheidias in this field of work, and to call it Aphrodite. But reasons have been adduced against this interpretation [a]. A beautiful bronze, of the pre-Pheidian style, has been recently acquired by M. Caraponos and published in the *Bulletin de Correspondance Hellénique* [b] under the name of Aphrodite. A female figure of tall slim maidenly form stands holding a dove in her left hand and in her right hand some object that has disappeared but was probably a flower ; the face is very earnest, and free from all sentiment, so far as one can judge from the photograph. The nobility and purity of the work, its naive unconscious grace, would give it an important place and an original value among Aphrodite-monuments, if the name were sure. A religious dedication of some kind it is undoubtedly, and the drapery with the folds of the chiton ποδήρης and its arrangement of the upper mantle strikingly recalls the Vesta Giustiniani ; the symbols also are appropriate to Aphrodite. But no certain representation of this period shows us an Aphrodite of these virginal forms, these half-developed features [c], and this girlish simplicity in the arrangement of the hair. It may be therefore that the bronze is a representation of a girl-priestess of Aphrodite, and dedicated to the goddess.

[a] See p. 666.

[b] 1891, Taf. 9 and 10, discussed, p. 461 ; height 27½ cent.

[c] I am following the account given by M. Lechat, *ib.* p. 467, not having seen the original.

We can discover more about the type of Aphrodite in the next period, the zenith of Greek religious sculpture, when Pheidias was working for Greece. His chryselephantine statue of the goddess at Elis has left no trace of itself in any copy or later work as far as we know[a]. But the Aphrodite on the Parthenon frieze reveals the style and spirit with which the Pheidian school handled this theme. The striking characteristics, which the mutilated original and Carrey's drawing present to us, are the dignity of the pose, the majesty of the ample forms, and the austere disposition of the drapery, the Ionic chiton leaving bare only the lower part of the arms, while the veil denotes the goddess of marriage. The face has disappeared. But a fragment in the Louvre may preserve for us an Aphrodite's head in the style of Pheidias (Pl. LIII). It has been described by Fröhner[b] as ' superbe sculpture grecque de l'école de Phidias.' And Overbeck supposes that it may have belonged to one of the figures on the Parthenon pediments. This conjecture is certainly far more reasonable than Stark's comparison of it with one of the Niobids : for it has no resemblance with any figure in the Niobe group, while no work that is not actually known to have come from the Parthenon recalls so vividly the style and forms of the Parthenon sculpture. It has, in fact, all the prominent forms of the Pheidian type of head : the great breadth of cheek and depth of skull, the full chin, the simple grandeur of the line of eyebrows, and the large circles of the eye-sockets, the striking breadth of the forehead and of the space between the eyes, the simplicity in the rendering of the hair. The lips are full, the upper high-arched. The eyes are gazing upward, and the whole countenance is full of thought and power without severity. For warmth of spiritual expression, perhaps, no head of ancient sculpture surpasses this.

[a] The type of the Aphrodite Oura-nia carved by Pheidias for Athens Prof. Furtwängler would discover in a statuette at Berlin, published in *Meister-werke,* p. 71, Fig. 24 : the drapery does not appear to be treated as we should expect in a temple-statue of this period, and the arrangement of the hair is not in accordance with the usual Pheidian manner ; but the figure seems in its main features to belong to this school.

[b] Fröhner, *Sculpture du Louvre,* 163.

PLATE LIII

PLATE LII

It is the head of a goddess, and the bright look on the face
and the faint smile speak of Aphrodite.

There is, perhaps, only one head in Europe that shows us
how the countenance of the goddess was treated by the sculpture of the fourth century in the period before Praxiteles ;
namely the head in Holkham Hall in Norfolk[a], a good
Graeco-Roman copy of a great original (Pl. LII). The skull
is strikingly deep, but the surface of the cheek is not so broad
as in the earlier type, while the sidewards inclination of the
head, which becomes from this time onward a common
characteristic of the goddess, is more marked. Yet it is free
from excessive or voluptuous sentiment, and the expression is
spiritual and noble. The hair is drawn away from the high
broad forehead in rippling lines, but a small crescent-shaped
tress falls on the cheek as is more usual in heads of the later
period. The eyesockets are rather large, the eyes somewhat
long, and the upper eyelid is slightly drawn down. The nose
and chin are large, and the lips slightly parted. In the forms
and expression the idea of love is purely and impressively
given, but still with some reserve and without too much self-
consciousness. The original was probably of the same period
as the very beautiful Kertsch vase in the Hermitage of
St. Petersburgh, on which is drawn the judgement of Paris
and the three goddesses [b] ; and the work of the sculptor has
many affinities with that of the vase-painter, who has given
his Aphrodite the same large and noble features and the
languid droop of the head.

The masterpiece of Praxiteles, the marble statue of the
goddess of Cnidus, is the most important monument of
the worship of Aphrodite. It is necessary first to examine
the statements made concerning it by ancient writers. The
records suffice to prove that this statue enjoyed a more
widely spread reputation than any of the other works of
Praxiteles, and there are passages in literature which describe
not only the outward motive but also the intrinsic character
of the work. The words in Lucian's treatise[c] tell us some-

---

[a] Michaelis, *Ancient Marbles*, p. 314.
[b] Reinach, *Antiquités du Bosphore Cimmérien*, Pl. 79.   [c] *Amores*, 13.

thing of the pose, and then go on to define certain formal excellencies in the work which helped to convey the highest impression of external beauty and charm. This, in Lucian's eyes and the eyes of the whole ancient world, was the perfect ideal of the undraped Aphrodite, and the nudity itself was part of the novelty of the representation. Usually, except where an Oriental type survived, she was represented with drapery in the older and more austere Hellenic art. She must, indeed, have been represented unclad, or nearly so, in the scene of her birth from the waters carved on the footstool of the Olympian Zeus, and we see in Carrey's drawing a figure that seems to be the naked goddess on the western gable of the Parthenon. But it was a much greater departure from religious convention to erect such a statue of a divinity in a temple for worship ; and the conservative Greeks of Cos, with more regard for religion than for art, rejected this wonder of the world. Was Praxiteles the first who made this change ? It is not at all certain, for Pliny[a] speaks of a famous Aphrodite statue by Scopas, naked and ' Praxiteliam illam antecedens,' a phrase which may mean 'surpassing in merit,' or ' preceding in time,' the famous Praxitelean work. It is true that in the context the words would seem to refer to artistic merit rather than to time ; but, in any case, we may believe *a priori* that any statue by Scopas was earlier than one which Praxiteles could only have carved when he was in the zenith of his power and at the height of his reputation.

At all events it was in the Praxitelean period that this innovation was made[b]. And we need not accuse Praxiteles of venturing in his handling of the religious subject to go beyond what the spirit of the age conceded. To embody the perfect ideal of the goddess for his generation, it had become necessary to show her unclothed ; and, if there had been no other reason, the formal excellencies of Praxiteles' art, his consummate power of giving life to the surface of the marble, would have prompted him to this.

[a] *N. H.* 36. 26.

[b] It has been assumed that a statue of Aphrodite, carved by Eucleides before 346 B.C. for the temple of Bura in Achaea, and mentioned by Pausanias (7. 25, 9) and Diogenes Laertius (3. 42), was undraped; but vide supra, p. 613.

PLATE LIV

To face page 712

Still less need we accuse him, as Brunn in his *Künstler-geschichte* has done, from the evidence of certain epigrams and other references in literature[a], of infusing into his work any predominant sensual quality. The anecdotes on which he lays overmuch stress prove nothing but that the statue was nude and surpassed all others in the Greek world in formal beauty. Praxiteles is not necessarily answerable for the sensual effect produced by his work upon certain minds. Brunn's examination of the epigrams aims at proving that they express a certain contrast between the loftier spiritual beauty of the Pheidian Athena (the Lemnian statue or the Parthenos) and the lower sensually fascinating beauty of the Cnidian : but it is difficult to see this clearly in the verses. One epigrammatist tells us that when you stand before the Cnidian you greet her as the queen of gods and men, and Pallas and Hera themselves would admit that the judgement of Paris was true : ' wrong-fully do we blame the Phrygian shepherd ' ; but when you stand before the Athena you call Paris a boor for withholding the palm from her. There is nothing here said about any difference of impression that the two statues produce upon the mind or senses ; we only gather that each in turn, when men gazed upon it, overpowered the judgement. We must not read between the lines ; we know that there was a marked difference between the spiritual character of a Pheidian work and one of the younger Attic school ; but the epigrams are silent about this. We have then the anecdotes of Athenaeus and Clemens Alexandrinus, who aver that the courtesan Phryne was his model. Literary gossip about artists is rarely of value ; but if these stories were true, they prove nothing concerning the impression and idea of the Cnidian statue ; for though we know something about Phryne's life, we know nothing of her face and expression. Athenagoras[b] speaks of the Aphrodite Hetaira, the ' courtesan-goddess in Cnidus '; but if the epithet refers to the worship of Aphrodite Hetaira that we hear of at Samos and elsewhere, the reference is entirely unhistorical; if it is merely vituperative, in such a

[a] Overbeck, *Schriftquellen,* 763, 1237–1240.
[b] *Leg. pro Christ.* 14.

context it has small value.   Both Clemens and Athenagoras are writing with intention.   On the other hand these facts must be weighed.   The statue was chosen as a monument of the state-religion of Cnidus, and reasons have been shown for believing that its official state-title was Εὔπλοια; and the goddess of the sea was another form of the ancient Ourania, who was much more than a goddess of human love.   And there is a passage in Lucian [a] where the statue is regarded as the very counterpart of Ourania herself; a statement which is interpreted by Brunn as if it only pointed the contrast between the actual Aphrodite in the heavens and her image on earth, but which is more naturally understood as signifying that the image represented Ourania, according to the meaning of the term current in Lucian's day, as the celestial divinity of pure love.

No doubt Praxiteles may not have intended this.   But how could Lucian, the most subtle art-critic in antiquity, have called her Ourania if that which was prominent in her form and face was the idea of sensual passion?   Of course nothing would so clearly reveal the inner intention of the work as the expression of the face; and Lucian alone tells us something of this.   He enumerates its characteristics in terms which refer mainly to spiritual expression and partly to certain physical forms.   No uncertainty attaches to the sense of the words τὸ φαιδρὸν καὶ κεχαρισμένον [b], denoting the radiant charm of the face.   When he speaks of the quality of τὸ ὑγρόν in the countenance, he refers to the dreamy or languishing expression of yearning imparted by the slight drawing-up of the lower eyelid, which we see in many heads of Aphrodite, and of Alexander the Great also.   If we insist that it must have added a sensual trait, how could it have appeared in the face of the ideal maiden Panthea [c], whose countenance and whole form were full of the very modesty of Sosandra herself?   But the meaning of ὑπερήφανον μειδιῶσα and σεσηρότι γέλωτι [d] is not quite clear at a glance.   It would hardly be in accordance either with the Greek construction or with the rhythm of the sentence to take ὑπερήφανον with κάλλιστον as meaning

[a] De Imag. 23.   [b] Imag. 6.   [c] Ib.   [d] Amores, 13.

'beautiful beyond measure'; we must take it with μειδιῶσα. If this should denote a disdainful and haughty smile, how could such a trait have been united with the radiant charm of the visage? Both σεσηρότι and ὑπερήφανον are words that would imply as a rule nothing attractive; yet it is clear from the context that they are here used in their rarer sense, the one to express the smile on the parted lips, the other in the sense of 'lofty' or 'sublime.' Both these usages are justified; and the countenance of the Hermes of Praxiteles, with its indefinable expression, may give us reason to suppose that the sentiment of his Aphrodite's face was equally baffling for ordinary words to explain, and that Lucian is therefore obliged to resort to far-fetched phrases.

The written evidence then does not warrant us in imputing a sensual character to this, the greatest of Praxiteles' works; the record tells us rather that this statue was in spiritual expression worthy of ranking with the Aphrodite of Alcamenes, with the Zeus and Athena of Pheidias, and the Hera of Polyclitus ; that what Pheidias had done for the type of Athena Praxiteles did for that of Aphrodite [a], both having created the perfect image that men might worship as the ideal form of these divinities.

We must also take account of the evidence afforded us by certain monuments ; in the first place by coins of Commodus and Caracalla, which of themselves contribute little or nothing to our knowledge of the intrinsic qualities of the work, as they possess no merit of style, but which help us to settle certain questions of motive and to discover other reproductions of the original. When we compare the figure on these coins with Lucian's account we can have no doubt that the coin-cutter has given us a mechanical but more or less accurate copy of the Cnidian statue; and they help us to fill up the gaps in his description (Coin Pl. B 50). The whole weight of the body was thrown on the right leg, and the left knee was slightly inclined inwards. The head appears on the coins altogether in profile, but this is probably a departure from the original made by the unskilled copyist, who may have tried unsuccess-

---

[a] Lucian, *Imag.* 23; Philostratus, *Vit. Apoll. Tyan.* 6. 19.

fully to represent thus the sideward and downward turn of the head, whereby the modesty of the Cnidian statue may have been partly expressed or the character of Aphrodite Εὔπλοια, surveying the sea beneath her, may have been conveyed.

But what is the meaning of the water-vase and the raiment which she holds above it? These would have been in place by the side of the statue, both as a necessary external support and as alluding to the goddess of the water; and it is inconceivable that the coin-cutter should himself have invented and added this detail, as there was no external necessity for it in the coin-representation. The positive evidence of the coins then counts more than the silence of Lucian, and we may suppose that the vase and the robe were part of the original idea, but that they were not placed so near the figure as to hide the left side; for Pliny says that the execution was equally admirable from whatever side the statue was viewed, implying that it was visible from every point of view[a]. If this motive, then, of the right hand holding the drapery which touches the vase is authentic, a certain part of the meaning of the whole work depends on the way in which we interpret it. Is the goddess laying it aside or is she raising it to clothe herself with it? That is to say, is she undraping herself to step down into the sea, or is she Aphrodite Ἀναδυομένη, the goddess just risen from the waves and not yet draped? The shamefaced gesture of the hand, the timidity expressed in her pose, would be equally appropriate on either interpretation; but the pose of the body which is displayed by the coin-figures, and by the Munich statue that will be mentioned directly, makes for the latter explanation. For her body inclines away from the vase, and this is natural if she is raising the drapery off it and drawing it towards her; whereas we usually incline towards the object upon which we place something. And again, the goddess rising from the sea was a common theme of Greek art and myth, and only slight allusions were needed to suggest it to the ordinary Greek's imagination; but neither art nor myth had much to say about the goddess stepping from the shore to bathe.

[a] *N. H.* 36. 20.

Among the numerous statues of Aphrodite that survive there are only two that, on the evidence of the coins, may be pronounced to stand in very close relation to the Praxitelean original—the statue in the Glyptothek of Munich, and one in the Vatican. The details of the composition are almost the same in both, with the exception that the drapery is held rather differently in the Vatican statue, in which the idea of Aphrodite ᾽Αναδυομένη is by no means so clearly expressed [a], and that its glance is more downward and sidelong. In both the pose of the limbs and the balance of the body is the same as on the coins. The hair of both is treated with the same simplicity and purity, being drawn away from the face and passing in light rippling waves into a knob at the back. Of the Munich statue much has been restored (Pl. LIV), namely, most of the upper part of the head, the nose, and the centre of the lips, half of the right fore-arm, the left arm from the bracelet downwards, the fingers of the left hand, the feet, and some parts of the vase and drapery. Nothing of the Vatican figure is new, except the left arm, and the right from the elbow downwards. Neither the one nor the other displays in the rendering of the surface of the body any striking excellence of style, and though the Vatican statue may be nearer to the original as regards the position of the vase, we cannot prove that in other respects it is a more faithful copy. The high value of both works lies in the rendering of the countenance, which more completely and more profoundly than any other monuments displays the ideal character of Aphrodite.

Both faces are free from all sensual expression, all coquetry and affectation, and both have a certain stamp of divinity. The yearning pensive sentiment is expressed in each, the eyes of the Vatican figure being fixed on the ground, those of the other gazing dreamily into the distance and slightly uplifted. The forms and expression display the χάρις, the

---

[a] Overbeck, in the *Geschichte der Griechischen Plastik*, and Michaelis, in the *Archäologische Zeitung*, 1876, declare that the pose of the Vatican figure and of the coin-figures proves that she is laying her robe aside; but they do not take into sufficient account the inclination of the figure.

spiritual grace of Praxitelean sculpture, but the countenance of the Munich statue alone shows the faint smile which was the masterly trait of the original, giving to the visage of the Cnidian goddess its radiant charm. The goddess and the woman are blended in these works as they were in the later worship.

The influence of the Praxitelean type on the whole predominates in the later monuments. Yet the religious sculpture after Praxiteles preserved in some of its representations of Aphrodite a certain tradition from the period before him. The most important work that illustrates this survival is the Melian statue, which will be described later : it is also illustrated by two Aphrodite heads in England, one belonging to the collection at Brocklesby Hall in Lincolnshire, the other in the possession of Lord Ronald Gower in London. The first is probably a good Graeco-Roman copy of a late fourth-century work (Pl. LV), for the hard lines of the throat and the shallow dry treatment of the parts about the eye betray the later hand ; and yet many of the forms are those of the early fourth-century type—the very broad cheek, the great breadth between the eyes, the rather austere arrangement of the hair. In the whole head there is a large vitality combined with a very serious expression, and in fact we could not be sure that this is the face of Aphrodite, if it were not for the pose of the head, the half-opened lips, and the holes for ear-rings in her ears. The forehead, which was once surmounted by a stephane, is extraordinarily high, and its height and triangular form remind us of the head of the Demeter of Cnidus.

The head belonging to Lord Ronald Gower (Pl. LVI) is an original Greek work, and unique among the Aphrodite heads in England ; it is of lifesize and of Parian marble, which has suffered much from corrosion, but not at all from the hand of the restorer, except that the eye-sockets, which were originally hollowed out for the insertion of eyeballs of metal, have now been filled up with plaster, and this has given a dull and lifeless look to this part of the face. Otherwise the face and forepart of the head is in perfect preservation, and the

PLATE LV

To face page 718

PLATE LVI

warmth and the purity of the Greek work is felt in the treatment of the lips and the parts about the mouth. The hair
shows the same graceful simplicity of arrangement as the
Cnidian head, being carefully drawn away from the forehead
and cheeks, and worked in fine rippling lines and gathered
in a knot on the neck. The forehead is high, the cheeks of
little depth, and the contour of the face suggests a period
in the fourth century a little later than the Praxitelean. But
the broad-ridged nose and the large chin are forms that recall
an earlier type, and the characteristic expression is not so
developed as in the Praxitelean masterpiece. The eyes were
not so narrow, the face is less full of yearning sentiment;
a faint trace of this is visible in the half-opened lips, and
though many of the usual traits that reveal the goddess, such
as the sidewards inclination of the head, are wanting, yet we
need not doubt but that this is Aphrodite, with a countenance
more austere and reserved than Praxiteles gave to his Cnidian
work. The impression on the features is rather one of deep
thought than of sentiment.

A certain degeneracy in religious sculpture that we can
trace from the beginning of the third century downwards
can be well illustrated by some of the statues of Aphrodite
that we have inherited from the Alexandrine period. Long
before any falling off in formal skill, we note the loss of
seriousness, the decay of imagination. Nearly all of the
crowd of Aphrodite statues in our museums are Graeco-
Roman, but three at least may be mentioned that belong to
the Greek period, though of later origin than those already
described. The Capitoline Venus is almost the best-preserved
statue of antiquity, having been immured in a cell during the
Middle Ages. There is far more reason for regarding it as
a Greek original of the third century B.C. than as a Graeco-
Roman work; for none of these show in the surface such finish,
warmth, and modulation. The glistening lustre of the surface,
the liquid transition from part to part in the handling of the
organism, are chief qualities of early Alexandrine sculpture[a].

[a] Cf. 'Eutychides fecit Eurotan in quo artem ipso amne liquidiorem plurimi
dixere,' Pliny, 34. 78.

The softness of each detail in the Capitoline statue is as remarkable as the rhythm of the whole, the fascinating undulation of the lines. Its formal merits, in fact, are far higher than those of the two copies of the Cnidian statue, but in spirit and idea it falls far below them. All is calculated for external and transitory effect ; the emphasis is on the flesh and surface, and there is no marking of the permanent structure of the organism nor of the forms of the skull which are clearly shown in the heads of the Cnidian type. Neither in the face nor in the whole form is there any deep sentiment expressed, any inward life revealed. The statue is, indeed, free from the vicious self-consciousness of the later Medicean Venus of Florence, but neither in the pose of the limbs nor in the countenance does the αἰδώς, the diffident modesty of the Cnidian, appear. The pose is without *naïveté*, and the action of the hands is full of reflection. There is nothing sensual in the face, but when we compare it with the Praxitelean, we feel the loss of imagination, of ideal character, here ; it is not so much that the expression is degraded, but it has become narrower and shallower : what is expressed in the mouth and large circles of the eyes is nothing more than a serious dignity. In certain details, also, we note the lack of purity and reserve ; the hair in the crobylus is arranged for the most effective display, and some of the luxuriant locks have escaped and lie on the cheek, and this lavish treatment of the hair and this crobylus rising above the forehead become characteristic of the later Aphrodite type. The face and body show more fullness and maturity of form. The Praxitelean ideal has been changed by the sentiment of the Alexandrine period, when the images of the divinities became part of the pageantry of the court. It is not the goddess, but the queen, that is presented to us with studied and brilliant elegance in the Capitoline statue.

A work of the same type, and probably of the same period as this, is the Aphrodite of Syracuse (Pl. LVIII). The head is missing, but it was evidently turned towards her right, as in the other statues of this type. The pose of the Cnidian original has been altered for this as for the Capitoline figure.

PLATE LVIII

The weight is thrown on the left leg, and both hands are used to screen her body, but in the Syracusan figure the left hand raises a portion of the drapery for this purpose [a], the rest of which is most artificially arranged as a sort of framework or shell for lower limbs. The modesty which was an inward quality of the Cnidian work becomes over expressed, or expressed by merely mechanical signs in the later sculpture, and is paraded in the Syracusan statue so as to lose all spiritual impressiveness.   All that we are struck with in this, as in the statue of the Capitoline, is the workmanship of the very warm and soft surface, and the articulation of the torso.

A fragment of great interest, as illustrating the sentiment of the later period, is the Aphrodite head at Smyrna, that may be attributed to the early part of the third century.   In certain details, but not in expression, it resembles the Castellani head in the British Museum—for instance, in the two crescent-shaped locks in the middle of the forehead.   The hair is arranged in the later luxuriant style with a touch of Alexandrine fashion ; it is not drawn away from the cheeks, but is allowed to cover most of the ears ; above the forehead appears the rather low crobylos.   The head shows the later proportions, being a high oval with more height than breadth. Neither in the expression, which is one of refined voluptuousness, nor in the relaxed features, is there any nobility or divine character.   The mouth and chin are comparatively small, and the cheek has little breadth ; the eyelids are large, as is usual in heads of Greek workmanship, but the eyeballs narrow and long, so as to give the languishing look of Aphrodite.

On the other hand, a few monuments have been preserved which prove that in some works of Alexandrine art the power of the older religious sculpture still survived.   The Castellani bronze head in the British Museum must have belonged to a statue of Aphrodite ; for the sideward turn of the head, the brightness of the face and its expression of yearning, are

[a] I have suggested in a paper in the *Hellenic Journal*, 1891, p. 58, that the right hand was drawing a strip of her drapery across her breasts : but this is impossible ; the marks between her breasts and on her left upper arm are due to the external supports that were riveted here to keep the right forearm in its position.

characteristic of her, although the eyes appear to have had nothing of the usual narrowness. And some of the forms of the older types of sculpture survive, for instance, the great breadth between the eyebrows. Yet the head is entirely of Alexandrine type; a large full oval, with considerable breadth of centre, and rather narrow width of cheeks; and a sure mark of the Alexandrine period is the prettiness of the two crescent-shaped locks on the forehead.

But no monument can show so strikingly how, in spite of decay, the older ideal style could survive in the representations of this divinity as the Melian statue in the Louvre[a].

This statue was found in the island of Melos in the year 1820, and fragments of other statues of the Herme form were discovered at the same time; also part of an upper left arm, a hand holding an object which is probably an apple, and a fragment of a basis with a large socket in the area of it, and on the face an inscription with the name of an artist of the Carian Antioch on the Maeander[b]. Now we have no accurate information as to the exact spot or position in which these fragments were found, and therefore their *provenance* does not oblige us to connect any of them with the statue itself. The most important of all the external evidence as to the date and motive of the work would be afforded by the block with the inscription, if we could prove that this was part of the statue's basis. For then we should know, looking at the square socket in this plinth, that some object such as a trophy, Herme, or pillar, stood at her left side and might have served as a support for her left arm, or might account for the pose and action of it; and, again, we should know that no other figure except possibly a Herme could be grouped with her on her left; and, lastly, that the work must at least be later than the foundation of the city on the Maeander (circ. 280–270 B.C.).

[a] For recent literature concerning this work, vide Ravaisson, Vénus de Milo (*Mémoire de l'Academie des inscriptions et belles lettres*, T. 34. 1, 116 pages); Furtwängler, *Meisterwerke*, pp. 367–401 (Engl. Ed.); Overbeck, *Geschichte d. griech. Plastik,* 4th ed., vol. 2, pp. 383–398.

[b] . . . ΑΝΔΡΟΣ . . . ΕΝΙΔΟΥ . . . ΙΟΧΕΥΣ ΑΠΟ ΜΑΙΑΝΔΡΟΥ ΕΠΟΙΗΣΕΝ.

PLATE LVII

To face page 722

The style of the writing belongs to the middle or first half of the second century B. C., if we can trust the copyist of the inscription. But the fragment cannot be immediately brought into evidence, for it has mysteriously disappeared. It is a gratuitous insult to suggest, as has been suggested, that the authorities of the Louvre deliberately destroyed it because it proved that their great acquisition did not belong to the best period of Greek sculpture. We must be content to depend on the records of those witnesses who saw it, and on the drawing made of it by the artist Debay.

Dr. Furtwängler has subjected the whole question to a very searching analysis in his *Meisterwerke*, and has come to the conclusion, from evidence that cannot easily be controverted, that the plinth with the inscription certainly belonged to the original work; and this view is gaining general acceptance. This, then, is the important point from which all theories as to the restoration of the statue should start.

Before discussing these, it is well to examine what remains of the statue. We see a female figure larger than the natural size naked to the waist, with her lower limbs enveloped in a peplos, which is very carefully arranged around the loins, and which is saved from falling by the disposition of the end of the garment over the left thigh, also by the drawing-up of the drapery under one of the folds on the right, where possibly the right hand was supporting it, and lastly by the inward inclination of the left knee : a studied but perfectly possible arrangement. The whole weight of the body is thrown upon the right leg, and inclines greatly to this side, so that the right shoulder is sunk below the level of the other. But her head is turned somewhat to her left and bent forward, and the direction of her right side is the same. The left upper arm appears to have been held almost straight out from the shoulder and slightly forward, and the elbow not to have been sharply bent, as we may judge from the fragment of a left arm which was discovered near the spot, and which, as some of the edges exactly correspond, certainly belonged to the statue. The right arm was held obliquely across the body. There are two possible explanations of such a pose : it may be energetic and dramatic, that is, she may be raising some heavy object, a shield for instance, or she may be partly resisting, partly yielding, to some force which bears upon her from her left : or it may be inactive, that is, she may be leaning with one or both of her hands grasping some support which frees her left side of any effort and allows her to recline as it were upon her right limbs. But there are no signs in the face of any energetic action ; the expression which has been very variously interpreted is certainly full of repose.

So far there appears no sure reason for giving to the figure any particular name. But the forms of the face and torso, considered together with the arrangement of the drapery, may help to solve the question. It is in the body where the chief excellence and charm of the work is found. The large manner of the great style is still preserved in the organism which is treated so as to reveal much of the main fabric, the surface showing the shadow of the bone-structure beneath. But there is also consummate ' veritas' in the surface itself, in the rendering of the folds of the skin ; the marble is lustrous and ' liquid,' and the breath and life are seen in the body as they are never seen in a Graeco-Roman work. The shallow modulations of the left side show the warmest workmanship. Certain irregularities may be discerned which prove that the sculptor worked from the living model. But the whole is a striking combination of natural truth with high ideal conception. The arrangement of the drapery may betray a certain study of effect, and does not obey the severe necessity which adjusts the drapery of the Parthenon figures. But none the less the style here also is large and dignified. The predominant quality of the whole is ' decor,' the union of beauty with dignity, which is the ideal that the Greek style of the best age chose for the feminine type ; and this quality accords with the expression of the face. Some writers have persuaded themselves that certain sensuous traits are marked upon it, especially by the treatment of the mouth and eyes. The eyeball is somewhat rounded in the centre, as we find in the heads of Scopas and, at a far later date than these, in the Pergamene heads ; and the corners of the eye are rather

PLATE LIX

narrow, but the lower eyelids are not drawn up sufficiently to give to the eyes that expression of yearning that the Greeks called ὑγρότης. As regards the whole expression many various and contradictory accounts have been given. Veit Valentin sees in the face a look of alarmed wonder and high scornful disdain [a] ; it suits his theory of restoration to discover such an expression, but his account is almost as untrue as that of those who find amorous desire in it. Even the forms of the head, though in some respects they betray the style of the later period, retain much of the nobility of an older type. We note the broad sweep of the eyebrow, the breadth of the upper part of the face, the purity in the arrangement of the hair, which is drawn severely away from the cheeks, and features that are not small nor over-delicate. Viewed from near or from far, the countenance appears free from human weakness or passion, and is stamped with an earnestness lofty and self-contained, almost cold. There is a distant interest in the eyes, which are fixed on no near object.

From all this we can conclude that the work is genuinely Greek, and that it is a goddess who is thus represented. But what goddess? The pose and expression would not be unsuitable either to Athena or to Hera, but neither of these two divinities could be represented with undraped body : nor would this strongly modulated face be appropriate to them. The imperious face and posture might suggest a Nike adorning a trophy, or a Muse playing on the lyre ; but there is no instance of a half-draped Nike or Muse except in the Graeco-Roman period. The drapery and the face confirm the belief that this is Aphrodite represented in forms not wholly alien to the Pheidian representation of her.

This conclusion may enable us to choose between various theories of restoration. Many of these can be dismissed without much consideration. We cannot, for instance, seriously consider whether this is the voluptuous goddess

[a] In his two treatises *die hohe Frau von Milo* and *Neues über die Venus von Milo*, in which he gives a subtle analysis of the pose, but suggests a purely impossible explanation (he supposes she is struggling to resist Ares who grasps her right wrist).

of pleasure tempting Heracles. And the distant and forward
gaze of her eyes is in itself sufficient to show that she cannot
be looking at her reflection in a mirror held in either of her
hands, nor can be pouring oil from a flask in her left hand
into her right ; and it is difficult to reconcile the calm
reposeful face with the supposition that Ares is present, and
that she is repelling his advances, even if Greek sculpture
of this period could represent divinities in such a situation.
Again, the Florentine group of Ares and Aphrodite laying
her hands on his shoulders shows the goddess in a pose
essentially different from the Melian ; in whose face there
is no expression that could at all suggest a love-scene.
This is admitted by some, who still maintain that Ares is
present not as the lover but as the divine husband, and
that the group represents the union of the austere divinities
of Thebes. But, if we believed this, we should not be a step
nearer towards explaining the peculiar pose of her arms, and
all theories are useless that fail to give some reasonable
account of this. No doubt the presence of a second person
would relieve the monotony of line on the left side of the
goddess, but her distant and strangely self-contained expression make us rather believe that if anything was placed
by her left side it was some inanimate object. Finally, the
strongest objection to the theory that a second person was
present is the evidence of the inscribed plinth ; for if this,
with its rectangular socket in the middle, really belonged to the
original work, as there is every reason to suppose, then nothing
could have been placed at Aphrodite's left side except a pillar
or a herme. May we then suppose, with Dr. Furtwängler, that
she was holding out an apple in her left hand and leaning with
her left arm on a column? There is some external evidence
that might seem to support this supposition ; for the fragment
of a hand holding an apple was found somewhere near the
statue. But it is of far too rough and coarse execution for us
easily to believe that it is part of the Melian figure. And
there are internal reasons against this theory: if she is holding
out the apple, she is holding it in a very remarkable manner.
Not unobtrusively, as in many older and later monuments, as

a permanent and silent symbol of the goddess of fruitfulness and marriage, but parading it in her left hand raised nearly to the level of her head ; held thus, it could only be a sign triumphantly displayed of her victory over her rivals. But the face is perfectly free from excitement or hint of display. Dr. Furtwängler, indeed, would restore the left arm quite differently, on the supposition that the elbow was bent and the fore-arm was resting on the pillar in such a way that the hand with the apple lay over the edge pointing to the ground. But his restoration is by no means convincing, and his theory depends on the assumption that the hand with the apple must be part of the work. In spite of his arguments, which do not rest on direct evidence, it is still reasonable to doubt whether such a hand could have belonged to such a statue [a].

As the left foot appears to be considerably higher than the right, and might be only touching the ground with the ball of the sole, it has been supposed that the balance of the whole figure would be very frail and uneasy unless both hands were occupied in grasping some support, and that this might well be a spear held free of her body on her left side ; hence we might account for the complicated pose of the various parts of the body. The spear, indeed, might be an attribute of the goddess, alluding to her romantic relations with Ares, or to her ancient Eastern character. But as the left arm was held almost straight out, the spear grasped by both hands must have produced a very ludicrous effect [b]. Nor can we imagine how the spear could be placed in relation to the pillar or herme. And that both hands should be used to support her balance is not necessary, when we consider that the plinth with the inscription was higher than the rest of the basis, and that thus the left foot, though higher than the other, could still be resting firmly on this raised part.

[a] Vide Overbeck, *op. cit.* p. 388.

[b] Keil (*Die Venus von Milo*, Hanover, 1882), who restores the figure on this theory, takes no notice of the fragment found of the left arm, which shows that the left elbow was very slightly bent ; and apart from this the figure of the goddess in his sketch suggests an athlete with a leaping-pole, about to take a leap.

Among the probable explanations of the mysterious figure —and perhaps probability is all that we can hope to attain— are two that commend themselves. The socket in the plinth would agree with the theory that by her left side stood a herme-representation of the goddess herself in the form of an archaic image, and that she is resting her left arm on the head of her own idol. Many analogies might be quoted for this combination of a younger type of a divinity with an older: the statuette of Artemis from Larnaka is a conspicuous instance. Or she may be holding a shield erect with the left hand, while its lower rim rests on the pillar. The right hand would then be steadying the lower part of it, or simply employed in keeping her drapery in its place. The motive of other cognate works does not, of course, give us a conclusive proof as to the motive of the Melian statue; but if this theory were correct, we should understand why other representations of Aphrodite with the shield show in general treatment a strong resemblance to this work. Thus the figure of the Venus of Capua in the Museum of Naples, the goddess who is probably using the shield of Ares as a mirror, and whose foot is on his helm, though it differs from the Melian in many important details of the pose, is a work derived from the same original. We find a similar figure with almost the same arrangement of drapery on the coins of the Roman colony of Corinth (Coin Pl. B 46). A terracotta figure at Carlsruhe of some beauty of style, possibly a Nike writing on a shield, is of the same type as the Melian. It is evident that some representation to which all these might be closely akin was known in the Alexandrine period; for the device of the goddess, whose drapery has slipped from her shoulder, and who is gazing at her reflection in the shield of Ares, is mentioned by Apollonius Rhodius [105 k] amidst the figures wrought on the shield of Jason [a].

[a] It must be also borne in mind that the 'Melian' motive appears in other representations than those of the shield-holding goddess: e.g. in a terracotta statuette in Vienna of Aphrodite with her left leg resting on a dolphin, and her body inclining slightly to her left: she is draped like the Melian statue, and has the same large and noble structure of torso, but the face and expression recall the Praxitelean style.

The goddess with the shield for her mirror is a *jeu d'esprit* of Alexandrine imagination, suggested perhaps by her older serious cult-relations with Ares. But the Melian statue must have a more serious significance : for if she is holding the shield on a support she is neither looking into it nor writing on it. What she is doing or what she is looking at we shall perhaps never discover. In the meantime we may believe that in the statue we have a great monument of Aphrodite worship, free from the triviality of much contemporary art.

The question as to its date is, of course, mainly decided by the inscription, but it may also be judged on purely internal evidence. Some critics of the last generation confidently attributed the work to Scopas or Alcamenes, merely because of its high ethical qualities and the large treatment of the forms and drapery. But this theory has never been supported by any real criticism. That the Melian goddess is more austere in respect of drapery, form, and expression than the Cnidian is no proof at all that this statue is earlier than the Praxitelean. The older type with its appropriate qualities was often preserved in a certain locality for certain reasons ; and a post-Praxitelean sculptor whose theme was Aphrodite was not bound to adhere to the type of Praxiteles, and he might attach himself to the severer style of the older Attic school. It may have been Praxiteles who brought into fashion the type of the undraped goddess, and before his epoch we may believe that the form of the fully-draped Aphrodite had become less austere, and representations of the half-draped figure, such as the Melian statue and the Venus of Arles, a Graeco-Roman copy of a possibly pre-Praxitelean original, may have come into vogue. But of course it is absurd to argue that therefore any statue of a half-clothed Aphrodite must be older than the Cnidian. In judging the date of any ancient monument the marks of the later style are more valuable as chronological evidence than those of an older style that may be found in it. The latter may be a survival, the former can scarcely be an anticipation. Thus in the treatment of the structure of the torso, we find in the Aphrodite of Melos much of the older ideal manner ; but at the same time we note the liquid and lustrous surface, and the high effect of 'veritas' or 'surface-truth' that Praxiteles was the first to achieve in a conspicuous degree. Again, the throat is longer than is usual in the earlier type, and the small head bears a proportion to the body that was not adopted before the time of Lysippus. It is the head that proves most conclusively that we must assign to the Melian statue a relatively late date in the history of Greek sculpture; for we find on it the workmanship of the later Alexandrine hand. There is no marking of the bone-structure; the cheeks lack breadth and fall away suddenly towards the centre, where the surface is deeply modulated, and strong shadows fall about the mouth and nose and in the deep eye-sockets. The Tegean heads of Scopas show a surface of face quite as varied in modulation, but the lines are firm and plastic. But here the deeply-shadowed face gives us the impression of forms unfixed and relaxed. And this is the contrast that this head presents to the head from Tralles now in Vienna, which in its pose and slope of its shoulders displays a marked likeness to this, but shows a severer scheme, more plastic firmness. In fact, the Melian head may attest the influence which was strong in the Alexandrine period of painting upon sculpture. It is probably a work of the second century B.C., somewhat earlier than the monuments of the second Pergamene style, with which it has very little affinity; the female head from Pergamon (circ. 170–160 B.C), with which it has been rather arbitrarily compared, shows a far greater departure from the plastic style, a far more mobile and picturesque handling of the features; and the Pergamene artists in their religious sculpture fall below the sculptor of the Aphrodite of Melos in spirit and imagination.

REFERENCES FOR CHAPTERS XXI–XXIII.

Local worships of Aphrodite.

In North Greece.

¹ Byzantium: Hesych. Miles. Constantinop. 16 ἀνωτέρω δὲ μικρὸν
τοῦ Ποσειδῶνος ναοῦ καὶ τὸ τῆς Ἀφροδίτης προσαγορεύεται τέμενος.

² Pharsalus: Aphrodite Πειθώ: Roehl, *Ins. Graec. Anti* 327
τα(φρ)οδίτηι τᾶ Πειθο(ι) (inscription of fifth century B. C.).

³ Larissa: Ἄφριος: Ussing, *Inscrip. Graec.* 8. 8 b (inscription of
Roman period) Μηνὸς Ἀφρίου. Cf. the name Ἀρφείη for Aphrodite in
oracle found at Callipolis in Chersonnese, Kaibel, *Hermes*, 19, p. 261.

⁴ Athenae. 589 B, Lais was slain in Thessaly by Thessalian
women in the temple of Aphrodite, ταῖς ξυλίναις χελώναις τυπτομένην
ἐν Ἀφροδίτης ἱερῷ· διὸ καὶ τὸ τέμενος κληθῆναι ἀνοσίας Ἀφροδίτης (from
Polemon).

⁵ At Metropolis in Histiaea: Strabo, 438 Ἀφροδίτη ἡ ἐν τῇ Μητροπόλει:
worshipped with swine-offerings there.

⁶ᵃ Epirus: *C. I. Gr.* 1823 (inscription of second century A.D.). At
Dodona: Carapanos *Dodone*, Pl. XXVI, 1 Ὠφελίων Ἀφροδίτᾳ ἀνέθηκε.

ᵇ In Aetolia, at Phistion: Collitz *Dialect-Inschr.* 1428ⁱ ἀπέδοτο
Λύκος . . . Ἀφροδίτᾳ Συρίᾳ Φιστυίδι σῶμα ἀνδρῆον . . . ἐπ᾽ ἐλευθερίᾳ.

⁷ Delphi: Plut. *Amat.* 23 (p. 769) ἡ . . . ἀναβλαστάνουσα καθ᾽ ἡμέραν
τιμὴ καὶ χάρις καὶ ἀγάπησις ἀλλήλων καὶ πίστις οὔτε Δελφοὺς ἐλέγχει ληροῦντας
ὅτι τὴν Ἀφροδίτην Ἅρμα καλοῦσιν.

⁸ Thespiae: Paus. 9. 27, 5 ἔστι δὲ καὶ ἑτέρωθι Ἀφροδίτης Μελαινίδος
ἱερόν.

⁹ Thebes: Paus. 9. 16, 3 Ἀφροδίτης Θηβαίοις ξόανά ἐστιν οὕτω δὴ ἀρχαῖα
ὥστε καὶ ἀναθήματα Ἁρμονίας εἶναί φασιν . . . καλοῦσι δὲ Οὐρανίαν, τὴν δὲ αὐτῶν
Πάνδημον, καὶ Ἀποστροφίαν τὴν τρίτην. Cf. ¹¹⁶.

¹⁰ Oropus: Paus. 1. 34, 3 Ὠρωπίοις ναός ἐστιν Ἀμφιαράου . . . παρέχεται
δὲ ὁ βωμὸς μέρη . . . τετάρτη δέ ἐστι τοῦ βωμοῦ μοῖρα Ἀφροδίτης καὶ Πανακείας
ἔτι δὲ Ἰασοῦς καὶ Ὑγιείας καὶ Ἀθηνᾶς Παιωνίας.

In Attica.

¹¹ Athens : ^a Paus. I. 14, 7 πλησίον (near the temple of Hephaestus beyond the Ceramicus) ἱερόν ἐστιν Ἀφροδίτης Οὐρανίας ... Ἀθηναίοις δὲ κατεστήσατο Αἰγεύς ... τὸ δὲ ἐφ᾽ ἡμῶν ἔτι ἄγαλμα λίθου Παρίου καὶ ἔργον Φειδίου.

^b Ἀφροδίτη ἐν κήποις : Paus. I. 19, 2 τὴν Ἀφροδίτην ἢ τοῦ ναοῦ (ἐν Κήποις) πλησίον ἔστηκε. ταύτης γὰρ σχῆμα μὲν τετράγωνον κατὰ ταὐτὰ καὶ τοῖς Ἑρμαῖς, τὸ δὲ ἐπίγραμμα σημαίνει τὴν Οὐρανίαν Ἀφροδίτην τῶν καλουμένων Μοιρῶν εἶναι πρεσβυτάτην. C. I. A. 273 f. l. 12, publication of temple accounts circ. 422 B. C., (Ἀφροδίτ)ης ἐν κήποις. Paus. I. 19. 2 ἄγαλμα Ἀφροδίτης τῆς ἐν Κήποις ἔργον ἐστὶν Ἀλκαμένους καὶ τῶν Ἀθήνησιν ἐν ὀλίγοις θέας ἄξιον.

^c Aphrodite Πάνδημος : Paus. I. 22, 3 Ἀφροδίτην τὴν Πάνδημον, ἐπεί τε Ἀθηναίους Θησεὺς ἐς μίαν ἤγαγε ἀπὸ τῶν δήμων πόλιν, αὐτὴν σέβεσθαι καὶ Πειθὼ κατέστησε. The worship attributed to Solon by Nikander : vide ¹¹⁷.

^d Temple of Ἀφροδίτη ἐφ᾽ Ἱππολύτῳ : Schol. Eur. *Hipp.* 25 ἐπὶ πέτρας τινὸς ἐν τῇ Ἀττικῇ ἀφ᾽ ἧς ἦν ἀποβλέπεσθαι τὴν Τροιζῆνα, Ἀφροδίτης ναὸν ἱδρύσασθαι τὴν Φαίδραν φασίν· ἐκάλεσε δὲ Ἀφροδίτην ἐφ᾽ Ἱππολύτῳ, ἣν καὶ Ἱππολυτίαν καλοῦσι. Hom. *Odyss.* 11. 320, Schol. Φαίδρα ἱερὸν Ἀφροδίτης ἐν Ἀθήναις ἱδρύσατο τὸ νῦν Ἱππολύτιον καλούμενον. C. I. A. I. 212 :

Ι Ι Ε Ξ Ε = Ἀφροδίτης ἐπὶ
ΟΟΛ Υ Τ Ο   Ἱππολύτῳ·

one of the inscriptions found on the Acropolis of Athens, referring to the accounts of temples. Eurip. *Hipp.* 30 :

πέτραν παρ᾽ αὐτὴν Παλλάδος κατόψιον
γῆς τῆσδε ναὸν Κύπριδος ἐγκαθίσατο,
ἐρῶσ᾽ ἔρωτ᾽ ἔκδημον· Ἱππολύτῳ δ᾽ ἔπι
τὸ λοιπὸν ὠνόμαζεν ἱδρῦσθαι θεάν.

^e Aphrodite Ἐναγώνιος, on inscription of Imperial period found in theatre at Athens, C. I. A. 3. 189.

^f Athenae. 571 C τῆς παρ᾽ Ἀθηναίοις καλουμένης Ἑταίρας Ἀφροδίτης ... ἑταίραν δὲ Ἀφροδίτην τὴν τοὺς ἑταίρους καὶ τὰς ἑταίρας συνάγουσαν. Hesych. *s. v.* ἑταίρας· ἱερὸν τῆς Ἀφροδίτης Ἀθήνησι.

^g Aphrodite Ψίθυρος at Athens, vide ¹¹⁸ i.

¹² Attic Demes : ^a Paus. I. 14, 7 δῆμος δέ ἐστιν Ἀθηναίοις Ἀθμονέων οἱ Πορφυρίωνα ἔτι πρότερον Ἀκταίου βασιλεύσαντα τῆς Οὐρανίας φασὶ τὸ παρὰ σφίσιν ἱερὸν ἱδρύσασθαι.

^b At Alopecae : C. I. Gr. 395, inscription second century A. D.

^c Temple of Aphrodite on the way between Athens and Eleusis :

Paus. 1. 37, 7. At Plotheia, sacrifice to Aphrodite : *C. I. A.* 2¹, 570.

ᵈ At Cephale : Isaeus, 2. 31 ἐκεῖνοι ὀμόσαντες ἡμῖν πρὸς τῷ βωμῷ τῷ τῆς 'Αφροδίτης Κεφαλῆσι. Cf. *Athen. Mittheil.* 1893, p. 209 ὅρος τεμένους 'Αφροδίτης Κεφαλῆθεν (circ. 400 B. C.).

¹³ Peiraeeus : ᵃ Paus. 1. 1, 3 πρὸς δὲ τῇ θαλάσσῃ Κόνων ᾠκοδόμησεν 'Αφροδίτης ἱερόν, τριήρεις Λακεδαιμονίων κατεργασάμενος περὶ Κνίδον. Schol. Arist. *Pax* 144 Καλλικράτης φησὶν ἢ Μενεκλῆς ἐν τῷ περὶ 'Αθηνῶν γράφων οὕτω, "ἔχει δὲ ὁ Πειραιεὺς λιμένας τρεῖς . . . εἰς μὲν ὁ Κανθάρου λιμὴν . . . εἶτα 'Αφροδίσιον."

ᵇ Aphrodite Εὔπλοια, vide Rhang. *Antiq. Hellén.* No. 1069 'Αργεῖος 'Αργείου Τρικορύσιος στρατηγήσας ἐπὶ τὸν Πειραιᾶ 'Αφροδίτῃ Εὐπλοίᾳ τύχῃ ἀγαθῇ ἀνέθηκεν. Inscription of latter part of fourth century B. C.

ᶜ Oriental worship of Aphrodite in the Peiraeeus : *C. I. A.* 2. 168, inscription B. C. 333–332, recording the leave given by the state to the men of Citium to found a temple to the goddess there. *Id.* 2. 627, inscription found in the Peiraeeus, . . . περὶ ὧν ἀπαγγέλλει ἡ ἱ(έ)ρεια τῆς Συρίας (θεοῦ) . . . περὶ τῶν θυ(σιῶν ὧν ἔθυεν) τῇ τε 'Αφροδίτει τεῖ Συρίᾳ, κ.τ.λ. (circ. 100 B. C.). *Id.* 3. 136 Μητρὶ Θεῶν εὐαντήτῳ ἰατρίνῃ 'Αφροδίτῃ ἀνέθηκεν (Roman-Imperial period).

On the Attic coast.

¹⁴ ᵃ On the promontory of Colias : Paus. 1. 1, 5 Κωλιάδος δέ ἐστιν ἐνταῦθα 'Αφροδίτης ἄγαλμα καὶ Γενετυλλίδες ὀνομαζόμεναι θεαί. Strabo, 398 τὸ τῆς Κωλιάδος 'Αφροδίτης ἱερόν, εἰς ὃν τόπον ἐκκυμανθῆναι τὰ τελευταῖα τὰ ἐκ τῆς περὶ Σαλαμῖνα ναυμαχίας τῆς Περσικῆς ναυάγιά φασιν. Various explanations given of the name Κωλιάς by the Scholiast on Arist. *Nub.* 52. Cf. Harpocr. and Suid. *s. v.* Κωλιάς : her name occurs on an inscription on a seat found in the Erechtheum, *C. I. A.* 3. 339. Cf. Aphrodite Καλιάς worshipped on Hymettus, Photius, p. 185, 21.

ᵇ Probably near Phalerum, Aphrodite ἐπιτραγία : Plut. *Thes.* 18 λέγεται αὐτῷ (Θησεῖ) τὸν μὲν ἐν Δελφοῖς ἀνελεῖν θεὸν 'Αφροδίτην καθηγεμόνα ποιεῖσθαι καὶ παρακαλεῖν συνέμπορον, θύοντι δὲ πρὸς θαλάσσῃ τὴν αἶγα θήλειαν οὖσαν αὐτομάτως τράγον γενέσθαι· διὸ καὶ καλεῖσθαι τὴν θεὸν 'Επιτραγίαν. *C. I. A.* 3. 335 'Αφροδίτης 'Επιτραγίας, inscription of Imperial period on seat found in the Erechtheum.

¹⁵ In Megara : ᵃPaus. 1. 43, 6 μετὰ δὲ τοῦ Διονύσου τὸ ἱερόν ἐστιν 'Αφροδίτης ναός, ἄγαλμα δὲ ἐλέφαντος 'Αφροδίτης πεποιημένον, Πρᾶξις ἐπίκλησιν· τοῦτό ἐστιν ἀρχαιότατον ἐν τῷ ναῷ. Πειθὼ δὲ καὶ ἑτέρα θεός, ἣν Παρήγορον ὀνομάζουσιν, ἔργα Πραξιτέλους.

ᵇ Paus. 1. 40, 6, near the Acropolis of Megara, πεποίηται 'Αφροδίτης 'Επιστροφίας ἱερόν.

¹⁶ Corinth : ᵃ Euripides, *Frag.* (Strabo, 379) ἥκω περίκλυστον προλιποῦσ᾽ Ἀκροκόρινθον, ἱερὸν ὄχθον, πόλιν Ἀφροδίτης : *ib.* ἡ κορυφὴ ναΐδιον ἔχει Ἀφροδίτης. Paus. 2. 5, 1 ἀνελθοῦσιν ἐς τὸν Ἀκροκόρινθον, ναός ἐστιν Ἀφροδίτης· ἀγάλματα δὲ αὐτή τε ὡπλισμένη καὶ "Ηλιος καὶ "Ερως ἔχων τόξον. Alciphron, 3. 60 φασὶ τὴν Ἀφροδίτην ἐκ Κυθήρων ἀνασχοῦσαν τὴν Ἀκροκόρινθον ἀσπάσασθαι· εἰ μὴ ἄρα τοῖς μὲν γυναίοις Ἀφροδίτη πολιοῦχος. . . . Plut. *de Malig. Herod.* 39 ἐν τῷ ναῷ τῆς Ἀφροδίτης, ὃν ἱδρύσασθαι Μήδειαν λέγουσι (at Corinth).

ᵇ Paus. 2. 2, 4, in a cypress-grove before the city, Βελλεροφόντου τέ ἐστι τέμενος καὶ Ἀφροδίτης ναὸς Μελαινίδος, καὶ τάφος Λαΐδος.

ᶜ Paus. 2. 2, 3 ἐν δὲ Κεγχρέαις Ἀφροδίτης τέ ἐστι ναὸς καὶ ἄγαλμα λίθου.

¹⁷ Corinthian colonies : ᵃ Corcyra : *C. I. Gr.* 1872 and 1873.

ᵇ Syracuse : Hesych. *s. v.* Βαιῶτις· Ἀφροδίτη παρὰ Συρακοσίοις.

¹⁸ Sicyon : Paus. 2. 10, 4 Ἀφροδίτης ἱερόν· ἐσίασι μὲν δὴ ἐς αὐτὸ γυνή τε νεωκόρος, ᾗ μηκέτι θέμις παρ᾽ ἄνδρα φοιτῆσαι, καὶ παρθένος ἱερωσύνην ἐπέτειον ἔχουσα· λουτροφόρον τὴν παρθένον ὀνομάζουσι· τοῖς δὲ ἄλλοις κατὰ ταὐτὰ καὶ ὁρᾶν ἀπὸ τῆς ἐσόδου τὴν θεὸν καὶ αὐτόθεν προσεύχεσθαι· τὸ μὲν δὴ ἄγαλμα καθήμενον Κάναχος Σικυώνιος ἐποίησεν . . . πεποίηται ἔκ τε χρυσοῦ καὶ ἐλέφαντος, φέρουσα ἐπὶ τῇ κεφαλῇ πόλον, τῶν χειρῶν δὲ ἔχει τῇ μὲν μήκωνα τῇ δὲ ἑτέρᾳ μῆλον.

¹⁹ Hermione : ᵃ Paus. 2. 34, 11 Ἀφροδίτης ναός ἐστιν ἐπίκλησιν Ποντίας καὶ Λιμενίας τῆς αὐτῆς.

ᵇ Paus. 2. 34, 11 καὶ ναὸς ἕτερός ἐστιν Ἀφροδίτης· αὕτη καὶ ἄλλας ἔχει παρὰ Ἑρμιονέων τιμάς, καὶ ταῖς παρθένοις καὶ ἢν γυνὴ χηρεύουσα πρὸς ἄνδρα μέλλῃ φοιτᾶν, ἁπάσαις πρὸ γάμου θύειν καθέστηκεν ἐνταῦθα. Cf. *C. I. Gr.* 1233.

²⁰ Epidauros : Paus. 2. 29, 1 Ἀφροδίτης ἱερὸν πεποίηται.

²¹ At Troezen : ᵃ Paus. 2. 32, 3, worship of Aphrodite Κατασκοπία, connected with Hippolytos : *ib.* § 1 ἑκάστη παρθένος πλόκαμον ἀποκείρεταί οἱ (Ἱππολύτῳ) πρὸ γάμου, κειραμένη δὲ ἀνέθηκεν ἐς τὸν ναὸν φέρουσα. Cf. Lucian, *De Dea Syr.* 60.

ᵇ Ἀφροδίτη ἐν Βήσσαις : inscription at Troezen third century B. C. Collitz, *Dialect-Inschriften*, 3364, l. 14.

²² Argos : Paus. 2. 19, 6, ᵃ prehistoric ξόανα Ἀφροδίτης καὶ Ἑρμοῦ . . . Ὑπερμνήστρα κριθεῖσα (for sparing her husband) ἐν τοῖς Ἀργείοις ἀποφεύγει καὶ Ἀφροδίτην ἐπὶ τῷδε ἀνέθηκε Νικηφόρον.

ᵇ Paus. 2. 23, 8 πλησίον τοῦ Διονύσου καὶ Ἀφροδίτης ναός ἐστιν Οὐρανίας. Hesych. *s. v.* Ἀκρία . . . Ἀφροδίτη προσαγορευομένη ἐν Ἄργει. Cf. ¹¹⁴ c.

ᶜ Aphrodite Τυμβωρύχος : Clem. Alex. *Protrept.* 33 P. ἑῶ δὲ Ἀργείους οἱ Ἀφροδίτην Τυμβωρύχον θρησκεύουσι.

²³ Tegea: Paus. 8. 53, 7, near the temple of Demeter and Core, (ναὸς) Ἀφροδίτης καλουμένης Παφίας· ἱδρύσατο αὐτὴν Λαοδίκη γεγονυῖα μὲν ... ἀπὸ Ἀγαπήνορος ... οἰκοῦσα δὲ ἐν Πάφῳ.

²⁴ Mantinea: Paus. 8. 6, 5, by a fountain about a mile from the city, Ἀφροδίτης ἱερὸν Μελαινίδος. *Id.* 8. 9, 6, near the theatre in the city, ναοῦ τε Ἀφροδίτης ἐπίκλησιν Συμμαχίας ἐρείπια καὶ ἄγαλμα ἐλείπετο ... τὸ δὲ ἱερὸν κατεσκευάσαντο τοῦτο οἱ Μαντινεῖς ὑπόμνημα ἐς τοὺς ἔπειτα τῆς ὁμοῦ Ῥωμαίοις ἐπ᾿ Ἀκτίῳ ναυμαχίας.

²⁵ Sparta: Paus. 3. 15, 10–11 ᵃ ναὸς ἀρχαῖος καὶ Ἀφροδίτης ξόανον ὡπλισμένης.

ᵇ Paus. 3. 15, 11 ναῶν δέ, ὧν οἶδα, μόνῳ τούτῳ καὶ ὑπερῷον ἄλλο ἐπῳκοδόμηται Μορφοῦς ἱερόν. ἐπίκλησις μὲν δὴ τῆς Ἀφροδίτης ἐστὶν ἡ Μορφώ, κάθηται δὲ καλύπτράν τε ἔχουσα καὶ πέδας περὶ τοῖς ποσί. Plut. *Instit. Lacon.* 239 A Ἀφροδίτην σέβουσι τὴν ἐνόπλιον καὶ πάντας δὲ τοὺς θεοὺς θήλεις καὶ ἄρρενας λόγχας ἔχοντας ποιοῦνται. Inscription from Sparta of Imperial period, mentioning ἡ ἱέρεια τῶν Μοιρῶν Λαχέσεων καὶ Ἀφροδίτης ἐνοπλίου, *C. I. Gr.* 1444. Cf. inscription of Imperial period found near Amyclae, *Eph. Arch.* 1892, p. 23: mentioning the ἱερεὺς Ἀφροδείτης Οὐρανίας. Lactantius, *Div. Instit.* 1. 20, the Lacedaemonian women armed themselves against the Messenians, propter huius facti memoriam aedem Veneri armatae simulacrumque posuerunt. *Anthol.* 9. 320 εἶπέ ποκ᾿ Εὐρώτας ποτὶ τὰν Κύπριν· ἢ λάβε τεύχη, ἢ ᾿ξιθι τᾶς Σπάρτας· ἁ πόλις ὁπλομανεῖ. Cf. Anth. Palud. 173 αἰδομένη δ᾿ ἄρα θεσμὰ μενεπτολέμοιο Λυκούργου φίλτρα φέρει Σπάρτῃ τεύχεσιν ἀγχεμάχοις.

ᶜ Paus. 3. 17, 5 ὄπισθεν δὲ τῆς Χαλκιοίκου ναός ἐστιν Ἀφροδίτης Ἀρείας· τὰ δὲ ξόανα ἀρχαῖα, εἴπερ τι ἄλλο ἐν Ἕλλησι.

ᵈ Aphrodite Ἀριοντία: Roehl, *Inscr. Gr. Ant.* 79.

ᵉ Paus. 3. 13, 9 ξόανον ἀρχαῖον καλοῦσιν Ἀφροδίτης Ἥρας· ἐπὶ δὲ θυγατρὶ γαμουμένῃ νενομίκασι τὰς μητέρας τῇ θεῷ θύειν.

ᶠ *Id.* 3. 12, 11 πρὸς δὲ τῇ Σκιάδι οἰκοδόμημά ἐστι περιφερές, ἐν δὲ αὐτῷ Διὸς καὶ Ἀφροδίτης ἀγάλματα ἐπίκλησιν Ὀλυμπίων. τοῦτο Ἐπιμενίδην κατασκευάσαι λέγουσι.

ᵍ *Id.* 3. 18, 1 τῶν δὲ ἀνδριάντων τοῦ Παυσανίου πλησίον ἐστὶν Ἀμβολογήρας Ἀφροδίτης ἄγαλμα. Cf. Plut. *Quaest. Conviv.* p. 654 C Λέγοντες ἐν τοῖς τῶν θεῶν ὕμνοις· ἀνάβαλε ἄνω τὸ γῆρας, ὦ καλὰ Ἀφροδίτη.

²⁶ Paus. 3. 18, 8 Πολύκλειτος δὲ Ἀφροδίτην παρὰ Ἀμυκλαίῳ καλουμένην. Cf. inscription found at Amyclae mentioned above.

²⁷ Megalopolis: ᵃ Paus. 8. 32, 2 ἐρείπια καὶ τῆς Ἀφροδίτης ἦν τὸ ἱερόν,

πλὴν ὅσον πρόναός τε ἐλείπετο ἔτι καὶ ἀγάλματα ἀριθμὸν τρία, ἐπίκλησις δὲ Οὐρανία, τῇ δέ ἐστι Πάνδημος, τῇ τρίτῃ δὲ οὐδὲν ἐτίθεντο.

b Paus. 8. 31, 3 ἔστι δὲ ἐντὸς τοῦ περιβόλου τῶν μεγάλων θεῶν καὶ ᾿Αφροδίτης ἱερόν . . . ἀγάλματα ἐν τῷ ναῷ Δαμοφῶν ἐποίησεν, ῾Ερμῆν ξύλου καὶ ᾿Αφροδίτης ξόανον· καὶ ταύτης χεῖρές εἰσι λίθου καὶ πρόσωπόν τε καὶ ἄκροι πόδες· τὴν δὲ ἐπίκλησιν τῇ θεῷ Μαχανῖτιν ὀρθότατα ἔθεντο, ἐμοὶ δοκεῖν· ᾿Αφροδίτης γὰρ ἕνεκα καὶ ἔργων τῶν ταύτης πλεῖσται μὲν ἐπιτεχνήσεις, παντοῖα δὲ ἀνθρώποις ἀνευρημένα ἐς λόγους ἐστίν.

²⁸ Phigaleia : Paus. 8. 41, 10, on Mount Cotilum above the temple of Apollo of Bassae, ᾿Αφροδίτη ἐστὶν ἐν Κωτίλῳ· καὶ αὐτῇ ναός τε ἦν οὐκ ἔχων ἔτι ὄροφον καὶ ἄγαλμα ἐπεποίητο.

²⁹ Psophis : Paus. 8. 24, 6 Ψωφιδίοις ἐν τῇ πόλει τοῦτο μὲν ᾿Αφροδίτης ἱερὸν ᾿Ερυκίνης ἐστὶν ἐπίκλησιν, ἧς ἐρείπια ἐφ' ἡμῶν ἐλείπετο αὐτοῦ μόνα.

Achaea.

³⁰ Patrae : ᵃ Paus. 7. 21, 10 ἐν Πάτραις οὐ πολὺ ἀπωτέρω τοῦ Ποσειδῶνος ἱερά ἐστιν ᾿Αφροδίτης· τὸ δὲ ἕτερον τῶν ἀγαλμάτων γενεᾷ πρότερον ἢ κατ' ἐμὲ ἁλιεῖς ἄνδρες ἀνείλκυσαν ἐν δικτύῳ· ἔστι δὲ καὶ ἀγάλματα τοῦ λιμένος ἐγγυτάτω . . . καὶ ᾿Αφροδίτης ἧς καὶ πρὸς τῷ λιμένι ἐστὶ τέμενος· λίθου μὲν πρόσωπον καὶ ἄκραι χεῖρες καὶ πόδες, ξύλου δὲ τὰ λοιπὰ εἴργασται.

b Paus. 7. 21, 11 : in a grove near the shore another temple of Aphrodite.

³¹ Aegium : Paus. 7. 24, 2 πρὸς θαλάσσῃ ᾿Αφροδίτης ἱερὸν ἐν Αἰγίῳ καὶ μετ' αὐτὸ Ποσειδῶνος.

³² Aegira : Paus. 7. 26, 7 τὴν δὲ Οὐρανίαν σέβουσι μὲν τὰ μάλιστα, ἐσελθεῖν δὲ ἐς τὸ ἱερὸν οὐκ ἔστιν ἀνθρώποις.

³³ᵃ Bura : Paus. 7. 25, 9 ναὸς ἐνταῦθα Δήμητρος· ὁ δὲ ᾿Αφροδίτης Διονύσου τέ ἐστι, καὶ ἄλλος Εἰλειθυίας λίθου τοῦ Πεντελησίου τὰ ἀγάλματα, ᾿Αθηναίου δὲ ἔργα Εὐκλείδου· καὶ τῇ Δήμητρί ἐστιν ἐσθής.

³³ Dittenberger, *Syll. Inscr. Graec.* 178, inscription from the Arcadian Orchomenos containing the oath of alliance between the Orchomenians and the Achaean league, ὀμνύω Δία ᾿Αμάριον, ᾿Αθανᾶν ᾿Αμαρίαν, ᾿Αφ(ροδ)ί(ταν καὶ τοὺ)ς θ(εοὺς πάντας).

³⁴ Elis : ᵃ Paus. 6. 20, 6 πλησίον τῆς Εἰλειθυίας ἐρείπια ᾿Αφροδίτης Οὐρανίας ἱεροῦ λείπεται, θύουσι δὲ καὶ αὐτόθι ἐπὶ τῶν βωμῶν.

b Paus. 6. 25, 2, at Olympia near the Agora a ναός and τέμενος of Aphrodite, τὴν μὲν ἐν τῷ ναῷ καλοῦσιν Οὐρανίαν, ἐλέφαντος δέ ἐστι καὶ χρυσοῦ, τέχνη Φειδίου, τῷ δὲ ἑτέρῳ ποδὶ ἐπὶ χελώνης βέβηκε· τῆς δὲ περιέχεται μὲν τὸ τέμενος θριγκῷ, κρηπὶς δὲ ἐντὸς τοῦ τεμένους πεποίηται καὶ ἐπὶ τῇ κρηπῖδι ἄγαλμα ᾿Αφροδίτης χαλκοῦν ἐπὶ τράγῳ κάθηται χαλκῷ· Σκόπα τοῦτο ἔργον, ᾿Αφροδίτην δὲ Πάνδημον ὀνομάζουσι.

ᶜ Near the Leonidaeum in the Altis : Paus. 5. 15, 3 Ἀφροδίτης βωμὸς καὶ Ὡρῶν μετ᾽ αὐτόν.

ᵈ Paus. 6. 26, 5 Θεῶν δὲ ἱερὰ ἐν Κυλλήνῃ Ἀσκληπιοῦ, τὸ δὲ Ἀφροδίτης ἐστί· τοῦ Ἑρμοῦ δὲ τὸ ἄγαλμα, ὃν οἱ ταύτῃ περισσῶς σέβουσιν, ὀρθόν ἐστιν αἰδοῖον ἐπὶ τοῦ βάθρου.

³⁵ Naupactos : Paus. 10. 38, 12 Ἀφροδίτη ἔχει μὲν ἐν σπηλαίῳ τιμάς· εὔχονται δὲ καὶ ἄλλων ἕνεκα, καὶ αἱ γυναῖκες μάλιστα αἱ χῆραι γάμον αἰτοῦσι παρὰ τῆς θεοῦ. At Oiantheia : *ib.* Ἀφροδίτης τε ἱερόν.

³⁶ Ambracia : *C. I. Gr.* 1798, 1799.

³⁷ Epirus : *C. I. Gr.* 1823, Imperial period.

³⁷ᵃ Corcyra : *C. I. Gr.* 1872, 1873.

Asia Minor, and coasts of the Black Sea.

³⁸ Phanagoria : Strabo, 495 Φαναγόρεια ... πόλις ἀξιόλογος ... καὶ τὸ Ἀπάτουρον τὸ τῆς Ἀφροδίτης ἱερόν : the name explained by a legend that Aphrodite τῶν γιγάντων ἕκαστον δεχομένη καθ᾽ ἕνα τῷ Ἡρακλεῖ παραδιδοίη δολοφονεῖν ἐξ ἀπάτης. Cf. inscription from Phanagoria 303 B. c., *C. I. Gr.* 2120.

³⁹ Panticapeum : *C. I. Gr.* 2108 G, 2109, inscriptions of third and second centuries B. c., θεᾷ Ἀφρο(δίτῃ) (Οὐ)ρανίᾳ Ἀπατούρῃ.

⁴⁰ In a city of Sarmatia an inscription ⊕Ε . . . ΑΓΑΤΟΡΟ (circ. 500 B. c.) on a relief representing Aphrodite with Eros and Ares ; its style is quite out of keeping with the date of the inscription, *C. I. Gr.* 2133.

⁴¹ Scythian goddess Ἀρτίμπασα identified with Ἀφροδίτη Οὐρανία Herod. 4. 59.

⁴² Amastris in Paphlagonia : *C. I. Gr.* 4150 C. Cf. *Catalogue of Greek Coins,* 'Pontus,' p. 84 (Brit. Mus.) Aphrodite on throne with calathos, veil, chiton, and peplos, sceptre in left hand, on right Nike holding out wreath : Pl. XIX ².

⁴³ Chalcedon : Hesych. *s. v.* ἐλεήμων. Ἀφροδίτη ἐλεήμων· ἐν Κύπρῳ καὶ Χαλκηδονίᾳ.

⁴⁴ At Abydos : Athenae. 572 E Πόρνης δὲ Ἀφροδίτης ἱερόν ἐστι παρὰ Ἀβυδηνοῖς, ὥς φησι Πάμφιλος.

⁴⁵ Troas : ᵃ *C. I. Gr.* 6165 ἀπὸ τῆς ἐν Τρῳάδι Ἀφροδίτης. Cf. Plut. *Lucull.* 12 εἰς δὲ Τρῳάδα καταχθεὶς ἐσκήνωσε μὲν ἐν τῷ ἱερῷ τῆς Ἀφροδίτης.

ᵇ Near Gargara an Aphrodision on a promontory called Πυρρά : Strabo, 606.

ᶜ Diffusion of the cult of Aphrodite Aeneas from the Troad. Dion. Halic. 1. 49, Aeneas and his followers, πρῶτον μὲν εἰς Θρᾴκην ἀφικόμενοι κατὰ τὴν χερρόννησον, ἣ καλεῖται Παλλήνη, ὡρμίσαντο ... μείναντες δὲ ... νεὼν 'Αφροδίτης ἱδρύσαντο ... καὶ πόλιν Αἴνειαν ἔκτισαν. *Id.* I. 50 ἔπειτα εἰς Κύθηρα ... ἱερὸν 'Αφροδίτης ἱδρύονται. *Ib.* in Zacynthos, θύουσιν 'Αφροδίτῃ πρὸς τῷ κατασκευασθέντι ἱερῷ θυσίαν : (many signs of this worship surviving in the island) Αἰνείου καὶ 'Αφροδίτης ὁ δρόμος, καὶ ξόανα τούτων ἔστηκεν ἀμφοτέρων ... εἰς Λευκάδα κατάγονται ... κἂν ταύτῃ πάλιν ἱερὸν 'Αφροδίτης ἱδρύονται, ... καλεῖται δὲ 'Αφροδίτης Αἰνειάδος. *Ib.* in Actium, 'Αφροδίτης Αἰνειάδος ἱερόν ... ἐν δὲ 'Αμβρακίᾳ ἱερὸν τῆς αὐτῆς θεοῦ καὶ ἡρῷον Αἰνείου. *Ib.* on the coast north of Buthrotum, ἱερὸν καὶ αὐτόθι τῆς 'Αφροδίτης ἱδρυσάμενοι. *Id.* I. 51, λιμὴν 'Αφροδίτης on the south-east coast of Italy where Aeneas landed. Temple at Eryx : Diod. Sic. 4. 83 Αἰνείας ὁ 'Αφροδίτης πλέων εἰς 'Ιταλίαν καὶ προσορμισθεὶς τῇ νήσῳ πολλοῖς ἀναθήμασι τὸ ἱερόν, ὡς ἂν ἰδίας μητρὸς ὑπάρχον, ἐκόσμησε. Dion. Halic. I. 53 τεκμήρια τῆς εἰς Σικελοὺς Αἰνείου τε καὶ Τρώων ἀφίξεως πολλὰ μὲν καὶ ἄλλα, περιφανέστατα δὲ τῆς Αἰνειάδος 'Αφροδίτης ὁ βωμὸς ἐπὶ τῇ κεφαλῇ τοῦ 'Ελύμου ἱδρυμένος, καὶ ἱερὸν Αἰνείου ἱδρυμένον ἐν Αἰγέστῃ. Paus. 3. 22, 11, Aphrodisias in South Laconia regarded as founded by Aeneas ; *id.* 8. 12, 9, Mount 'Αγχισία in Arcadia near Orchomenos where Anchises was buried, πρὸς δὲ τοῦ 'Αγχίσου τῷ τάφῳ ἐρείπιά ἐστιν 'Αφροδίτης ἱεροῦ. Statue of Aeneas at Argos, *id.* 2. 21, 1. Schol. *Il.* 2. 820 πλάττουσιν αὐτὴν ('Αφροδίτην) καὶ ἔφιππον, ὅτι ὁ Αἰνείας ὁ υἱὸς αὐτῆς πλεύσας μέχρι τῆς δύσεως μετὰ τοῦτο ἵππῳ ἐπέβη καὶ τὴν μητέρα ἐτίμησε τοιούτῳ ἀγάλματι. Cf. [119] m, *Iliad*, 20. 293– 300. Cf. Acesilaus (Schol. *Il.* 20. 308–309), Müller, *Frag. Hist. Graec.* 1, p. 103, No. 26. Festus, p. 269 (Müller) ait quidem Agathocles complures esse auctores qui dicant Aenean sepultum in urbe Berecynthia. Schol. *Aen.* 2. 717 Atticus (Penates) dicit ex Samothracia in Italiam devectos.

[46] At Pergamum : Polyb. 17. 2 τὸ τῆς 'Αφροδίτης ἱερὸν ... καὶ τὸ Νικηφόριον, ἃ κατέφθειρε (Φίλιππος). *C. I. Gr.* 3542 ἐπηκόῳ θεᾷ 'Αφροδίτῃ (first century B. C. ?).

[47] a At Smyrna : 'Αφροδίτη Οὐρανία, late Roman sepulchral relief from Smyrna at Verona, dedicated to the ἀρχιέρεια 'Αφροδίτης Οὐρανίας. *C. I. Gr.* 3157.

b Aphrodite Στρατονικίς : *C. I. Gr.* 3137, treaty between Smyrna and Magnesia ad Sipylum (third century B. C.), l. 83 ἀναθέτωσαν Σμυρναῖοι μὲν (τὴν ὁμολογίαν) ἐν τῷ τῆς 'Αφροδίτης τῆς Στρατονικίδος ἱερῷ. Cf. Tac. *Ann.* 3. 63 Smyrnaeos oraculum Apollinis, cuius imperio Stratonicidi Veneri templum dicaverint, referre.

[48] Ephesos : a Athenae. 573 A Εὐάλκης ἐν τοῖς 'Εφεσιακοῖς καὶ ἐν 'Εφέσῳ φησὶν ἱερὰ ἱδρῦσθαι ἑταίρᾳ 'Αφροδίτῃ.

ᵇ Serv. Virg. *Aen.* 1. 720 Apud Ephesios Venerem Automatam dixerunt vel Epidaetiam.

⁴⁹ At Erythrae : ᵃ Aphrodite Πάνδημος, in inscription concerning the sale of priesthoods (circ. 270 B.C.): Dittenberger, *Sylloge*, 370, l. 57.

ᵇ Ἀφροδίτη Πυθόχρηστος *ib.* l. 75.

ᶜ Ἀφροδίτη ἡ ἐν Ἐμβάτῳ (a district of Erythrae), l. 40.

Caria.

⁵⁰ Miletus : Posidippos, *Anth. Pal.* 12. 131 :

> ἁ Κύπρον, ἅ τε Κύθηρα καὶ ἁ Μίλητον ἐποιχνεῖς
> καὶ τὸ καλὸν Συρίης ἱπποκρότου δάπεδον.

Cf. Theocr. 28. 4 :

> πόλιν ἐς Νείλεος ἀγλαάν
> ὅπᾳ Κύπριδος ἷρον καλάμω χλῶρον ὑπ᾽ ἀπάλω.

⁵¹ At Mylasa : *C. I. Gr.* 2693 f Ἀφροδίτης Στρατείας ἱερεύς, inscription from second century B.C.

⁵² At Oecus : Theocr. 7. 116 Οἰκεῦντα ξανθᾶς ἕδος αἰπὺ Διώνας.

⁵³ At Aphrodisias : rights of asylum given to the temple of Aphrodite there in a letter from Antony (37 B.C.), *C. I. Gr.* 2737. Cf. 2782, &c., an ἀνθηφόρος of the goddess of Aphrodisias mentioned in 2822. Cf. Tac. *Ann.* 3. 62 Aphrodisiensium civitas Veneris . . . religionem tuebantur.

⁵⁴ At Cnidos : Paus. 1. 1, 3 Κνίδιοι τιμῶσιν Ἀφροδίτην μάλιστα, καὶ σφίσιν ἔστιν ἱερὰ τῆς θεοῦ. τὸ μὲν γὰρ ἀρχαιότατον Δωρίτιδος ᵃ, μετὰ δὲ τὸ Ἀκραίας ᵇ, νεώτατον δὲ ἦν Κνιδίαν οἱ πολλοί, Κνίδιοι δὲ αὐτοὶ καλοῦσιν Εὔπλοιαν ᶜ. Inscription dedicated to Aphrodite and Hermes found in Cnidus, Newton, *Halicarnassus*, n. 31 : vide series of Aphrodite heads on Cnidian coins, *Choix de medailles grecques du cabinet de M. Imhoof-Blumer*, 4. 127–135.

⁵⁵ At Halicarnassus : *Bull. de Corr. Hell.* 1880, p. 400.

Pamphylia.

⁵⁶ At Aspendos on Mount Castnium : hence Aphrodite Καστνία in Lycophron, 403. Strabo, 437–438 Καλλίμαχος μὲν οὖν φησιν ἐν τοῖς ἰάμβοις τὰς Ἀφροδίτας (ἡ θεὸς γὰρ οὐ μία) τὴν Καστνιῆτιν ὑπερβάλλεσθαι πάσας τῷ φρονεῖν, ὅτι μόνη παραδέχεται τὴν τῶν ὑῶν θυσίαν.

Cilicia.

⁵⁷ At Aegae : *C. I. Gr.* 4443, dedication to Ἀφροδίτη Εὔπλοια together with Poseidon Ἀσφάλειος (first century B.C.).

The islands.

⁵⁸ Rhodes: worshipped with Apollo and Asclepios there, *Bull. de Corr. Hell.* 1880, p. 139.

⁵⁸ᵃ At Cos: vide inscription in *Revue des Études Grecques*, 1891, p. 361 : and Paton and Hicks, *Inscriptions of Cos*, No. 387. Cf. mime of Herondas, 1. 26, 62, Aphrodite called ἡ θεός. Head of Aphrodite on tetradrachm of Cos, *Musée Hunter*, p. 142. 1. Cf. ¹¹⁷ h, ¹¹⁴ f.

⁵⁹ Crete: the Cretans claimed this island to be the original home of the Aphrodite worship: Diod. Sic. 5. 77 διὰ δὲ τὴν ἐπιφάνειαν καὶ τὴν ἐπὶ πλεῖον ἐπιδημίαν αὐτῆς τοὺς ἐγχωρίους ἐξιδιάζεσθαι τὴν θεόν, καλοῦντας Ἀφροδίτην Ἐρυκίναν καὶ Κυθέρειαν καὶ Παφίαν, ἔτι δὲ καὶ Συρίαν.

ᵃ Ancient Ἀφροδίσιον in the territory of the Latii, *C. I. Gr.* 2554 : Aphrodite mentioned in the federal oath sworn by the men of Hierapytnia, *C. I. Gr.* 2555.

ᵇ In Lyctos and Dreros: Cauer, *Delect.*² 117.

ᶜ At Cnossus under the title Ἄνθεια, Hesych. *s. v.*

⁶⁰ Delos: Callimach. *Del.* 307 ἱρὸν ἄγαλμα Κύπριδος ἀρχαίης ἀριήκοον, ἥν ποτε Θησεὺς εἵσατο σὺν παίδεσσιν, ὅτε Κρήτηθεν ἀνέπλει. Paus. 9. 40, 3 Δηλίοις Ἀφροδίτης ἐστὶν οὐ μέγα ξόανον . . . κάτεισι δὲ ἀντὶ ποδῶν ἐς τετράγωνον σχῆμα· πείθομαι τοῦτο Ἀριάδνην λαβεῖν παρὰ Δαιδάλου. Plut. *Theseus*, 21 τῷ θεῷ θύσας καὶ ἀναθεὶς τὸ Ἀφροδίσιον, ὃ παρὰ τῆς Ἀριάδνης ἔλαβεν. *Bull. de Corr. Hell.* 1882, 23, l. 189, inventory of temple-property (circ. 180 B.C.), Ἀφροδισίων τῷ χορῷ λαμπάδες. *Ib.* l. 131 Ἀπόλλωνι Ἀφροδίτη. Worshipped with Isis there in later times : vide inscription in Ἀθηναῖον, 4, p. 458, No. 7 Ἴσιδι Σωτείραι Ἀστάρτει Ἀφροδίτηι καὶ Ἔρωτι Ἀρφοκράτει Ἀπόλλωνι Ἀνδρόμαχος Φανομάχου (ὑπὲρ ἑαυτοῦ) καὶ γυναικὸς καὶ τέκνων χαριστήριον.

ᵃ At Aegina : *Quaest. Graec.* 44, Plut. Paus. 2. 29, 6 πλησίον δὲ τοῦ λιμένος ἐν ᾧ μάλιστα ὁρμίζονται ναός ἐστιν Ἀφροδίτης.

Cyprus.

⁶¹ Paphos: Hom. *Od.* 8. 362 :

ἡ δ' ἄρα Κύπρον ἵκανε φιλομμειδὴς Ἀφροδίτη
ἐς Πάφον, ἔνθα τέ οἱ τέμενος βωμός τε θυήεις.

Paus. 8. 5, 2 Πάφου τε Ἀγαπήνωρ γέγονεν οἰκιστὴς καὶ τῆς Ἀφροδίτης κατεσκευάσατο ἐν Παλαιπάφῳ τὸ ἱερόν· τέως δὲ ἡ θεὸς παρὰ Κυπρίων τιμὰς εἶχεν ἐν Γολγοῖς καλουμένῳ χωρίῳ. Strabo, 683 Παλαίπαφος, ὅσον ἐν δέκα σταδίοις ὑπὲρ τῆς θαλάττης ἱδρυμένη, ὕφορμον ἔχουσα καὶ ἱερὸν ἀρχαῖον τῆς Παφίας Ἀφροδίτης. Tac. *Ann.* 3. 62 Exin Cyprii tribus delubris, quorum vetustissimum Paphiae Veneri auctor Aerias, post filius

eius Amathus Veneri Amathusiae . . . posuissent. *Id. Hist.* 2. 3
fama recentior tradit a Cinyra sacratum templum, deamque ipsam
conceptam mari huc adpulsam. Sed scientiam artemque haruspicum
accitam, et Cilicem Tamiram intulisse . . . mox . . . tantum Cinyrades
sacerdos consulitur. Hostiae ut quisque vovit sed mares deliguntur :
certissima fides haedorum fibris. Sanguinem arae obfundere vetitum :
precibus et igne puro altaria adolentur . . . simulacrum deae non effigie
humana, continuus orbis latiore initio tenuem in ambitum metae
modo exsurgens ; et ratio in obscuro. *ib.* Conditorem templi regem
Aerian vetus memoria, quidam ipsius deae nomen id perhibent (? Ἀφροδίτη ᾿Αρεία). Cf. Max. Tyr. 8. 8. For connexion of Aphrodite worship
with the Cinyradae in Cyprus, vide *Philologus* 24. 226. Cf. Serv. *Aen.*
1. 720 Apud Cyprios Venus in modum umbilici vel ut quidam volunt
metae colitur. Inscriptions found on site of Paphos, e.g. *C. I. Gr.*
Ἀφροδίτῃ Παφίᾳ ἡ πόλις Παφίων (in the time of Ptolemy Euergetes II).
C. I. Gr. 2640 Ἀφροδίτης καὶ Διὸς Πολιέως καὶ Ἥρας (third century B.C.).

[62] Γολγοί, ? older name of the site of the Paphian temple (vide
Neubauer, *Comm.* Mommsen, 673, etc.). Cf. Steph. Byz. *s. v.* Γολγοί·
πόλις Κύπρου . . . λέγεται καὶ Γόλγιον οὐδετέρως· ἀφ᾽ οὗ Γολγία ἡ Ἀφροδίτη.
Theocr. 15. 100 Δέσποιν᾽, ἃ Γολγόν τε καὶ Ἰδάλιον ἐφίλασας Αἰπεινάν τ᾽
Ἔρυκα, χρυσῷ παίσδοισ᾽ Ἀφροδίτα. Schol. *ib.* Γολγός· πόλις Κύπρου,
ὠνομασμένη ἀπὸ Γολγοῦ τινὸς Ἀδώνιδος καὶ Ἀφροδίτης. Catull. 64. 96
Quaeque regis Golgos, quaeque Idalium frondosum.

[63] Citium : vide supra [13e]. *C. I. A.* 2. 168 ; *C. I. Gr.* 2641.

[64] Amathus : Paus. 9. 41, 2 ἔστι δὲ Ἀμαθοῦς ἐν Κύπρῳ πόλις· Ἀδώνιδος
ἐν αὐτῇ καὶ Ἀφροδίτης ἱερόν ἐστιν ἀρχαῖον : vide supra [61] (Tac. *Ann.* 3. 62).
Catull. 36. 14 Colis quaeque Amathunta quaeque Golgos. Hesych.
s.v. κάρπωσις· θυσία Ἀφροδίτης ἐν Ἀμαθοῦντι (κάρπωσις = burnt-offering :
vide Stengel, *in Hermes*, 1892, p. 161) ; grave of Ariadne there, Plut.
Thes. 20 καλεῖν δὲ τὸ ἄλσος Ἀμαθουσίους ἐν ᾧ τὸν τάφον δεικνύουσιν Ἀριάδνης Ἀφροδίτης. Cf. [110k].

[65] The promontory Olympus on the north-east of Cyprus : Strabo,
682 ἔχουσα Ἀφροδίτης Ἀκραίας ναὸν ἄδυτον γυναιξὶ καὶ ἀόρατον. *Ib.* ἄκρα
Πηδάλιον, ἧς ὑπέρκειται λόφος . . . ἱερὸς Ἀφροδίτης. *Id.* 683 Ἀρσινόη ὁμοίως
πρόσορμον ἔχουσα καὶ ἱερὸν καὶ ἄλσος. In 682 he mentions the locality
Ἀφροδίσιον καθ᾽ ὃ στενὴ ἡ νῆσος.

[66] Hesych. Ἔγχειος (?) Ἀφροδίτη Κύπριοι. Cf. [43].

[67] Aphrodite παρακύπτουσα in Cyprus, [110g].

[68] Cythera : Paus. 3. 23, 1 τὸ ἱερὸν τῆς Οὐρανίας ἁγιώτατον καὶ ἱερῶν
ὁπόσα Ἀφροδίτης παρ᾽ Ἕλλησίν ἐστιν ἀρχαιότατον· αὐτὴ δὴ ἡ θεὸς ξόανον
ὡπλισμένον. Cf. *Il.* 15. 432 Κυθήροισι ζαθέοισι. Cf. [99b].

⁶⁹ In Cranaë off Gythium : Paus. 3. 22, 1 ἱερόν ἐστιν Ἀφροδίτης ἐν τῇ ἠπείρῳ Μιγωνίτιδος, καὶ ὁ τόπος οὗτος ἅπας καλεῖται Μιγώνιον. Τοῦτο μὲν δὴ τὸ ἱερὸν ποιῆσαι λέγουσιν Ἀλέξανδρον.

⁷⁰ Amorgus : C. I. Gr. 2264 Οὐρανίᾳ τῇ ἐν ἀσπίδι (inscription circ. 100 A.D.). Cf. Plut. Cleom. 17 and 21, district outside Argos called ἡ ἀσπίς.

⁷¹ Anaphe : C. I. Gr. 2477.

⁷² Ceos : Inscr. Graec. Antiq. (Roehl) 397 Θεοκύδης Ἀρισταίχμου Ἀφροδίτῃ ἀνέθηκεν ἄρξας. Ἀφροδίτῃ Κτήσυλλα Anton. Liber. Transf. 1 οἱ δὲ θύουσιν ἄχρι νῦν Ἰουλιῆται μὲν (a family in Ceos) Ἀφροδίτῃ, Κτήσυλλαν ὀνομάζοντες, οἱ δὲ ἄλλοι Κτήσυλλαν Ἑκαέργην.

ᵃ Gyaros : vide ¹¹⁰ f.

⁷³ ? Lemnos : Schol. Ap. Rhod. 1. 614, the legend of the Lemnian women despising Aphrodite.

ᵃ Lesbos : inscription to Aphrodite-Peitho, and Hermes, published by Keil, Philologus Supplem. 2. 579 ὅ κε θέλῃ θύειν ἐπὶ τῷ τᾶς Ἀφροδίτας τᾶς Πειθῶς καὶ τῷ Ἑρμᾷ.

⁷⁴ Paros : Inscr. Graec. Antiq. (Roehl) 405 Ἀφροδίτης.

⁷⁵ Samos : Athenae. 572 F Ἄλεξις ὁ Σάμιος ἐν δευτέρῳ Ὡρῶν Σαμιακῶν τὴν ἐν Σάμῳ Ἀφροδίτην, ἣν οἱ μὲν ἐν καλάμοις καλοῦσιν, οἱ δὲ ἐν ἕλει, ἀττικαί (φησιν) ἑταῖραι ἱδρύσαντο αἱ συνακολουθήσασαι Περικλεῖ, ὅτε ἐπολιόρκει τὴν Σάμον. Ἀφροδίτη Κουροτρόφος at Samos, ¹¹⁸i.

⁷⁶ Samothrace. Inscription (? of fourth century B.C.) in Conze Reise auf den Inseln des Thrakischen Meers, p. 69, Taf. 16. 10 Ἀφροδίτῃ Καλιάδι.

Sicily.

⁷⁷ Syracuse. ᵃΒαιῶτις : Hesych. s. v. Ἀφροδίτη παρὰ Συρακοσίοις.

ᵇ ? Καλλίπυγος : Athenae. 554 C, E.

⁷⁸ Acrae : C. I. Gr. 5424 προστατεύσαντες Ἥρᾳ καὶ Ἀφροδίτᾳ. Ib. 5425.

⁷⁹ Panormus : C. I. Gr. 5553 Κλεαγόρας Ἀφροδίτῃ ἀνέθηκε τράπεζαν. Sappho (Strabo, 40) ἤ σε Κύπρος ἢ Πάφος ἢ Πάνορμος.

⁸⁰ Messana : C. I. Gr. 5615, dedication to Aphrodite by temple-officials.

⁸¹ Catana : C. I. Gr. 5652 ἱερατευούσης θεᾶς Ἀφροδίτας.

⁸² Segesta : C. I. Gr. 5543 ἱερατεύουσαν Ἀφροδίτᾳ Οὐρανίᾳ.

⁸³ Eryx : Paus. 8. 24, 6 ἔστι γὰρ καὶ ἐν τῇ Σικελίᾳ τῆς Ἐρυκίνης ἱερὸν ἐν τῇ χώρᾳ τῇ Ἔρυκος ἁγιώτατον ἐκ παλαιοτάτου καὶ οὐκ ἀποδέον πλούτῳ τοῦ

ἱεροῦ τοῦ ἐν Πάφῳ. Diod. Sic. 4. 83 : the temple founded and enriched by Eryx, τὴν ἐξ αἰῶνος ἀρχὴν λαβὸν οὐδέποτε διέλιπε τιμώμενον : its prestige was great among the Sicanians and Carthaginians, τὸ δὲ τελευταῖον ʽΡωμαῖοι πάσης Σικελίας κρατήσαντες ὑπερεβάλοντο πάντας τοὺς πρὸ αὐτῶν ταῖς εἰς ταύτην τιμαῖς . . . οἱ μὲν γὰρ καταντῶντες εἰς τὴν νῆσον ὕπατοι καὶ στρατηγοὶ . . . ἐπειδὰν εἰς τὸν ῎Ερυκα παραβάλωσι, μεγαλοπρεπέσι θυσίαις καὶ τιμαῖς κοσμοῦσι τὸ τέμενος, καὶ τὸ σκυθρωπὸν τῆς ἐξουσίας ἀποθέμενοι μεταβάλλουσιν εἰς παιδιὰς καὶ γυναικῶν ὁμιλίας μετὰ πολλῆς ἱλαρότητος, μόνως οὕτω νομίζοντες κεχαρισμένην τῇ θεῷ ποιήσειν τὴν ἑαυτῶν παρουσίαν. Aelian. Nat. Hist. 10. 50 ἀνὰ πᾶν ἔτος καὶ ἡμέραν πᾶσαν θύουσι τῇ θεῷ καὶ οἱ ἐπιχώριοι καὶ οἱ ξένοι . . . ἕως δὲ καὶ ὑπολάμπει καὶ ἐκεῖνος (ὁ βωμὸς) οὐκ ἀνθρακιάν, οὐ σποδόν, οὐχ ἡμικαύστων τρύφη δᾴδων ὑποφαίνει, δρόσου δὲ ἀνάπλεώς ἐστιν καὶ πόας νεαρᾶς, ἥπερ οὖν ἀναφύεται ὅσαι νύκτες· τά γε μὴν ἱερεῖα ἑκάστης ἀγέλης αὐτόματα φοιτᾷ, καὶ τῷ βωμῷ παρέστηκεν. Cf.[114f.] Polyb. 1. 55 τούτου (῎Ερυκος) ἐπ᾽ αὐτῆς μὲν τῆς κορυφῆς οὔσης ἐπιπέδου, κεῖται τὸ τῆς ᾽Αφροδίτης τῆς ᾽Ερυκινῆς ἱερόν, ὅπερ ὁμολογουμένως ἐπιφανέστατόν ἐστι τῷ τε πλούτῳ καὶ τῇ λοιπῇ προστασίᾳ τῶν κατὰ τὴν Σικελίαν ἱερῶν. Strabo, 272 οἰκεῖται καὶ ὁ ῎Ερυξ λοφὸς ὑψηλός, ἱερὸν ἔχων ᾽Αφροδίτης τιμώμενον διαφερόντως ἱεροδούλων γυναικῶν πλῆρες τὸ παλαιόν, ἃς ἀνέθεσαν κατ᾽ εὐχὴν οἵ τε ἐκ τῆς Σικελίας καὶ ἔξωθεν πολλοί. For Aphrodite worship in Sicily, vide also Aphrodite-Aeneas, [45c].

[84] Argyros: Ampelii Liber, *Memor.* 8. 16 Argyro est fanum Veneris super mare : ibi est lucerna super candelabrum posita lucens ad mare sub divo.

[85] For Aphrodite-worship in Italy and along the Adriatic, vide Catullus, 36. 11 :

> Nunc o caeruleo creata ponto
> Quae sanctum Idalium Uriosque apertos,
> Quaeque Ancona Cnidumque harundinosam
> Colis quaeque Amathunta, quaeque Golgos,
> Quaeque Durrachium Adriae tabernam.

(See Robinson Ellis's note on ʽUrios,' *Commentary on Catullus,* p. 98.)

[86] At Naples : *C. I. Gr.* 5796. Cf. Add. 3, p. 1255.

[87] At Rome, worship of Aphrodite of Eryx before the Colline gate : Strabo, 272. Cf. Serv. Virg. *Aen.* 1. 720 Est et Erycina (Venus) quam Aeneas secum advexit.

[88] In Spain, at Saguntum : Polyb. 3. 97, 6 τὸ τῆς ᾽Αφροδίτης ἱερόν.

[89] At Cyrene : vide Plautus, *Rudens* (Act 1, sc. 1, l. 6), for the worship and temple of Venus Cyrenensis.

744   GREEK RELIGION.

⁹⁰ Naucratis : Athenae. 675 F–676 A (quoting from the book of Polycharmus of Naucratis, περὶ Ἀφροδίτης) κατὰ δὲ τὴν τρίτην πρὸς ταῖς εἴκοσιν ὀλυμπιάδα Ἡρόστρατος πολίτης ἡμέτερος . . . προσσχών ποτε καὶ Πάφῳ τῆς Κύπρου ἀγαλμάτιον Ἀφροδίτης σπιθαμιαῖον ἀρχαῖον τῇ τέχνῃ ὠνησάμενος ᾔει φέρων εἰς τὴν Ναύκρατιν· καὶ . . . ἐπεὶ χειμὼν αἰφνίδιον ἐπέπεσε . . . κατέφυγον ἅπαντες ἐπὶ τὸ τῆς Ἀφροδίτης ἄγαλμα, σώζειν αὐτοὺς αὐτὴν δεόμενοι. ἡ δὲ θεός, προσφιλὴς γὰρ τοῖς Ναυκρατίταις ἦν, αἰφνίδιον ἐποίησε πάντα τὰ παρακείμενα αὐτῇ μυρρίνης χλωρᾶς πλήρη ὀδμῆς τε ἡδίστης ἐπλήρωσε τὴν ναῦν . . . καὶ ὁ Ἡρόστρατος ἐξορμήσας τῆς νεὼς μετὰ τοῦ ἀγάλματος ἔχων καὶ τὰς αἰφνίδιον αὐτῷ ἀναφανείσας χλωρὰς μυρρίνας ἀνέθηκεν ἐν τῷ τῆς Ἀφροδίτης ἱερῷ, θύσας τε τῇ θεῷ καὶ ἀναθεὶς τῇ Ἀφροδίτῃ τἄγαλμα.

⁹¹ At Tentyra : Strabo, 815 (οἱ Τεντυρῖται) τιμῶσιν Ἀφροδίτην· ὄπισθεν δὲ τοῦ νεὼ τῆς Ἀφροδίτης Ἴσιδος ἔστιν ἱερόν.

⁹¹ᵃ Zephyrium, near Alexandria : Strabo, 800 ἄκρα ναΐσκον ἔχουσα Ἀρσινόης Ἀφροδίτης. Cf. Athenae. 318 D.

ᵇ Aphrodite Ζηρυνθία in Thrace (? Hekate) : Et. Mag. p. 411. 30 Ζηρυνθία· Ἀφροδίτη ἐν Θράκῃ. Ζήρυνθον γὰρ ἄντρον ἐν Θράκῃ . . . Λυκόφρων.

Hellenic Aphrodite ?

⁹² Daughter of Dione and Zeus : Hom. Il. 5. 312 Διὸς θυγάτηρ Ἀφροδίτη. Cf. Ib. 370 ; Eur. Hel. 1098 Κόρη Διώνης Κύπρι. Dione identified with Aphrodite in Theocr. 7. 116 : vide ⁵². Cf. Serv. Virg. Aen. 3. 466.

⁹³ Connected with Hebe : C. I. Gr. 2138 θεὰν Κωλιάδα εἰς Ἀβαῖον ἐποίησα Ἄλτιμος (circ. 500 B.C.). Cf. C. I. Gr. 214, worship of Hebe near that of Aphrodite Κωλιάς on Attic promontory opposite Aegina. At Sparta, vide ²⁵ᵍ. Hesiod, Theog. 16, 17 :

καὶ Θέμιν αἰδοίην, ἑλικοβλέφαρόν τ' Ἀφροδίτην,
Ἥβην τε χρυσοστέφανον καλήν τε Διώνην.

⁹⁴ With the Charites and Horae : Pau̯s. 6. 24, 7, statues of the Charites at Elis, with some emblems of Aphrodite, Χάριτας δὲ Ἀφροδίτῃ (οἰκείας) μάλιστα εἶναι θεῶν. Aristoph. Pax, 456 Ἑρμῇ, Χάρισιν, Ὥραισιν, Ἀφροδίτῃ, Πόθῳ. Cf. Homer, Il. 18. 382 :

Χάρις λιπαροκρήδεμνος
καλὴ τὴν ὤπυιε περικλυτὸς ἀμφιγυήεις

with Odyss. 8. 270.

Il. 5. 338 :

ἀμβροσίου διὰ πέπλου, ὅν οἱ Χάριτες κάμον αὐταί.

Odyss. 8. 362 :

ἡ δ' ἄρα Κύπρον ἵκανε φιλομμειδὴς Ἀφροδίτη . . .
ἔνθα δέ μιν Χάριτες λοῦσαν καὶ χρῖσαν ἐλαίῳ.

Hom. *Hymn Apoll.* l. 194

αὐτὰρ ἐϋπλόκαμοι Χάριτες καὶ εὔφρονες ῟Ωραι
'Αρμονίη θ' ῞Ηβη τε Διὸς θυγάτηρ τ' 'Αφροδίτη
ὀρχεῦντ', ἀλλήλων ἐπὶ καρπῷ χεῖρας ἔχουσαι.

Hom. *Hymn to Aphrodite,* 6. 11 :

ὅρμοισι χρυσέοισιν ἐκόσμεον, οἷσί περ αὐταὶ
῟Ωραι κοσμείσθην χρυσάμπυκες.

Hesiod, *Op.* 73 :

ἀμφὶ δέ οἱ Χάριτές τε θεαὶ καὶ πότνια Πειθὼ
ὅρμους χρυσείους ἔθεσαν χροΐ (the creation of Pandora).

Athenae. 682 F (quoting from the Cypria), ἡ δὲ σὺν ἀμφιπόλοισι φιλομμειδὴς 'Αφροδίτη πλεξαμένη στεφάνους εὐώδεας ἄνθεα γαίης . . . ἂν κεφαλαῖσιν
ἔθεντο θεαὶ λιπαροκρήδεμνοι, Νύμφαι καὶ Χάριτες ἅμα δὲ χρυσέη 'Αφροδίτη καλὸν
ἀείδουσαι κατ' ὄρος πολυπιδάκου ῎Ιδης.

[95] Aphrodite with Hephaestos : *Odyss.* 8. 266–369. Cf. Ap.
Rhod. 3. 36. Lucian, *Deor. Dial.* 15 πῶς οὐ ζηλοτυπεῖ ἡ 'Αφροδίτη τὴν
Χάριν ἢ ἡ Χάρις ταύτην ;

[96] Aphrodite with Ares : *Il.* 5. 311–364 ; 21. 416. Pindar, *Pyth.*
4. 87 Χαλκάρματος πόσις 'Αφροδίτης. Hes. *Theog.* 933 :

αὐτὰρ ῎Αρηϊ
ῥινοτόρῳ Κυθέρεια Φόβον καὶ Δεῖμον ἔτικτε . . .
'Αρμονίην θ', ἣν Κάδμος ὑπέρθυμος θέτ' ἄκοιτιν.

Temple of Ares at Athens : Paus. 1. 8, 4 near the βουλευτήριον
ἔνθα ἀγάλματα δύο . . . 'Αφροδίτης κεῖται. Joint temple of Ares and
Aphrodite on the road from Argos to Mantinea : Paus. 2. 25, 1
κατὰ μὲν δὴ τοῦτο 'Αφροδίτης κεῖται ξόανον, πρὸς δὲ ἡλίου δυσμὰς ῎Αρεως.
? Ares worshipped with Aphrodite in Crete, the two deities being
mentioned side by side in the public oaths taken by the men of Latus
and Hierapytna. *C. I. Gr.* 2554 and 2555.

[97] Hesiod, *Theog.* 201 :

τῇ δ' ῎Ερος ὡμάρτησε καὶ ῎Ιμερος ἕσπετο καλὸς
γεινομένῃ τὰ πρῶτα θεῶν τ' ἐς φῦλον ἰούσῃ. Cf. [118]k.

[98] Cic. *de Deor. Nat.* 3. 23 Venus prima Coelo et Die nata cuius
Eli delubrum vidimus, altera spuma procreata, ex qua et Mercurio
Cupidinem secundum natum accepimus, tertia Iove nata et Dione,
quae nupsit Volcano. Sed ex ea et Marte natus Anteros dicitur,
quarta Syria Cyproque concepta, quae Astarte vocatur, quam Adonidi
nupsisse proditum est. Amp. *Lib. Mem.* 9 Veneres quattuor ; prima
Coeli et Diei filia, secunda quae ex spuma nata esse dicitur Aetheris et
Oceani filia, tertia quae Volcano nupsit quae cum Marte se miscuit : unde
Cupido natus esse dicitur, quarta Cypri et Syriae filia quam Adon habuit.

746　　　　GREEK RELIGION.

Oriental Aphrodite.

⁹⁹ᵃ Aphrodite Οὐρανία: Paus. 1. 14, 7 πρώτοις ἀνθρώπων Ἀσσυρίοις κατέστη σέβεσθαι τὴν Οὐρανίαν, μετὰ δὲ Ἀσσυρίους Κυπρίων Παφίοις καὶ Φοινίκων τοῖς Ἀσκάλωνα ἔχουσι. Luc. de Dea Syr. 33, description of the goddess of Hierapolis, ἔχει δέ τι καὶ Ἀθηναίης καὶ Ἀφροδίτης καὶ Σεληναίης καὶ Ῥέης καὶ Ἀρτέμιδος καὶ Νεμέσιος καὶ Μοιρέων· χειρὶ δὲ τῇ μὲν ἑτέρῃ σκῆπτρον ἔχει, τῇ ἑτέρῃ δὲ ἄτρακτον καὶ ἐπὶ τῇ κεφαλῇ ἀκτῖνας τε φορέει καὶ πύργον καὶ κεστόν, τῷ μούνην τὴν Οὐρανίην κοσμέουσι.

ᵇ At Cythera, ⁶⁸: Paus. 3. 23, 1. Herod. 1. 105 τῆς Συρίης ἐν Ἀσκάλωνι πόλι . . . τῆς οὐρανίης Ἀφροδίτης τὸ ἱρόν. ἔστι δὲ τοῦτο τὸ ἱρὸν . . . πάντων ἀρχαιότατον ἱρῶν ὅσα ταύτης τῆς θεοῦ. καὶ γὰρ τὸ ἐν Κύπρῳ ἱρὸν ἐνθεῦτεν ἐγένετο, ὡς αὐτοὶ λέγουσι Κύπριοι· καὶ τὸ ἐν Κυθήροισι Φοίνικές εἰσιν οἱ ἱδρυσάμενοι ἐκ ταύτης τῆς Συρίης ἐόντες. Id. 1. 131 ἐπιμεμαθήκασι δὲ οἱ Πέρσαι καὶ τῇ Οὐρανίῃ θύειν, παρά τε Ἀσσυρίων μαθόντες καὶ Ἀραβίων· καλέουσι δὲ Ἀσσύριοι τὴν Ἀφροδίτην Μύλιττα. Cf. Artemis, ¹³².

ᶜ Religious prostitution in the worship of Mylitta at Babylon: Herod. 1. 199 sub fin. ἐνιαχῇ δὲ καὶ τῆς Κύπρου ἐστὶ παραπλήσιος τούτῳ νόμος. The same rites in the worship of the goddess at Byblos: Lucian de Dea Syr. 6. In Lydia and Locris: Athenae. 516 A οὐ μόνον δὲ Λυδῶν γυναῖκες ἄφετοι οὖσαι τοῖς ἐντυχοῦσιν, ἀλλὰ καὶ Λοκρῶν τῶν Ἐπιζεφυρίων, ἔτι δὲ τῶν περὶ Κύπρον (quoting from Clearchus περὶ βίων). Justin. 21. 3 speaks of this practice among the Locrians, and (18. 5) in Cyprus. At Eryx ⁸³: in Armenia in the worship of Anaitis, Strabo, 532 τὰ τῆς Ἀναΐτιδος (ἱερὰ) διαφερόντως Ἀρμένιοι τετιμήκασι . . . καὶ θυγατέρας οἱ ἐπιφανέστατοι τοῦ ἔθνους ἀνιεροῦσι παρθένους, αἷς νόμος ἐστὶ καταπορνευθείσαις πολὺν χρόνον παρὰ τῇ θεῷ μετὰ ταῦτα δίδοσθαι πρὸς γάμον, οὐκ ἀπαξιοῦντος τῇ τοιαύτῃ συνοικεῖν οὐδενός.

ᵈ Paus. 3. 8, 4 οἱ Ἀράβιοι Διόνυσον θεὸν μοῦνον καὶ τὴν Οὐρανίην ἡγεῦνται εἶναι.

ᵉ Herodian, Ab Exc. Div. Marc. 5. 6 τῆς Οὐρανίας τὸ ἄγαλμα μετεπέμψατο, σεβόντων αὐτὸ ὑπερφυῶς Καρχηδονίων τε καὶ τῶν κατὰ τὴν Λιβύην ἀνθρώπων . . . Λίβυες μὲν οὖν αὐτὴν Οὐρανίαν καλοῦσι, Φοίνικες δὲ Ἀστροάρχην ὀνομάζουσι, σελήνην εἶναι θέλοντες.

ᶠ Herod. 4. 59 (the Scythians) ἱλάσκονται . . . Ἀπόλλωνά τε καὶ Οὐρανίην Ἀφροδίτην . . . Οὐρανίη δὲ Ἀφροδίτη, Ἀρτίμπασα. Cf. 4. 67 οἱ Ἐνάρεες (a Scythian tribe) οἱ ἀνδρόγυνοι τὴν Ἀφροδίτην σφι λέγουσι μαντικὴν δοῦναι.

ᵍ In Corinth: Strabo, 378 τὸ τῆς Ἀφροδίτης ἱερὸν οὕτω πλούσιον ὑπῆρξεν ὥστε πλείους ἢ χιλίας ἱεροδούλους ἐκέκτητο ἑταίρας, ἃς ἀνετίθεσαν τῇ θεῷ ἄνδρες καὶ γυναῖκες. Pind. Frag. 87:

Πολύξεναι νεανίδες, ἀμφίπολοι Πειθοῦς ἐν ἀφνείᾳ Κορίνθῳ,
αἵτε τᾶς χλωρᾶς λιβάνου ξανθὰ δάκρυα θυμιᾶτε,
πολλάκι ματέρ᾽ ἐρώτων Οὐρανίαν πτάμεναι νόημα ποττὰν ᾽Αφροδίταν
. . . . σὺν δ᾽ ἀνάγκᾳ πᾶν καλόν.

Athenae. 573 C νόμιμόν ἐστιν ἀρχαῖον ἐν Κορίνθῳ . . . ὅταν ἡ πόλις εὔχηται περὶ μεγάλων τῇ ᾽Αφροδίτῃ, συμπαραλαμβάνεσθαι πρὸς τὴν ἱκετείαν τὰς ἑταίρας ὡς πλείστας καὶ ταύτας προσεύχεσθαι τῇ θεῷ καὶ ὕστερον ἐπὶ τοῖς ἱεροῖς παρεῖναι . . . καὶ οἱ ἰδιῶται δὲ κατεύχονται τῇ θεῷ, τελεσθέντων περὶ ὧν ἂν ποιῶνται τὴν δέησιν, ἀπάξειν αὐτῇ τακτὰς ἑταίρας.

h At Thebes, ⁹.

i At Athens, ¹¹a.

k In the Peiraeeus, ¹³d.

l At Argos, ²².

m At Megalopolis, ²⁷.

n At Aegira, ³².

o At Panticapaeum, ³⁹. *C. I. Gr.* 2108 G, 2109.

p At Smyrna, ⁴⁷a. *C. I. Gr.* 3157.

q Polemon, *Frag.* 42 (Schol. *Oed. Col.* 100) ᾽Αθηναῖοι . . . νηφάλια μὲν ἱερὰ θύουσιν . . . ᾽Αφροδίτῃ Οὐρανίᾳ.

r At Olympia: Paus. 6. 25, 1 τὴν μὲν ἐν τῷ ναῷ καλοῦσιν Οὐρανίαν ἐλέφαντος δέ ἐστι καὶ χρυσοῦ, τέχνη Φειδίου, τῷ δὲ ἑτέρῳ ποδὶ ἐπὶ χελώνης βέβηκε. Cf. ⁴.

s Xenophon, *Symp.* 8. 9 ἑκατέρᾳ (᾽Αφροδίτῃ) χωρὶς βωμοί τε καὶ ναοὶ καὶ θυσίαι, τῇ μὲν Πανδήμῳ ῥᾳδιουργότεραι, τῇ δὲ Οὐρανίᾳ ἁγνότεραι.

t Plato, *Sympos.* 180 D ἡ . . . πρεσβυτέρα καὶ ἀμήτωρ Οὐρανοῦ θυγάτηρ, ἣν δὴ καὶ Οὐρανίαν ἐπονομάζομεν· ἡ δὲ νεωτέρα Διὸς καὶ Διώνης, ἣν δὴ Πάνδημον καλοῦμεν.

u Lucian, *Dialog. Meretr.* 7. 1 θῦσαι μὲν τῇ Πανδήμῳ λευκὴν μηκάδα, τῇ Οὐρανίᾳ δὲ τῇ ἐν Κήποις δάμαλιν.

v Artemid. *Oneirocr.* 2. 37 (᾽Αφροδίτη Οὐρανία) μάλιστα ἀγαθὴ περὶ γάμους καὶ κοινωνίας καὶ πρὸς τέκνων γονήν.

w *Orphic Hymn,* 55. 5 :
καὶ κρατέεις τρισσῶν μοιρῶν, γεννᾷς δὲ τὰ πάντα,
ὅσσα τ᾽ ἐν οὐρανῷ ἐστι καὶ ἐν γαίῃ πολυκάρπῳ
ἐν πόντου τε βυθῷ.

x Epigram, *Anth. Pal.* 1. 297 εἰς ἄγαλμα τῆς Οὐρανίας ᾽Αφροδίτης·
ἡ Κύπρις οὐ πάνδημος, ἱλάσκεο τὴν θεὸν εἰπὼν
Οὐρανίαν.

y Appuleius, *Met.* 11. 2 Caelestis Venus quae primis rerum

748   GREEK RELIGION.

exordiis sexuum diversitatem generato amore sociasti et aeterna subole genere humano propagato nunc circumfluo Paphiae sacrario coleris : the moon is addressed in his prayer as Regina Caeli, Caelestis Venus.

ᶻ Stobaeus, *Physica*, κεφ. θ. περὶ Ἀφροδίτης Οὐρανίας καὶ Ἔρωτος θείου.

¹⁰⁰ Aphrodite Ὀλυμπία at Sparta, ²⁵ᶠ.

¹⁰¹ Aphrodite Ἀφρογενής, poetical title, cf. *C. I. Gr.* 5956 : Hesiod, *Theog.* 191 :

τῷ δ᾽ ἔνι κούρη
ἐθρέφθη· πρῶτον δὲ Κυθήροισι ζαθέοισιν
ἔπλητ᾽, ἔνθεν ἔπειτα περίρρυτον ἵκετο Κύπρον :

cf. ³.   Anacreon, 54 :

χαροπῆς ὅτ᾽ ἐκ θαλάσσης
δεδροσωμένην Κυθήρην
ἐλόχευε πόντος ἀφρῷ.

¹⁰² Ἀστερία : Cram. *Anecd. Paris.* 1. 319 Ἀφροδίτην ἄν τις εἴπῃ τὴν τοῦ πάντος αἰσθητοῦ φύσιν τούτεστι τὴν πρωτογενῆ ὕλην, ἣν καὶ Ἀστερίαν καὶ Οὐρανίαν καλεῖ τὰ λόγια. Aphrodite with Zeus Ἀμάριος and Athena Ἀμαρία on an inscription of the Achaean league, *Rev. Arch.* 1876, p. 102. Cf. the legend in Hesiod, *Theog.* 988 about Phaethon, son of Kephalos, and Eos whom Aphrodite carried off καί μιν ζαθέοις ἐνὶ νηοῖς νηοπόλον μύχιον ποιήσατο δαίμονα δῖον. Strabo, 732 Πέρσαι . . . τιμῶσι καὶ Ἥλιον, ὃν καλοῦσι Μίθρην καὶ σελήνην καὶ Ἀφροδίτην.

¹⁰³ Πασιφάη, goddess worshipped at Thalamae in Laconia : χαλκᾶ ἕστηκεν ἀγάλματα ἐν ὑπαίθρῳ τοῦ ἱεροῦ (Ἰνοῦς) τῆς τε Πασιφάης καὶ Ἡλίου τὸ ἕτερον . . . Σελήνης δὲ ἐπίκλησις, καὶ οὐ Θαλαμάταις ἐπιχώριος δαίμων ἐστὶν ἡ Πασιφάη. Cf. Cic. *de Div.* 1. 43. Arist. *Mirab.* 133, referring to the cows of Geryon, τὰς δ᾽ ἐδάμασσε πόθῳ Πασιφάεσσα θεά. Πασιφάη connected with Apollo and Daphne by Plutarch, *Agis,* 9. Jo. Lyd. *de Mens.* 4. p. 89 (ἡ Ἀφροδίτη) καλεῖται δὲ πολλαχοῦ καὶ Πασιφάη.

¹⁰⁴ Aphrodite-Ariadne at Amathus in Cyprus ⁶¹ : Plut. *Thes.* 20 οἱ μὲν γὰρ ἀπάγξασθαί φασιν αὐτὴν ἀπολειφθεῖσαν ὑπὸ τοῦ Θησέως. *Ib.* at the sacrifice to Ariadne, κατακλινόμενόν τινα τῶν νεανίσκων φθέγγεσθαι καὶ ποιεῖν ἅπερ ὠδίνουσαι γυναῖκες. Grave of Ariadne in Naxos : two different sacrifices there, *ib.* τῇ μὲν γὰρ ἡδομένους καὶ παίζοντας ἑορτάζειν, τὰς δὲ ταύτῃ δρωμένας θυσίας εἶναι πένθει τινὶ καὶ στυγνότητι μεμιγμένας. Naxos, sacred to Dionysos and Aphrodite Ariadne : *Orphic Hymn to Aphrodite*, 55, l. 22 ἢ νύμφαις τέρπῃ κυανώπισιν ἐν χθονὶ Δία. At the feast of ὠσχοφόρια at Athens : Plut. *Thes.* 22 ἐπιφωνεῖν ἐν ταῖς σπονδαῖς, Ἐλελεῦ, Ἰοὺ Ἰού, τοὺς παρόντας· ὧν τὸ μὲν σπένδοντες ἀναφωνεῖν καὶ

παιωνίζοντες εἰώθασι, τὸ δὲ ἐκπλήξεως καὶ ταραχῆς ἐστι. Boys dressed up as girls : *ib.* φωνὴν καὶ σχῆμα καὶ βάδισιν ὡς ἔνι μάλιστα παρθένοις (ὁμοιού- μενοι) . . . φέρουσι (τοὺς ὀσχοὺς) Διονύσῳ καὶ ᾽Αριάδνῃ χαριζόμενοι διὰ τὸν μῦθον ἢ μᾶλλον ὅτι συγκομιζομένης ὀπώρας ἐπανῆλθον. At Argos in the temple of Dionysos Κρήσιος : Paus. 2. 23, 8 ᾽Αριάδνην ἀποθανοῦσαν ἔθαψαν ἐνταῦθα . . . πλησίον δὲ τοῦ Διονύσου καὶ ᾽Αφροδίτης ναός ἐστιν Οὐρανίας. Hesych. *s. v.* ᾽Αριδῆλαν τὴν ᾽Αριάδνην Κρῆτες. Ariadne, mother of Tauropolis, Schol. ap. Rhod. 3. 997.

Armed Aphrodite.

[105]a At Corinth with Helios, [16].

b Aphrodite Συμμαχία at Mantinea, [24].

c Aphrodite ῾Ωπλισμένη ᾽Αρεία, ᾽Αριοντία at Sparta, [25].

d At Mylasa : ᾽Αφροδίτη Στρατεία, [51].

e ῎Εγχειος ᾽Αφροδίτη in Cyprus, [66].

f In Cythera : ξόανον ὡπλισμένον, [68].

g At Amorgus : Aphrodite Οὐρανία ἡ ἐν ἀσπίδι, [70].

h Vide epigrams, *Anth. Plan.* 171–177.

i Plut. *Sulla,* 19, the names of Ares, Nike, and Aphrodite inscribed on Sulla's trophy after Chaeronea, ὡς οὐχ ἧττον εὐτυχίᾳ κατορθώσας ἢ δεινότητι καὶ δυνάμει τὸν πόλεμον. Cf. Plutarch, *Parall.* 37, statue of Aphrodite Νικηφόρος sent to Rome by Fabius Fabricianus.

k Ap. Rhod. 1. 742 :

ἑξείης δ᾽ ἤσκητο βαθυπλόκαμος Κυθέρεια
῎Αρεος ὀχμάζουσα θοὸν σάκος· ἐκ δέ οἱ ὤμου
πῆχυν ἐπὶ σκαιὸν ξυνοχὴ κεχάλαστο χιτῶνος
νέρθεν ὑπὲκ μαζοῖο· τὸ δ᾽ ἄντιον ἀτρεκὲς αὐτὼς
χαλκείῃ δείκηλον ἐν ἀσπίδι φαίνετ᾽ ἰδέσθαι.

l Porph. *de Abst.* 2. 56 ἐθύετο καὶ ἐν Λαοδικείᾳ τῇ κατὰ Συρίαν τῇ ᾽Αθηνᾷ κατ᾽ ἔτος παρθένος, νῦν δὲ ἔλαφος.

m Aphrodite Στρατονικίς at Smyrna, [47].

n Aphrodite Στρατηγίς at Paros : Le Bas, *Îles,* 2062, dedication ᾽Αφροδίτῃ Στρατηγίδι.

[106] Maritime Aphrodite a at Byzantium, [1].

b In Attica, [13a]. Aphrodite Κωλιάς, [14a]. At Aegina, [60a].

c At Hermione : Aphrodite Ποντία καὶ Λιμενία, [19a].

d At Patrae, [30a].

750   GREEK RELIGION.

^e Aegium, ³¹.

^f On south-east coast of Italy: Λιμὴν Ἀφροδίτης, ⁴⁵c.

^g Aphrodite Ἀκραία on the promontory of Olympos in Cyprus, ⁶⁵.

^h Aphrodite Εὔπλοια at Aegae in Cilicia with Poseidon Ἀσφάλειος, ⁵⁷. At Cnidos, ⁵⁴ : *C. I. Gr.* 4443, 7309. Aphrodite Εὔπλοια worshipped at Mylasa, inscription published in Μουσ. καὶ Βιβλιοθ. Σμύρνης, 1875, p. 50. At Naucratis, ⁹⁰.

ⁱ Aphrodite Κατασκοπία at Troezen, ²¹.

^k Plut. p. 983 F (*De Sollert. Anim.*) Ἀφροδίτην ὁμοῦ κατὰ θάλασσαν ποιουμένην αὐτῆς ἱερὰ καὶ ἀδελφὰ καὶ μηδὲν φονευομένῳ χαίρουσαν.

^l Plut. *Crassus*, 17, the goddess at Hierapolis in Syria, ἣν οἱ μὲν Ἀφροδίτην, οἱ δὲ Ἥραν, οἱ δὲ τὴν ἀρχὰς καὶ σπέρματα πᾶσιν ἐξ ὑγρῶν παρασχοῦσαν αἰτίαν. Ampel. *Lib. Mem.* 2. 32 Bello gigantum Venus perturbata in piscem se transfiguravit. Lucian, *de Dea Syr.* §§ 45, 46, lake with sacred fish near the temple of the goddess, κατὰ μέσον αὐτῆς (τῆς λίμνης) βωμὸς λίθου ἀνέστηκεν.

^m Λευκοθέα : ? a marine Aphrodite, akin to Dictynna and Derketo.

ⁿ Ἔφιππος? referring to the sea : Schol. *Il.* 2. 820 πλάττουσι δὲ αὐτὴν καὶ ἔφιππον, ὅτι ὁ Αἰνείας ὁ υἱὸς αὐτῆς, πλεύσας μέχρι τῆς δύσεως μετὰ τοῦτο ἵππῳ ἐπέβη καὶ τὴν μητέρα ἐτίμησε τοιούτῳ ἀγάλματι.

^o Bion, *Id.* 9. 1 :

Ἄμερε Κυπρογένεια, Διὸς τέκος ἠδὲ θαλάσσης.

^p *Anth. Pal.* 10, 21 Κύπρι γαληναίη (? referring to the sea-goddess). *Ib.* 9. 143 Ἱλάσκευ τὴν Κύπριν· ἐγὼ δέ σοι ἢ ἐν ἔρωτι οὔριος ἢ χαροπῷ πνεύσομαι ἐν πελάγει. Lucret. 1. 6 :

Te, dea, te fugiunt venti te nubila caeli
adventumque tuum.

^q Aphrodite Ναυαρχίς associated with Poseidon Σωσινέως on inscription found at Kertsch (of Roman period), *Rev. Arch.* 1881, p. 238.

^r Ἡγεμόνη : Hesych. *s. v.* Ἄρτεμις καὶ Ἀφροδίτη· καὶ ναῦς τις οὕτω καλεῖται : but cf. ¹¹⁷i.

^s Himer. *Or.* 1. 20 τὴν Ἀφροδίτην ἐκ μέσου τοῦ πελάγους ἀνεῖσαν ἔτι τὸν ἀφρὸν μετὰ τὴν θάλασσαν ἐξ ἄκρων πλοκάμων στάζουσαν.

Aphrodite, goddess of vegetation.

^{107a} Ἄνθεια at Cnossus, ⁵⁹.

^b Ἀφροδίτη ἐν Καλάμοις at Samos, ⁷⁵.

^c Sacrifice of herbs to Aphrodite at Eryx, ⁸³.

ᵈ Aphrodite Ἱεροκηπίς in Paphos: Baudissin, *Studien zur Semit. Relig.* 2. 210. Strabo, 683, in Cyprus near Paphos, μικρὸν ἀπὸ θαλάσσης καὶ ἡ Ἱεροκηπία. Cf. ¹¹ᵇ.

ᵉ At Hierapolis: Lucian, *de Dea Syr.* 49 (ἑορτὴν) οἱ μὲν πυρὴν οἱ δὲ λαμπάδα καλέουσι· θυσίην δὲ ἐν αὐτῇ τοιήνδε ποιέουσι· δένδρεα μεγάλα, ἐκκόψαντες ἐν τῇ αὐλῇ ἑστᾶσι· μετὰ δὲ ἀγινέοντες αἶγας τε καὶ ὄϊας καὶ ἄλλα κτήνεα ζῳὰ ἐκ τῶν δενδρέων ἀπαρτέουσι . . . τὰ δὲ αὐτίκα πάντα καίονται.

ᶠ Ἀοῖα: Hesych. δένδρα κοπτόμενα καὶ ἀνατιθέμενα τῇ Ἀφροδίτῃ . . . πρὸς ταῖς εἰσόδοις.

ᵍ Pomegranate sacred to Aphrodite in Cyprus: Athenae. 84 C, quoting from Antiphanes, τὴν γὰρ Ἀφροδίτην ἐν Κύπρῳ δένδρον φυτεῦσαι τοῦτό φασιν ἓν μόνον.

ʰ Plutarch, 756 E ζείδωρον αὐτὴν Ἐμπεδοκλῆς εὔκαρπον δὲ Σοφοκλῆς ἐμμελῶς πάνυ καὶ πρεπόντως ὠνόμασαν.

ⁱ Her worship connected with that of the Horae at Olympia, Paus. 5. 15, 3. Cf. ⁹⁴.

Aphrodite and Adonis as divinities of vegetation and death.

¹⁰⁸ ᵃ Cf. Ovid. *Metam.* 10. 512 (Adonis born from the myrtle-tree). Apollod. 3. 14, 3–4 Ἡσίοδος αὐτὸν (Ἄδωνιν) Φοίνικος καὶ Ἀλφεσιβοίας λέγει· Πανύασις δέ φησι Θείαντος βασιλέως Ἀσσυρίων, ὃς ἔσχε θυγατέρα Σμύρναν· αὕτη κατὰ μῆνιν Ἀφροδίτης, οὐ γὰρ αὐτὴν ἐτίμα, ἴσχει τοῦ πατρὸς ἔρωτα . . . θεοὶ δὲ κατοικτείραντες αὐτὴν εἰς δένδρον μετήλλαξαν, ὃ καλοῦσι σμύρναν . . . τοῦ δένδρου ῥαγέντος γεννηθῆναι τὸν λεγόμενον Ἄδωνιν.

ᵇ Gardens of Adonis: Plato, *Phaedr.* 276 B πότερα σπουδῇ ἂν θέρους εἰς Ἀδώνιδος κήπους ἀρῶν χαίροι θεωρῶν καλοὺς ἐν ἡμέραισιν ὀκτὼ γιγνομένους. Theophr. *Hist. Plant.* 6. 7, 3 ἐν ὀστράκοις ὥσπερ οἱ Ἀδώνιδος κῆποι σπείρεται τοῦ θέρους. Hesych. *s. v.* Ἀδώνιδος κῆποι: ἐν τοῖς Ἀδωνίοις εἴδωλα ἐξάγουσι καὶ κήπους ἐπ᾽ ὀστράκων, καὶ παντοδαπὴν ὀπώραν, οἶον ἐκ μαράθρων καὶ θριδάκων παρασκευάζουσιν αὐτῷ τοὺς κήπους· καὶ γὰρ ἐν θριδακίναις αὐτὸν κατακλινθῆναι ὑπὸ Ἀφροδίτης φασίν (? the Κύπριαι θυσίαι mentioned by Plato, p. 738 C, to be referred to the Adonis Aphrodite worship at Athens).

ᶜ Paus. 6. 24, 7 ῥόδον μὲν καὶ μυρσίνην Ἀφροδίτης τε ἱερὰ εἶναι καὶ οἰκεῖα τῷ ἐς Ἄδωνιν λόγῳ. Theocr. *Id.* 15. 112:

πὰρ μὲν ὀπώρα κεῖται, ὅσα δρυὸς ἄκρα φέροντι,
πὰρ δ᾽ ἁπαλοὶ κᾶποι, πεφυλαγμένοι ἐν ταλαρίσκοις
ἀργυρέοις.

ᵈ Plut. *Alcib.* 18 Ἀδωνίων εἰς τὰς ἡμέρας ἐκείνας (at the time of the departure of the Sicilian expedition in the summer) καθηκόντων πολλαχοῦ νεκροῖς ἐκκομιζομένοις ὁμοία προὔκειντο ταῖς γυναιξί, καὶ ταφὰς ἐμιμοῦντο κοπτόμεναι καὶ θρήνους ᾖδον. Hesych. *s.v.* καθέδρα· θυσία ᾿Αδώνιδος. Sapph. *Fr.* 62:

> κατθνάσκει, Κυθέρη, ἅβρος ῎Αδωνις, τί κε θεῖμεν;
> καττύπτεσθε κόραι καὶ κατερείκεσθε χιτῶνας.

e Arist. *Pax*, 419:

> πάσας τε τὰς ἄλλας τελετὰς τὰς τῶν θεῶν
> μυστήρι᾿ Ἑρμῇ, Διπόλει᾿, ᾿Αδώνια.

Lysistr. 387:

> ἆρ᾿ ἐξέλαμψε τῶν γυναικῶν ἡ τρυφὴ
> χὠ τυμπανισμὸς χοἰ πυκνοὶ Σαβάζιοι . . .
> ἔλεγεν δ᾿ ὁ μὴ ὥρασι μὲν Δημόστρατος
> πλεῖν εἰς Σικελίαν, ἡ γυνὴ δ᾿ ὀρχουμένη,
> αἰαῖ ῎Αδωνιν, φησίν, ὁ δὲ Δημόστρατος
> ἔλεγεν ὁπλίτας καταλέγειν Ζακυνθίων·
> ἡ δ᾿ ὑποπεπωκυῖ᾿, ἡ γυνὴ ᾿πὶ τοῦ τέγους,
> κόπτεσθ᾿ ῎Αδωνιν, φησί.

f Cratinus Βουκόλοι, fr. 2:

> ὃς οὐκ ἔδωκ᾿ αἰτοῦντι Σοφοκλέει χορὸν
> τῷ Κλεομάχου δ᾿, ὃν οὐκ ἂν ἠξίουν ἐγὼ
> ἐμοὶ διδάσκειν οὐδ᾿ ἂν εἰς ᾿Αδώνια.

g Dittenb. *Syllog. Inscr. Graec.* 427 ἔδοξε τοῖς θιασώταις (τῆς ᾿Αφροδίτης) ἐπειδὴ Στέφανος . . . τὴν πομπὴν τῶν ᾿Αδωνίων ἔπεμψε κατὰ τὰ πάτρια, B.C. 302–1, found in the Peiraeeus.

h Athenae. 456 A–B Πλάτων ἐν τῷ ᾿Αδώνιδι χρησμὸν δοθῆναι λέγων Κινύρᾳ ὑπὲρ τοῦ ᾿Αδώνιδος τοῦ υἱοῦ . . . λέγει δὲ ᾿Αφροδίτην καὶ Διόνυσον· ἀμφότεροι γὰρ ἤρων τοῦ ᾿Αδώνιδος. Cf. the oracle given to the Rhodians, Socrates, *Hist. Eccl.* iii. 23:

> ῎Αττιν ἱλάσκεσθαι θεὸν μέγαν ἁγνὸν ῎Αδωνιν
> εὔβιον, ὀλβιόδωρον, εὐπλόκαμον Διόνυσον.

Plut. *Sertorius,* 1 δυεῖν ῎Αττεων γενομένων ἐμφανῶν, τοῦ μὲν Σύρου, τοῦ δὲ ᾿Αρκάδος, ἑκάτερος ὑπὸ συὸς ἀπώλετο. *Orph. Hymn,* 56, Adonis addressed with epithets of Bacchus, Εὐβουλεῦ . . . κούρη καὶ κόρε . . . δικέρως. Firm. Mat. ed. Halm, p. 120 in sacris Phrygiis quae matris deum dicunt, per annos singulos arbor pinea caeditur et in media arbore simulacrum iuvenis subligatur.

i Argos: Paus. 2. 20, 6 οἴκημα ἔνθα τὸν ῎Αδωνιν αἱ γυναῖκες ᾿Αργείων ὀδύρονται.

k Samos: Athenae. 451 B Δίφιλος ἐν Θησεῖ τρεῖς ποτε κόρας Σαμίας φησὶν ᾿Αδωνίοισι γριφεύειν παρὰ πότον.

l At Alexandria in Caria: Steph. Byz. *s.v.* πρὸς τῷ Λάτμῳ τῆς Καρίας ἐν ᾗ ᾿Αδώνιον ἦν ἔχον Πραξιτέλους ᾿Αφροδίτην.

ᵐ Cyprus : ? at Golgoi, ⁶².

ⁿ At Amathus, ⁶⁴.

ᵒ Byblos: Lucian, *de Dea Syr.* 6 εἶδον δὲ καὶ ἐν Βύβλῳ μέγα ἱρὸν
Ἀφροδίτης βυβλίης, ἐν τῷ καὶ τὰ ὄργια ἐς Ἄδωνιν ἐπιτελέουσιν, ἐδάην δὲ καὶ
τὰ ὄργια· λέγουσι γὰρ δὴ ὧν τὸ ἔργον τὸ ἐς Ἄδωνιν ὑπὸ τοῦ συὸς ἐν τῇ
χώρῃ τῇ σφετέρῃ γενέσθαι καὶ μνήμην τοῦ πάθεος τύπτονταί τε ἑκάστου ἔτεος
καὶ θρηνέουσι καὶ τὰ ὄργια ἐπιτελέουσιν . . . ἐπεὰν δὲ ἀποτύψωνταί τε καὶ
ἀποκλαύσωνται πρῶτα μὲν καταγίζουσι τῷ Ἀδώνιδι ὅκως ἐόντι νέκυϊ, μετὰ δὲ
τῇ ἑτέρῃ ἡμέρῃ ζώειν τέ μιν μυθολογέουσι καὶ ἐς τὸν ἠέρα πέμπουσι καὶ τὰς
κεφαλὰς ξυρέονται ὅκως Αἰγύπτιοι ἀποθανόντος Ἄπιος. Cf. Strabo, 755
ἡ . . . Βύβλος . . . ἱερά ἐστι τοῦ Ἀδώνιδος. Luc. *op. cit.* 8, the river called
Adonis in the territory of Byblos, ἑκάστου ἔτεος αἱμάσσεται . . . καὶ
σημαίνει τοῖς Βυβλίοις τὰ πένθεα· μυθέονται ὅτι ταύτῃσι τῇσιν ἡμέρῃσιν ὁ
Ἄδωνις ἀνὰ τὸν Λίβανον τιτρώσκεται καὶ τὸ αἷμα ἐς τὸ ὕδωρ ἐρχόμενον
ἀλλάσσει τὸν ποταμὸν καὶ τῷ ῥόῳ τὴν ἐπωνυμίην διδοῖ.

ᵖ Antioch : Ammian. Marcell. 22. 9, 15 evenerat autem isdem
diebus annuo cursu completo Adonea ritu veteri celebrari, amato
Veneris, ut fabulae fingunt, apri dente ferali deleto, quod in adulto
flore sectarum est indicium frugum . . . ululabiles undique planctus
et lugubres sonus audiebantur.

ᑫ Sestos : Musaeus τὰ καθ᾽ Ἥρω, 42 :

Δὴ γὰρ Κυπριδίη πανδήμιος ἦλθεν ἑορτή,
τὴν ἀνὰ Σηστὸν ἄγουσιν Ἀδώνιδι καὶ Κυθερείῃ.

l. 47 :

οὐδὲ γυνή τις ἔμιμνεν ἐνὶ πτολίεσσι Κυθήρων.

ʳ Alexandria in Egypt: Theocr. *Id.* 15 : departure of Adonis, l. 150 :

νῦν μὰν Κύπρις ἔχοισα τὸν αὐτᾶς χαιρέτω ἄνδρα,
ἀῶθεν δ᾽ ἀμές νιν ἅμα δρόσῳ ἀθρόαι ἔξω
οἰσεῦμες ποτὶ κύματ᾽ ἐπ᾽ αἰόνι πτύοντα.

ll. 143–144 :

ἵλαθι νῦν φίλ᾽ Ἄδωνι, καὶ ἐς νέωτ᾽ εὐθυμήσαις,
καὶ νῦν ἦνθες, Ἄδωνι, καὶ ὅκκ᾽ ἀφίκῃ, φίλος ἥξεις.

ˢ Apollod. *Bibl.* 3. 14, 5 (Ἄδωνιν) Ἀφροδίτης διὰ κάλλος ἔτι νήπιον,
κρύφα θεῶν, εἰς λάρνακα κρύψασα, Περσεφόνῃ παρίστατο. ἐκείνη δὲ ὡς
ἐθεάσατο οὐκ ἀπεδίδου. κρίσεως δὲ ἐπὶ Διὸς γενομένης, εἰς μοίρας διῃρέθη ὁ
ἐνιαυτός· καὶ μίαν μὲν παρ᾽ ἑαυτῷ μένειν τὸν Ἄδωνιν μίαν δὲ παρὰ Περσεφόνῃ
παρέταξε, τὴν δὲ ἑτέραν παρ᾽ Ἀφροδίτην.

ᵗ Schol. Theocr. 5. 92 τὴν ἀνεμώνην Νίκανδρός φησιν ἐκ τοῦ Ἀδώνιδος
αἵματος φυῆναι.

754   GREEK RELIGION.

¹⁰⁹a Aphrodite mourning for Adonis: Macrob. *Sat.* 1. 21, 5 simulacrum huius deae in monte Libano fingitur capite obnupto, specie tristi faciem manu laeva intra amictum sustinens: lacrimae visione conspicientium manare creduntur (he explains this as the image of winter) . . . sed cum sol emersit ab inferioribus partibus terrae . . . tunc est Venus laeta.

b Bion, *Id.* 1. 4:

μηκέτι πορφυρέοις ἐπὶ φάρεσι, Κύπρι, κάθευδε,
ἔγρεο, δειλαία, κυανόστολε, καὶ πλατάγησον
στάθεα.

l. 32 :

ὥρεα πάντα λέγοντι καὶ αἱ δρύες, αἳ τὸν Ἄδωνιν,
καὶ ποταμοὶ κλαίοντι τὰ πένθεα τᾶς Ἀφροδίτας.

c Eus. *Praep. Evang.* 1. 28 (speaking of the Phoenicians) κλαυθμὸν καὶ ἔλεος καὶ οἶκτον βλαστήματι γῆς ἀπιόντι καθιέρουν.

Chthonian Aphrodite.

¹¹⁰a Plaut. *Mercator*, scaena supposita, Act 4 *sub fin.* :

Diva Astarte, hominum deorumque vis vita salus,
rursus eadem quae est pernicies mors interitus.

b Hesych. *s. v.* Εὐμενής· Ἀφροδίτη.

c Ἀφροδίτη Παφίᾳ Εὐβούλᾳ, inscription of the later Ptolemaic period : *Hell. Journ.* 1888, p. 223.

d Plut. *Quaest. Rom.* 269 B καὶ γὰρ ἐν Δελφοῖς Ἀφροδίτης Ἐπιτυμβίας ἀγαλμάτιόν ἐστι, πρὸς ὃ τοὺς κατοιχομένους ἐπὶ τὰς χοὰς ἀνακαλοῦνται. He compares Venus Libitina of Rome.

e Clem. Alex. *Protrept.* 33 P. Ἀργείους, οἳ Ἀφροδίτην τυμβωρύχον θρησκεύουσι.

f Aphrodite Μελαινίς, at Corinth, Thespiae and Mantinea ^{16, 8, 24}. ? Μυχεία: Suidas, *s.v.* Μυχαίτατον; cf. inscr. found in Gyaros, Ἀφροδείτῃ (Μ)υχίᾳ: *Bull. de Corr. Hell.* 1877, p. 357.

g Aphrodite Παρακύπτουσα = Aphrodite Γοργώ: Plut. *Amat.* 766 D τί γὰρ ἂν λέγοι τις Εὐξύνθετον καὶ Λευκομάντιδα τὴν ἐν Κύπρῳ Παρακύπτουσαν ἔτι νῦν προσαγορευομένην; ἀλλὰ τὴν Γοργοῦς ἴσως ποινὴν οὐκ ἀκηκόατε τῆς Κρήσσης παραπλήσια τῇ Παρακυπτούσῃ παθούσης· πλὴν ἐκείνη μὲν ἀπελιθώθη παρακύψασα τὸν ἐραστὴν ἰδεῖν ἐκκομιζόμενον. Ovid, *Metam.* 14. 759 :

dominae sub imagine signum
servat adhuc Salamis : Veneris quoque nomine templum
Prospicientis habet.

Anton. Liber. 39, gives the love-story without any reference to the cult from which it arose.

ʰ Aphrodite Λαθρίη : Meineke, *Del. Epigr.* p. 115.

ⁱ Hesych. *s. v.* Ἐρινννς· δαίμων καταχθόνιος ἢ ᾿Αφροδίτης εἴδωλον.

ᵏ Clemens Rom. *Homil.* 5. 23 (τάφος τις δείκνυται) ᾿Αφροδίτης ἐν Κύπρῳ.

ˡ Inscription quoted by the author of Arist. *Mirab. Auscult.* 145, perhaps from the Ismenion of Thebes :

Ἡρακλέης τεμένισσε Κυθήρᾳ Φερσεφαάσσᾳ
Γηρυονεὺς ἀγέλην ἤδ᾿ Ἐρύθειαν ἄγων
τὰς δὲ δάμασσε πόθῳ Πασιφάεσσα θεά.

ᵐ Plutarch, *Coniug. Praecep.* 138 D οἱ παλαιοὶ τῇ ᾿Αφροδίτῃ τὸν Ἑρμῆν συγκαθίδρυσαν. Cf. ²², ²⁷, ⁵⁴, ⁷³ᵃ.

¹¹¹ ᵃ Apollod. 3. 14. 4 Κινύρας . . . γήμας Μεθάρνην κόρην Πυγμαλίωνος Κυπρίων βασιλέως . . . ἐγέννησεν . . . ᾿Αδωνιν.

ᵇ Clem. Alex. *Protrept.* p. 51 P. ὁ Κύπριος ὁ Πυγμαλίων ἐκεῖνος ἐλεφαντίνου ἠράσθη ἀγάλματος—τὸ ἄγαλμα ᾿Αφροδίτης ἦν καὶ γυμνὴ ἦν—. . . Φιλοστέφανος ἱστορεῖ.

ᶜ Πυγμαίων Hesych. *s. v.* ὁ ᾿Αδωνις παρὰ Κυπρίοις.

¹¹² ᵃ Aphrodite connected with the Moirae and the Erinyes : Schol. Soph. *O. C.* 45 Ἐπιμενίδης Κρόνου φησὶ τὰς Εὐμενίδας ἐκ τοῦ καλλίκομος γένετο χρυσῆ ᾿Αφροδίτη, Μοῖραι τ᾿ ἀθάνατοι καὶ Ἐρίνυες αἰολόδωροι.

ᵇ Connected with Nemesis at Rhamnus : Pliny, *N. H.* 36, 17. Cf. inscription on a seat in the Attic theatre : *C. I. A.* 3. 289 Ἱερεὺς Οὐρανίας Νεμέσεως· also at Sparta, ²⁵.

Male Aphrodite.

¹¹³ ᵃ Macrob. *Sat.* 3. 8 Signum etiam eius est Cypri barbatum corpore sed veste muliebri, cum sceptro et natura virili et putant eandem marem ac feminam esse. Aristophanes eam ᾿Αφρόδιτον appellat . . . Philochorus quoque in Atthide eandem affirmat esse Lunam, et ei sacrificium faciunt viri cum veste muliebri, mulieres cum virili, cum eadem et mas aestimatur et femina.

ᵇ Serv. Virg. *Aen.* 2. 632 Est etiam in Cypro simulacrum barbatae Veneris, corpore et veste muliebri, cum sceptro et natura virili, quod ᾿Αφρόδιτον vocant, cui viri in veste muliebri, mulieres in virili veste sacrificant. Cf. Firm. Mat. *De errore prof. relig.* p. 80, ed. Halm.

ᶜ Cf. Catull. 68. 51 duplex Amathusia.

ᵈ Hesych. *s. v.* ᾿Αφρόδιτος· ὁ δὲ τὰ περὶ ᾿Αμαθοῦντα γεγραφὼς Παιάνισον (? leg. Παίων ὡς) ἄνδρα ἐσχηματίσθαι ἐν Κύπρῳ λέγει.

756 GREEK RELIGION.

ᵉ Jo. Lyd. *De Mens.* 4, p. 89 Παμφυλοὶ καὶ πώγωνα ἔχουσαν ἐτίμησαν Ἀφροδίτην ποτέ.

ᶠ Plut. *De Mul. Virt.* 4, p. 245 F (at Argos) μέχρι νῦν τὰ Ὑβριστικὰ τελοῦσι γυναῖκας μὲν ἀνδρείοις χιτῶσι καὶ χλαμύσιν, ἄνδρας δὲ πέπλοις γυναικῶν καὶ καλύπτραις ἀμφιεννύντες.

ᵍ Cf. Schol. *Il.* 2. 820, the women at Rome, εὐξαμένας τῇ Ἀφροδίτῃ ἀνατριχωθῆναι, τιμῆσαί τε αὐτὴν ἀγάλματι κτένα φέρουσαν καὶ γένειον ἔχουσαν, διότι καὶ ἄρρενα καὶ θήλεα ἔχει ὄργανα.

ʰ Cram. *Anecd. Paris,* 1. 320 ὡς καὶ αὐτὴ ἡ Ἀφροδίτη τήν τε τοῦ ἄρρενος καὶ τοῦ θήλεος ἔχουσα φύσιν.

ⁱ Theophrast. *Char.* περὶ δεισιδαιμονίας· καὶ εἰσελθεῖν εἴσω στεφανοῦν τοὺς Ἑρμαφροδίτους ὅλην τὴν ἡμέραν.

Animals sacrificed to Aphrodite.

¹¹⁴ ᵃ Swine offered at Castniae in Pamphylia, ⁵⁶: at Metropolis in Thessaly, ⁵.

ᵇ Jo. Lyd. *De Mens.* 4, 45. Bonn. Ed. p. 80 ἐτιμᾶτο ἡ Ἀφροδίτη τοῖς αὐτοῖς οἷς καὶ ἡ Ἥρα· ἐν δὲ τῇ Κύπρῳ πρόβατον κωδίῳ ἐσκεπασμένον (? leg. ἐσκεπασμένοι) συνέθυον τῇ Ἀφροδίτῃ· ὁ δὲ τρόπος τῆς ἱερατείας ἐν τῇ Κύπρῳ ἀπὸ τῆς Κορίνθου παρῆλθέ ποτε. εἶτα δὲ καὶ σύας ἀγρίους ἔθυον αὐτῇ διὰ τὴν κατὰ Ἀδώνιδος ἐπιβουλήν.

ᶜ Athenae. 96 A, quoting from Antiphanes' Κορινθία· ἐν τῇ Κύπρῳ δ' οὕτω φιληδεῖ ταῖς ὑσίν (Ἀφροδίτη) ... ὅτι δ' ὄντως Ἀφροδίτῃ ὗς θύεται μαρτυρεῖ Καλλίμαχος ἢ Ζηνόδοτος ἐν ἱστορικοῖς ὑπομνήμασι γράφων ὧδε "Ἀργεῖοι Ἀφροδίτῃ ὗν θύουσι, καὶ ἡ ἑορτὴ καλεῖται ὑστήρια."

ᵈ Arist. *Acharn.* 794 ἀλλ' οὐχὶ χοῖρος τἀφροδίτῃ θύεται. At Hierapolis θύουσι δὲ βόας ἄρσενάς τε καὶ θήλεας καὶ αἶγας καὶ ὄιας· σύας δὲ μούνας ἐναγέας νομίζοντες οὔτε θύουσιν οὔτε σιτέονται ... ὀρνίθων τε αὐτέοισι περιστερὴ χρῆμα ἱρότατον, καὶ οὐδὲ ψαύειν αὐτέων δικαιεῦσι Luc. *De Dea Syr.* 54.

ᵉ Paus. 2. 10. 4 τῶν ἱερείων τοὺς μηρούς θύουσι πλὴν ὑῶν to Aphrodite at Sicyon.

ᶠ Ael. *De Nat. Anim.* 10. 50 εἰ γοῦν ἐθέλοις θῦσαι ὄιν, ἰδού σοι τῷ βωμῷ παρέστηκεν ὄις ... εἴτε αἶγα εἴτε ἔριφον (referring to the worship at Eryx). At Cos, goats offered to Aphrodite: Paton and Hicks, *Inscriptions of Cos,* no. 369; an ἔριφος θήλεια, *ib.* no. 401.

ᵍ Aphrodite Ἐπιτραγία, in Attica, ¹⁴ᵇ; at Elis, ³⁴; cf. ⁹⁹ᵘ. Tac. *Hist.* 2. 3 (in Cyprus) hostiae ut quisque vovit, sed mares deliguntur;

certissima fides haedorum fibris. Plaut. *Poenul.* sex agnos immolavi Veneri.

ʰ Jo. Lyd. *De Mens.* 4, 44. p. 79 ἱερούργουν δὲ αὐτῇ χῆνας καὶ πέρδικας, ὅτι αἱ μὲν τοῖς ὕδασι χαίρουσι (πελαγία δὲ ἡ ʼΑφροδίτη).

ⁱ Empedocles ap. Porph. *de Abstinent.* 2. 21 :

> ἀλλὰ Κύπρις βασίλεια . . .
> τὴν οἵ γʼ εὐσεβέεσσιν ἀγάλμασιν ἱλάσκοντο
> γραπτοῖς τε ζῴοισι μύροισί τε δαιδαλεόσμοις
> σμύρνης τʼ ἀκράτου θυσίαις λιβάνου τε θυώδους
> ξουθῶν τε σπονδὰς μελιττῶν ῥιπτοῦντες ἐς οὖδας.

(For emendations in the text vide Bernays, *Theophrastus Schrift über Frömmigkeit*, p. 178.)

ᵏ Theocr. 27. 63 ῥέξω πόρτιν Ἔρωτι καὶ αὐτᾷ βοῦν ʼΑφροδίτᾳ. Cf. ʼΑφροδίτη Ταυροπόλος Schol. Dionys. *Perieg.* 609.

ˡ Ἱερεῖον τῇ ʼΑφροδίτῃ ἥδιστον· οἶσθα γάρ που τὸ περὶ τοῦ λαγῶ λεγόμενον, ὡς πολὺ τῆς ʼΑφροδίτης μέτεστιν αὐτῷ.

¹¹⁵ a *Hom. Hymn to Aphrod.* 1-6 ; Aesch. *Danaides* (Athenae. 600 A):

> ἐρᾷ μὲν ἁγνὸς οὐρανὸς τρῶσαι χθόνα,
> ἔρως δὲ γαῖαν λαμβάνει γάμου τυχεῖν,
> ὄμβρος δʼ ἀπʼ εὐνάεντος οὐρανοῦ πεσὼν
> ἔκυσε γαῖαν· ἡ δὲ τίκτεται βροτοῖς
> μήλων τε βοσκὰς καὶ βίον Δημήτριον,
> δενδρῶτις ὥρα δʼ ἐκ νοτίζοντος γάμου
> τέλειός ἐστι· τῶν δʼ ἐγὼ παραίτιος.

Imitated by Euripides, *Frag.* 890; Athenae. 599 F.

ᵇ Soph. *Frag.* 678 (Stobaeus, 63. 6):

> ὦ παῖδες ἦ τοι Κύπρις οὐ Κύπρις μόνον,
> ἀλλʼ ἐστὶ πολλῶν ὀνομάτων ἐπώνυμος.
> ἔστιν μὲν Ἅιδης, ἔστι δʼ ἄφθιτος βίος,
> ἔστιν δὲ λύσσα μαινάς, ἔστι δʼ ἵμερος
> ἄκραντος, ἔστʼ οἰμωγμός· ἐν κείνῃ τὸ πᾶν
> σπουδαῖον ἡσυχαῖον ἐς βίαν ἄγον.

ᶜ Eur. *Hipp.* 447 :

> φοιτᾷ δʼ ἀνʼ αἰθέρʼ, ἔστι δʼ ἐν θαλασσίῳ
> κλύδωνι Κύπρις, πάντα δʼ ἐκ ταύτης ἔφυ.

ᵈ Eur. *Med.* 835 :

> Κηφισοῦ ῥοὰν
> τὰν Κύπριν κλῄζουσιν ἀφυσσαμέναν
> χώρας καταπνεῦσαι μετρίας ἀνέμων

ἡδυπνόους αὔρας, ἀεὶ δ' ἐπιβαλλομέναν
χαίταισιν εὐώδη ῥοδέων πλόκον ἀνθέων
τᾷ σοφίᾳ παρέδρους πέμπειν ἔρωτας,
παντοίας ἀρετᾶς συνεργούς.

Aphrodite as a city-goddess.

116 a Jo. Lyd. *De Mens.* 4, p. 91 οἱ Φοίνικες 'Αστάρτην τὴν σφῶν πολιοῦχον.

b Aesch. *Sept.* 140 :

Κύπρις ἅτε γένους προμάτωρ
ἄλευσον· σέθεν γὰρ ἐξ αἵματος
γεγόναμεν.

c At Paphos [61], in Achaea [33] : Aphrodite Συμμαχία at Mantinea, [24].

117 a Aphrodite Πάνδημος : Xen. *Symp.* 8. 9, [99] s.

b Plat. *Symp.* 180 D, [99] t.

c Paus. 6. 25. 1, [99] r.

d *Anthol.* 1. 297, [99] x.

e At Thebes, [9].

f At Megalopolis, [27].

g At Erythrae, [49] a.

h At Cos : Paton and Hicks, *Inscriptions of Cos*, no. 401 'Αφροδίτῃ
Πανδάμῳ ἔριφον θήλειαν.

i At Athens : Athenae. 569 D Νίκανδρος ὁ Κολοφώνιος ἱστορεῖ ἐν
τρίτῳ Κολοφωνιακῶν φάσκων αὐτὸν (Σόλωνα) καὶ Πανδήμου 'Αφροδίτης ἱερὸν
πρῶτον ἱδρύσασθαι ἀφ' ὧν ἠργυρίσαντο αἱ προστᾶσαι τῶν οἰκημάτων.
Harpocr. *s. v.* Πάνδημος 'Αφροδίτη· 'Απολλόδωρος ἐν τῷ περὶ θεῶν πάνδημόν
φησιν 'Αθήνησι κληθῆναι τὴν ἀφιδρυθεῖσαν περὶ τὴν ἀρχαίαν ἀγορὰν διὰ τὸ
ἐνταῦθα πάντα τὸν δῆμον συνάγεσθαι τὸ παλαιὸν ἐν ταῖς ἐκκλησίαις, ἃς ἐκάλουν
ἀγοράς. *Bull. de Corr. Hell.* 1889, p. 161, inscription found on the
south-west side of the Acropolis fourth century B.C., τόνδε σοι, ὦ
μεγάλη σεμνὴ Πάνδημε 'Αφροδίτη, . . . Μενεκράτεια Δεξικράτους 'Ικαριέως
θυγάτηρ ἱέρεια τῆς 'Αφροδίτης τῆς Πανδήμου. *Ib.* p. 163, inscription 284
B. C., . . . ὅπως ἂν οἱ ἀστυνόμοι . . . ἐπιμέλειαν ποιῶνται τοῦ ἱεροῦ τῆς
'Αφροδίτης τῆς Πανδήμου κατὰ τὰ πάτρια, found on the same spot as the
above (published also in *Delt. Arch.* 1888, p. 188). Cf. *Delt. Arch.*
1891, p. 127, inscription of latter part of third century B. C., ἡ βουλὴ
ἡ ἐπὶ Διονυσίου ἄρχοντος ἀνέθηκεν 'Αφροδίτει ἡγεμόνῃ τοῦ δήμου καὶ Χάρισι.
Athenae. 659 D Μένανδρος ἐν Κόλακι . . . μάγειρον ἐν τῇ τῆς Πανδήμου
'Αφροδίτης ἑορτῇ ποιεῖ ταυτὶ λέγοντα

. . . . θεοῖς ὀλυμπίοις εὐχώμεθα
ὀλυμπίαισι πᾶσι πάσαις
. . . . διδόναι σωτηρίαν
ὑγίειαν ἀγαθὰ πολλὰ . . .

[118] a Connected with the clan and with marriage: Ἀφροδίτη Ἀπατούρη, [38] and [39].

b Children consecrated to Aphrodite at Paphos: *C. I. Gr.* 2637 (second century A. D.).

c Aphrodite Ἥρα at Sparta, [25] e.

d Artemidor. *Oneirocrit.* [99] v.

e Aphrodite Ἄρμα at Delphi, [7].

f Aphrodite Νυμφία: Paus. 2. 32, 7, on the road between Troezen and Hermione, Ἀφροδίτης ἱερὸν Νυμφίας ποιήσαντος Θησέως, ἡνίκα ἔσχε γυναῖκα Ἑλένην. Cf. [19].

g Aphrodite Γενετυλλίς: Arist. *Nub.* 52 Schol. Γενετυλλὶς ἡ τῆς γενέσεως ἔφορος Ἀφροδίτη. *Lysistr.* 2 Schol. Γενετυλλὶς γυναικεία θεὸς περὶ τὴν Ἀφροδίτην. Lucian, *Pseudol.* 11 εἰπὲ γάρ μοι πρὸς Πανδήμου καὶ Γενετυλλίδων καὶ Κυβήβης. *Erotes*, 42 πᾶς θεὸς ἐπιτρίβων τοὺς γεγαμηκότας, ὧν ἐνίων οἱ κακοδαίμονες ἄνδρες οὐδὲ αὐτὰ ἴσασι τὰ ὀνόματα, Κωλιάδας, εἰ τύχοι, καὶ Γενετυλλίδας ἢ τὴν Φρυγίαν δαίμονα καὶ τὸν δυσέρωτα κῶμον ἐπὶ τῷ ποιμένι· τελεταὶ δὲ ἀπόρρητοι καὶ χωρὶς ἀνδρῶν ὕποπτα μυστήρια καὶ—τί γὰρ δεῖ περιπλέκειν; διαφθορὰ ψυχῆς. Alciphron, 3. 11 ποῦ γὰρ ἐγὼ κατ᾽ ἀγρὸν ἱδρύσω Κωλιάδας ἢ Γενετυλλίδας; οἶδ᾽ ἀκούσας ἄλλα τινὰ δαιμόνων ὀνόματα, ὧν διὰ τὸ πλῆθος ἀπώλισθέ μου τῆς μνήμης τὰ πλείονα (cf. Hekate, [23] k).

h Aphrodite Θαλάμων: Hesych. *s. v.* ἄνασσα, Ἀφροδίτη.

i Κουροτρόφος: Athenae. 441 F (from Plato) πρῶτα μὲν ἐμοὶ γὰρ Κουροτρόφῳ προθύεται πλακοῦς ἐνόρχης. *Anth. Pal.* 6. 318 Κύπριδι Κουροτρόφῳ δάμαλιν ῥέξαντες ἔφηβοι χαίροντες νύμφας ἐκ θαλάμων ἄγομεν. In Samos at the feast of Ἀπατούρια Homer πορευόμενος γυναιξὶ Κουροτρόφῳ θυούσαις ἐν τῇ τριόδῳ. Cf. Athenae. 592 [a], who identifies Κουροτρόφος with Aphrodite.

k Stobaeus, 67. 20 Ποῦ μὲν γὰρ Ἔρως παραγένοιτ᾽ ἂν δικαιότερον ἢ ἐπὶ νόμιμον ἀνδρὸς καὶ γυναικὸς ὁμιλίαν; ποῦ δὲ Ἥρα; ποῦ δὲ Ἀφροδίτη; cf. Diod. Sic. 5. 73.

Aphrodite as goddess of beauty and love.

[119] a Μορφώ at Sparta, [25] b: Hesych. *s.v.* Μορφώ· ἡ Ἀφροδίτη.

b Ἀποστροφία: in Thebes, [9]. Cf. Ἐπιστροφία in Megara, [15] b.

c Ἀνδροφόνος or ἀνοσία in Thessaly, [4]: Plut. 768 A ἔτι νῦν τὸ ἱερὸν Ἀφροδίτης ἀνδροφόνου καλοῦσιν.

d Aphrodite Πειθώ in Pharsalus [2]: cf. inscription from Lesbos, [73 a]. Hesiod, *Works and Days*, l. 73—description of Pandora's creation, [94]. Περσεθέα: ἡ Ἀφροδίτη Hesych. *s.v.* ? leg. Πεισιθέα.

e Μανδραγορῖτις: Hesych. *s.v.* ἡ Ἀφροδίτη. Μαχανῖτις at Megalopolis, [27 b].

f Μιγωνῖτις in Cranae south of Laconia, [69].

g Πρᾶξις Aphrodite at Megara, [15].

h Παρακύπτουσα at Cyprus, [110 g].

i Ψίθυρος: Harpocr. *s. v.* ψιθυριστής. Ἑρμῆς ἐτιμᾶτο Ἀθήνησι καὶ ψίθυρος Ἀφροδίτη καὶ Ἔρως ψίθυρος.

Βαιῶτις at Syracuse, [77 a].

k *Fragment of Homeric hymn to Aphrodite,* 10 (Baumeister):

Κυπρογενῆ Κυθέρειαν ἀείσομαι, ἥ τε βροτοῖσι
μείλιχα δῶρα δίδωσιν, ἐφ᾽ ἱμερτῷ δὲ προσώπῳ
αἰεὶ μειδιάει καὶ ἐφ᾽ ἱμερτὸν φέρει ἄνθος.
χαῖρε, θεά . . . .
. . . . δὸς δ᾽ ἱμερόεσσαν ἀοιδήν.

Cf. fragment 6. 19. Ἔρως as the personification of human love: Plato, *Sympos.* 119 C βωμῶν καὶ θυσιῶν οὐδὲν γίνεται περὶ αὐτοῦ. Eur. *Hipp.* 539.

l Apollod. 3. 14, legend of the daughters of Cinyras, ἀλλοτρίοις ἄνδρασι συνευναζόμεναι διὰ μῆνιν Ἀφροδίτης.

m Ἱπποδάμεια: ἡ Βρισηῒς καὶ Ἀφροδίτη Hesych. *s. v.*

n Firm. Mat. *De errore profan. relig.* p. 78 ed. Halm (Phryges qui Pessinunta incolunt) . . . mulieris divitis ac reginae suae amorem quae fastus amati adulescentis tyrannice voluit ulcisci, cum luctibus annuis consecrarunt.

o Firm. Mat. p. 80 Assyrii et pars Afrorum aerem nomine Iunonis vel Veneris virginis—si tamen Veneri placuit aliquando virginitas—consecrarunt.

[120] Aphrodite Ἑταίρα: a Athenae. 571 C τῆς παρὰ τοῖς Ἀθηναίοις καλουμένης ἑταίρας τῆς Ἀφροδίτης, περὶ ἧς φησὶν ὁ Ἀθηναῖος Ἀπολλόδωρος ἐν τοῖς περὶ θεῶν οὕτως " ἑταίραν δὲ τὴν Ἀφροδίτην τὴν τοὺς ἑταίρους καὶ τὰς ἑταίρας συνάγουσαν·" τοῦτο δ᾽ ἐστὶ φίλας. Photius *s. v.* Ἑταίρας Ἀφροδίτης· ἱερὸν Ἀθήνησιν ἀπὸ τοῦ συνάγειν ἑταίρους καὶ ἑταίρας. At Ephesus, [48].

b Aphrodite Πόρνη at Abydos, [44].

c Cf. Clem. Alex. *Protrept.* p. 33 P. οὐχὶ Ἀφροδίτη περιβασίη μὲν Ἀργεῖοι, ἑταίρᾳ δὲ Ἀθηναῖοι καὶ καλλιπύγῳ θύουσιν Συρακούσιοι; ἣν Νίκανδρος ὁ ποιητὴς καλλίγλουτόν που κέκληκεν. Vide Hesych. *s. v.* Περιβασώ and Τρυμαλῖτις, epithets of Aphrodite.

d Aphrodite Καλλίπυγος: Athenae. 554 C–E ἱδρύσαντο Ἀφροδίτης ἱερὸν καλέσασαι καλλίπυγον τὴν θεόν, ὡς ἱστορεῖ καὶ Ἀρχέλαος ἐν τοῖς ἰάμβοις.

COIN PLATE B

e Aphrodite Λύκαινα : *Orphic Hymn*, 54. 11, ? meaning of title.

f Dedications by hetaerae in Pharos in the Adriatic : *C. I. Gr.* 1837 D, E. Philetairos in the Κυνηγίς (Athenae. 572 D) :

> οὐχ ἐτὸς ἑταίρας ἱερόν ἐστι πανταχοῦ
> ἀλλ' οὐχὶ γαμετῆς οὐδαμοῦ τῆς Ἑλλαδος ;

Aphrodite identified with women.

[121] a Aphrodite 'Αρσινόη near Alexandria, [91] a.

b Aphrodite Βελεστίχη : Plut. 753 E ἡ δὲ Βελεστίχη, πρὸς Διός, οὐ βάρβαρον ἐξ ἀγορᾶς γύναιον ; ἧς ἱερὰ καὶ ναοὺς 'Αλεξανδρεῖς ἔχουσιν, ἐπιγράψαντος δι' ἔρωτα τοῦ βασιλέως, 'Αφροδίτης Βελεστίχης.

c Aphrodite Λαμία : Athenae. 253 B Θηβαῖοι κολακεύοντες τὸν Δημήτριον, ὥς φησι Πολέμων, . . . ἱδρύσαντο ναὸν 'Αφροδίτης Λαμίας. Cf. 'Αφροδίτη Λέαινα *id.* 253 A.

d Aphrodite Πυθιονίκη at Athens : Athenae. 595 A–C Θεόπομπος ἐν τῇ πρὸς 'Αλέξανδρον ἐπιστολῇ τὴν 'Αρπάλου διαβάλλων ἀκολασίαν φησίν . . . ἦν πάντες ᾔδεσαν ὀλίγης δαπάνης κοινὴν τοῖς βουλομένοις γινομένην, ταύτης ἐτόλμησεν ὁ φίλος εἶναι σοῦ φάσκων ἱερὸν καὶ τέμενος ἱδρύσασθαι, καὶ προσαγορεῦσαι τὸν ναὸν καὶ τὸν βωμὸν Πυθιονίκης 'Αφροδίτης, ἅμα τῆς τε παρὰ θεῶν τιμωρίας καταφρονῶν.

Aphrodite in Orphic literature.

[122] *Hymn* 54, lines 1–8 :

> Οὐρανίη, πολύυμνε, φιλομμειδὴς 'Αφροδίτη,
> ποντογενής, γενέτειρα θεά, φιλοπάννυχε, σεμνή,
> νυκτερίη, ζεύκτειρα, δολοπλόκε, μῆτερ ἀνάγκης,
> πάντα γὰρ ἐκ σέθεν ἐστί, ὑπεζεύξω δέ τε κόσμον,
> καὶ κρατέεις τρισσῶν μοιρῶν, γεννᾷς δὲ τὰ πάντα,
> ὅσσα τ' ἐν οὐρανῷ ἐστι και ἐν γαίῃ πολυκάρπῳ,
> ἐν πόντου τε βυθῷ· σεμνὴ Βάκχοιο πάρεδρε,
> τερπομένη θαλίῃσι, γαμοστόλε, μῆτερ ἐρώτων.

ll. 22, 23 :

> ἢ νύμφαις τέρπῃ κυανώπισιν ἐν χθονὶ Δίᾳ,
> θυιὰς ἐπ' αἰγιαλοῖς ψαμμώδεσιν ἅλματι κούφῳ.

Frag. 28. 4 :

> πόλεμος μὲν Ἄρης, εἰρήνη δ' ἐστ' 'Αφροδίτη.